Encyclopedia of
American Spy Films

Garland Reference Library of the Humanities
(Vol. 1187)

Encyclopedia of
American Spy Films

Larry Langman
David Ebner

Garland Publishing, Inc.
New York & London   1990

Library of Congress Cataloging-in-Publication Data

Langman, Larry.
An encyclopedia of American spy films / by Larry Langman, David Ebner.
p.   cm. — (Garland reference library of the humanities ; vol. 1187)
Includes bibliographical references (p.
ISBN 0-8240-5533-0 (alk. paper)
1. Spy films—United States—Catalogs.   I. Ebner, David.
II. Title.   III. Series.
PN1995.9.S68L36   1990
016.79143'658—dc20   90-3577

Printed on acid-free, 250-year-life paper

MANUFACTURED IN THE UNITED STATES OF AMERICA

"What a charming evening we might have had if
you had not been a spy and I a traitor."
"Then we might never have met."

Dishonored   (1931)

"Tell me, in all the world, who is the most
secret agent?"
"Anyone who manages to stay secret."
"But there is an even more ideal agent. One who
doesn't know he is an agent."

Telefon   (1977)

Contents

Preface

The authors of this encyclopedia have tried to bring together in one volume virtually every American-produced film from the early silent period to the late 1980s concerning spies, government operatives and undercover agents. The book includes more than 1,000 films and about 100 historical, biographical and film-related entries.

Obviously, certain problems arose regarding criteria for selection of films. We have included, in addition to spy dramas, comedies, serials and other films depicting customs, immigration, treasury and other government agents who have gone under cover to accomplish their missions. We have omitted industrial or corporate espionage dramas since they are far removed from national security or the movie audience's conception of intrigue and sabotage.

We were concerned also with what constitutes an "American film," especially those which appeared after World War II. Some American studios produced films overseas while others cooperated with foreign studios in joint productions. We resolved the dilemma by incorporating these hybrid works into the book. Foreign films which were released by American companies and featured major American talent presented another problem. However, to keep the book comprehensive, we decided to include many of these as well. Others, such as *The Guns of Navarone*, which has several American players but is listed as a British production, have been omitted.

The spy film, like other genres, is not always clearly delineated. It often blends with comedies, musicals and westerns. To avoid the sin of omission, we have found a niche for these schizophrenic productions. Our main regret is that certain foreign classics such as Hitchcock's *The 39 Steps* and *The Lady Vanishes* or the entertaining British-produced James Bond series had to be omitted. However, they have been fully discussed in other books. To have included foreign spy films would have defeated our original purpose and would have required additional years of research. On a more positive note, we are certain that both the film buff and scholar will discover a number of new films and find our historical entries entertaining and informative.

How the Book Is Arranged

All entries are listed alphabetically. Two or more films with the same title are listed chronologically. Each film entry includes its release date, releasing company, director, screenwriter and five or more major players. Unfortunately, several more obscure early silent works do not list any director or screenwriter, and we were unable to locate these credits in the standard film sources. Some pre-1914 films run only 15 or 30 minutes (one or two reels). These have been identified with quotation marks. All other full-length features, serials and documentaries appear in italics. When several films suggest a specific historical event, such as the Palmer raids, the topic is treated as a separate entry to avoid repeating the same information, and a cross-reference appears at the end of the film entry.

Acknowledgments

Any work of this scope requires the hands and ideas of several people. We would like to thank the following for their unending help: film enthusiast Paul Gold for his relevant materials; film collector Joseph A. Molinari for allowing us access to his thousands of films; former U.S. government agent Harry Friedman for his wealth of experience; and historian Ed Borg for his historical notes.

Introduction

Why a book about spy films? Whereas westerns, horror films and comedies provide sufficient entertainment, they do not offer the particular type of insight into human nature that the spy genre does. For instance, the main character in a war drama is often part of a squad, platoon or other unit, while the secret agent often works alone, surrounded by a hostile environment. In the detective film or western, the hero, although he may be a loner, can at least be himself. The spy, on the other hand, must hide his own identity and always be on guard against betrayal from within and without if he wishes to survive. In no other situation does the main character face such constant danger or sense of insecurity as the undercover agent—the quintessential outsider.

Also, suspense is heightened for us by the knowledge that the fate of our country or the world hangs upon the actions of the lone agent. Will captured O.S.S. agent James Cagney in *13 Rue Madeleine* (1946), undergoing brutal torture by the Gestapo, reveal the time and place of the Normandy invasion? In *The Manchurian Candidate* (1962) we find ourselves making the long climb with Frank Sinatra to an almost ceiling-high booth at Madison Square Garden, hoping that he can prevent Laurence Harvey, under hypnosis, from assassinating a Presidential nominee. Sometimes the hero-agent himself literally hangs precariously from some precipice or familiar monument, as Robert Cummings does from the Statue of Liberty in *Saboteur* (1942) and Cary Grant, from Mount Rushmore, in *North by Northwest* (1959), both Hitchcock suspense thrillers.

Adventure films, romances, historical dramas, comedies, mysteries and westerns appeared on screen before the spy film and have been more popular. The espionage film incorporates many characteristics of the above types, sometimes even merging with them. In *Raiders of the Lost Ark* (1981) Steven Spielberg added high adventure to Indiana Jones' mission for U.S. intelligence. Hitchcock imbued the genre with the elements of wit and suspense. Spies Marlene Dietrich in *Dishonored* (1931) and Greta Garbo in *Mata Hari* (1932) raised the element of romance to new heights when they chose love over duty. The spy film merged with the historical drama as early as 1909 in the silent short "Benedict Arnold and Major André" and in a string of Civil War films. Buster Keaton in his classic *The General* (1927) and Red Skelton in *A Southern Yankee* (1948) blended espionage and comedy. Spies infiltrated the detective series, especially during World II in such entries as *Enemy Agents Meet Ellery Queen* and *Sherlock Holmes and the Secret Weapon*, both released in 1942. Even the western, the most structured of all genres, was occasionally modified to fit contemporary themes. The legendary cowboy star William S. Hart in *The Border Wireless* (1918) battled German spies along the Mexican border during World War I, and popular Roy Rogers in the World War II horse opera *King of the Cowboys* (1943) uncovered a gang of Nazi saboteurs.

Spy films, because of their international plots, have occasionally strayed from pure escapism to social and political commentary, often to the detriment of many innocent groups. The Japanese war scare of 1907 resulted in a string of anti-Japanese films that lasted for a decade, bringing almost irreparable harm to the Japanese-American community. By the time World War I exploded, the spy film had already entered the world of propaganda and politics. Its unfavorable image of Germans and Prussians prejudiced the public against millions of loyal German-Americans. Spy dramas and comedies sympathized with the British, French and Belgians and attacked pacifists. The postwar years, during the Red Scare of 1919–1920, were witness to anti-Bolshevik and anti-labor dramas along with plots about U.S. government agents smashing counterfeit, smuggling and drug rings. The advent of sound helped the spy films, which depended more upon dialogue than war films or westerns. The espionage drama of the 1930s, often harking back to the Civil War and World War I, focused its attentions on romance rather than politics.

While the U.S. was engaged in tracking down and arresting foreign agents before entering World War II, Hollywood studios, always aware of topical issues, kept many of its players, especially those with foreign accents, such as Sig Rumann, Otto Preminger and Conrad Veidt, busily employed in a string of spy dramas and comedies.

Films released prior to America's entry into the conflict usually hesitated to identify the national origins of their foreign spies. Occasionally, political pressure on Hollywood studios came from the most unexpected places. Neal Gabler in his book, *An Empire of Their Own: How the Jews Invented Hollywood*, writes that many considered Joseph P. Kennedy, the American ambassador to Great Britain, a Nazi sympathizer. The father of the future President John F. Kennedy met with a number of Jewish movie executives and producers in 1940 and warned them against producing anti-Nazi movies. Gabler discovered a letter in the Roosevelt Library from Douglas Fairbanks, Jr. to President Roosevelt, written in 1940, in which the actor indicates that Kennedy warned the industry's movers and shakers that "anti-semitism was growing in Britain and that the Jews were being blamed for the war. . . ." Fairbanks continued, in his letter to Roosevelt, to describe Kennedy's emphasis upon "the fact that the film business was using its power to influence the public dangerously and that we all, and the Jews in particular, would be in jeopardy, if they continued to abuse that power."

The studios, attempting to remain neutral, did not want to alienate any of their lucrative foreign markets. American audiences, however, drew the obvious conclusions. The foreign accents of these nefarious agents often suggested their Teutonic backgrounds. *Cipher Bureau* (1938) features Leon Ames as the head of the counter-espionage cipher bureau, an agency set up to foil hostile nations from sending secret messages to their agents in the U.S. Anna Sten portrays a young refugee seeking American citizenship in *Exile Express* (1939), a low-budget drama. About to be deported, she escapes from the train journeying from the West Coast to the East. Foreign spies, who need her assistance in deciphering a secret formula, pursue her. *Foreign Correspondent* (1940), Hitchcock's highly suspenseful and exciting drama of political intrigue on the eve of World War II, was his second American film. Joel McCrea, as an American reporter sent to Europe in August of 1939 to uncover the truth about the threat of war, becomes entangled in an international spy ring whose members are posing as part of a peace organization. In *The Devil Pays Off* (1941) J. Edward Bromberg, as a former navy man, uncovers a plot involving a shipping tycoon who plans to sell his fleet to a potential enemy of the U.S. Teenagers break up a spy ring in *Down in San Diego* (1941), a World War II comedy drama set chiefly around a naval base.

When the war clouds gathered once again over Europe in 1939, the genre, formally responding with *Confessions of a Nazi Spy* (1939), returned to politics and propaganda. However, once America entered the conflict, Hollywood produced a flood of spy dramas, comedies and musicals, many of which were hurriedly made. The dramas tended to emphasize the melodramatic, and the bulk of these only proved how little the movie capital, eager to blend purpose with entertainment, understood the realities of wartime espionage.

Dozens of spy films released after Japan's attack on Pearl Harbor dealt with threats of espionage and sabotage on the home front—with more than 75 released in 1942 alone. Most of these dramas differentiated between U.S. and Axis intelligence preparations. American agencies usually acted defensively, sending out their operatives only to halt a rash of sabotage acts or prevent the theft of vital documents or a secret weapon. On the other hand, aggressive and well-entrenched German and Japanese agents were often seen in prewar America laying the foundation for future espionage. Once the U.S. entered the conflict, films showed these enemy networks unleashing their attacks upon defense plants, munitions dumps, shipyards and other military targets. *Joe Smith, American* (1942) features Robert Young as a World War II airplane technician who is captured and tortured by German agents. *Busses Roar* (1942) takes place chiefly aboard a bus and concerns the transport of a bomb that is to be used to ignite an oil field as a beacon for a Japanese submarine. *Dangerously They Live* (1942) has Nazi spies kidnapping a British agent on a secret mission in New York. An innocent man gets mixed up in a murder and a sinister spy ring in *Fly by Night* (1942), a low-budget Hitchcock-type drama.

During the remaining war years, the spy drama blended with other types—with mixed results. Several westerns began to appear. In *Cowboy Commandos* (1943), for example, Nazi agents are on the verge of dynamiting a western mine that is producing a rare ore. There were musicals such as *Ship Ahoy* (1942) and horror films like *Revenge of the Zombies* (1943), each harboring spies bent on destruction. Several short documentaries dealt with espionage at home. "While America Sleeps" (1939), for instance, explains how enemy agents operate. "For the Common Defense" (1942) tells of a South American spy network's link to American gangsters. And in "Keep 'Em Sailing" (1942) an F.B.I. agent exposes sabotage attempts directed at U.S. cargo ships.

The Cold War following World War II generated an increased production in films which pitted Eastern bloc agents against those of the West. For the most part, these were earnest, if heavy-handed, attempts to illustrate the evils of Communism from Hollywood's point of view. The forces of good and evil in these dramas were as clearly delineated as they were in the old-fashioned gangster movies of the 1930s. In fact, David A. Cook, in his 1981 study, *A History of Narrative Film*, labels these anti-Communist thrillers a sub-type of the gangster film. He equates the spy with the conventional gangster and the international Red conspiracy with the familiar syndicate of the gangster genre.

The striking success of Britain's James Bond films of the early 1960s, with their satiric tone and glib hero, had a marked effect upon Hollywood. Bond clones began tumbling out of U.S. studios at a rate that almost sated the public's appetite for the genre by 1970. The following list of American espionage-related films between 1966 and 1972 shows the rise and sudden collapse of the genre:

1966:	19 releases
1967:	10
1968:	13
1969:	6
1970:	5
1971:	3
1972:	2

After reaching its nadir in the early 1970s, the spy movie was repackaged and regained some of its former popularity by the 1980s. The earlier films of the 1960s were light, satirical and sexually implicit. Those espionage films that followed were made to adapt to the new trends favored by contemporary audiences—added emphasis on sex and nudity, heightened violence and a more cynical amoral hero. The forces of darkness included, along with the conventional Soviet rogues, incompetent military officials and arrogant C.I.A. and F.B.I. agents. Life was cheap to these new villains, who appeared as early as the 1950s in such films as *North by Northwest* (1959). They often sacrificed innocent civilians to meet their own goals. The F.B.I. and C.I.A. chiefs were frequently depicted as paranoid and more dangerous than the enemy they sought to destroy, in effect, showing us once again that the spy film reflects the moral ambiguities of contemporary society. Lines between good and evil in these films are often blurred.

Throughout its history, the spy film benefited at least one segment of the Hollywood community—actresses. They rarely played the lead in war, detective, crime or western films. With a woman as the main character of a spy plot, the danger and suspense elements increased audience interest as well as box office receipts. The female spy, more vulnerable than her male counterpart with whom she more often than not fell in love, allowed the writers to expand the romantic interest. Such major screen personalities as Marion Davies in *Operator 13* (1934), Myrna Loy in *Stamboul Quest* (1934), Marlene Dietrich in *Dishonored* (1931) and Greta Garbo in *Mata Hari* (1932) brought style and class to the spy film.

Hollywood generally kept pace with national and international events in portraying the shifting face of the enemy agent. Complications began to set in after the Communists wore out their villainous welcome upon the screen in the 1980s. General Secretary Gorbachev's glasnost helped to end the career of the Soviet spy in films. Seeking new sinister and sadistic villains to fill the void, screenwriters and directors experimented with Middle East terrorists (*The Delta Force*), paranoid and ambitious mavericks of the military-industrial complex (*Dreamscape*) and racial extremists and bigots (*Betrayed*). By the end of the decade, film studios had settled upon their latest force of evil—the drug lord. The large-scale drug dealer made an ideal bogeyman. Here was no blurred foe, but a clear menace whom virtually all audiences could hate. The drug lord presented no threat to foreign film markets, as did dramas about terrorists, since the plot could remain apolitical.

Spy films, with their themes of war, loyalty and paranoia, have occasionally provoked controversy, as with the blatantly anti-Japanese *Patria* (1916), the Cold War drama *My Son John* (1952) and the more recent covert-action dramas such as *Invasion U.S.A.* (1985), and have sometimes been labeled as fascist films because of their suggested paranoia, military fantasy and pathological individualism.

Like other kinds of film, the spy drama has its established conventions—the lone and outnumbered hero, the many known and unknown dangers facing him, the kind stranger who helps him but may turn out to be an informer, the strange setting, the urgency of his mission, the knowledge that his country or superiors are depending upon him to succeed, and always the threat of death that awaits him if he fails. Nevertheless, the structure of genre films does not have to be restrictive; it has its advantages. These familiar basic elements give the screenwriter and director the freedom to focus on style, nuances and themes. Genres generate myths which in turn help to define and unite a society. They also give their audiences a sense of order and clarity in a world that is often more chaotic than intelligible. Regardless of how an audience interprets each film, the spy drama may help us to understand a particular historical period, or it may convey the fears and aspirations of a generation. Above all, the more thought-provoking films act as cautionary tales, warning us of false prophets, enemies both real and imaginary, and possible dangers to our democratic processes.

Abbreviations

AA	Allied Artists
AE	Associated Exhibitors
AI	American International
APD	Allied Producers and Distributors Corporation
APR	Associated Producers
ARC	American Releasing Company
Avco	Avco Embassy
BFB	Brody-Freed-Brandchild
BV	Buena Vista
Cin.	Cinerama Releasing Corporation
Col.	Columbia
CU	Commonwealth United
EL	Eagle Lion
FBO	Film Booking Offices
FN	First National
GN	Grand National
MGM	Metro Goldwyn Mayer
Mon.	Monogram
NC	Nation Cinema Pictures
NG	National General Pictures
Par.	Paramount
PDC	Producers Distributing Corporation
PRC	Producers Releasing Corporation
RC	Robertson-Cole
Rep.	Republic
RKO	RKO Radio Pictures
S-L	Sawyer and Lubin
TCF	Twentieth Century-Fox
U	Universal
UA	United Artists
UI	Universal-International
WB	Warner Brothers
WW	Sono Art-Worldwide

Sources

André, John. *Major André's Journal.* New York: New York Times, 1968.

Bailey, Anthony. *Major André.* New York: Farrar, Straus, Giroux, 1987.

Bailey, Thomas A. *The American Pageant.* 2nd ed. Boston: D.C. Heath, 1961.

Barbour, Alan G. *Saturday Afternoon at the Movies.* New York: Bonanza Books, 1986.

Becket, Henry S. A. *The Dictionary of Espionage.* New York: Stein and Day, 1986.

Binion, Rudolph. *Defeated Leaders: The Political Fate of Caillaux, Jouvenal, and Tardieu.* Morningside Heights, NY: Columbia University Press, 1960.

Blitzer, Wolf. *Territory of Lies: The Exclusive Story of Jonathan Jay Pollard.* New York: Harper & Row, 1989.

Boylan, Brian Richard. *Benedict Arnold: The Dark Eagle.* New York: W.W. Norton, 1973.

Chambers, Whittaker. *Witness.* New York: Random House, 1952.

——. *Odyssey of a Friend: Whittaker Chambers' Letters to William F. Buckley, Jr., 1954–1961.* New York: Putnam, 1970.

Christensen, Terry. *Reel Politics.* New York: Basil Blackwell, 1987.

Clayton, Aileen. *The Enemy is Listening.* New York: Ballantine Books, 1982.

Currey, Cecil B. *Edward Lansdale: The Unquiet American.* Boston: Houghton Mifflin, 1989.

Dunan, Marcel, ed. *Larousse Encyclopedia of Modern History.* New York: Crescent Books, 1987.

Dunlop, Richard. *Donovan, America's Master Spy.* Chicago: Rand McNally, 1982.

Dupuy, R. Ernest, and Trevor N. Dupuy, eds. *Encyclopedia of Military History.* New York: Harper & Row, 1986.

Eames, John Douglas. *The MGM Story.* New York: Crown Publishers, 1979.

——. *The Paramount Story.* New York: Crown Publishers, 1985.

Epstein, Edward Jay. *Deception: The Invisible War Between the KGB and the CIA.* New York: Simon & Schuster, 1989.

Eudes, Dominic. *The Kapetanios: Partisans and Civil War in Greece, 1943–49.* London: New Left Books, 1972.

Film Daily Year Book of Motion Pictures (annually). New York: Distributed by Arno Press, 1970.

Gabler, Neal. *An Empire of Their Own: How the Jews Invented Hollywood.* New York and London: Anchor Books, Doubleday, 1989.

Gouzenko, Igor. *This Was My Choice.* London: Eyre and Spottiswoode, 1948.

Hanchett, William. *The Lincoln Murder Conspiracies.* Urbana, IL: University of Illinois Press, 1983.

Hanson, Patricia King, ed. *The American Film Institute Catalogue of Motion Pictures Produced in the U.S.: Feature Films 1911–1920.* Berkeley: University of California, 1988.

Hirschhorn, Clive. *The Universal Story.* New York: Crown Publishers, 1983.

——. *The Warner Bros. Story.* New York: Crown Publishers, 1979.

Howe, Russell. *Mata Hari, The True Story.* New York: Dodd, Mead, 1986.

Isenberg, Michael T. *War on Film: The American Cinema and World War I, 1914–1941.* East Brunswick, NJ: Associated University Presses, 1981.

Jewell, Richard B., and Vernon Harbin. *The RKO Story.* New York: Crown Publishers, 1982.

Johns, Phillip. *Within Two Cloaks: Missions*

with S.I.S. and S.O.E.. London: Kimber, 1979.

Keller, William Walton. *The Liberals and J. Edgar Hoover: Rise and Fall of a Domestic Intelligence State.* Princeton, NJ: Princeton University Press, 1989.

Kessler, Ronald. *Spy vs. Spy: Stalking Soviet Spies in America.* New York: Charles Scribner's Sons, 1988.

Knightley, Phillip. *The Second Oldest Profession: Spies and Spying in the Twentieth Century.* New York: W. W. Norton, 1986.

———. *The Master Spy: The Story of Kim Philby.* New York: William Morrow & Co., 1989.

Kohn, George C. *Dictionary of Wars.* Garden City, NY: Anchor Books, 1987.

Langer, William L., ed. *Encyclopedia of World History.* Leicester, Eng.: Harrap/Galley Press, 1987.

Langguth, A. J. *Patriots: The Men Who Started the Revolution.* New York: Simon & Schuster, 1988.

Langman, Larry, and Edgar Borg. *Encyclopedia of American War Films.* New York: Garland Publishing, 1989.

Lord Boothby. "Philby & Co.," *Books and Bookmen*, v.18, n.10 (July 1973), p. 45.

MacDonald, Callum. *The Killing of Reinhard Heydrich.* New York: The Free Press, 1989.

Maltin, Leonard. *The Great Movie Shorts.* New York: Bonanza Books, 1972.

Martin, James Joseph. *Men Against the State: The Expositors of Individualist Anarchism in America.* New York: Libertarian Book Club, 1953.

Masterman, J. C. *The Double-Cross System in the War of 1939 to 1945.* New Haven, CT: Yale University Press, 1972.

McCormick, Donald. *The Master Book of Spies.* New York: Franklin Watts, 1974.

Meeropol, Robert and Michael. *We Are Your Sons: The Legacy of Ethel and Julius Rosenberg.* Boston: Houghton Mifflin, 1975.

Mendelsohn, John, ed. *Covert Warfare.* 18 vols. New York: Garland Publishing, 1988.

Miller, Don. *B Movies.* New York: Ballantine Books, 1987.

Miller, Nathan. *Spying in America: The Hidden History of U.S. Intelligence.* New York: Paragon House, 1989.

Morris, Richard B., ed. *Encyclopedia of American History.* New York: Harper & Row, 1982.

New York Times Film Reviews (1913–1980). New York: Quadrangle Books, Inc.

Ogden, August Raymond. *The Dies Committee: A Study of the Special House Committee for the Investigation of Un-American Activities, 1938–1944.* Washington, DC: The Catholic University of America Press, 1945.

O'Reilly, Kenneth. *Hoover and the Un-Americans: The F.B.I., H.U.A.C. and the Red Menace.* Philadelphia: Temple University Press, 1983.

Posner, Steve. *Israel Undercover: Secret Warfare and Hidden Diplomacy in the Middle East.* Syracuse, NY: Syracuse University Press, 1987.

Pratt, Julius W. *A History of United States Foreign Policy.* New York: Prentice-Hall, 1955.

Roosevelt, Kermit. *War Report of the OSS.* New York: Walker, 1976.

Rowan, Richard Wilmer. *The Pinkertons: A Detective Dynasty.* Boston: Little, Brown, 1931.

Rubenstein, Leonard. *The Great Spy Films.* Secaucus, NJ: The Citadel Press, 1979.

Schlesinger, Arthur M., ed. *Almanac of American History.* New York: Bramhall House, 1986.

Seale, Patrick, and Maureen McConville. *Philby: The Long Road to Moscow.* London: Hamish Hamilton, 1973.

Shindler, Colin. *Hollywood Goes to War.* Boston: Routledge & Kegan Paul, 1979.

Siepman, Kate, ed. *Benet's Reader's Encyclopedia.* 3rd ed. New York: Harper & Row, 1987.

Sinclair, Andrew. *The Red and the Blue: Cambridge, Treason and Intelligence.* Boston: Little, Brown, 1986.

Spears, Jack. *Hollywood: The Golden Era.* New York: Castle Books, 1971.

Tadmor, Joshua. *The Silent Warriors.* New York: Macmillan, 1969.

Troy, Thomas F. *Donovan and the C.I.A.: A History of the Establishment of the Central Intelligence Agency.* Frederick, MD: Aletheia Books, 1981.

Tuchman, Barbara W. *The Guns of August.* New York: Macmillan, 1962.

United States Congress. Hearings Before the Committee on Un-American Activities, Eighty-Fourth Congress. First Session. *Investigation of Communist Activities.* 2 vols. Washington, DC: U.S. Government Printing Office, 1955.

Variety Film Reviews 1907–1984. New York: Garland Publishing, 1986.

Volkman, Ernest. *Warriors of the Knight: Spies Soldiers and American Intelligence.* New York: William Morrow & Co., 1985.

Ward, Christopher. *The War of the Revolution.* New York: Macmillan, 1952.

West, Nigel. *Molehunt: Searching for Soviet Spies in MI15.* New York: William Morrow & Co., 1989.

West, W. J. *Truth Betrayed.* London: Duckworth, 1987.

Witcover, Jules. *Sabotage at Black Tom: Imperial Germany's Secret War in America, 1914–1917.* Chapel Hill, NC: Algonquin Books, 1989.

Wood, Robin. *Hitchcock's Films.* New York: Castle Books, 1969.

The
Encyclopedia

A

Abbott and Costello in the Foreign Legion (1950), U. *Dir.* Charles Lamont; *Sc.* John Grant, Martin Ragaway, Leonard Stern; *Cast includes:* Bud Abbott, Lou Costello, Patricia Medina, Walter Slezak, Douglas Dumbrille, Leon Belasco.

Abbott and Costello journey to Algiers to convince a former wrestler to return to the U.S. in this broad comedy. They soon become entangled in an intrigue between local natives and the Foreign Legion, which the duo are tricked into joining. Some of the better comic routines include the pair's escape across the desert while Arab horsemen are in hot pursuit and Lou's innocent purchase of several thinly clad slave girls. Walter Slezak portrays their tough sergeant-traitor while Patricia Medina plays a spy in the employ of a villainous sheik (Douglas Dumbrille). ■

Above Suspicion (1943), MGM. *Dir.* Richard Thorpe; *Sc.* Keith Winter, Melville Baker, Patricia Coleman; *Cast includes:* Joan Crawford, Fred MacMurray, Conrad Veidt, Basil Rathbone, Reginald Owen, Richard Ainley.

Joan Crawford and Fred MacMurray play American newlyweds in England who are about to honeymoon in Europe on the eve of World War II in this adaptation of Helen MacInnes' novel. The British secret service enlists the couple's aid in obtaining plans from an agent concerning a German secret weapon. They reluctantly agree and are soon embroiled in intrigue, narrow escapes, and murder in France and Germany before they accomplish their mission and return safely. George Sanders, as a Gestapo agent, befriends the couple but suspects them of espionage.

The film offers typical Hollywood humor of the period. In one scene in a German bookstore, MacMurray is accosted by a Nazi soldier. "Heil Hitler," the non-English-speaking representative of the Third Reich salutes. "Nuts to you, dope," MacMurray replies. In another scene in a museum, a German guide describes to Joan Crawford some of the more interesting historical torture devices on display, adding that modern methods are more proficient. "Totalitarian manicure?" she suggests. This was Crawford's last film for MGM after working at the studio for 17 years. Conrad Veidt succumbed to a heart attack after completing the film. ■

Ace of Hearts, The (1921), Goldwyn. *Dir.* Wallace Worsley; *Sc.* Ruth Wightman; *Cast includes:* Lon Chaney, Leatrice Joy, John Bowers, Hardee Kirkland, Raymond Hatton.

Anarchists plan to cleanse society and thereby improve the world by murdering off wealthy industrialists in this intriguing drama. The cabal, after deciding upon its next victim, uses a deck of cards for the selection of the assassin. Whoever receives the ace of hearts must perform the killing.

Two members, Henry and John, both love Lillith, another member of the group. John gets the fatal card and agrees to plant a bomb under the table of the victim who happens to frequent the restaurant in which John is a waiter. When he arrives at the restaurant and sees his intended prey, he prepares to carry out his assignment, but then notices a young couple at an adjoining table and realizes the explosion will also kill these innocent lovers. Placing human life above the aims of his secret society, he declines to activate the bomb.

When his fellow conspirators learn of his failure, they vote to kill him. Henry, meanwhile, also has second thoughts as the cards are being dealt out. Disillusioned with the group and its destructive aims, he decides to

Lobby card with Humphrey Bogart, posing as an American traitor, joining Mary Astor on voyage to Panama. *Across the Pacific* (1942).

set off the bomb in the meeting place, thereby killing off the entire society. Lon Chaney portrays Henry. Leatrice Joy plays Lillith. See Anarchists in the U.S. ∎

Across the Pacific (1926), WB. *Dir.* Roy Del Ruth; *Sc.* Darryl Zanuck; *Cast includes:* Monte Blue, Myrna Loy, Jane Winton, Walter McGrail, Charles Stevens, Edgar Kennedy.

Set in the Philippines following the Spanish-American War, the drama concerns a group of rebel islanders who are on the verge of overthrowing the democratic regime. The U.S. government assigns one of its agents (Monte Blue) to uncover the leader. Blue romances a local native (Myrna Loy) so that he can learn the whereabouts of the insurrectionist chief. The film, based on a novel by Charles E. Blaney, concludes with an action-filled battle between the dissidents and American troops. Edgar Kennedy provides the comic relief. Warner Brothers used the title again in 1942 but for an entirely different story. See Philippines. ∎

Across the Pacific (1942), WB. *Dir.* John Huston; *Sc.* Richard Macauley; *Cast includes:* Humphrey Bogart, Mary Astor, Sydney Greenstreet, Charles Halton, Sen Yung, Keye Luke.

The strategic Panama Canal is the subject of this World War II drama starring the three principals of director John Huston's previous hit, *The Maltese Falcon* (1941). The story opens several weeks before Japan's attack on Pearl Harbor. U.S. Army intelligence suspects a known agent, Dr. Lorenz (Sydney Greenstreet), who is sympathetic to the Japanese, is involved in some kind of conspiracy involving the Panama Canal. Humphrey Bogart portrays an American agent posing as a court-martialed army officer assigned to learn the doctor's plans. "Something big is brewing," Bogart's superior explains. "We have reason to believe they'll be boiling over soon. . . . They're sure to involve the Canal. Lorenz may or may not be the key man. It's up to you to find out."

Bogart arranges for passage aboard a Japanese freighter sailing from Canada to the Panama Canal. On board are Dr. Lorenz and an American woman (Mary Astor). Lorenz soon strikes up a friendship with Bogart and discreetly offers the American money for his knowledge of military installations at the Canal. Meanwhile Bogart becomes romantically involved with Astor, who in reality is the daughter of a drunken Panamanian plantation owner under the power of Japanese agents, and is the lure for Bogart as he temporarily joins forces with the espionage network. After a short stopover in New York, the vessel continues on its course to the Panama Canal. Once the boat docks and Bogart delivers the schedule of U.S. military flights over the Canal to Lorenz, the doctor grows suspicious of Bogart. He discontinues his dealings with the American, knocks him unconscious and has Bogart's Panama contact murdered so that the flight schedule cannot be changed.

Lorenz and his minions depart for a plantation where preparations have been made for a hidden, secretly assembled airplane to bomb the Canal. Bogart follows but is captured and held at gunpoint while the Japanese pilot gets ready to carry out his mission. Bogart disarms his captor, proceeds to the nearby small airstrip, gains control of a machine gun and destroys the plane. He then takes the doctor prisoner. It is December 6, 1941.

Released early in the war, the film contains little in the way of propaganda or patriotic speeches that were soon to become prevalent in similar releases. "You guys have been looking for a war, haven't you?" Bogart remarks to his captor in one of the final scenes. "That's right," the guard replies. "That's why we're starting it." "You might start it," Bogart returns, "but we'll finish it."

Huston left the film before its conclusion when he was called for active service. Vincent Sherman completed the direction in the taut Huston style which included the rather implausible escape by Bogart. The film is based on "Aloha Means Goodbye," a short story by Robert Carson. See Panama Canal. ■

Action in Arabia (1944), RKO. *Dir.* Leonide Moguy; *Sc.* Philip MacDonald, Herbert Biberman; *Cast includes:* George Sanders, Virginia Bruce, Lenore Aubert, Gene Lockhart, Robert Armstrong, Michael Ansara.

Nazi agents attempt to stir up an Arab revolt and plan to destroy the Suez Canal in this World War II action drama. George Sand-

ers, as a savvy American reporter in Damascus, manages to foil the villainous plot while romancing Virginia Bruce, who plays a secret agent. The story is set in 1941, with Sanders at first attempting to solve the murder of a fellow journalist. The implausible plot of this routine film allows Sanders, a dashing, sophisticated pre-James Bond hero, to frequent gambling casinos and charm worldly women in one sequence and, in another, to steal a German airplane to frustrate the efforts of spies Gene Lockhart and Alan Napier. ■

Action of the Tiger (1957), MGM. *Dir.* Terence Young; *Sc.* Robert Carson; *Cast includes:* Van Johnson, Martine Carol, Herbert Lom, Gustavo Rocco, José Nieto, Helen Hayes.

A wealthy and attractive Frenchwoman hires an American adventurer and his motor launch to help her rescue her blind brother, a political prisoner being held in Albania, in this slow-paced Cold War drama. Martine Carol, as the sister, at first has difficulty persuading Carson, the American (Van Johnson) "who'll do anything for money." Carson, a contraband runner, is busily engaged working with his Albanian partner (José Nieto) to smuggle children out of Communist Albania. Taken in by Carol's charm and beauty, he reluctantly agrees to help her.

The remainder of the episodic plot consists of the pair's attempts to lead the brother and a host of children across the border to Greece while Albanian soldiers relentlessly pursue them. The motley group are helped by an Albanian peasant who pleads with Johnson to take his small children to England. A small band of shepherds give them food, but soldiers suddenly attack the camp, ruthlessly kill the elderly shepherd leader and capture the fugitives. Local anti-Communist bandits attack the small convoy and rescue Johnson and his party. The bandit chief, who desires Carol for his woman, sacrifices his life to help them cross the border to Greece.

The stereotyped characters hamper the plausibility of the yarn. Johnson's derring-do—his shoot-outs with the soldiers, his climbing a mountain to drop grenades on border guards—is unconvincing. Albanian Communists slap old women and prisoners and kill innocent peasants at random. Local peasants are quick to turn over their children to the American so that they can find a better life in the West. Some plot elements are unclear. Why does Johnson's Albanian contact at first help him and then, appearing in military uniform, pursue his American friend? Why is the blind brother a prisoner, why is he left unguarded and why is he so relentlessly hunted down?

The film, lensed chiefly in Spain, allows for large vistas of rugged mountains and glimpses into some native customs. The lines from Shakespeare's *Henry V*, tacked on at the end as if an afterthought, explain little about the plot:

> In peace there's nothing so becomes a man
> As modest stillness and humility:
> But when the blast of war blows in our ears,
> Then imitate the action of the tiger. . . .

If Albania was to be used as background for a Cold War film, other incidents, some based on actual events, may have served the cause better. Early in the Cold War, for example, several attempts were made by British and American agents to infiltrate Soviet territory—all resulting in failure. One joint British-American operation designed to land agents in Albania ended in disaster when the agents were killed as soon as they arrived. But perhaps these incidents were rejected as film plots since they could not serve Western propaganda. ■

Adele (1919), U. *Dir.* Wallace Worsley; *Sc.* Jack Cunningham; *Cast includes:* Kitty Gordon, Mahlon Hamilton, Wedgewood Nowell, Joseph Dowling.

In this World War I romantic drama a nurse and her sweetheart both go to France, she to help with the wounded and he to fight for his country. Mahlon Hamilton, as the young hero, is wounded and placed in the hospital where Adele (Kitty Gordon), the nurse, has been assigned. But the Germans attack and capture the wounded and the nurses. A German officer among the invaders promises to save the young man's life if Adele will spy for the enemy. She agrees, but when she confronts the English captain, she confides to him the agreement she made with the German. He then gives her useless information about some obsolete cannon that he can afford to sacrifice. Meanwhile, the captain orders a successful counterattack, and the British retake the town and the hospital. After the war Adele and her fiancé marry. The plot includes the typical—though late—anti-Hun sentiment when Adele is forced to kill the German officer after he tries to attack her. The film is based on the 1915 novel *The Nurse's Story* by Adele Bleneau. ■

Advance to the Rear (1964), MGM. *Dir.* George Marshall; *Sc.* Samuel A. Peeples, William Bowers; *Cast includes:* Glenn Ford, Stella Stevens, Melvyn Douglas, Jim Backus, Joan Blondell, Andrew Prine.

A pigheaded Union colonel causes a multitude of problems for his troops in this Civil War comedy. Melvyn Douglas, as the commander of a company of misfits, insists on making all the military decisions. But they usually turn out to be disasters. Glenn Ford portrays a sensible-minded captain who is frustrated by his eccentric colonel. Stella Stevens, as a Confederate spy, provides the romance. Joan Blondell plays a madam whose group of prostitutes provide the customary diversions for the troops. Veteran character player Alan Hale portrays a sergeant. One of the highlights of the farce is a comical battle between the Yankees and the Confederates. The film was adapted from the novel *The Company of Cowards* by Jack Schaeffer, who also authored *Shane*. ■

Adventures of Kitty Cobb, The (1914), Warner. *Cast includes:* Marian Swayne, Jack Hopkins, Howard Missimer, Maggie Weston, Ida Darling.

Foreign agents attempt to steal the plans for a new weapon developed by a private inventor in this simple drama. The scientist, played by Jack Hopkins, has been working on his project for the U.S. government. Kitty Cobb (Marian Swayne), the inventor's sweetheart, has been employed as a secretary to his mother. Kitty prevents the theft by the spies, but they kidnap her and take her to their hideaway. The inventor, with the help of an acquaintance, locates the hide-out and, after a brawl with the enemy agents, manages to rescue Kitty. Howard Missimer portrays the chief spy. The film is based on James Montgomery Flagg's cartoon character and book by the same name. ■

Adventures of Tartu, The (1943). See *Tartu* (1943). ■

Adventures of the Flying Cadets (1943) serial, U. *Dir.* Ray Taylor, Lewis D. Collins; *Sc.* Morgan B. Cox, George H. Plympton, Paul Huston; *Cast includes:* Johnny Downs, Bobby

Jordan, Ward Wood, Billy Benedict, Eduardo Ciannelli, Robert Armstrong, Jennifer Holt.

Cadets at a school for future pilots tangle with Nazi agents and other criminals in this 13-chapter World War II serial designed chiefly for juvenile audiences. The quartet of cadets, played by Johnny Downs, Bobby Jordan, Ward Wood and Billy Benedict, handle the action-filled adventures that concern, in part, several killings of those who hold the secret to a cache of gold. Veteran character actor Eduardo Ciannelli once again plays an archvillain who hatches the plot that entangles the stalwart young heroes. See Serials. ∎

Affair in Trinidad (1952), Col. *Dir.* Vincent Sherman; *Sc.* Oscar Saul, James Gunn; *Cast includes:* Rita Hayworth, Glenn Ford, Alexander Scourby, Valerie Bettis, Torin Thatcher, Howard Wendell.

Murder, skullduggery and intrigue dominate this weak plot which centers around a local Trinidad dive and its inhabitants. Rita Hayworth, as a sultry entertainer, agrees to work as an undercover agent for the local police who suspect that spies were responsible for her husband's death. Alexander Scourby portrays a notorious international criminal who heads the spy ring and desires Hayworth. Torin Thatcher, as the local police inspector, suspects Scourby of having something to do with the murder. Glenn Ford, as the victim's brother, appears at the café to investigate his brother's suspicious death. Ford and Hayworth fall for each other, but she cannot reveal her true feelings while working for Thatcher. She allows Scourby to develop his interest in her—much to the consternation of Ford. The law finally catches up with Scourby and his underlings, allowing Ford and Hayworth's love to blossom. ∎

After Tonight (1933), RKO. *Dir.* George Archainbaud; *Sc.* Jane Murfin, Albert LeVino, Worthington Minor; *Cast includes:* Constance Bennett, Gilbert Roland, Edward Ellis, Sam Godfrey, Mischa Auer.

A romantic drama set chiefly in Vienna during World War I, the plot describes the various dangers a spy must face in the course of his or her work. The foreword, in part, underscores this as it pays tribute to these shadow warriors: "While others receive the plaudits of those they have saved, the spy risks his or her all and lives or dies without glory."

Constance Bennett portrays a secret Russian agent operating in Austria. Several times she just barely escapes capture as her fellow agents are caught or shot. Gilbert Roland, as an Austrian captain who heads his country's counterespionage agency, is assigned to smash a Russian spy network. The agents have been highly successful at crippling Austria's war plans and at evading capture. Predictably, Bennett, posing as a nurse, and Roland, whom she had met earlier on her journey to Vienna, fall in love. Roland eventually suspects her of spying and he sets up a trap in which she hands over a secret message. However, her assistant, who has been masquerading as a gypsy street vendor, helps her to escape. Bennett and Roland meet again after the armistice and renew their relationship.

The hackneyed plot was handled infinitely better at least twice during the previous year (*Mata Hari* with Greta Garbo and *Dishonored* with Marlene Dietrich) and numerous other times during the previous decade. When the film lost money at the box office, the studio heads wrongfully placed most of the blame on Bennett's lack of public appeal and dismissed her.

Hollywood's treatment of the Russians in films dealing with World War I was, at best, ambiguous. More often than not the officers and leaders were pictured as vain authoritarians or heavy drinkers, a bellicose lot who indulged in pillaging and rape. (*Bavu* (1923) and Cecil B. DeMille's *The Volga Boatman* (1926) are but two examples.) The Russian masses were portrayed as a people misled by their rulers. Only a handful of films, including *After Tonight* and such antiwar dramas as *The Case of Sergeant Grischa* (1930), depicted Russians in a sympathetic light.

But the major subject matter of *After Tonight* concerns the art of spying, with the film's sympathies resting with the spy. Secret messages are written in invisible ink, sewed into coat linings or inserted into hollow coins. Captured spies go bravely to their death rather than turn informant. In one scene, after a spy is shot by a firing squad, Bennett says to Roland: "It seems so terribly unfair. He was doing the best for his country—just as you are doing." "Yes," Roland adds, "but he probably sent hundreds of men to their death." "So does the man behind the machine-gun," Bennett retorts. "He isn't shot when he's caught." Part of the foreword makes a case for the exigencies of the secret agent: "While nations have armies and navies, while there is greed, hatred and selfish ambition among men, there will be work for and great need of the Spy." ■

Against All Flags (1952), U. *Dir.* George Sherman; *Sc.* Aeneas MacKenzie, Joseph Hoffman; *Cast includes:* Errol Flynn, Maureen O'Hara, Anthony Quinn, Alice Kelley, Mildred Natwick, Robert Warwick.

An English naval officer is dishonorably dismissed from the service so that he can go under cover and carry out his mission as a spy in this early-18th-century swashbuckling sea tale told tongue-in-cheek. Errol Flynn, as the secret agent, gains the confidence of pirate chieftains Anthony Quinn and Maureen O'Hara. His plan is to reach their fortifications and sabotage their defense guns so that an English warship can enter the port and put an end to the pirates' escapades. However, Quinn suspects Flynn whose life is saved by O'Hara. A romance develops between the attractive buccaneer and the newcomer. But Flynn almost loses his standing with O'Hara who quickly displays her jealousy when he rescues a Mogul princess (Alice Kelley) from the pirates' clutches. Once at the fortress he sabotages the cannon so that an English ship can pass in safety and clean things up. Flynn is then rewarded with O'Hara's love for a happy ending. ■

Agent From H.A.R.M. (1966), U. *Dir.* Gerd Oswald; *Sc.* Blair Robertson; *Cast includes:* Mark Richman, Wendell Corey, Carl Esmond, Barbara Bouchet, Martin Kosleck, Rafael Campos.

Originally produced as a television pilot, this minor drama concerns a plot by a crazed archvillain to annihilate America's population by using alien spores that turn people into fungi. Mark Richman, as the title character, portrays another James Bond clone—dapper, sexually active, witty and expert in the art of espionage. He is assigned by his superior (Wendell Corey) to question an alien scientist (Carl Esmond) working in the area of spores. After some cat-and-mouse play, Esmond confides that a recent meteorite contains an unusual species of spores that can transform humans into fungi. The scientist, who is hard at work trying to produce an antidote, adds that an enemy agent (Martin Kosleck) and his minions plan to spray the

lethal spores on America's food crops. Richman then proceeds through some not-too-clever sleuthing to hunt down the agents. Barbara Bouchet, who has won the confidence of the scientist by posing as his long-lost niece, actually works for Kosleck. Although Richman foils the diabolical plot in time, the scientist has injected himself with the antidote, which proves ineffective against the spores. In the mortuary Richman writes on the heroic dead man's identification label: "Human Being." ■

Air Raid Wardens (1943), MGM. *Dir.* Edward Sedgwick; *Sc.* Martin Rackin, Jack Jevne, Charles Rogers, Harry Crane; *Cast includes:* Laurel and Hardy, Edgar Kennedy, Jacqueline White, Stephen McNally, Donald Meek.

Stan and Ollie, in their own unique way, help the war effort on the home front in this slight World War II comedy. After they are rejected for military service by their local draft board, the boys, as two incompetent businessmen, become air raid wardens, positions they handle with their usual ineptness. However, they accidentally manage to capture a nest of Nazi agents. Unfortunately, even with the help of four screenwriters and support from veteran character player Edgar Kennedy, the film provides few laughs. It marked the beginning of their decline for this comic duo. ■

Alaska Patrol (1949), Film Classics. *Dir.* Jack Bernhard; *Sc.* Arthur Hoerl; *Cast includes:* Richard Travis, Helen Westcott, Jim Griffith, Emory Parnell, Selmer Jackson.

Richard Travis portrays a U.S. Navy intelligence officer who masquerades as a spy to snare a network of enemy agents in this low-budget drama. Much of the plot occurs aboard a freighter off the coast of Alaska where Travis cavorts with villains Emory Parnell and Raif Harolde. Helen Westcott plays a government secretary. An otherwise fairly routine espionage tale, the film rates a cut above average because of its documentary-like approach. ■

Alias the Lone Wolf (1927), Col. *Dir.* Edward H. Griffith; *Sc.* Dorothy Howell, Edward H. Griffith; *Cast includes:* Bert Lytell, Lois Wilson, Ned Sparks, Paulette Duval, William V. Mong.

Based on Louis Joseph Vance's fictional

Robin Hood of crime, this weak drama about a gang of jewel thieves features Bert Lytell as the title character. Lytell, working for the U.S. Secret Service, masquerades as an underworld character in an effort to expose a group of jewel smugglers. Operating alone as usual and outnumbered by the miscreants, the Lone Wolf eventually exposes the gang, including a young woman (Paulette Duval), who are attempting to smuggle the contraband into the country. Ned Sparks provides some comedy relief. ∎

Alien Enemy, An (1918), Panalta. *Dir.* Wallace Worsley; *Sc.* Monte M. Katterjohn; *Cast includes:* Louise Glaum, Thurston Hall, Mary Jane Irving, Albert Allardt, Charles C. Hammond, Jay Morley.

A World War I drama, the film concerns a young woman whose American parents were killed by a sadistic Prussian officer when she was very little. Adopted by a kindly German family, the orphan (Louise Glaum) is never told about her original parents. When World War I erupts, German agents persuade her to spy for them. She meets and falls in love with an American (Thurston Hall) involved in the war effort, and they soon marry. Dissatisfied with her espionage assignment even before she had met Hall, she now gives it up entirely.

The Prussian (Albert Allardt) who had killed her parents learns that her husband has been assigned to go to France. He threatens to tell her husband about her espionage activities if she doesn't steal secret documents. Glaum gives the agent false papers, but her husband suspects her of spying and leaves her. Later, he discovers the truth, and Glaum avenges her parents' death by killing their murderer. The couple are then reunited. The film has patriotic scenes of American troops liberating French villages and sequences of a prisoner-of-war camp where Germans attempt to escape. Glaum plays a dual role, that of a mother and daughter. ∎

All Through the Night (1941), WB. *Dir.* Vincent Sherman; *Sc.* Leonard Spigelgass, Edwin Gilbert; *Cast includes:* Humphrey Bogart, Conrad Veidt, Kaaren Verne, Jane Darwell, Frank McHugh, Jackie Gleason, Judith Anderson.

Humphrey Bogart stars in this World War II comedy drama about spies and hoodlums in New York City's Yorkville district. The plot involves Nazi spies who plan to blow up a battleship in a local harbor. When Bogart, a small-time Broadway gambler, learns that his supplier of cheesecake, a German-American baker, has been murdered by Nazi spies, he decides to investigate. Clues lead him to a nightclub singer (Kaaren Verne) who, because of her European relatives, is forced to act as a liaison for the killers. Bogart seems romantically interested in Verne, but continues to pursue the killers. He and his Broadway cronies later discover a hidden room and a gang of spies led by Conrad Veidt. Bogart and his pals then infiltrate the spies' headquarters, uncover a plot to blow up a battleship and capture the enemy agents after a wild fist fight. The villainous Veidt and one of his henchmen (Peter Lorre) escape. When Veidt orders Lorre to go on with the sabotage mission, the underling refuses. The master spy kills Lorre in cold blood and pilots an explosive-filled speedboat toward the targeted battleship. But Bogart foils Veidt's plot.

The blend of drama and comedy mixes pleasantly as Bogart and his Broadway rival, played by Barton MacLane, do a spoof of gangster movies. Comic highlights include a midnight search of a suspicious warehouse and a brawl between Bogart and his cronies and a group of Nazi sympathizers. The film, which effectively evokes the German-American Yorkville section of New York, offers a large cast of comics, including a young Jackie Gleason, Phil Silvers and William Demarest. Also, several character players who specialized in spy and Nazi roles, appeared in the film, including Martin Kosleck, Hans Schumm and Otto Reichow. ∎

Amazing Impostor, The (1919), Pathé. *Dir.* Lloyd Ingraham; *Sc.* Frank Howard Clark; *Cast includes:* Mary Miles Minter, Edward Jobson, Margaret Shelby, Carl Stockdale, Allan Forrest, Henry Barrows.

A young innocent brings upon herself a series of misadventures aboard a train in this comedy about jewel thieves, Bolshevik spies and the search for romance. Mary Miles Minter, as the whimsical daughter of a chewing gum mogul, dreams of a more romantic life in an effort to escape the reality of her father's mundane business. She meets a Russian countess during a train journey and is impressed by the aristocratic woman. The countess, however, actually is a jewel thief. Minter allows herself to be taken in by the bogus countess and exchanges identities with her. The result of the switch is that Minter is chased by other thieves who want the jewels and by two Bolshevik agents who think she is carrying important documents. Meanwhile, Allan Forrest, as an amateur sleuth, is attracted to her and tries to help her out of some of her predicaments. The culprits are arrested, Minter reveals her true identity and the young couple profess their love for each other. See Red Scare of 1919–1920. ∎

Amazing Lovers (1922), Jans. *Dir.* B.A. Rolfe; *Sc.* Charles A. Logue; *Cast includes:* Diana Allen, Marc MacDermott.

Diana Allen, as a French secret service agent, is assigned to uncover an international counterfeit ring in this routine drama. A gang of counterfeiters, operating in New York, is turning out bogus French money. An unscrupulous banker is collaborating with the gang for his own ends; he seeks huge potential profits as a result of the falling exchange rate.

The French branch of the gang sends Allen to the U.S. to transport the counterfeit money back to France. Meanwhile, the leader of the gang falls in love with her. While they are in America, the gang leader has a falling out with the banker and kills him. To protect Allen from deportation, the gang leader then arranges a marriage between Allen and a young American who, under the influence of alcohol, believes he has committed the murder. Allen ultimately effects the arrest of the entire outfit. The title refers to her hasty marriage to the dupe who, it turns out, is actually her husband. ∎

Ambassador, The (1984), Cannon. *Dir.* J. Lee Thompson; *Sc.* Max Jack; *Cast includes:* Robert Mitchum, Ellen Burstyn, Rock Hudson, Fabio Testi, Donald Pleasence, Heli Goldenberg.

A U.S. ambassador, against all odds, attempts to reconcile the monumental differences between Israeli and Palestinian students in this intelligent drama of intrigue and frustration. Robert Mitchum, as the idealistic and patient ambassador, neglects his own marriage as he goes about pursuing peace between the two dissident factions. Two such meetings end in bloody violence. Rock Hudson, as Mitchum's security adviser, has his hands full rescuing the ambassador whom he has warned of the dangers in such a mission. Ellen Burstyn, as Mitchum's alcoholic wife,

meanwhile is having an affair with a P.L.O. terrorist.

Mitchum faces opposition from both Israeli and Palestinian leaders who prefer that he not meddle in their politics. They are also prepared to sabotage his efforts at bringing together those with open minds. Israeli intelligence officers obtain films of his wife's liaison and turn them over to the Palestinians, who in turn plan to use them to blackmail Mitchum. Again, Hudson intervenes to prevent Mitchum and his wife from gaining acceptance and recognition from students representing both factions. The film was adapted from Elmore Leonard's novel *52 Pick Up* which was remade in 1986 into another film using the original title. ∎

Ambush Bay (1966), UA. *Dir.* Ron Winston; *Sc.* Marve Feinberg, Ib Melchior; *Cast includes:* Hugh O'Brian, Mickey Rooney, James Mitchum, Pete Masterson, Harry Lauter, Greg Amsterdam.

A Japanese-American secret agent sacrifices her own life to help the success of the Allied invasion of the Philippines in this World War II action drama. A patrol of nine marines is sent on a secret mission in the Philippines to contact a Japanese who has vital information concerning General MacArthur's proposed invasion. The leathernecks meet stiff resistance as they traverse the jungle and lose several of their buddies and their native guide before they locate their contact. To their surprise, the person is a young Japanese woman (Tisa Chang) from California. She informs the patrol that the enemy has mined the location of the landing. With their radio destroyed and their number reduced to two, the pair are forced to destroy the mines before the American ships reach the mine field.

The film has an abundance of heroics. Hugh O'Brian, as a tough, determined sergeant, takes command of the patrol when its officer is killed the first day. O'Brian dies manning a machine gun while giving his fellow marine time to detonate the mine field. Mickey Rooney portrays an experienced combat marine who voluntarily goes to his death blowing up several Japanese soldiers while cracking a joke. Wounded in a previous gun battle, he waits for the enemy to approach, holds out two grenades and quips: "Guess what I got for you. Baked potatoes. You can eat these with the jackets on them."

As the Japanese discharge their rifles into him, he tosses the grenades into their midst. The Japanese-American spy who aids the remnants of the patrol offers herself to the leader of the pursuing Japanese, thereby giving the marines a chance to escape. When the Japanese officer discovers her ploy, he kills her. James Mitchum, as a green private, narrates the tale and is the only survivor in this routine drama.

The film ends with a voice-over of General MacArthur's "I shall return" speech to the Filipinos as the camera focuses on Mitchum waiting on the shore for a submarine to pick him up. Although MacArthur's words were (and still are) very poignant, they have little to do with the actual film, which relies more on heroics and bravado than on realism or historical perspective. See Philippines. ∎

Ambushers, The (1967), Col. *Dir.* Henry Levin; *Sc.* Herbert Baker; *Cast includes:* Dean Martin, Senta Berger, Janice Rule, James Gregory, Albert Salmi, Kurt Kaszner.

The weakest entry in the Matt Helm series, the film once again stars Dean Martin as the cool secret agent who is assigned by his agency chief to locate Janice Rule. It seems she has been kidnapped by the sinister Albert Salmi. Senta Berger, as a fellow agent from another country, provides some of the romantic interest for Martin. Character actor Kurt Kaszner portrays a humorous henchman, a Mexican beer mogul, working for Salmi. Beverly Adams repeats her role as Martin's secretary. Double-entendres, some gadgetry and a costly production again proliferate, but this time around the film, based on the novel by Donald Hamilton, suffers in acting, repetition and inept plot resolution. ∎

American Buds (1918), Fox. *Dir.* Kenean Buel; *Sc.* Kenean Buel; *Cast includes:* Jane Lee, Katherine Lee, Albert Gran, Regina Quinn, Lucille Southerwaite.

A light World War I comedy about two young orphans and their misadventures, the film features the Lee sisters as two mischievous children placed in an orphan asylum located near an army camp. They become entangled in a romantic triangle concerning the colonel's daughter and her two suitors. The Lee children resolve the predicament when they expose one of the men as a spy. All turns out well for the girls when the colonel discovers that they are the children of his missing daughter. Jane and Katherine Lee, popular silent screen performers of the period, made several comedies involving spies. ∎

American Civil War: intelligence and covert actions. It is difficult to separate the wheat from the chaff in dealing with espionage during the Civil War. Although a number of spy accounts, including those of Emma Edmonds and Elizabeth Van Lew, were published after the war, their veracity is greatly in doubt. In a similar vein, the credit claimed by Belle Boyd, a Confederate agent, for informing General "Stonewall" Jackson of Northern unpreparedness at Royal Front, Virginia, and thus enabling the Southern general to defeat his adversaries, is suspect; apparently, Jackson already possessed this information before Boyd approached him.

Nevertheless, Hollywood, inspired by the actual activities of several real-life agents such as Pauline Cushman, leaped at the opportunity to dramatize the exploits of female spies during the Civil War. Two Civil War films reenact the undercover work of Cushman, a Union spy. Selig released *Pauline Cushman, the Federal Spy* in 1913. MGM's 1934 drama *Operator 13* starred Marion Davies as a Union spy who works alongside Cushman, portrayed by Katherine Alexander, who has a secondary role in the film.

Other films relied more heavily on fictitious plots. In "The Girl Spy Before Vicksburg" (1911), a silent drama, the heroine disguises herself as a member of a Union munitions convoy and destroys the powder wagon. The incidents may well have been based on the published memoirs of Loreta Janeta Velasquez, a Confederate spy who often impersonated men during her undercover activities. In *Madam Who?* (1918) a young Confederate woman, willing to sacrifice her life for the South, engages in the dangerous act of espionage. Betty Compson in *Court Martial* (1928) portrays the leader of a group of Southern marauders. *Virginia City* (1940) features Miriam Hopkins as a Confederate spy. She falls in love with Errol Flynn, a Union officer trying to prevent a wagon train loaded with gold from reaching Confederate lines. In the comedy *Advance to the Rear* (1964) Stella Stevens portrays a Confederate spy.

Allan Pinkerton, intelligence chief for General McClellan who was in charge of the Army of the Potomac in 1861–1862, liked to have people think of his organization as the "Secret

Service." In so doing, Pinkerton encouraged the impression that his unit was a highly centralized, national department of the Union government. Nevertheless, Pinkerton did manage to snare a number of Confederate spies, including Rose Greenhow, who allegedly had alerted Confederate General Beauregard of a threatening Union attack and thus enabled the general to defeat the North at the First Battle of Bull Run. Pinkerton had counterespionage agents in the Washington area and was able to keep that city relatively free of Southern spies. Three films set during the Civil War period portray Pinkerton busy at his espionage work. In *Hands Up* (1926), a silent comedy, Raymond Griffith, a gifted silent screen comic, plays a Southern spy assigned to prevent a gold shipment from reaching President Lincoln. Meanwhile, Pinkerton sends a Union spy to make certain the shipment gets through. In *Operator 13* (1934) Pinkerton solicits the services of a Union woman (Marion Davies) to spy on the South. And in *The Tall Target* (1951), about a plot to assassinate newly elected President Lincoln, Pinkerton is portrayed in a cameo role.

Neither of the adversaries in the Civil War had substantial secret information concerning the other side. The Confederacy had just been born, but the Union, despite experiences in the War of 1812 and the Mexican War of 1846–1848, had failed to establish an effective intelligence organization. The terrain, railroad lines, industrial output, natural resources and population were known to both sides. Officers in the Northern and Southern armies were familiar with each other and many of them had been classmates at West Point. Intelligence was thus looked upon as an informal, haphazard undertaking.

After President Lincoln dismissed General McClellan in 1863, General Hooker assumed command of the Army of the Potomac and appointed Col. George Sharpe to take charge of his Bureau of Military Information. It was this agency that later grew, under General Grant, into a modern intelligence service.

The South had, in the Knights of the Golden Circle, a convenient subversive movement. The Knights, although originally organized as a social institution, had undergone a political transformation. They supported the institution of slavery and were decidedly pro-South. They had been organized in the South but, by the time of the Civil War, had spread to several Northern states. With Southern encourage- ment, the Knights sabotaged the Northern war effort and engaged in espionage. They attempted to run weapons into Kansas and Missouri to aid Confederate raiding parties there. The Knights cooperated with the group of Northern Democrats known as Copperheads, who were opposed to the war.

The Northwest Conspiracy was the most daring scheme undertaken by the Knights and Copperheads. The idea was to encourage, with the assistance of the Copperheads and the Sons of Liberty, as the Knights were now known, the defection from the Union of several Western states which would then establish a Northwest Confederacy sympathetic to the South. The plan never reached fruition, thanks to the penetration of the Sons of Liberty by Union agents. The Northwest Conspiracy provided the basis for much of the plot of *Operator 13* (1934), a romantic drama starring Gary Cooper and Marion Davies as spies for the South and North, respectively. Other spy dramas have dealt more generally with Southern conspiracies in the West. In *The Copperhead* (1920), for example, Lionel Barrymore portrays a Union agent whom President Lincoln has secretly assigned to infiltrate the Copperheads. In *Rebel City* (1953) Southern sympathizers stir up trouble in Kansas. Finally, *The Black Dakotas* (1954) concerned a Confederate agent who attempts to incite Indian troubles in the West to divert Union troops from the battlefield.

Espionage agents utilized modern technology for the first time during the Civil War. Balloons were used for reconnaissance purposes. Thaddeus Lowe demonstrated to President Lincoln the use of these balloons in 1861. He flew over Washington in his balloon and reported, via a telegraph wire, what he observed to the War Department, which telegraphed the results to President Lincoln. Lowe eventually developed seven reconnaissance balloons from which he was able to direct federal fire against Confederate positions. The Confederates used several balloons but were never able to develop their potential because they lacked the technology of the North. See Andrews' Raid, Pauline Cushman, Northwest Conspiracy. ■

American Guerrilla in the Philippines

(1950), TCF. *Dir.* Fritz Lang; *Sc.* Lamar Trotti; *Cast includes:* Tyrone Power, Micheline Presle, Tom Ewell, Bob Patten, Tommy Cook, Jack Elam.

A small group of American and native forces carry out behind-the-lines covert operations against the invading Japanese from 1942 until General MacArthur's return to the Philippines in this World War II action drama. Tyrone Power, as a U.S. ensign, and a fellow sailor, played by Tom Ewell, take refuge in the jungle after their PT boat is destroyed. At first, they make several attempts to rejoin American forces. Micheline Presle, as the wife of a French plantation owner, tries to persuade the Americans to join forces with Filipino guerrillas against the Japanese. But Power is determined to rejoin U.S. forces. After several setbacks, he makes contact with an American colonel who orders Power back to Leyte. "What General MacArthur wants is a spy service—intelligence—a people's army ready to act when we're ready and not before," the colonel explains. "You'll be in charge of radio operations on Leyte."

The film, adapted from Ira Wolfert's novel, includes several rousing action scenes involving suspenseful encounters between the guerrillas and the enemy troops. See Philippines. ∎

American Revolution: intelligence and covert actions.

The American revolutionaries throughout the war were faced by a British army superior in firepower and numbers as well as a world-class naval power. To effectively meet the challenge, the Americans made extensive use of espionage agents, many of whom were working for the Patriot cause prior to the outbreak of hostilities. The British side similarly used spies; however, the British had to develop their espionage network during the course of the war.

The Sons of Liberty were organized in 1765 in Boston in opposition to the Stamp Act which had been passed by the British Parliament earlier that year. Whereas previous tax levies by the Crown had fallen disproportionately on different sections of the colonies, the Stamp Act affected everyone by imposing a uniform tax on newspapers, legal papers, dice and cards. In so doing, the Stamp Act unified the Colonists against Great Britain.

The Sons of Liberty formed a paramilitary organization throughout the colonies. They rioted, attacked stamp agents and destroyed the stamps. They then struck at British forts in North and South Carolina and, by means of terror, forced all the stamp agents to resign. Faced with this mounting violent and costly opposition, Parliament revoked the Stamp Act the following year. *The Howards of Virginia* (1940), a historical drama set during the American Revolution, reenacts several historical incidents, including the Stamp Act riots.

In reaction to Parliament's step backward, the Sons of Liberty evolved from a militant organization into a clandestine espionage network. It soon merged with a newer organization, the Committees of Correspondence. The Committees, like their predecessor, began in that hotbed of revolution that was called Boston. Sam Adams was one of the leading radicals who organized the Committees in 1772. They were instrumental in swaying public opinion against the Crown. Very often they functioned as an illegal, secret government by enforcing their will on the local population. The Committees of Correspondence accelerated the growth towards revolution. One of their strategies was the development in 1775 of a more militant arm, the Committees of Safety, which seized British arms depots and organized armed militias. D. W. Griffith's epic drama *America* (1924) brings to life numerous historical figures, including Samuel Adams, and depicts his role as a leader of the Revolution. The historical drama *Johnny Tremain* (1957) also recounts Adams' role in the intrigues of the period.

Paul Revere, a messenger for the Committees of Correspondence and Safety, was one of several members who kept tabs on British army maneuvers in the greater Boston area. Revere and other members warned local Patriot militias of any sudden hostile British moves. On April 16, 1775, Dr. Joseph Warren assigned Revere to warn local Patriots against the impending British seizure of arms at Concord, Massachusetts. The weapons were moved from Concord in time. Revere was on the road again on April 18, warning local militias against a second British march against Concord. He was captured and then released *sans* horse; in the meantime, another Patriot rider completed Revere's celebrated midnight ride to Concord. Revere's famous ride was depicted in more than half a dozen films. One of the earliest was "The Midnight Ride of Paul Revere" (1907), a short Edison production directed by film pioneer Edwin S. Porter. *Washington at Valley Forge* (1914), *Cardigan* (1922), *Janice Meredith* (1924), *America* (1924) and *Johnny Tremain* (1957) are other films which include the historical ride.

After the actual outbreak of war, General Washington, needing a more professional reconnaissance unit, turned to Lt. Col. Thomas Knowlton, a veteran of the French and Indian Wars. Knowlton's Rangers, as they were known, scouted behind enemy lines and provided significant intelligence regarding the geography of the territory in dispute. Joshua Mersereau, a native of New York City, along with his two sons and brother, reported British troop movements on Staten Island directly to Washington. They deliberately leaked disinformation to British intelligence.

Captain Benjamin Tallmadge ran another espionage apparatus known as the "Culper Ring"; he also reported directly to Washington. His most celebrated case was the capture of Major André, the British Colonel who conspired with Benedict Arnold. Robert Townsend, a clothing merchant who worked as an espionage agent for Tallmadge, reported all the gossip among the British troops who entered his clothing store and coffee shop. The reports were written either in invisible ink or cryptograms. "Benedict Arnold and Major André" (1909), a short silent drama, is one of a handful of films to reenact the collusion between Arnold and André. Washington himself was the head of the Patriot's intelligence network. Hercules Mulligan, one of his New York spies, learned of two British assassination attempts on Washington and thus saved his life.

In the winter of 1777, the Continental Army, bivouacking in Morristown, New Jersey, was badly demoralized. At the time, it only required a determined British assault to break the back of the Revolution. Washington planted disinformation with British intelligence that he was planning to attack them on two fronts— in New York City and Philadelphia—and thus convinced the British to regroup in defensive positions. The British similarly relied on secret agents. However, even though the Loyalists supplied the crown with valuable intelligence nuggets, there was no organized espionage network in existence at the outbreak of hostilities.

Benjamin Church, an army doctor, was a double agent who worked for the Committees of Correspondence in Boston but whose real allegiance lay with the British. He provided the British with precise information regarding weapons caches and movement of troops.

He was so successful in deceiving the Patriots that, in 1775, he was placed in charge of the Continental Army's hospital in Cambridge, Massachusetts. Unfortunately for Dr. Church, his female agent was intercepted and questioned by George Washington. She revealed that Church was an informant for Gage. Church was tried and convicted of collaborating with the enemy. He served time in prison and was eventually permitted to leave the country. The doctor portrayed by George Sanders in The Scarlet Coat (1955) may well have been based on Church. In this historical drama the doctor, working for the British, tries to convince British officers that a wealthy Tory actually is a Colonial spy.

Joseph Galloway was in the perfect position for a British spy, for he had been a delegate to the First Continental Congress in 1774 and was privy to information at the source. It was at the First Continental Congress that Galloway became a British agent. He delivered secret maps of Pennsylvania to General William Howe and claimed that he had provided key information responsible for British success against Washington at Brandywine in 1779. Galloway generally exaggerated his own importance, especially when he claimed to have fielded a network of 80 spies. It does appear that he was able to provide details of American fortifications at Valley Forge and notes of the debates inside the Continental Congress. He furnished British Admiral Richard Howe with maps of the Delaware River as well as Patriot fortifications along that river. The British appointed Galloway Chief of Police of Philadelphia during their tenure of that city in 1777–1778. This British agent had a very active imagination and at various times made plans to kidnap Patriot government officials, including the entire Continental Congress. None of these plans ever bore fruit. Following the Revolution, Galloway escaped to Great Britain and remained there until his death in 1803.

The individual British espionage agents in the New England and Middle states were organized into a comprehensive network by Major André, who was special assistant to General Clinton. He was at the point of achieving the most spectacular coup of the war—the defection of General Benedict Arnold together with the surrender of West Point—when he was caught and hanged in 1780. These incidents are reenacted in the historical drama The Scarlet Coat (1955).

Washington's agents were able to deceive British General Clinton into believing that Continental troops were planning an attack on the British stronghold of New York City. Clinton naturally remained in New York and was unable to assist Cornwallis at Yorktown, Virginia, where the actual attack took place. The combined French and American forces thus defeated Cornwallis on October 19, 1781. Minor skirmishes continued, but the British defeat at Yorktown marked the virtual end of the war. Great Britain turned to its interests on the Continent and signed the Peace of Paris which recognized American independence. See George Washington. ■

Amsterdam Kill, The (1977), Golden Harvest. *Dir.* Robert Clouse; *Sc.* Robert Clouse, Gregory Tiefer; *Cast includes:* Robert Mitchum, Bradford Dillman, Richard Egan, Leslie Nielsen, Keye Luke, George Chung.

U.S. drug enforcement agencies in Hong Kong and Amsterdam learn that several international narcotics dealers have been assassinated. Both agencies conclude that a major trafficker is seeking to gain control of the market. Robert Mitchum, as a former narcotics agent who was dismissed for receiving a payoff, becomes involved when a Chinese drug lord (Keye Luke) asks Mitchum to meet with him in Amsterdam. The American, drifting aimlessly in London, agrees to the meeting and learns that Luke wants to retire from the illicit trade. He is willing to inform on the key dealers and their operations in return for a large sum of money and asylum.

Mitchum arranges the deal with his friend (Bradford Dillman) who now heads the Hong Kong branch of the U.S. Drug Enforcement Agency. Several busts, coordinated with the Hong Kong police, fail to turn up any major dealers. It seems that there is a leak in security. Mitchum, treated with contempt by both U.S. and local officials, returns in disgust to Amsterdam where his contact is murdered. Following several beatings and captures, Mitchum gains possession of Luke's notebook containing the vital information he needs. He finally tracks down the key figures in the conspiracy, which include the chief of the Amsterdam U.S. agency (Leslie Nielsen) and Dillman in Hong Kong. ■

Anarchists in the U.S. The anarchists insinuated themselves into the general labor mayhem of the last two decades of the nineteenth century. Although primarily a political movement, the American anarchists identified themselves with the labor movement in its struggle with the capitalists; in so doing, they managed to join the mainstream of American labor in a manner they were unable to do previously.

The struggle for the eight-hour workday was one of the major causes of the labor movement at the end of the nineteenth century. During the course of that struggle, the workers in Chicago in 1886 were locked out of their jobs and opposed by the police; by armed strikebreakers who had been deputized as law officers with weapons; and by the Pinkertons, a private police force. During one battle between the strikers and their opponents two strikers were shot dead by the police. August Spies, the German-born editor of Chicago's anarchist newspaper *Die Arbeiter Zeitung*, called for revenge and scheduled a mass protest meeting the next day in Haymarket Square. The police intervened during the protest on May 4, 1886; someone threw a bomb into the middle of the police lines, killing seven policemen. There was no evidence linking anyone to the bomb attack. Nevertheless, in the pervasive climate of fear by the ruling classes of the time, eight anarchists were found guilty and sentenced to death. Three of the defendants had their sentences commuted to terms in jail, one committed suicide and the other four, including Spies, were hanged in 1887. Screen comic Buster Keaton incorporated some of the Haymarket riot events into his 1922 comedy *Cops*. He had a crazed anarchist toss a bomb into the midst of a police officers' parade.

Undoubtedly the key event in the anarchist movement in the United States was the assassination of President McKinley in 1901 by the son of Polish immigrants, Leon Czolgosz. Czolgosz was a laid-off laborer and self-educated anarchist who attended chapter meetings in Chicago where he heard the radical Emma Goldman speak. He was convinced that all rulers were evil and that it was right to kill them to improve the lot of the common man.

Outraged by the murder of President McKinley, the American public united in its abhorrence of the anarchists. The popular media uniformly lashed out at the violent and terrorist character of the anarchist movement. Its vision of a society free from the constraints of the State was, naturally, ignored, and emphasis was placed on the anarchists' rejection of church, family, marriage and statutes. The anarchist became the quintessence of evil in the world; *Harper's Weekly* went so far as to suggest that Satan himself was the ultimate anarchist.

President Theodore Roosevelt, who succeeded McKinley, in his speech before Congress in 1901, insisted that anarchists were more depraved than ordinary criminals; whereas other criminals were the products of unfortunate social conditions, anarchists consciously rejected the opportunities offered in this country and intentionally committed violence against innocent victims. Roosevelt suggested that anarchist writings be prohibited, that anarchists themselves be deported and that Congress bar the immigration of anarchists into this country. Congress in 1903 heeded the President's call and passed legislation barring the immigration of anarchists.

Nevertheless, the anarchist movement in the U.S. survived. Its principles were adopted by the International Workers of the World (I.W.W.), the most radical union in the first decade of the 20th century. The union called several strikes, incurred the wrath of employers and the American Federation of Labor and faded into relative obscurity after World War I. Washington enacted further anti-anarchist legislation in 1918 and in the following years deported many foreign-born anarchists and troublemakers.

The movie industry was generally antagonistic in its portrayals of anarchists and their causes. Several early silent films focused on the more flagrant actions of the movement, exploiting the sensational bombings that appeared in the headlines. In *The Bomb Throwers* (1915), for example, terrorists threaten the life and family of an honest district attorney. After convincing Tony, a poor Italian immigrant widower, that the D.A. was responsible for his wife's death, they hand him a bomb to be placed under the home of their victim. In *The Ace of Hearts* (1921), with Lon Chaney, anarchists plan to cleanse society—and thereby improve the world—by assassinating wealthy industrialists. Their main weapon— the bomb. In *A Ship Comes In* (1928), with Rudolph Schildkraut and Louise Dresser, an anarchist conceals a bomb in a cake which explodes and wounds a judge. *Safe for Democracy* (1919) attacks members of the International Workers of the World, a radical union of the period, equating them with foreign agents trying to subvert war production. On the comic side, Buster Keaton, in his two-reeler "The High Sign" (1922), focuses on an organization of assassins who hire Keaton as their emissary.

For most of the 1920s and through the 1930s Hollywood relegated the image of the anarchist to an unsympathetic comic figure— a wild-eyed, bearded, scruffy individual—often with bomb in hand. ■

André, John (1750–1780). André was born into a Swiss merchant family that had settled in London. He studied mathematics at the University of Geneva and the University of Gottingen prior to purchasing a lieutenant's commission in the Seventh Regiment of Foot in 1771. Sent to Canada during the American Revolution, he was captured by Washington's troops in 1775 and incarcerated. He was released in a prisoner swap within a year.

He was moved to Philadelphia where he served as intelligence officer for General Gray. It was in that capacity that he was to become involved, through Elizabeth Shippen, a wealthy local Tory, with Benedict Arnold. Shippen eventually married Arnold.

When the British were forced out of Philadelphia, André's superiors appointed him to intelligence duties with General Clinton in New York City where he ran Clinton's espionage network. He soon began negotiating a major coup with American General Benedict Arnold for the surrender of West Point. André had a meeting with Arnold on the evening of September 21, 1780, in Haverstraw, New York. Unfortunately for him and, ultimately, Arnold, André was unable to return to the British ship which had brought him to the meeting; he disguised himself as a civilian and attempted to pass through Continental lines. André was once again captured, but this time with more dire consequences.

When the Colonists carefully examined his possessions, they discovered several of General Arnold's documents. Arnold learned of André's arrest and escaped to New York City where he received the protection of Britain's General Clinton. The Americans proposed to exchange André for Arnold, but General Clinton refused. An American military court tried André for spying and sentenced him to death by hanging. André's request to be shot as a soldier was rejected and he was hanged in 1780.

André's military exploits appeared in only a handful of minor but generally accurate historical spy dramas. "Benedict Arnold and Major André" (1909) reenacts the highlights in the ignoble military career of Benedict Arnold. These include a meeting with General George Washington, the collusion between Arnold and Major André, the latter's finish upon a scaffold and Arnold's death in England. In *The Scarlet Coat* (1955), with Cornel Wilde, Michael Wilding and George Sanders, Wilding portrays Major John André, a British officer, who develops a fondness for his adversary, a fictitious American spy and double agent (Cornel Wilde) who is trying to uncover a traitor (Benedict Arnold). ■

Andrews' Raid (also known as the Great Locomotive Chase). This bold raid behind Confederate lines on April 22, 1862, carried out by a small force of Northern soldiers, began the tradition of awarding the Congressional Medal of Honor, the nation's highest military award, for unusual bravery.

A squad of 22 Union soldiers under James J. Andrews volunteered to penetrate Confederate lines and cut rail communication between Marietta, Georgia, and Chattanooga, Tennessee. The troop of spies, dressed in civilian clothes, seized a train pulled by a locomotive named *The General* and headed west to destroy bridges and other communication links on the line. Confederate forces discovered the plan and chased the Northerners in another locomotive named *Texas* for a distance of about 90 miles and captured the hijackers after *The General* had used all its fuel. Andrews and seven of his troop were executed as spies. The remainder, after surviving internment in prisoner-of-war camps, were the first to be awarded the Congressional Medal of Honor.

The historic raid inspired two silent films and a Walt Disney feature. "Railroad Raiders of '62" (1911), a short drama by Kalem studio, presented a generally accurate account of the incident. Buster Keaton, in his highly acclaimed comedy classic *The General* (1927), retained the framework of the original raid but added many inventive gags. Walt Disney Studios produced *The Great Locomotive Chase* (1956), a fictionalized but colorful version of the incident. ■

Angry Hills, The (1959), MGM. *Dir.* Robert Aldrich; *Sc.* A. I. Bezzerides; *Cast includes:* Robert Mitchum, Elisabeth Mueller, Stanley Baker, Gia Scala, Theodore Bikel, Sebastian Cabot.

An American war correspondent, carrying vital information about members of the Greek underground, attempts to escape from Greece while he is pursued by the Gestapo in this World War II drama set in 1941 on the eve of Nazi occupation. Robert Mitchum, as the reporter who agrees to help the Greek resistance by delivering a list of Greek agents to British intelligence, becomes the target of the Nazis who want the list of names while anti-Nazi forces try to assist him in his escape. Elisabeth Mueller portrays an undercover Greek agent and mistress to a Gestapo chief. Stanley Baker plays the head of the Gestapo in Athens and Mueller's lover. Gia Scala, as a poor villager, nurses Mitchum back to health, helps him make contact with the Greek underground and falls in love with him. Theodore Bikel, as a vicious and cowardly Greek collaborator, offers his pretty half-sister to German officials as a means of furthering his own career.

The clever dialogue and finely etched characterizations are a notch above the average espionage drama in this work based on Leon Uris' novel. "You journalists," Donald Wolfit, as an intellectual, anti-Fascist Greek patriot, muses about Mitchum's profession, "I envy you. The world's in flames, you stand apart as if you were gods. The folly of man is no more to you than a news item." Marius Goring, as a hypochondriac German officer, ponders cynically about his nation's military successes. "The Fuhrer leads us from victory to victory," he says to Gestapo chief Stanley Baker. "And each victory leads us further away from home. A few more such victories and we may never return." Baker gives a sympathetic and humane portrayal of the Gestapo chief who abhors violence—an interpretation often employed by Hollywood in World War II dramas produced after the conflict. ■

Apocalypse Now (1979), UA. *Dir.* Francis Ford Coppola; *Sc.* John Milius, Francis Ford Coppola; *Cast includes:* Marlon Brando, Martin Sheen, Robert Duvall, Fred Forrest, Sam Bottoms.

Director Francis Coppola's epic about the Vietnam conflict and its effects on its participants consciously draws upon Joseph Conrad's 1911 novella *Heart of Darkness*. Both works concentrate chiefly on a river journey that ultimately leads into a world of darkness, terror and death in which the pivotal character of each exclaims: "The horror! The horror!"

Martin Sheen portrays a U.S. intelligence officer sent into Cambodia by his superiors to "terminate" the command of Kurtz (Marlon Brando), a megalomaniac American officer whose military tactics are disapproved of by the top brass. "There's a conflict within every human heart between the rational and the irrational," a superior officer explains to Sheen, "but the good does not always triumph." During his trip on the river Sheen encounters an enigmatic colonel (Robert Duvall) who commands a squadron of helicopters. Duvall, a surfing enthusiast, orders a helicopter raid on a Viet Cong village while his loudspeakers blast out Wagner's *Die Walkure*. Before he engages in surfing, he orders one last napalm attack on some nearby enemy mortar positions. "I love the smell of napalm in the morning," Duvall admits.

When Sheen finally arrives at Brando's camp, he witnesses corpses dangling from trees, scattered skulls and crucified bodies. Sheen meets with the renegade leader who leads a private army of tribesmen. Brando, seen mostly in shadows, engages in some arcane commentary and concludes that "we must make friends with moral terror," that "it is judgment that defeats us." Using a knife, Sheen carries out his assignment. This final sequence has been attacked by audiences and critics alike as muddled and incomprehensible.

Throughout most of the film, however, Coppola transcends the realistic world of warfare to evoke a surrealistic environment of mist and darkness symbolizing conspiracy and evil. When he uses lights, as in a night sequence at a U.S.O. station along the river, they represent a carnival world of fantasy for the soldiers and the crew of Sheen's patrol boat. "Beautiful," says one of the sailors, "it's just beautiful." The film is less a depiction of the Vietnam War than it is of a nightmarish and ironic vision of horror and death.

Brando's character, aside from Conrad's source, may well have been based in part on the unusual exploits of Anthony Poe, a World War II marine veteran and C.I.A. paramilitary specialist and intelligence officer. He played a role in the covert war in Laos in the 1960s where he trained and commanded warriors of several tribes against North Vietnamese and Pathet Lao forces in the region. Operating virtually independently, his unorthodox military tactics made him into an almost mythical figure, one that struck fear into the hearts of his enemies. Strange tales of his exploits began to emerge. When the media exposed his C.I.A. affiliations, he shifted his base to Thailand. See Vietnam War: Intelligence and Covert Actions. ∎

Appointment in Berlin (1943), Col. *Dir.* Alfred E. Green; *Sc.* Horace McCoy, Michael Hogan; *Cast includes:* George Sanders, Marguerite Chapman, Onslow Stevens, Gale Sondergaard, Alan Napier.

George Sanders portrays a double agent in this World War II drama. Discharged from the Royal Air Force because of his outspoken views against the Munich Pact, he is secretly enlisted into the British secret service. He collaborates with German agents and is sent to Berlin where he broadcasts anti-British propaganda. His programs, however, are so written as to transmit vital information to the British War Office. When the Nazis finally figure out that he is a British agent, Sanders makes a run for freedom. Two women (Marguerite Chapman and Gale Sondergaard) who help him escape from the Nazis are executed. Sanders himself is killed while attempting to escape in a German plane. The clever plot twists and their dramatic execution help to lift this drama above the ordinary. Curiously, it is a rather pessimistic wartime tale, considering the period in which it was made and released. See German Intelligence: World War II. ∎

Arabesque (1966), U. *Dir.* Stanley Donen; *Sc.* Julian Mitchell, Stanley Price, Pierre Marton; *Cast includes:* Gregory Peck, Sophia Loren, Alan Badel, Kieron Moore, Carl Duering, John Merivale.

An American exchange professor in England becomes embroiled in a web of intrigue and murder when he is called upon to decipher a seemingly harmless document written in hieroglyphics in this mildly entertaining drama. Gregory Peck, as a scholar in ancient languages at Oxford, translates the message which is coveted by several shadowy Middle East groups. The paper somehow leads to murders and an impending assassination of a Middle Eastern political leader (Carl Duering). Sophia Loren, as a seductive Arab, helps Peck although he is not certain about her role in the unfolding intrigue. Alan Badel and Kieron Moore portray two of several villains in this film adaptation of Gordon Cotler's novel *The Cipher*. ■

Arctic Flight (1952), Mon. *Dir.* Lew Landers; *Sc.* Robert Hill, George Bricker; *Cast includes:* Wayne Morris, Lola Albright, Alan Hale, Jr., Carol Thurston, Phil Tead, Tom Richards.

A Communist spy, posing as an American businessman, takes aerial pictures of strategic Alaskan sites which he intends to deliver to the Russians in this drama set during the Cold War. Alan Hale, Jr., as the enemy agent masquerading in the guise of a tourist, hires Alaskan bush pilot Wayne Morris to take him on a scenic flight where he photographs various sites. Later, when Morris discovers his passenger's true purpose, he tries to alert the few other inhabitants of the isolated region. At first they ignore his suspicions. Finally, they join Morris in trying to prevent Hale from crossing into Russian territory. Morris catches up to Hale and a fight ensues in which Hale loses the important photos and his identification. He manages to escape into Russian territory but is shot by the border guards when he fails to show any identification. The film was adapted from "Shadow of the Curtain," a story by Ewing Scott.

The film almost anticipates an actual Cold War incident between the Soviet Union and the U.S. that was to occur in 1954 in that region. A U.S. intelligence patrol, stationed on an ice island near the North Pole and assigned to monitor Soviet activities, found itself drifting toward Soviet territory. See *Ice Station Zebra* (1968). ■

Argyle Secrets, The (1948), Film Classics. *Dir.* Cyril Endfield; *Sc.* Cyril Endfield; *Cast includes:* William Gargan, Marjorie Lord, Ralph Byrd, Jack Reitzen, John Banner, Barbara Billingsley.

A collection of documents that contain evidence of treason by some well-known Americans during World War II becomes the focus of a reporter and various blackmailers in this

Enemy agents threaten reporter William Gargan, who has a list of American traitors during World War II. *The Argyle Secrets* (1948).

drama set in postwar U.S. William Gargan, as the journalist, wants the papers so that he can expose the traitors who collaborated with the Nazi regime. Meanwhile, assorted agents representing different extortion rings, are also after the documents. Several murders are committed before the intrigue comes to a halt. Marjorie Lord portrays one of the blackmailers. Ralph Byrd, better known for his portrayals of Dick Tracy in serials and feature films, plays the local police detective. ■

Arizona Bushwhackers (1968), Par. *Dir.* Lesley Selander; *Sc.* Steve Fisher; *Cast includes:* Howard Keel, Yvonne De Carlo, John Ireland, Marilyn Maxwell, Scott Brady, James Craig.

Howard Keel portrays a Confederate prisoner of war who agrees to work for the Union as a frontier lawman but privately welcomes the opportunity to spy for the South. More a western than a Civil War drama, the film deals with the efforts of a Confederate prisoner to reestablish law and order in a crooked frontier town. With the Union busy fighting the war and prison camps overcrowded with captured Southerners, President Lincoln permits several Confederates who take an oath to the Union to leave the wretched conditions of incarceration and work as lawmen in the West. Keel is assigned to end the corruption in a town controlled by a dishonest sheriff (Barton MacLane) and a villainous saloon owner (Scott Brady). Yvonne De Carlo, as a milliner, helps Keel in his spying. John Ireland plays Keel's rebel-hating deputy. ■

Armored Command (1961), AA. *Dir.* Byron Haskin; *Sc.* Ron W. Alcorn; *Cast includes:* Howard Keel, Tina Louise, Warner Anderson, Earl Holliman, Burt Reynolds.

An attractive Nazi spy employs her sexual charms in an attempt to gather information concerning a strategic Allied position in this routine World War II action drama. The spy, played by Tina Louise, ensnares an innocent American sergeant (Earl Holliman) and a private (Burt Reynolds) who brawl for her affections. But her scheme is thwarted in the nick of time by a battle-hardened colonel (Howard Keel). During the ensuing battle, the spy vindictively shoots Reynolds and in turn is killed by Holliman. The film provides an exciting climactic battle sequence.

This was Reynolds' second feature film (*Angel Baby*, released the same year, was his first) following a successful career in television. ■

Arms and the Girl (1917), Paramount. *Dir.* Joseph Kaufman; *Sc.* Charles E. Whittaker; *Cast includes:* Billie Burke, Thomas Meighan.

In this comedy-drama based on the 1916 play by Grant Stewart and Robert Baker, Billie Burke portrays a young American woman on vacation in Belgium as World War I erupts. She misses her train and becomes entangled in military matters as Germans enter the town where she is staying. At first accused of spying, she is freed, but another American, an engineer, is suspected of the same offense and sentenced to death by a firing squad. Posing as the condemned man's fiancée, she comes to his rescue. The sentimental German general orders them married while her real fiancé arrives.

This was one of the earliest films to treat World War I lightly. A comedy film in the midst of the Great War was a risky business as casualty reports, newspaper accounts and newsreels were revealing in graphic terms that the war, now in its third year, had turned into a "bloody slaughterhouse." Burke, a Broadway comedy star, made her second screen appearance in this film which received mixed reviews.

Paramount decades later reworked the plot for *Arise, My Love* a 1940 romantic drama set during the Spanish Civil War. Finding a fellow American (Ray Milland) about to be executed, Claudette Colbert, as a journalist, poses as his wife and effects his release. A sentimental Spanish officer falls for her story—until he discovers too late that Milland is a bachelor. ■

Arms and the Woman (1916), Pathé. *Dir.* George Fitzmaurice; *Sc.* Ouida Bergere; *Cast includes:* Mary Nash, Lumsden Hare, H. Cooper Cliffe, Robert Broderick, Rosalind Ivan.

A World War I drama set in the U.S. before and during the conflict, the plot concerns a young Hungarian immigrant who demonstrates her love for her adopted country. At first an impoverished entertainer in a sleazy New York bar, she attracts the attentions of a steel magnate who eventually marries her. When war erupts, she tries to stop her husband from selling arms to Germany. Meanwhile, German spies are operating within the borders of the U.S. They are trying to make deals with munitions merchants. The wife becomes involved in frustrating these plots as well. See German Intelligence: World War I. ■

Arnold, Benedict (1741–1801). No other figure in American history has become as infamous a traitor as Benedict Arnold. During the American Revolution he attempted to surrender the fort at West Point, on New York's Hudson River, to the British. An intensely ambitious man, Arnold seemed to have acted out of feelings of frustration and revenge for what he felt was a lack of appreciation for his military competence and bravery.

Within a few weeks after being posted to the command of West Point in the summer of 1780, Arnold reopened contact with Major John André, an aide to British General Clinton, and delivered plans to the British officer detailing the fort's weaknesses. André, however, was captured on the way to New York with the information and Arnold, upon hearing of the seizure of the courier, fled to a British warship in the Hudson River. André was shortly thereafter hanged as a spy because he was wearing civilian clothes when he was captured. The short silent film "Benedict Arnold and Major André" (1909) portrays these events fairly accurately.

The British rewarded Arnold for his treachery with a commission as brigadier general and pension payments for him and his family. For the remainder of the American Revolution, Arnold served the British, leading raids against the Americans in Virginia and Connecticut.

Prior to the West Point incident, Arnold had compiled a record of near brilliance as a commander in the Patriot cause. He defeated the British at Fort Ticonderoga and on Lake Champlain in upstate New York. He was wounded in an unsuccessful winter invasion of Quebec (1775–1776) and played an important role in the American victory at Saratoga (1777). Earlier in 1777, Arnold was passed over for promotion by Congress in favor of less senior and accomplished officers despite Washington's appeal in Arnold's favor. He did get his promotion to major general later in the war, but the incident seemed to have scarred him. After the Revolution, Arnold and his family lived in Canada and London where he died a man scorned by the people of England.

Only a small number of films recount Arnold's exploits. "Benedict Arnold" (1909), a short Vitagraph drama, covers his attempt to turn over West Point to the British and his narrow escape. In "The Capture of Fort Ticonderoga" (1911) Arnold is depicted as a hero at that historical confrontation. A generally fictitious dramatization of Arnold's traitorous actions occurs in *The Scarlet Coat* (1955), with Cornel Wilde as an American spy, Michael Wilding as Major André and Robert Douglas as Arnold. ■

Arrest Bulldog Drummond (1938), Par.

Dir. James Hogan; *Sc.* Stuart Palmer; *Cast includes:* John Howard, Heather Angel, H. B. Warner, Reginald Denny, E. E. Clive, Jean Fenwick.

International agents steal a secret destructive device in this low-budget drama set in England. John Howard, as the renowned amateur sleuth Bulldog Drummond, becomes enmeshed in the plot while preparing for his marriage to Heather Angel. He accidentally chances upon the corpse of the inventor of the secret device. Putting aside his personal plans, he swings into action to solve the case. As anticipated, he recovers the invention and unmasks the murderer after undergoing a series of stirring adventures including a suspenseful island chase. The film is based on the novel by H. C. McNeile. ■

As in a Looking Glass (1916), World. *Dir.*
Frank H. Crane; *Cast includes:* Kitty Gordon, F. Lumsden Hare, Frank Goldsmith, Gladden James, Louise Bates, J. Malcolm Dunn.

English actress Kitty Gordon portrays an adventuress who leaves Europe for the U.S. to escape her oppressive lover and a string of wealthy men with whom she has had affairs. In Washington she meets a government worker, played by F. Lumsden Hare. A foreign agent blackmails her into stealing naval plans from the American with whom she has fallen in love. Instead of betraying Hare, she elopes with him. Enemy agents find the couple, steal the plans and force her to accompany them to their leader. She manages to destroy the vital papers and is fatally shot. She lives long enough to telephone her husband and confess all.

Although the film was released before America's entry into World War I, it already reflected the entrenched anti-German sentiments of many filmmakers and their audiences. Earlier films with this view were quickly criticized by politicians and some movie critics. But by the time this drama was released, the Prussian-as-secret-agent had become the established norm. The film was adapted from Francis Charles Phillips' 1887 novel and play. ■

Assassination (1987), Cannon. *Dir.* Peter
Hunt; *Sc.* Richard Sale; *Cast includes:* Charles Bronson, Jill Ireland, Stephen Elliott, Jan Gan Boyd, Randy Brooks, Erik Stern.

Mysterious assassins make various attempts on the life of the First Lady in this political thriller. Jill Ireland, as the adventurous wife of the President, dislikes being followed around by members of the U.S. Secret Service, especially Charles Bronson, who portrays a dedicated, professional agent. A senator-friend (Michael Ansara) of the President removes Bronson from his assignment. After several attempts on her life, Ireland agrees that the situation is serious. Bronson returns to foil other attempts and finally unravels the plot. The President, when he decided to run for the office, was a bachelor—a definite political handicap. So he entered into the loveless marriage, agreeing to allow Ireland to get a quiet divorce at a later date and go her own way. However, the ambitious Ansara, thinking the divorce could hurt the President's chances for reelection, schemes to have her killed. A widowed President, Ansara concludes, stands a better chance for reelection than a divorced President. Jan Gan Boyd portrays Bronson's sexy partner. The film ends with Bronson's resignation from the secret service.

The convoluted plot is too unbelievable to be taken seriously. Bronson and Ireland fail to bring any sparks to their early confrontation, although off screen they are husband and wife. Feeble attempts at comic relief fall flat as Ireland continually presents security problems for Bronson and his crew of agents. "Oh, boy," he says in frustration at Ireland's antics, "am I going to miss Nancy Reagan." To the film's credit, it has less violence and gore than some of Bronson's previous action dramas. See U.S. Secret Service. ■

Assignment in Brittany (1943), MGM. *Dir.* Jack Conway; *Sc.* Anthony Veiller, William H. Wright, Howard Emmett Rogers; *Cast includes:* Jean Pierre Aumont, Susan Peters, Richard Whorf, Margaret Wycherly, Signe Hasso, Reginald Owen.

Pierre Aumont, who later changed his name to Jean Pierre, plays a dual role in this World War II drama based on the novel by Helen MacInnes. As a French agent recently returned to England after a successful mission against the Nazis in North Africa, Aumont is transferred by his commander to the British for another secret assignment. He is to impersonate his look-alike, a wounded French soldier, for the purpose of locating a secret Nazi submarine base hidden somewhere on the coast of France. "If we continue to lose ships at this rate," an English officer explains, "we'll lose the war. For the past two months not a ship has gotten into England without running into a gauntlet of Nazi submarines." "And I'm to find this base?" Aumont replies. "You've got to find it," the officer says with all the gravity of the typical World War II drama.

Aumont parachutes into France and journeys to his look-alike's village where he is accepted by the soldier's sweetheart (Susan Peters) and his mother (Margaret Wycherly). After a confrontation with a French traitor and contact with the French underground, he finds the camouflaged submarine base. But he is captured by the Gestapo before he can relay the information to the British. French patriots effect his escape, after which he wires the location of the base to England. A successful British Commando raid follows.

The film gets caught up in its own earnest attempts at presenting a patriotic message. An elderly restaurant owner, brutally tortured by Gestapo chief George Coulouris, goes to his death without exposing Aumont.

A group of hostages, including women and children, are shot as they sing the "Marseillaise," already used more effectively in *Casablanca* (1942). The plot contrivances of the masquerading hero almost being exposed by the mother and former sweetheart of the real French collaborator whom he is impersonating and his romance with a true daughter of the cause have been seen on the screen too many times before. ■

Assignment—Paris (1952). Col. *Dir.* Robert Parrish; *Sc.* William Bowers; *Cast includes:* Dana Andrews, Marta Toren, George Sanders, Audrey Totter, Sandro Giglio, Donald Randolph.

An American reporter in Paris attempts to expose a plot by East bloc countries against the West in this Cold War drama. Dana Andrews, as the journalist, is sent to Budapest to investigate a link between the Hungarian dictator and Tito. He obtains a picture as proof of the plot and smuggles it out of the country. But he is caught and made to confess that he is a spy. He manages to escape to safety. Marta Toren plays a fellow reporter with whom Andrews falls in love. George Sanders, as a journalist in charge of the Paris office, is also in love with Toren. The film, based on "Trial by Terror," a short story by Pauline and Paul Gallico, presents a fair depiction of the difficulties of newspaper work under the censorship procedures of Communist countries. See Cold War. ■

Atlantic Convoy (1942), Col. *Dir.* Lew Landers; *Sc.* Robert Lee Johnson; *Cast includes:* Bruce Bennett, Virginia Field, John Beal, Larry Parks, Lloyd Bridges.

Iceland is the location of this World War II drama. John Beal plays a meteorologist who is suspected of supplying Nazi submarines with information about American shipping. Although he rescues an injured American pilot and several children in a daring airplane landing, he is unable to cast off suspicions of collaborating with the enemy. He eventually absolves himself when he leads the U.S. air patrol to the location of a German submarine. Virginia Field provides the romance in this low-budget but well-paced film. ■

Atomic City, The (1952), Par. *Dir.* Jerry Hopper; *Sc.* Sydney Boehm; *Cast includes:* Gene Barry, Lydia Clarke, Lee Aaker, Michael Moore, Nancy Gates, Milburn Stone.

Bruce Bennett (2nd from left) plots out the course of a German U-boat preying upon Allied shipping in World War II. *Atlantic Convoy* (1942).

Spies kidnap the son of an American nuclear scientist in this taut Cold War drama. The parents (Gene Barry and Lydia Clarke) are contacted by telephone and told to deliver the formula for the H-bomb in exchange for their son. The boy's father turns over a useless formula to stall for time while the F.B.I. steps in to investigate. Clues eventually lead the officers to an old Santa Fe dwelling site where the boy is being held captive. Regardless of the outcome of the caper, the kidnappers plan to kill their prisoner to prevent him from identifying them. The boy manages to escape his captors through a small opening in the cave but finds himself in a precarious position on edge of a cliff. However, he is rescued in time and the enemy agents are captured. Milburn Stone is the hard-nosed, professional F.B.I. chief in charge of the case.

Director Jerry Hopper, in a semi-documentary style, takes his cameras directly to the Los Alamos plant where the plot begins. He then examines the life-threatening work the scientists are engaged in and the poten-tially hazardous conditions their families are exposed to. Hopper then goes into the streets of Los Angeles on the trail of the kidnappers and finally to the ancient Indian cliff dwelling.

The film emphasizes the importance of keeping the nation's nuclear secrets out of the hands of potential enemies. "Our job," points out the F.B.I. chief to the distraught father, "is to keep the bomb at home and to apprehend the kidnappers and to bring your son home safely." "That's the order of their importance, isn't it?" Barry responds. "One, two, three. Tommy is Number Three." Later, at F.B.I. headquarters, Stone addresses his team of agents assigned to the case about rounding up every spy. "You're probably asking yourselves, 'What about the boy? Isn't getting Tommy Addison back safely more important?' I'm giving you my answer to that officially. No. No matter how callous that may seem, your first job is to locate and apprehend the spies." The title refers to Los Alamos where the residents live under tight security and the fear of radiation accidents. ∎

Avalanche Express (1979), TCF. *Dir.* Mark Robson; *Sc.* Abraham Polonsky; *Cast includes:* Robert Shaw, Lee Marvin, Linda Evans, Maximilian Schell, Mike Connors, Joe Namath.

The C.I.A. uses a high-ranking Soviet defector to ensnare a dangerous Soviet agent in this unexciting Cold War drama based on Colin Forbes' novel. Lee Marvin, as an unorthodox C.I.A. agent, cooks up the scheme to transport the defector (Robert Shaw) by train. Marvin is confident that Maximilian Schell, a major Russian agent engineering a biological warfare scheme, will make an attempt on the defector's life. As Marvin anticipated, Schell's spies try several times to eliminate Shaw, who is guarded aboard the train by American agents. However, Marvin accomplishes his mission despite the typical obstacles, including the avalanche mentioned in the title. Unfortunately, the film production suffered more serious setbacks. Producer-director Mark Robson died during filming, followed by Robert Shaw, who suffered a fatal heart attack during post-production work. See Central Intelligence Agency. ∎

B

Back at the Front (1952), U. *Dir.* George Sherman; *Sc.* Lou Breslow, Don McGuire, Oscar Brodney; *Cast includes:* Tom Ewell, Harvey Lembeck, Mari Blanchard, Barry Kelley, Vaughn Taylor, Richard Long.

A sequel to the previous year's *Up Front* (1951), the film continues the comic adventures of Willie and Joe, characters created by cartoonist Bill Mauldin. Tom Ewell portrays Willie, and Harvey Lembeck replaces David Wayne as Joe. The two G.I.s are recalled to active duty and shipped to Japan although the boys have exploited every devious trick to avoid going. Following some comic military mishaps, they get leave which takes them to Tokyo. It isn't long before they become entangled with a gang of smugglers selling arms to North Korea. They are chased by M.P.s, tempted by a voluptuous spy (Mari Blanchard) and threatened by the chief smuggler (Russell Johnson) before they emerge as heroes. Their general decides to send the improbable heroes back to the States before they do more harm.

William Henry Mauldin, who saw service in Italy during World War II, became the most popular U.S. Army cartoonist of the war. His work, featuring his lovable characters Willie and Joe, was published in *Stars and Stripes*, the official weekly army newspaper, and captured the dour humor of life at the front. ■

Back to Bataan (1945), RKO. *Dir.* Edward Dmytryk; *Sc.* Ben Barzman, Richard Landau; *Cast includes:* John Wayne, Anthony Quinn, Beulah Bondi, Fely Franquelli, Richard Loo.

American and Filipino guerrillas battle the ruthless Japanese in this World War II action drama. The film, which opens with the withdrawal of U.S. forces from the Philippines, features John Wayne as an American colonel who stays behind to help organize native resistance against the invaders. Anthony Quinn, as a Filipino patriot who believes the Americans have permanently abandoned his homeland, is reluctant at first to join the struggle against the Japanese. But he later fights alongside Wayne.

The Japanese try to persuade the Filipinos that the U.S. is their enemy. When this fails to end the armed resistance, the invaders unleash a reign of terror on the civilian population. The guerrillas, meanwhile, keep up their attacks and ambushes, inflicting substantial damage on the Japanese. The resistance contributes substantially to the defeat of the enemy when American troops land at Leyte.

Quinn's sweetheart (Fely Franquelli) collaborates with the Japanese as a radio personality—similar to that of the infamous Tokyo Rose. Her pro-Japanese propaganda broadcasts are transmitted to Filipino troops and civilians. "Why do you fight?" she announces. "This is not your war. America brought you into it." However, in reality she is working as an agent for the U.S., secretly broadcasting military information to the Allies and guerrillas.

Several sequences reflect Hollywood's heavy-handed use of propaganda during the war years. Vladimir Sokoloff, as a local native school principal, is brutally hanged by the Japanese when he refuses to lower the American flag outside his schoolhouse. Another sequence re-creates, in part, the infamous death march forced upon captured American and Filipino troops by the Japanese. Later, a young Filipino boy sacrifices his life to save Wayne and his guerrilla force. "I'm sorry I didn't learn to spell 'liberty,'" the little patriot says before he dies. His teacher, witnessing her pupil's death, remarks: "Who ever learned it so well." A voice-over recites General MacArthur's tribute to the guerrillas: "These inadequately armed patriots have fought the enemy for two years. Their names and deeds shall be enshrined in the hearts our two peoples."

The drama is an interesting blend of fact and fiction. It reenacts several actual incidents besides the death march, one of which includes the liberation of the Cabanatuan prison camp where, among others, American soldiers, sailors and marines were held as prisoners of war. Some of these men were later used in the production of the film. See Philippines. ■

Background to Danger (1943), WB. *Dir.* Raoul Walsh; *Sc.* W. R. Burnett; *Cast includes:* George Raft, Brenda Marshall, Sydney Greenstreet, Peter Lorre, Osa Massen, Kurt Katch.

A World War II drama set in Turkey, the film stars George Raft as an American agent in a battle of wits against Nazi and Russian agents. Germany, looking for an excuse to march into neutral Turkey, is trying to persuade the Turks that the Russians plan to invade their country. "Our task," explains Sydney Greenstreet, as one of Germany's top agents, "is to present Turkey with a match that will inflame the people against Russia." Raft gains possession of false Nazi documents showing that Russia is planning to invade Turkey. He then becomes the target both of Nazi agents, who want to publish the documents in the Turkish press, and Russian spies, who want to destroy them.

Two popular character actors, Greenstreet and Peter Lorre, enliven the film with their characterizations. Greenstreet, as a malevolent Nazi operative who enjoys fine music and good conversation while dispensing torture only as a last resort, has the more colorful role and delivers the best lines in the film. "In international diplomacy," he explains to a subordinate, "the shortest distance between two points is never a straight line." Lorre portrays an eccentric, vodka-gulping Russian agent who, when frustrated, sits on the floor and exclaims: "I want my vodka!" Brenda Marshall, as Lorre's assistant, provides the love interest for Raft in this tale based on the novel *Uncommon Danger* by Eric Ambler. ■

Baltimore Plot. See *The Tall Target* (1951). ■

Bamboo Prison, The (1954), Col. *Dir.* Lewis Seiler; *Sc.* Edwin Blum, Jack DeWitt; *Cast includes:* Robert Francis, Dianne Foster, Brian Keith, Jerome Courtland, E. G. Marshall, Earle Hyman.

This Korean War film suggests that some American prisoners of war held by the Communists and who turned collaborator were actually agents working for the U.S. government. The story takes place during the peace negotiations at Panmunjon. Robert Francis portrays one such U.S. intelligence agent at a prison camp who is despised by his fellow inmates for cooperating with the enemy. Brian Keith plays another prisoner and fellow spy. E. G. Marshall, as a Communist, masquerades as a priest in the camp to spy on the prisoners.

One of the earliest Korean War films to explore the fate of American prisoners of war, the drama suggests one of the major differences between this conflict and World War II. Americans were confronted with torture and brainwashing by the North Koreans; dissension arose among the prisoners as some suspected others of going over to the enemy. After the war, some were accused of collaborating with the Communists. See Brainwashing; Korean War. ■

Bancroft, "Brass." A fictional U.S. Secret Service agent, Bancroft was portrayed by Ronald Reagan in a series of routine action dramas—*Secret Service of the Air* (1939), *Code of the Secret Service* (1939), *Smashing the Money Ring* (1939) and *Murder in the Air* (1940). Not exactly an early James Bond type, "Brass" was a dedicated, no-nonsense agent who volunteered to go under cover to expose an illegal operation, was quick with his fists and had his share of romances. The economic plots were fast-paced and generally a cut above the usual B feature. W. H. Moran, former chief of the U.S. Secret Service, provided much of the material on which the films were based. Reagan, who fitted the role rather well, received good support from several regulars, including John Litel, James Stephenson and Eddie Foy, Jr. as his comic sidekick. Although there were many film series about detectives, some of whom occasionally battled attempts at espionage and sabotage, this was the only series about a Secret Service agent. ∎

Barbary Pirate (1949), Col. *Dir.* Lew Landers; *Sc.* Robert Libbot, Frank Burt; *Cast includes:* Donald Woods, Trudy Marshall, Lenore Aubert, Stefan Schnabel, Ross Ford, John Dehner.

An army officer is sent to Tripoli to help stop Barbary pirates from attacking American shipping in this drama set in the days following the American Revolution. It seems that a secret agent in the U.S. is collaborating with the pirates. Donald Woods portrays the gallant hero who allows himself to get caught, cultivates a friendship with Yusof, the Bey of Tripoli (Stefan Schnabel), and uncovers the traitor in Washington who has been supplying the pirates with information concerning the cargo of American ships. Trudy Marshall, whom Woods rescues, provides the romance. The low-budget film provides a fair amount of action as Woods battles his way to freedom.

Although characters and plot are completely fictitious, the basic premise is based on historical events. Barbary pirates did indeed prey upon American as well as European shipping. The U.S. paid annual tributes to several North African Muslim states for safe passage. However, unlike the film, the piracy continued, resulting in the Tripolitan War of the early 1800s.

Open warfare between the U.S. and the Barbary States broke out in 1800. President Jefferson decided to send a naval squadron to blockade Tripoli. The naval blockade was partly successful, but an American overland raid on the city failed. Commodore Edward Preble, commanding another squadron in 1803–1804, renewed the blockade even more vigorously and even attacked shipping and fortifications in Tripoli harbor. In 1805 Tripoli signed a peace treaty with the U.S. that ended the payment of American tribute. The U.S., still a newcomer among Western nations, gained prestige as a naval power as a result of the war. However, other Barbary States continued to exact payments from the U.S. until the Algerine War (1816). ∎

Batman, The (1943) serial, Col. *Dir.* Lambert Hillyer; *Sc.* Harry Fraser, Norman McLeod, Leslie Swabacker; *Cast includes:* Lewis Wilson, Douglas Croft, J. Carrol Naish, Shirley Patterson, William Austin, Charles Middleton.

This was the first screen appearance of Batman and Robin, the dynamic duo heroes of the comic-book world, created by Bob Kane. In this 15-chapter World War II serial Lewis Wilson and Douglas Croft, as Batman and Robin respectively, battle the sinister Dr. Daka, a Japanese superspy portrayed humorously by J. Carrol Naish. Daka heads the "League of the New Order," an organization made up of former scientists, engineers and industrialists who have served prison terms. His goal, when not foiled by our heroes— who seem to succumb to Daka's minions after each encounter—is to wreak destruction upon America's war potential. Daka's secret laboratory, located within and below a carnival museum in an abandoned section of California's "Little Tokyo," contains an array of high-tech apparatus which he readily employs against his victims. He also controls a group of zombie-like subjects whom he directs by remote control. Of a more conventional nature is a trapdoor he maintains which leads to a pit of hungry alligators. Needless to say, he falls victim to his own device in the final episode.

One scene shows a section of the abandoned Little Tokyo as a narrator states: "This was part of a foreign land transplanted bodily to America. . . . The wise government rounded up the shifty-eyed Japs." Except for this racist allusion to America's wartime enemy, the serial deals chiefly with fist fights and chases more in tune with gangster melodramas than with tales of espionage. A sequel followed in 1949 titled *Batman and Robin* with Robert Lowery handling the role of Batman and Johnny Duncan as his sidekick. ∎

Beast of Yucca Flats, The (1961), Crown. *Dir.* Coleman Francis; *Sc.* Coleman Francis; *Cast includes:* Tor Johnson, Douglas Mellor, Larry Aten, Barbara Francis, Bing Stafford, Linda Bielima.

A rare hybrid of the horror and spy genres, this weird little film centers on a scientist who is pursued by Communist agents. Tor Johnson portrays a Soviet scientist who has defected to the U.S. He carries secret data about Soviet moon tests. Two Soviet agents, ordered to retrieve his notes, pursue him into Yucca Flats, used as a test area for atomic bombs. Johnson's companion, a U.S. agent, empties his gun at the agents while the scientist continues his escape into the desert. The scientist's body becomes contaminated by local radioactivity from an atomic blast in the distance. The explosion has killed the two pursuers and soon transforms Johnson into a frightening creature. He then begins to attack anyone who comes within his range. Two highway patrolmen hunt for him and eventually kill him with two bullets. At least one critic called the film a "non-movie." ∎

Beasts of Berlin (1939), PDC. *Dir.* Sherman Scott; *Sc.* Shephard Straube; *Cast includes:* Roland Drew, Steffi Duna, Greta Granstedt, Alan Ladd, Lucien Prival, Vernon Dent.

A strong anti-Nazi drama, one of the earliest to be released during World War II, the film concerns a group of German underground resisters who struggle against the Nazi party in their land. Several sequences concern the problems of an anti-Nazi spy who is a member of Germany's Storm Troopers. There are scenes showing the brutal methods that the Gestapo employs to gather information, break men's spirits and terrorize the population. Other sequences describe the inhuman treatment of prisoners in Hitler's concentration camps. The plot of the film itself does not equal the importance of its message—that of a national policy of brutality which at first jars and then angers the conscience of decent and compassionate people.

The film was originally called *Goose Step*—the title of Shephard Straube's story from which it was adapted. It was later changed to *Hitler—Beast of Berlin*, before it assumed its present title. Producers Distributing Corporation, a new kid on the block, scheduled this drama as its first release. To avoid controversy, the studio softened the title to the final one. This, however, was only the beginning of its problems. Fearing an outcry from the numerous German Bund branches in the nearby states, the New York board of censors decided to ban the film. The company was forced to delete some material before the ban was lifted. When the drama finally premiered in New York, the critics, surprised at its candor, praised its outspokenness and avoided pointing out its weak plot elements and poorly conceived German settings. Despite its faults, it was the first Hollywood feature to openly attack the Nazi techniques and atrocities that later were to become a familiar mainstay of World War II propaganda films. ∎

Behind Closed Doors (1929), Col. *Dir.* R. William Neill; *Sc.* Howard J. Green; *Cast includes:* Virginia Valli, Gaston Glass, Otto Matieson, Andre De Segurola.

Virginia Valli portrays a secret service agent in this weak drama of intrigue about two opposing factions of a fictitious European country. It seems that the Royalists, who wish to have their monarchy restored, must deliver some important documents into the hands of a rich American woman. The Republicans, however, are aware of their opponents' plans and plan to prevent the delivery of the papers. They assign one of their agents (Gaston Glass) to journey to the U.S. to accomplish this. A romance develops between Valli and Glass, who eventually surrenders the secret papers. ∎

Behind the Eight Ball (1942), U. *Dir.* Edward F. Cline; *Sc.* Stanley Roberts, Mel Ronson; *Cast includes:* Harry Ritz, Al Ritz, Jimmy Ritz, Carol Bruce, Dick Foran, Grace McDonald.

Enemy agents disrupt a rural theatrical group in this World War II minor musical. Carol Bruce, as the inspiration behind a straw-hat musical comedy, has ideas of taking the show to New York. Meanwhile, a couple of spies have ideas of their own concerning the use of the same barn where the show is being staged. They plan to use the structure for transmitting their secret messages. The Ritz Brothers add their zany antics to the goings-on, which include a murder. The trio eventually tangle with the spies. ∎

Behind the Mask (1932), Col. *Dir.* John Francis Dillon; *Sc.* Jo Swerling, Dorothy Howell; *Cast includes:* Jack Holt, Constance Cummings, Boris Karloff, Claude King, Bertha Mann, Edward Van Sloan.

Jack Holt, as a U.S. Secret Service agent, goes under cover to expose a drug syndicate in this weak drama that attempts to blend horror and intrigue. Edward Van Sloan, as a crazed surgeon whose operations all intentionally end in failure, is the mastermind of a drug ring. He uses the coffins of his murdered patients to store the drugs. Holt poses as an escaped convict to work his way into the private hospital and Sloan's employ. Although he is captured at one point and placed on the operating table, he manages to escape the mad doctor's clutches and break up the illegal proceedings. Constance Cummings pro-

German spies don't seem to appreciate the humor of the Ritz Brothers (without hats) in this World War II musical comedy. *Behind the Eight Ball* (1942).

vides some of the love interest. The film is based on the story "In the Secret Service" by Jo Swerling. ■

"Benedict Arnold and Major André" (1909), Vitagraph. *Dir.* J. Stuart Blackton; *Sc.* Charles Kent; *Cast includes:* William Humphrey, Charles Kent.

A short drama based on historical events during the American Revolution, the film re-enacts the highlights in the ignoble military career of Benedict Arnold. These include a meeting with General George Washington, the collusion between Arnold and Major André, the latter's end upon a scaffold and Arnold's death in England. Some of these incidents were dramatized once again five decades later in *The Scarlet Coat* (1955). See John André; Benedict Arnold; American Revolution: Intelligence and Covert Actions. ■

Berlin Correspondent (1942), TCF. *Dir.* Eugene Forde; *Sc.* Steve Fisher, Jack Andrews; *Cast includes:* Virginia Gilmore, Dana Andrews, Mona Maris, Martin Kosleck, Sig Rumann, Kurt Katch.

This World War II drama takes place in Berlin prior to America's entry into the war. Dana Andrews, as an American radio correspondent, comes into possession of highly secret Nazi war information. Constantly under guard by Nazis, especially while he is broadcasting, he has a difficult time getting the information out of the country. Eventually he steals a plane and, taking with him a converted Nazi sympathizer (Virginia Gilmore), escapes to England. Martin Kosleck, who virtually made a career impersonating Germans, portrays a high-ranking Nazi official who suspects Andrews. ■

Berlin Express (1948), RKO. *Dir.* Jacques Tourneur; *Sc.* Harold Medford; *Cast includes:* Merle Oberon, Robert Ryan, Charles Korvin, Paul Lukas, Robert Coote, Roman Toporow.

A group of unrepentant Nazis continues to create mayhem in strife-torn Germany in this

Roman Toporow, Paul Lukas, Robert Coote, Charles Korvin and Robert Ryan join forces to track down a gang of unpatriated Nazi conspirators in post-World War II Germany. *Berlin Express* (1948).

post-World War II drama. The story chiefly takes place aboard a Berlin train carrying passengers from various countries. Earlier, the French secret service has intercepted a carrier-pigeon message with cryptic writing and notifies their British, American and Soviet counterparts. However, none of the agents can decipher the message. On board the train a hand grenade kills one of the travelers, allegedly the head of a fact-finding commission to unify Germany. The others learn that the Nazi underground killed the wrong man. Paul Lukas, as the German statesman traveling incognito, is the target. He is eventually kidnapped, leading some of the other passengers—an American agricultural expert, an English instructor, a French businessman, a secretary and a Russian officer—to join forces in an attempt to rescue him amid the eerie, bombed-out landscape of Frankfurt. The city has been reduced to a "world of rubble under strict military control," according to the narrator. The film handles the obvious theme of international cooperation among the four powers with restraint and subtlety.

Robert Ryan, as the American, tracks down the leaders of the neo-Nazi group but is captured along with Lukas' secretary. Robert Coote, the Englishman, helps in the search. Merle Oberon, as Lukas' French secretary, motivates the manhunt for her employer by appealing to the group's humanity. Charles Korvin, as the French businessman who joins the others, in reality is the leader of the Nazis and tries to kill Lukas after the Nazi gang is annihilated by the U.S. military police. Roman Toporow, as the Russian soldier who

joins in the search, is suspicious of his Western counterparts but in the final scenes learns to trust them.

Jacques Tourneur, whose work as a director began in silent films, enhanced this thriller with a rich visual style that was relatively uncommon in Hollywood films of the period. A narrator introduces the drama and the main characters. Possibly the only weak point in the plot is the cabal's motive. According to the film, the Nazis are trying to prevent the unification of Germany, with Lukas, their target, a respected German statesman who has worked out a viable plan for this reunification. One would think that the defeated Nazis would welcome unification whereas the Allied powers would be suspicious of such as plan, but perhaps these neo-Nazis preferred the unification on their own, totalitarian terms. See Nazi Subversion: Post-World War II. ∎

Berlin via America (1918), Fordart. *Dir.* Francis Ford; *Sc.* Elsie Van Name; *Cast includes:* Francis Ford, Edna Emerson, Jack Newton, George Henry, Ed Dorhan, George Jones.

Actor-director Francis Ford, brother of director John Ford, portrays an American flier employed by the U.S. Secret Service in this World War I drama. Posing as a traitor to his country, he casts doubts in the minds of his mother and sweetheart about his loyalty. However, his plan works; he gains the confidence of Prussian spies and is transported to Germany where he joins Baron von Richthofen's Flying Circus. He soon emerges as one of their leading aces while secretly dropping messages to the Allies concerning imminent enemy advances. Other Germans suspect him of being a double agent and have him arrested. He is sentenced to be shot but is rescued after an Allied bombardment routs the enemy. His sweetheart (Edna Emerson), now a nurse, attends to his wounds which he received during the shelling.

The patriotic fervor of the period permitted a character who used stealth and deception for the Allied cause to be considered a hero. However, when a foe used similar tactics to aid his country's cause, he was branded as vile and treacherous. To emphasize this type of morality even more strongly, film studios used their most popular leading men as "friendly" spies while utilizing their tradiional "heavies" as enemy agents. ∎

Best Man, The (1919), Hodkinson. *Dir.* Thomas Heffron; *Sc.* Arthur F. Statter; *Cast includes:* J. Warren Kerrigan, Lois Wilson, Fred Montague, Alfred Whitman, Frances Raymond, Clyde Benson.

Based on Grace Livingston Hill's 1913 novelette, the drama concerns an important secret government code that has been stolen and must be recovered. J. Warren Kerrigan portrays a U.S. Secret Service agent who is assigned this difficult task. He accomplishes this by impersonating the individual (Clyde Benson) who has arrived from England to break the code.

Lois Wilson, as the daughter of a deceased father, is compelled to enter into a marriage with Benson to protect the dead man's reputation from slander. Not having seen Benson for years, she assumes that Kerrigan, the secret agent posing as Benson, is the man she is to marry. Dedicated to completing his mission regardless of the sacrifice, Kerrigan goes through with the wedding ceremony and the couple board a train for their honeymoon. Wilson slowly develops a liking for Kerrigan, and they begin to fall in love. The spies, still determined to get the code, have boarded the same train. Nevertheless, Kerrigan delivers the important document to officials in Washington, and the spies are apprehended. ■

Betrayal From the East (1945), RKO. *Dir.* William Berke; *Sc.* Kenneth Gamet, Aubrey Wisberg; *Cast includes:* Lee Tracy, Nancy Kelly, Richard Loo, Abner Biberman, Regis Toomey, Philip Ahn.

Japanese spies seek to obtain a blueprint of the Panama Canal defenses in this routine World War II drama adapted from Alan Hynd's book. Lee Tracy plays a failing carnival barker and ex-soldier who is hired by the secret agents to steal the plans. Instead, he reports to U.S. Army intelligence to reveal the scheme. A counterplot is immediately deployed to entrap the spies in this predictable tale which includes a rousing scrap between Tracy and the head of the Japanese spy ring. Nancy Kelly portrays the female lead while Abner Biberman and Richard Loo play two of the sinister Japanese agents. Possibly the only unique angle in the plot is the death of the two principals who foil the enemy plans. In an obvious but unsuccessful attempt to imbue the plot with a semblance of authenticity, the studio hired the popular writer Drew

Pearson to narrate the prologue and epilogue. See Panama Canal. ■

Betrayed (1954), MGM. *Dir.* Gottfried Reinhardt; *Sc.* Ronald Millar, George Froeschel; *Cast includes:* Clark Gable, Lana Turner, Victor Mature, Louis Calhern, O. E. Hasse, Wilfrid Hyde-White.

Betrayal within the Dutch underground provides the background for this World War II drama. Set in Holland during the Nazi occupation, the film depicts the story of an underground leader (Victor Mature) who causes the deaths of his fellow resistance fighters. His traitorous actions come about when he learns that the underground has condemned his mother for collaborating with the Germans. Seeking revenge upon the Dutch citizenry, he secretly notifies German intelligence about future raids by the resistance. This results in the deaths of many partisans.

Clark Gable portrays a Dutch intelligence agent who helps to expose the traitor. Earlier in the film he is seen working undercover and transmitting messages to the British. He is captured and interrogated by the head of German intelligence, who offers him a chance to work as a double agent for the Nazis. "For men like us," the German explains, "there's no higher achievement than to be the master spy—the double agent." Gable, however, refuses, hinting it is a question of character. "The spy has no character," the German persists. "He only assumes one." Fortunately for Gable, he is rescued by the Dutch underground before the Nazis have a chance to dispense with him.

Lana Turner, as a Dutch widow who volunteers to serve as a secret agent for the British, falls in love with Gable, who has escaped to England. He suspects her motives but soon falls for her. Later, while she is operating under cover in Holland, Gable learns that there is a traitor in her unit and accuses her of collaborating with the Nazis. But he later uncovers the real collaborator—the underground leader.

When the film was completed, Gable left MGM after spending almost a quarter of a century with the studio. He continued to work—at a more profitable percentage basis—for other studios during his last few remaining years.

The spy drama includes a sequence involving British paratroopers who have become surrounded at Arnheim. The film has some members of the Dutch resistance leading the besieged troops out of trap. Actual events reveal a different story.

The strategy for the Battle of Arnheim (September 17–26, 1944) was developed by a joint Anglo-American military team. Dubbed "Operation Market Garden," the plan was to outflank the German army stationed along the Rhine and drive through Holland in a quick movement into north Germany. American paratroopers were assigned the task of capturing the bridges at Nijmegen and Grove while the First British Airborne Division was slated to capture the bridge on the Lower Rhine at Arnheim. The British Second Army was then scheduled to penetrate German lines some fifty-odd miles in an effort to join their paratroopers at the bridge at Arnheim.

Unfortunately for the Allied forces that took part in the operation, Market Garden was destined to end in a debacle. British intelligence, which had earlier broken Germany's major code, and the Dutch resistance reported that two enemy panzer divisions were in Arnheim. Nevertheless, Britain's Field Marshal Montgomery elected to ignore the report and its confirmation and proceeded with the operation. In addition, German Field Marshal Model was accidentally passing through Arnheim at the time of the initial British paratrooper landings. He managed to organize the German armored forces who were retreating from the Allied invasion at Normandy and beat the British First Airborne Division in a bloody encounter at the bridge. The British Second Army, unable to penetrate the German lines, could not assist their besieged comrades. Operation Market Garden resulted in failure and the Allies were denied a quick victory in the West. See Operation Nordpol. ∎

Betrayed (1988), MGMUA. *Dir.* Costa-Gavras; *Sc.* Joe Eszterhas; *Cast includes:* Debra Winger, Tom Berenger, John Heard, Betsy Blair, John Mahoney, Ted Levine.

Debra Winger portrays an F.B.I. agent who goes under cover to help expose a neo-Fascist paramilitary organization operating in the U.S. in this suspenseful drama. Tom Berenger plays a Midwestern farmer whom Winger is assigned to investigate as a possible suspect in the killing of a controversial radio talk-show host. Posing as a tractor driver, Winger wins Berenger's confidence, and they soon fall in love. Winger reports to her superiors

that Berenger, a widower with two children, is a hard worker, a good father and a decent American. She believes the F.B.I. is mistaken about him. But John Heard, who portrays the agent in charge of the investigation and Winger's former lover, requests that she continue to probe into Berenger's background. She reluctantly returns to her assignment.

Berenger, who has fallen in love with Winger, begins slowly to confide in her. "One thing for sure," he says casually while they are driving in his truck, "we're going to kill the hell out of Z.O.G.—Zionist Occupation Government." Shortly after this, he takes her hunting one night with his friends, except that their quarry is a captured black man whom they soon kill in cold blood. Winger, shaken by the experience, reports back to Heard and asks to be taken off the assignment. "I'm in too deep," she pleads. "Maybe my loyalties are all screwed up." But once again Heard persuades her to return.

She later learns that Berenger is the "point man" for an ambitious politician and part of a right-wing movement plotting to assassinate political leaders, blacks and others they believe are threats to the American way of life. Finally, Winger is forced to kill Berenger as he is about to assassinate a political candidate. She then decides to resign from the F.B.I. "Stay with us," Heard says. "We're your family. We'll protect you." But Winger is determined. "The bureau was my family. I trusted you. You used me. You betrayed me." She then leaves.

Although much of the plot is far-fetched, the film offers a disturbing picture of frustrated, decent people who allow their fears to be exploited by others, such as the white-supremacy group in the film. "It's self-defense," one farmer explains. "We've got to protect ourselves." Another local inhabitant confides to Winger: "The bank took my farm, Vietnam took my son." These are the voices of a defeated, embittered people. Their search for a better America is desperate. They are willing to join any group and murder anyone who they think is threatening their country. They even resort to teaching hate and prejudice to their children to bring about their fantasy. See Federal Bureau of Investigation. ∎

Better 'Ole, The (1926), WB. *Dir.* Charles Reisner; *Sc.* Darryl F. Zanuck, Charles Reisner; *Cast includes:* Syd Chaplin, Doris Hill,

Harold Goodwyn, Jack Ackroyd, Edgar Kennedy, Charles Gerrard, Tom McGuire.

A World War I comedy based on the English cartoon characters of Captain Bruce Bairnsfather, the film stars Charlie Chaplin's half-brother, Syd Chaplin, as a happy-go-lucky English soldier. He and his army cronies, played by Harold Goodwyn and Jack Ackroyd, go through a series of misadventures while in the front lines. By the time this farce ends—and following a string of funny gags—the Germans are routed. Chaplin's major, who is actually a German spy, is caught and Syd wins sergeant's stripes. An English film version of the cartoonist's characters, bearing the same title, appeared in 1919. ■

Beyond the Last Frontier (1943), Rep. *Dir.* Howard Bretherton; *Sc.* John K. Butler, Morton Grant; *Cast includes:* Eddie Dew, Smiley Burnette, Lorraine Miller, Bob Mitchum, Harry Woods, Ernie Adams.

Dual spying adds a slight note of originality to this otherwise conventional western about a gang of border smugglers running contraband into Texas. Eddie Dew portrays a Texas Ranger who has gone under cover and becomes a member of the gang. Meanwhile, the outlaws have installed their own spy among the Rangers, causing complications for Dew and the forces of law and order. The remainder of the horse opera chiefly concerns the two undercover agents hunting for each other among the hills. Smiley Burnette portrays Dew's merry sidekick. Lorraine Miller, as the female lead, has mostly a decorative role. Bob (Robert) Mitchum was shortly to become a major screen personality, particularly scoring with the critics as an officer in the highly acclaimed World War II drama *The Story of G.I. Joe* (1945). ■

Bhowani Junction (1956), MGM. *Dir.* George Cukor; *Sc.* Sonya Levien, Ivan Moffat; *Cast includes:* Ava Gardner, Stewart Granger, Bill Travers, Abraham Sofaer, Francis Matthews, Marge Maitland.

Communist espionage and sabotage plague India during its last chaotic days under British rule in this post-World War II drama. Ava Gardner, an an Anglo-Indian, returns to an India marked by turbulence as the British prepare to withdraw. Communist agents are busy inciting the huge crowds against the soldiers. Stewart Granger, as an English colonel assigned to guard Bhowani Junction, a major

rail line, against Communist sabotage, narrates the tale. "The Communist underground," he says in a voice-over, "was ready to turn genuine passive resistance into a bloodbath." Granger eventually falls in love with Gardner. Peter Illing, as a Communist leader, rescues Gardner after she kills a British officer who has tried to rape her. At one point Gardner believes she loves another half-caste (Bill Travers) who is in charge of the local rail link. Granger and Travers in the climactic sequence prevent a train from being wrecked by Communist terrorists. Granger then observes that the important passenger—the target of the saboteurs—is Gandhi.

Throughout the drama Gardner faces the dilemma of choosing between her European and Indian roots. She is encouraged by Francis Matthews, as an Indian, to return to her native heritage. In this sense she personifies the turmoil India faced in choosing its political future. An Indian nationalist loyal to Gandhi says of the Communist insurgents: "Their masters and their minds are in Moscow. They want to reduce India to anarchy so they can take over." The dreams and hopes of the Indians are echoed in the words of one of her supporters: "Our country will open like a flower once the British are gone and our country is free." The film, based on the novel by John Masters, captures the teeming throngs and upheaval of the period but fails to develop the complex social and political issues. ■

Big Jim McLain (1952), WB. *Dir.* Edward Ludwig; *Sc.* James Edward Grant, Richard English, Eric Taylor; *Cast includes:* John Wayne, Nancy Olsen, James Arness, Alan Napier, Veda Ann Borg, Gayne Whitman.

John Wayne portrays an investigator for the House Un-American Activities Committee delving into Communist subversion in Hawaii in this Cold War drama. His fellow operative, played by James Arness, is murdered. Wayne finally gets enough evidence on the Communists and, after a fist fight with the gang, its members are brought to trial. But they hide behind the Fifth Amendment, thereby escaping the full sentence of the law. Nancy Olsen portrays a doctor's secretary who falls in love with Wayne in this routine film.

The unabashed anti-Communist propaganda that dominates the film is accompanied by a glorified tribute to those congressmen who served on the House Un-American Activities Committee. The opening shot of the Capitol is accompanied by a voice-over extolling the work of H.U.A.C., which was then busy ferreting out party members and fellow travelers in the film industry. John Wayne, at the time, presided over The Motion Picture Alliance for the Preservation of American Ideals, an organization opposed to Communist influence in Hollywood. See Cold War. ■

Big Noise, The (1944), TCF. *Dir.* Malcolm St. Clair; *Sc.* W. Scott Darling; *Cast includes:* Stan Laurel, Oliver Hardy, Doris Merrick, Arthur Space, Veda Ann Borg, Bobby Blake.

Laurel and Hardy, employed as janitors at a detective agency in this World War II comedy, impersonate private eyes when they learn that a scientist needs guards to protect a superbomb that he has constructed. At the inventor's home, they soon become involved with a gang of thieves plotting to steal the secret weapon. The pair run off with the bomb and hide in a radio-controlled plane that is being used for target practice. The boys spot a Japanese submarine, unload the bomb on the enemy vessel and bail out.

The critics unanimously panned the film, finding few laughs and a rehash of the team's old routines. Even Stan and Ollie's fans consider this padded feature to be one of their worst. Not only were their visual gags mediocre, but their verbal material— never their forte in their best works—was particularly deficient. However, some of their lines manage to capture the comic potential of the duo. "I think Mr. Hartley (the scientist) is just a little bit cracked," Stan confides to Ollie. "All inventors are like that," Hardy explains, "they're eccentric. They're not like you and me. They're different." The film introduced the popular song of the period, "Mairzy Doats," and had the dubious distinction of anticipating the atom bomb (the secret weapon in the plot).

As Laurel and Hardy began to fade from the screen, Abbott and Costello, who also starred in wartime comedies (*Buck Privates, In the Navy, Buck Privates Come Home*), rose to take their place and remained unchallenged as the top comedy team during World War II. Unlike Stan and Ollie, they lacked the characterizations that made their audiences care about them as real people, but they provided enough laughs to keep them in the forefront of screen comedy. ■

Birds Do It (1966), Col. *Dir.* Andrew Marton; *Sc.* Arnie Kogen, Art Arthur; *Cast includes:* Soupy Sales, Tab Hunter, Arthur O'Connell, Edward Andrews, Doris Dowling, Beverly Adams.

Soupy Sales portrays a secret agent assigned by the government to Cape Kennedy to prevent dust from interfering with the missile program in this zany slapstick comedy. It seems that the space program has been suffering setbacks; dust was found to be responsible for rocket misfires. Sales, as "miniscule molecular particle surveillance monitor," immediately begins operations to correct the problem. However, enemy agents, led by Tab Hunter, try to sabotage the janitor's efforts. The highlight of the film occurs when Sales, subjected to negative ionization, starts to fly. Arthur O'Connell portrays a screwball professor. Beverly Adams, as O'Connell's defiant daughter, provides some romantic interest. Doris Dowling, as a muddled Congresswoman, engages in some political spoofing. ■

Birth of a Race, The (1918), State Rights. *Dir.* John W. Noble; *Sc.* George F. Wheeler, Rudolph De Cordova, John W. Noble, Anthony P. Kelly; *Cast includes:* Louis Dean, Harry Dumont, Carter B. Harkness, Doris Doscher, Charles Graham, Ben Hendricks.

This patriotic film's theme—the development of democracy and the dangers it faces from the tyrannical powers in Europe—was changed because of the perils of World War I. Originally conceived as a sympathetic "race story of the Negro," the work was intended as a reply to the racist innuendoes of D. W. Griffith's *The Birth of a Nation* (1915). However, in its final form it remains a drama of family dissension, German spies and eventual family reconciliation.

A German-American steel magnate and his son Oscar side with the Kaiser during World War I while George, another son, joins the Allied forces. The industrialist's daughter (Gertrude Braun), as an American nurse, works in a hospital in France which is overrun by Germans. She is abused by her own brother Oscar, who fails to recognize her. George, a patient in the hospital, kills his brother. When he returns to the U.S., he discovers a German spy trying to steal secret documents that belong to George's father. George then kills the enemy agent. The father, realizing the mistake he has made, shifts his sympathies to America. The opening prologue consists of biblical and historical scenes showing the emergence of the democratic idea and includes the creation, the crucifixion of Christ, the discovery of the New World, the signing of the Declaration of Independence and the American Civil War. ■

Black Dakotas, The (1954), Col. *Dir.* Ray Nazarro; *Sc.* Ray Buffum, DeVallon Scott; *Cast includes:* Gary Merrill, Wanda Hendrix, John Bromfield, Noah Beery, Jr., Howard Wendell, Robert Simon.

During the Civil War, a Confederate agent, sent by the South, attempts to stir up Indian troubles in the West to divert Union troops from the battlefield in this routine drama. Southerner Gary Merrill disrupts President Lincoln's plan to make peace with the Sioux so that Union troops can be redeployed to fight against the South. Merrill, however, turns crooked and decides to keep the gold earmarked for the Indians. Wanda Hendrix, as the daughter of a Rebel spy, provides the romantic interest. The hero of this routine film is played by John Bromfield, a stage line owner. The plot allows for several battles between the Indians and the cavalry. See American Civil War: Intelligence and Covert Actions. ■

Black Dragons (1942), Mon. *Dir.* William Nigh; *Sc.* Harvey Gates; *Cast includes:* Bela Lugosi, Joan Barclay, Clayton Moore, George Pembroke, Robert Frazer, Stanford Jolley.

Possibly the most implausible spy tale to emerge from World War II, this inept drama stars Bela Lugosi as a Nazi doctor bent on a trail of revenge after he is betrayed by the Axis powers. One of Hitler's best surgeons before the war, Lugosi is sent to Japan where he alters the facial features of six members of the secret Black Dragon society so that they appear to be Caucasians. Their assignment is to journey to the U.S. as saboteurs and disrupt war production. When he completes the face-lifts, Lugosi is locked up to safeguard the plot. He escapes and, in retaliation, pursues and murders each secret agent. Clayton Moore, who later gained popularity as The Lone Ranger, plays the male romantic lead while Joan Barclay provides the lone feminine interest. ■

Black Legion. Although most Americans instantly recognize the Ku Klux Klan, the Black Legion, a clone organization, is hardly recalled at all. It fed on the fears and frustrations of working men and women who felt threatened by aliens and other minority groups.

The Black Legion experienced a surge in membership in the 1930s during the years of the Great Depression and, at its peak, claimed a membership of five million—chiefly in Michigan and Ohio. Like the Klan, it was antagonistic to blacks, Jews and Catholics. Its members were sworn to secrecy and pledged blind obedience to their leaders. For some strange psychological quirk, the Legion dressed in black robes and hoods in contradistinction to the Klan which dressed in white. Both groups' members underwent secret rites which strengthened control over the individual by the group.

A new member had to affirm "The object of this Order is to promote, protect, and preserve Protestantism; to create and guard the welfare of the Protestant people socially as well as politically." At one time, there was talk of setting up a Protestant dictatorship in the United States. This world view was reinforced by whippings, beatings and occasional shootings. What ultimately led to the public exposure of the Black Legion and the prosecution of a number of its members was the murder in 1936 of Charles Poole, a Detroit W.P.A. employee. The reasons for his murder are still unclear, but its historical significance lay in the subsequent publicity and prosecutions that the murder provoked. Investigations revealed that twenty men took part in the killing.

The Detroit prosecutor in the case, Duncan McCrea, was himself revealed to have been a member of the group when his own investigators uncovered an old Black Legion membership card with McCrea's name on it. McCrea, however, stoutly denied membership in the organization. The public exposure and reaction was so severe that the attorney general of Michigan, David Crowley, ordered every prosecutor in the state to track Black Legion activities. Subsequent investigations revealed a widespread network of members throughout twelve states and women's auxiliaries. Public disgust, coupled with strict prosecution of the murderers, led to the eventual disintegration of the organization.

Hollywood occasionally used the term

"Black Legion" in dramas before the 1930s, but it usually referred to a nebulous fictitious secret criminal or spy organization, such as in the World War I drama *Who Was the Other Man?* (1917). The film told about a "Black Legion" of clandestine Germans. However, only a handful of Hollywood dramas have attempted to expose, or even dramatize, the activities of the real-life organization. *Black Legion* (1936), directed by Archie Mayo and featuring Humphrey Bogart, left little to the imagination when it revealed the inner workings of a violent group of superpatriots. The hooded members use floggings, beatings and bombs to intimidate and terrorize their alien neighbors in the name of Americanism. The robed bigots are finally brought to justice at a sensational murder trial after they order the killing of one of their victims. *Legion of Terror* (1936), with Bruce Cabot and Marguerite Churchill, gave a fairly accurate portrayal of some of the Black Legion's more clandestine activities. The plot deals with a secret terrorist organization, known as the Legion of Terror, that threatens a local community. The gang engages in various criminal acts, including mailing bombs to U.S. Congressmen.

Other films with similar themes appeared occasionally during the following decades. In *Violence* (1947) a secret organization, calling itself "United Defenders" and specializing in spreading disorder and brutality, caters to discontent World War II veterans. Masquerading as patriots, the group exploits its members by having them commit acts of violence. *Storm Warning* (1951), with Ginger Rogers, Ronald Reagan and Doris Day, explored the extreme right and racist activities of the K.K.K. in a small Southern community. Reagan portrays a district attorney trying to prosecute a Klan member for murdering a reporter in a town sympathetic to the Klan. *Betrayed* (1988), with Debra Winger and Tom Berenger, examines a neo-Fascist paramilitary organization operating in the U.S. Winger portrays an undercover F.B.I. agent who learns that Berenger is a "point man" for an ambitious politician and part of a right-wing movement plotting to assassinate political leaders, blacks and others they believe are threats to the American way of life. ■

Black Moon Rising (1986), New World. *Dir.* Harley Cokliss; *Sc.* John Carpenter, Desmond Nakano, William Gray; *Cast includes:* Tommy Lee Jones, Linda Hamilton, Robert Vaughn, Richard Jaeckel, Lee Ving, Bubba Smith.

Tommy Lee Jones portrays a professional thief who sometimes takes on special assignments for the U.S. government in this action drama that cares more about cars than people. Jones breaks into the offices of a Las Vegas corporation under government investigation on several counts and steals a cassette containing its tax records. He then hides the cassette in the Black Moon, a souped-up, experimental car. However, an attractive car thief (Linda Hamilton) soon steals the vehicle with the cassette. Her boss (Robert Vaughn), the crazed head of the car theft gang, indulges in random homicide. Lee, therefore, has his hands full for the remainder of the film as he tries to retrieve the cassette while being pursued both by police and Mafia minions. The emphasis is on the Black Moon, which can sprout wings, is impervious to external harm and can travel at high speeds. ■

Black Parachute, The (1944), Col. *Dir.* Lew Landers; *Sc.* Clarence Upson Young; *Cast includes:* John Carradine, Osa Massen, Larry Parks, Jeanne Bates, Jonathan Hale.

Espionage and guerrilla warfare are the ingredients of this World War II drama set in an unnamed Nazi-occupied country whose citizens take up arms against the invaders. Larry Parks portrays an American agent sent into the country by parachute to rescue its king who is held hostage by the Nazis. He joins forces with the local underground in their struggle against the Nazis. Parks finally succeeds in his mission so that the king can broadcast against the ruthless occupiers. Osa Massen portrays a German spy while John Carradine plays a ruthless Nazi general responsible for the king's downfall in this tale in which all the Germans are stereotyped as monstrous caricatures. ■

Black September. The Black June and Black September Palestinian terrorist groups are portrayed by Yasir Arafat, the leader of the P.L.O., as splinter radical factions over whom he has no control. In this manner, Arafat can function on two levels: he can talk of peace but surreptitiously continue to order assassinations and conduct acts of blackmail. The Western press, because of a combination of fear of the P.L.O. and a psychological need to identify with the revolutionary "mystique," has swallowed the P.L.O. chief's line.

The reality probably is that Arafat does influence these splinter groups.

Black September was born in the Kingdom of Jordan. In 1970 the Palestinian presence was causing major problems for King Hussein, and in September of that year he unleashed the Jordanian army on Al-Fatah within the kingdom; thousands of Palestinians were killed and hence the name Black September was adopted. Supposedly as a result of this massacre, Abu Daoud and a group of his supporters split with the mainstream P.L.O. The radical leader opposed the P.L.O.'s search for a political option in solving the Palestinian problem and adopted the *nom de guerre* Black September.

In subsequent years it took responsibility for numerous killings. In 1971 Black September assassinated the Prime Minister of Jordan, Wafsi Tell, who was held responsible for the decision to send the Jordanian army against the Palestinians the previous year. In 1972 the group hijacked a Belgian airliner at Lod Airport in Israel and later that same year murdered eleven Israeli athletes at the Olympic games in Munich. The following year, 1973, was a particularly violent one for the group: the American ambassador and a Belgian diplomat were murdered at the Saudi Arabian embassy in the Sudan; the Israeli embassy in Bangkok was seized; and an attack was made at the Athens airport during which five people were killed and over fifty others were injured.

Syria's response to the Palestinians in Lebanon was similar to that of the Jordanians. In June 1976 the Syrians, together with their Christian allies, launched an attack on the Palestinian terrorists in Lebanon and defeated them. A new splinter group—Black June—was formed by the remnants of the Palestinians. Members of this group attacked a hotel in Damascus and took hostages in an attempt to force the release of jailed P.L.O. members in Syria. The Syrians responded by counterattacking the hotel, killing the leader of the group and hanging its other three members.

Black September eventually merged with Black June and the Abu Nidal terrorists whose leader was Sabri Khalil al-Banna. In 1977 several members of the newly merged group assassinated the foreign minister of the United Arab Emirates who was then negotiating in Abu Dhabi.

Following the merger, Abu Nidal possibly took control of the group. Born Sabry al Banna in 1937 in the city of Jaffa in what today is Israel, Abu Nidal attended the best school in Jerusalem, the Islamic Al Rhoda. He subsequently joined the Baath party and then switched to Al-Fatah. Abu Nidal made a public show of breaking with the latter organization in 1974 and formed his own Fatah Revolutionary Council.

Abu Nidal organized commercial subsidiaries of his terrorist group throughout the Arab world and in Europe. He maintained one such organization, S.A.S. Foreign Trade and Investment Company, in Warsaw. One branch, Zibado Foreign Trade Consultants, was established in East Berlin, and others were founded in Bulgaria, Cyprus, Turkey, Italy, Belgium, Austria and Spain. At times, depending upon the political climate, he was able to set up business fronts in Syria and Iraq.

"Business" consisted of blackmailing various wealthy Arab families and governments such as Saudi Arabia, the United Arab Emirates, Kuwait and Jordan. To make his point, Abu Nidal ordered the murders of two United Emirate diplomats in Bombay in 1982 and a Kuwaiti diplomat in Madrid and the Jordanian ambassadors in New Delhi and Rome the same year. He won his argument, and the Arab governments have been paying him ever since. His commercial establishments shipped arms to both Iraq and Iran. It has been estimated that all of these endeavors have earned Abu Nidal a fortune of over $200 million.

Reports suggest that, as a result of the latest warming trends between Egypt and Libya, Abu Nidal has been placed under house arrest in a compound near Tripoli in Libya where he now lives. President Mubarak of Egypt had asked Colonel Qadafi for the extradition of Abu Nidal or his incarceration as a condition for the improvement of relations between the two countries. House arrest, apparently, was Qadafi's compromise. Abu Nidal is being temporarily shelved because he is an embarrassment to the "peace process" between Israel and the Arabs.

Several films depict hijackings, assassinations and other acts of international terrorism closely associated with those of Black September. Ironically, the one film, *Black Sunday* (1977), that calls the Arab terrorists by name, has an entirely fictitious plot. The other dramas simply label the terrorists as

Arab extremists but base their actions on incidents for which members of Black September have taken credit. In *The Next Man* (1976), for example, Arab terrorists dispatch one of their paid international agents to assassinate several moderate Arabs, including a Saudi Arabian diplomat who proposes making peace with Israel in exchange for technological development. *The Delta Force* (1986) concerns the hijacking of an airplane by a violent faction of Arab terrorists. They divert the flight from Athens to New York and detour the plane filled with American passengers to Beirut. In *Terminal Entry*, released the same year, a Middle East terrorist leader orders dozens of suicide hit squads to the U.S. to assassinate major political leaders. *Death Before Dishonor* (1987) deals with a radical terrorist organization that assassinates an Israeli ambassador and his family in Cyprus, kidnaps a U.S. colonel and threatens to bomb a U.S. embassy. In many of these films, the terrorist theme is exploited simply to introduce the action and violence that dominate the plot. ∎

Black Sunday (1977), Par. *Dir.* John Frankenheimer; *Sc.* Ernest Lehman, Kenneth Ross, Ivan Moffat; *Cast includes:* Robert Shaw, Bruce Dern, Marthe Keller, Fritz Weaver, Steven Keats, Bekim Fehmiu.

International terrorists plot a mass slaughter of the Super Bowl stadium audience in this tense drama based on Thomas Harris' novel. The Black September movement, known for its ruthless killing of Israeli athletes at the Munich Olympics, hopes to force the U.S. to end its military and economic aid to Israel. So its leaders dispatch one of its chief activists, played by Marthe Keller, to carry out the wholesale killing at the stadium. Bruce Dern, as a mentally disturbed former Vietnam prisoner of war, pilots the television blimp which hovers over the stadium. He falls for Keller's charms and agrees to help her. Robert Shaw, as an Israeli guerrilla who accidentally discovers part of the terrorist plan, links up with F.B.I. agents to prevent the impending disaster. Fritz Weaver portrays the government agent who works closely with Shaw. Steven Keats, as Shaw's highly emotional fellow Israeli agent, is staunchly anti-Arab. Bekim Fehmiu portrays the terrorist leader.

The film goes beyond the usual superficialities of this type of action drama by introducing better characterizations and some balanced sympathies behind the terrorist motivations. For instance, Shaw, although completely dedicated to foiling the plot and capturing the terrorists, understands the frustrations of the terrorists and their cause. Again, an Arab official who reluctantly helps Shaw by giving him material on the violent background of Keller's life, concludes: "She is your creation."

Following the massacre of the Israeli Olympic athletes in 1972 by the Palestinian terrorists known as Black September, Israel fielded a counterterrorist group, the Wrath of God. Its function was to identify, seek out and kill members of the Black September group as well as other Arab terrorists in Europe. More than 12 Black September leaders fell victim to the Wrath of God, which was reportedly dissolved as a result of protests from various European governments. See Mossad. ∎

Black Tom explosion. See German Intelligence: World War I. ∎

Blackhawk (1952) serial, Col. *Dir.* Spencer Bennet, Fred F. Sears; *Sc.* George H. Plympton, Royal K. Cole, Sherman L. Lowe; *Cast includes:* Kirk Alyn, Carol Forman, John Crawford, Michael Fox, Don Harvey, Rick Vallin.

Blackhawk and his brotherhood of daring airmen battle a network of enemy agents from an unspecified country in this 15-chapter serial aimed chiefly at a juvenile audience and based on comic-book characters created by Reed Crandall and Charles Cuidera. An unseen mastermind of the spy ring sends out his minions to commit various acts of sabotage in the U.S., thereby keeping our superheroes busy dashing about. Kirk Alyn heads the Blackhawks who, at one point, are infiltrated by one of the spies impersonating a twin brother. Carol Forman and Rick Vallin portray two of the chief saboteurs. Some of the cast appeared in *Superman*, an earlier Columbia serial starring Alyn as the man of steel. ∎

Blindfold (1966), U. *Dir.* Philip Dunne; *Sc.* Philip Dunne, W. H. Menger; *Cast includes:* Rock Hudson, Claudia Cardinale, Jack Warden, Guy Stockwell, Brad Dexter, Anne Seymour.

A major American scientist becomes the target of both U.S. Secret Service agents and

Rock Hudson (r.) leads Claudia Cardinale and others out of a nest of spies. *Blindfold* (1966).

an international spy ring in this comedy drama. It seems that both sides of the Cold War, the East and West, are in the "business" of gathering the best scientific brains available. "What we're up against," a Central Intelligence Agency general explains, "is nothing less than an international black market in brains . . . scientific geniuses bought, sold, traded—if necessary, kidnapped."

Rock Hudson, as a distinguished New York psychiatrist, is enlisted by a general in the C.I.A. (Jack Warden) to treat a disturbed scientist whom the agency has kidnapped. Meanwhile, an international spy ring is interested in kidnapping the scientist from the C.I.A. Guy Stockwell portrays the chief spy. Claudia Cardinale, as the victim's sister, becomes embroiled in the plot when she receives a phone call from her brother. She at first accuses Hudson of being involved with the spies. They eventually join forces to help free the scientist who falls into the hands of the spies.

Hudson, who had been blindfolded during his trips to where the man was being held captive, retraces his journey by analyzing the sounds he had heard earlier—a device used in a previous spy drama. (In *Joe Smith, American*, released in 1942, a World War II airplane technician, captured and tortured by German agents, later retraces for the F.B.I. the journey to the spies' hide-out.)

Blindfold encompasses several comedy devices, including satire, gags and slapstick, the last being the weakest. In one particular sequence, for example, Hudson fights off a gang of thugs with the contents of a fire extinguisher, spraying them and Cardinale with streams of whipped cream. The satirical elements are more comical than the slapstick. Jack Warden, as the no-nonsense C.I.A. general, takes special pride in the secrecy of the operation. "Our security must be airtight—a work of art," he repeatedly warns Hudson. The film, based on Lucille Fletcher's novel, also pokes fun at the police, exemplified by Brad Dexter's portrayal of a slow-witted detective. ∎

Blockade (1928), RKO. *Dir.* George B. Seitz; *Sc.* Harvey Thew; *Cast includes:* Anna Q. Nilsson, Wallace MacDonald, James Bradbury, Sr., Walter McGrail.

Rumrunning during the Prohibition era serves as the subject of this inept action drama set off the coast of Florida. Anna Q. Nilsson, as a special undercover agent for the U.S. Revenue Service, masquerades as a young socialite in an attempt to expose the smugglers. Wallace MacDonald portrays a young business executive who is on a fishing vacation in Florida. He becomes entangled with the band of criminals and Nilsson, with whom he soon falls in love. Posing as a hijacker, Nilsson infiltrates the gang and makes short work of rounding them up. The film includes scenes of hijacking in the vicinity of the islands off Florida. Of course, the hero and heroine end up in each other's arms in the final scene. ∎

Blockade (1938), UA. *Dir.* William Dieterle; *Sc.* John Howard Lawson; *Cast includes:* Madeleine Carroll, Henry Fonda, Leo Carrillo, John Halliday, Vladimir Sokoloff, Reginald Denny.

Producer Walter Wanger's superficial drama of the Spanish Civil War attempts to depict the devastation thrust upon cities and the suffering of civilian populations as a result of modern warfare. Airplanes rain down disaster on military targets and civilians with equal destruction. Submarines impose a tight blockade while spies inform the undersea vessels of the position of supply ships.

Amid the chaos emerges a romantic plot involving Madeleine Carroll, whose father is an international spy, and Henry Fonda, who portrays a peasant soldier fighting for his country. Once Carroll witnesses the misery she has helped to bring about, she reveals the location of the spies to Fonda. Meanwhile, high-ranking military officers are in collusion with enemy agents. Fonda pleads for peace in this antiwar film that manages to remain neutral. "Where is the conscience of the world that it allows the killing and maiming of civilians to go on?" he asks.

Although the film was cautious not to side with either the Loyalists or Franco's forces, it met with much controversy. The Hays Office, Hollywood's self-governing censorship committee, suggested numerous changes in the script to avoid antagonizing foreign nations. At its release it received the support of Amer-ican Communists while the Catholic press and the Knights of Columbus condemned it. In New York City demonstrators gathered in front of Radio City Music Hall, protesting the showing of the film. *Blockade*, with all its ambiguity and artificiality, was the first significant film to deal with the war in Spain. *The Last Train From Madrid*, released the previous year, was even more nebulous about the conflict, simply using the war only as background for a weak drama. One decade later, *Blockade* was used against screenwriter John Howard Lawson when he was brought before the House Un-American Activities Committee investigating Communist influence in Hollywood. Excerpts from the film were used in *The Good Fight*, a 1984 documentary about the Spanish Civil War. ∎

Lobby card showing newspaperman James Cagney, who possesses a secret document, battling the chief of the Japanese secret police. *Blood on the Sun* (1945).

Blood on the Sun (1945), UA. *Dir.* Frank Lloyd; *Sc.* Lester Cole; *Cast includes:* James Cagney, Sylvia Sidney, Rosemary De Camp, Wallace Ford, Robert Armstrong, John Emery.

James Cagney portrays a tough American newspaper editor in pre-World War II Japan who discovers a Japanese plot for world conquest. The film concerns the search by Japanese police to retrieve the controversial plan before it is made public. Finally, it is up to Cagney to smuggle the important document out of the country in this tense drama. Sylvia Sidney, as a double agent, is employed by Japanese officials to recover the plans from Cagney. In reality, she is working for the Chinese who want to expose the Japanese militarists.

In the final moments Cagney must run a gauntlet of Japanese secret police waiting to stop him from entering the American embassy. A bullet wounds him, but an American official comes out of the embassy in time to save the editor's life. Embarrassed by his failure, the head of the Japanese secret police tries to smooth over the incident. The self-righteous embassy official declares: "The United States Government doesn't settle for a deal." Colonel Tojo (Robert Armstrong), another Japanese official who had tried to kill Cagney, offers his hand in friendship. "You have saying, 'Forgive your enemies.' I am willing," he says. "Sure, forgive your enemies," Cagney replies defiantly, "but first get even."

Released during the last months of World War II, the drama joins the long list of anti-Japanese propaganda films of that period. The infamous Tanaka Plan, or Tanaka Memorial, that the film centers around, was an actual document stolen in 1927. Exposed in the international press, it included detailed maps and other information that revealed Japan's secret plans involving a future war with China, Korea and the U.S. It even told of Japan's plot to bomb America's naval base at Pearl Harbor. The plan was so outlandish at the time that no one treated it seriously. See Pearl Harbor. ∎

Blue Envelope Mystery, The (1916), Vitagraph. *Dir.* Wilfred North; *Sc.* Helen Duey; *Cast includes:* Lillian Walker, John D. Bennet, Bob Hay, Charles Kent, Josephine Earle, Harry Northrup.

A stenographer carrying a secret formula is kidnapped by spies in this comedy drama unfolded in flashback. Lillian Walker, as the heroine-victim, had been raised in society. A suitor, more interested in her fortune than her love, abandons her when he discovers that her deceased father had left her penniless. Obtaining a position with an inventor, Walker is entrusted with delivering her employer's latest discovery to government officials in Washington. Kidnapped by enemy agents, she foils their attempts to locate the formula. They never learn that she has hidden it in her hat. The film, adapted from the novel *The Blue Envelope* by Sophie Kerr, ends with the heroine's marriage to the inventor. ∎

Blue Thunder (1983), Col. *Dir.* John Badham; *Sc.* Dan O'Rannon, Don Jakoby; *Cast includes:* Roy Scheider, Malcolm McDowell, Warren Oates, Candy Clark, Daniel Stern, Paul Roebling.

A Los Angeles police helicopter pilot and Vietnam War veteran foils a military conspiracy in this far-fetched but action-packed drama. Roy Scheider, as the pilot, and Daniel Stern, as a rookie cop and Scheider's assistant, test-drive "Blue Thunder," a technologically advanced super-helicopter designed to combat terrorism. Packed with special artillery and eavesdropping devices, the secret vehicle is a marvel of modern technology as it cruises above the city on its maiden run. During the trial period Scheider accidentally overhears a conversation about a military conspiracy, including references to the death of a councilwoman who had been slain earlier in the film.

The tape of the conversation, which Scheider made, also implicates Malcolm McDowell, who portrays a member of the team that is introducing the specially equipped helicopter. Scheider and McDowell have remained mortal enemies since their days in Vietnam. In an attempt to retrieve the incriminating tape, McDowell has Stern murdered. Scheider then commandeers the copter to help him unmask the entire conspiracy which involves highly placed politicians as well as McDowell. Although the film chiefly focuses on action, there are some ideological allusions concerning the abuses of the Military Industrial Complex. Candy Clark, as Scheider's girlfriend, helps him recover the hidden tape, which they then turn over to a local television station. Warren Oates, who died shortly after the film was released, portrays Scheider's hard-nosed superior. The film is dedicated to him. ∎

Blue, White and Perfect (1941), TCF. *Dir.* Herbert I. Leeds; *Sc.* Samuel G. Engel; *Cast includes:* Lloyd Nolan, Mary Beth Hughes, Helene Reynolds, George Reeves, Steve Geray, Henry Victor.

One of the earliest American films to be released following Japan's attack on Pearl Harbor, the drama concerns a plot concocted by enemy agents to steal industrial diamonds. Lloyd Nolan, as Michael Shayne, a fictional detective created by Brett Halliday, immediately gets on the case which takes him aboard a Honolulu-bound liner. Employed as a private investigator for an airplane plant, he is assigned to recover the diamonds which are necessary as cutting tools. Mary Beth Hughes portrays the sleuth's fiancée. Although he had earlier promised her that he would quit his sleuthing, he embarks on the mysterious voyage. By the time the vessel docks at Honolulu, Shayne has solved the case and retrieved the precious stones. ■

Body and Soul (1931), Fox. *Dir.* Al Santell; *Sc.* Jules Furthman; *Cast includes:* Charles Farrell, Elissa Landi, Humphrey Bogart, Myrna Loy, Donald Dillaway.

A weak World War I romantic drama, the film concerns friends in the Royal Flying Corps whose lives are affected by espionage agents operating in England. Humphrey Bogart portrays one of the fliers who marries before being shipped to France where he soon becomes involved in another romance. He dies during an attack on an observation balloon. Charles Farrell, who is aboard the plane, is forced to land. Back in England, he meets Bogart's widow (Elissa Landi). She is under suspicion as an enemy agent who is responsible for the deaths of several fliers. However, the real spy (Myrna Loy) is ultimately revealed. The film is based on the play *Squadrons* by A. E. Thomas which, in turn, had been adapted from "Big Eyes and Little Mouth," a short story by Elliott White Springs. Myrna Loy, before appearing as the leading lady in sophisticated and screwball comedies and the popular "Thin Man" series, practically made a career portraying spies during her early years in Hollywood. ■

Bomb Throwers, The (1915), Pathé. *Cast includes:* Edwin August.

Local Communists threaten the life and family of an honest district attorney in this little drama. After one of their members, a dangerous terrorist, is jailed through the efforts of the D.A., the remainder of the gang seek revenge. They convince Tony, a poor Italian immigrant widower, that the D.A. was responsible for his wife's death. They hand him a bomb to be placed under the home of their victim. Tony discovers in time that the terrorists have lied to him. He hurtles the bomb at a shed where they are hiding, thereby killing the gang and saving the D.A. and his family.

The film gained unexpected publicity at the time of its release. Newspapers were carrying sensational stories of a Communist conspiracy to blow up St. Patrick's Cathedral. A live bomb was actually found inside the New York church. Several suspects were arrested and convicted. See Anarchists in the U.S.; Palmer Raids. ■

Bombay Clipper (1942), U. *Dir.* John Rawlins; *Sc.* Roy Chanslor, Stanley Rubin; *Cast includes:* William Gargan, Irene Hervey, Charles Lang, Maria Montez, Lloyd Corrigan, Mary Gordon.

Millions of dollars' worth of industrial diamonds, necessary for England's war effort, becomes the focal point of this drama set during World War II. An American foreign correspondent (William Gargan) and his wife (Irene Hervey), as passengers aboard a plane traveling from Bombay to San Francisco, find themselves entangled in a hijacking. Truman Bradley, as the head of a group of international spies, forcibly takes over control of the clipper. His target is the large supply of diamonds that are aboard. They are India's gift to embattled Britain. Gargan soon springs into action and disarms the master spy, thereby rescuing the other innocent passengers and the important cargo. ■

Bombs Over Burma (1942), PRC. *Dir.* Joseph H. Lewis; *Sc.* Milton Raison, Joseph H. Lewis; *Cast includes:* Anna May Wong, Noel Madison, Leslie Denison, Nedrick Young, Dan Seymour, Frank Lackteen.

The Burma Road and China's heroic struggle against the Japanese are the backgrounds of this weak World War II drama. Anna May Wong, formerly associated with major films, portrays a schoolteacher who is requested by the Chinese government to work as a secret agent. It seems that spies, operating along the Burma Road, are trying to stop the shipment of essential supplies. One agent is transmitting information to the Japanese about convoys traveling the Burma Road. The low-budget film, suspiciously similar to *Shanghai Express* (1932) in its structure and array of characters, provides very little action and few scenes of the war.

Joseph H. Lewis, whose creative use of the camera and sense of film rhythm later gained him a cult following among some critics as an *auteur* director, manages some interesting effects within his limited budget. Several scenes have no dialogue, depending entirely on visual storytelling—an artistic technique reminiscent of the silent era and often neglected with the advent of sound. See Burma. ■

Bond, James. The fictitious British spy, James Bond, also known as 007, has had a marked and lasting influence on American spy films. Created by novelist Ian Fleming, a former British intelligence officer, Bond received a boost in popularity in the U.S. when President Kennedy acknowledged that Fleming's espionage novels were his favorite escape books. The author's works, which originally met with only modest acceptance, now soared in sales.

Films inevitably followed. Sean Connery was the first British film actor to portray the suave spy who enjoyed a dry martini almost as much as going to bed with a voluptuous woman. Whether the sardonic agent was being chased by an oddball villain or lured by an exotic *femme fatale*, he managed to keep his urbanity. But he was just as likely to kill a foe in cold blood and follow the act with a quip.

The James Bond films, beginning in 1962 and made chiefly in England, had big budgets and consisted of elaborate gadgetry, huge sets, foreign locales and a parade of sexy women. The scripts offered stylish action and witty one-liners. With names like Honeychile, Solitaire and Pussy Galore, the women were often equally beautiful and dangerous—in and out of bed, but the archvillains and their henchmen were even more strange. Dr. No, Goldfinger, Odd Job and Jaws presented diabolical and unpredictable perils for 007, yet Bond, behind the wheel of his speedy and specially equipped Aston Martin or using some newly developed weapon, foiled them all.

Each film broke previous box-office records and prompted other studios to try to cash in on this latest screen phenomenon. Several American clones soon followed. Dean Martin starred as Matt Helm in *The Si-*

lencers (1966), *Murderers' Row* (1966), *The Ambushers* (1967) and *The Wrecking Crew* (1968). James Coburn portrayed Derek Flint in *Our Man Flint* (1966) and *In Like Flint* (1967). Both of these superspies imitated many of Bond's traits but failed to surpass him. Some U.S. productions stretched plot credibility, added more technological gadgetry and introduced sexier scenes. But the James Bond series has retained its popularity (although the later entries suffered from lack of freshness) for more than 25 years.

Several actors played Bond, each in a slightly different way. Roger Moore gave a more flippant interpretation. George Lazenby appeared in one film and played down Bond's macho and womanizing characteristics. Timothy Dalton's more recent portrayals add a darker, more brooding tone to the character. Many fans of the series prefer Connery and consider his Bond the definitive one. The following lists the Bond films chronologically and the actor who portrays the legendary 007.

> *Dr. No* (1962) Connery
> *From Russia With Love* (1963) Connery
> *Goldfinger* (1964) Connery
> *Thunderball* (1965) Connery
> *You Only Live Twice* (1967) Connery
> *On Her Majesty's Secret Service* (1969) Lazenby
> *Diamonds Are Forever* (1971) Connery
> *Live and Let Die* (1973) Moore
> *Man With the Golden Gun* (1975) Moore
> *The Spy Who Loved Me* (1977) Moore
> *Moonraker* (1979) Moore
> *For Your Eyes Only* (1981) Moore
> *Octopussy* (1983) Moore
> *Never Say Never Again* (1983) Connery
> *A View to a Kill* (1985) Moore
> *The Living Daylights* (1986) Dalton
> *Licence to Kill* (1989) Dalton ■

Bond Between, The (1917), Par. Dir. Donald Crisp; Sc. George Beban; Cast includes: George Beban, John Burton, Nigel de Brullier, Colin Chase, Eugene Pallette, Vola Vale.

A U.S. Secret Service agent, assigned to investigate a suspected art smuggler, instead finds herself helping him prove his innocence in this drama. Colin Chase, as the suspect, is an impoverished art student studying in Paris who returns to his father in New York when World War I erupts. An unscrupulous art dealer (Eugene Pallette) dupes the unsuspecting Chase into transporting stolen paintings to the U.S. The Secret Service, thinking that Chase is a dealer-smuggler, delegates an agent (Vola Vale) to find evidence against him. Meanwhile, Pallette, who is now in New York, plans to steal several valuable paintings from a museum where Chase's father is employed as a night watchman. Vale, who has befriended the young artist, informs him of the possible theft. Chase tries to foil Pallette's scheme but is himself arrested. Pallette is eventually caught and the father and son rewarded. Chase and Vale, who have fallen in love, decide to marry. ∎

Bonds of Honor (1919), Haworth. *Dir.* William Worthington; *Sc.* Francis Guinan; *Cast includes:* Sessue Hayakawa, Tsuri Aoki, Marin Sais, Dagmar Gadowsky, Herschell Mayall.

A World War I drama set in Japan, the film concerns a respectable Japanese family torn apart by a weak-willed son. The young man's wasted life brings shame and dishonor to his twin brother and father. Sessue Hayakawa portrays a dual role, that of a devoted and helpful son, and his twin who spends most of his time in a gambling house. Their father is a government official who is in the midst of developing secret war plans. A German agent befriends the young gambler who soon mounts up huge debts. The spy persuades his victim to borrow his father's plans so that they can be photographed. The gambler agrees, but upon returning the papers, he is caught by his father. He is told that he must take his own life to protect the family from dishonor. He rejects the harsh sentence and decides to escape across the border into Russia. The father then charges his other son to bring the fugitive to justice. This was a particularly unusual setting and subject for an American film. ∎

Boots (1919), Famous Players. *Dir.* Elmer Clifton; *Sc.* M. M. Stearns; *Cast includes:* Dorothy Gish, Richard Barthelmess, Fontine La Rue, Edward Peil, Kate V. Toncray, Raymond Cannon.

A young maid saves the lives of two world leaders in this spy comedy. Dorothy Gish, as a servant at an old English inn, reads romantic novels to brighten her dull and cheerless life. She likes a young student (Richard Barthelmess) who is a boarder at the inn. Unknown to her, he is actually a Scotland Yard detective who has another guest, a sculptress, under surveillance. When Gish sees the student and the sculptress together, she grows disillusioned with her private world of romance and decides to get rid of all her novels. She takes them to the cellar where she discovers an underground passageway which connects the inn to the rooms where President Wilson meets with King George.

Meanwhile, Bolsheviks devise a plot to kill the two world leaders. Gish accidentally stumbles across the conspiracy led by the sculptress who is actually a Bolshevik. Our heroine manages to foil the assassination attempt and marry the Scotland Yard investigator who professes his love for her. The title refers to Gish's name.

Following the Russian Revolution, the Bolsheviks were considered a potential threat in Great Britain. England's Secret Intelligence Service (S.I.S.), founded in 1909, considered the Soviets the chief danger to the empire and allocated its operating funds accordingly. S.I.S. operatives sought to recruit agents throughout Europe and the Soviet Union in an effort to gain information about Russian spies planted in England and Soviet plans concerning Britain. This inordinate fear of the Communists dominated S.I.S. policy well into the 1930s when Nazi Germany finally replaced the Soviet Union as the number one villain. ∎

Border Incident (1949), MGM. *Dir.* Anthony Mann; *Sc.* John C. Higgins; *Cast includes:* Ricardo Montalban, George Murphy, Howard da Silva, James Mitchell, Arnold Moss, Teresa Celli.

U.S. and Mexican immigration agencies combine forces to smash a smuggling operation that is transporting illegal aliens into the U.S. in this drama whose subject matter is as timely and relevant today as it was in the late 1940s. Ricardo Montalban, as a Mexican agent, and George Murphy, who represents U.S. authorities, decide to join the gang in an effort to break up the smuggling activities from within. They temporarily succeed in their masquerade, but Murphy's cover is exposed and he is brutally murdered. It is then left to Montalban to end the illegal operations, which he does expeditiously in a climactic shoot-out. The gang, whose members include Arnold Moss and Alfonso Bedoya—the latter famous for his bandit role in *The Treasure of the Sierra Madre* ("I don't have to show you no stinkin' badges")—is led by chief villain Howard da Silva. ∎

Border Wireless, The (1918), Artcraft. *Dir.* William S. Hart; *Sc.* C. Gardner Sullivan; *Cast includes:* William S. Hart, Wanda Hawley, Charles Arling, James Mason, E. von Ritzen, Berthold Sprotte.

An embittered outlaw, transformed by love and patriotism, turns hero in this World War I drama. William S. Hart, usually associated with westerns, turns to crime after his parents' death. He blames the railroad for evicting his parents from their ranch. Although an outlaw, he rescues a pretty telegrapher (Wanda Hawley) from a gang of bandits and soon falls in love with her. When war erupts, Hart decides to enlist, but a local German spy informs the authorities that Hart is an outlaw. Under the guise of working a mine near the Mexican border, German spies operate a wireless station and are about to transmit to their countrymen the location of General Pershing's troop ship that is sailing for France. Hart foils their plan and destroys the wireless equipment. Authorities then allow him to enlist. Before he leaves for France, he confesses his love to Hawley and promises to marry her when he returns. ■

Borderline (1950), U. *Dir.* William A. Seiter; *Sc.* Devery Freeman; *Cast includes:* Fred MacMurray, Claire Trevor, Raymond Burr, Roy Roberts, José Torvay, Morris Ankrum.

A Los Angeles policewoman and a federal agent are assigned to break up a narcotics operation in Mexico in this drama filled with improbable incidents. The federal narcotics agency asks Claire Trevor, as the L.A. officer, to gather evidence against the drug ring. She poses as a chorus girl and makes contact with the head smuggler. However, a rival gang bursts into the room, seizes the drugs and takes Trevor along with them.

Meanwhile, Fred MacMurray, as an undercover government agent, is masquerading as one of the competitors. Not knowing each other's true identity, MacMurray and Trevor both head for California to capture the chief villain. A romance blossoms, although each is troubled with the thought of handing the other over to the authorities. However, the smuggling racket is smashed, and they learn the truth about each other. Raymond Burr portrays one of the smugglers. MacMurray, on loan to Universal for this production, was a Paramount contract player for most of his film career, specializing in sophisticated and farcical comedies. ■

Borrowed Plumage (1917), Triangle. *Dir.* Raymond B. West; *Sc.* J. G. Hawks; *Cast includes:* Bessie Barriscale, Arthur Maude, Dorcas Matthews, Barney Sherry, Wallace Worsley, Tod Burns.

An American naval officer is reunited with his Irish sweetheart in this silent drama set during the American Revolution. An American warship suddenly appears off the Irish coast. The young officer (Arthur Maude), who is familiar with the area, is assigned to go ashore and reconnoiter. Meanwhile, a local earl and his family abandon their castle when they learn about the nearby American vessel. They leave behind their kitchen maid (Bessie Barriscale), the American's former girlfriend, to attend to their estate. Playfully wearing her mistress' fancy clothes, she is mistaken for the earl's wife by local militiamen.

When the American officer arrives and sees his former sweetheart entertaining the soldiers, he enters, posing as an Irish gentleman. The English soon discover his true identity, arrest him for impersonating a civilian and sentence him to death as a spy. The maid, to save the man she loves, signals the American ship. A small but hectic battle ensues between the Americans and the British troops, and the officer is rescued. He takes his sweetheart with him to America. ■

Bowery Battalion (1951), Mon. *Dir.* William Beaudine; *Sc.* Charles Marion; *Cast includes:* Leo Gorcey, Huntz Hall, Donald MacBride, Virginia Hewitt, Russell Hicks, William Benedict.

Another in the Bowery Boys comedy series, this entry uses the framework of a service comedy with the young roughnecks mixing it up with a gang of spies. Some of the boys take an air raid drill seriously and enlist in the army. Leo Gorcey, as their perpetual leader, tries to discourage them and maneuvers to get them released. But he, too, ends up in uniform. The usual comic antics involving military drills and barracks discipline follow, with Huntz Hall, as Gorcey's stooge, grabbing most of the laughs.

Meanwhile, enemy agents try to steal military secrets from the army base. Virginia Hewitt portrays an attractive spy posing as an innocent secretary. The agents kidnap Gorcey, thinking he can supply them with important information. His pals help to rescue him, tangling with the spies in a spirited free-for-all. The boys win medals for their heroism and are then tossed into the guardhouse for leaving the camp without permission. ■

Bowery Blitzkrieg (1941), Mon. *Dir.* Wallace Fox; *Sc.* Sam Robbins; *Cast includes:* Leo Gorcey, Bobby Jordan, Huntz Hall, Warren Hull, Charlotte Henry.

The East Side Kids engage in their typical low comedy as they clash with foreign agents in this entry. A low-budget production, the slapstick comedy features several performers who were popular in silent films, including "Sunshine Sammy" Morrison and Jack Mulhall. Charlotte Henry, who had played the title character in an early sound adaptation of *Alice in Wonderland*, provides the love interest in this routine film. ■

Boys From Brazil, The (1978), TCF. *Dir.* Franklin J. Schaffner; *Sc.* Heywood Gould; *Cast includes:* Gregory Peck, Laurence Olivier, James Mason, Lilli Palmer, Uta Hagen, Steven Guttenberg.

The threat of future Hitler-cloned dictators forms the central theme of this far-fetched drama based on Ira Levin's novel. Gregory Peck portrays the infamous Josef Mengele, the cold-blooded World War II concentration-camp doctor. Having taken refuge somewhere in South America, he is busy working on a bizarre experiment. The mad doctor has successfully turned out "little Hitlers" from the dictator's tissue. A secret organization made up of former Nazi officers sends one of its members (James Mason) to Mengele's jungle laboratory to postpone his project. It seems that a well-known hunter of war criminals named Leiberman is snooping around. But Mengele refuses to postpone his work.

Laurence Olivier, as the elderly Jewish Nazi-hunter, learns about Peck's diabolical experiments. He asks a European journalist, an old acquaintance, to help him gather information on Mengele. The reporter scoffs at the old man. Leiberman reminds his friend about Mengele, "the chief doctor of Auschwitz, who killed 2 1/2 million people, experimented with children—Jewish and non-Jewish—using twins, mostly, injecting blue dies into their eyes to make them acceptable Aryans, amputating limbs and organs from thousands without anesthetics. . . . "

In the final implausible scenes, Leiberman confronts his adversary who has just killed an innocent father to duplicate similar conditions to those of Hitler's youth. Mengele, holding a gun on Leiberman who has been wounded in a struggle with the doctor, boasts about his clones. He explains that there are 94 boys, "exact genetic duplicates" of Hitler. The dead man's young son returns from school and, learning that Mengele has killed his father, orders the family dogs to attack the doctor. Mengele dies as a result of the attack.

Following this bloody sequence, a member of the Young Jewish Defenders, a radical group, visits Leiberman, who is recuperating from his gunshot wounds. He wants the list of Hitler clones so that his organization can kill the young boys. "I will not slaughter the innocent, and neither shall you," Leiberman says as he burns the list of names. The last scene shows the boy, whose father has been murdered by the doctor, interested in gory photographs of Mengele—suggesting that perhaps he will mature into another Hitler. Although many critics attacked much of the film as silly, they singled out Olivier's remarkable performance. See Latin America; Josef Mengele; Nazi Subversion: Post-World War II. ■

Brainwashing. The term gained prominence during the Korean War and referred to the Chinese Communists' treatment of prisoners. Interrogators used physical abuse, drugs, isolation and other disorientation techniques to psychologically manipulate their victims' minds. Brainwashing may have accounted for the disturbing number of American prisoners of war who collaborated with their guards or signed anti-U.S. statements.

Of the handful of American films that examine the subject of brainwashing—usually superficially—most exploit it for purposes of propaganda. *Prisoner of War* (1954) depicts American intelligence officers dropping a volunteer (Ronald Reagan) into North Korea to check on a series of stories emanating from behind enemy lines about the brutal treatment of captured soldiers. *The Bamboo Prison* (1954) tries to cover up the acts of those American prisoners who cooperated with the Communists by suggesting that some who turned collaborator were actually agents working for the U.S. Government. Perhaps the most chilling drama about brainwashing is *The Manchurian Candidate* (1962). It recounts the collective nightmare of a group of former prisoners of war. Frank Sinatra and Laurence Harvey portray army buddies who, along with other captives, have been brainwashed during their internment in a North Korean prison camp. Harvey has been programmed to carry out a series of assassinations in the U.S.

Several films with plots indirectly related to the Korean War depict ex-P.O.W.s hurting from the effects of brainwashing. In *The Destructors* (1968) John Ericson portrays a Korean War hero who has temporarily turned traitor as a result of Communist brainwashing. In *The Fearmakers* (1958) Dana Andrews portrays a Korean War veteran who has suffered from Communist brainwashing techniques while a prisoner of war. ■

Brass Target (1978), UA. *Dir.* John Hough; *Sc.* Alvin Boretz; *Cast includes:* Sophia Loren, John Cassavetes, George Kennedy, Robert Vaughn, Patrick McGoohan, Max von Sydow.

A fictionalized version of General Patton's death at the hands of assassins is added to this drama about a contrived plot concerning the theft of Nazi Germany's gold. The film opens with the theft of the gold bullion from a U.S. army train. The crime results in the murder of 59 U.S. soldiers. The scene then shifts to a pugnacious General Patton (George Kennedy), whose blatant anti-Communist ideology leads to heated confrontations with Russian military officers. Patton, forced to investigate the theft, is killed when he persists in uncovering all those involved in the conspiracy.

A cynical major and veteran of the O.S.S. (John Cassavetes) has been assigned to the investigation by the Criminal Investigation Division of the army. The major, who was responsible for more than one hundred successful O.S.S. missions during the war, wants only to return to the States. Forced to handle the gold theft investigation, he determines to wrap up the case quickly and efficiently. He soon discovers a complex web of conspiracy, intrigue and betrayal. Colonel Rogers (Robert Vaughn), who, along with several other American officers in occupied Germany, schemes to seize the gold that the Third Reich plundered during the war. They are abetted by U.S. Colonel McCauley (Patrick McGoohan), the former head of the Office of Strategic Services. Sophia Loren portrays the lover of Max von Sydow, the professional assassin hired by Vaughn.

The dialogue attempts to illuminate char-acter, theme and a general atmosphere of cynicism, disillusionment and corruption— similar to several postwar dramas of the period. "The O.S.S.," muses Colonel McCauley, "used to be the greatest thing during the war. But you know what? Since then the only thing we are now is a bunch of thieves and murderers." "I wish the war had never ended," former O.S.S. agent Cassavetes adds, thinking how easy it had been to identify the good and evil forces. Later, Cassavetes contrasts his investigative methods with those of the C.I.D., which he describes as ponderous and too structured. "Me?" he explains. "I'm a Sicilian. To me, everything's a conspiracy. Everyone makes deals." And still later, when he meets an old war ally, Max von Sydow, he jokes, "The war was made to order for you. You stole from both sides with equal grace." But von Sydow remains unmoved. "What was the greater immorality," the former secret-agent-turned-professional-killer replies, "my petty crimes or the war itself?" Cassavetes wants von Sydow to help him find the assassin who is planning to kill Patton, not realizing that his acquaintance is that same assassin. "You could never see past your morality," von Sydow says, adding, "Some men have to be killed."

Cassavetes finally succeeds in unmasking all the entangled elements of the conspiracy and corruption, including killing von Sydow, who tries to escape. But he fails to locate the missing gold or prevent the assassination of the general. In reality, Patton was killed in an automobile accident. The film is based on the novel *The Algonquin Project* by Frederick Nolan in which the character who is murdered is fictional. See Nazi Subversion: Post-World War II. ■

Brave Warrior (1952), Col. *Dir.* Spencer G. Bennet; *Sc.* Robert F. Kent; *Cast includes:* Jon Hall, Christine Larson, Jay Silverheels, Michael Ansara, Harry Cording James Seay.

An American agent is assigned to uncover traitors who are inciting the Indians in this action drama set on the eve of the War of 1812. Jon Hall portrays the government representative who tries to prevent the Indians from joining the British cause. Jay Silverheels, as Tecumseh, chief of the Shawnees, helps Hall. Christine Larson provides the love interest for Hall. In attempting to depict the conflict between American and British sympathizers of the period, the film stretches historical facts. Actually, the Shawnee sided with the British against the Americans during the War of 1812. Also, Chief Tecumseh was firmly antagonistic toward the fledgling nation. See War of 1812: Intelligence and Covert Actions. ■

Breakheart Pass (1976), UA. *Dir.* Tom Gries; *Sc.* Alistair MacLean; *Cast includes:* Charles Bronson, Ben Johnson, Jill Ireland, Richard Crenna, Charles Durning, Roy Jenson.

Conspirators, in collusion with a band of Indians and a gang of outlaws, plot to overrun a U.S. Army post and make off with its gold and silver cache in this fast-paced action drama set chiefly aboard a train in the West of the late 1800s. Charles Bronson, as a U.S. Secret Service agent, poses as a criminal in the custody of a marshal. Richard Crenna, as a seemingly concerned territorial governor, in reality is the leader of the conspiracy. Ben Johnson portrays the marshal and Crenna's secret partner. Charles Durning, as a railroad supervisor in charge of the train, is also part of the conspiracy. Jill Ireland plays Crenna's girlfriend who is unaware of the intrigue. Ed Lauter, as an upright army officer aboard the train, allegedly is on a mission to deliver medical supplies to the army post grappling with a deadly epidemic.

Crenna, as governor, concocts a story that a remote army post is in the midst of a diphtheria epidemic and needs an immediate shipment of medical supplies. He commissions a train to transport the supplies and a doctor to the fort. The cases, however, contain rifles for Crenna's Indian friends and dynamite to blow up the fort. The doctor and others are systematically murdered as the train speeds toward its destination. The last few cars of the train, which hold the army troop replacements, is mysteriously disengaged on an incline. The cars roll backward out of control, pick up momentum and finally plunge into a ravine, killing all the soldiers aboard.

Working under cover through most of the film, Bronson eventually discovers the hidden rifles and dynamite and exposes the conspiracy. He slows down the train by dynamiting the tracks in several places and sends the major to the fort to bring back the troops. The Indians and gang of outlaws are either driven off or killed, as are the chief conspirators. The

film was adapted from Alistair MacLean's novel. ■

Bribe, The (1949), MGM. *Dir.* Robert Z. Leonard; *Sc.* Marguerite Roberts; *Cast includes:* Robert Taylor, Ava Gardner, Charles Laughton, Vincent Price, John Hodiak, Samuel S. Hinds.

A U.S. federal officer is assigned to spy on a war-surplus racket operated from a Latin American island in this bland drama. Clues lead Robert Taylor, as the agent, to Ava Gardner, who is connected with the gang of racketeers. Taylor faces the dilemma between love and duty after falling in love with Gardner. However, plot incidents work out so that Taylor is able to smash the racket and rescue the reformed Gardner. Vincent Price portrays the gang leader. John Hodiak, as a former pilot, works as a mechanic for the gang to raise enough money for himself and his wife to move elsewhere. Charles Laughton portrays a down-at-the-heels beachcomber who acts as contact man for the racketeers. The film is based on Frederick Nebel's short story. See Latin America. ■

Bright Shawl, The (1923), FN. *Dir.* John S. Robertson; *Sc.* Edmund Goulding; *Cast includes:* Richard Barthelmess, Dorothy Gish, Luis Alberni, Mary Astor, André de Beranger, Edward G. Robinson.

The drama, based on a story by Joseph Hergesheimer, is set in Cuba during the 1870s when it was ruled by Spain. Richard Barthelmess portrays a wealthy American who, out of sympathy for the oppressed Cuban masses, accompanies his friend, a Cuban patriot (André de Beranger), to the strife-torn country. Barthelmess aids a group of revolutionaries plotting against the tyrannical colonial rulers. He passes information that he receives from a dancer (Dorothy Gish), who has fallen in love with him, to the rebel leader. However, the American is actually in love with his friend's sister, played by Mary Astor. Meanwhile, a Spanish spy, upon learning how the information is being leaked, endangers Beranger's entire family. But Barthelmess and those under suspicion are able to escape to the U.S.

The film, of course, is fictitious although there are instances of Americans deliberately traveling to Cuba to fight for its independence from Spain. Thomas Jordan (1819–1895), an American newspaper editor and former Confederate intelligence officer, had provided General Beauregard with enough vital military information he obtained from a Confederate spy to help the general achieve victory at the first Battle of Bull Run. Later, advocating that Cuba be annexed for economic and military reasons, he journeyed to the Spanish-held island in 1869 to command Cuban insurgents who were fighting for their independence. However, after several defeats he escaped from Cuba and headed back to the U.S.

Cuba's Ten Years' War (1868–1878), one of several revolutions, was begun by Carlos Manuel del Castillo, a rich planter and lawyer. The civil war ended badly for the rebels who were promised sweeping reforms and other concessions, none of which were fulfilled by Spain. Once again, dissent from the colonists was met with a firm despotic fist. The United States, still reeling from its own civil strife, did not intervene in Cuba until decades later. ■

British Agent (1934), WB. *Dir.* Michael Curtiz; *Sc.* Laird Doyle; *Cast includes:* Leslie Howard, Kay Francis, William Gargan, Philip Reed, Irving Pichel, Walter Byron.

A drama set in the early stages of the Russian Revolution, the film stars Leslie Howard as the British consul-general in strife-torn Russia. He is determined to keep Russia in World War I although the country, burdened with a revolt at home, is seeking to make peace with Germany. England at first unofficially assigns Howard this task so that military pressure may continue on Germany during World War I. Howard promises officials of the Communist regime that England will provide money and munitions. However, his superiors never respond to his requests for further instructions, and Howard is betrayed by his own government. Although his life is in danger, Howard continues his own crusade against the Communists.

Early in the film Howard saves the life of Lenin's secretary (Kay Francis), and the two fall in love. But their political differences threaten their relationship. "There'd be no more wars if nations would mind their own business," Francis remarks in reference to England's interference in Russia's plan to withdraw from the conflict. "And abandon their friends?" Howard questions. "If England had starved in the trenches," she explains, "as Russia had, and fought with shells

filled with sawdust, I'd like to know what she'd do." "Shall I tell you?" Howard replies. "She'd go on fighting—for humanity."

Howard is captured and placed in a structure to be blown up. Francis joins him, but at the last moment news reaches the soldiers that Stalin is recovering from a gunshot wound and they go off to celebrate. The lovers are spared. Several historical figures portrayed on screen include Lenin, Trotsky and Lloyd George.

The film exemplifies early Hollywood's anti-Communist approach. Revolutionary forces are pictured as ill-bred rabble who murder the innocent. In the autobiography by R. H. Bruce Lockhart, the wartime British diplomat on whose experiences the story is based, there is no such dedication or obsession on the part of the author, whom Howard portrays, to continue the campaign against Bolshevism. Howard's betrayal by his own country anticipates the cynical plots of several Cold War films, including *The Spy Who Came in From the Cold* (1965), starring Richard Burton.

The plot of *British Agent* has some basis in fact. Britain's newly established Secret Intelligence Service (S.I.S.) during World War I had several agents in Russia whose role there was a dual one. Their chief job was to keep Russia's armies busy on the eastern front battling the Germans. Secondly, the agents were assigned to foil their German counterparts' attempts to instigate a separate peace between the czarist government and the Central Powers.

The incident involving the assassination attempt on Lenin's life is fairly accurate. Fanny Kaplan, a fanatical Socialist, shot him on August 18, 1918, seriously wounding the Russian leader. Russian-born Sidney Reilly, a member of Britain's S.I.S. and a fanatical anti-Bolshevik, claimed the plot was part of a larger scheme—the Lettish Plot—aimed at inciting an uprising that would overthrow the Communists and replace them with an anti-Bolshevik regime. The entire plot collapsed, forcing Reilly to flee Russia. ■

British Intelligence (1940), WB. *Dir.* Terry Morse; *Sc.* Lee Katz; *Cast includes:* Boris Karloff, Margaret Lindsay, Maris Wrixon, Holmes Herbert, Bruce Lester, Leonard Mudie.

Based on Anthony Paul Kelly's successful 1918 play about intrigue and German spies operating in England during World War I, the film stars Boris Karloff as a master spy who cleverly installs himself as an employee in the home of a high-ranking British cabinet minister. Margaret Lindsay, a double agent, poses as a German spy to learn the identity of the leader of the enemy agents who has been relaying all British military strategy to Berlin. The film features a climactic air raid of zeppelins over London intent on destroying British military headquarters.

This is the third screen version of Kelly's play, the other two released in 1926 and 1930 under the original title, *Three Faces East*. The 1930 adaptation featured Erich von Stroheim as the head of the German spy network. He received top billing over Constance Bennett and garnered the best reviews from the critics.

Although set during World War I, the drama has enough updated dialogue to mark it as a World War II propaganda film. "We are destined to conquer the world," a German officer announces to Lindsay early in the film. "A new leader will arise," he continues. "I will not live to see it, but one day Germany will rule the world." In the final scene, after British intelligence smashes the German spy network, the cabinet minister asks the chief of intelligence: "These sacrifices. . . . Do you think they will eventually mean something to mankind?" "We want to help humanity," the chief replies, facing the camera. "We fight wars only because we crave peace so ardently, and we pray that each war will be the last. But always in the strange scheme of things some maniac with a lust for power arises and . . . destroys the peace and tranquillity we've created. . . . We hate war . . . but when war comes we must and will fight on and on."

Not unlike other major studios, Warner remade many of its old silent and early sound properties and embellished them with updated material, slick production values and fresh faces. One slight addition that someone at the studio thought would be clever gave this third version an ironic touch. A fumbling German corporal wore a Chaplinesque mustache and had some of his dark hair fall over one eye. ∎

British intelligence: World War I. Great Britain's intelligence community achieved several memorable coups during the war, including the exposure of the infamous Zim-mermann Telegram and the cracking of German codes in the Admiralty's celebrated Room 40. British intelligence deployed its services not only against the Central Powers but to promote its interests in neutral U.S. The British used German-speaking expatriates to infiltrate the German intelligence network. Emanuel Voska, one such Slavic agent, supplied the American press with sensational stories of German subversion in America.

Immediately upon the onset of war in 1914 the British severed the two telegraph cables linking Germany to North and South America. Berlin was thus compelled to contact its agents via radio; naturally, Britain intercepted and decoded the secret German messages. British naval intelligence sifted through and edited the German material and then forwarded it either to Col. Edward House, President Wilson's close confidant, or to the American ambassador in London.

The most spectacular intelligence coup of the war was the Zimmermann Telegram. German Foreign Minister Zimmermann in 1917 contacted his country's minister in Mexico, von Eckhardt, with the proposal of a German-Mexican military alliance. In return for its cooperation, Mexico would regain its lost states of New Mexico, Texas and Arizona. The British passed the intercepted telegram to Washington, and its subsequent publication severely prejudiced American public opinion against Germany.

In 1915 a U.S. Secret Service agent retrieved a briefcase crammed with documents that Dr. Heinrich Albert, the German commercial attaché, had forgotten on a train. The Germans' bogus companies in the U.S. were exposed and, although nothing illegal could be discovered, the Secretary of the Treasury disclosed the story to the press. These revelations added damage to the already poor German image in the U.S. *The Eagle's Eye*, a 1918 serial, describes some of Dr. Albert's wartime espionage activities.

Robert Fay, a demolitions specialist, was arrested in 1915 and linked to suspected German bombings in the U.S. Captain Franz von Papen was suspected of being Fay's "control" and was declared *persona non grata* by the U.S. government. Von Papen received an American safe-conduct pass which allowed him to travel through Great Britain on his way home to Germany. Although the British permitted von Papen safe passage, they confiscated his luggage which contained check stubs and various other papers revealing the extent of German subversion in North America.

American film studios produced many World War I spy dramas set in England or British possessions. Virtually all the heroes and heroines were American performers and the plots were similar to other American espionage films. The lack of characterization blurred differences between films set in either country. Therefore, dramas with either American or English locales were practically indistinguishable. Furthermore, writers and directors offered few details concerning the *modus operandi* of British intelligence. The films, subsequently, were chiefly entertainments with a smattering of propaganda. *Shell 43* (1916), for example, concerns a British spy (H. B. Warner) who poses as an American war correspondent. He has a German pass that allows him to move freely on the battlefield. In the final scene he heroically sacrifices his own life to destroy a strategic enemy position.

The bulk of British- and American-oriented espionage dramas appeared in 1918. *Inside the Lines* (1918) features Lewis Stone as an English officer who foils a plot by German spies to blow up Gibraltar and cripple a large part of the English navy anchored there. In *The Great Love* (1918) German spies plot the destruction of an English munitions factory. *The Man Who Wouldn't Tell* (1918) concerns a nest of German spies and members of the British secret service who are on the enemy agents' trail. In *Patriotism* (1918) Allied officials suspect a spy, operating along the coast of Scotland, has been sending signals to German submarines.

Some filmmakers, probably to make their works more palatable to American audiences, blended American characters into their plots. *Who Goes There?* (1917), for example, takes place in Belgium during the war. An American of Belgian descent (Harry Morey) is captured by the Germans and forced to bring back from England a female spy (Corinne Griffith) who has a secret code. If he does not return with her, a group of Belgian hostages will be killed. He carries out the mission but turns over the code to British agents. *Love in a Hurry* (1919) concerns a young American's involvement with German agents operating in England.

Post-World War I films continued along similar paths but focused more on romance and less on anti-German propaganda. Set in England at the beginning of World War I, the drama *Shadows of Suspicion* (1919) concerns British and German spies searching for secret papers. An Englishman (Ben Lyon) educated in Germany becomes a double agent working for England in *The Great Deception* (1926). He travels between the two countries providing German headquarters with false information while supplying Britain with valuable intelligence. *Three Faces East* (1926) concerns a network of German spies operating in London during World War I, the chief of whom poses as a butler employed in the home of an important British war official. *True Heaven* (1929) features George O'Brien as an English officer first stationed in Belgium where he falls in love with Lois Moran who is a spy for the Germans. Later, he is assigned as a spy to infiltrate German headquarters. The lovers meet again and spend the night together. Torn between her love for her country and her feelings for the Englishman, she succumbs to the former and reports him to her superiors.

Spy films released during the sound era in the 1930s were more sophisticated in character development, dialogue and theme. *British Agent* (1934), set in the early stages of the Russian Revolution, has Leslie Howard as the British consul-general in strife-torn Russia falling in love with Lenin's secretary (Kay Francis). He is assigned to keep Russia in World War I although the country is seeking to make peace with Germany because of a debilitating revolt at home. In *Lancer Spy* (1937) George Sanders plays a dual role. He is a German officer captured by the British and sent to England; there a British look-alike (also Sanders) studies the German's every move to impersonate him. Finally, an escape is arranged and the English surrogate makes it to Berlin where he is to learn the latest military strategy of the enemy. *British Intelligence* (1940), a remake of *Three Faces East* (1926), deals with German spies operating in England during the war. Boris Karloff portrays a master spy who cleverly installs himself as an employee in the home of a high-ranking British cabinet minister.

By the 1950s American studios like Universal and Allied Artists began churning out numerous routine historical action adventures, adding color and some fading film stars to their productions. Allied Artists' *The*

Royal African Rifles (1953), for example, features Louis Hayward as a British navy officer in East Africa. He is on the trail of a shipment of rifles and machine guns stolen from his ship, weapons sorely needed by British colonial troops. German agents, who are behind the scheme, hope to tie up British troops with a native uprising. ■

British intelligence: World War II.

Although British intelligence had the skilled help of Hollywood and such fictional characters as Bulldog Drummond, the Lone Wolf and Sherlock Holmes in World War II, it needed little assistance from external sources. With the exception of Ireland, British intelligence (MI5) from 1939 to 1945 penetrated virtually all German covert operations within the British Isles. London was also able to feed disinformation about the impending invasion of Europe to the Nazis, who remained unaware that their own agents were under constant surveillance. In fact, the British uncovered and caught virtually every German spy, sometimes effectively turning these captives into double agents. This feat went unequaled by any other Allied or Axis power during the war.

The spectacular success by British intelligence did not come about by accident or coincidence. It was accomplished in part by anticipating an armed conflict and establishing a counterspy network in advance. Britain began its intricate intelligence operations as early as 1936 as a move to neutralize future German attempts at espionage and sabotage. One of London's key operatives was an English double agent whom the Germans trusted implicitly. Using a wireless that the Germans supplied, he soon began turning over vital codes and names of German spies to intelligence. One particular film that suggests London's prewar intelligence activities is *Golden Earrings* (1947). Operating in Germany with a fellow British agent on the eve of World War II, Ray Milland and his companion are dispatched on a secret mission to get the formula of a revolutionary poison gas from an anti-Nazi German scientist.

Several pre-World War II spy films, although entirely fictitious, hinted of enemy activities in England. Hollywood's Bulldog Drummond series, with its stereotyped characters, escapist plots and studio sets, is typical. In *Bulldog Drummond at Bay* (1937) international agents attempt to steal the secret

of a robot airplane. *Bulldog Drummond's Revenge* (1937) concerns enemy operatives trying to steal a new type of explosive developed by English scientists. And in *Bulldog Drummond in Africa* (1938) spies kidnap Scotland Yard Inspector Nielson, sending Bulldog Drummond to Africa to rescue his friend. Typical of the period, these minor films rarely identified the nationalities of the spies or the countries behind the schemes.

By 1940 Germany, confident in its own spy network, decided to expand its covert operations in England. It sent in more agents by way of boat and parachute, using either Ireland or Scotland as an entry point. Unaware that their established fellow agents were being tracked by the British, the new arrivals contacted their associates and thus revealed their own identity. Intelligence often gave captured German agents a choice: either face a firing squad or provide the British with information. A branch of Britain's MI5, the XX Committee or Double Cross Committee, concentrated on converting prisoners into double agents. Most captured agents found little future in sacrificing their lives for the Fatherland. Some agents, however, received the death penalty, which served a dual propaganda role. First, it convinced the English people that internal intelligence was not only on the job but effective; second, it proved to the German high command that their other agents were safely entrenched and transmitting important information.

Rarely did American films show this face of the war. However, in *Decision Before Dawn* (1951) Oskar Werner, as a captured Luftwaffe medic disillusioned with Hitler, acts as a secret agent for the Allies. Although he loves his country, the idealistic German officer abhors the government that has led Germany down the road to destruction. He volunteers to return to Germany as a spy in the belief that by ending the war sooner he will be saving lives.

Few American films about espionage in England before and during the war years even touched upon the numerous successes of MI5. Instead, they focused on familiar and routine plots. In *Counter-Espionage* (1942), for example, the Lone Wolf, played by Warren William, hunts down a Nazi spy network in wartime London while protecting secret military plans. *The Gorilla Man* (1942) has Nazi spies in England trying to prevent a commando, recently returned from a mission on the continent, from delivering military information. In *The Hour Before the Dawn* (1944), a representative patriotic film of the period, Veronica Lake, as a Nazi agent stationed in England, marries conscientious objector Franchot Tone as a cover for her clandestine activities. Following a German air raid aimed at a nearby airfield, he sheds his pacifist views, kills his wife after he learns that she is a spy and enlists in the Royal Air Force. *Secrets of Scotland Yard* (1944) explores some of the methods employed by Scotland Yard to break enemy codes and shows the dangers its agents face. The plot includes a traitor working within the bureau—a unique film element for the war years but anticipating the infiltration of real-life spies Kim Philby, Donald Maclean and Guy Burgess who worked for the Soviets. In Fritz Lang's masterful *Ministry of Fear* (1944) Ray Milland gets mixed up with a network of spies who are transmitting military secrets to Germany. The agents are using a seemingly worthy organization, "Mothers of the Free Nations," run by an Austrian refugee, as their front.

A. Conan Doyle's famous detective characters, played by Basil Rathbone and Nigel Bruce, were updated to help the British war effort. In *Sherlock Holmes and the Secret Weapon* (1942) both the British government and Nazi agents are after a secret bombsight. Holmes, relying upon disguise, makes sure that the enemy does not get the weapon. *The Voice of Terror* (1942) concerns a Nazi radio broadcast that is terrorizing the English citizenry. Holmes is hired by the British Inner Council to capture the Nazi agent responsible for the "voice of terror" broadcasts. The Inner Council was a thinly disguised title for Prime Minister Winston Churchill's wartime Inner Circle, as later described by John Colville, Churchill's private secretary, in his 1981 book *Winston Churchill and His Inner Circle*.

One well-known and highly successful ploy by British intelligence concerned Operation Overlord, better known as the Normandy invasion. British agents found an actor who closely resembled Field Marshal Montgomery. Clifton James, a lieutenant in the Royal Army Pay Corps, followed Montgomery for a week and closely watched all his mannerisms and gestures. James was able to duplicate Montgomery's twitching of the left cheek, his tense look and his rigid stance. The actor was soon clothed in Montgomery's battle gear, flying jacket and ribbons. British

intelligence flew the impostor to Gibraltar where he was given a highly visible reception followed by a public drive to Government House. Naturally, British intelligence made certain that James was not playing to an empty house and that German agents had full view of the proceedings. James was escorted to the army air base where he was flown to Algiers; he met with the Allied Commander-in-Chief, General Wilson, and then disappeared. This deception is mentioned in the film *36 Hours* (1964) and inspired the Danny Kaye comedy *On the Double* (1961) in which the comic is called upon to impersonate a British general whom he happens to resemble. The action takes place on the eve of the Normandy invasion in which the general plays a strategic role. Finally, a British drama, *I Was Monty's Double*, appeared in 1958.

Thanks to this subterfuge and other ruses such as naval maneuvers off the British coast near Calais as well as false radio signals and phony military bases, the Germans were kept guessing about the location of the Allied invasion.

A handful of films skirted with other actual incidents before turning to flights of fancy. *Nightmare* (1942) at least provides a semblance of plausibility by introducing a Nazi spy whose fellow agents are being parachuted into Scotland. In *Count Five and Die* (1958) British and U.S. intelligence forces devise a plan to baffle the Germans about the actual location of the Allied invasion of Europe.

The true exploits of British agents, volunteers in London's Special Operations Executive, operating in Axis-controlled France, Italy and other countries, unfortunately, have largely remained neglected by Hollywood. Such books as *Watch for Me by Moonlight* by Evelyn Le Chene and *When the Moon Rises* by Tony Davies, which recount the tense experiences of British spies in France and Italy respectively, would make excellent films. ∎

British spy films. The spy genre as we know it today has its roots in the gangster film and the thriller. The former provided the conflict between the forces of good and evil, with the undercover agent replacing the detective, the foreign spy the criminal, and the international conspiracy substituting for the mob. The thriller, meanwhile, supplied the essential components of tension and suspense. The icons and myths of the spy genre can be traced directly to the 1930s and the British practitioners who molded it into its present form. Here can be found the finely honed iconography of codes, formulas, secret weapons and disguise. Lone agents are willing to sacrifice their lives while deadly enemy spies work for unnamed, aggressive powers. These films perpetuate the myths that a nation can be saved by the simple intervention of an embattled lone hero; that external forces are responsible for many of society's problems; and that all covert government operations are inherently initiated for the citizens' benefit, inspired by democratic ideals and carried out with a sense of morality. This contrasts sharply with contemporary American dramas which often portray C.I.A. agents and their superiors as corrupt, self-serving manipulators.

Alfred Hitchcock, the acknowledged master of suspense, directed a string of entertaining British spy films during the 1930s, many receiving critical acclaim. The Man Who Knew Too Much (1934), about an assassination plot, has such unforgettable moments as the disturbing murder at a Swiss hotel and the disquieting assassination attempt at Albert Hall. The 39 Steps (1935) develops one of the director's favorite themes—a man falsely charged with murder who has to prove his innocence. The Secret Agent (1936) has a perverse plot about a British secret service agent who, in his pursuit of a foreign spy, wrongly kills an innocent man. Sabotage (1936), which focuses on a crazed anarchist who is trying to blow up London, has the disorienting scene in which a boy, unknowingly delivering a bomb for the anarchist, is blown up, along with other passengers on an omnibus. The Lady Vanishes (1938), a suspenseful tale about European espionage set chiefly aboard a train, reflects Hitchcock's concern about his country's refusal to acknowledge the dangers of Nazi Germany. The director imbued these spy films with creative editing, inspired wit and personal ingenuity. By using theaters and national institutions as settings, he dramatized how an orderly world can easily be toppled into a condition of chaos and turmoil. His films consistently challenged the creative talents of other directors.

Other British spy films of the 1930s made worthwhile contributions to the genre. Victor Saville's I Was a Spy (1933) reenacts the ac-

tual experiences of Martha McKenna, a young Belgian nurse during World War I who volunteered to spy for the Allies after witnessing German atrocities in her homeland. Harold Young's The Scarlet Pimpernel (1934), about the Reign of Terror that followed the French Revolution, suggested that one determined Englishman, infused with a sense of justice and the spirit of liberty, can defeat the forces of totalitarianism in a land gone mad. Both Saville's Dark Journey (1938) and Michael Powell's The Spy in Black (1939) concerned a British female as a double agent during World War I, with Conrad Veidt as a German villain in these better-than-average dramas.

Britain, fighting for its life during World War II, cut back on its production of dramas and concentrated its talents on war documentaries. Its spy films in these years—Carol Reed's Night Train to Munich (1940), Leslie Howard's Pimpernel Smith (1941) and Michael Powell's Forty-Ninth Parallel (1941)—although well made, were generally burdened with excessive heroics and propaganda, as were those made in the U.S.

The Cold War brought a resurgence of British spy films, most notably in the 1960s and 1970s. Reed led off with his moody The Man Between and his sardonic spy spoof Our Man in Havana, both 1960. Martin Ritt turned out the cynical The Spy Who Came In From the Cold (1965), based on John Le Carre's successful novel. Sidney J. Furie introduced the first in the Harry Palmer series, The Ipcress File (1965), with Michael Caine portraying the unlikely and stoic secret agent. Michael Anderson's The Quiller Memorandum (1966), about neo-Nazis operating in Europe, had a screenplay by Harold Pinter. American director Sidney Lumet, working in Britain, made The Deadly Affair (1967), a seedy tale about a British agent's suicide, also based on a Le Carre novel. Fred Zinnemann's The Day of the Jackal (1973), based on Frederick Forsyth's novel, took advantage of several scenic European locales as it unfolded an assassination plot on de Gaulle's life.

Terence Young's Dr. No (1962), the first of the James Bond films, and its many sequels profoundly influenced the next generation of spy movies. The series offered the right blend of sex, wit and suspense, a personable Bond (Sean Connery), a bevy of seductive women, fascinating villains and high-tech weapons and cars—all of which led to record grosses at the box office and a succession of imitators both in theaters and on television. American studios were quick to respond with their own series (Matt Helm, Derek Flint, television's Napoleon Solo) and single entries but found the Bond films formidable competition.

The series, with its enigmatic hero, agent 007, who is "licensed to kill," coupled with political events and exposés involving double agents and questionable intelligence practices, contributed to the moral ambiguities and cynical tone that filtered into the spy genre by the 1970s. Cyril Frankel's *Permission to Kill* (1975) revealed the dark side of spying. John Mackenzie's *The Fourth Protocol* (1987) has two K.G.B. agents assigned to set off an atomic bomb in England. Each agent has secret orders to assassinate the other when the mission is accomplished. British agent Michael Caine, who foils the plot, learns to his surprise that the head of the K.G.B. and the chief of British intelligence have been collaborating on the entire operation. See James Bond. ∎

Bugle Sounds, The (1941), MGM. *Dir.* S. Sylvan Simon; *Sc.* Cyril Hume; *Cast includes:* Wallace Beery, Marjorie Main, Lewis Stone, George Bancroft, Henry O'Neill.

Wallace Beery stars as an old-time cavalry sergeant who resists the transition from mount to mechanization in this sentimental service drama sprinkled with comedy. When sabotage occurs at his army camp, Beery is suspected because of his dislike for armored vehicles. But eventually he is vindicated when the real spies are caught. Marjorie Main provides some of the laughter as a shrewish woman who knows how to handle the stubborn sergeant. Venerable character actor Lewis Stone portrays the camp colonel. ∎

Bulldog Drummond at Bay (1937), Rep. *Dir.* Norman Lee; *Sc.* James Parrish, Patrick Kirwan; *Cast includes:* John Lodge, Dorothy Mackaill, Victor Jory, Claud Allister, Hugh Miller, Leslie Perrins.

International agents attempt to steal the secret of a robot airplane in this weak drama that lacks the charm and wit of previous entries in the series based on author H. C. McNeile's personable detective. The agents, who represent the "mystery man of Europe," an ominous international arms dealer, kidnap the inventor of the new weapon when they fail to obtain it through legitimate means.

John Lodge (c.), as Bulldog Drummond, shares information with Scotland Yard about a scheme by international agents to steal Britain's military secrets. *Bulldog Drummond at Bay* (1937).

John Lodge, as the gentleman sleuth Bulldog Drummond, gets into the act and manages to foil the gang's plot. Dorothy Mackaill plays the female lead. Claud Allister, as Drummond's sidekick, contributes some slight comic relief. Victor Jory and Hugh Miller portray the villains. The continental arms dealer apparently is based on the shadowy affairs of Basil Zaharoff, an infamous figure of the period. See British Intelligence: World War II; Sir Basil Zaharoff. ∎

Bulldog Drummond in Africa (1938), Par. *Dir.* Louis King; *Sc.* Garnett Weston; *Cast includes:* John Howard, Heather Angel, H. B. Warner, J. Carrol Naish, Reginald Denny, E. E. Clive.

When a gang of spies kidnaps Scotland Yard Inspector Nielson, Bulldog Drummond follows the trail to Africa to rescue his friend in this routine drama. The story begins on the eve of Drummond's wedding. His bride-to-be, played by Heather Angel, pays a visit to the inspector (H. B. Warner) and witnesses his abduction. She returns to Drummond, tells him what she has seen and both set off for the wilds of Africa. A series of perils threaten both Drummond and his party and the inspector. First, the spies place a time bomb on Drummond's plane to prevent him from following them. Later, the amateur sleuth rescues his inspector friend who has been tied to a stake in a lion pit. Reginald Denny, as Drummond's friend, and E. E. Clive, as the detective's valet, provide the comic relief in this tale based on characters created by H. C. McNeile. See British Intelligence: World War II. ∎

Bulldog Drummond's Revenge (1937), Par. *Dir.* Louis King; *Sc.* Edward T. Lowe; *Cast includes:* John Barrymore, Louise Campbell, John Howard, E. E. Clive, Reginald Denny, Frank Puglia.

Enemy agents steal a new type of explosive developed by English scientists in this routine drama, one of the entries in the Bulldog Drummond detective series. John Howard, as the gentleman-sleuth, makes it his business to uncover the plot and regain the secret weapon. John Barrymore, as Colonel Nielson, a Scotland Yard officer, assists Drummond. Louise Campbell provides some slight romantic entanglement for Howard. E. E. Clive, as Drummond's valet, is partly responsible for the comic relief in this suspenseful tale that depends more on action than on actual sleuthing.

Barrymore played in only three of Paramount's eight entries in the "Drummond" series which ran from 1937 to 1939. He inherited the Nielson role from Sir Guy Standing, who died in 1937 after appearing in *Bulldog Drummond Escapes* the same year. Barrymore, whose success onstage was repeated in silent films, even without benefit of his superb voice, was rushed into numerous talkies when sound arrived. Then in his 50s, the former romantic lead and swashbuckling hero of the silents began to show signs of memory loss while his once-famous profile reflected his intemperate past life. He was soon relegated to either roles of self-parody or those of secondary characters. However, he imbued even these parts with his personal charm and wit. He died in 1942. See British Intelligence: World War II. ■

Bullet for Joey, A (1955), UA. *Dir.* Lewis Allen; *Sc.* Geoffrey Homes, A. I. Bezzerides; *Cast includes:* Edward G. Robinson, George Raft, Audrey Totter, George Dolenz, Peter Hanson, Peter Van Eyck.

A Communist secret agent hires a former American gangster to kidnap an atomic physicist in this routine Cold War drama. Peter Van Eyck, as the Communist mastermind behind the kidnapping plot, employs the talents of a deported gangster (George Raft) to help kidnap the physicist (George Dolenz) and smuggle him out of Canada. Edward G. Robinson, as a Royal Canadian Mounted Police inspector, is on the job to foil the plot. When Raft becomes aware of the political ramifications of the Communists' eventual

American gangster George Raft (c.) negotiates with Communist agent Peter Van Eyck (r.) to kidnap an atomic physicist. *A Bullet for Joey* (1955).

goals, he sacrifices his life to help Robinson and the physicist. Audrey Totter portrays Raft's former girlfriend. ■

Bullin' the Bullsheviki (1919), State Rights. *Dir.* Frank P. Donovan; *Sc.* Joe Farnham, Frank P. Donovan; *Cast includes:* Marguerite Clayton, Patsy De Forest, Billy Ruge, Edward Elkus, George Humbert, Pearl Shepard, Louise Fazenda.

A young American woman journeys to Russia to wipe out Bolshevism in this zany comedy. Marguerite Clayton portrays Lotta Nerve, the determined American Joan of Arc who, along with two spies masquerading as a horse, decides to save the world from the Bolsheviks. Once in Russia, she encounters Lean Itsky (Billy Ruge), a Trotsky-like leader who takes the pretty American to a hotel room and begins to undress her. Lotta rejects his advances and sends her two secret agents to summon an army. Meanwhile she steals Itsky's military plans. She reports to the battlefield and sends an ultimatum to Itsky that he and his followers take a bath and seek employment. Following a battle which claims most of the Bolsheviks, Itsky and his key staff surrender. They are court-martialed and shot to the cheers of the troops and Lotta. See Red Scare of 1919–1920. ■

Burden of Proof, The (1918), Select. *Dir.* Julius Steger; *Sc.* S. M. Weller; *Cast includes:* Marion Davies, Mary Richards, Eloise Clement, John Merkyl, L. Rogers Lytton, Willard Cooley.

A marriage is almost torn apart when the husband suspects his wife of collaborating with German spies in this World War I domestic drama. John Merkyl portrays the husband who discovers that important documents entrusted to him by the U.S. government have been stolen from his desk. An investigation by the chief of the Department of Justice reveals that the wife (Marion Davies) has sent a letter to a German. He intercepts the letter in time and finds the missing papers and a note from the wife which reads: "I cannot depart without sending you this as a token of our gratitude."

The husband, upon reading this, rushes to his wife and accuses her of betraying his trust and her country. However, the problem is soon resolved when he learns the truth. She had innocently written the letter, but a German spy gained access to their home, stole the secret papers and placed them into the wife's harmless letter. The spies are rounded up and the husband asks for his wife's forgiveness. The film was adapted from the 1877 play *Dora* by Victorien Sardou. ■

Burma. Col. William J. Donovan, who headed the O.S.S. during World War II, first became interested in establishing a paramilitary operation in Burma in 1942. Gen. Joseph Stilwell, who first opposed such an operation, finally agreed. He assigned Capt. Carl Frederick Eifler, an intelligence officer, to head Detachment 101, a paramilitary force, and operate behind enemy lines in Burma. "The next thing I want to hear out of you," Stilwell ordered, "are some loud booms from behind Jap lines."

Eifler led his group, the first of its kind, against the Japanese forces, sabotaging their communications and supply lines. Detachment 101 also provided tactical support to U.S. air and ground forces. Capt. Roger Hilsman, Jr., a fellow intelligence and covert operations officer, led a battalion of Kachin (Burmese tribesmen) guerrillas in jungle fighting against the Japanese for one year. The entire Burmese operation was considered a great success.

Few World War II spy films dealt with the Burmese sector or O.S.S. involvement in covert operations in that region. *Burma Convoy* (1941), a low-budget drama, concerned enemy agents trying to thwart American trucks

from delivering war matériel to the Chinese along the Burma Road. In *Bombs Over Burma* (1942) Anna May Wong portrays a schoolteacher who is requested by the Chinese government to work as a secret agent. Spies, operating along the Burma Road, are tying to stop the shipment of essential supplies. One agent is transmitting information to the Japanese about convoys traveling the Burma Road. In *Half Way to Shanghai* (1942), a low-budget drama set in Burma in 1942 before the Japanese invasion, Nazi agents attempt to get maps of Chinese defenses and ammunition depots. ■

Burma Convoy (1941), U. *Dir.* Noel Smith; *Sc.* Stanley Rubin, Roy Chanslor; *Cast includes:* Charles Bickford, Evelyn Ankers, Frank Albertson, Cecil Kellaway, Willy Fung, Keye Luke.

A minor drama set during the Sino-Japanese War about a group of brave truck drivers who transport munitions to Chinese troops from Rangoon to Chungking over the Burma Road, the film stars Charles Bickford who is in charge of the operation. He is plagued with hijacking and ambushes as he tries to unravel how the guerrillas know the schedules in advance. It seems a Eurasian spy ring is at the bottom of all his problems. His younger brother, played by Frank Albertson, had been mixed up with the agents and was found murdered. Bickford avenges his brother's death. ■

Busses Roar (1942), WB. *Dir.* D. Ross Lederman; *Sc.* George R. Bilson, Anthony Coldeway; *Cast includes:* Richard Travis, Julie Bishop, Charles Drake, Eleanor Parker, Elisabeth Fraser, Richard Fraser.

A low-budget World War II drama that takes place chiefly aboard a bus, the film concerns the transport of a bomb that is to be used to ignite an oil field as a beacon for a Japanese submarine. A large portion of the film is devoted to a saboteur and his efforts at a bus terminal to place the explosive on the bus bound for San Francisco. The U-boat will use the light as a marker while it shells strategic shore positions. Needless to say, the plan is foiled in the nick of time. ■

American trucker Charles Bickford (l.) suspects Turhan Bey (c.) as part of a sabotage plot to prevent supplies from reaching Chinese troops during the Sino-Japanese War. *Burma Convoy* (1941).

C

Caillaux Case, The (1918), Fox. *Dir.* Richard Stanton; *Sc.* Adrian Johnson; *Cast includes:* Henry Warwick, Madeline Travers, George Majeroni, Eugene Ormonde, Frank McGlynn, Philip Van Loan.

Based on an actual sensational contemporary French trial involving spies and traitors, the drama, set during World War I, presents the incidents and courtroom scenes in semi-documentary style. Joseph Caillaux, the French minister of finance, and Henriette marry after both get divorces from their spouses. Caillaux advances to premier and plots a conspiracy with Bolo Pasha to have the French and Germans join forces. An editor discovers the plot but is killed by the premier's wife before he can print the story. Henriette is acquitted. But when new evidence comes to light, Pasha is executed and the premier is charged with treason and imprisoned.

At the time that the film was released, the French courts had already sentenced some of the traitors while others were awaiting final judgment. Newspaper accounts of the trial described the rage of the French people toward the defendants. Frank McGlynn, who portrays Kaiser Wilhelm, went on to impersonate other historical figures on the screen, playing Abraham Lincoln numerous times.

Joseph Caillaux's political career spanned over four decades during the most turbulent of times in post-revolutionary French history. He was elected to the French Chamber of Deputies in 1898 as a member of the Radical Party and served in various capacities in a number of French governments through 1940.

After serving as Minister of Finance under Clemenceau, Caillaux himself was elected premier in 1911. His most notable achievement was the negotiated settlement of the Moroccan crisis during which he ceded some North African territory to the German colony of Cameroon and for which he was generally criticized.

Premier Georges Clemenceau personally arranged the arrest of Caillaux during World War I for the latter's strong advocacy of a negotiated settlement with Germany. Caillaux was eventually found guilty of communicating with the enemy during wartime and was imprisoned.

At the end of the war, when the passions generated by that conflict had cooled, Caillaux was pardoned, had his rights restored and was elected to the Senate. He served once again as Finance Minister in the 1920s. He was instrumental in toppling the Popular Front government in 1937 and, in 1940, voted to confer extraordinary powers on the head of the Vichy government, Marshal Petain. ■

Cairo (1942), MGM. *Dir.* W. S. Van Dyke II; *Sc.* John McLain; *Cast includes:* Jeanette MacDonald, Robert Young, Ethel Waters, Reginald Owen, Grant Mitchell.

MGM moved its singing star Jeanette MacDonald out of costume musicals and into an implausible comedy-drama (with several patriotic songs) set in World War II England and Egypt—with mixed results. She portrays an American movie actress in England who hires Robert Young as her butler. Young, a Yankee reporter assigned to cover the war in North Africa, suspects MacDonald of being a Nazi agent and accepts the position to keep an eye on her. He engages in virtually every pratfall that can be attributed to a bumbling butler.

The plot ultimately takes the couple to Cairo. Young follows a group of spies to their hidden desert lair where they have surreptitiously assembled an airplane. MacDonald manages to open a secret pyramid by reaching the musical note of high C. Ethel Waters, as MacDonald's maid, sings several songs and adds to the comedy. Mona Barrie portrays a Nazi spy. The film added little to the careers of the above performers. ■

Victor McLaglen (l.) and rival Edmund Lowe fight over Binnie Barnes in a cafe' where spies are stealing military secrets. *Call Out the Marines* (1942).

Call Out the Marines (1942), RKO. Dir.

Frank Ryan, William Hamilton; *Sc.* Frank Ryan, William Hamilton; *Cast includes:* Victor McLaglen, Edmund Lowe, Binnie Barnes, Paul Kelly, Robert Smith, Dorothy Lovett.

Victor McLaglen and Edmund Lowe, who made a series of comedies based on the characters they originally played in Raoul Walsh's silent war film *What Price Glory?* (1926), repeat their roles as a pair of brawling leathernecks in this World War II routine service comedy that includes a few songs. The film opens at a racetrack where the old service pals meet after an absence of several years. McLaglen is a sanitation worker complete with white uniform and cart; Lowe, more dapper but also down on his luck, pushes a wheelchair for an elderly gentleman. The buddies exchange a few tall tales, meet and brawl over a café hostess (Binnie Barnes) and rejoin the marines as sergeants.

Hoping to buy stolen military plans, enemy agents frequent the café, which is close to a marine base. Barnes, as a contact for the spies, arranges the purchase for a package of secrets which a marine offers for a large sum of cash. Lowe and McLaglen stumble upon the plot and pursue the agents who are soon caught

and arrested. Paul Kelly, as a U.S. Marine major, works under cover as the café owner in an effort to unmask the entire spy network.

A minor wartime entertainment, the film offers comedy based on old-fashioned pratfalls and Mack Sennett-type chases. Songs like "Call Out the Marines" and "Hands Across the Border" echo the patriotism and propaganda often embedded in World War II films. In one scene in the café the lights dim, a projection screen is lowered and newsreels are shown of American fighter planes flying in formation, warships ready for action and platoons of marching marines. ■

Called to the Front (1914), Apex. *Cast includes:* Arthur Finn.

A drama set during World War I, the plot concerns a U.S. Secret Service officer and wireless operator (Arthur Finn) who must deliver important documents to the Russians. During the course of his mission he is wounded. His sweetheart, a fellow wireless operator, manages to rescue him. Several realistic battle sequences heighten the tension in this otherwise routine film. ■

Calling All Marines (1939), Rep. *Dir.* John H. Auer; *Sc.* Earl Felton; *Cast includes:* Donald Barry, Helen Mack, Warren Hymer, Robert Kent, Cy Kendall, Leon Ames.

A routine drama about a recruit who at first rejects the traditions of the marine corps but comes around in time to accept them, the film stars Donald Barry as a hoodlum in the employ of spies. He joins the marines to steal the plans for a new aerial torpedo but is exposed and jailed. The international gang captures him to stop him from talking, but he escapes. He then helps to bring about their demise in a climactic gun battle in the hills where the spies are blown to bits. Helen Mack provides the romantic interest in this low-budget film. ■

Calling Philo Vance (1940), WB. *Dir.* William Clemens; *Sc.* Tom Reed; *Cast includes:* James Stephenson, Margot Stevenson, Henry O'Neill, Edward Brophy, Ralph Forbes, Donald Douglas.

Enemy agents seek to steal the plans for a new bomber design in this drama that mixes international intrigue with the detective genre. James Stephenson, as the title character—a supersleuth created by writer S. S. Van Dine—is called into the case. He methodically and analytically solves two murders, including that of the inventor, and bags the culprits. Comic character player Edward Brophy, as a slow-witted detective, and James Conlon, as a grumbling city medical examiner, provide some laughs in an otherwise dull tale.

As with other series based on fictional detectives—such as the Charlie Chan, Bulldog Drummond and the Lone Wolf dramas—the Philo Vance series joined the trend of occasionally immersing its sleuth in international intrigue during World War II. Writers turned out plots that had the popular detectives battling spies instead of the conventional criminals and murderers. The film is based on the short story by S. S. Van Dine. See Detectives and Spies. ■

Capricorn One (1978), WB. *Dir.* Peter Hyams; *Sc.* Peter Hyams; *Cast includes:* Elliott Gould, James Brolin, Brenda Vaccaro, Sam Waterston, O. J. Simpson, Hal Holbrook.

This thriller about America's first manned space flight to Mars that turns out to be a hoax offers an interesting premise. However, the drama soon deteriorates into a series of implausible incidents. Head of the space agency Hal Holbrook is forced to cancel the flight because of some defective parts. Knowing that the cancellation will damage the space program, he decides to set up a mock landing to fool the President, politicians and public. He persuades the three astronauts (James Brolin, Sam Waterston, O. J. Simpson) to go along with the scheme. "We are not your enemy," he explains when they voice their opposition. "We're all working for the same thing." Brolin, the chief astronaut, has strong reservations at first, as do his fellow spacemen. "If the only way to keep something alive is to become everything I hate," he states, "I don't know if it's worth keeping alive." Finally, Holbrook is forced to play his trump card. He reveals that a covert organization representing business and other interests has threatened the lives of the astronauts' families if they do not cooperate. He explains that the program has gotten out of his hands—that more powerful forces have taken charge.

The hoax goes off smoothly during the next several months until problems arise during the reentry of the capsule. Holbrook is forced to announce that the astronauts died when the capsule burned up. Consumed by his ambitious scheme which he tries to keep alive,

he orders the astronauts, who have been kept hidden all these months, to be killed. They escape, but only Brolin manages to stay alive in the desert wastes following a relentless pursuit by a network of agents commanded by Holbrook. Meanwhile a curious reporter (Elliott Gould) investigates the project after his friend, who had been working on the flight, has disappeared. Gould becomes the target of several assassination attempts but eventually rescues Brolin. They appear at a funeral tribute to the lost astronauts, exposing Holbrook and the entire conspiracy. ■

Captain Carey, U.S.A. (1950), Par. *Dir.* Mitchell Leisen; *Sc.* Robert Thoeren; *Cast includes:* Alan Ladd, Wanda Hendrix, Francis Lederer, Joseph Calleia, Celia Lovsky, Richard Avonde.

Alan Ladd, as an O.S.S. agent during World War II, returns to Italy after the war and unmasks a traitor responsible for several deaths. In particular, Ladd would like to avenge the deaths of Giulia, a young Italian woman he had fallen in love with and a fellow O.S.S. agent. The film opens during the war, with Ladd and his friend, operating behind enemy lines in a small Italian village, hiding out in an abandoned villa from German troops. As the two agents are transmitting their information to headquarters, German troops break in. Ladd realizes they have been betrayed. His friend is killed and Ladd is seriously wounded. Before he passes out, he hears another gunshot and thinks they have killed Giulia (Wandra Hendrix).

Upon his return to Italy for a visit, he discovers that she is still alive and married to a baron (Francis Lederer) who wields political influence and power. Disappointed, Ladd resigns himself to her marriage and loses interest in hunting for the traitor. "When you lose something you thought was valuable," he muses, "you bleed a little and forget it." A villager whose son was wrongly killed as the betrayer and whose husband was murdered before he could reveal to Ladd what he knew about the real traitor, convinces Ladd to continue his search. But Ladd runs into hostility in the village. The inhabitants blame him for the deaths of 28 of their relatives who were shot by the Germans as an act of reprisal. He is soon embroiled in strange events as several witnesses are murdered to prevent him from learning the identity of the traitor. He finally learns that Giulia's husband is the traitor.

The baron, to free Giulia's brother from a prison camp, made a deal with the Nazis to reveal the hiding place of the O.S.S. team. The baron is killed in a struggle with Ladd. The film was adapted from the novel *After Midnight* by Martha Alband. See Office of Strategic Services. ■

Captain Courtesy (1915), Bosworth-Par. *Dir.* Hobart Bosworth; *Cast includes:* Dustin Farnum, Herbert Standing, Winifred Kingston, Courtenay Foote, Jack Hoxie.

A spy betrays an American-style Robin Hood in this romantic drama set in old California when that territory was ruled by Mexico. Dustin Farnum portrays the son of American settlers who were killed when he was a young boy. Vowing revenge, he masquerades as Captain Courtesy, an elusive defender of Americans' rights in the territory. He robs the rich Mexicans and turns over his spoils to his fellow countrymen. A renegade American (Courtenay Foote) sees the masked hero at a local mission and informs the Mexican authorities who soon dispatch some troops. Captain Courtesy rides out, finds a troop of American cavalrymen and leads them back to the mission in time to save the besieged American settlers. The American traitor and spy, the hero learns, was the person responsible for his parents' death. But the young woman he loves stops him from taking revenge. The film was adapted from the 1906 novel by Edward C. Carpenter. ■

Communist spies try to steal a U.S. space capsule after its re-entry from orbit in the Cold War drama *Capture That Capsule!* (1961).

Capture That Capsule! (1961), Riviera. *Dir.* Will Zens; *Sc.* Will Zens, Jan Elblein; *Cast includes:* Richard Miller, Dick O'Neil, Richard Jordahl, Pat Bradley, Carl Rogers, Dorothy Schiller.

Communist spies try to steal a U.S. space capsule after its reentry from orbit in this Cold War drama devoid of credibility. As the inept enemy agents carry out their plot, they are unaware that the capsule is only a decoy set up by American secret agents to trap the Communists. So the chases and death serve little purpose. A weak plot, inane dialogue and stereotyped characters hamper any illusion of reality. ■

Careful, Soft Shoulders (1942), TCF. *Dir.* Oliver H. P. Garrett; *Sc.* Oliver H. P. Garrett; *Cast includes:* Virginia Bruce, James Ellison, Aubrey Mather, Sheila Ryan, Ralph Byrd.

A World War II spy comedy drama with Washington society as a background, the film features Virginia Bruce as a bored socialite who gets involved with Nazi spies. As a lark, she announces at a social function that she would not mind meeting some foreign spies. Aubrey Mather, as a secret agent, takes Bruce at her word and, posing as a double agent, tries to use her to obtain strategic navy plans. James Ellison, as the target of the spies, becomes emotionally involved with Bruce. They are captured by the spy ring but manage to escape and expose the group. Although a low-budget film, it provides sufficient originality and freshness as well as an interesting picture of early wartime Washington. ■

Carolina Cannonball (1955), Rep. *Dir.* Charles Lamont; *Sc.* Barry Shipman; *Cast includes:* Judy Canova, Andy Clyde, Ross Elliott, Sig Ruman, Leon Askin, Jack Kruschen.

Enemy agents attempt to steal America's first atomic-powered guided missile but are unprepared for their run-in with Judy Canova in this zany comedy. When the guided missile lands somewhere in a deserted area in the West, the foreign spies hope to retrieve it before U.S. officials locate the secret weapon. Near the site is Roaring Gulch, an abandoned town where Judy Canova and her grandfather (Andy Clyde), the only inhabitants, run a steam-powered trolley shuttle. As expected, they mix it up with the intruders. U.S. special agent Ross Elliott follows the spies to the missile site in this comedy which depends chiefly on slapstick. Released during the Cold War, the film was attacked by at least one critic who thought it was in bad taste to make light of such a serious situation when the U.S. was on edge about Communist espionage. ■

Casablanca (1942), WB. *Dir.* Michael Curtiz; *Sc.* Julius and Philip Epstein, Howard Koch; *Cast includes:* Humphrey Bogart, Ingrid Bergman, Paul Henreid, Claude Rains, Conrad Veidt, Sydney Greenstreet, Peter Lorre, S. Z. Sakall.

This drama of love and redemption takes place during World War II, prior to Pearl Harbor, in Casablanca, a Moroccan seaport where international intrigue and a flourishing black market dominate the lives of many of its inhabitants. Rick (Humphrey Bogart), a cynical, disillusioned American in self-exile, runs a café. One day Ilsa (Ingrid Bergman), Rick's former sweetheart, enters his café with her husband, Victor Laszlo (Paul Henreid), a leader of anti-Nazi resistance. That night, while sitting alone and drinking heavily, Rick ponders: "Of all the gin joints in all the towns in all the world—she walks into mine." Ilsa, in desperation, turns to Rick to help her husband who is being sought by the Gestapo. At first he refuses, but when she promises to stay with him, he reluctantly decides to help them both. Rick outwardly professes a lack of interest in her that reassures Victor of his wife's devotion. Providing the couple with special letters of transit, Rick arranges for their flight out of Casablanca. He then walks down that familiar tarmac with his friend, Renault (Claude Rains), a witty and charmingly corrupt Vichy police captain. Their lost ideals rekindled, the two men join the Allies in their fight against totalitarianism as Rick announces: "Louie, I think this is the beginning of a beautiful friendship."

The film has rightfully earned its reputation as a classic. It tells a highly romanticized story that captivates its audiences. Rarely has a cast been so well chosen to play the rich assortment of characters. The anti-Nazi propaganda that permeates the work is not only unobtrusive, it is essential to the characters and the plot. For example, when someone warns Laszlo that he and other leaders like him will be caught, he replies defiantly: "Thousands will rise in their places." And when Laszlo says to Rick, "Welcome back to the fight. This time I know our side will win," the audience empathizes with both men. In one inspiring scene in the café, which has become a microcosm of the embattled nations of Europe, several Nazi officers

break into a chorus of "Die Wacht am Rhein" but are drowned out when Laszlo leads the French patrons in a stirring rendition of the "Marseillaise."

The film opened only weeks after Allied forces landed in French North Africa (November 8, 1942). This was followed by the Casablanca conference between Roosevelt and Churchill on January 23, 1943—two fortuitous events that no doubt heightened interest in the film. The historical conference contributed to the allegorical speculations about the role of Rick, the neutral American who remains uninvolved until the appropriate moment and then enters the fight. "I stick my neck out for nobody," he announces early in the film. When he allows a young refugee couple, desperate for exit visas, to win at one of his gambling tables, the wife cries: "He is an American. You see, America must be a wonderful place." When the arrogant Col. Strasser (Conrad Veidt), recently arrived from Berlin, dismisses Rick as "just another blundering American," Renault is quick to correct this assessment. "We mustn't underestimate American blundering," he adds. "I was with them when they blundered into Berlin in 1918." American isolationism is suggested in Rick's casual musings: "I bet they're asleep in New York. I bet they're asleep all over America." The film is so affecting that no one cares that historically there never were any "letters of transit." Romantic drama at its best, *Casablanca* was what America needed in the gloomy period of the war when the Allies were fighting desperately to hold back the encroaching tide of totalitarianism. See Vichy France. ■

Central Intelligence Agency. Perhaps the most controversial and least understood agency in the history of the country, the C.I.A. was founded in 1947 to integrate intelligence activities of several government departments for national security interests. Functioning in an advisory capacity to the National Security Council, the C.I.A. has no law enforcement powers or internal security role. The N.S.C. may assign other functions to the agency relating to security. The C.I.A., which is strictly prohibited from operating within the nation's borders, came under fire in the 1970s for violating this constraint.

Gen. William J. Donovan, who headed the Office of Strategic Services (O.S.S.) during World War II, conceived the idea in 1943 for a postwar, permanent agency responsible for gathering and coordinating intelligence. He sent a memorandum in 1944 to President Roosevelt suggesting an official intelligence agency. Donovan's proposal met with stiff opposition from rival departments and bureaus, including the State, War and Navy Departments and the Federal Bureau of Investigation. F.B.I. Director J. Edgar Hoover, particularly, believed that the functions Donovan suggested fell under the aegis of the F.B.I., which had the experience and manpower for such tasks. The final blow to Donovan's plan came when it was revealed in the press and quickly attacked as a government scheme to institute an "American Gestapo."

However, Donovan's dream came to fruition in 1947 after Congress passed the National Security Act and President Truman signed it on July 26. The establishment of the National Security Council and its subagency, the C.I.A., saw the light of day not out of reverence for Donovan's vision but from the political necessities of the growing Cold War. The National Security Act defined the duties of the C.I.A. At the same time, President Truman introduced his Truman Doctrine which stated that the U.S. would help non-Communist countries struggling against Communist domination.

The C.I.A.'s functions include the clandestine gathering of foreign intelligence; covert action; counterintelligence operations outside the U.S.; and the development of technical systems which help in the gathering of information, such as reconnaissance satellites. It is from these areas that so many American spy films have derived their plots.

Most spy dramas and comedies in which the C.I.A. plays a role depict the agency in an unfavorable light. Those rare films which are sympathetic to the agency focus chiefly on action and preclude any political content. Since Hollywood is known more for reflecting attitudes and opinions than for originating them, unfavorable news stories may well have influenced the studios, directors and writers to draw negative conclusions about the C.I.A. and its activities.

C.I.A. chiefs often are shown as manipulative, deceptive and sometimes even depraved. One such chief in The Killer Elite (1975), in contracting a private company to protect an Asian national, explains his agency's expediency: "We don't want Chong killed in the U.S. Right now we can't afford the publicity." Robert Redford, as a "reader," a low-level researcher for the C.I.A., uncovers a plot within the organization in Three Days of the Condor (1975). It seems that its chief, played by John Houseman, has his own ideas about how best to protect the interests of the U.S. In Good Guys Wear Black (1978) the former head of a Vietnam commando rescue team is drawn into a U.S. government conspiracy in this action-oriented drama set after the Vietnam War. Chuck Norris, as a karate expert, had been abandoned, along with his special small force, on their last mission for the C.I.A. In Hopscotch (1980), an above-average comedy, a disgruntled C.I.A. agent (Walter Matthau) who has been relegated to a dreary filing job decides to expose the espionage game and unmask its chief players. Ned Beatty portrays the up-tight, obnoxious C.I.A. chief who precipitates the problem. Another arrogant C.I.A. chief in The Kidnapping of the President (1980) demands that his agency handle the abduction of a U.S. President. He frustrates the more expert efforts of secret service chief William Shatner, who is burdened with negotiating with terrorists while he is trying to free the President. A C.I.A. boss in Target (1985) in reality is a double agent who has killed the wife and children of a German citizen to protect his own cover.

Hitchcock's North by Northwest (1959) offers a particularly intriguing portrayal of a callous C.I.A. supervisor (Leo G. Carroll). Torn between sacrificing individual lives or permitting foreign powers to steal America's secrets, he justifies his ruthlessness as a necessary means toward winning the Cold War. To protect his own undercover agent, he allows enemy assassins, who mistake innocent Cary Grant for a C.I.A. member, to pursue Grant. Later, Grant confronts Carroll and rebukes him for endangering others, musing that losing the Cold War may be preferable to Carroll's extreme methods. "I'm afraid," the paranoid C.I.A. chief replies, "we're already doing that."

Lower-echelon agents frequently are arrogant and treacherous, sometimes even coldblooded killers. In Blindfold (1966), a comedy drama with Rock Hudson and Claudia Cardinale, a major American scientist becomes the target of a kidnapping plot by both C.I.A. agents and an international spy ring. Mark Gordon in Don't Drink the Water (1969), a farce based on Woody Allen's stage play, portrays a C.I.A. agent who looks more like an underworld hit man than a hero. Ruthless U.S. secret agent William DeVane in *Marathon Man* (1976) is part of a covert plot by the C.I.A. to cover up the activities of a villainous, escaped Nazi war criminal who occasionally informs on his fellow Nazis. In *Hot and Deadly* (1984) a recent C.I.A. recruit quickly becomes disillusioned with the agency, especially its cold-blooded tactics, when he witnesses his partner callously murder an innocent bystander.

Other dramas and comedies criticize the C.I.A. in general. In the satirical *The President's Analyst* (1967) James Coburn portrays a psychiatrist who is chosen to act as the U.S. President's personal analyst. The film aims its barbs at several institutions, including, among others, the F.B.I. and C.I.A. Burt Young in *The Killer Elite* tries to enlighten his friend (James Caan), both of whom occasionally take on assignments for the C.I.A., about the type of work they are involved in. "I know the rationale—self-defense, God and country, another assignment in the national interest. Damn it, you're so busy doing their dirty work, you don't know who the bad guys are." In *Wrong Is Right* (1982) the intelligence agency comes under heavy fire as an amoral group of misfits ready to manipulate anyone to gain its ends. The C.I.A. in *The Osterman Weekend* (1983) convinces an influential television interview host (Rutger Hauer) to spy on his friends who are suspected of being Soviet agents in this convoluted drama about the invasion of privacy. In *The Falcon and the Snowman* (1985), based on actual incidents, Timothy Hutton, as a troubled employee of a U.S. security agency, accidentally stumbles across C.I.A. messages. "Every day I get these misrouted cables," he confides to a friend, "the C.I.A.'s secret mail. Details of covert actions that have nothing to do with national security. Manipulations of foreign press, political parties, whole economies...." The documentary *On Company Business* (1980) explores the agency's interference in various European strikes and covert operations in other parts of the globe, particularly Latin America.

However, a handful of films cast the C.I.A. in a favorable light. In *The Girl in the Kremlin* (1957) a frustrated sister (Zsa Zsa Gabor) appeals to an ex-C.I.A. officer (Lex Barker) to help her find her twin who has vanished. Burt Reynolds, as a C.I.A. agent in *Operation CIA* (1965), is sent to Saigon during the Vietnam War to investigate the murder of a fellow agent. *Solomon King* (1974) concerns a C.I.A. agent helping a former Green Beret fighter carry out a raid against insurgents in a Middle East sheikdom. In *Rosebud* (1975), with Peter O'Toole and Richard Attenborough, a C.I.A. agent helps to rescue five rich young girls held captive by P.L.O. terrorists. *Avalanche Express* (1979), a Cold War drama with Robert Shaw and Lee Marvin, shows the agency using a high-ranking Soviet defector to ensnare a dangerous Soviet agent. Ken Wahl, as a C.I.A. superspy in *The Soldier* (1982), hopscotches around the globe in an effort to ply his brand of professional tactics against the villains, although the results end in violence and bloodshed. ∎

Chairman, The (1969), TCF. *Dir.* J. Lee Thompson; *Sc.* Ben Maddow; *Cast includes:* Gregory Peck, Anne Heywood, Arthur Hill, Alan Dobie, Conrad Yama, Keye Luke.

Gregory Peck portrays an American Nobel prizewinner who, while teaching in London, is asked by his government to journey to Communist China on a secret mission in this implausible Cold War drama. After receiving a highly enigmatic letter from his former Chinese instructor (Keye Luke), Peck reluctantly agrees to make the dangerous trip. Soviet Russia, Britain and the U.S., in a combined effort, want him to gather information about a secret, highly advanced food-growing process developed by the Chinese. For this purpose, Peck has a special transmitter implanted into his skull. He is, however, unaware that the device contains a deadly explosive element that can be activated at any time.

Once in mainland China, Peck meets his old professor and the man's daughter (Francisca Tu) and is soon introduced to the Chinese Communist Party chairman. The wily chairman admits that his scientists are confronted with an enzyme problem that is holding up the special food-production experiment, hinting that Peck may be able to solve the dilemma. Peck strongly suggests that the discovery should be available to all nations, but the chairman is ambiguous in his reply. After some frustration on Peck's part in finding the necessary formula, his former professor dies and leaves the American a book which also contains the secret molecular structure. Peck then rushes to the Soviet border to escape the Chinese who have grown suspicious. Back in England, those tuned in on Peck's movements fear that he will be captured and agree to detonate the implanted explosive. But at the last moment Peck is rescued by Russian troops.

Anne Heywood portrays a fellow professor with whom Peck is romantically involved. Arthur Hill, as a military attaché, exemplifies the military establishment whose aims conflict with those of the scientific community. Conrad Yama portrays the clever and witty chairman. The film was adapted from Jay Richard Kennedy's novel. ∎

Chambers, Whittaker. See *The Trials of Alger Hiss* (1980). ∎

Charge of the Lancers (1954), Col. *Dir.* William Castle; *Sc.* Robert E. Kent; *Cast includes:* Paulette Goddard, Jean Pierre Aumont, Richard Stapley, Karin Booth, Charles Irwin, Ben Astar.

Romance blooms between a gypsy and a French captain during the Crimean War in this routine drama. Paulette Goddard portrays the passionate gypsy while Jean Pierre Aumont appears as the captain. The lovers are caught by the Russians, but they manage to spy upon the enemy and rescue a British officer (Richard Stapley). Karin Booth, as a Russian agent, masquerades as an English nurse. Goddard and Aumont return with their vital information which helps the British to capture the Russian naval base at Sebastopol. Historical records report that the introduction of a new type of cannon played the principal role in the battle. ∎

Charlie Chan in Panama (1940), TCF. *Dir.* Norman Foster; *Sc.* John Larkin; *Cast includes:* Sidney Toler, Jean Rogers, Lionel Atwill, Mary Nash, Sen Yung, Kane Richmond.

Another Hollywood detective temporarily steps out of his conventional domestic crime series to perform his patriotic duty in this World War II spy-detective drama. Charlie Chan, working in league with U.S. intelligence, foils a plot to blow up a portion of the Panama Canal and trap a U.S. fleet passing through during maneuvers. The Chinese detective also uncovers a mysterious German spy. The film, in part, is a remake of *Marie Galante* (1934), which, ironically, has a secret agent of Japan joining forces with those of the U.S. and England to prevent the destruction of the Panama Canal. See Panama Canal.

Other Hollywood sleuths, including Sherlock Holmes (*Voice of Terror*, etc.) and Ellery Queen (*Enemy Agents Meet Ellery Queen*), tackled Nazi and Japanese agents during the war years. These diversions added a little spark to each series and no doubt contributed to the patriotism of the period. See Detectives and Spies. ∎

Charlie Chan in the Secret Service (1944), Mon. *Dir.* Phil Rosen; *Sc.* George Callahan; *Cast includes:* Sidney Toler, Gwen Kenyon, Mantan Moreland, Marianne Quon, Arthur Loft, Benson Fong.

Secret plans are stolen from an inventor in this below-average detective-spy entry in the popular series featuring the world-famous Chinese sleuth created by Earl Derr Biggers. Sidney Toler, as Charlie Chan, recently recruited as a U.S. government agent, is appointed to solve the murder of the inventor and recover the missing documents. Mantan Moreland, as Chan's chauffeur, and Benson Fong, as Tommy, one of the detective's sons, are around for comic relief and to offer some dubious aid to Chan. However, since most of the incidents take place in the inventor's home, the film takes on a claustrophobic atmosphere. This was the first in the detective series to be produced by Monogram, which acquired the rights from 20th Century-Fox. See Detectives and Spies. ∎

Chasing Danger (1939), TCF. *Dir.* Ricardo Cortez; *Sc.* Robert Ellis, Helen Logan; *Cast includes:* Preston Foster, Lynn Bari, Wally Vernon, Henry Wilcoxon, Joan Woodbury, Harold Huber.

A spy ring secretly supplies munitions to Arab tribes in their revolt against their French rulers in this pre-World War II comedy drama set chiefly in the Moroccan desert. Preston Foster, as an American newsreel cameraman, and Wally Vernon, as his comic sidekick, somehow get themselves entangled in this political intrigue and have to do some fast explaining to extricate themselves from several tight situations. Henry Wilcoxon portrays a French secret service agent who is on the trail of the arms-smuggling spies. Lynn Bari and Joan Woodbury provide the romantic interests in this occasionally comical tale directed deftly by former actor Ricardo Cortez. ∎

Chasing Trouble (1940), Mon. *Dir.* Howard Bretherton; *Sc.* Mary McCarthy; *Cast includes:* Frankie Darro, Marjorie Reynolds, George Cleveland, Alex Callam, Mantan Moreland, Lillian Elliott.

Enemy agents sabotage various important U.S. installations until they are apprehended in this low-budget drama set during World War II but before America's entry into the conflict. The saboteurs, operating out of a flower store, send their deadly explosives to utilities and other vital locations by hiding the bombs in special bouquets. Frankie Darro, as a delivery boy for the shop, helps to expose the gang. Interested in handwriting analysis, Darro uses his hobby to track down the saboteurs.

Monogram found a niche for youthful-looking Frankie Darro, then in his twenties, and placed him in a series of similar action dramas during 1940 and into early 1941. Darro, usually employed at some menial job, would become entangled in a mystery and end up playing detective. Howard Bretherton directed these unartistic but moderately entertaining films. ∎

Checkmate (1973), J.E.R. *Dir.* Lem Amero; *Sc.* LaRue Watts; *Cast includes:* Diana Wilson, An Tsan Hu, Don Draper, J. J. Coyle, Caren Kaye, Kurt Mann.

Madame Chang, a female version of the infamous Fu Manchu, cooks up a plot to blackmail the major world powers in this amateurishly produced drama. Chang, portrayed by An Tsan Hu, has her sexy underlings seduce the top secret agents of four nations in her effort to gain access to a nuclear-armed satellite. Each victim possesses one key to the weapon which will allow the power-crazed Chang to demand four billion dollars from the countries. Diana Wilson, doing a poor imitation of a James Bond-type of superspy, puts an end to Chang's delusions of grandeur. ∎

Chetniks (1943), TCF. *Dir.* Louis King; *Sc.* Jack Andrews, E. E. Paramore; *Cast includes:* Philip Dorn, Anna Sten, John Sheppard, Virginia Gilmore.

This World War II film pays tribute to Yugoslavia's heroic General Draja Mihalovich and his brave guerrillas who fought against their Nazi occupiers. In this straightforward drama the general, played by Philip Dorn, and his band are shown outwitting the invaders at almost every turn. They ambush an Italian supply column and eventually capture an entire town held by the enemy after the general's wife (Anna Sten) and child are caught and held as hostage.

The film was based on contemporary news reports filtering out of Nazi-occupied Europe as well as biographical information supplied by officials of the Yugoslavian Embassy in the United States. The Chetniks, fighting under the monarchist Mihailovich and representing Serbian nationalism, were highly regarded in the West. But they soon found themselves out of favor with the Allies, who instead recognized Marshall Tito and his partisans. Britain's Special Operations Executive (S.O.E.), a major intelligence agency, early in the war feared helping European pro-Communist resistance forces which could pose a general threat during the postwar years. Therefore, the S.O.E. eagerly sought out royalist or conservative resistance fighters whom it was willing to furnish with extensive arms and equipment against the Nazis. However, after extensive and angry internal quarrels, the British late in the war selected Tito's Communist guerrillas. ∎

China Gate (1957), TCF. *Dir.* Samuel Fuller; *Sc.* Samuel Fuller; *Cast includes:* Gene Barry, Angie Dickinson, Nat King Cole, Paul DuBov, Lee Van Cleef, George Givot.

The French Indo-China War provides the background for this action drama about a patrol of French Legionnaires assigned to blow up a secret Communist ammunition dump. The munitions are hidden in one of many tunnels in the northern hills, and the only one who can lead the soldiers through the mined and booby-trapped areas is "Lucky Legs" (Angie Dickinson), a Eurasian double agent posing as a Red sympathizer. She refuses to go unless the French commander promises to arrange for her five-year-old son to be sent to America. The officer agrees.

Gene Barry, as an American mercenary now fighting with the Legionnaires, had been married to Lucky in the past but left when he learned that their baby had been born with Chinese features. Abandoned in Asia by the only man she ever loved and burdened with the child, she was forced to survive by any means available. When she discovers that Barry is the explosives expert on the mission, she again refuses to go. But Barry convinces her to lead the patrol for the sake of the child. Their romance is rekindled during the journey. Although the objective is accomplished, Dickinson is killed in the explosion when she heroically rewires the charge cut by the Communists. The last scene shows Barry taking his son to the States.

Director-writer Samuel Fuller, who had been the first upon the screen with a 1951 Korean War film (*The Steel Helmet*), again scooped Hollywood with this tale of the French Indo-China War set in 1954. As in several of his other war dramas, he presents a gritty film. Those on the patrol find little glory in war. One Legionnaire is killed suddenly while he is joking about his former job as a traffic cop in Paris. Another dies painfully of a broken back when he accidentally falls off a precipice. "Let there be a heaven," he utters before he dies as his fellow soldiers look on, "or it will kill me to have to come back here again." Nat King Cole portrays an American volunteer who had fought in Korea and wants to continue the struggle against Communism. In one scene he steps on a booby trap and a spike goes completely through his foot.

The major characters have become hardened and cynical as a result of war. Dickinson, who collaborates with the enemy and sells them liquor, doesn't care which side wins. Barry, toughened by the Korean War and his disillusioned marriage, tells the others on the mission that the objective is more important than any one man's life. When one Hungarian volunteer has nightmares during the journey, Barry suggests that the captain kill him to protect the mission. But Barry relents grudgingly upon the captain's insistence and gives the tormented soldier one more chance.

Released during the Cold War, the film echoes the hard line against the Communists. A French priest in Indo-China tells how the Reds, labeling him a capitalist collaborator, cut off one of his legs. Opening scenes show the plight of starving villagers whose homes have been relentlessly bombed and turned into rubble. A French soldier during the mission proudly announces: "This time the Foreign Legion mercenary is not fighting for money or for the French government alone. This time he's fighting for the whole western world against a common enemy." ∎

China Girl (1942), TCF. *Dir.* Henry Hathaway; *Sc.* Ben Hecht; *Cast includes:* Gene Tierney, George Montgomery, Lynn Bari, Victor McLaglen, Alan Baxter.

Japanese agents plot the destruction of China in this World War II drama set in Mandalay and China during the Sino-Japanese War, prior to Japan's attack on Pearl Harbor. George Montgomery, as an American newsreel cameraman, falls in love with a young Chinese woman (Gene Tierney) educated in the U.S. Meanwhile, Japanese planes bomb China's cities. When Tierney is killed during one of the raids, Montgomery wreaks revenge upon the Japanese planes with a machine gun. Lynn Bari and Victor McLaglen portray spies, with Bari falling for Montgomery. The film has several exciting war scenes in an otherwise routine tale. ∎

China Passage (1937), RKO. *Dir.* Edward Killy; *Sc.* Edward L. Hartmann, J. Robert Bren; *Cast includes:* Constance Worth, Vinton Haworth, Leslie Fenton, Gordon Jones, Alex Craig, Dick Elliott.

Constance Worth, as a U.S. Government agent, is assigned to uncover a diamond smuggling operation in this atmospheric drama. The mysterious doings, including murder, take place in Shanghai and then move aboard a San Francisco-bound liner. An American soldier of fortune (Vinton Haworth), who has had some experience in sleuthing, takes command of the investigation involving a diamond theft and murder aboard the vessel. At first unaware of Worth's real identity, he falls in love with her during the voyage. Dick Elliott's drunken antics provide some comic relief in an otherwise bland film. ∎

China Slaver, The (1929), Trinity. *Dir.* Frank Mattison; *Sc.* L. V. Jefferson, Cecil Burtis Hill; *Cast includes:* Sojin, Albertino Valentino, Jim Aubrey, Bud Shaw, Opal Baker.

A band of Chinese narcotics smugglers who also trade in white slavery use a remote island for their operations in this dated melodrama. Sojin, a popular oriental performer of the 1920s, portrays the despotic ruler and leader of the gang. All is going well for the miscreants until an innocent little Chinese stowaway appears and disrupts the lucrative illegal doings. The intruder happens to be a special agent of the Chinese secret service. ∎

Soldier of fortune Vinton Haworth investigates an international diamond-smuggling operation and several murders in *China Passage* (1937).

China Venture (1953), Col. *Dir.* Don Siegel; *Sc.* George Worthing Yates, Richard Collins; *Cast includes:* Edmond O'Brien, Barry Sullivan, Jocelyn Brando, Leo Gordon, Dayton Lummis, Leon Askin.

A small group of U.S. Marines and sailors is assigned by Navy intelligence the task of bringing in a downed Japanese admiral on the China coast for questioning in this suspenseful drama set during World War II. The Americans successfully reach the admiral (Philip Ahn) who was hurt in the plane crash. Their journey back, however, is fraught with a variety of problems, including battles with Japanese and Chinese guerrillas. An internal conflict arises when a battle-hardened marine captain (Edmond O'Brien) clashes with his inexperienced superior navy officer (Barry Sullivan). Ultimately, the latter proves himself by his sacrifice to stay behind to hold off the advancing Japanese.

The plot involving a Japanese admiral may well have been inspired by an actual incident. Admiral Yamamoto Isoruku, commander of the Japanese fleet, visited several bases at the front. The admiral, who had

planned the sneak attack on Pearl Harbor, used the wireless to transmit his itinerary in code to the various commanders. U.S. forces, having earlier broken the Japanese code, intercepted the message. On April 18, 1943, American airmen shot down the plane transporting Yamamoto, who died in the crash. See U.S. Intelligence: World War II. ■

Chinatown Squad (1935), U. *Dir.* Murray Roth; *Sc.* Dore Schary, Ben Ryan; *Cast includes:* Lyle Talbot, Valerie Hobson, Hugh O'Connell, Andy Devine, E. Alyn Warren, Leslie Fenton.

San Francisco's Chinatown provides the setting for this weak drama that weaves together a tale of mystery and international intrigue. An agent of the Chinese Communists, who has journeyed to the U.S. to purchase airplanes for his cause, is mysteriously murdered. Lyle Talbot, as a former policeman who has been dismissed from the force, is currently employed as a chauffeur of a sightseeing bus. Determined to solve the murder and get his old job back, he becomes involved in the investigation. Valerie Hobson portrays the female lead. Character actor Andy Devine handles the comic relief. ∎

C.I.A. See Central Intelligence Agency. ∎

Chief code-breaker Leon Ames (c.) tries to break the latest code used by a local spy ring in this pre-World War II drama. *Cipher Bureau* (1938).

Cipher Bureau (1938), GN. *Dir.* Charles Lamont; *Sc.* Arthur Hoerl; *Cast includes:* Leon Ames, Charlotte Wynters, Joan Woodbury, Don Dillaway, Tenen Holtz.

A pre-World War II drama, the film features Leon Ames as the head of the counter-espionage cipher bureau, an agency set up to foil hostile nations from sending secret messages to their agents in the U.S. Ames' naive brother, a navy lieutenant, is deceived by a female spy, but he manages at the last moment to turn against the alien agents. The marines are called in to round up the network of spies.

No foreign nation is identified, but the accents of the spies strongly suggest that they are of German origin. Hollywood attempted to remain neutral during the rise of Nazi and Fascist forces in Europe on two counts. First, the American public was in no mood to become entangled in another foreign war. The second reason was purely monetary—the studios did not want to alienate any lucrative foreign market. Therefore, it seems rather surprising that a film released during this period would even hint at anything anti-German. Hitler's invasion of Poland in 1939 and the release of *Confessions of a Nazi Spy*, Warners' hard-hitting anti-Nazi propaganda exposé, brought Hollywood's fence-straddling to an end. ∎

Civil War. See American Civil War: Intelligence and Covert Actions. ∎

Claws of the Hun, The (1918), Par. *Dir.* Victor Schertzinger; *Cast includes:* Charles Ray, Jane Novak, Robert McKim, Melbourne McDowell, Dorcas Matthews, Mollie McConnell.

German spies attempt to steal secret papers from an American munitions plant with the help of a consulting engineer in this World War I drama. Charles Ray, as the son of the plant owner, is prevented by his mother from enlisting in the military. Rejected by his sweetheart and buddies as a slacker, he nevertheless helps to foil the plot and capture the traitorous employee. In the end, he is given permission to enlist. Jane Novak portrays the female lead. The film was noted for its better production values than those found in other similar works of the period. See German Intelligence: World War I. ∎

Cleopatra Jones and the Casino of Gold (1975), WB. *Dir.* Chuck Bail; *Sc.* William Tennant; *Cast includes:* Tamara Dobson, Stella Stevens, Tanny, Norman Fell, Albert Popwell, Caro Kenyatta.

Tamara Dobson repeats her Cleopatra Jones role of a street-smart black heroine and undercover agent out to smash international drug operations in this action drama set chiefly in Hong Kong. Stella Stevens, as the main villain, runs her illegal drug trade from a Macao gambling house. Tanny portrays Dobson's Chinese confidant. Norman Fell plays Dobson's boss who runs the secret agency she works for. Albert Popwell and Caro Kenyatta are only two of the drug traffickers whom Dobson, as superheroine, has to tackle in this cliché-ridden film which borders on camp. ∎

Clipped Wings (1953), AA. *Dir.* Edward Bernds; *Sc.* Charles R. Marion, Elwood Ullman; *Cast includes:* Leo Gorcey, Huntz Hall, Bernard Gorcey, Renie Riano, Todd Karns, June Vincent.

Another entry in the popular Bowery Boys comedy series, this film has some of the young gang members mixing it up with a spy ring. Leo Gorcey and Huntz Hall, as his stooge, visit a pal who is in a guardhouse. Thinking they are signing a pass to see him, they find themselves in uniform. Their buddy, an army lieutenant, is actually working for the F.B.I. in an attempt to ferret out a group of enemy agents. Gorcey and Hall become involved in the spy hunt and accidentally help to capture the culprits. The Bowery Boys engage in their usual antics, with most of the laughs and low comedy stemming from Hall. In this entry, for example, he is mistakenly assigned to a women's barracks where he creates mayhem. ■

Cloak and Dagger (1946), WB. *Dir.* Fritz Lang; *Sc.* Albert Maltz, Ring Lardner, Jr.; *Cast includes:* Gary Cooper, Lilli Palmer, Robert Alda, Vladimir Sokoloff, J. Edward Bromberg, Ludwig Stossel.

Gary Cooper portrays an American scientist whom the Office of Strategic Services conscripts near the end of World War II to journey to Europe to learn the extent of Nazi experiments with atomic energy. "There was a time," Cooper says when he is first approached about the assignment, "when I thought I wanted to be some kind of secret agent. I gave it up when I was eight." Rather reluctantly, he travels to Switzerland to interview a Hungarian physicist and try to prevent her from returning to her homeland. When he learns that the woman scientist has been killed by the Nazis, he realizes he must then go to Italy, which is swarming with enemy troops, to persuade another scientist to defect.

He meets and falls in love with an Italian partisan (Lilli Palmer) who at first treats him with disdain because of his amateur standing as a secret agent and his lack of anti-Fascist commitment (anticipating her similar role in the 1962 drama *The Counterfeit Traitor*). But she is soon attracted to the American and helps him to reach another scientist (Vladimir Sokoloff) held prisoner by the Nazis. The Italian tells Cooper that he can't leave because the Nazis are holding his daughter hostage. The American promises to rescue the daughter, but when he does, the young captive admits that the real daughter was killed by the Nazis. A gunfight ensues between Allied agents and enemy troops as Cooper, Sokoloff and Palmer escape to an awaiting plane to take them to freedom. Palmer, the dedicated freedom fighter and anti-Fascist, decides to remain behind. Cooper heads for home with the freed scientist, pledging to return to her. The drama is based in part on *Cloak and Dagger*, a book about the O.S.S. coauthored by Corey Ford, an O.S.S. officer, and Alistair MacLean.

Director Fritz Lang, who adds the proper suspense, tension and atmosphere to the drama, never accomplished his original goal. When he was assigned to the film, he intended to bring out the gravity and implications of nuclear weapons, but the scenes alluding to these issues were cut from the final version. Virtually all that remains of his original intention is the cynical comment by Cooper, who is disturbed about the applications of modern science: "The energy contained in this apple can destroy the world. And yet we cannot create one small apple." This scene and the ending at the airfield have been parodied in *Top Secret!* (1984).

The book is based on the exploits of Michael Burke (1918–1987), a World War II covert operations officer who infiltrated behind German lines in Italy to carry out several missions. In 1943 Burke and his fellow agents successfully smuggled several Italian weapons experts out of the country, including scientist Dr. Carlo Calosi and Admiral Eugenio Minisini. The two men then went to work for the U.S. Navy where they helped to develop an anti-torpedo device. After the war Burke acted as technical adviser on the above film and then remained for several years at Warner as a screenwriter. ■

Cloak and Dagger (1984), U. *Dir.* Richard Franklin; *Sc.* Tom Holland; *Cast includes:* Henry Thomas, Dabney Coleman, Michael Murphy, Christina Negra, John McIntire, Jeanette Nolan.

An 11-year-old boy with a fanciful imagination accidentally discovers a plot by enemy agents to smuggle American secrets out of the country in this entertaining drama that blends intrigue with the theme of father-son relationships. Henry Thomas, as the youngster who has conjured up his own superhero in his imaginary adventures, has withdrawn into a videogame world following his mother's death. He has also adopted the hero of the game, Jack Flack, as his fantasy-father. His real, hard-working father (Dabney Coleman, who doubles as the boy's fictitious hero) tries to help the boy distinguish between reality and fantasy. "Heroes don't just shoot people," he explains to his son. "They put supper on the table."

When the boy witnesses a murder by enemy spies, no one will believe his tale about the crime and secret papers hidden in a videocassette. Neither does his father, who has lived with his son's world of fantasy. Little Henry, supported only by his young girlfriend (Christina Negra) and his imaginary hero-father, is left to his own devices as he attempts to expose the spies. Michael Murphy portrays the chief villain. John McIntire and Jeanette Nolan pose as a pair of innocent senior citizens who in reality are part of the conspiracy. The drama, which borrows some suspense elements from Hitchcock (a missing finder for identification purposes, an apparently harmless elderly couple, a midnight airplane flight, etc.), is a loose adaptation of the 1949 film *The Window*, with Bobby Driscoll as the young boy. ∎

Virginia Gilmore comforts cameraman Alan Baxter, who has film clips of an ex-Nazi living in New York City. *Close-Up* (1948).

Close-Up (1948), EL. *Dir.* Jack Donohue; *Sc.* John Bright, Max Wilk; *Cast includes:* Alan Baxter, Virginia Gilmore, Richard Kollmar, Loring Smith, Phil Huston, Russell Collins.

A gang of ex-Nazis undercover in New York tries to destroy newsreel clips which prove damaging evidence against one of its members in this slow-paced drama. Alan Baxter, as the cameraman who took the pictures which can prove that the former Nazi is currently in the city, becomes the target of some of the gang members. Virginia Gilmore portrays an associate of the gang who helps to effect Baxter's capture. However, the culprits soon learn that all Baxter possesses is a copy of the newsreel; the original eventually reaches the local police. Richard Kollmar, as the chief villain, plots to have the negatives and the original destroyed to protect his cover. The drama was shot in New York City for authenticity and was one of the first of many post-World War II films to use location shooting there. See Nazi Subversion: Post-World War II. ∎

Clue, The (1915), Par. *Dir.* James Neill; *Sc.* Margaret Turnbull; *Cast includes:* Blanche Sweet, Gertrude Keller, Edward Mackay, Sessue Hayakawa, Page Peters.

Two shadowy Russian emigrés, a member of the Japanese secret service and two innocent young women make up the chief characters of this convoluted drama. The film offers some suspense; a couple of murders and a mysterious map desired by the Japanese but in the possession of the Russians. Blanche Sweet portrays one of the young Americans whom a Russian tries to woo. Sessue Hayakawa, as the Japanese agent assigned to steal the coveted map, eventually blows up the room inhabited by the Russian with the map. He had earlier killed the other Russian. Hayakawa himself dies but lives long enough to see the map consumed by fire. See Japanese War Scare of 1907. ∎

Code of the Secret Service (1939), WB. *Dir.* Noel Smith; *Sc.* Lee Katz, Dean Franklin; *Cast includes:* Ronald Reagan, Rosella Towne, Eddie Foy, Jr., Moroni Olsen, Edgar Edwards, Jack Mower.

The U.S. Secret Service goes after a gang who has made off with a set of treasury banknote engraving plates in this drama dominated by implausible plot incidents. Ronald Reagan, as "Brass" Bancroft, one of the service's top agents, and Eddie Foy, Jr., as his comic sidekick and assistant, trail the gang to their hideaway in the remote hills of Mexico. After a chain of exciting experiences the duo finally retrieves the valuable plates and capture the leader of the gang. Rosella Towne provides some slight romantic interest for Reagan in a tale that is supposedly based on an actual case history from the files of the secret service. See "Brass" Bancroft; U.S. Secret Service. ∎

Cold War. Shortly after World War II ended, tensions began to mount between the Western powers and the Soviet Union and its satellite nations. The term "Cold War" gradually signified this growing feeling of animosity between the Western capitalist democracies and the Communist bloc. The West had become increasingly alarmed at the Soviet's increasing expansionism and power near the end of the war and shortly thereafter. During World War II, the U.S.S.R. seized the three Baltic nations of Latvia, Estonia and Lithuania. Sections of Poland, Rumania and Czechoslovakia were also incorporated into the Soviet Union.

Helped by the presence of Soviet troops, Communist governments were installed in Eastern Europe and in parts of Germany and Korea. Contact between the people in Soviet-dominated areas and the West quickly diminished, leading Winston Churchill, in his 1946 speech at Fulton, Missouri, to say that an "iron curtain" had descended across Eastern Europe. At the same time, the West became fearful of the spread of Communism in Asia where China had become part of the Communist bloc. The Cold War was fought in several ways—through military alliances such as N.A.T.O. and the Warsaw Pact, by supporting opposing sides in domestic strife as occurred in Greece and China, through economic aid and trade programs such as the Marshall Plan, and by spying.

The almost obsessive dependence upon agents and double agents, intelligence and disinformation, defection and debriefing, precipitated the world's most sophisticated secret intelligence empires. This unique war was fought not by soldiers but by spies, and the battlefields were the war-scarred cities of Europe. The generally heightened tension sometimes erupted into shooting wars such as the Korean War, the Vietnam War and the Afghanistan guerrilla war.

As films about World War II diminished in number, dramas involving the new conflict began to appear on the screen. Hollywood, always seeking fresh material, had a field day with the variety of possible plots. Melodramas of intrigue, torture, treachery, defection and escape were peopled by separated lovers yearning to be reunited, traitors selling out their countries and refugees with relatives at home forced to spy on their newly adopted country. Federal agents, often played by Hollywood's most rugged or romantic leads, swung into action to prevent the flow of military secrets to the East. Many of the plots ended up as reworkings of old material. A few were so didactic that they became ludicrous. Others bordered on panic and paranoia as they tried to warn Americans of the dangers of subversion and the impending downfall of democracy and freedom.

Occasionally, actual incidents were turned into screen dramas. *Guilty of Treason* (1950) is based on the Josef Cardinal Midszenty case of 1949. The cardinal (Charles Bickford) clashes with Hungarian Communist authori-

ties and is incarcerated. The trial, with its attempts to discredit the Primate of Hungary, inflamed western public opinion. *I Was a Communist for the FBI* (1951), made chiefly to assuage the House Un-American Activities Committee, is based on the true story of Matt Cvetic, who posed as a Red for nine years. Frank Lovejoy, as the double agent, exposes various Communist plots before the H.U.A.C. By 1953, films like *Flight to Tangier* were beginning to suggest that the Soviets were planting "sleepers"—secret agents who became U.S. citizens and waited sometimes for years to carry out their subversive activities.

Berlin became the focus of a new crisis beginning in 1958 that culminated in the construction of the Berlin Wall in 1961 by the East German Communist government. The western-controlled portion of the city was suddenly sealed off from the Communist zone with a barrier of concrete and barbed wire. The wall effectively closed an escape route to the West for refugees from Communism. It cut one of the few open lines of communication between people in the two zones and prevented peoples in Eastern Europe from witnessing the contrast in living conditions between Communist and Western societies. *Escape From East Berlin* (1962) reenacts the true experiences of a handful of East Germans who in 1962 tunneled their way under the Berlin Wall, only months before the film was released. Unpredictably and spectacularly, the wall, which was the basis of this film and a symbol of oppression and isolation, crumbled as a result of the East Germans' rush to freedom in the last weeks of 1989. In its wake also lay the virtual collapse of the Cold War spy film genre.

The bulk of the Cold War films resembled routine dramas with the typical traitors, foreign agents and military secrets at stake. These melodramatic elements recalled a string of familiar plots about earlier conflicts. *Walk a Crooked Mile* (1948), for instance, concerns Soviet agents trying to steal America's atomic secrets. They are assisted by a traitorous American scientist. F.B.I. agent Dennis O'Keefe joins forces with Scotland Yard investigator Louis Hayward to uncover the culprits. The following year *Project X*, a low-budget drama, has Soviet agents once again trying to get their hands on atomic secrets. This time they are done in by one of their own party members who cooperates with U.S. government investigators. In *Walk*

East on Beacon (1952) George Murphy, as an F.B.I. chief, foils a Soviet plan to steal scientific information from a refugee scientist who is threatened with the death of his son. The film is based on an article written by J. Edgar Hoover, head of the F.B.I. at the time. That same year John Wayne, as the title character in *Big Jim McLain*, a special investigator for the House Un-American Activities Committee, hunts down Communist subversives in Hawaii. In *Security Risk* (1954), a low-budget drama, a federal agent (John Ireland) gets involved in the murder of an atomic scientist, whose killer wants to sell secrets to the Communists. In *Five Steps to Danger* (1956) Sterling Hayden gets entangled with Soviet spies who are trying to steal the secrets of America's ballistics missiles.

Many Cold War features take place in European cities whose exotic structures and suspicious-looking inhabitants add to the tangled webs of intrigue. Tyrone Power in *Diplomatic Courier* (1952) is assigned by U.S. intelligence to contact an agent in Salzburg. Hildergarde Neff masquerades as a Soviet spy so that she can go to America. Patricia Neal poses as a dizzy American tourist but actually is a Russian spy in this convoluted plot. In *Assignment—Paris*, released the same year, Dana Andrews, as an American reporter working in Paris, is sent to Budapest to expose a plot against the West by the Iron Curtain countries. In *The Steel Fist*, also released in 1952, a student (Roddy MacDowell) somewhere behind the Iron Curtain precipitates a labor riot and is forced to hide from the police. The underground helps him to cross the border to the West. Clark Gable, as an American reporter, tries to smuggle his Russian wife (Gene Tierney) out of the Soviet Union in *Never Let Me Go* (1953). In *Guerrilla Girl*, released the same year, a former Greek officer (Helmut Dantine) during World War II returns to his homeland only to discover that Communist revolutionaries are plotting to take over the country. In *Night People* (1954), shot on location in Germany, an American officer (Gregory Peck) stationed in West Berlin rescues a G.I. captured by the Communists. Former Nazis have joined the Communists and work to subvert the West in this drama. A spurious document detailing an alliance between the U.S. and the Soviet Union in the event of trouble with China is the subject of *The Kremlin Letter* (1970). Location shots include Mexico, Rome, New York and Finland, the last substituting for Russian settings.

Europe was not the only area to serve as a background for Cold War dramas. In *Target Hong Kong* (1952) an American soldier of fortune (Richard Denning) disrupts a Communist plot to take over Hong Kong. The following year George Brent, as an American intelligence agent in *Tangier Incident*, journeys to that exotic city to stop the transfer of atomic secrets to the Communists by a trio of traitorous scientists. *The Ugly American* (1963), loosely based on the episodic novel by William J. Lederer and Eugene Burdrick, stars Marlon Brando as the new ambassador to a fictitious Southeast Asian country plagued by intrigue, espionage and internal strife. The film underscores the general confusion and ignorance of American politicians and an indifferent public concerning underdeveloped countries. "We can't hope to win the Cold War," Brando warns, "unless we remember what we are for as well as what we are against."

Dramas often cautioned their audiences about the evils of Communism. In *I Married a Communist* (1949), which lapses into an old-fashioned gangster melodrama, Robert Ryan, as an ex-Communist, is warned by his former party bosses that no one "quits" the party. They want him to foment labor trouble. A shoot-out resolves the plot. *The Red Danube*, released the same year, is less sensational but just as melodramatic in dealing with escapees from the East in postwar Vienna. The Soviets demand that they be sent to the Eastern bloc for repatriation. Some of the refugees, including Janet Leigh as a ballerina, prefer suicide to a life under Communism. *The Red Menace* (1950), another drama, shows how a variety of naive Americans are duped by Communists. The victims, all believing that Communism can change a country's social ills, include a disillusioned veteran, a young black student, an impoverished girl and a refugee.

My Son John (1952), one of the most controversial films of the period, concerns a young American (Robert Walker) from a good home who befriends Communists. He is suspected by the F.B.I. of associating with Communist spies. His parents (Helen Hayes and Dean Jagger), whose two other sons are about to embark for Korea, cannot believe that their boy John is a traitor. The drama ends with John's murder and the playing of his previ-

U.S. government agent Andrea Dromm holds off a member of a gang of assassins in the comedy *Come Spy With Me* (1967).

ously recorded confession. Several critics and other viewers attacked the film as bordering on paranoia in its anti-Communist zeal. They saw it as an endorsement of religious conformity, anti-intellectualism and guilt by association.

The flood of Cold War films that followed World War II turned into a trickle by the 1980s. Those that occasionally show up on movie screens, such as *Rocky IV* (1985), in which Sylvester Stallone boxes a Russian giant, and *Red Dawn* (1984), about a Communist invasion of the U.S., are grotesques of the genre. They tend to deal chiefly in violence for its own sake and are almost completely devoid of any discussion of ideologies or issues. See Defection, Soviet Spies in the U.S. ■

Come On In (1918), Par. *Dir.* John Emerson; *Sc.* John Emerson, Anita Loos; *Cast includes:* Ernest Truex, Shirley Mason, Charles De Planta, Joseph Burke, Renault Tourneur.

A World War I comedy starring Ernest Truex, the film tells of a patriotic young man's abortive attempts to enlist in the army. It seems that he is a half-inch too short.

Strolling in a park, he becomes involved in a fight with a German who smashes a bottle on his head. Ernest feels his head and dashes to the nearest draft board. He passes the height requirement because of the bump on his head. Once in the service he continually moves up in rank due to a series of humorous misadventures in which he is able to display his peculiar style of bravery. In one sequence he rescues his colonel who has been captured by German agents. One of the spies has married the colonel's daughter whom Ernest loves. Our hero manages to have the bridegroom arrested before the honeymoon. This film was Ernest Truex's screen debut. ■

Come Spy With Me (1967), TCF. *Dir.* Marshall Stone; *Sc.* Cherney Berg; *Cast includes:* Troy Donahue, Andrea Dromm, Albert Dekker, Mart Hulswit, Valerie Allen, Dan Ferrone.

A weak comedy with bland songs designed to exploit the popularity of the spy genre during the late 1960s, the film concerns a plot to assassinate a group of foreign statesmen planning a conference aboard an aircraft carrier somewhere in the Caribbean. When two U.S.

agents are mysteriously killed, intelligence selects pretty blonde Andrea Dromm to investigate. Her superiors suspect that the deaths are related to the upcoming meeting. Dromm poses as a diver and enters a local contest. She meets Troy Donahue whose charter boat is to be used for the competition. Meanwhile an enemy agent (Albert Dekker) who has been placing explosives in strategic areas is observing the skin divers. He ends up abducting another diver whom he suspects of spying on him. Realizing his error, he then kidnaps Dromm as well. U.S. agents then descend upon Dekker's hide-out, rescue the two young women and render the explosives harmless. Dromm is then free to return to her romance with Donahue. ■

Commando (1985), TCF. *Dir.* Mark L. Lester; *Sc.* Steven de Souza; *Cast includes:* Arnold Schwarzenegger, Rae Dawn Chong, Dan Hedaya, Vernon Wells, James Olsen, David Patrick Kelly.

A retired leader of a special covert U.S. strike force comes out of his world of seclusion to rescue his kidnapped daughter in this ludicrous, overly violent drama. Arnold Schwarzenegger portrays Matrix, the former superagent, whose daughter is kidnapped by Bennett, a fellow agent working for General Arius, a deposed dictator. Bennett wants Matrix to assassinate the present Democratic president of a fictitious Latin American country so that the dictator can return. Once in the country, Matrix eludes the dictator's henchmen and begins to search for his daughter. Following a series of violent incidents, he learns that the general is holding his daughter captive at an island fortress. Matrix arrives at the stronghold in time to save his daughter after annihilating a host of the general's men as well as the dictator. He then confronts Bennett. "The man I trusted for five years wants me dead," Matrix had stated earlier. He kills Bennett in a knife fight after goading him into it. "Think of sticking your knife into my flesh . . . and twisting it," Matrix utters. "You don't want to deny yourself that pleasure."

The politically oriented suggestions that the retired Matrix has become disillusioned with violence, that the general is a depraved right-wing dictator and that U.S. covert action forces helped to install the democratically elected president appear too simplistic. Also, any attempt at presenting a thought-provoking idea is quickly canceled by the heavy emphasis on action and violence. See Latin America. ■

Commando Squad (1987), Trans World. *Dir.* Fred Olen Ray; *Sc.* Michael D. Sonye; *Cast includes:* Kathy Shower, Brian Thompson, William Smith, Robert Quarry, Sid Haig.

Kathy Shower portrays a narcotics agent working out of Los Angeles in this violence-oriented drama about a cocaine operation based in Mexico. "Here in L.A. we have a saying: 'A friend is someone who stabs you in the front,'" she narrates in a string of pseudo-cynical aphorisms as the titles appear on the screen. An undercover agent who obviously relishes her dangerous assignments, she moves catlike through the sleazy city streets and alleys bustling with drug dealers. "Once you know the world is corrupt," she announces, explaining her credo, "—and you know deep down in your bones—then things become simple, clear."

After wrapping up one narcotics case, she reports to her chief who informs her that most of the cocaine is coming from a major smuggling operation across the border. The agency has lost five operators in its attempt to break up the gang. The chief has lost contact with Shower's former partner (Brian Thompson), the latest agent to disappear in Mexico. Upon hearing this, she decides to postpone her vacation and take the assignment. Once again, she dons a disguise that fools nobody and shows up in a cheap Mexican bar filled with deadbeats.

The remainder of the film deals with her battles against members of the gang of smugglers and her rescue of Thompson, who has been held captive and continually beaten. The leader of the operation turns out to be Morgan Denny (William Smith), a former agent. Thompson captures him after a brutal fight. "Everyone's in it for their own gain," Shower concludes. "But then there is such a thing as loyalty. That's looking out for the people that belong to you. Morgan forgot that." ■

Confessions of a Nazi Spy (1939), WB. *Dir.* Anatole Litvak; *Sc.* Milton Krims, John Wesley; *Cast includes:* Edward G. Robinson, Francis Lederer, George Sanders, Paul Lukas, Henry O'Neill, James Stephenson.

A strong, didactic anti-Nazi propaganda drama and one of the earliest World War II

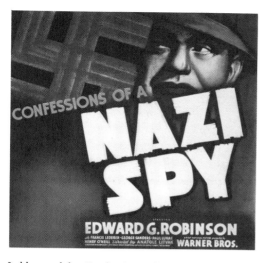

Lobby card for *Confessions of a Nazi Spy* (1939), the first major film to expose the Nazi spy network in the U.S.

spy films, the story opens in 1938 in the United States while in Germany Hitler's war machine gears up to smash its way across Europe. Through German-American organizations such as the Bund, Nazi spies organize a network of agents and collaborators in defense plants, the military services and other occupations who gather classified information that is relayed back to Germany. Edward G. Robinson, as a tough, no-nonsense F.B.I. agent, uncovers the key members of the nest of spies who are quickly brought to trial and found guilty. But before the trial ends, the audience is exposed to the Nazi agents' attacks on the U.S. Constitution, the ideals of democracy and those who believe in free speech. Americans of German descent who disagree with the Hitler's New Order are either beaten up by thugs or sent back to German concentration camps.

Although the message was bold for its time, the film is heavy-handed in its presentation. The one-dimensional spies lack plausibility at times; the strong-arm men in their employ are stereotypes; and the preachy voice-overs during lengthy newsreel shots of Nazi troops on the march and invading other countries are unnecessary and redundant. Even the prosecutor (Henry O'Neill) at the climactic trial faces the camera as he recites his cautionary summary: "There are those who will say we have nothing to fear—that we are immune—that we are protected by vast oceans from the bacteria of aggressive dictatorships

and totalitarian states. But we know and have seen the mirror of history in Europe this last year—the invasions of Poland, Norway and Denmark by Nazi Germany and Russia." He concludes: "America is not simply one of the remaining democracies. America is democracy!"

While the film lauds the American democratic ideals over Nazi Germany, it remains a product of its time. There are no blacks or other racial minorities in the New York street scenes, stores, offices or plants. No characters of other religious groups appear. Only two types dominate the American landscape of this film: white Anglo-Saxon Protestants—the good guys, and the Nazis—the bad guys.

The film is based in part on "Storm Over America," a series of articles by Leon Turrou, a former F.B.I. agent who used material from the spy trials of 1937 in which four people were convicted. The trials established that a link existed between Germany and the German-American Bunds, rallies and special youth camps that were popular in the United States in the 1930s. Probably the most forceful propaganda film of the period, it was careful to point out that most Americans of German ancestry were loyal, law-abiding citizens. See Federal Bureau of Investigation; German Intelligence: World War II; U.S. Intelligence: World War II. ■

Confidential Agent (1945), WB. *Dir.* Herman Shumlin; *Sc.* Robert Buckner; *Cast includes:* Charles Boyer, Lauren Bacall, Peter Lorre, Katina Paxinou, Victor Francen, Dan Seymour.

Based on Graham Greene's novel of intrigue, the film concerns a war-weary representative of Republican Spain sent to England to prevent the Fascists from purchasing coal. The year is 1937, and although the story has for its background the Spanish Civil War, the entire film takes place in England. Charles Boyer, as a former Spanish concert pianist whose wife was "killed by order of the Fascists," is dedicated to his country's struggle against totalitarian forces. He has volunteered for the assignment in England where he is followed and hounded by Fascist agents trying to stop him from completing his mission. "You're more of an idealist than I am," his counterpart, a ruthless Fascist leader (Victor Francen) admits. "All I want back is my estate." Boyer refuses to negotiate. "It would be a great loss if you died for some vague, impossible dream," his adversary continues. "No," Boyer replies, "a very small price if it would help prevent a rotten Fascist world you want—a private little world that would protect your privileges." Boyer meets the daughter of a wealthy lord, played by Lauren Bacall, who decides to befriend Boyer and assist him. He is beaten up, shot at and robbed of his identification papers, but he manages to prevent the Fascist forces from obtaining the coal.

Although Warner Brothers made this film six years after the end of the war in Spain, the studio had been in the forefront of anti-Nazi and anti-Fascist propaganda films such as *Confessions of a Nazi Spy* (1939). Greene has filled his story with a host of odd and interesting characters. Dan Seymour, as an eccentric Indian, is making a life-long study of human nature. "I am a mass observer," he announces. Katina Paxinou and Peter Lorre portray Spanish Loyalists who have betrayed the cause and sold out to the enemy. "Idealism is a luxury I cannot afford," Paxinou says as she, too, tries to prevent Boyer from completing his assignment. She pushes an innocent 14-year-old girl out of a window to frame Boyer for the murder. Lorre works as an instructor for a school specializing in disseminating a newly developed international language. The owner of the institution claims that "all this hate, all these wars we read about . . . they're all due to misunderstanding." In an interview with Boyer, the man admits: "The Civil War in your country upset us greatly." "Yes," Boyer retorts impatiently, "it upset us, too." Herman Shumlin, who also directed the World War II drama *Watch on the Rhine* (1943), captures not only the horror and cruelty of the distant war in Spain, but the malevolent nature of totalitarianism as well. ▪

Conspiracy (1939), RKO. *Dir.* Lew Landers; *Sc.* Jerome Chodorov; *Cast includes:* Allan Lane, Linda Hayes, Robert Barrat, Charles Foy, J. Farrell MacDonald.

A mythical Central American country is the background for intrigue and revolution in this action drama. Allan Lane portrays an American radio operator forced to flee from his ship when a passenger is murdered and his life is threatened. On shore he meets a revolutionary, played by Linda Hayes. Lane hides out in a local café run by a fellow American. Lane experiences several close

American radio operator Allan Lane (l.), masquerading as an officer in a fictitious Latin American country, helps revolutionaries Linda Hayes and Robert Barrat to overthrow a hated dictator. *Conspiracy* (1939).

calls as he is chased by secret police and a speedboat. The intricate and sometimes confusing plot is resolved when the dictator who controls the small nation is toppled from office and democracy and order are restored to the country. This low-budget film is not related to a 1930 release bearing the same title.

With the forces of totalitarianism on the march in Europe in the late 1930s, Hollywood studios by 1939 began to tackle—albeit often indirectly, as in the above film—such political issues as Fascism and Nazism while singing the praises of democracy. RKO, which released *Conspiracy*, also turned out *They Made Her a Spy* the same year while Warner produced *Confessions of a Nazi Spy*. ▪

Conspirators, The (1944), WB. *Dir.* Jean Negulesco; *Sc.* Vladimir Posner, Leo Rosten; *Cast includes:* Hedy Lamarr, Paul Henreid, Sydney Greenstreet, Peter Lorre, Victor Francen, Vladimir Sokoloff.

Set in Lisbon during World War II, this drama of intrigue stars Hedy Lamarr as a young French woman married to a German official and Paul Henreid as a Dutch guerrilla leader hunted by the Nazis for his sabotage activities. Lamarr, working as an agent against the Nazis, witnesses the murder of one of her contacts in an alley. To escape the police, she enters a nearby cafe and sits at Henreid's table. Henreid, who has just arrived in Lisbon, is on his way to England to enlist in the air force after performing several acts of sabotage in his German-occupied country. He welcomes the beautiful and mysterious stranger at his table. "I'm told Lisbon is a strange city," he says nonchalantly, "a city of echoes and shadows. A hundred eyes watch your every move." After some small talk, she quietly disappears into the night.

When another agent about to return to Holland on a secret mission is killed, Henreid, known as the "Flying Dutchman," is accused of the crime. Anti-Nazi secret agents operating in Lisbon at first suspect Henreid of killing one of their members. Later, after the agents uncover the real murderer, Henreid volunteers to go in the dead agent's place. Lamarr, who has fallen in love with Henreid, promises to wait for him.

Sydney Greenstreet, as a flamboyant writer and leader of the network of agents, runs a local Lisbon shop that houses a secret upstairs room. "I love melodrama," he confides to Henreid as he leads him up a hidden staircase. "You see, I used to be a writer before the war. I now deal in living characters." Peter Lorre portrays another member of the group. Victor Francen, as a chief of the German legation, plays a double agent. Working for the Germans while masquerading as a member of the band of agents, he is finally exposed and killed. Henreid, as the archetypal freedom fighter, played a similar role in the classic World War II romantic drama *Casablanca* (1942), which also featured Greenstreet and Lorre. *The Conspirators* is based on the novel by Frederic Prokosch. See Lisbon; Operation Nordpol. ∎

Convoy (1927), FN. *Dir.* Joseph C. Boyle; *Sc.* Willis Goldbeck; *Cast includes:* Lowell Sherman, Dorothy Mackaill, Lawrence Gray, William Collier, Ian Keith, Gail Kane.

A World War I sea drama, the film centers on a young woman, portrayed by Dorothy Mackaill, who is called upon by the U.S. Secret Service to uncover a spy. It seems that someone is leaking information to the enemy about troop transport departures. The young heroine is told to stay with the suspected agent day and night. During the course of the story her brother is killed in battle and his body is returned home. The film provides several sea battles, although most of the story is dominated by the melodramatic spy element. ∎

Copperhead, The (1920), Par. *Dir.* Charles Maigne; *Sc.* Charles Maigne; *Cast includes:* Lionel Barrymore, William Carlton, Frank Joyner, Richard Carlyle, Ann Cornwall.

Based on Frederick Landis' 1893 novel which was adapted for the stage in 1918 by Augustus Thomas, the Civil War drama stars Lionel Barrymore in the role of Milt Shanks, a die-hard Southern sympathizer. Residing in a small Illinois town, he enrages the other citizens with his outspoken views and his stance as a conscientious objector during the Civil War. The film version carries the story into the next century and the year 1904, introducing Theodore Roosevelt. It is at that time that Shanks confides to his granddaughter that President Lincoln had secretly assigned him to infiltrate the Copperheads, Northerners who advocated the cause of the South. Barrymore had played the role on stage in 1918 and received high acclaim for his performance. He revived the work in 1926, after which he signed with MGM where he remained for the next 28 years. See American Civil War: Intelligence and Covert Actions. ∎

Copperheads. The term, now used as political insult, was first applied during the American Civil War (1861–65) to Northern and Western peace-Democrats and others who favored making peace with the Confederacy for philosophical or commercial reasons. The expression, based on the actions of a copperhead snake that strikes from secrecy, originally denoted one who tries to hurt a cause through secret action. In some cases, Copperhead groups functioned as semisecret societies whose members assisted deserters and committed occasional acts of terrorism. Others openly adopted the title and even wore badges, made from a copper penny, to identify themselves as part of a political movement.

One such secret Copperhead society, the Knights of the Golden Circle, operated in Indiana. Governor Oliver P. Morton assigned Brigadier General Henry B. Carrington, in charge of that state's military recruitment in 1862, to investigate subversive Copperhead activities. Carrington, in turn, recruited a Union soldier to infiltrate the Golden Circle society. The undercover agent eventually uncovered the Northwest Conspiracy, a Confederate plot to foment revolution among several Northern states and have them join the Confederacy. Several conspirators were arrested, tried and convicted. But the U.S. Supreme Court overturned the convictions on the grounds that military tribunals did not have the authority to try civilians in non-combat areas.

In modern American politics, the term "Copperhead" is sometimes used pejoratively to describe one who secretly or openly favors an enemy cause. The term was used as late as 1941 by President Roosevelt, in referring to the isolationist views of Charles Lindbergh, who the President claimed was hindering America's attempts to help the beleaguered Western allies fighting the forces of fascism.

The controversial Copperheads are rarely mentioned in Civil War-related films. However, they played a major role in at least two dramas, *The Copperhead* (1920) and *Rebel City* (1953), the latter a low-budget drama about Southern sympathizers who stir up trouble in Kansas. See also American Civil War: Intelligence and Covert Actions. ∎

Cornered (1945), RKO. *Dir.* Edward Dmytryk; *Sc.* John Paxton; *Cast includes:* Dick Powell, Walter Slezak, Micheline Cheirel, Nina Vale, Morris Carnovsky, Luther Adler.

This post-World War II drama concerns high-ranking Nazis who have escaped prosecution by the Allies and have settled in Argentina where they are busy planning the next war. Dick Powell portrays a Canadian soldier who is in pursuit of Marcel Jarnac (Luther Adler), one of these Nazis. Jarnac was responsible for the murder of Powell's French bride during the war. Powell's search takes him to Buenos Aires where he discovers a nest of international agents and unrepentant German officers including his wife's killer. In a brutal climax, Powell beats Jarnac to death with his bare fists.

This bleak, depressing film includes several fascinating characters. A shadowy, amoral figure (Walter Slezak) deals with both sides, the hunters and the hunted, for his own profit. A corrupt *femme fatale* (Nina Vale) aligns herself with the pro-Nazi movement in Argentina. An idealistic Argentine lawyer (Morris Carnovsky) is the leader of a group of private citizens bent on exposing neo-Nazi movements wherever they turn up. Perhaps the most unsavory character is that of the cold-blooded killer Jarnac, who is planning for the next war. He has begun by gaining control of various profit-making industries in South America.

The dialogue enhances the theme of dark forces lurking in the shadows, waiting for the right opportunity to spring upon the inno-cent. "They are even more than war criminals fleeing a defeated nation," Carnovsky warns Powell, whose blind vengeance is interfering with the lawyer's determination to bring the plotters to justice. "They do not consider themselves defeated. We must destroy not only the individuals but their friends, their very means of existence, wherever they start to entrench themselves. . . . " Jarnac, arrogant and dangerous, boasts of his successful methods and ridicules the ways of the Western democracies to his captive Powell, whom he intends to kill. "You attack the wrong things in the wrong way. You attack the evil in men. We accept it. . . . Wherever you create misery and discontent, there you will find us at work. . . . " But the overconfident Jarnac soon pays with his life for his crimes against humanity. See Latin America; Nazi Subversion: Post-World War II. ∎

Count Five and Die (1958), TCF. *Dir.* Victor Vicas; *Sc.* Jack Seddon, David Pursall; *Cast includes:* Jeffrey Hunter, Nigel Patrick, Annamarie Duringer, David Kossoff, Rolf Lefebvre, Larry Burns.

British and U.S. intelligence forces devise a plan to baffle the Germans about the actual location of the Allied invasion of Europe in this drama of intrigue set in England during World War II. Jeffrey Hunter portrays an American agent assigned to work closely with British intelligence. Nigel Patrick plays Hunter's British superior officer. Annamarie Duringer, as a Dutch underground agent, turns out to be a double agent working for the Nazis. Duringer is killed before she can spoil the elaborate scheme to deceive the Nazi military defense forces. The title refers to the cyanide capsule distributed to secret agents which they can take to prevent them from giving information to the enemy if they are captured and tortured. See British Intelligence: World War II; Operation Overlord. ∎

Counter-Espionage (1942), Col. *Dir.* Edward Dmytryk; *Sc.* Aubrey Wisberg; *Cast includes:* Warren William, Eric Blore, Hillary Brooke, Thurston Hall, Fred Kelsey, Forrest Tucker.

Columbia studios during World War II occasionally pressed their in-house sleuth, the Lone Wolf, into service against enemy agents instead of such run-of-the-mill adversaries as domestic criminals. Other Hollywood studios did likewise with Sherlock Holmes, Ellery Queen and other free-lance detectives. In this routine war drama the Lone Wolf, played by Warren William, hunts down a Nazi spy network in wartime London and protects secret military plans. Eric Blore, as the detective's sidekick, provides the comic relief while Hillary Brooke adds the romantic interest. See British Intelligence: World War II; Detectives and Spies. ■

Counterfeit (1919), Par. *Dir.* George Fitzmaurice; *Sc.* Ouida Bergere; *Cast includes:* Elsie Ferguson, David Powell, Helene Montrose, Charles Kent, Charles Gerard.

Elsie Ferguson portrays a government agent who masquerades as a member of the "fast set" in this drama set in Newport. She has been assigned to expose a counterfeiting ring that is passing bogus bills among the rich. David Powell, as Stuart Kent, a wealthy young man, falls for the pretty stranger who has joined his social set until he suspects her to be one of the counterfeiters. She soon disposes of the criminals and wins back Kent's love in this harmless tale. ■

Counterfeit (1936), Col. *Dir.* Erle C. Kenton; *Sc.* William Rankin, Bruce Manning; *Cast includes:* Chester Morris, Margot Grahame, Lloyd Nolan, Marian Marsh, Claude Gillingwater, George McKay.

Chester Morris, as an agent of the U.S. Treasury Department, poses as a criminal so that he may be accepted by a gang of counterfeiters in this action drama. The culprits successfully kidnap a government engraver to help them in their scheme. Lloyd Nolan portrays the sinister leader of the gang. Marian Marsh, as another kidnap victim of the counterfeiters, provides the romantic interest for Morris, although she doesn't know his true identity. Marian's sister (Margot Grahame) is Nolan's sweetheart. Once Morris' cover is exposed, he and Marsh find their lives threatened by Nolan. However, a last-minute attack by a horde of Treasury agents and local policemen upon the stronghold of the criminals saves the couple. George McKay, as one of the gang members, provides a minimum of comic relief.

Versatile Lloyd Nolan successfully worked both sides of the law in numerous action dramas in which he played detective and other heroic roles as well as villains. One of his best-remembered characters was that of the F.B.I. chief in the critically acclaimed spy drama *The House on 92nd Street* (1945). ■

U.S. Secret Service agent Jack Lord poses as a hired gun as he chases after a gang of counterfeiters. *The Counterfeit Killer* (1968).

Counterfeit Killer, The (1968), U. *Dir.* Josef Leytes; *Sc.* Harold Clements, Steven Bochco; *Cast includes:* Jack Lord, Shirley Knight, Jack Weston, Charles Drake, Joseph Wiseman, Don Hammer.

A U.S. Secret Service agent poses as an underworld hired gun so that he can infiltrate a gang of counterfeiters in this drama. Jack Lord portrays the government agent whose undercover disguise gets him accepted into the bogus-money ring. His mission is to solve a rash of murders and to expose the illegal operation. Joseph Wiseman proves menacing as the leader of the gang. Mercedes McCambridge portrays a barmaid at a waterfront saloon where most of the film unfolds. Shirley Knight, as a waitress, falls in love with Lord who is busy gathering evidence against Wiseman. Jack Weston, as a pawnshop owner, is in league with the counterfeiting gang. Charles Drake plays a fellow agent. ■

Counterfeit Traitor, The (1962), Par. *Dir.* George Seaton; *Sc.* George Seaton; *Cast includes:* William Holden, Lilli Palmer, Hugh Griffith, Erica Beer, Werner Peters, Eva Dahlbeck.

William Holden portrays a Swedish-American businessman who is persuaded to pose as a Nazi sympathizer while he spies for the Allies in this literate World War II romantic drama. Blackmailed by Allied agents, he reluctantly agrees to cooperate. In the desirable position of a Swedish citizen and well known in the oil industry, he is free to travel frequently from Stockholm to Germany. He cautiously maneuvers himself into the enemy's confidence, a deception that proves fruitful. He furnishes vital facts concerning German oil refineries and advances in jet aircraft to British and U.S. intelligence.

Lilli Palmer, as the unhappy wife of a Nazi officer, is actually working under cover for the Allies. She meets Holden and falls in love with him. A devout Catholic, she volunteers her services out of religious and moral principles, and is caught in a chilling scene when she confesses to a Nazi whom she believes is a priest. At first Holden, who is involved in espionage primarily to protect his business ventures, cannot understand her reasons. "If I don't help, I lose my self-respect," she explains. "Haven't you opposed something because its wrong—morally wrong?" Referring to the victims of Nazi camps, Holden replies, "I suffer for them—" "But not with them," she interjects. "That's the difference." When she is executed by the Germans, Holden looks on helplessly from his prison cell.

Hugh Griffith, as a witty and shrewd chief of British intelligence, forces Holden into service. Early in the film he has little sympathy for the businessman's precarious masquerade. "How does a person get to be so cold-blooded?" Holden asks. "Watching German planes bomb London helps enormously," Griffith replies sarcastically.

Holden, whose motives for aiding the Allies are purely self-serving at the beginning of the venture, is transformed into a staunch anti-Nazi after he witnesses the brutality and violence of the Third Reich. In one of many poignant scenes, he is forced, while in Stockholm, to insult a Jewish friend in front of a group of Nazis. At first filled with remorse, he later receives a letter from the man indicating he understood Holden must have had a reason. The location shooting in various European cities, imaginative suspense and memorable scenes all add to the drama and realism.

The film, based on a story by Alexander Klein, was in turn taken from the true experiences of a Swedish agent. Eric Siegfried Erickson's real life closely corresponded to the portrayal of him in *The Counterfeit Traitor*. Born in 1889 and the son of Swedish immigrants, he worked for the Standard Oil Company in oil exploration in Texas. When World War I broke out, he joined the U.S. Army and served as an officer; after the war,

Erickson enrolled in Cornell University and graduated as an engineer in 1921.

The young engineer returned to the oil industry and was assigned to the Far East for several years. He then moved to Sweden where he became the supervisor of Texas Oil interests in that country. Erickson, always displaying his restless quality, left Texas Oil and opened his own oil-importing business. In 1936, he became a Swedish citizen. His business interests took him throughout Europe; he regularly visited Nazi Germany. The American ambassador to the Soviet Union, Lawrence Steinhardt, noted Erickson's potential and recruited him as an espionage agent for the U.S.

Erickson spoke fluent German and regularly met with Nazi government officials and magnates of German heavy industry during the normal course of business. To all outward appearances, the oil executive became a Nazi sympathizer. He had close working relationships with Germany's Himmler and Goring. Erickson's performance as a Nazi supporter alienated many of his friends. Nevertheless, he persisted and provided the U.S. with much valuable information concerning German oil production and development. His undercover work enabled the Allies to engage in pinpoint bombing of German oil fields and refining installations throughout the war.

Following the defeat of the Axis powers, President Truman invited Erickson to the White House and publicly paid all the honors due this heroic individual. ∎

Counterspy Meets Scotland Yard (1950),
Col. *Dir.* Seymour Friedman; *Sc.* Harold R. Greene; *Cast includes:* Howard St. John, Amanda Blake, Ron Randell, June Vincent, Fred Sears, John Dehner.

The second in the series of dramas based on the radio program and characters created by Phillips H. Lord, this film concerns strange doings at a missile compound. Once again, Howard St. John portrays David Harding, counterspy, who joins forces with a Scotland Yard investigator to bring the spy ring to justice in this routine yarn. Ron Randell enacts the Englishman who takes over for a murdered counterspy agent. ∎

Court Martial (1928), Col. *Dir.* George B.
Seitz; *Sc.* Anthony Coldeway; *Cast includes:* Jack Holt, Betty Compson, Doris Hill, Pat Harmon, Frank Lackteen.

A Civil War drama about a group of Southern guerrillas, the film stars Jack Holt as a Union officer appointed by President Lincoln to bring in the leader (Betty Compson) of the marauders. Holt, working under cover, gains the confidence of the gang members, falls for the leader and saves her life during a cavalry battle. In turn, she rescues Holt when the other members discover his secret mission. When he returns to his post, he is court-martialed for aiding the leader instead of capturing her. As he is about to face the firing squad, Compson appears. Although mortally wounded by a member of her own gang, she is determined to save Holt's life.

The plot of the film may be pure fiction, but the depiction of organized guerrilla bands terrorizing Union communities behind the lines is based on fact. Several groups, including Mosby's Raiders, Morgan's Raiders and Coleman's Scouts proved very effective in disrupting Union communications, carrying out acts of sabotage and diverting much-needed Northern troops from the front lines. Some of these guerrillas continued to operate throughout the conflict. See American Civil War: Intelligence and Covert Actions; John Hunt Morgan; John Singleton Mosby. ■

Cowboy Commandos (1943), Mon. *Dir.* S. Roy Luby; *Sc.* Elizabeth Beecher; *Cast includes:* Ray Corrigan, Dennis Moore, Max Terhune, Evelyn Finley, Johnny Bond, Bud Buster.

Nazi agents are on the verge of dynamiting a western mine that is producing a rare ore in this World War II propaganda western. Ray Corrigan, as a local sheriff, and his two pals (Dennis Moore and Max Terhune) have the job of stopping acts of sabotage that are plaguing a local mine. The spy ring has been preventing shipments of the much-needed ore for the war effort from reaching its destination. Following the obligatory gun and fist fights, the trio round up the nest of vipers before they carry out their final plan of blowing up the entire mine. Evelyn Finley, as a trick rider, plays the female lead. Propaganda elements include a war-bond drive presented within the context of the plot and the song "I'll Get the Fuhrer Sure As Shootin'." ■

Crack-Up, The (1936), TCF. *Dir.* Malcolm St. Clair; *Sc.* Charles Kenyon, Sam Mintz; *Cast includes:* Peter Lorre, Brian Donlevy,

Helen Wood, Ralph Morgan, Thomas Beck, Kay Linaker.

Peter Lorre, as a master international spy, poses as a dimwitted airport loiterer who amuses the local employees in this strange drama. His masquerade is part of his plan to eventually steal the blueprints for an experimental airplane. Brian Donlevy, as an ace test pilot, accepts money from a fellow worker to steal the same blueprints for a spy ring. In reality, he intends to betray the gang. He escapes from the spies by boarding another plane whose other passengers include its designer, a copilot and Lorre. The plane is forced down into the sea as a result of a terrible storm. As the sea begins to swallow the airship, Lorre reveals his true identity. When they are confronted with the reality of their perilous situation, the doomed men decide to turn over the one life preserver to the youngest passenger—the copilot. Lorre then places the coveted blueprints into the copilot's pocket. The plane slips beneath the sea with its three victims as the one survivor remains afloat.

The plane that the men are on, the *Wild Goose*, is a large craft that resembles the infamous "Spruce Goose" which Howard Hughes later designed and vowed to turn into a success. He was only able to fly it for a short distance before it became a failed dream and a museum piece. ■

"Crime Does Not Pay." MGM produced a high-quality series of two-reel dramatized documentaries from 1935 to 1947 called "Crime Does Not Pay." Although the majority of the entries were concerned with exposing various illegal activities, several released during World War II dealt with the threat of spies. "While America Sleeps" (1939), for instance, explains how enemy agents operate. "For the Common Defense" (1942) tells of a South American spy network's link to American gangsters. In "Keep 'em Sailing" (1942) an F.B.I. agent exposes sabotage attempts directed at U.S. cargo ships.

The series produced five or six entries each year and proved to be an effective training ground for several directors and performers. In addition, the series won two Academy Awards. The two-reelers chiefly dealt with exposing a variety of rackets, ranging from shoplifting to smuggling. Occasionally, such topics as drunk driving were covered. ■

Draftee Eric Linden accepts an assignment to help expose an enemy spy ring that has infiltrated his own company. *Criminals Within* (1941).

Criminals Within (1941), PRC. *Dir.* Joseph Lewis; *Sc.* Arthur Hoerl; *Cast includes:* Eric Linden, Ann Doran, Constance Worth, Donald Curtis, Weldon Heyburn, Ben Alexander.

Enemy aliens seek to steal a secret formula known only to five chemists in this inept drama set before America's entry into World War II. The spies slay one of the scientists, hoping to obtain the list of his assistants. Eric Linden, as an army draftee, becomes embroiled in the intrigue and soon discovers a nest of spies in his own company. Ann Doran, as an inquisitive reporter, becomes romantically involved with Linden. Constance Worth portrays one of the enemy agents. ■

Crimson Wing, The (1915), V.L.S.E. *Dir.* E. H. Calvert; *Cast includes:* E. H. Calvert, John Cossar, Ruth Stonehouse, Beverly Bayne, Bryant Washburn, Betty Scott.

A French spy's jealousy leads to tragic results in this World War I romantic drama based on a novel by Hobart C. Chatfield-Taylor. Ruth Stonehouse, as a French actress, casts off the romantic advances of John Cossar, who portrays the French spy. She enlists as a Red Cross nurse and discovers her old flame, a German army officer (E. H. Calvert), wounded in battle. She hides him in her aunt's home and begins to nurse him back to health. When Cossar discovers the wounded German, he threatens to report him as an enemy spy unless Stonehouse marries him. She consents to the Frenchman's terms, provided that the officer first regains his strength. The nurse then commits suicide rather than marry Cossar. The German muses about the end of the war when he can return to his own childhood sweetheart, the daughter of a French general. ■

Crooked Streets (1920), Par. *Dir.* Paul Powell; *Sc.* Edith Kennedy; *Cast includes:* Ethel Clayton, Jack Holt, Clyde Fillmore, Clarence Geldart, Josephine Crowell, Frederick Starr.

A British secret service agent, assigned to investigate opium smuggling in China, rescues a young American woman from the clutches of a gang dealing in "white slavery" in this action drama. Jack Holt portrays the British hero who challenges the gang leader to a boxing match, with the victor winning the woman captive. Ethel Clayton, as the heroine, poses as a tourist accompanying an antiquarian in China. Both seem interested in antiques. Actually, she is an agent of the U.S. Internal Revenue Service. The two agents fall for each other, and Holt unmasks the antiquarian as the head of the smuggling ring. The couple then sail away on their honeymoon. ■

Cross-Up (1958), UA. *Dir.* John Gilling; *Sc.* John Gilling, Willis Goldbeck; *Cast includes:* Larry Parks, Constance Smith, Lisa Daniely, Cyril Chamberlain.

A London-based international counterfeiting ring pursues an American journalist who possesses a list of the gang's agents in this minor drama. Larry Parks, as the correspondent, becomes involved with a young woman (Lisa Daniely) who is an agent of the counterfeiting ring. He obtains a diary from her during a struggle in which she is accidentally shot. The book contains coded entries of all the agents in various countries. Cyril Chamberlain, as the leader of the gang, sends out his minions to retrieve the diary, but Parks proves an elusive adversary. Constance Smith, as Parks' secretary, rounds out the chief principals in the small cast.

Larry Parks, an obscure actor in low-budget films, scored a hit impersonating the famous mammy singer in *The Jolson Story* (1946). He appeared in only a handful of films when his screen career suddenly came to a crashing halt. He was blacklisted by the studios as a result of his appearance before the House Un-American Activities Committee where he admitted his connections with subversive groups. Unable to find work in Hollywood, he journeyed to England where he made this film. He died in 1975 at age 61, neglected by the film world and virtually forgotten by his fans. ■

Crucible of Life, The (1918), General Enterprises. *Dir.* Capt. Harry Lambert; *Cast includes*: Grace Darmond, Jack Sherrill, Frank O'Connor, Winifred Harris, Edwin Forsberg.

The leader of a gang of burglars who is of German descent is in reality a German agent in this complex drama set during World War I. At first he involves a reckless young man in several thefts. He is then assigned by Germany to enlist in the Allied army in France where he can be of further use as a spy. The young American whom he had earlier misled into a life of crime is in the same outfit and catches the spy signaling to the German trenches. Following a fierce struggle, the spy is subdued. The film is based on the 1879 play *Fairfax* by Bartley Campbell. ■

Cuba (1979), UA. *Dir.* Richard Lester; *Sc.* Charles Wood; *Cast includes*: Sean Connery, Brooke Adams, Jack Weston, Hector Elizondo, Denholm Elliott, Martin Balsam.

Set in Cuba during the final days of the Batista regime, the plot concerns the military's last-gasp attempt to bolster a crumbling system already decaying from corruption, mismanagement and police brutality. Sean Connery portrays the lone British mercenary whom Batista hires to defeat Castro's guerrillas. Serving as Batista's spokesman, a genial but incompetent general (Martin Balsam) puts his country's fate in Connery's hands and feels confident that the Englishman's arrival will turn the desperate situation in favor of the present government.

What Connery observes is a lackadaisical and untrained army, a population cowering in fear of the police and military, and a wealthy class ignorant and unconcerned about Cuba's current plight. Fidel Castro's agents are everywhere—factory workers smuggle weapons to guerrillas in the countryside, hotel employees secretly make payoffs to gun runners, others plot and carry out random assassinations. Connery realizes the situation is hopeless.

Unfortunately, the film lacks unity. The plot constantly shifts its focus upon various characters and incidents—Connery and his special mission, a married couple going through a strained relationship, the rural guerrillas preparing for an all-out assault, a young ambitious roughneck trying to estab-

lish himself with Castro's forces by taking on all assignments requiring assassination. In addition, there are cuts to the aristocrats trying to maintain their lavish rituals while ignoring the poverty and upheaval about to engulf them.

Most of the characters are unsympathetic types, lacking vitality and action. They simply move through the scenes and observe. Connery witnesses the chaos, barely reacting to each new crisis. "Soldiering has changed," he muses to a Cuban officer. "It's—not as clean as it was." Brooke Adams, as the rich wife of a philandering husband, had had an affair with Connery years earlier. When Connery suggests that she leave Cuba with him, she confides that she cannot give up her luxuries and aristocratic way of life. A decent young Cuban officer assigned to work with Connery observes the corruption of his superiors, witnesses the beatings and killings of civilians by his soldiers and the police, sees the indifference of the aristocracy—and does nothing. "You're too late," is all he says to Connery. Jack Weston portrays a crass American businessman trying to turn a profit out of the political and economic turmoil engulfing Cuba.

Some of the dialogue is moderately interesting, especially in the confrontational scenes between Balsam, as the venal general, and Connery. "Tell me what your favorite weapon is," Balsam inquires. "Brains," the mercenary replies. When the general asks Connery what methods he will use against the guerrillas, the latter responds: "Harry and kill." Balsam doesn't understand the simplicity of the words. He then repeats them and smiles. Ironically, this is the same method Castro has been using so effectively against the government.

Later, Connery comments: "You only defeat someone like Castro if you're right." "Is Castro right?" the general returns. "That's not the point," Connery explains. "Does Cuba think he's right?" The flustered general, who was a corporal before Batista promoted him, changes the subject. "I expect to be called 'general.'" "It's important," Connery acknowledges before leaving the general's presence, "to call people what they are— sir." ■

Cup of Fury, The (1920), Goldwyn. *Dir.* T. Hayes Hunter; *Sc.* E. Richard Schayer; *Cast includes*: Helene Chadwick, Rockcliffe Fellowes, Frank Leigh, Clarissa Selwyn, Kate Lester, Herbert Standing.

A German spy in the U.S. during World War I plots to sabotage a shipyard in this drama adapted from Rupert Hughes' novel. Sydney Ainsworth, as the enemy agent, tries to get an employee (Helene Chadwick) at the shipyard to help him. But the patriotic young woman reveals his scheme to the shipbuilder (Rockcliffe Fellowes) who had hired her, and, together, they prevent the saboteur from causing any destruction. Chadwick, who had come under suspicion because of her adopted parents' suicide after they had been accused of treason, is cleared of any charges. The film ends with the launching of the next completed vessel which bears her name. ■

Cushman, Pauline (1835–1893). One of the Union's successful spies in the Civil War, the actress Pauline Cushman came close to losing her life when her ruse was discovered. In 1863, as part of her disguise, she was banished from the North as a supposed Confederate sympathizer. She did important undercover work for the Union in Kentucky and Tennessee before she was apprehended in possession of valuable Southern papers. After being court-martialed and sentenced to hang, she was saved when the Confederates, in a hasty retreat from Shelbyville, Tennessee (June 1863), inadvertently left her behind. Cushman made a postwar career of lecturing about her spy experiences. Plagued by personal problems, she took her own life.

Two Civil War films portray her exploits. Selig released *Pauline Cushman, the Federal Spy* in 1913. MGM's 1934 Civil War drama *Operator 13* starred Marion Davies as a Union spy who works alongside Pauline Cushman, portrayed by Katherine Alexander. Cushman's activities, unfortunately, are confined to the first half of the film and take a back seat to the fictitious escapades of Davies. ■

Custard Cup, The (1923), Fox. *Dir.* Herbert Brenon; *Sc.* G. Marion Burton; *Cast includes:* Mary Carr, Myrta Bonillas, Miriam Battista, Jerry Devine, Ernest McKay.

A U.S. Secret Service agent poses as a member of a counterfeit gang so that he can get enough evidence to put the culprits behind bars. The drama centers around the "custard cup," a series of tenements constructed in an oval shape. Mary Carr portrays a widow and mother who has lost her family during a flu epidemic. She is hired to manage the building development to help support her new family—three adopted children. The counterfeiters, operating in the vicinity, have been exploiting the caretaker to help them in their illegal dealings. He does not realize he is being used by them. The secret service operator eventually effects the arrest of the gang. Harry Sedley portrays the gang leader. ■

Customs Agent (1950), Col. *Dir.* Seymour Friedman; *Sc.* Russell S. Hughes, Malcolm Stuart Boylan; *Cast includes:* William Eythe, Marjorie Reynolds, Griff Barnett, Howard St. John, Jim Backus, Robert Shayne.

U.S. Customs goes after a gang of drug smugglers and its Chinese-American connection in this drama enhanced slightly by its semi-documentary trappings. William Eythe (who began his undercover career in 1945 in Henry Hathaway's highly successful *House on 92nd Street*) portrays a customs agent who, following some complex maneuvering in China, gains the confidence of the gang. The smugglers have been stealing streptomycin, diluting it and selling it illegally. Eythe tracks down the leaders of the gang (Griff Barnett and Howard St. John) in California where the obligatory showdown ensues. Marjorie Reynolds, who portrays a seductress working for the smugglers, almost ensnares Eythe. ■

D

Dan (1914), Par. *Sc.* Hal Reid; *Cast includes:* Lew Dockstader, Lois Meredith, Gale Kane, Beatrice Clevener.

A Civil War drama, the film tells the story of Dan, a black slave who sacrifices his own life to save that of his master's son. The young man, a Confederate officer, is captured by Union troops and sentenced to death as a spy. Dan gains access to the tent where the prisoner is being held and persuades him to blacken his face to facilitate his escape. In the morning the black servant is executed in place of his white master. Lew Dockstader, the famous white minstrel entertainer who appeared chiefly in blackface, was especially selected for the title role, and he blended the appropriate mixture of drama and comedy into the character of Dan.

The film, released in the early days of World War I, was timely for its war background and battle scenes. Although the subject matter concerning the servant and his overzealous loyalty to his master is offensive and disagreeable to today's audiences, contemporary moviegoers were exposed to large doses of "racist" dramas and comedies not only about blacks, but American Indians. Stereotypes of ethnic groups, most notably Italians and Jews, were popular subjects of derision chiefly in comedies. ∎

Danger in the Pacific (1942), U. *Dir.* Lewis D. Collins; *Sc.* Walter Doniger, Maurice Tombragel; *Cast includes:* Leo Carrillo, Andy Devine, Don Terry, Louise Allbritton, Turhan Bey.

A British intelligence agent is assigned to track down a cache of Nazi arms hidden somewhere on a Pacific island in this low-budget World War II drama. Leo Carrillo, as the agent, and his pals Don Terry and Andy Devine, who handles the comic relief, face various dangers, including headhunters, before they locate the arsenal. They finally call in the Royal Air Force to help them escape. Turhan Bey plays the villain who has stored the arms for eventual use by the Axis. Louise Allbritton, as a rich sportswoman, supplies the romance for Terry, who made a series of action dramas with Carrillo and Devine during this period. Carrillo was better known for his comic character portrayals in a string of comedies and dramas in which he invariably fractured the English language. ∎

Dangerous Days (1920), Goldwyn. *Dir.* Reginald Barker; *Sc.* Mary Roberts Rinehart; *Cast includes:* Lawson Butt, Clarissa Selwynne, Rowland Lee, Barbara Castleton, Ann Forrest.

A German spy conspires to cripple the production of American munitions manufacturers in this drama that takes place on the eve of World War I. Rudolph (Frank Leigh), a German secret agent, wants his brother Herman to plant a bomb at a steel plant where he is employed. To motivate his brother, Rudolph concocts a story about the owner's son trying to take advantage of Herman's daughter. Herman believes his brother and plants the explosive. His daughter learns of the plot and tries to warn the owner. But she is killed in the explosion.

The plot was considered dated by contemporary critics when the film was released. One reviewer wrote that the story was reminiscent of something "a long time ago." The war had been over for two years. Movie audiences that had lined up to see the latest war drama only a few years earlier, all but disappeared whenever a new combat film was released. Studios, caught with a backlog of

British intelligence agent Leo Carrillo (r.) and his two buddies Andy Devine and Don Terry are temporary prisoners of Nazi agents who have hidden an arsenal of weapons on a Pacific island. *Danger in the Pacific* (1942).

these features after the Armistice, were forced to edit out battle scenes, change their titles and announce for each that "this is NOT a war picture." The film was adapted from Mary Roberts Rinehart's novel of the same name. ■

Dangerous Hours (1920), Par. Dir. Fred Niblo; *Sc.* C. Gardner Sullivan; *Cast includes:* Lloyd Hughes, Barbara Castleton, Claire Du-Brey, Jack Richardson, Walt Whitman.

An anti-Bolshevik propaganda film set during the post-World War I years, the drama concerns Russian agents sent to the U.S. to foment industrial unrest. Lloyd Hughes portrays an unsuspecting American who is duped by Communist agitators. To further their own destructive ends, the Reds exploit his popularity among his fellow workers. But Hughes eventually gets wise to their purpose and turns against the revolutionaries. When they plan to set off a bomb, he tosses it at them. See Labor Unrest; Red Scare of 1919–1920. ■

Dangerous Partners (1945), MGM. Dir. Edward L. Cahn; *Sc.* Marion Parsonnet; *Cast includes:* James Craig, Signe Hasso, Edmund Gwenn, Audrey Totter, Mabel Paige.

A young couple trying to bilk an insurance company out of a large sum of money is pursued by a Nazi agent in this routine World War II drama. James Craig and Signe Hasso portray the two desperate lovers who find a will and decide to pose as the recipients of the inheritance. Meanwhile, Edmund Gwenn, as an enemy spy who needs the money to leave the United States, catches up with them. But government agents intercede in time to capture him. The film, one of several to mix the crime and spy genre, was adapted from "Paper Chase," a story by Oliver Weld Bayer. ■

Dangerously They Live (1942), WB. Dir. Robert Florey; *Sc.* Marion Parsonnet; *Cast includes:* John Garfield, Nancy Coleman, Raymond Massey, Lee Patrick, Moroni Olsen.

Nazi spies kidnap a British agent on a secret mission in this World War II drama of intrigue set in New York. Nancy Coleman, as the British heroine, is abducted by Nazi agents on her way to Grand Central Station before she can deliver an important message. But the taxi she is in crashes, and she is rushed to a hospital by ambulance and attended by an intern (John Garfield) who takes a personal interest in her case. Once in the hospital, she confides her true identity to Garfield, who doesn't believe her. The spies show up, with Moroni Olsen posing as her father. Coleman at first feigns amnesia, resulting in Garfield's insisting that she remain in the hospital a little longer. When Olsen leaves, Coleman insists that the visitor is not her father. Garfield appears skeptical. "The world has turned upside down," she explains. "Words don't mean what they're meant to mean. People are not what they should be."

When Olsen returns with a famous psychiatrist (Raymond Massey), she allows them to take her away, hoping she can learn more about their operations. To reassure her, Olsen permits Garfield to accompany her. Once in the lair of the spies, he realizes she is telling the truth. The psychiatrist, who turns out to be the leader of the spy ring, threatens to kill Garfield unless she reveals the exact course of a Canadian convoy on its way to England. She pleads for the life of Garfield, who is being held captive, claiming he is an innocent victim. "Hostages don't have to know, they only have to die," Massey replies, his words anticipating the wave of terrorist films that flooded the screens in the 1970s and 1980s. She then reveals the information about the convoy which he then transmits to a pack of U-boats. Unknown to him, she has disclosed the wrong coordinates. Garfield escapes from his captor and gets the drop on Massey and Olsen. Coleman proceeds to signal the Canadians, giving them the location of the German submarines. Canadian bombers then find and sink the U-boats. The film is based on the story "Remember Tomorrow" by Marion Parsonnet. ∎

Daniel (1983), Par. *Dir.* Sidney Lumet; *Sc.* E. L. Doctorow; *Cast includes:* Timothy Hutton, Mandy Patinkin, Lindsay Crouse, Edward Asner, Ellen Barkin, Julie Bovasso.

Set in the turbulent 1960s and based on E. L. Doctorow's *The Book of Daniel*, the drama deals with how the children of convicted spies confront their heritage. The fictionalized characters are drawn from events surrounding the controversial Julius and Ethel Rosenberg case of the early 1950s in which the couple were tried and given death sentences for turning over atomic secrets to the Russians. Timothy Hutton, as Daniel, the graduate-student son of the condemned spies, is forced to shed his general detachment when his politically active sister attempts suicide. He begins to search the past for the truth behind his parents' conviction. Mandy Patinkin and Lindsay Crouse appear in flashback sequences as Daniel's father and mother. Edward Asner, as a family friend, acts as their defense attorney.

Using flashbacks to capture the events in his parents' lives, the film explores various personal and political incidents ranging from the Depression years of the 1930s through the early 1950s, all perceived through the son's fragile emotions. Although Daniel tries to determine whether his parents were actually guilty or the innocent casualties of anti-Communist hysteria during the Cold War, the script, sidestepping the controversy, leaves the issue unanswered. Instead, the film ends on an upbeat note with Daniel casting off his political and social indifference and demonstrating the spirit of his parents' activism.

The Julius and Ethel Rosenberg case turned into one of the most controversial trials of the 1950s. When Russia in 1949 announced to a surprised world that it had exploded an atomic bomb, it broke America's nuclear monopoly. U.S. intelligence had assumed that the Russians would not have that capability until 1952. The trauma of that announcement sent tremors through the U.S. and unleashed a search for spies who may have helped the Russians jump the three-year gap.

Convinced that the Russians had planted a "mole" in America's nuclear research project during World War II, the F.B.I. tracked down a succession of spies and Soviet agents. David Greenglass, who had worked for the army as a machinist on the Manhattan Project in Los Alamos, New Mexico, was arrested and charged with revealing the details of the trigger which had been used to explode the first atomic bomb. Facing a possible death sentence if convicted, Greenglass admitted that he had been recruited into the Communist Party and espionage work by his sister, Ethel Rosenberg, and her husband, Julius. The latter was an electrical engineer, had served in the U.S. Army Signal Corps during

World War II and was a Communist Party member for many years.

The F.B.I. closed in, arrested the Rosenbergs and charged them with heading a Soviet intelligence network in the U.S. They were accused of reporting to Anatoly Yakovlev, a member of the Soviet mission in New York City. Morton Sobell, another electrical engineer, was arrested together with the Rosenbergs and charged with spying. Sobell, however, was not linked to atomic espionage.

The Rosenbergs were brought to trial in the spring of 1951, convicted and sentenced to death. They continued to insist upon their innocence up to the last moment. Despite appeals, they were executed in 1951—the first American spies killed during peacetime. Greenglass and Sobell received long jail terms. Rosenberg adherents to this day continue to insist that the couple were victims of a hysterical Red hunt in the wake of the Russian atomic bomb explosion. The Rosenbergs' two children, Robert and Michael Meeropol, in their book *We Are Your Sons* make a strong case for their parents' innocence. ∎

Daredevil, The (1918), Mutual. *Dir.* Francis Grandon; *Sc.* J. Clarkson Miller; *Cast includes:* Gail Kane, Norman Trevor, W. W. Crimans, Roy Applegate, Duncan McRae, Henry Sedley.

The daughter of a U.S. Army officer killed in France, posing as a young man, effects the capture of German spies in this World War I drama based on Maria Thompson Davies' novel. Gail Kane, as Roberta Carruthers, the young orphan, is forced to live with her uncle, her only living relative. Learning that her uncle expects a nephew, not a niece, Roberta dons men's clothing and changes her name to Bob. She is accepted in this fashion by her uncle and soon attains a position as translator for Governor Falkner (Norman Trevor). In this capacity she uncovers a plot by German secret agents and soon foils it. She then divulges her true identity to the delight of the governor who promptly falls in love with her and proposes marriage. ∎

Dark Road, The (1917), Triangle. *Dir.* Charles Miller, J. G. Hawks; *Sc.* John Strongly, John Lynch; *Cast includes:* Dorothy Dalton, Robert McKim, Jack Livingston, Jack Gilbert, Walt Whitman, Lydia Knott.

In this World War I drama an ambitious temptress marries an English captain for his position and wealth. When the officer (Jack Livingston) leaves for the front, his wife Cleo (Dorothy Dalton) moves in with his relatives at a country estate where she quickly becomes romantically involved with her husband's young cousin (Jack Gilbert). He, too, soon departs for military duty. She next takes up with an art connoisseur (Robert McKim) who in reality is a German spy. He learns from her husband's letters about secret troop movements and relays the information to German headquarters. When his superior officers discover that the captain was the cause of the leak, they give him a chance to clear his name. He tracks down the source to the spy's home and finds his wife in the man's arms. She dies during the ensuing struggle in which the spy is taken prisoner. ∎

Dark Star, The (1919), Par. *Dir.* Allan Dwan; *Sc.* Robert W. Chambers; *Cast includes:* Marion Davies, Norman Kerry, Matt Moore, Dorothy Green, Ward Crane, George Cooper.

Marion Davies portrays the daughter of an American missionary who finds herself entangled with German spies in this World War I drama set in Europe. She unknowingly gains access to vital plans about the locations of Turkish fortresses. She turns them over to a friend (Norman Kerry), who in reality is a French secret agent. When German spies learn that he possesses the plans, they follow him and Davies aboard a vessel and tie up the couple. The spies then arrange for the pair to be blown up along with the secret information. But Davies soon foils their plot. The film ends in a Paris café where Kerry rescues Davies from the clutches of the spies who perish in the fracas.

The title refers to a star or evil planet. A metallic substance that has fallen from the planet has been shaped into a statuette in the the image of Erik, Prince of Darkness. The plans which become the center of the plot are hidden in the image. Davies' father, unaware of the importance of the object, returns with it to America where, following his death, it becomes the property of his daughter. The film, based on the 1917 novel by Robert W. Chambers, received poor reviews and ultimately failed at the box office. The two leads made several other war films during the next decade. Director Allan Dwan went on to turn out many large-scale productions during the sound era. ∎

German spy Julie Andrews entertains Allied officers in London while gathering information from them in the World War I spoof *Darling Lili* (1970).

Darling Lili (1970), Par. *Dir.* Blake Edwards; *Sc.* Blake Edwards, William Peter Blatty; *Cast includes:* Julie Andrews, Rock Hudson, Jeremy Kemp, Lance Percival, Michael Witney, Jacques Marin.

Julie Andrews portrays the title character, an English entertainer who is actually a German spy, in this World War I comedy drama that failed at the box office. She meets and falls in love with an American air squadron commander, played by Rock Hudson. Jeremy Kemp, as her contact and German intelligence officer, masquerades as her Swiss relative. Lance Percival, as Hudson's flying buddy who is usually intoxicated, contributes to the comedy relief. The film captures the flavor of the period, including such nostalgic numbers as "Pack Up Your Troubles in Your Old Kit Bag and Smile," "It's a Long, Long Way to Tiperary" and "Keep the Home Fires Burning," all sung by Andrews. Action sequences include aerial dogfights which have little to do with the basic plot. ■

Daughter Angele (1918), Triangle. *Dir.* William Dowlan; *Sc.* George Elwood Jenks; *Cast includes:* Pauline Starke, Walt Whitman, Lule Warrenton, Gene Burr, Philo McCullough, Myrtle Rishell.

Traitors signal to German submarines in this World War I drama starring Pauline Starke. She poses as an orphan girl to gain entrance into the mansion of her real grandfather to help uncover the villainous goings-on. U.S. intelligence suspects the spies are operating from this location and sends in one of its agents who soon captures the culprit and wins the hand of Starke. Walt Whitman portrays the elderly grandfather who has not seen his grandchild in years. Lule Warrenton, as the old man's housekeeper, attempts to steal his fortune. Her son, played by Gene Burr, turns out to be the traitor flashing vital information to enemy submarines. ■

Daughter of Destiny (1918), FN. *Dir.* George Irving; *Cast includes:* Madame Petrova, Thomas Harding, Anders Randolf,

Robert Brodrick, Henri Leone, Richard Garrick.

A World War I drama set in a mythical European kingdom, the film concerns the romantic affairs of an American ambassador's daughter. Madame Petrova, as the title character and daughter, believes her husband, a German spy posing as an artist, has been killed in battle. She accompanies her father to Belmark where she falls in love with that nation's crown prince. The remainder of the complex plot deals with her giving up her lover so that he may marry a princess, America's entering the war against Germany, and a German agent trying to keep the kingdom from declaring war against his country.

Released during the war, the film is blatantly anti-German. One agent, in an attempt to disrupt a patriotic rally, throws a bomb during a crowd scene when he thinks the leaders of Belmark are about to side with the U.S. against Germany. The drama even proposes that all the German leaders be executed. ■

Daughter of Shanghai (1937), Par. *Dir.* Robert Florey; *Sc.* Gladys Unger, Garnett Weston; *Cast includes:* Anna May Wong, Philip Ahn, Charles Bickford, Larry Crabbe, Cecil Cunningham, J. Carrol Naish.

Concerned with putting an end to an illegal alien-smuggling operation, the U.S. Department of Justice assigns one of its Chinese agents to the case. Philip Ahn portrays the special agent. The smugglers, operating from their base in San Francisco, have contacts as far as a tropical island. Anna May Wong, as the Chinese-American daughter of one of the gang's victims, seeks revenge upon those who murdered her father to stop him from exposing their scheme. She soon joins forces with Ahn and a romance develops between the two. She journeys to the island where the smugglers are operating and masquerades as a café entertainer. She soon learns enough to help Ahn uncover the entire operation. ■

David Harding, Counterspy (1950), Col. *Dir.* Ray Nazarro; *Sc.* Clint Johnston, Tom Reed; *Cast includes:* Willard Parker, Audrey Long, Howard St. John, Raymond Greenleaf, Harlan Warde, Alex Gerry.

Espionage and murder plague a torpedo plant in this drama. Willard Parker portrays a naval officer who is appointed to fill in for a fellow officer who was murdered. Working for Harding (Howard St. John), chief of the government counterspies, Parker woos the widow (Audrey Long) who happens to be one of the enemy agents. Eventually, the spies are rounded up. The title character, created by Phillips H. Lord, was based on a popular radio program of the period. ■

Davis, Sam. See *Sam Davis, The Hero of Tennessee* (1915). ■

Dawn Express, The (1942), PRC. *Dir.* Albert Herman; *Sc.* Arthur St. Claire; *Cast includes:* Michael Whalen, Ann Nagel, William Bakewell, Constance Worth, Hans von Twardowski, Jack Mulhall.

Nazi agents attempt to steal the secret of a new type of gasoline known as "Formula 311" in this low-budget World War II drama. Michael Whalen portrays a chemist working for the government on this clandestine project when two fellow scientists are murdered. Whalen volunteers to help the U.S. Secret Service capture the spy ring by masquerading as a traitor. The villains are finally done in, and so is the film with such dialogue as "This is bigger than you or I" and "Follow that plane." Ann Nagel portrays the female lead. The film has been released under the alternate title *Nazi Spy Ring*. ■

Dawn of the East (1921), Par. *Dir.* Edward H. Griffith; *Sc.* E. Lloyd Sheldon; *Cast includes:* Alice Brady, Kenneth Harlan, Michio Itow, America Chedister, Betty Carpenter.

A former Russian countess, now happily married to an American diplomat, is threatened with exposure of her past if she does not steal political documents from her husband in this routine drama. Alice Brady, as the harassed wife, had entered into a nominal marriage while working as a dancer in a Shanghai café years earlier. It was there that she met an unscrupulous Chinese royalist (Michio Itow) who offers her a proposition. If she marries a Chinese suitor, she will receive a large sum of money and the marriage will not be binding. She agrees to these terms and, with part of the dowry, escapes to the U.S.

Later, the royalist suddenly appears and threatens to tell her current husband about her former marriage unless she steals from his possession important papers referring to Chinese affairs. She refuses. He then sends for her former husband. Brady convinces the duped Chinese that he had been swindled by the royalist. The man kills the instigator, destroys all evidence of the previous marriage and returns to his homeland. ■

Day of the Dolphin (1973), Avco. *Dir.* Mike Nichols; *Sc.* Buck Henry; *Cast includes:* George C. Scott, Trish Van Devere, Paul Sorvino, Fritz Weaver, Jon Korkes, Edward Hermann.

Conspirators plot to kill the U.S. President by using dolphins to blow up his yacht in this diverting but slow-paced drama. Fritz Weaver, as a senior executive of a foundation which is conducting advanced research with dolphins, heads the conspirators. Jon Korkes, working for Weaver, kidnaps two dolphins. One is to carry explosives to the President's yacht. Paul Sorvino, posing as writer, in reality is a U.S. secret agent assigned to investigate Weaver's activities. George C. Scott, as a marine scientist working with the dolphins, eventually foils the assassination plot. He sends out the second dolphin to intercept the bomb-carrying one. The explosives are then placed on the plotter's yacht. Trish Van Devere portrays Scott's wife. The film was adapted from Robert Merle's novel. ■

Innocent U.S. government worker Reedy Talton prowls the dark world of espionage as he tries to extricate himself from charges of treason. *Dead to the World* (1962).

Dead to the World (1962), UA. *Dir.* Nicholas Webster; *Sc.* John Roeburt; *Cast includes:* Reedy Talton, Jana Pearce, Ford Rainey, Casey Peyson, John McLiam, John Dorman.

A State Department employee is charged with betraying his country when officials discover that secrets have been transmitted to Communist Bulgaria in this minor drama. Reedy Talton portrays the innocent U.S. government worker who comes under fire from the authorities, especially since the family re-

ceiving the information is the one who helped Talton during World War II. To complicate matters further, he is suspected of killing an influential politician (Leon B. Stevens). The remainder of the plot concerns Talton's efforts to prove his innocence. Jana Pearce helps him uncover the actual traitor. The film is based on *State Department Murders*, a novel by Edward Ronns. ■

Deadline for Murder (1946), TCF. *Dir.* James Tinling; *Sc.* Irving Cummings, Jr.; *Cast includes:* Paul Kelly, Kent Taylor, Sheila Ryan, Jerome Cowan, Renee Carson, Joan Blair.

A secret U.S. government report about international oil deposits leads to a series of murders in this drama of intrigue. Kent Taylor, as a good-natured gambler, volunteers to help a friend (Joan Blair) and soon finds himself enmeshed in a robbery and murder plot. Blair calls upon Taylor to retrieve a government document that her stepson, in a moment of weakness, gave to a seductress. As Taylor hunts down the coveted paper, he discovers that each person who has possessed it has been murdered. The trail of suspicion finally leads to a conspiracy brewed by Jerome Cowan and Renee Carson. Paul Kelly, as a detective, enters the case in the nick of time to collar Cowan as the murderer. Sheila Ryan portrays a newspaper reporter in this well-paced tale. ■

Deadly Game, The (1941), Mon. *Dir.* Phil Martinelli; *Sc.* Wellyn Totman; *Cast includes:* Charles Farrell, June Lang, John Miljan, Bernadine Hayes, David Clarke.

One of the many B features turned out by Monogram during World War II, this routine drama concerns a G-man posing as a Nazi agent. Predictably, the hero ultimately ensnares an entire spy network. June Lang has the role of female lead. Charles Farrell, who receives top billing here, starred in such major productions as the silent *Seventh Heaven* (1927), a romantic drama with World War I as background. Released only months before America's entry into the war, the film anticipates the flow of low-budget home-front Nazi spy dramas that were to saturate the nation's movie screens during the next few years. ■

Death Before Dishonor (1987), New World. *Dir.* Terry J. Leonard; *Sc.* John Gatliff, Lawrence Kubik; *Cast includes:* Fred Dryer,

Brian Keith, Joanna Pacula, Paul Winfield, Muhamad Bakri, Kasey Walker.

This pointless and excessively violent drama pits a gung-ho U.S. Marine sergeant against an extremist Arab terrorist group operating in the Middle East. Crosscutting between a marine reconnaissance training school in the U.S. and a radical terrorist organization which has just unleashed one of its teams to assassinate an Israeli ambassador and his family in Cyprus, the film then moves to Jemal, a fictitious Arab country friendly to the West but threatened by an impending military coup. In an attempt to force the Americans to leave before he strikes against the government, the terrorist leader orders the capture of a U.S. colonel and the bombing of the U.S. embassy.

These acts, especially that of taking his commanding officer hostage, arouse the anger of Fred Dryer, who portrays the frozen-faced, humorless U.S. sergeant determined to hunt down the kidnappers. Following a succession of blunders on his part, Israeli intelligence agents operating in Jemal contact Dryer and invite him and two of his marines to join them in a raid on the terrorist headquarters. The climactic battle results in the rescue of the hostage and the destruction of the terrorist group.

Paul Winfield, as the cautious U.S. ambassador to Jemal, prefers going "by the book" and rebukes Dryer for engaging in combat in a foreign land. Brian Keith portrays the U.S. colonel in charge of embassy security who hangs tough when he is taken hostage. Joanna Pacula plays an Israeli secret agent posing as a photojournalist. The Americans are portrayed as naive dabblers in the intrigues of the Middle East while the Israelis are depicted as the more knowledgeable. "These rebels," the Mossad leader enlightens Dryer before the climactic firefight, "are not a rag-tag army. What the Russians didn't give them, you probably sold them."

The film sheds little light on the political issues that have engulfed the region in war and terrorism for several decades. Instead, it offers several scenes of explicit violence. The terrorists use a power drill to torture their captives. New recruits to Dryer's unit must undergo their rite of passage, which include drinking a helmet full of beer and having gold insignia hammered into their chests until blood flows. Perhaps the most unintentionally revealing bit of dialogue that questions

the integrity of the film occurs when Winfield says to the photojournalist: "The reality is the United States does not and will not negotiate with terrorists."

Despite the film's obvious fictitious plot, the kidnapping of an American military officer may have been based on the 1981 incident in which the ultra-left Red Brigades kidnapped Brig. Gen. James Dozier in Italy. However, unlike the melodramatics depicted in the film, General Dozier was rescued in 1982 by the Italian police. The "Delta Force" of the film was fashioned after America's efforts to establish an elite counterterrorist unit early during the Reagan administration. Bruised by a series of terrorist acts and humiliated by the failure in 1980 of the operation called Desert One to free the American hostages in Teheran, the Pentagon sought to develop a counterterrorist unit to strike swiftly around the globe. Again, unlike the super-efficient force portrayed in the film, the real-life group soon found itself engulfed in secrecy (operating largely without the knowledge either of Congress or the military) and virtually neutralized as the result of the Iran-Contra affair. ∎

Decision Before Dawn (1951), TCF. *Dir.* Anatole Litvak; *Sc.* Peter Viertel; *Cast includes:* Richard Basehart, Gary Merrill, Oskar Werner, Hildegarde Neff, Dominique Blanchar, O. E. Hasse.

Allied intelligence uses prisoners of war as spies during the last days of World War II to speed the end of the conflict in this grim drama about conflict of loyalties. Oskar Werner, as a captured Luftwaffe medic disillusioned with Hitler, acts as a secret agent for the Americans. Although he loves his country, the idealistic German officer abhors the government that has led Germany down the road to destruction. After seeing the brutal killing of a fellow prisoner of war by fanatical Nazis, he volunteers to return to Germany as a spy in the belief that by ending the war sooner he will be saving lives.

Werner is assigned to locate the position of a Panzer division endangering an Allied advance. His movements behind the lines provide plenty of suspense as he gathers the necessary information. Although he completes his mission, he is killed while saving an Allied officer's life. Richard Basehart, as the officer, manages to get the information back to headquarters. Gary Merrill portrays the chief of Allied intelligence. The scenes inside Germany near the end of the war show a country in ruins and a defeated people stunned by the devastation which surrounds them.

This was one of the earliest postwar films to hint that there were some anti-Nazi Germans who voluntarily endangered their lives to help overthrow Hitler's Third Reich. As such, it was unique in exploring the ambivalent feelings in its main character who sees himself both as a defender of his country and a traitor—a tragic figure who is torn between causing immediate harm to his fellow countrymen and helping to bring peace by shortening the war. The film was adapted from the novel *Call It Treason* by George Howe. See British Intelligence: World War II. ■

Defection. Incidents involving defection have been recorded long before the term "defector" came into general use during the Cold War. During the American Revolution, for example, Major John André, a British spy who was special assistant to Britain's General Clinton, was at the point of achieving the most spectacular coup of the war—the defection of General Benedict Arnold together with the surrender of West Point—when he was caught and hanged in 1780. These incidents are reenacted in the historical drama *The Scarlet Coat* (1955).

The Civil War offered another example of defection, but on a much larger scale. One of the most ambitious undertakings of the South involved the Copperheads and was known as the Northwest Conspiracy. The idea was to encourage the defection from the Union of several Western states which would then establish a Northwest Confederacy sympathetic to the South.

However, it was not until the post-World War II period that the defector became a familiar subject both in newspapers and on screen. Hollywood's image of the defector— one who has renounced his or her country and who may posses knowledge that other nations covet—has been entirely subjective. If he escaped from behind the Iron Curtain to shed the oppressive chains of totalitarianism, he was a sort of hero and was embraced by the West. If he abandoned his democratic roots and went over to the Communists, he was portrayed as a traitor. So much for objectivity.

Sometimes the screen hero masqueraded as a defector but in reality was a double agent.

This added complications to the plot and possible confusion for the audience. But in an age of paranoia and an obsession with Communism, these shifting allegiances with their fuzzy morality only underscored the times we were living in. In *Three Days of the Condor* (1975) a C.I.A. chief (John Houseman), formerly with the O.S.S. during World War II, is asked by a younger agent: "Do you miss that kind of action?" "No," Houseman replies mournfully, "I miss that kind of clarity."

The Iron Curtain (1948) was one of the earliest Cold War films about defection. Seeking a better life for their child, a Russian clerk (Dana Andrews) working in Canada and his wife (Gene Tierney) decide to turn themselves in to Canadian authorities. They immediately reveal the inner apparatus of a Soviet spy network functioning in Canada. The film is based on the experiences of Igor Gouzenko, whose revelations made headlines in 1946. *Operation Manhunt* (1954), a highly fictionalized drama of the defector's exploits in Canada, served as a pseudo-sequel. The Soviets assign one of their secret agents to assassinate Gouzenko. Harry Townes portrays Gouzenko, who remains firm in his convictions although he knows he is being hunted. The assassin, played by Jacques Aubuchon, at first stalks his victim diligently but then ends up also defecting.

An obligatory characteristic of these early defection dramas was to denigrate the stifling existence of Communist life while extolling the virtues of freedom. In *Man on a Tightrope* (1953) a Czechoslovakian circus owner (Fredric March), fed up with Communist bureaucracy and oppression, plots to smuggle his entire enterprise across the border to the West. The genre reached its height of absurdity with *Jet Pilot* (1957) in which a Soviet flier (Janet Leigh) defects to the West and falls in love with an American air force colonel (John Wayne). Leigh shoots down her fellow pilots and strafes ground troops while making her escape. Implausibility mounts when army officials learn that she is actually a spy. They arrange for Wayne to pose as a defector and for the couple to escape to Russia. But when Wayne undergoes tough scrutiny at the hands of the Communists, Leigh arranges for their escape back to the U.S.

Occasionally, a Cold War drama reversed the plot by having an American turn defector. *The Thief* (1952) concerns a Washington-based American nuclear scientist in this unusual film which has no spoken dialogue but retains its sound effects. Ray Milland portrays the defector who, working with foreign agents, photographs certain secret papers and turns the film over to the enemy. When government officials discover a security leak, Milland and his cohorts scheme to leave the country.

Later defection films played down political themes and concentrated on action and suspense. In Hitchcock's *Torn Curtain* (1966) Paul Newman, as an important American physicist, poses as a defector to obtain Communist defense secrets from his East German counterpart. Newman and his assistant (Julie Andrews) face the usual dangers before he accomplishes his mission. In *Ice Station Zebra* (1968) American and British agents at the North Pole clash with Russian troops. Rock Hudson, as a nuclear submarine commander, is assigned to retrieve a space capsule that has landed on the North Pole. Ernest Borgnine portrays a Russian defector who accompanies the secret mission. *Avalanche Express* (1979), a Cold War drama with Robert Shaw and Lee Marvin, shows the agency using a high-ranking Soviet defector to ensnare a dangerous Soviet agent.

The defection theme, as with most genres, deteriorated into comedies and self-parodies. In the comedy *The Wicked Dreams of Paula Schultz* (1968) Elke Sommer, as a major East German athlete preparing for the Olympic Games, eludes a lecherous propaganda minister and defects to the West. She accomplishes this feat by pole-vaulting over the Berlin Wall. C.I.A. and Communist agents soon get involved in her defection.

Meanwhile, in the world of reality and political intrigue the subject of defectors took on a more ominous tone. One of the most radical experiments introduced by the C.I.A. during the Vietnam War was the Phoenix Program. Vietcong defectors, encouraged by an offer of amnesty, were often persuaded to identify their ex-comrades, who were then arrested and often shot.

Contrary to popular belief, defectors to the West are not generally encouraged or enthusiastically welcomed. They require large expenditures of funds, for they must be debriefed, given new names at a new location and provided a subsidy for a few years. However, the value of a defector depends chiefly upon his rank or position in the Soviet Union. Military officers with the rank of colonel or higher and K.G.B. agents take priority. They must all undergo a period of isolation and questioning; in some cases, they are subjected to drugs to help determine their reliability.

The most perverse example of excessive abuse on the part of the C.I.A. involved the defector Yuri Nosenko, a K.G.B. officer. In 1964 he escaped to the U.S. carrying an abundance of vital information. The C.I.A., however, suspected that he might have been a plant—a double agent—sent to spread disinformation and discredit previous fellow defectors. The C.I.A., obsessed with cracking Nosenko's credibility, secretly transferred him to a remote area in Virginia, removed all his clothes and tossed him into a small cell without windows. He remained a prisoner for more than three years in this vault-like cell and was under constant surveillance. Every few days he was wired to a lie detector and questioned unceasingly. He was subjected to a series of actions designed to disorient him. Unable to wring a confession from him, Nosenko was finally released. In all those years of incarceration in which he was subjected to physical and mental suffering, he was never officially accused of a crime or put on trial. ∎

Defense Play (1988), Trans World. *Dir.* Monte Markham; *Sc.* Aubrey Solomon, Steve Greenberg; *Cast includes:* David Oliver, Susan Ursitti, Monte Markham, Eric Gilliom, William Frankfather, Patch Mackenzie.

Soviet agents plot to sabotage an important U.S. military missile launching in this late Cold War drama. A young Soviet secret agent (Eric Gilliom), trained in Russia to pass for an American, infiltrates a special project at a campus physics laboratory working closely with the U.S. military space program. The Soviet plan is to destroy a much-touted launching and have it look like an accident. The failure will discredit the military and cut off funding.

Young Scott Denton (David Oliver), the son of an air force colonel, is fascinated with the experimental lab after meeting the professor's daughter (Susan Ursitti). When the professor (Terrance Cooper) suspects one of his three young assistants of tampering with his experiments, the Soviet agent kills him. While the police call the death an accident, Scott claims the professor was murdered. He and Susan take it upon themselves to investigate. They finally come up with proof that Gilliom, one of the assistants, is using a false name. Gilliom, the undercover spy, escapes to a small boat off shore where his superior is stationed. Still intent on carrying out the destruction of the missile which is about to be launched, Gilliom fires a remote-controlled bomb to the site. Young Scott, using another computer, intercepts and destroys the flying bomb with another remote-controlled weapon and the launching goes off without a hitch.

The contrived drama has one interesting sequence. Opening scenes show a typical crowded American bar filled with young people who are busily engaged in drinking, talking and dancing. When one young patron who has had too much to drink begins to brawl with another, the lights suddenly brighten and the music and talking stop. A Soviet officer enters from a glass booth. The officer contrasts sharply with the casual dress of the young people. He rebukes the intoxicated patron in Russian. The room, we discover, is actually a simulation of an American establishment used to train Soviet agents to act and speak like Americans. ∎

Delta Force, The (1986), Cannon. *Dir.* Menahem Golan; *Sc.* James Bruner, Menahem Golan; *Cast includes:* Chuck Norris, Lee Marvin, Martin Balsam, Joey Bishop, Robert Forster, Lanie Kazan.

A special force of U.S. agents is assigned to rescue the passengers of an airplane that has been hijacked by deranged Arab terrorists in this action drama. The kidnappers, members of an extremist Palestinian faction, have diverted the Athens-to-New York flight and detoured the plane filled with American passengers to Beirut. The terrorists release the women and children while taking all others to a secluded location in the city. Members of the Delta Force penetrate the hiding place with the help of a Greek Orthodox priest who is also an undercover agent for Israeli intelligence. The infiltrators rescue the Americans by entering through sewer pipes but learn that another group of captives has been taken away by the Arab leader (Robert Forster). A Delta Force major pursues the terrorist chief, kills him and effects the release of the prisoners.

Chuck Norris, known chiefly for superhero roles in action-oriented films, portrays the American major who precipitates most of the battles against the hijackers. He is determined, after the fiasco to save the captured Americans during the Iranian hostage crisis, that this time the operation will succeed. Lee Marvin portrays the commander in charge of the Delta Force commissioned to rescue the hostages. Several passengers are portrayed by major screen personalities. Shelley Winters and Martin Balsam are a Jewish-American couple, with Balsam as a concentration camp survivor. George Kennedy portrays a Catholic priest. Lanie Kazan and Joey Bishop, as another Jewish couple, are in the midst of celebrating their 25th wedding anniversary. Robert Forster, as the Arab leader, is a menacing figure willing to go to any lengths to achieve recognition for his cause. ∎

Desert Bride, The (1928), Col. *Dir.* Walter Lang; *Sc.* Elmer Narris; *Cast includes:* Betty Compson, Allan Forrest, Edward Martindel, Otto Matiesen, Roscoe Karns.

Allan Forrest portrays the chief of the French intelligence service who frustrates the military plans of a belligerent Arab chieftain in this silent desert melodrama. The native leader (Otto Matiesen) plots to recover his much-needed ammunition that Forrest has seized. Betty Compson, as the niece of an army officer, portrays an adventurous young woman. A climactic battle ensues with the desert warriors temporarily gaining the upper hand. But the soldiers arrive in the nick of time and subdue the dissidents. ∎

Desert Song, The (1943), WB. *Dir.* Robert Florey; *Sc.* Robert Buckner; *Cast includes:* Dennis Morgan, Irene Manning, Bruce Cabot, Victor Francen, Lynne Overman, Gene Lockhart.

In this updated version of the well-known operetta, Nazi spies scheme to build a railroad in French Morocco in 1939, using Riffs as slave laborers. Dennis Morgan, as an American expatriate who had fought against Franco's Fascists in Spain, works as a piano player in Morocco. Disguised as the Red Rider, he organizes the natives in an uprising against their oppressors. Following a series of desert battles and the unmasking of a German agent, he finally succeeds in gaining freedom for the Riffs and foiling the Nazi scheme. Irene Manning, portraying the female lead, contributes some of the singing. The original songs are retained in this screen version that includes four new numbers. Other adaptations of the play include a 1929 musical and a 1956 rendition with Kathryn Grayson and Gordon MacRae, both of which adhere more closely to the original plot. ■

Destructors, The (1968), Feature Film Corp. *Dir.* Francis D. Lyon; *Sc.* Arthur C. Pierce; *Cast includes:* Richard Egan, Patricia Owens, John Ericson, Michael Ansara, Joan Blackman, David Brian.

A U.S. intelligence agency member becomes involved in a plot by enemy agents to steal a secret laser ray gun in this inept Cold War drama. Richard Egan, as the agent, suspects a plot is afoot after a factory is blown up and some laser rubies are missing. These items, he concludes, are essential for the operation of the ray gun. Michael Ansara, as the chief villain, has a swimsuit business which he uses as a front. John Ericson, as one of Ansara's cohorts, is a Korean War hero who has temporarily turned traitor as a result of Communist brainwashing. Joan Blackman portrays a young woman who is in love with Ericson. However, the climax reveals that she is actually part of the spy operation. See Brainwashing. ■

Detectives and spies. Hollywood sleuths on occasion turned their attentions from conventional criminals to tackle enemy agents. Louis Joseph Vance's fictional hero, "The Lone Wolf," for example, had a long screen history, beginning in the silents. In *The False Faces* (1919), set during World War I and starring Henry B. Walthall as the detective, he learns that German spies intend to increase their activities in the United States. Jack Holt portrays the Robin Hood-type sleuth in *The Lone Wolf* (1924), which concerns some coveted secret papers that contain military plans of the U.S. Columbia studios again pressed their in-house sleuth, the Lone Wolf, into service against enemy agents during World War II. He came out of retirement for *The Lone Wolf Spy Hunt* (1939), in which Warren William as the title character foils a Washington spy network from stealing secret anti-aircraft plans. In *Counter-Espionage* (1942) William, again playing the "Wolf," hunts down a Nazi spy network in World War II London while protecting secret military plans. In *Passport to Suez* (1943) William, as a double agent, joins a Nazi spy ring in Egypt as a ploy to retrieve stolen plans concerning the Suez Canal.

Jack Boyle's popular fictional character Boston Blackie, a former criminal who works on the side of the law, had a long screen life. In the World War I drama *The Silk-Lined Burglar* (1919) Sam De Grasse, as the regenerated miscreant, plies his safe-cracking talents to assist a young woman in obtaining evidence against a suspected German spy. Lionel Barrymore, as Boston Blackie in *A Face in the Fog* (1922), becomes entangled in an international plot to restore the monarchy in Bolshevik Russia. During the sound era Chester Morris took over the role. He becomes implicated in a murder in *Meet Boston Blackie* (1941), and to prove his innocence he exposes an entire spy ring.

Basil Rathbone and Nigel Bruce became the most popular team to portray A. Conan Doyle's Sherlock Holmes and Dr. Watson. *The Voice of Terror* (1942) concerns a Nazi radio broadcast that is terrorizing the English citizenry. In *Sherlock Holmes and the Secret Weapon* (1942), about a new bombsight, Holmes employs a series of disguises to elude the enemy while Dr. Watson remains baffled by his friend's methods. Dr. Moriarty, Holmes' archenemy, is again on the loose in this updated version of Doyle's story titled "The Dancing Men." Holmes and Watson then travel to the U.S. to take on an international spy ring in *Sherlock Holmes in Washington* (1943). *Pursuit to Algiers* (1945), another of the updated Sherlock Holmes entries of the 1940s, involves a threat against a young king's life by an unnamed enemy although there are hints that totalitarian forces are behind the plot.

MGM purchased the rights to all the Nick Carter stories, updated the material from its pre-World War I background to the World War II period and featured dapper Walter Pidgeon as the master sleuth in the new series. The undistinguished first entry, *Nick Carter, Master Detective* (1939), directed by Jacques Tourneur, deals with spies trying to steal secret plans from an airplane factory. Comic character actor Donald Meek portrays the detective's assistant. Rita Johnson plays an airline stewardess. The detective series differed from others in that Carter was usually engaged in tracking down enemy agents and saboteurs rather than run-of-the-mill criminals and murderers. For example, in *Phantom Raiders* (1940), the second entry, saboteurs are busy attacking ships in the Panama Canal region before Carter puts a stop to their activities. The third and final entry, *Sky Murder*, also released in 1940, again concerned foreign spies.

Other detectives also took on an array of enemy agents. In *Charlie Chan in Panama* (1940), the Hawaiian sleuth, working in league with U.S. intelligence, foils a plot to blow up a portion of the Panama Canal and trap a U.S. fleet passing through during maneuvers. The film, in part, was a remake of *Marie Galante* (1934), which, ironically, had a secret agent of Japan joining forces with those of the U.S. and England to prevent the destruction of the Panama Canal. In *Enemy Agents Meet Ellery Queen* (1942) William Gargan, portraying the master sleuth, exposes a spy ring interested in industrial diamonds for precision instruments, the coveted goal of both Nazi and Free Dutch agents. These diversions added a little spark to each series and no doubt contributed to the patriotism of the period. ■

Devil Makes Three, The (1952), MGM.

Dir. Andrew Marton; *Sc.* Jerry Davis; *Cast includes:* Gene Kelly, Pier Angeli, Richard Rober, Richard Egan, Claus Clausen.

A secret plot hatched in 1947 in post-World War II Germany to resurrect the Nazi Party provides the basis for this drama. Gene Kelly portrays a U.S. Army officer who returns to occupied Germany to visit a family that helped him during the war. As a flier during the conflict, he was captured after his plane was shot down. He then escaped from a prisoner-of-war camp and found refuge with the anti-Nazi family.

He discovers that the couple had been killed in a bombing raid and their daughter (Pier Angeli), who currently works as a bar girl, is engaged in smuggling. U.S. intelligence then asks him to spy for the agency and help track down the neo-Nazi underground and their gold shipments. Kelly at first refuses to cooperate. The neo-Nazis, who are shipping looted gold across the border to help finance their new secret army, are waiting for the occupation to end before they rise up. Following several suspenseful chases, Kelly and the authorities close in on the leader of the ring. The film, made on location, utilizes such locales as Munich, Salzberg and Berchtesgaden. See Nazi Subversion: Post-World War II. ■

Devil Pays Off, The (1941), Rep. *Dir.* John

H. Auer; *Sc.* Lawrence Kimble, Malcolm S. Boyle; *Cast includes:* J. Edward Bromberg, Osa Massen, William Wright, Abner Biberman.

An ex-serviceman, cashiered from the navy, redeems himself when he prevents the sale of American ships to an unnamed foreign power in this World War II drama. J. Edward Bromberg, as the former navy man, uncovers a plot involving a shipping tycoon who plans to sell his fleet to a potential enemy of the U.S. Osa Massen portrays his wife.

Many films dealing with international intrigue and released before America's entry into the war employed a nebulous, unidentified foreign enemy. This technique had been used previously in relation to World War I and in numerous silent adventure films concerning Central and South America. In the case of the World War II features, the German accents of the villains telegraphed their national origin. World War I silent films had to depend on characters' German-sounding names flashed upon the screen on title cards. ■

Devil's Chaplain, The (1929), Rayart. *Dir.*

Duke Worne; *Sc.* Arthur Hoerl; *Cast includes:* Josef Swickard, Virginia Brown Faire, Cornelius Keefe, Wheeler Oakman, George MacIntosh, Boris Karloff.

A dethroned king of a fictitious European country seeks sanctuary in the U.S. in this minor drama. Josef Swickard, as the ruler, becomes the target of a band of spies trying to assassinate him. A top agent of the U.S. Secret Service (Cornelius Keefe), assigned to protect the king, rescues him on several occasions. Virginia Browne Faire, as the king's fiancée, accompanies him to the States and falls for Keefe. Swickard is finally restored to the throne. His fiancée, however, decides to remain in the U.S. with her new-found love. ■

Dick Tracy's G-Men (1939) serial, Rep.

Dir. William Witney, John English; *Sc.* Barry Shipman, Franklyn Adreon, Rex Taylor, Ronald Davidson, Sol Shor; *Cast includes:* Ralph Byrd, Irving Pichel, Ted Pearson, Phylis Isley, Walter Miller, George Douglas.

A master international spy threatens the security of the U.S. in this 15-chapter serial based on the adventures of the title character created by comic strip artist Chester Gould. The chief villain, played by Irving Pichel, plots various acts of sabotage, including the destruction of the Panama Canal, and it is up to Dick Tracy, the popular detective, and his band of G-men, to stop the sinister Zarnoff. Missing from this serial are the familiar characters of Pat Patton, Junior and Tess Trueheart, well known to the readers of the strip. Ralph Byrd impersonated the famous sleuth in several serials and features, alternating with Morgan Conway. ∎

Die Hard (1988), TCF. *Dir.* John McTiernan; *Sc.* Jeb Stuart, Steven De Souza; *Cast includes:* Bruce Willis, Alan Rickman, Alexander Godunov, Bonnie Bedelia, Reginald Veljohnson, William Atherton.

Twelve terrorists take over an unfinished building in Los Angeles and hold about 30 party guests hostage in this suspenseful but unbelievable drama. Alexander Godunov portrays Hans Gruber, a member of a radical West German group of terrorists who has been expelled from the organization. Gruber, heading his own faction, devises a complex plan to steal $600 million from a Japanese industrialist's almost impregnable vault. They seize control of the Nakatomi Building and hold the group hostage. To cover their real intent—the theft of the negotiable bearer bonds—they demand from the police and F.B.I. who have surrounded the edifice the release of several political prisoners in Ireland, Canada and Sri Lanka. Meanwhile, one of Gruber's underlings, a computer expert, is busy trying to break the various codes to the Nakatomi's vault.

Gruber, however, faces an unexpected obstacle. A New York cop, played by Bruce Willis, who had come to the party to see his estranged wife, was in another room when the terrorists burst in. Making his way to freedom within the confines of the edifice, he manages to fight off Gruber's men who are sent to kill him. The terrorists pay a heavy price in their attempt on Willis' life. The police officer, though, has his own problems. The police department officials don't believe his estimates of the situation. The F.B.I. agents ignore his warnings and send men to their death in an effort to storm the building. Finally, Willis, short on weaponry and outnumbered, finds himself alone in his battle against Gruber and his men.

Aside from the tightly woven suspense, well-mounted action sequences, and superhuman efforts of Willis who eventually annihilates the entire gang, the director has added a note of ironic humor concerning the timely issue of terrorists. A local television studio has brought in an expert on terrorism to analyze the crisis in progress. Supercilious and self-assured, the guest begins to explain the typical stages of a terrorist situation. "The hostages and the terrorists go through a sort of transference and a projection of dependency. A strange sort of trust and bond develops. We've had situations where the hostages have embraced their captors . . ." As he spouts his erudition, the scene shifts to show one of the terrorists dragging the corpse of one of his victims. ∎

Dies Committee. See *Murder in the Air* (1940). ∎

Dimension 5 (1966), Feature Film Corp. *Dir.* Franklin Adreon; *Sc.* Arthur C. Pierce; *Cast includes:* Jeffrey Hunter, France Nuyen, Harold Sakata, Donald Woods, Linda Ho, Robert Ito.

A secret agent and his Hong Kong assistant prevent the Communist Chinese from destroying Los Angeles in this routine science fiction drama. Jeffrey Hunter, as the American agent working for the fictional Espionage, Inc., learns from a captured spy that a Chinese group known as Dragon secretly plans to transport aboard a ship bound for the U.S. sections of an H-bomb. He enlists the aid of his assistant (France Nuyen) and together they travel into the near future and steal aboard the suspected vessel. They discover hidden in the rice shipment the parts of the bomb. But they are captured by the chief villain (Harold Sakata) and his minions. Linda Ho, as one of Sakata's agents and a friend of Hunter, decides to free the captives. The Communist agents are annihilated, and the hero and heroine return by way of their time-converter belts to the present. ∎

Diplomacy (1916), Par. *Dir.* Sidney Olcott; *Sc.* Hugh Ford; *Cast includes:* Marie Doro, Elliott Dexter, Edith Campbell Walker, George Majeroni, Frank Losee, Russell Bassett.

Based on *Dora*, Victorien Sardou's 1877 drama of international intrigue, the film concerns a young member of the English diplomatic corps who suspects his wife of having been a secret agent for a foreign power. Elliott Dexter, as the suspicious husband, earlier was rejected as a suitable mate for the daughter (Marie Doro) of an impoverished marquise (Edith Campbell Walker). He was accepted only after he obtained a position with the diplomatic service and had increased his financial status through wise investments. Soon after the wedding he gains access to information that leads him to believe that his wife, as a foreign agent, had betrayed him. However, all is resolved by the end of the drama. The film, set in several European locales, was remade a decade later starring Neil Hamilton and Blanche Sweet in the principal roles. ■

Diplomacy (1926), Par. *Dir.* Marshall Neilan; *Sc.* Benjamin Glazer; *Cast includes:* Neil Hamilton, Blanche Sweet, Arlette Marchal, Matt Moore, Gustav von Seyffertitz, Earle Williams.

International treaties, stolen documents and murder dominate this tale of intrigue during a diplomatic conference in Deauville. Neil Hamilton portrays an American diplomat who has lost an important document. Blanche Sweet plays his attractive wife. Possession of the coveted document results in one act of torture, one shooting and two murders of members of the diplomatic service. Matt Moore, masquerading as a buffoonish character, turns out to be a U.S. Secret Service agent who salvages the conference. Earle Williams portrays a British diplomat. The film, based on the play *Dora* by Victorien Sardou, ends with a tribute to all secret service agents who protect and defend the integrity of international law and diplomacy. An earlier screen version of Sardou's play appeared in 1916. ■

Diplomatic Courier (1952), TCF. *Dir.* Henry Hathaway; *Sc.* Casey Robinson, Liam O'Brien; *Cast includes:* Tyrone Power, Patricia Neal, Stephen McNally, Hildegarde Neff, Karl Malden.

Spies and counterspies dominate this tangled web of intrigue set in Europe during the Cold War. Tyrone Power, as a diplomatic courier, is assigned by U.S. intelligence to contact an agent in Salzburg and get some secret papers. Power arrives at the depot, but his contact, Sam, an acquaintance from the past, refuses to recognize or acknowledge Power, who notices that the agent is being followed. Power follows Sam aboard another train, but before he can receive the important document, Sam is killed and his body thrown from the train.

The remainder of the film concerns Power's efforts to retrieve the document. An American C.I.D. colonel (Stephen McNally) is assigned to work with Power in finding the document. In Trieste, he tracks down a young woman (Hildegarde Neff), whom the murdered agent had contacted on the train and who is suspected of being a Soviet spy. Power confronts her with his suspicions. "I worked with them because Sam told me to," she admits. "For four years I worked for Sam as an agent—a spy, if you prefer." Later, the colonel explains the contents of the document. "Sam was bringing out with him the complete Communist timetable, including the date, for the invasion of Yugoslavia."

When the convoluted plot finally untangles, Power discovers that Neff has only been masquerading as a Soviet agent as a ploy to get to America. The couple eventually reunite. Patricia Neal, as a dizzy American tourist, is, in reality, a Russian spy who uses her sexual charms on Power. The Communists, it seems, want to get the document before it falls into western hands. The film, adapted from the novel *Sinister Errand* by Peter Cheyney, touches upon several contemporary themes. Neff, one of the countless uprooted Europeans, is written off by the American colonel as "just another casualty in this Cold War." Neal, as a sexually starved American, uses her role as Soviet spy to satisfy her personal needs while serving Moscow. Power, who sees himself as a "postman, not an intelligence man," represents the uninformed American who learns only from bitter experience about Soviet ruthlessness and the world of international intrigue. See Cold War. ■

Dishonored (1931), Par. *Dir.* Josef von Sternberg; *Sc.* Daniel Rubin; *Cast includes:* Marlene Dietrich, Victor McLaglen, Lew Cody, Warner Oland, Barry Norton.

Marlene Dietrich portrays an Austrian agent who chooses romance over duty in this World War I drama. When her husband, an Austrian captain, is killed in the war, she turns to prostitution. An Austrian intelligence chief (Gustav von Seyffertitz), noticing her at her trade in the dark streets of Vienna, believes she would make an effective agent. "I need a woman who knows how to deal with men," he explains. In a relatively short

Lobby card showing Austrian spy Marlene Dietrich about to make the fatal error of allowing her Russian enemy and lover, Victor McLaglen, to escape. *Dishonored* (1931).

time she becomes one of his top spies, known as X-27.

After exposing an Austrian officer (Warner Oland) as a double agent and traitor, she proceeds to her next assignment— the capture of a Russian spy (Victor McLaglen). She finally traps the infamous agent known as "The Fox." The only problem is that she has fallen in love with him. At the last minute, before his execution, she helps him to escape. For placing love before her loyalty to her country, she must face a firing squad. Before going to her death, she rejects her prison clothes for the attire she wore as a secret agent for her country. "Could you let me die in a uniform of my own choosing?" she requests of a visiting priest. "Any dress I was wearing when I served my countrymen, not my country," she explains. The sympathetic holy man brings her the outfit she wore as a prostitute. Standing emotionlessly before the firing squad, she performs her last two gestures—she lights a cigarette and adjusts her garter.

The film is a weak drama, but Dietrich brings romance and vitality to her role as the worldly and sensual spy, dominating most of the scenes. "I'm not afraid of life, although I'm not afraid of death either," she states to a policeman early in the film. Her appearance at secret service headquarters suggests that of a visiting dignitary; all the officers in the room are struck by her presence. When Oland, the Austrian double agent, relinquishes his sword to her, he says, "What a charming evening we might have had if you had not been a spy and I a traitor." "Then," she responds, "we might never have met." ■

Disraeli (1929), WB. *Dir.* Alfred E. Green; *Sc.* Julian Josephson; *Cast includes:* George Arliss, Joan Bennett, Florence Arliss, Anthony Bushell, David Torrence, Ivan Simpson.

Possession of the Suez Canal becomes the target of both Russia and England in this tale of international intrigue set in 1874 England. George Arliss, as Benjamin Disraeli, gives another of his film impersonations of historical figures. The film opens with Disraeli's efforts to have England purchase the Suez Canal from bankrupt Egypt. But his country's statesmen and leaders reject the move, labeling him an "undisciplined politician" and a "dangerous visionary."

Convinced that Russia is prepared to purchase the Canal as a stepping stone to India, Disraeli schemes to raise the money privately for the venture. Meanwhile, the Russian embassy unleashes several spies to report on Disraeli's every move. His secretary is one such agent whom Disraeli soon discovers. The secretary's wife, posing as a wealthy woman of position, is another spy who wins the confidence of Disraeli's wife so that she can be present at Disraeli's social functions. Following a series of setbacks, Disraeli appeals to a young lord's patriotism and idealism to join him in his efforts. At first the young man is hostile toward the statesman. But Disraeli is tenacious in winning him over. "Now is Russia's opportunity to snap up India," he explains. "With India lost, the whole fabric crumbles and England sinks into insignificance." The young man agrees to work as Disraeli's secretary and is soon sent to Cairo to purchase the Canal. The film ends with Queen Victoria's appreciation of Disraeli's coup.

The literate script and Arliss' trouping transcend the staginess of the script based on the play by Louis N. Parker.

Benjamin Disraeli, the Prime Minister who represented the epitome of British imperialism in the latter part of the nineteenth century, had his eye on the Suez Canal ever since its opening in 1869. Travel through the new Canal reduced the journey between Great Britain and India, which was previously routed around the Cape of Africa, by thousands of miles.

In 1875 the majority of shares of the Suez Canal Company were owned by French nationals and the Khedive of Egypt who had mortgaged them until 1895. In November 1875, the Khedive, who was perhaps the most conspicuous consumer of his time, was badly in need of money. He was in deep negotiations for the sale of his shares when Disraeli, who viewed the Suez Canal as a political and military asset, learned of the situation. Negotiations soon began between the French foreign minister, who, along with other French leaders, viewed the Canal as a commercial liability, and the British foreign

secretary. On November 23 the Khedive acceded to sell his shares to the Government of Great Britain for four million pounds.

Disraeli still had to find the money for the Khedive and, since Parliament was not in session, he had to borrow the funds. The Prime Minister turned to one of the few private British bankers able to provide the capital at short notice—Baron Rothschild—who immediately supplied the cash. Despite the public's conception that Disraeli had snared a controlling interest for Great Britain in the Suez Canal Company, this was not the case. The Khedive's mortgaged shares amounted to somewhat less that half of the total and did not entitle him to voting rights until 1895. Nevertheless, Disraeli's purchase would henceforth provide Great Britain with a legitimate vested claim in the operation of the Suez Canal. ■

Docks of New York (1945), Mon. *Dir.* Wallace Fox; *Sc.* Harvey Gates; *Cast includes:* Leo Gorcey, Huntz Hall, Billy Benedict, Bud Gorman, Gloria Pope, Carlyle Blackwell, Jr.

The perennial East Side Kids find themselves entangled in a plot involving a European princess, foreign agents and a gang of jewel thieves in this comedy. The boys' misadventures begin when they find a necklace. They then become the target of murderers and police and, at one point, are arrested and put behind bars. After they are released, Muggs (Leo Gorcey), Gimpy (Huntz Hall) and their pals swing into action and end up capturing the villains. Cy Kendall portrays the leader of the killers. Carlyle Blackwell, Jr. and Gloria Pope provide the love interest. ■

Doing Their Bit (1918), Fox. *Dir.* Kenean Buel; *Sc.* Kenean Buel; *Cast includes:* Jane Lee, Katherine Lee, Franklyn Hanna, Gertrude Le Brandt, Alex Hall, Beth Ivins.

A comedy drama set during World War I, the film opens in Ireland where two children are left orphans when their father dies in battle in France. The two young sisters (Jane and Katherine Lee) are shipped to America to live with an uncle who owns a munitions plant. The kids soon help to expose a group of spies who are plotting against the factory.

Released several months prior to the Armistice, the film is unique in one sense and representative in another. Except for Charlie Chaplin's *Shoulder Arms*, released the same year, and several others, war comedies were not usually made until after the conflict. But the film was typical of the home-front films. It emphasized the patriotic role of women who did their bit at home while their men bravely manned the trenches in France. ■

Domino Principle, The (1977), Avco. *Dir.* Stanley Kramer; *Sc.* Adam Kennedy; *Cast includes:* Gene Hackman, Candice Bergen, Richard Widmark, Mickey Rooney, Edward Albert, Eli Wallach.

A shadowy international organization specializing in political intrigue recruits amoral types to carry out its biddings, including assassination, in this slow-paced drama. Gene Hackman, as a potentially violent ex-con, attracts some of the leaders of the secret group. Judging him as a likely candidate for future assassinations, they hire him for a particularly important job. After he is trained for his imminent assignment, which includes practice in executing his intended victim by helicopter, he suddenly realizes that he has been designated to kill the President. When he refuses to carry out the assignment, he in turn is killed by members of the group. Candice Bergen portrays his bewildered wife. Mickey Rooney, as his alleged pal who served time with him, in reality is in the employ of the organization. The film, adapted from the novel by Adam Kennedy, is representative of several dramas of the period which reflected overtones of betrayal, cynicism and conspiracy. ■

Don Winslow of the Coast Guard (1943) serial, U. *Dir.* Ray Taylor, Lewis D. Collins; *Sc.* Paul Huston, George Plympton, Griffin Jay; *Cast includes:* Don Terry, Walter Sande, Elyse Knox, Philip Ahn, June Duprez, Edgar Dearing.

The stalwart U.S. Navy officer Don Winslow once again battles "The Scorpion," the master spy who is plotting with the Japanese in this 13-chapter serial, a sequel to *Don Winslow of the Navy* (1942). While Winslow, played again by Don Terry, and the Coast Guard are trying to keep the Pacific coast free of enemy submarines and acts of sabotage, the enemy is trying to prevent U.S. war materiel from reaching the South Pacific. Navy brass transfers Winslow to the Coast Guard to foil the sinister Scorpion (Nestor Paiva) and his underlings. Walter Sande returns in his role as Winslow's sidekick. See Serials. ■

Don Winslow of the Navy (1942) serial, U. *Dir.* Ray Taylor, Ford Beebe; *Sc.* Paul Huston, Griffin Jay; *Cast includes:* Don Terry, Walter Sande, John Litel, Wade Boteler, Samuel S. Hinds, Claire Dodd.

Don Terry, as the popular comic strip character Don Winslow, battles a sinister spy ring operating from a Pacific island in this 12-chapter World War II serial. Walter Sande, as Winslow's buddy, shares the perilous situations thrust upon the two seamen each week as they seek to expose the Scorpion (Kurt Hutch), the elusive mastermind behind the gang of enemy agents. The Japanese leader dispatches his plots by way of his chief henchman, played by John Litel. Claire Dodd and Anne Nagel decorate the screen in an otherwise all-male cast. Wade Boteler portrays a U.S. Navy intelligence expert, and the venerable character actor Samuel H. Hinds is in charge of Uncle Sam's Pacific fleet in this action-packed serial designed chiefly for juveniles. See Serials. ■

Donovan, William J. "Wild Bill" (1883– 1959). A graduate of Columbia University and a lawyer, he got his nickname "Wild Bill" as a result of heroic service as an officer with the famous 69th New York regiment in World War I that earned him several medals. George Brent portrayed the role of Donovan, a major character, in *The Fighting 69th* (1940). Donovan was appointed in 1941 by President Franklin D. Roosevelt to head the Office of Strategic Services (O.S.S.), the agency responsible for espionage, intelligence and sabotage during World War II. He staffed his organization with a wide range of people that included bankers, lawyers, actors, college professors and even acrobats. Donovan welded the disparate group into an effective organization that conducted many successful operations behind enemy lines during World War II in Europe and the Far East. He was an effective administrator and displayed an ability to inspire unswerving loyalty from his staff. His unorthodox methods often put him in conflict with regular military personnel and career civil servants. He was given the rank of major general for his work.

Although he was never impersonated as a major character in a Hollywood film, he has been mentioned in several dramas, including *Scorpio* (1973) and *Three Days of the Condor* (1975), as an almost legendary figure. See Office of Strategic Services; U.S. Intelligence: World War II. ■

Don't Drink the Water (1969), Avco. *Dir.* Howard Morris; *Sc.* R. S. Allen, Harvey Bullock; *Cast includes:* Jackie Gleason, Estelle Parsons, Joan Delaney, Richard Libertini, Michael Constantine, Avery Schrieber.

An American family is held hostage in an Iron Curtain country in this farce based on Woody Allen's stage play. Jackie Gleason, as a Newark kosher caterer traveling reluctantly with his wife and daughter in Europe, cannot get excited about the sites of the old world. "If you like ruins," he mutters about his family's anticipated stop in Greece, "take a look at my business when you get back." At one point he is mistaken for a spy when he goes about snapping pictures. As hostages in Communist Vulgaria, the family has some madcap misadventures as they seek asylum in the American embassy.

All the comic trappings are unleashed in this romp, including chases, slapstick, one-liners and oddball characters. Estelle Parsons, as Gleason's featherbrained wife, adds to the nonsense. When their plane is hijacked to a Communist country, she radiates with joy for "a last chance to see an enslaved nation before the tourists take over." Joan Delaney portrays their sexually aware teenage daughter. "Danger really turns me on," she confides to an ambassador's bumbling son. "Do you know how many babies were born during the blitz?" Richard Libertine, as a loony priest who has lived within the confines of the U.S. embassy for six years as a political refugee, practices magic ineptly as he prances about the building. Mark Gordon portrays a C.I.A. agent who looks more like an underworld hit man. Michael Constantine, as a member of Vulgaria's secret police, organizes spontaneous student protests using middle-aged citizens. See Central Intelligence Agency. ■

Doomed Battalion, The (1932), U. *Dir.* Cyril Gardner; *Sc.* Luis Trenker, Carl Hartl; *Cast includes:* Tala Birell, Luis Trenker, Victor Varconi, Albert Conti, Henry Gordon, Henry Armetta.

A World War I drama shot on location in the Austrian Tryrol, the plot concerns an Austrian battalion holding a vital mountain-top stronghold that is being mined by an attacking Italian army. The doomed defenders are ordered to hold their position at all costs. Victor Varconi, as the commander of the Italian soldiers, stations himself at the home of his old friend, currently a scout (Luis Trenker) fighting with the besieged troops. Trenker skis down the mountain and penetrates the enemy lines to learn the exact time the Italians plan to set off the explosions. He is the last hope for the soldiers guarding the stronghold.

The film had been made previously in Germany with Trenker as its author and in the same role. Perhaps this explains why Austrians are portrayed as heroic figures in the film—an unusual role for them in a Hollywood production. It was remade again in 1940 as *Ski Patrol.* The incident involving the undermining of an enemy position with explosives was based on an actual event that occurred during the war, except that the victims were the Italians. The Germans dug a tunnel beneath the Italian trenches and blew them up, killing the occupants. A similar situation appeared in the 1936 World War I drama *The Road to Glory,* directed by Howard Hawks. ■

Double agents. The clandestine activities of double agents throughout history have been well documented. They have also fascinated movie audiences since the early silent period. Some present and former members of official intelligence organizations make a distinction between the double agent and the penetration agent. They define the former as a citizen of a third country who provides information to agents of two other or opposing countries. The penetration agent, on the other hand, is a member of one government intelligence service who works undercover for another government. Kermit Roosevelt, in his book *War Report of the OSS* (1976), describes double agents as ". . . captured agents who would be persuaded to continue their activities for the enemy. . . ." We have taken the broader, more popular definition of the term.

Generally, the real-life exploits of these men and women who played the most dangerous espionage game of all proved more exciting than their fictitious counterparts. Some of their exploits have been tapped as plots for intriguing films. Others have yet to be discovered.

The double agent in American history appears as early as the American Revolution. Benjamin Church, an army doctor during the

Revolution, was a double agent who worked for the Committee of Correspondence in Boston but whose real allegiance lay with the British. He provided the British with precise information regarding weapons caches and movement of troops. A handful of films cover this period. In *The Scarlet Coat* (1955), for instance, Cornel Wilde portrays a fictitious American spy and double agent who is trying to uncover the traitorous Benedict Arnold.

World War I provided a stream of spy plots about double agents, some based on actual personalities, others purely figures of fantasy. Francis Ford portrays an American flier employed by the secret service in the World War I drama *Berlin via America* (1918). Posing as a traitor to his country, he gains the confidence of Prussian spies and is transported to Germany. He soon begins dropping messages by air to the Allies concerning imminent enemy advances. Ben Lyon, as an Englishman educated in Germany, becomes a double agent working for England in *The Great Deception* (1926). He travels between the two countries providing German headquarters with false information while supplying Britain with valuable intelligence. Dolores Del Rio, as a German agent in the World War I drama *Lancer Spy* (1937), aids an English double agent (George Sanders) with whom she has fallen in love.

Women played double agents more often than men. Dolores Cassinelli in the World War I drama *Lafayette, We Come!* (1918) portrays a young Frenchwoman who, as a double agent, has dealings with German spies, but in reality works for the Americans. Margaret Lindsay, as a double agent in the World War I drama *British Intelligence* (1940), poses as a German spy to learn the identity of the leader of the enemy agents relaying British military strategy to Berlin. In *Mata Hari* (1985) the famed *femme fatale* is arrested as a German spy and volunteers her services as a double agent for the French.

World War II created the same fears for both the Allied and Axis countries concerning double agents. J. Edgar Hoover, as chief of the Federal Bureau of Investigation, had been authorized in 1937 by President Roosevelt to conduct anti-subversive surveillance. The F.B.I. enlisted a number of German expatriates, including William Sebold. Sebold had been born in Germany and, under F.B.I. tutelage, became a double agent. As a result of his activities, the F.B.I. in 1940 arrested 32 German agents operating in the U.S. and brought German espionage here to a halt.

The British, meanwhile, uncovered and caught virtually every German spy, sometimes effectively turning these captives into double agents. This feat went unequaled by any other Allied or Axis power during the war. Britain began its intricate intelligence operations as early as 1936. One of London's key operatives was an English double agent whom the Germans trusted implicitly. Using a wireless that the Germans supplied, he soon began transmitting vital codes and names of German spies.

Ironically, one valuable "walk-in" during World War II, Dr. Fritz Kolbe, a German foreign ministry official, was rejected by British intelligence as a possible double agent. Kolbe, a professed anti-Nazi, was determined to turn over his large stack of copies of secret documents and telegrams to the Allies. He handed them to the Americans, instead, and soon proved to be one of the most useful secret agents ever to fall into the hands of American intelligence.

Hollywood cranked out many World War II dramas about double agents during the conflict. George Sanders in *Appointment in Berlin* (1943) portrays such an operative. Secretly enlisted into the British secret service, he collaborates with German agents and is sent to Berlin where he broadcasts anti-British propaganda. His programs, however, are so written as to transmit vital information to the British War Office. Warren William, as the Lone Wolf, plays a double agent in *Passport to Suez* (1943). He joins a Nazi spy ring in Egypt in an effort to retrieve stolen plans concerning the Suez Canal. Richard Quine portrays a double agent in the World War II drama *We've Never Been Licked* (1943). As a student at Texas A & M, he becomes unpopular when he takes up the Japanese cause. Quine journeys to Japan and broadcasts Japanese propaganda to the U.S. and elsewhere. In reality, he secretly sends military information to American intelligence. Victor Francen, as chief of the German legation in Lisbon, plays a double agent in the drama *The Conspirators* (1944). Working for the Germans while masquerading as a member of an anti-Nazi spy ring, he is finally exposed and killed.

The double-agent formula proved so successful that it was continued well after the war. Richard Conte in *13 Rue Madeleine*

(1946), portrays a Nazi officer who secretly trains with the O.S.S. to learn the location of the forthcoming Allied invasion of France. Clark Gable in *Betrayed* (1954) portrays a Dutch intelligence agent who is captured and interrogated by the head of German intelligence. He is offered a chance to work as a double agent for the Nazis. "For men like us," the German explains, "there's no higher achievement than to be the master spy—the double agent." Gable, however, refuses. In *The Enemy General* (1960) Van Johnson, as an O.S.S. agent, is assigned to smuggle a Nazi officer, who in reality is a double agent, out of Europe and escort him safely to England. Robert Goulet portrays a double agent who infiltrates the Nazi organization by posing as an American traitor in *I Deal in Danger* (1966).

Women once again played an important role as double agents in post-World War I spy dramas. Constance Bennett portrays an American double agent in the World War II drama *Madame Spy* (1942). Sylvia Sidney, as a double agent in *Blood on the Sun* (1945), set in Japan during the 1920s, is employed by Japanese officials to recover important stolen plans from newspaper reporter James Cagney. In reality, she is working for the Chinese who want to expose the Japanese militarists. Patricia Morison, as a nightclub singer in the Cold War drama *Sofia* (1948), is a double agent who exchanges information with both Western and East bloc spies. Anita Bjork portrays a double agent working for the Communists in the Cold War drama *Night People* (1954). Angie Dickinson in *China Gate* (1957), a drama about the French Indo-China War, portrays a Eurasian double agent posing as a Red sympathizer. Annamarie Duringer, as a Dutch underground agent in *Count Five and Die* (1958), a suspense drama set in World War II, turns out to be a double agent working for the Nazis. Danielle Aubry plays a French spy in the Vietnam War suspense drama *Operation CIA* (1965). In reality, she is a double agent working with local terrorists. Diane Keaton, as a double agent in *The Little Drummer Girl* (1984), has as her Israeli mission to locate and help annihilate a dangerous Palestinian terrorist (Sami Frey).

The Cold War witnessed the almost obsessive dependence upon agents and double agents, intelligence and disinformation, defection and debriefing—all of which precipitated the world's most sophisticated secret intelligence empires. *I Was a Communist for the FBI* (1951) was based on the true story of Matt Cvetic, who posed as a Communist for nine years. Frank Lovejoy, as the double agent, exposes various Communist plots before H.U.A.C. Gene Barry, as an American C.I.A. agent, is assigned to ferret out a British double agent operating in England in the drama *Subterfuge* (1969). Lee Remick portrays a double agent working for the U.S. in the suspense drama *Telefon* (1977). She joins forces with Charles Bronson, as a Soviet agent, both of whom are trying to stop a plot involving a war between the two world powers. A C.I.A. boss in *Target* (1985) in reality is a double agent who has killed the wife and children of a German citizen to protect his own cover.

The C.I.A.'s paranoia about double agents may best be demonstrated by its abusive treatment of the defector Yuri Nosenko, a K.G.B. officer. In 1964 he escaped to the U.S. carrying an abundance of vital information. The C.I.A., however, suspected that he might have been a plant to spread disinformation and discredit previous fellow defectors. The agency secretly transferred him to a remote area in Virginia, removed all his clothes and tossed him into a small cell without windows where he remained a prisoner for more than three years. Unable to wring a confession from him, Nosenko was finally released. In all those years he was never officially accused of a crime or put on trial. ■

Teenager Dan Dailey and his sister Bonita Granville are confronted by enemy agents interested in a local naval base in this World War II drama. *Down in San Diego* (1941).

Down in San Diego (1941), MGM. *Dir.* Robert Sinclair; *Sc.* Harry Clark, Franz Spencer; *Cast includes:* Ray McDonald, Bonita

Granville, Dan Dailey, Leo Gorcey, Joe Sawyer.

Teenagers break up a spy ring in this below-average World War II comedy drama set
chiefly around a naval base. Ray McDonald
and Bonita Granville are teamed up as the
romantic leads. Dan Dailey, as Granville's
brother, gets into trouble in this weakly plotted film that depends too heavily on chases,
repetitious dialogue and a silly juvenile love
story before the enemy agents are finally
caught. Among the several veteran character
actors who try to help things along are tough-
guy Joe Sawyer and the venerable Henry
O'Neill in his 100th screen role. The film was
originally titled *Young Americans*. ■

Dr. Goldfoot and the Bikini Machine

(1965), AI. *Dir*. Norman Taurog; *Sc*. Elwood
Ullman, Robert Kaufman; *Cast includes:* Vincent Price, Frankie Avalon, Dwayne Hickman, Susan Hart, Jack Mullaney, Fred Clark.

Vincent Price portrays a mad scientist out
to control the world in this zany spoof of the
spy film genre. To accomplish his wild
dream, he sets up a laboratory where he turns
out female androids—human-looking robots
that are used to seduce important men.
Frankie Avalon, as a neophyte secret agent,
eventually puts an end to Price's ambitious
scheme. Fred Clark portrays Avalon's frantic,
bureaucratic boss. Susan Hart, as one of
Price's manufactured creatures, tries to ensnare a rich playboy (Dwayne Hickman). Jack
Mullaney portrays the scientist's wacky assistant who works in the laboratory filled
with esoteric apparatus. An inept Italian-pro-
duced sequel, *Dr. Goldfoot and the Girl
Bombs*, with Vincent Price and Fabian, appeared later the same year. ■

Draft 258 (1918), Metro. *Dir*. W. Christy Ca-
banne; *Sc*. June Mathis; *Cast includes:* Mabel
Taliaferro, Walter Miller, Earle Brunswick,
Eugene Borden, Sue Balfour, William H.
Tooker.

A World War I propaganda film, the story
concerns the lives of a variety of humble people. An Italian vendor adopts a Belgian war
orphan whose family was killed by the Germans. A mother breaks up a pacifist meeting
that her son is attending. Slackers are shown
hastily marrying to avoid answering their
country's call to duty. Enemy conspirators
who plot to disrupt the draft by dissuading

young men from fighting are rounded up by
the American cavalry. ■

Assassin David Patrick Kelly (l.) enters a nightmare
of the President of the U.S. (Eddie Albert) while
Dennis Quaid (r.) prepares to protect the Commander in Chief. *Dreamscape* (1984).

Dreamscape (1984), TCF. *Dir*. Joe Ruben;
Sc. David Loughery, Chuck Russell, Joe
Ruben; *Cast includes:* Dennis Quaid, Max
von Sydow, Christopher Plummer, Eddie Albert, Kate Capshaw, David Patrick Kelly.

An extreme right-wing government official
who heads a special "covert intelligence" operation hatches a far-fetched plot to assassinate the U.S. President in this science fiction
drama. In charge of a clandestine government
program involving dream experiments,
Christopher Plummer conspires to use the
consciousness of one of the subjects to infiltrate the nightmares of the Chief Executive
(Eddie Albert) and kill him. The President
has been having recurring nightmares about
nuclear devastation which he believes he
will be responsible for. "It's my responsibility," he confides to Plummer, whom he considers a close friend, "to bring the world back
from the brink. This nuclear madness has to
end. I'm going to make a disarmament deal
with the Russians."

The ultra-conservative Plummer realizes
he must find a way to stop the President. He
later expresses his discontent to the scientist
(Max von Sydow) in charge of the program.
"He's going to emasculate our nuclear deterrent and bring our whole damn country to its
knees." Ruthless in his goal, he has his special agents kill a snooping writer who suspects Plummer's motives in bringing the
President to the scientist's campus laboratory
and later orders the scientist's death. Plum-

mer selects one of his underlings (David Patrick Kelly), a mentally unstable psychopath who has been working with the scientist, to enter the President's dream and assassinate him. However, Dennis Quaid, as an ex-psychic who reluctantly has returned to the dream program, discovers the plot and also enters the President's nightmare. Quaid and Kelly, representing the forces of good and evil respectively, confront each other in the hellish, apocalyptic world that the President has conjured up, and the battle results in Kelly's death. Kate Capshaw portrays the scientist's assistant in this drama that concentrates on the phenomenon of "dreamlinking," the psychic overlapping of one's consciousness onto another sleeping person's subconscious. ■

U.S. Navy intelligence agent Don Terry (r.) protects Ona Munson from spies in the Congo who are interested in a rare metal. *Drums of the Congo* (1942).

Drums of Fu Manchu (1940) serial, Rep. *Dir.* William Witney, John English; *Sc.* Franklyn Adreon, Morgan L. Cox, Ronald Davidson, Norman S. Hall, Barney A. Sarecky, Sol Shor; *Cast includes:* Henry Brandon, William Royle, Robert Kellard, Gloria Franklin, Olaf Hytten, Tom Chatterton.

Henry Brandon, as the infamous and sinister Fu Manchu, seeks his usual quest of world domination in this 15-chapter serial based on the fictional characters created by Sax Rohmer. Heading a secret network of agents, all fanatic followers of his cause, Fu Manchu attempts to ignite a war in Central Asia. His usual nemesis, Sir Nayland Smith, played by William Royle, has his hands full trying to foil his archenemy. Luana Walters provides some romantic interest in this better-than-average serial. See Serials. ■

Drums of the Congo (1942), U. *Dir.* Christy Cabanne; *Sc.* Roy Chanslor; *Cast includes:* Ona Munson, Stuart Erwin, Peggy Moran, Don Terry, Richard Lane, Jules Bledsoe.

A U.S. Navy intelligence officer searches for a rare and precious metal in Africa's Congo in this routine World War II drama.

However, Don Terry, as the American, faces several obstacles. Enemy agents would also like to get their hands on this particularly hard substance. Aside from several clashes with the spies, Terry is confronted with the savage beasts who lurk in the jungle around him. Ona Munson, as an African doctor who elects to help Terry, provides the romantic element. Richard Lane and Peggy Moran portray enemy spies determined to prevent Terry and Munson from accomplishing their mission. Stuart Erwin supplies some comedy relief. ■

Dugan of the Dugouts (1928), Anchor. *Dir.* Robert Roy; *Sc.* Robert Roy; *Cast includes:* Pauline Garon, Danny O'Shea, Ernest Hilliard, J. P. McGowan, Sid Smith.

A World War I comedy drama about a young man who joins up because his sweetheart likes a particular sergeant, the film features Danny O'Shea as the hapless hero. Danny wants to be a sergeant just like his rival, getting salutes, giving orders and winning back his girl. Events swing around in his favor when the sergeant is arrested as a spy. Several laughs are interspersed throughout this minor feature. ■

E

Eagle and the Hawk, The (1950), Par. Dir. Lewis R. Foster; *Sc.* Geoffrey Homes, Lewis R. Foster; *Cast includes:* John Payne, Rhonda Fleming, Dennis O'Keefe, Thomas Gomez, Fred Clark, Frank Faylen.

Agents of Napoleon III, as part of their plot to make Maximilian the emperor of Mexico, attempt to instigate the followers of Juarez to declare war on Texas in this action drama set in 1863. John Payne, as a Texas Ranger, is assigned to escort a government agent, played by Dennis O'Keefe, into Mexico. O'Keefe's job is to foil the impending attack on the Lone Star State. They try to warn a patriotic Mexican general (Thomas Gomez), a staunch supporter of Juarez, that the chief foreign agent (Fred Clark) is using the general to carry out French interests, not Mexican. When the two Americans try to get proof of their charges, Payne is captured by Clark. O'Keefe rescues him but is himself seriously hurt in the attempt. He takes his own life, leaving Payne to carry on for him. Rhonda Fleming, as Clark's wife, falls in love with Payne and assists him in exposing her husband's plot to the general. Clark tries to make a getaway but is followed by Payne and the general, the latter sacrificing his life to bring Clark to justice. "He would have been a great man," another loyal Mexican says to Payne about the dead general. "He was a patriot," Payne replies. "Could he have been any greater?" The film was adapted from the story "A Mission to General Houston" by Jess Arnold.

Although the basic plot is pure fiction, the historical background has some basis in fact. When Emperor Maximilian of Mexico died before a firing squad on June 19, 1867, outside Queretaro, Mexico, several hopes died with him. His death ended his naive and con-

tradictory goals of establishing a liberal Mexican monarchy based on conservative support and foreign arms. Also buried with Maximilian was the grandiose scheme of French Emperor Napoleon III to rebuild a French empire in the New World.

The Austrian Archduke Ferdinand Maximilian came to the throne of Mexico as a result of the machinations of Mexican conservatives and Napoleon III of France, a nephew of the French military leader. Mexicans opposed to the liberal reforms of Juarez convinced both Maximilian and Napoleon III that a strong monarchy would gain the support of many Mexicans tired of the disorder that plagued their country. Napoleon saw an opportunity to extend his influence in North America and offered the throne to Maximilian. Maximilian was crowned Emperor of Mexico in 1864 after French troops had driven Juarez and his republican forces out of the capital.

Maximilian's collapse was due as much to events outside Mexico as to his inability to rally popular support. The U.S., which had been involved in its own Civil War at the time, considered France's action as a violation of the Monroe Doctrine. With the end of the American Civil War in 1865, the U.S. threatened military intervention in Mexico unless France withdrew. Meanwhile, Napoleon III faced the growing threat of a European war and withdrew his troops from Mexico by March 1867. Though given the opportunity to leave with them, Maximilian determined to stay with his small native army and fight for his beliefs. Juarez easily defeated the military remnants of his monarchist opponents. Maximilian was captured and executed after a military trial. Again, *Juarez* portrays him as a tragic figure.

Several other films deal with this turbulent period. Maximilian's tragic story is faithfully covered in *Juarez* (1939) with Brian Aherne as the emperor and Paul Muni as Juarez, the Mexican revolutionary who defeated him. The drama captures much of the historical and personal conflict of the period. *Stronghold* (1952), a contrived love story involving Americans in Mexico, has no connection to historical events. George Macready portrays Maximilian in *Vera Cruz* (1954), a cynical and fictitious tale about trust and betrayal during the Juaristas' attempts to free their country from the emperor's grip. ■

Eagle of the Sea (1926), Par. *Dir.* Frank Lloyd; *Sc.* Julian Josephson; *Cast includes:* Ricardo Cortez, Frances Vidor, Sam De Grasse, Andre Beranger, Mitchell Lewis, Guy Oliver.

This early-19th-century tale of intrigue involves a plot to free Napoleon from his exile on the island of St. Helena as well as instigate another war between England and the U.S. so that Spain can gain control of New Orleans. Sam De Grasse portrays the Spanish agent who has helped to hatch the scheme. He tries to hire a notorious pirate, Captain Sazarac (Ricardo Cortez), to lead the mission, but the latter has no interest in plotting against the U.S. When De Grasse's niece (Frances Vidor), who has overheard her uncle's offer, threatens to expose him, he has her kidnapped and taken aboard a merchant ship. The pirate follows in his ship and rescues her after a sea battle with a Spanish galleon.

According to the script, the pirate had years earlier helped Andrew Jackson defeat the English at the Battle of New Orleans in the War of 1812. Pardoned by Jackson, the pirate and his crew later resorted to their former occupation—much to the dismay of General Jackson. In these respects the character Sazarac seems to be drawn from the real-life pirate Jean Lafitte. The film was adapted from the novel *Captain Sazarac* by Charles Tenney Jackson. ■

Eagle's Eye, The (1918) serial, Wharton. *Dir.* George A. Lessey, Wellington Playter; *Cast includes:* King Baggot, Marguerite Snow, William N. Bailey, Florence Short, Bertram Marburgh, Paul Everton.

This World War I serial told the story (in 20 chapters) of German spies operating within the borders of the U.S. The plot dealt with the efforts of the "Criminology Club," made up of a group of loyal Americans, to combat the various plots of German agents working under cover. Besides depicting virtually all the possible acts of espionage and sabotage enemy agents are capable of carrying out, the lengthy serial, in its patriotic fervor, unfavorable characterizations of such German figures as Franz von Papen and Heinrich Albert—previously exposed as secret agents. Based on a story by William J. Flynn, a former U.S. Secret Service chief, the serial was banned by one film chain (Loews) which considered some of the sequences slanderous to loyal German-Americans. See British Intelligence: World War I; German Intelligence: World War I. ■

Eagle's Wing, The (1916), Bluebird. *Dir.* Rufus Steele; *Sc.* Maud Grange; *Cast includes:* Grace Carlyle, Vola Smith, Herbert Rawlinson, Charles Hill Mailes, Rodney Ronous, Charles Gunn.

Foreign agents supply information to their respective countries about America's military preparedness in this World War I propaganda drama. When the two spies (Charles Gunn, Albert McQuarrie) learn that a defense bill recently passed by Congress will leave the U.S. vulnerable to invasion for at least two years, they report the news to their own unnamed powers. However, the President of the U.S. has his own ideas and devises a plan that will place the nation on an almost instant war footing. The spies, learning about this new development, quickly contact their governments, recommending them not to invade.

Although the United States officially remained neutral, its citizens had already chosen sides in the war that raged in Europe. Stories of Prussian atrocities in Belgium, German subversion in the U.S. and a procession of anti-German and preparedness films in local theaters drove most Americans into the arms of the English and French. The U.S. government gave the film studio permission to include several scenes depicting the manufacture of munitions. Allegedly, members of President Woodrow Wilson's Cabinet and National Defense Council saw the film when it was shown in Washington, D.C. ■

Earhart, Amelia. See *Flight for Freedom* (1943). ■

Eiger Sanction, The (1975), U. *Dir.* Clint Eastwood; *Sc.* Hal Dressner, Warren B. Murphy, Rod Whitaker; *Cast includes:* Clint Eastwood, George Kennedy, Vonetta McGee, Jack Cassidy, Heidi Bruhl, Thayer David.

Clint Eastwood portrays a retired mountain climber and former assassin who is called back to duty by a secret intelligence agency for another assignment in this well-paced revenge drama set chiefly in Switzerland. His mission, which he accepts, includes eliminating two killers who have murdered one of Eastwood's fellow agents. He slays one, but the other proves more difficult to locate and identify. The only clue is that he is a member of an international mountain-climbing team. To complete his task, he journeys to Arizona to practice for the climbing. He then returns, finds his prey and, after some suspenseful dueling with the enemy agent, accomplishes his task. Vonetta McGee, as another fellow agent, falls in love with Eastwood. George Kennedy portrays Eastwood's Arizona friend and ranch owner. Jack Cassidy plays the troublesome agent whose murderous career Eastwood finally ends. The film is based on Trevanian's novel. ■

Eleventh Hour, The (1923), Fox. *Dir.* Bernard J. Durning; *Sc.* Louis Sherwin; *Cast includes:* Shirley Mason, Charles "Buck" Jones, Richard Tucker, Alan Hale, Walter McGrail.

Cowboy star Buck Jones puts aside his western paraphernalia in this drama to portray an undercover agent for the U.S. Secret Service. He maneuvers his way into a network of alien agents headed by a power-hungry prince who is seeking to steal the formula for a powerful explosive. The prince (Alan Hale), who owns a submarine and other means of transportation, unleashes his villainous underlings against the inventor of the explosive and his niece (Shirley Mason).

Meanwhile, the scientist, who has unknowingly squandered his niece's inheritance, falls under the power of his partner who has his own ulterior motive. He desires to wed the pretty niece. However, Jones foils the entire plot and rescues the heroine who has fallen into the hands of the villain. The film was adapted from the play by Lincoln J. Carter. ■

Elusive Isabel (1916), Bluebird. *Dir.* Stuart Paton; *Sc.* Raymond L. Schrock; *Cast includes:* Florence Lawrence, Sydney Bracey, Harry Millarde, Wallace Clarke, William Welsh.

The U.S. Secret Service uncovers a plot on the part of Latin-speaking countries to take control of the U.S. Harry Millarde, as a secret service agent, is assigned to foil the conspiracy, whose members are meeting secretly in the States. Florence Lawrence, as a secret agent working for the cabal, falls in love with Millarde, who manages to prevent the conspirators from carrying out its plans. The original novel was written by Jacques Futrelle, one of the passengers who perished aboard the Titanic. ■

Emergency Landing (1941), PRC. *Dir.* William Beaudine; *Sc.* Martin Mooney; *Cast includes:* Forrest Tucker, Carol Hughes, Evelyn Brent, Emmett Vogan, William Halligan, George Sherwood.

Enemy agents harass an airplane plant in this unexceptional drama that takes place before America's entry into World War II. William Halligan, as an airplane magnate and owner of the plant, has to contend with domestic problems as well. Forrest Tucker, as a test pilot, helps his pal, another airman who has developed a radio-controlled aircraft, get a test flight. The experiment ends in failure, and the plane crashes. A skittish heiress (Carol Hughes) enters the scene and promises to help the two fliers. The plot involving the enemy agents drops into the background as the two friends are forced to deal with Hughes' whims. ■

Emperor's Candlesticks, The (1937), MGM. *Dir.* George Fitzmaurice; *Sc.* Monckton Hoffe, Harold Goldman; *Cast includes:* William Powell, Luise Rainer, Robert Young, Maureen O'Sullivan, Frank Morgan, Henry Stephenson.

Intrigue, missing documents and kidnapping all play a role in this lavishly produced romantic drama set chiefly in pre-World War I Vienna. The film opens in Vienna at a gala masked ball where Polish patriots plot the kidnapping of a young Russian grand duke (Robert Young), the son of the czar, whom they intend to exchange for the release of a Polish political prisoner who has been sentenced to die in 15 days. Young is led into the kidnappers' hands by the prisoner's attractive daughter (Maureen O'Sullivan) and forced to write a note to his father, the emperor, to release the condemned man. The young duke, who has come to Vienna in search of romance and adventure, understands little of the political conflict between his country and Poland. "You and your father," one of his Polish captors (Douglas Dumbrille) exclaims, trying to enlighten him, "and your father's father for 150 years have throttled our country, have tortured and imprisoned us!" But the bulk of the film focuses on romance rather than politics.

William Powell, as a Polish secret agent posing as a debonair aristocrat, is assigned to smuggle the letter into Russia past the Russian secret police. Meanwhile, Luise Rainer, as a Russian spy, is assigned by her superior to deliver secret papers condemning Powell to death as soon as he crosses the Russian border. Both Powell and Rainer are passengers on the same train bound for St. Petersburg. For reasons of safety and unknown to each other, they hide their documents in a pair of candlesticks, each containing a secret compartment. Complications arise when the candlesticks are stolen. The two spies, after some cat-and-mouse games, eventually join forces in searching for their respective documents. At the same time, they fall in love with each other. After some desperate situations, events turn out favorably for the couple, who are pardoned by the czar himself. "There is one thing that moves us deeply," he says when the two spies are summoned before him, "the bravery and generosity of love. It is because these qualities are so evident in this room that has seen so much of qualities far different that you are pardoned." The film, based on a novel by Baroness Orczy, evokes a charming world of royalty that came crashing down with the advent of World War I. ∎

Enemy Agent (1940), U. *Dir*. Lew Landers; *Sc*. Sam Robins, Edmund L. Hartman; *Cast includes*: Richard Cromwell, Helen Vinson, Robert Armstrong, Marjorie Reynolds, Jack Arnold, Russell Hicks.

When secret agents of a foreign power steal the army's new bombsight, the F.B.I. is called in on the case in this World War II drama. At first, the investigators accuse an innocent defense plant draftsman, played by Richard Cromwell, but by the end of the tale they are on the trail of the real culprits. The film concludes with an offbeat sequence in which the F.B.I. members pose as half-drunk college students. They force their way into the home of the chief of the spies and begin a football game. When the rest of the enemy agents are summoned, the F.B.I. boys round them all up.

Released during World War II but before America's entry into the conflict, this film and many others of the period hesitated to identify the national origins of their foreign spies. The studios, attempting to remain neutral, did not want to alienate any of their lucrative foreign markets. American audiences, however, drew the obvious conclusions. The foreign accents and names of these nefarious agents often suggested their Teutonic backgrounds.

The plot concerning the theft of the bombsight approximates an actual incident during the war. Perhaps the most important bombsight mentioned during World War II was the legendary Norden bombsight—a secret device heavily guarded by the U.S. military and much coveted by Nazi agents. Hermann Lang, an inspector at the Norden factory, one night removed the plans for the bombsight and copied them. He then turned the copy over to Nikolaus Ritter, the head of a German spy ring in America. Ironically, the German air force gained little benefit from its most prized acquisition. The Germans did not install the device in their bombers in time for their heavy raids over Britain. Later, the Luftwaffe made little use of the bombsight since its bombers were chiefly assigned a supportive and defensive role over Germany. ∎

William Gargan as master sleuth Ellery Queen gets a less-than-enthusiastic reception from suspected spy Gale Sondergaard in the World War II drama *Enemy Agents Meet Ellery Queen* (1942).

Enemy Agents Meet Ellery Queen (1942), Col. *Dir*. James Hogan; *Sc*. Eric Taylor; *Cast includes*: William Gargan, Margaret

O.S.S. agent Van Johnson (c.) makes contact with the French Resistance as Jean-Pierre Aumont operates the secret wireless in the World War II drama *The Enemy General* (1960).

Lindsay, Charles Grapewin, Gale Sondergaard, Gilbert Roland, Sig Ruman.

When World War II erupted, the Hollywood studios enlisted the aid of its detectives, ordinarily busy in their series foiling common criminals and murders, to uncover German and Japanese spies lurking in every corner of the nation. William Gargan, portraying master sleuth Ellery Queen, employs his skills in exposing a spy ring in this low-budget second feature. Industrial diamonds for precision instruments are the coveted goal of both Nazi and Free Dutch agents. Margaret Lindsay plays his secretary. See Detectives and Spies. ■

Enemy General, The (1960), Col. *Dir.* George Sherman; *Sc.* Dan Pepper, Burt Picard; *Cast includes:* Van Johnson, Jean-Pierre Aumont, Dany Carrel, John Van Dreelen, Hubert Noel.

Spies and counterspies dominate this action drama set during World War II. Van Johnson, as an American agent in the Office of Strategic Services, is assigned to smuggle a Nazi officer out of Europe and escort him safely to England. The German, played by John Van Dreelen, has a record of murder and other crimes. He was responsible for the death of Johnson's fiancée and other innocent French citizens. When Johnson, who considers his assignment repugnant from the start, discovers that the Nazi is actually a counterspy planning to give the Allies false information, he kills him. See U.S. Intelligence: World War II. ■

Enter the Dragon (1973), WB. *Dir.* Robert Clouse; *Sc.* Michael Allin; *Cast includes:* Bruce Lee, John Saxon, Jim Kelly, Shih Kien, Bob Wall, Ahna Capri.

Martial-arts expert Bruce Lee portrays a secret agent who, operating under cover, joins an Oriental combat competition as a ploy to investigate the illegal activities of an international criminal. The action-oriented drama is set chiefly on an island off the Chinese coast. John Saxon plays an American contestant skilled in martial arts, as does Jim Kelly. Shih Kien, as the master villain who controls gangs of murderous thugs, has sponsored the brutal contest at his island fortress. Ahna Capri and Betty Chung provide the female interest in this film which concentrates more on the personal combat battles than on the plot.

Bruce Lee, who died on July 20, 1973, shortly after completing the film, was the leading exponent of the various types of Oriental self-defense, including karate, judo and kung fu. He had made about a half-dozen of these popular violent dramas from his home base in Hong Kong. This was his first work for an American company. ■

Erickson, Eric S. See *The Counterfeit Traitor* (1962). ■

Escape (1940), MGM. *Dir.* Mervyn LeRoy; *Sc.* Arch Oboler, Marguerite Roberts; *Cast includes:* Norma Shearer, Robert Taylor, Conrad Veidt, Alla Nazimova, Felix Bressart, Albert Basserman.

Norma Shearer, as the mistress of a Nazi general, helps an American (Robert Taylor) get his mother out of Germany in this pre-World War II drama set in 1936 and based on a popular novel by Ethel Vance. Taylor, a naive American, journeys to Nazi Germany to locate his missing mother. She had returned earlier to her native homeland to settle some real estate accounts but had been arrested and sentenced to death for wanting her funds in United States dollars. Taylor is frustrated by the bureaucracy he encounters in his search for information. A chance meeting with Shearer, a countess whose lover is a ruthless general (Conrad Veidt), offers Taylor a spark of hope. Through other convoluted sources he learns that his mother is in a concentration camp awaiting execution. A suspenseful escape is planned and carried out with the help of some anti-Nazi Germans.

Although released before America's entry into World War II and during a period when the U.S. remained officially neutral, the film was another in a series of anti-Nazi Hollywood works that helped to underscore the harshness and brutality of Hitler's regime, a belief that many Americans already shared as a result of newspaper articles and personal experiences that daily filtered out of Nazi-occupied lands. The opening scenes show Taylor's mother being held in a concentration camp awaiting her death sentence. A young doctor who had operated on her visits the aging actress and boasts of the power and goals of the new Germany. "Our children will thank us for the world we are making for them," he exclaims. His patient remains un-

impressed. "For a world filled with the seed of a new hate?" she responds. "For a world in ruins?"

Taylor's mother is played by Alla Nazimova, whose screen debut occurred almost a quarter of a century earlier in *War Brides* (1916), a powerful antiwar drama released before America's entry into World War I. In 1944 she portrayed Paul Henreid's mother in another wartime drama, *In Our Time.* Conrad Veidt, a native of Germany, had fled that country with his Jewish wife in 1929. He portrayed Nazis in several Hollywood features (*All Through the Night, Casablanca*) before his death in 1943. ■

Don Murray tries to stop distraught East Berliner Christine Kaufmann from escaping to the West in the Cold War drama *Escape From East Berlin* (1962).

Escape From East Berlin (1962), MGM. *Dir.* Robert Siodmak; *Sc.* Gabrielle Upton, Peter Berneis, Millard Lampell; *Cast includes:* Don Murray, Christine Kaufmann, Werner Klemperer, Ingrid Van Bergen, Bruno Fritz, Maria Tober.

Based on an actual 1962 incident, this didactic Cold War drama, set in 1961, recounts how a handful of East Germans tunneled their way under the Berlin Wall to freedom. Don Murray portrays an East German who works as a chauffeur for a Communist major and his sex-starved wife. Murray, who is content with his life in East Berlin, is surrounded by friends and family who voice their dissatisfaction with their drab existence under Communism. His best friend confides to him that he will try to escape. Murray, who tries unsuccessfully to dissuade his friend, watches helplessly as the young man is shot to death after driving a truck through the wall and getting himself entangled in a web of barbed wire.

The dead man's sister (Christine Kaufmann) seeks out Murray to learn what has happened to her brother. Murray, who can't bring himself to tell her the truth, says he escaped to the West. She is elated and confides to him that she, too, wants to leave. "I want to get away from everybody who accepts this world as if it were right and normal," she exclaims. Under pressure from the young woman and his family, Murray reluctantly agrees to help them all escape. Since their house is close to the Berlin Wall, he devises a plan to tunnel through to the other side. The remainder of the film shows Murray, his family, and some close friends who have joined them, experiencing several narrow escapes. A suspenseful finale has soldiers storming the house just as the group of 28 men, women and children make their way to freedom.

The gloomy drama, with its emphasis on walls, barbed wire and omnipresent guards, has few light moments to relieve its somber tone. It contains the typical propaganda elements often found in other Cold War films of the period. It opens with newsreel shots of the Berlin Wall being built and East Germans trying to escape through the barbed wire, over the wall and by jumping out of windows that lead to the Western sector. Simultaneously, a voice-over announces, in part: "A new phase is added to the archives of infamy—the Berlin Wall, dividing not only Berlin, but the free world from the prison state of Communism." Another sententious remark is tacked on to the end of the film. "It is man's nature to escape confinement," the words scroll up slowly. "Millions remain imprisoned but 28 more human beings cherish anew the happiness of being free—to cross a street; to stroll in any direction; to talk above a whisper." See Cold War. ■

Escape From Hong Kong (1942), U. *Dir.* William Nigh; *Sc.* Roy Chanslor; *Cast includes:* Leo Carrillo, Andy Devine, Marjorie Lord, Don Terry, Gilbert Emery.

Three American buddies become entangled with German agents and a female undercover agent for British intelligence in Hong Kong in this World War II action drama. Don Terry plays the hero and Marjorie Lord the heroine, whom Terry at first suspects of being a Nazi spy. Leo Carrillo and Andy Devine portray Terry's pals. The boys clean up the spy network and, taking Lord with them, escape in a speedboat as the Japanese bomb Hong Kong—on December 7. Carrillo and Devine teamed up in a string of action dramas during the early 1940s, joined by Don Terry or Dick Foran who served as the male romantic lead. ■

Espionage (1937), MGM. *Dir.* Kurt Neumann; *Sc.* Manuel Seff, Leonard Lee, Ainsworth Morgan; *Cast includes:* Edmund Lowe, Madge Evans, Paul Lukas, Leonid Kinsky, Ketti Gallian, Skeets Gallagher.

A sophisticated international munitions magnate's (Paul Lukas) business activities attract reporters as well as assassins in this pre-World War II drama. Two foreign correspondents (Edmund Lowe, Madge Evans) board the same European train as Lukas to get a scoop. Also tracking the arms manufacturer is an American Communist assassin in the employ of Russia. Lukas, however, surprises his pursuers when they learn that the object of his mysterious rail journey is to quietly marry his true love and retire from the munitions business. Added to the spying element are satirical barbs aimed at capitalism and Communism in this adaptation of Walter Hackett's stage play. ■

Brenda Marshall, as a former German spy now married to a U.S. diplomat, confronts Nazi agent James Stephenson (l.) about her predicament. *Espionage Agent* (1939).

Espionage Agent (1939), WB. *Dir.* Lloyd Bacon; *Sc.* Warren Duff, Michael Fessier, Frank Donaghue; *Cast includes:* Joel McCrea, Brenda Marshall, Jeffrey Lynn, George Bancroft, Stanley Ridges.

A generally conventional drama set on the brink of World War II, the film stars Joel Mc-

Crea as a career diplomat who discovers that his wife (Brenda Marshall), whom he had recently met overseas, is a former German spy. At a Washington party, a German agent (Martin Kosleck), who knows about her past, asks her to gather information from her husband's private papers. She reveals this incident and her entire past to McCrea who then reports these facts to his superiors. Having no other recourse in lieu of his sensitive position, they force his resignation.

The plot is steeped in espionage and planned sabotage as McCrea and his wife go about uncovering a Geneva-based German spy network bent on crippling American industry when and if necessary. Much time is spent in explaining the vital work of the State Department.

The main theme the film strongly suggests is that the U.S. is ill-prepared to deal with subversive activities, especially those involving spies and saboteurs. "Will we as a nation ever learn the difference between tolerance and stupidity?" warns a State Department officer (Stanley Ridges) in 1915 following a rash of sabotage attacks. Later, on the eve of World War II, an American foreign correspondent (George Bancroft), in a reference to the ease with which spies and saboteurs can enter the U.S., comments: "Isolation is a political policy, not a brick wall around a nation." Finally, the head of a German spy ring mocks the laxity of U.S. security. "The fact remains," he announces to his cohorts, "that no effective counter-espionage measures have been able to get through their Congress." According to the film, Congress revised the nation's laws concerning espionage as a result of McCrea and his wife's undercover work in Geneva. The film is based on the story "Career Man" by Robert Henry Buckner. ■

Eternal Temptress, The (1917), Par. *Dir.* Emile Chautard; *Sc.* Eve Unsell; *Cast includes:* Lina Cavalieri, Mildred Counselman, Elliott Dexter, Alan Hale, Edward Fielding, Hallen Mostyn.

This silent romantic drama, set in Italy during World War I, has as its theme the power of women over men. The internationally famous actress, Lina Cavalieri, portrays the beautiful temptress who enchants a young American, played by Elliott Dexter, with her feminine charms. Meanwhile, Austrian secret agents, bent on getting their hands on vital documents stored in the American embassy, plot to use

the American, who is blinded by love, as their tool. So enthralled with Cavalieri is the young man that he is willing to steal the papers. The siren, however, who has herself fallen for Dexter, saves him from betraying his country. A preface introduces the theme of the drama by depicting various historical examples of famous men whom women have ensnared in their web of passion. ■

Ever in My Heart (1933), WB. *Dir.* Archie Mayo; *Sc.* Bertram Millhauser; *Cast includes:* Barbara Stanwyck, Otto Kruger, Ralph Bellamy, Ruth Donnelly, Frank Albertson.

A tear-jerker about a happily married couple before World War I, the film depicts how world events can affect the lives of two innocent people. Barbara Stanwyck, as the daughter of a New England family with a rich heritage, marries a professor of German background (Otto Kruger). When war breaks out, American anti-German sentiment turns against the otherwise close couple. Their child dies of an illness, friends cancel social engagements and Kruger is dismissed from his teaching job. Hounded because of his heritage, he sends his wife to live with her relatives and he returns to Germany where he becomes a spy for his homeland. The following year Stanwyck, while serving as a Red Cross worker in France, sees Kruger dressed in an American uniform and studying the latest troop movements. After they spend the night together, he begins to leave to report that the Rainbow Division is moving toward the Argonne. Torn between love and duty, Stanwyck thinks of her brother who is a flier fighting somewhere in France and of the lives of the thousands of American troops marching into the battle. She decides to poison the wine without his knowledge. They toast their enduring love and die in each other's arms.

This was one of the few films about the war to show the plight of German-Americans who had to face a daily barrage of anti-German propaganda. During the war years, newspaper accounts and films continually told of German atrocities that befell the Belgian populace, all of which incited the American public against their fellow citizens of German heritage. ■

Evil That Men Do, The (1984), ITC Releasing Corp. *Dir.* J. Lee Thompson; *Sc.* David Lee Henry, John Crowther; *Cast includes:* Charles

Bronson, Theresa Saldana, Joseph Maher, José Ferrer, René Enriquez, John Glover.

A retired professional killer takes on one last assignment against a sadistic villain who is protected, in part, by U.S. government agents in this simplistic revenge action drama set in Guatemala. Charles Bronson portrays the hired gun who reluctantly gives up his soft island life to do battle with the forces of evil. Joseph Maher, as the diabolical Moloch, specializes in violence and torture from his fortress base in Guatemala. He is also councilor to several Central American self-styled dictators. An unnamed American agency, which suspiciously resembles the C.I.A., is obsessed by the growth of Communism in the region. Its chiefs see Moloch as a deterrent and therefore defend his methods. Theresa Saldana portrays the wife of a man who has been brutally tortured and murdered by Moloch's underlings. She rebukes Bronson on moral grounds for the unorthodox and violent methods he employs to get to the archvillain. However, since this is a Bronson film, the script, based on the novel by R. Lance Hill, is more concerned with action than issues. ■

Executive Action (1973), NG. *Dir.* David Miller; *Sc.* Dalton Trumbo; *Cast includes:* Burt Lancaster, Robert Ryan, Will Geer, Gilbert Green, John Anderson, Paul Carr.

A disturbing but unsuccessful semi-documentary drama about the Kennedy assassination, the film suggests the President's death was the result of a conspiracy on the part of a group of ruthless businessmen. Burt Lancaster, as a powerful industrialist and leader of the cabal, decides, along with his cronies, that President Kennedy must be eliminated. Robert Ryan and Will Geer portray Lancaster's close collaborators and fellow businessmen. Ed Lauter, as the person in charge of the three riflemen, directs the actual assassination. James MacColl gives a chilling performance as Lee Harvey Oswald's look-alike. Oscar Oncidi impersonates Jack Ruby. This was actor Robert Ryan's last film.

The Kennedy assassination left in its wake a wide spectrum of conjecture, including several theories of conspiracy. An official inquiry did little to quell speculations about the shocking death of a relatively young, idealistic and internationally popular President who was shot in the presence of his attractive wife. The subject, therefore, was ripe for Hollywood treatment. The viewpoint of screenwriter Trumbo, a survivor of the wrath of the House Un-American Activities Committee hearings and the Hollywood blacklist, is that of a right-wing conspiracy. The plotters single out Kennedy's interest in reaching a detente with the Soviets, his support of the Civil Rights movement, and the possibility that he may pull out the troops from Vietnam.

The term "executive action" has been used by the C.I.A. as a euphemism for assassination. Although the C.I.A. has never acknowledged carrying out an assassination, the agency has made attempts—as the result of Presidential directives—on the lives of Cuba's Fidel Castro and the Congo's Patrice Lumumba. These were some of the revelations of the Church Committee—a Senate committee initiated in 1975 to investigate U.S. intelligence activities. At the end of the committee hearings, an order was issued to all U.S. intelligence departments forbidding assassination as one of their options against foreign leaders. ■

Exile Express (1939), GN. *Dir.* Otis Garrett; *Sc.* Edwin Justus Mayer, Ethel LaBlanche; *Cast includes:* Anna Sten, Alan Marshall, Jerome Cowan, Jed Prouty, Walter Catlett.

Anna Sten portrays a young refugee seeking American citizenship in this World War II drama. About to be deported, she escapes from the train journeying from the West Coast to the East. Foreign spies, who need her assistance in deciphering a secret formula, pursue her. Alan Marshall, as a sympathetic reporter, comes to her aid. The couple, of course, become romantically involved. Comic relief is supplied by Jed Prouty, Walter Catlett and, as a local deputy sheriff, Vince Barnett. ■

Exposed (1983), MGM/UA. *Dir.* James Toback; *Sc.* James Toback; *Cast includes:* Nastassia Kinski, Rudolf Nureyev, Harvey Keitel, Ian McShane, Bibi Anderson, Ron Randall.

An American fashion model becomes romantically involved with a French terrorist in this enigmatic drama which mixes the world of art and culture with that of violence and terror. Nastassia Kinski, as a student dropout after her college professor lover ends their affair, seeks her fortune in New York City. Unable to succeed as a pianist, she gains fame and wealth as a model. Rudolf Nureyev, as a serious French violinist and devoted ter-

Scientist Reginald Denny (2nd from r.) outwits Nazi spy ring members Reginald Sheffield, Katherine Emery, Stanley Ridges and Steven Geray in this World War II detective drama. *Eyes in the Night* (1942).

rorist, meets Kinski at an exhibit, and they soon become lovers.

Nureyev then returns to France on a personal mission. He intends to kill a dangerous and violent terrorist (Harvey Keitel) whose indiscriminate bombings and assassinations Nureyev deplores and considers counterproductive to his own political goals. Kinski follows him to France and innocently falls in with Keitel's terrorist group. She has been led to Keitel's forces by a professional and cold-blooded terrorist-bomber (Bibi Anderson) working in league with Keitel. However, he allows Kinski to leave before his climactic showdown with Nureyev. ∎

Eye of the Needle (1981), UA. *Dir.* Richard Marquand; *Sc.* Stanley Mann; *Cast includes:* Donald Sutherland, Kate Nelligan, Ian Bannen, Christopher Cazenove, Faith Brook, Barbara Ewing.

Donald Sutherland portrays a top Nazi spy and ruthless killer in this drama set during World War II. Installed in England by the Nazis during the early years of the war, Suther-

land is discovered operating a secret short-wave radio by his kindly landlady. He expeditiously murders her and continues his espionage work. The scene shifts to 1944 on the eve of the Allied invasion of Hitler's fortress Europe. Sutherland, still operating under cover, photographs a fake airfield in eastern England to convince the German high command that the invasion will take place somewhere other than Normandy. Aware that his discovery can affect the outcome of the war, he makes contact with a U-boat to take him back to Germany.

While waiting on an isolated island for his rendezvous, he meets a couple residing there. The husband (Christopher Cazenove) is a paraplegic—the result of an earlier car accident. His wife (Kate Nelligan), dutiful but sexually unfulfilled, soon becomes romantically involved with Sutherland. At first unaware of his true identity, she eventually has to choose between love and duty—including killing her new-found lover who is about to leave on his secret mission. The film is based on Ken Follett's novel. ∎

Eyes in the Night (1942), MGM. *Dir.* Fred Zinnemann; *Sc.* Guy Trosper, Howard Emmett Rogers; *Cast includes:* Edward Arnold, Ann Harding, Donna Reed, Katherine Emery, Horace McNally, Allen Jenkins.

Nazi spies try to get possession of a secret formula from a scientist in this World War II detective drama based on Baynard Kendrick's novel *Odor of Violet*. Edward Arnold portrays a canny blind detective who, with his very clever seeing-eye dog, seems to overcome every predicament. Donna Reed, as the young, precocious daughter of the scientist (Reginald Denny), is an aspiring actress at a local summer stock playhouse who unknowingly falls in with a group of spies. Stanley Ridges, as the scientist's butler, is actually in charge of the spies who are trying to break into the scientist's safe that contains the much-wanted formula. Arnold discovers the spy ring while he is investigating the murder of Reed's fiancé. Ann Harding, as Reed's stepmother, calls upon her friend, Arnold, to solve the killing. Allen Jenkins, as the detective's assistant, supplies the slight comic relief in this offbeat tale that blends detective elements with the spy genre. ■

F

Face in the Fog, The (1922), Par. *Dir.* Alan Crosland; *Sc.* John Lynch, Jack Boyle; *Cast includes:* Lionel Barrymore, Seena Owen, Lowell Sherman, George Nash, Louis Wolheim, Mary MacLaren.

Russian agents, the U.S. Secret Service, a reformed criminal-hero and a Grand Duchess all play a role in this drama of mystery and intrigue. Lionel Barrymore, as Boston Blackie, a former thief who is now an amateur detective, becomes entangled in an international plot. A blind beggar slips a packet into Blackie's pocket and is then cold-bloodedly murdered. Once at home, Blackie discovers that the contents consist of valuable jewels. A U.S. Secret Service agent, on the trail of the jewel thieves, enters into the plot. It seems that the jewels belong to a Russian duchess (Seena Owen) who plans to use them to finance a campaign to overthrow the present Russian government. Agents of her country are bent on obtaining the jewels and preventing her subversive activities. The unfortunate beggar was one of her servants. Eventually the foreign spies are rounded up, and Blackie returns the valuables to their rightful owner.

The basis of the plot may have stemmed from a post-World War I incident in England involving the czar's diamonds. Russian agents allegedly sold the diamonds to subsidize a pro-labor newspaper in England. Members of various British intelligence agencies, virtually all of whom were infected at the time with a fear of Bolshevik subversion, were quick to investigate every suspicious move on the part of Russians residing in England. See Detectives and Spies; Red Scare of 1919–1920; U.S. Secret Service; Federal Bureau of Investigation. ■

U.S. secret agent Rory Calhoun seeks refuge during World War II with Italian partisans, including Marina Berti, who is suspected of collaborating with the enemy. *A Face in the Rain* (1963).

Face in the Rain, A (1963), Embassy. *Dir.* Irvin Kershner; *Sc.* Hugo Butler, Jean Rouverol; *Cast includes:* Rory Calhoun, Marina Berti, Niall McGinnis, Massimo Giuliani.

An American agent who has parachuted behind enemy lines into Italy is forced to spend most of his time fleeing from the pursuing Nazis in this routine World War II drama. Rory Calhoun portrays the American who never gets the opportunity to set up operations. After he seeks refuge with one of his contacts, a professor, he learns that the man's wife is the mistress of a German officer. Much of the film is taken up with chases across rooftops, etc. See Jedburgh Operations; U.S. Intelligence: World War II. ■

Fair Lady (1922), UA. *Dir.* Kenneth Webb; *Sc.* Dorothy Farnum; *Cast includes:* Betty

Blythe, Thurston Hall, Robert Elliott, Gladys Hulette, Florence Auer.

Betty Blythe, as Countess Margherita, the heroine of this complicated little drama set in New Orleans, becomes entangled with a Mafia gang. An Italian secret service agent (Macey Harlam), assigned to expose the crime syndicate and its chief, poses as Count Modena. Thurston Hall portrays Caesar Maruffi, an Italian banker who is actually the head of the ring. Norvin Blake, as the hero, has little to do with the drama. Intrigues, fist fights and car chases help to round out the plot until the gang leader is finally exposed. The film is based on Rex Beach's novel *The Net*. ■

Fair Pretender, The (1918), Goldwyn. *Dir.* Charles Miller; *Cast includes:* Madge Kennedy, Tom Moore, Robert Walker, Paul Doucet, Wilmer Walter, Emmett King.

A young aspiring actress recovers important documents stolen by a German spy in this World War I comedy drama. Madge Kennedy, as a resourceful stenographer for a theatrical producer, poses as a widow at a social function to prove to her employer that she has acting talent. She meets a playwright (Tom Moore) at the house party but doesn't know that he has never sold a play. The stenographer is suddenly faced with a crisis when her supposedly dead husband returns. Treating the situation lightly, he doesn't expose her but asks her to leave the party. The young playwright leaves with her and, following several escapades, they retrieve a secret document and effect the capture of a German spy. The young couple fall in love and his play is performed. ■

Falcon and the Snowman, The (1985), Orion. *Dir.* John Schlesinger; *Sc.* Steven Zallian; *Cast includes:* Timothy Hutton, Sean Penn, David Suchet, Lori Singer, Pat Hingle, Dorian Harewood.

Two young men from wealthy families sell U.S. government secrets to the Russians in this drama based on actual incidents in the lives of Chistropher Boyce and Andrew Daulton Lee. Timothy Hutton, as Boyce, is at odds with his family, especially his domineering father (Pat Hingle), a retired F.B.I. agent. Boyce's only interest is his pet falcon, and his closest friend is Lee (Sean Penn), a small-time drug dealer who has had his own falling-out with his family. Boyce's father gets

his son a job with a California government agency which handles secret documents. Young Boyce, torn between work and school, takes the job. On his days off he journeys to Mexico where Lee maintains an apartment for his drug operations. Lee invites Boyce to join him in his drug-smuggling business, jokingly spelling out his philosophy: "He who dies with the most toys wins." But Boyce turns down the offer.

Back at his high-security job, Boyce accidentally receives a secret message, intended only for C.I.A. personnel, about covert operations in Australia. The message implicates the C.I.A. in infiltrating an Australian union for the purpose of breaking an impending strike. Boyce, disturbed that the U.S. is involved in illegal foreign activities, tells Lee about what he has discovered. "Every day I get these misrouted cables," he says, "the C.I.A.'s secret mail. Details of covert actions that have nothing to do with national security. Manipulations of foreign press, political parties, whole economies. . . ." The two friends, after some quibbling about how to handle the situation, decide to sell the information to Soviet agents at the Russian embassy in Mexico.

Boyce's purpose in exposing the C.I.A. activities, according to the film, is to neutralize the agency's effects on world events. Lee, on the other hand, is interested only in the money which he needs to feed his growing dependence on drugs and his expensive life style. After supplying a steady stream of codes and other information to the Russians, Boyce, more naive than his partner, grows disillusioned with the results of his traitorous acts and decides to quit. "There's not going to be any reconciliation," he says to Lee about the Russians. "They're just as paranoid and dangerous as we are. I can't imagine why I thought they'd be any different." But Lee, desperately in need of funds, insists they continue. His carelessness in contacting the enemy leads to his arrest. Eventually Boyce is arrested. Both were tried and convicted in 1974. Boyce was sentenced to 40 years' imprisonment, and Lee received a life sentence. The film is based on Robert Lindsey's book.

The incidents involving the exchange of government secrets and the trial took place before the C.I.A. operations were exposed as a result of Congressional hearings in 1975. The agency's director, Richard Helms, was almost indicted as a result of an 18-month Congressional investigation. Other shocking revelations began to appear in books by former C.I.A. agents. The documentary *On Company Business* (1980) explored the agency's interference in various European strikes and covert operations in other parts of the globe, particularly Latin America. See Central Intelligence Agency. ∎

Falcon's Adventure, The (1946), RKO. *Dir.* William Berke; *Sc.* Aubrey Wisberg, Robert E. Kent; *Cast includes:* Tom Conway, Madge Meredith, Edward Brophy, Robert Warwick, Myrna Dell, Steve Brodie.

International agents try to steal a scientist's formula for synthetic industrial diamonds in this well-paced drama which blends the detective genre with that of intrigue. Another entry in the "Falcon" series, this tale places the dapper sleuth, played by Tom Conway, in the midst of a plot involving theft, murder and intrigue after he foils the kidnapping of a young Brazilian woman (Madge Meredith). When her scientist-father is killed, the police suspect the Falcon. He again falls under suspicion when a second scientist's life comes to an untimely end in Florida. To save his own neck, the private sleuth is forced to solve the mystery. It seems that the top man of an industrial diamond syndicate, who wanted the formula destroyed to protect his own interests, is behind all the skullduggery. Chunky character actor Edward Brophy adds some comedy relief as the Falcon's sidekick. ∎

Falcon's Brother, The (1942), RKO. *Dir.* Stanley Logan; *Sc.* Stuart Palmer, Craig Rice; *Cast includes:* George Sanders, Tom Conway, Jane Randolph, Don Barclay, Cliff Clark, Edward Gargan.

German agents concoct an assassination plot against a Latin American diplomat in an attempt to disrupt relations between the intended victim's country and the U.S. in this offbeat entry in the popular "Falcon" detective series. Tom Conway portrays Tom Lawrence, the brother of the famed American detective, Gay Lawrence, better known as the Falcon (George Sanders).

Arriving in the U.S., Conway becomes entangled in a murder and the assassination plot. He discovers that enemy agents have been using the covers of magazines featuring models as a means of communicating with fellow agents. Decoding the latest magazine cover as a clue, he and a plucky reporter (Jane

Randolph) visit a small community where the spies have entrenched themselves in preparation for the assassination. Conway and his female companion are captured, brought into an abandoned church and tied up as the plane carrying the important statesman lands. The visitor is escorted through a gate as the assassins take aim. Conway, although bound, manages to pull a nearby rope which rings the church bells. The Falcon arrives upon the scene, hears the signal and push the foreign emissary out of harm's way as a concealed rifle cracks the stillness. The bullet misses its intended target but kills the private detective. Police officers who have pursued the Falcon then round up the gang of spies following a brief gun battle. After his brother's death, Conway, about to leave the U.S., receives a threatening phone call from another foreign agent telling him to leave the country or he will end up like his brother. Conway decides to stay and replace his brother as the Falcon. Edward Gargan, as a slow-witted policeman, tries to bring some comic relief to the detective-spy tale.

The film is unusual in that Conway, as the screen brother of the Falcon, was the real-life brother of Sanders. The plot angle of Sanders' death was designed to replace Sanders, who was bowing out of the popular Falcon series for the studio, with another suave actor. See Latin America. ∎

Fall In (1943), UA. *Dir.* Kurt Neumann; *Sc.* Eugene Conrad, Edward E. Seabrook; *Cast includes:* William Tracy, Joe Sawyer, Robert Barrat, Jean Porter, Arthur Hunnicutt, Rebel Randall.

Another weak entry in the series of service comedies starring youthful, moon-faced William Tracy and contentious Joe Sawyer, the film once again features the pair as rival sergeants in their typical antics in and around an army training camp. This time they become involved with a group of local hillbillies as well as a network of spies in a script that depends heavily on slapstick. ∎

Fall of a Nation, The (1916), National Films. *Dir.* Bartley Cushing; *Sc.* Thomas Dixon; *Cast includes:* Arthur Shirley, Lorraine Huling, Flora MacDonald, Percy Standing, Paul Willis, Philip Gastrock.

A preparedness drama depicting the invasion of the United States by Germany with the help of a traitor, the film quickly became a popular success despite its dramatic deficiencies and inept acting. A millionaire, obsessed with the desire for power, secretly plots with Germany to land troops and weapons on American shores. Major cities fall to the invaders who commit a variety of atrocities upon the defenseless citizens.

A prologue shows the birth of the republic as well as numerous battle scenes, all realistically staged, and extols the benefits of democracy while condemning the European political regimes of kings and royalty. In its preparedness zeal, the drama berates such antiwar critics as a thinly veiled William Jennings Bryan, played by Percy Standing, as well as religious leaders who countenance neutrality. One sequence depicts a naive, almost simple-minded minister who is assigned to try to restrain the invaders by greeting them with kindness. He is quickly taken prisoner. Thomas Dixon, the screenwriter and author of the original novel, also wrote the novel and play *The Clansman*, which became the basis for D. W. Griffith's 1915 screen masterpiece, *The Birth of a Nation*.

Although the film was attacked by many movie critics and Washington politicos, it scored at the box office. It was released almost on the heels of *The Battle Cry of Peace* (1915), another strong preparedness drama. Both helped to turn the tide against the pacifist movement (not an especially strong force even at its peak) which was supported by such productions as *Civilization* (1916). Pacifism, *The Fall of a Nation* suggested, was akin to disloyalty and cowardice. ■

Fallen Sparrow, The (1943), RKO. *Dir.* Richard Wallace; *Sc.* Warren Duff; *Cast includes:* John Garfield, Maureen O'Hara, Walter Slezak, Patricia Morison, Martha O'Driscoll.

The Spanish Civil War looms in the background of this suspenseful drama starring John Garfield as a former member of the Lincoln Brigade and veteran of that conflict. He had been captured and tortured during the war. It seems that he had gained possession of a Nazi flag lost in battle by a German battalion. Certain high officials, who are willing to kill for it, want the standard returned. Unable to extract the whereabouts from Garfield, they allow him to escape, hoping he will lead them to the flag. In New York his close friend is murdered, and Garfield links the death to the Nazis, particularly to their sadistic leader,

played menacingly by Walter Slezak. One of Slezak's agents (Maureen O'Hara) tries to gain information from Garfield, who later learns that she is working for the Nazis. He turns her over to the F.B.I. and remarks to a nearby detective: "Another sparrow has fallen."

The camera work, low-key lighting and sound effects are especially effective in dramatizing Garfield's paranoia and fear of his pursuing enemies, both real and imagined. Memories of the torture he had experienced in Spain still haunt Garfield, who has not fully recovered psychologically from his wartime ordeal. Footsteps heard in another room may conjure up untold terrors, for they remind him of the sound of his sadistic torturer's approaching clubfoot.

Very few Hollywood films dealt with the controversial Spanish Civil War. Those that did, such as *Blockade* (1938), steered clear of specific social and political causes, opting instead for some nebulous statements about destruction. *The Fallen Sparrow*, released during World War II, remains an anti-Nazi drama rather than an attack on Franco's Fascism. The film is based on the novel by Dorothy B. Hughes. ■

False Faces, The (1919), Par. *Dir.* Irvin Willat; *Sc.* Irvin Willat; *Cast includes:* Henry B. Walthall, Mary Anderson, Lon Chaney, Milton Ross, Thornton Edwards.

Henry B. Walthall portrays the fictional hero the Lone Wolf in this World War I drama based on Louis Joseph Vance's 1918 novel. The film opens somewhere in the trenches of France where Walthall makes his way back to Allied lines. Learning that a network of German spies will accelerate its activities in the U.S., he sails for America to foil the plot. There is much foul play aboard the vessel involving a wounded war hero and his sister who is actually an English operative carrying a secret message. German spies then make an attempt on Walthall's life, but he manages to survive. After the ship docks in New York City, the gang, operating from an innocent-looking building which it owns, plots further conspiracies. Walthall eventually helps to round up the enemy agents, including their leader, played by Lon Chaney, and recovers the message that has fallen into the hands of the chief spy. Mary Anderson, as the British agent, also provides the romance in this suspenseful tale.

Aside from the opening combat sequences, the film has scenes of German submarine warfare while the hero crosses the Atlantic. The plot structure is reminiscent of a conventional serial with its melodramatic events unfolding quickly and economically.

The city dwelling where the gang takes refuge recalls the actual notorious Manhattan town house where German-Americans, allied to Germany, assembled during the war for social and conspiratorial reasons. Run by its owner, a former opera singer, the "safe house" would often echo the sounds of revelry and then suddenly grow silent as the guests, German agents and saboteurs, hovered ecstatically over new explosive devices and plots. See Detectives and Spies; German Intelligence: World War I. ■

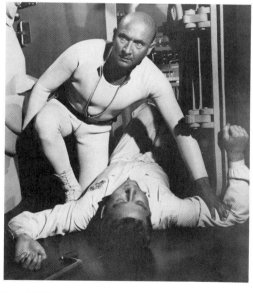

Donald Pleasence portrays a spy aboard a miniaturized submarine injected into a patient's body where a team of doctors hopes to remove a blood clot in the science fiction drama *Fantastic Voyage* (1966).

Fantastic Voyage (1966), TCF. *Dir.* Richard Fleischer; *Sc.* Harry Kleiner, David Duncan; *Cast includes:* Stephen Boyd, Raquel Welch, Edmond O'Brien, Donald Pleasence, Arthur O'Connell, William Redfield.

A miniaturized submarine transports a group of scientists inside the body of a former Iron Curtain captive in this original and suspenseful Cold War science-fiction drama.

The patient, an important scientist suffering brain damage, is rushed from the Communist bloc to a special laboratory in the U.S. The only way to save his life is to operate from inside his body. A special military unit known as the Combined Miniature Deterrent Forces, which reduces the physical size of troops and equipment, shrinks a submarine and its crew of five so that they can be injected into the patient's bloodstream to remove a blood clot.

Thus begins a strange journey past nerve fibers, blood vessels and other elements of the human body that treats the submarine as it would any other "invader." The miniature vessel, therefore, comes under attack by antibodies, adding more obstacles to the crew members who have only one hour to complete their mission before they return to their original size. Another factor threatens the voyage. Aboard the sub is a Soviet spy bent on sabotaging the project.

Stephen Boyd, as a U.S. agent who rescued the scientist from the East, is assigned to accompany the special crew. Donald Pleasence portrays the commander, an expert in circulatory systems, who navigates the vessel. Arthur Kennedy, as the doctor in charge of repairing the brain damage, is the chief suspect. Raquel Welch portrays his assistant. Edmond O'Brien and Arthur O'Connell, as worried officers of the special miniature force, add to the general tension. ■

Fastest Guitar Alive, The (1967), MGM. *Dir.* Michael Moore; *Sc.* Robert E. Kent; *Cast includes:* Roy Orbison, Sammy Jackson, Maggie Pierce, Joan Freeman, Lyle Bettger.

Two undercover Confederate agents steal a fortune in gold from the Union to help the cause of the South in this weak musical comedy set during the last days of the Civil War. Roy Orbison and Sammy Jackson portray the two spies who rob the San Francisco mint and head for the South with the gold. They then unexpectedly experience a series of misadventures with a medicine show composed entirely of women, a band of crooks and an eccentric Indian. Meanwhile, the South has surrendered and the two heroes are branded as thieves. To save themselves, they must figure out a way to return the gold without anyone knowing it. As expected, all turns out well for the pair. ■

Fat Spy, The (1965), Magna. *Dir.* Joseph Cates; *Sc.* Matthew Andrews; *Cast includes:* Phyllis Diller, Jack E. Leonard, Brian Donlevy, Johnny Tillotson, Jayne Mansfield, Lauree Berger.

An inept comedy involving twin brothers, a search for a fountain of youth and a group of singing teen-agers add up to a plotless fiasco. Comedian Jack E. Leonard, in a dual role, portrays one twin wearing a hairpiece and his counterpart. He is the "spy" of title, sent to snoop on youths who journey to an island searching for a lost treasure. Comedienne Phyllis Diller is seeking the same island which she thinks contains the Fountain of Youth. Veteran character actor Brian Donlevy, as a broomstick tycoon, sends his daughter (Jayne Mansfield) to assist Leonard. The interesting cast members make this film an interesting curio for at least one viewing. ■

Fathom (1967), TCF. *Dir.* Leslie Martinson; *Sc.* Lorenzo Semple, Jr.; *Cast includes:* Tony Franciosa, Raquel Welch, Ronald Fraser, Greta Chi, Richard Briers, Tony Adams.

North Atlantic Treaty Organization agents attempt to recover a nuclear trigger device mechanism capable of destroying the world in this fast-paced comedy thriller. Shapely Raquel Welch portrays "Fathom," an American parachutist in Europe for a sky-diving competition, who thinks she is helping the British when she agrees to participate in the search for the device lost off the coast of Spain. In reality, she has been hired to recover a priceless piece of stolen jewelry. Tony Franciosa, as a suspicious American, romances Welch, who is pursued by a bull, an international spy and other assorted villains before the plot comes to a successful conclusion. The scenery and sky-diving stunts add interest to the mayhem. ■

F.B.I. See Federal Bureau of Investigation. ■

FBI Story, The (1959), WB. *Dir.* Mervyn LeRoy; *Sc.* Richard L. Breen, John Twist; *Cast includes:* James Stewart, Vera Miles, Murray Hamilton, Larry Pennell, Nick Adams, Diane Jergens.

This episodic film dramatizes the history of the Federal Bureau of Investigation through the experiences of one of its agents, played by James Stewart. In addition to the F.B.I.'s investigations of the Ku Klux Klan, John Dillinger and the Barker gang, the film also covers the exposés of Nazi spies and the German-American Bundists in America during World War II.

The drama is humanized through Stewart, a dedicated agent who is torn between his devotion to the Bureau and his desire to provide a better life for his family. At one point the frustrated and disillusioned Stewart contemplates resigning, but he is encouraged to remain when J. Edgar Hoover takes over and inspires his agents with a love of justice. Stewart and his wife (Vera Miles) face their share of tragedy. His friend and fellow agent (Murray Hamilton) is killed by gangsters and, later, his son (Buzz Martin) is killed in action during World War II. The film was adapted from the book by Don Whitehead. ■

Fearmakers, The (1958), UA. *Dir.* Jacques Tourneur; *Sc.* Elliot West, Chris Appley; *Cast includes:* Dana Andrews, Dick Foran, Mel Torme, Marilee Earle, Veda Ann Borg, Kelly Thorsden.

Agents of an unnamed foreign power take over a Washington, D.C., public-opinion polling firm and use it for their own political ends in this unusual drama of international intrigue and subversion. Dana Andrews, as a Korean War veteran who has suffered from Communist brainwashing techniques while a prisoner of war, returns to find that his polling agency has been sold to another person (Dick Foran). Andrews' former partner has met with a mysterious accident. Andrews, after discovering that the firm now is manipulating data to further political causes and selected political candidates, decides to expose the bogus results and those behind the plot. Strongly patriotic and determined to get his company back, he struggles against the foreign agents and eventually succeeds. Marilee Earle provides some romance for the war veteran in this offbeat tale based on the novel by Darwin L. Teilhet. See Brainwashing. ■

Federal Agent (1936), Rep. *Dir.* Sam Newfield; *Sc.* Barry Barringer; *Cast includes:* Willam (Bill) Boyd, Charles A. Browne, Irene Ware, George Cooper, Lenita Lane, Don Alvarado.

Foreign agents are trying to steal the secret of a newly developed chemical explosive in this weak drama. The U.S. government assigns one of its agents, played by William Boyd, to the case. Boyd is more than willing to capture the spies since they were also re-

Foreign agents, determined to influence American politics, forcefully take over the public-opinion polling company owned by Korean War veteran Dana Andrews (2nd from l.). *The Fearmakers* (1958).

sponsible for the murder of his friend, a fellow agent. Using the latest in contemporary sleuthing apparatus such as a transcription machine and a wireless to help in the capture, Boyd brings about the demise of the culprits. Irene Ware portrays a mysterious woman whom Boyd at first finds an interesting challenge. He later becomes romantically involved with her.

Boyd, who starred in silent films during the 1920s, made a series of action and adventure dramas during the early 1930s, playing such macho types as stunt men, soldiers and carnival barkers. His most famous role, however, was that of Hopalong Cassidy, a western character created by Clarence E. Mulford in a series of short stories and novels. Boyd, whose screen career had declined with the advent of sound, agreed to play Hopalong, introducing the cowboy hero to movie audiences in 1935. He continued to play Hoppy in more than 50 films—one of the longest-running and most popular western film series. Boyd and Cassidy repeated their success on television in the 1950s. ■

Federal Agent at Large (1950), Rep. *Dir.* George Blair; *Sc.* Albert DeMond; *Cast includes:* Dorothy Patrick, Robert Rockwell,

Kent Taylor, Estelle Rodriguez, Thurston Hall, Frank Puglia.

Gold smugglers operating in Mexico become the target of a U.S. Treasury investigation in this drama. Kent Taylor, as a government agent, poses as a gangster so that he can infiltrate the gang. The smugglers, Taylor learns, cleverly hide the gold in Aztec pottery which an archaeologist (Robert Rockwell), one of their collaborators, then easily transports through customs across the border. Dorothy Patrick, as the tough leader of the gang, reveals a tender side to her nature when she succumbs to Taylor's charms. She ends up testifying as a friendly witness of the government. Frank Puglia portrays a Mexican who at first is employed by the smugglers but is soon convinced to help the authorities. ■

Federal Bureau of Investigation. Some of the F.B.I.'s greatest successes occurred at the beginning of World War II. Its crackdown on enemy agents operating in the U.S. was so effective that no major incidents of sabotage were reported for the duration of the conflict. Also, F.B.I. agents in South America during the war, working either under cover as attachés of U.S. embassies or as members of private companies, foiled German operations in Argentina, Chile, Brazil and Mexico. The agency even thwarted a pro-German coup in Bolivia against the pro-British government. By the end of World War II, the F.B.I. had helped to apprehend more than 400 Axis agents and put out of commission two dozen secret radio transmitters.

Another major triumph for the agency took place during the Cold War. Convinced that the Russians had planted a "mole" in America's nuclear research project during World War II, the F.B.I. tracked down a succession of spies and Soviet agents. The film *Daniel* (1983) concerns the agency's efforts during this period.

The Bureau of Investigation—the precursor of the F.B.I.— was created in 1908 by Charles Bonaparte, the U.S. Attorney General. Attorney General Harlan Stone reorganized the Bureau of Investigation as the F.B.I. in 1924 and appointed J. Edgar Hoover director. Hoover was subsequently reappointed to the position by all attorneys general and Presidents until his death in 1972.

Many critics claim that during his 48-year tenure, Hoover shaped the F.B.I. to conform to his own personal ideology. The Bureau gathered material and reported it to the Attorney General and to the various U.S. Attorneys' offices throughout the country. The U.S. Attorneys then decided upon what action to take. Hoover concentrated the Bureau's resources on Communist subversion and the more highly publicized criminal cases including the capture of John Dillinger. He was criticized for not devoting enough attention to white-collar crime and to the growth of the Mafia. Hoover, however, was oblivious to criticism and continued to attempt to emasculate America's political left; in addition, in the 1960s, he sought to discredit the black-power movement and Dr. Martin Luther King in particular. Hoover was reported to have maintained dossiers on leading politicians, including attorneys general and Presidents, who were naturally reluctant to confront him.

The Bureau, under Hoover, expanded its scientific apparatus and offered its laboratory, fingerprint and computer facilities to police departments throughout the country. Several films, including *The House on 92nd Street* (1945) and *Walk East on Beacon* (1952), use a semi-documentary approach to reveal some of the agency's methods.

The F.B.I. has primary jurisdiction in cases involving violation of federal law. The Bureau ordinarily does not engage in external espionage nor does it enter narcotics, tax fraud, security fraud or customs violations cases. With the passage of the Federal Civil Rights acts in the 1960s, the F.B.I. expanded its investigative role into civil rights violations. This has been clearly dramatized in *Mississippi Burning* (1989), with Gene Hackman and Willem Dafoe as F.B.I. agents investigating the murders of three civil rights workers. (However, many critics complained that the film fabricated the Bureau's role in that case.) Congressional passage of anti-racketeering laws similarly brought the full weight of the Bureau into the fight against organized crime.

In 1968 Congress, possibly as a reaction to Hoover's past authoritarian control over the agency, passed legislation that the director be appointed by the President with the advice and consent of the Senate, replacing the old method of selection by the Attorney General. There are now approximately between 7,000 and 8,000 agents, the majority of whom have legal or accounting backgrounds.

Hollywood dramas have depicted the F.B.I. and its operatives carrying out a wide range of investigations. Unlike most films about the C.I.A., F.B.I. productions almost invariably depicted the agency and its members favorably. Espionage films with F.B.I. agents as heroes became popular in the 1930s. In *Navy Spy* (1937), for example, the F.B.I. rescues a U.S. Navy lieutenant (Conrad Nagel) who is kidnapped by foreign agents. Nagel possesses a secret formula that is coveted by a foreign power. Several serials featured F.B.I. agents as their heroes. In *Robinson Crusoe of Clipper Island* (1937) Mala portrays a Polynesian-born F.B.I. operative whom his superiors assign to investigate an unidentified dirigible that has crashed on a remote Pacific island. He battles hostile islanders and an international spy ring.

By the end of the decade several factors effected many of these films: production values increased, plots and characters became more realistic and World War II served as background. *Confessions of a Nazi Spy* (1939) best exemplifies these changes. Edward G. Robinson, as an F.B.I. chief, uncovers the key members of a nest of Nazi spies who are quickly brought to trial and found guilty. When secret agents of a foreign power steal the army's new bombsight in *Enemy*

Agent (1940), the F.B.I. is called in on the case. George Reeves, as an F.B.I. agent, and Marjorie Weaver, as a journalist, pursue an escaped German flier from a Canadian prisoner-of-war camp and get mixed up with a murderous spy ring in *Man at Large* (1941). Sometimes the subgenre would revert to its B format, as in the minor drama *Secret Enemies* (1942), about F.B.I. agents closing in on a Nazi spy network operating out of a New York hotel. In *They Came to Blow Up America* (1943) F.B.I. agent George Sanders poses as a loyal Nazi to help capture enemy saboteurs who have landed on America's shores. A few wartime documentaries appeared about the work of the Bureau. In "Keep 'Em Sailing" (1942), for instance, an F.B.I. agent exposes sabotage attempts directed at U.S. cargo ships.

Hollywood produced a string of films about the Cold War, including several involving the F.B.I. Agent Dennis O'Keefe joins forces with Scotland Yard investigator Louis Hayward in *Walk a Crooked Mile* (1948) to uncover Soviet agents trying to steal America's atomic secrets. *I Was a Communist for the FBI* (1951), made chiefly to assuage the House Un-American Activities Committee, was based on the true story of Matt Cvetic, who posed as a Communist for nine years. Frank Lovejoy, as the double agent, exposes various Communist plots before H.U.A.C. at a time when that committee was actively investigating the entertainment industry. Milburn Stone portrays an F.B.I. chief who rescues the kidnapped son of a nuclear scientist in *The Atomic City* (1952). Many of these seemed like the old-fashioned police dramas, with federal agents replacing detectives and Communists substituting for gangsters. At the end of the decade in which the Cold War dominated international events and sparked a series of related films, Warner Brothers released *The FBI Story* (1959), a fairly interesting history of the Bureau, starring James Stewart as a dedicated agent who witnesses the growth of the agency over the years.

When the James Bond spy films captured American audiences in the early 1960s, American studios began to broaden the themes of its espionage dramas. The films offered more violence and sex at the expense of characterization and realism. An F.B.I. agent in *Hell's Bloody Devils* (1970), a violent action drama, infiltrates a neo-Nazi organization that has links to the Las Vegas Mafia.

F.B.I. members and an Israeli secret agent prevent international terrorists from carrying out the mass murder of a Super Bowl audience in *Black Sunday* (1977). Arnold Schwarzenegger, as a former F.B.I. agent dismissed for roughing up a suspect, is coaxed to unofficially help his former chief in exposing a leak in the agency in *Raw Deal* (1986). A local policeman and an F.B.I. agent join forces to smash a drug operation that is supporting a right-wing paramilitary group in the action drama *The Wild Pair* (1987).

Comedies involving F.B.I. agents have occasionally appeared, but it was not until the 1980s that writers and directors began to satirize aspects of the Bureau. In the slapstick comedy *Clipped Wings* (1953) a pal of the Bowery Boys is actually working for the F.B.I. and trying to ferret out a group of enemy agents. Leo Gorcey and Huntz Hall become involved in the spy hunt and accidentally help to capture the culprits. *Die Hard* (1988), which is a tense drama, nevertheless pokes satirical fun at F.B.I. agents as part of its comic relief. ∎

Federal Fugitives (1941), PRC. *Dir.* William Beaudine; *Sc.* Martin Mooney; *Cast includes:* Neil Hamilton, Doris Day, Victor Varconi, Charles Wilson, George Carleton, Lyle Latell.

Saboteurs attack America's war production in this inept World War II drama. Released before the country's entry into the world conflict, the film concentrates on the home front where agents cause a series of fatal airplane crashes. Neil Hamilton portrays the hero who pursues the culprits. At one point he is almost killed, but the *femme fatale* who has led him into a trap falls in love with him and saves his life. Victor Varconi, as the leader of the spies, meets his end by falling down an elevator shaft. Doris Day, who went on to star in a series of musicals and romantic comedies, provides the love interest. ∎

Fifth Column, The. The term *fifth column* derives from the Spanish Civil War (1936–1938) when one of Franco's generals, during a radio address, announced: "We have four columns advancing upon Madrid. The fifth column will rise at the proper time." The term became synonymous with traitorous or subversive elements within a city or nation who undermine the spirit or resistance of its population in favor of its enemy. It also prompted a 1940 play of the same name by Ernest Hemingway. Several spy films, released before World War II, conveyed the activities of fifth columnists operating in varying degrees in European countries and the U.S. For example, in *Blockade* (1938), producer Walter Wanger's superficial drama about the Spanish Civil War, high-ranking military officers are seen in collusion with enemy agents.

Since the bulk of World War II spy films came from the U.S., America became the major target of the dreaded fifth columnists. The dramas were chiefly cautionary films aimed at the citizenry. *Confessions of a Nazi Spy* (1939), the first major American anti-Nazi propaganda drama, shows how, through German-American organizations such as the Bund, Nazi spies organize a network of agents and collaborators in defense plants, the military services and other occupations; they busily gather classified information that is relayed back to Germany. In *Spy Ship* (1942) Irene Manning portrays a fifth columnist who sells U.S. shipping secrets to the enemy.

Other films depict the devastating effects of fifth columnists in Europe. In the comedy drama *Once Upon a Honeymoon* (1942), for instance, Austrian nobleman Walter Slezak, working in secret for the Third Reich, helps to bring about the fall of Czechoslovakia, Poland and other countries, peaceful lands which he visits disguised as a statesman and soon subverts through his treachery and lies.

Hollywood, demonstrating a fear of fifth columnists that bordered almost on paranoia, released some films that warned of Nazi activities extending into the postwar years. In the World War II drama *The Master Race* (1944) Nazi leaders begin their strategy for the next war as Allied armies push toward Berlin. George Coulouris portrays a high Nazi official and advocate of German supremacy who orders his military staff to go underground and cause turmoil among the liberated nations of Europe until the Nazis are strong enough to rise again. Journeying to an American-occupied Belgian village where he poses as a patriot, he soon starts to spread dissension and unrest among the villagers before he is exposed. *Cornered* (1945), a post-World War II drama, concerns high-ranking Nazis who have escaped prosecution by the Allies and have settled in Argentina where they are busy planning the next war.

The threat of these sympathizers and enemy agents compelled President Franklin D. Roosevelt, on May 26, 1940, during one of his radio fireside chats, to address the American people on this issue. "We know of new methods of attack," he warned, "the Trojan Horse, the fifth column that betrays a nation unprepared for treachery. Spies, saboteurs and traitors are the actors in this new tragedy." ∎

Fighting Blade, The (1923), FN. *Dir.* John Robertson; *Sc.* Josephine Lovatt; *Cast includes:* Richard Barthelmess, Lee Baker, Morgan Wallace, Bradley Barker, Dorothy Mackaill.

Richard Barthelmess portrays Karl, a famous Dutch swordsman, who serves as a spy for Oliver Cromwell in this 17th-century costume drama of intrigue. The anti-Royalist leader sends Karl on a secret mission to get the layout of a particular castle. Posing as a mercenary soldier, Karl is allowed to enter. But his disguise is soon uncovered. He is arrested and sentenced to hang the next morning. He manages to escape and hide in the room of Thomasine (Dorothy Mackaill), an heiress and ward of the villainous earl of the castle. Karl then returns to Cromwell and leads the troops against the earl.

Meanwhile the earl, who has plans to force Thomasine to marry him, orders an elaborate wedding feast. His ward, now in love with Karl, proceeds with the ritual against her will. Cromwell and his troops, led by Karl, arrive in time to stop the wedding and take control of the castle. The film was adapted from the novel by Beulah Marie Dix. ∎

Fighting Eagle, The (1927), PDC. *Dir.* Donald Crisp; *Sc.* Douglas Z. Doty; *Cast includes:* Rod LaRocque, Phyllis Haver, Sam De Grasse, Max Barwyn, Julia Faye.

Political intrigue and spying in the Napoleonic era dominate this drama. Phyllis Haver portrays a countess who is admired by Emperor Napoleon Bonaparte. A member of her country's secret service, she has been assigned to bring back important papers from Spain. The treacherous Tallyrand (Sam De Grasse), meanwhile, threatens the success of her mission with his machinations. She recruits a young country innkeeper (Rod LaRocque) to help her complete her journey. Much of the film concentrates on the LaRocque character, a boastful figure who rises from a humble soldier to colonel. Max Barwyn impersonates Napoleon, and Julia Faye portrays Josephine in this uneven tale. ■

Fighting O'Flynn, The (1949), UI. *Dir.* Arthur Pierson; *Sc.* Douglas Fairbanks, Jr., Robert Thoeren; *Cast includes:* Douglas Fairbanks, Jr., Helena Carter, Patricia Medina, Richard Greene, Arthur Shields, J. M. Kerrigan.

A romantic adventure set in early-19th-century Ireland, the film stars Douglas Fairbanks, Jr. as the title character who comes home to Ireland to claim a castle willed to him by a late relative. In the end, he wins the love of a viceroy's daughter and saves his country from a French invasion. Fairbanks, a soldier of fortune and a likable rogue, dashes about with panache and humor, somewhat in the acrobatic tradition of his father, as he foils the plans of a traitorous officer (Richard Greene). Greene, a spy for Napoleon, is attempting to clear the way for the French general to gain control of Ireland from where he intends to invade England.

The woman Fairbanks falls in love with (Helena Carter), who is in danger and about to confide in him, asks: "Are you loyal to your king?" "My king?" he questions. "I'm an Irishman, and every Irishman is his own king." Later, during a conversation with Greene, Fairbanks, who has uncovered his rival's plot, is asked the price of his silence. "An Irishman silent?" Fairbanks laughs. This tone continues through most of the plot of this lilting adventure based on the novel *The O'Flynn* by Justin Huntly McCarthy. ■

Fire Over Africa (1954), Col. *Dir.* Richard Sale; *Sc.* Robert Westerby; *Cast includes:* Maureen O'Hara, Macdonald Carey, Binnie Barnes, Guy Middleton, Hugh McDermott, James Midburn.

A smuggling operation somewhere in Tangier forces customs officers and international police, frustrated in their attempts to uncover the ring, to bring in some of their top secret agents in this far-fetched drama filmed on location. Maureen O'Hara, as one of the special agents assigned to break up the smuggling racket, soon falls for Edmond O'Brien, portraying one of the gang. In reality, he is another agent working on the same case. Operating separately, they smash the smuggling ring, but only after O'Brien is shot several times. However, he manages to return to battle against the culprits.

Incidents and dialogue follow conventional patterns. "Your worries are over," announces a U.S. spokesman to other officials concerned about the illegal smuggling. "I've got just the gal. She's on her way here now. We'll keep this thing real secret." ■

Firefly of France, The (1918), Par. *Dir.* Donald Crisp; *Sc.* Margaret Turnbull; *Cast includes:* Wallace Reid, Ann Little, Charles Ogle, Raymond Hatton, Winter Hall.

A World War I drama, the film involves stolen plans belonging to France, German spies, car chases, a gunfight in a chateau and a love story with Wallace Reid and Ann Little as the principals. Reid portrays a young American who journeys to France to join the Lafayette Escadrille. He encounters a mysterious young woman (Ann Little) as well as several German spies. The "Firefly" of the title is a flier, a shadowy figure who initially disappears with the French plans. The French fear that he or the papers have fallen into enemy hands while newspaper stories suggest that he might be a traitor. The film is based on the 1918 novel by Marion Polk Angellotti. ■

Firefox (1982), WB. *Dir.* Clint Eastwood; *Sc.* Alex Lasker, Wendell Wellman; *Cast includes:* Clint Eastwood, Freddie Jones, David Huffman, Warren Clarke, Ronald Lacey, Kenneth Colley.

A U.S. pilot is assigned to secretly infiltrate Soviet military defenses in an effort to steal a highly advanced jet fighter in this slow-paced Cold War drama based on Craig Thomas' novel. Clint Eastwood, who also directed, portrays the stalwart retired American air ace whose mission it is to appropriate the super high-speed jet replete with weapons technology activated by the pilot's thoughts. After a long and detailed exposition showing Eastwood undergoing rigorous training in Great Britain for the special task before him, the second half of the drama consists of his efforts to escape in the cockpit of the plane. On his tail is another jet, a clone flown by a Soviet ace. A climactic battle between the two sleek planes finally ensues, with the predictable results. ■

First Comes Courage (1943), Col. *Dir.* Dorothy Arzner; *Sc.* George Sklar, Lewis Meltzer, Melvin Levy; *Cast includes:* Merle Oberon,

Brian Aherne, Carl Esmond, Fritz Leiber, Erville Alderson, Erik Rolf.

A World War II drama about resistance fighters in Nazi-occupied Norway, the film centers around a Norwegian (Merle Oberon) whose romance with a Nazi officer is only a ploy on her part to extract military information which is transmitted to England. A British commando (Brian Aherne) sent to Norway is captured and meets Oberon, whom he had met before the war. A commando strike force comes to the rescue of the pair, but Oberon volunteers to remain and continue her spy work. A slight twist in an otherwise routine drama occurs when the German officer and Oberon marry. After Aherne kills the husband, Oberon decides that her status as a widow of a Nazi officer will help her covert activities. The film was adapted from the novel *The Commandos* by Elliott Arnold. See Operation Nordpol. ∎

Japanese prison camp commandant Richard Loo attempts to take advantage of one of his prisoners of war, Barbara Hale, in the World War II drama *First Yank Into Tokyo* (1945).

First Yank Into Tokyo (1945), RKO. *Dir.* Gordon Douglas; *Sc.* J. Robert Bren, Gladys Atwater; *Cast includes:* Tom Neal, Barbara Hale, Marc Cramer, Richard Loo, Keye Luke.

Tom Neal portrays an American bomber pilot who volunteers to help rescue an American engineer held captive in Japan in this World War II drama. Army intelligence selects Neal because he has lived in Japan before the war. Doctors give him a facelift to make him look Japanese. They caution him that the operation will permanently alter his face. He agrees and, after a short stay in the hospital, is sent off to enemy territory. Neal not only rescues the engineer (Marc Cramer) but his girl-

friend (Barbara Hale) as well. A nurse on Bataan, she was captured and imprisoned by the Japanese when the peninsula fell.

The familiar propaganda elements that accompanied many films of the period are present. Scenes of Japanese atrocities, almost obligatory in World War II dramas, include those committed against American prisoners of war. Richard Loo, as a one-dimensional, sadistic, prison-camp officer, orders numerous punishments and boasts of Japanese dreams of conquest. "Your country is an overripe plum," he announces to an American prisoner. "It will be shaken to the earth by the wind sweeping from Japan." The American is quick to respond: "We know how to handle big winds."

A shot of the atom bomb exploding ends the story. This was a last-minute addition since the film, made before the bomb was announced, was released a month or so after the war. According to the original script, the U.S. needed the engineer for his invention of a new type of gun that would bring the war to a speedier end. Last-minute editing changed the weapon to the atom bomb, thereby making this the first film to deal with the A-bomb. ∎

Five Fingers (1952), TCF. *Dir.* Joseph L. Mankiewicz; *Sc.* Michael Wilson; *Cast includes:* James Mason, Danielle Darrieux, Michael Rennie, Walter Hampden, Oscar Karlweiss, Herbert Berghof.

A sophisticated spy thriller set in Turkey during World War II, the drama features James Mason as a valet to the British ambassador. Suave, persuasive and clever, Mason performs his job efficiently while in his off-duty hours he discreetly sells the Germans secret documents which he has photographed. To help him, he enlists the aid of a penniless Polish countess (Danielle Darrieux) who is desperate for money but proud. The Nazis, thinking Mason is a British agent, don't act on the information they purchase. Instead, they send a member of the Gestapo to Ankara to investigate their informant's authenticity. The newcomer poses as a Swiss businessman but gives himself away as he departs at a banquet in the countess's home. "How charmingly you Swiss click your heels," she remarks. "An old Swiss custom?" Meanwhile, the British, suspecting a leak at the Ankara embassy, dispatch their top counterintelligence agent (Michael Rennie) to investigate. He delights in the challenge, especially in insignificant gossip. "Counterespionage is the highest form of gossip," he announces to the British ambassador, portrayed by veteran actor Walter Hampden. John Wengraf, as the aristocratic and cynical German ambassador von Papen, grows impatient with the blundering Berlin officials who refuse to believe the documents are authentic. "Half-witted paranoiac gangsters!" he exclaims when he reads reports of a British raid on a German fuel depot that could have been prevented had Berlin acted upon Mason's information. The film ends with Mason's escape and retirement in South America, but he soon discovers that all the funds the Germans paid him are in counterfeit bills.

The screenplay is based on a true story that unfolded in Turkey in 1944. Elias Basna, an Albanian valet to the British ambassador, gained access to various plans, photographed them and sold them to members of the German embassy, chiefly Franz von Papen (1879–1969), a German diplomat and secret service officer. Among the more important information Basna turned over to von Papen were records of the wartime conferences between President Roosevelt and Prime Minister Churchill. Ironically, after the war Basna discovered that the money he received was counterfeit. A former employee of the German embassy, L. C. Moyzisch, described the events in a book titled *Operation Cicero*. See German Intelligence: World War II. ■

Five Graves to Cairo (1943), Par. *Dir.* Billy Wilder; *Sc.* Charles Brackett, Billy Wilder; *Cast includes:* Franchot Tone, Anne Baxter, Akim Tamiroff, Erich von Stroheim, Peter Van Eyck, Fortunio Bonanova.

A suspenseful World War II drama set in North Africa in 1942 after the fall of Tobruk, the film features Franchot Tone as a British corporal, the lone survivor of a tank crew, who seeks refuge in a hotel in a North African town. German troops, led by Field Marshal Rommel (Erich von Stroheim), arrive almost at the same time. Tone impersonates a German agent in an effort to get Rommel's African campaign plans.

Well-rounded characterizations add to the suspense and tone of the film. The anxious hotel owner (Akim Tamiroff) is worried that Tone will be discovered by the Nazis. Fortunio Bonanova, as a happy-go-lucky Italian general whom the Germans treat with scorn,

dismisses the insults. "Can a nation that belches understand a nation that sings?" he remarks. Anne Baxter, as a French maid whose brother is a prisoner in Germany, at one point is willing to betray Tone to help her brother. Peter Van Eyck portrays a smug, arrogant German lieutenant, a professional soldier who enjoys his work.

The obligatory war propaganda of the period intrudes occasionally. Tone, who is about to leave for British-held Cairo with Rommel's strategic plans, pleads the Allied cause. "It's not one brother that matters," Tone reminds Baxter, "it's a million brothers. It's not just one prison gate. . . . It's all their gates that must go." After he leaves, the Nazis execute her after she refuses to give them any information about Tone. When Tone returns to the hotel several months later following General Montgomery's counterattack, he learns of her death. Tamiroff leads him to the cemetery where she is buried. "We're after them now," he says, kneeling at her grave, "British, French and American. We're after them now, coming from all sides. We're going to blast the blazes out of them!"

Regardless of the propaganda, director-writer Billy Wilder and cowriter Charles Brackett have tried not to stereotype Rommel as just another Nazi villain. He is shown treating captured British officers with respect at a dinner party. But this may have been to promote his own vanity rather than to display any signs of warmth. The hotel setting and the variety of characters suggest a microcosmic interpretation: the arrogance of the two German officers, the humane Italian general's paradoxical attitudes about the Nazis and war in general, the French maid's flirting with collaboration, the double agent's British coolness and restraint. On the other hand, the didactic speeches, villainous German lieutenant, exaggerated courage of Baxter under fire and buffoonish portrayal of the Italian mark the film as a product of its time. The title refers to five locations in Egypt where the Germans, before the war, have secretly buried huge supplies of fuel in anticipation of a future war. ■

Five Guns West (1955), ARC. *Dir.* Roger Corman; *Sc.* R. Wright Campbell; *Cast includes:* John Lund, Dorothy Malone, Touch Connors, Bob Campbell, Jonothon Haze, Paul Birch.

A Confederate deserter, who has in his possession the names of undercover agents and a supply of gold, becomes the target of a manhunt in this Civil War drama. Southern authorities, in an effort to capture him, pardon five murderers (presumably the only men they can spare), swear them into service and assign them to the task. Their mission is to overtake the deserter at a way station operated by Dorothy Malone and her uncle (James Stone). The quintet, however, have other plans. They intend to keep the gold for themselves after killing the deserter. Unknown to the plotters, the Confederate army has secretly placed among them an officer (John Lund) to make certain they carry out their original mission. Lund, after indulging in a little romance with Malone, finally reveals his true identity and has to battle it out with the others to save the prisoners, Malone and her uncle. ■

Five Steps to Danger (1956), UA. Dir. Henry B. Kesler; Sc. Henry B. Kesler; *Cast includes*: Ruth Roman, Sterling Hayden, Werner Klemperer, Richard Gaines, Charles Davis, Jeanne Cooper.

Secret ballistics missiles are the subject of this Cold War drama. Sterling Hayden plays an innocent on vacation who becomes entangled with Soviet spies (Werner Klemperer, Richard Gaines). They would like to lay their hands on information concerning the missiles. Ruth Roman plays the female lead in this routine espionage story. ■

Flame of Stamboul (1951), Col. Dir. Ray Nazarro; Sc. Daniel B. Ullman; *Cast includes*: Richard Denning, Lisa Ferraday, Norman Lloyd, Nestor Paiva, George Zucco, Donald Randolph.

The defense plans for the Suez Canal become the target of an international thief and his agents in this low-budget tale of intrigue set in Egypt. Richard Denning, as a U.S. intelligence agent, is assigned to track down George Zucco, who portrays the "The Voice," the notorious mastermind behind the plot. Lisa Ferraday, as a local cabaret dancer, is involved in the scheme to steal the secret plans from an Egyptian official. Denning, a no-nonsense agent, is efficient at bringing the spy network to justice after he discovers their hide-out. ■

Flame of the Desert (1919), Goldwyn. Dir. Reginald Barker; Sc. Charles Logue; *Cast includes*: Geraldine Farrar, Lou Tellegen, Alec Francis, Edythe Chapman, Casson Ferguson, Macey Harlam.

Espionage and rebellion pervade this romantic drama set during the Sanusi Anti-British Revolt in colonial Egypt. Lady Isabella (Geraldine Farrar), an Englishwoman, falls in love with a sheik (Lou Tellegen), who is actually an English lord in disguise. His acceptance by other Egyptian leaders places him at their conference tables where he is able to learn of their plot to overthrow British rule. Farrar follows the bogus sheik to Egypt and becomes embroiled in the uprising which is quickly suppressed by the alert British. She is rescued by the lord and is awarded a medal, which is presented by the man she loves. Farrar is surprised to discover that the sheik is an Englishman.

The Sanusi Anti-British Revolt (1915–1917) was inspired by Turkish propaganda during World War I. Muslim kinship was used as a means to generate attacks on the British, who were then Turkey's enemy. Sanusi desert tribes in Egypt revolted against the British, who at the time controlled the country. The British, at first unsuccessful, eventually drove the Sanusi out of Egypt and into Libya's eastern province of Cyrenaica in 1917. ■

Flames of Chance (1918), Triangle. Dir. Raymond Wells; Sc. Harvey Gates, Elizabeth Haas; *Cast includes*: Jack Mulhall, Margery Wilson, Anna Dodge, Wilbur Higbee, Percy Challenger, Ben Lewis.

In this World War I spy story set in a German prisoner-of-war camp, Jack Mulhall portrays one of the captives who receive letters of encouragement from a New York stenographer. When one of the letters accidentally is held near a lamp, Mulhall notices secret writing on it. He realizes that the supposedly innocent mail is being used by spies in America to send messages to Germany. During a routine prisoner exchange he is selected for release from the camp because of a major wound. He heads for the United States where he eventually uncovers the spy, the young woman's boss. See German Intelligence: World War I. ■

Flight for Freedom (1943), RKO. *Dir.* Lothar Mendes; *Sc.* Oliver H. P. Garrett, S. K. Lauren; *Cast includes:* Rosalind Russell, Fred MacMurray, Herbert Marshall, Eduardo Ciannelli, Walter Kingsford.

Rosalind Russell portrays an American aviatrix in this fictionalized biography of Amelia Earhart that begins during World War II and flashes back to the early 1930s. The opening scenes include a voice-over that pays tribute to the contributions of the aviatrix. The flashback begins with Russell meeting another famous flier (Fred MacMurray), and they fall in love in spite of the warning of her instructor (Herbert Marshall) to stay away from aviators. The first half of the drama deals with the pilots' romantic complications and Russell's desire to break previous flying records.

The second half introduces international intrigue as MacMurray accidentally discovers a secret Japanese submarine base on a Japanese mandated island in the Pacific. Intelligence officers of the U.S. Navy, suspecting that the Japanese may have similar bases on other islands, ask Russell to volunteer her services for her country. They invent a ploy in which Russell, a world-famous pilot, will announce that she is lost somewhere in the Pacific, thereby initiating a search for her plane by the navy. U.S. planes, in reality, will be photographing all the Japanese islands for military installations while Russell hides out on a remote island.

Russell is summoned to Washington and presented with the secret plan. "We want you to do a job for us," a navy commander announces. "A job so big that I have no hesitation in saying that the safety of our country may well depend on its successful outcome." He then continues, "We know that for years the Japanese have been arming and fortifying the mandated islands in preparation for war against the United States. To protect ourselves, we must know the exact details and scope of these preparations."

Russell agrees and flies to New Guinea where a Japanese hotel clerk repeats the entire plan to her, warning her that a Japanese ship will be standing by where she is to land. The Japanese will then reveal to the world that she has been located, thereby negating the U.S. Navy search for her. Russell decides to make the journey anyway, deliberately crashing her plane into the Pacific so that the U.S. can carry out its reconnaissance.

Amelia Earhart (1898–1937), the American aviatrix, pioneered women's involvement in flight. She had several noteworthy accomplishments to her credit when she suddenly disappeared on July 2, 1937, near the South Pacific island of Howland. She was on the last third of an around-the-world flight. Unsubstantiated rumors repeatedly surfaced for many years afterward that she was forced down by the Japanese and crashed on a South Seas island because she allegedly discovered that Japan had built bases on mandated former German Pacific islands. At the time of her disappearance, Earhart and Lieutenant Commander Fred Noonan were flying a twin-engine Lockheed on the way back to the U.S. Two of the more recent biographies about Earhart appeared in 1989— *Amelia Earhart* by Doris L. Rich and *The Sound of Wings* by Mary S. Lovell. Both books explore the speculation that she might have been a spy assigned to reconnoiter Japanese military bases in the Caroline Islands and conclude that the conjecture has no basis in fact.

Earhart, born in Atchison, Kansas, served as a military nurse in Canada during World War I and then did social work in Boston before taking up flying. She was the first woman to cross the Atlantic by air (1928) as a passenger on a flight from Newfoundland to Wales. She married publisher George Putnam in 1931 but continued to use her own name in succeeding aerial endeavors. In 1932 she became the first woman to negotiate a solo crossing of the Atlantic. Among her solo exploits was a flight from Hawaii to California in 1935. During the early 1930s she also served as an officer of one of the early airlines to offer regular air service between Washington, D.C., and New York. ∎

Flight to Nowhere (1946), Golden Gate/Screen Guild. *Dir.* William Rowland; *Sc.* Arthur V. Jones; *Cast includes:* Alan Curtis, Evelyn Ankers, Micheline Cheirel, Jack Holt, Jerome Cowan, Hoot Gibson.

A map that reveals uranium deposits on a South Pacific island becomes the focus of intrigue and murder at a Death Valley hotel in this weak drama. A former U.S. intelligence agent (Alan Curtis) who has turned charter pilot is talked into helping his former bureau solve the murder of a Korean courier and the mystery of the missing map. After transporting a suspicious group of passengers to the hotel in Death Valley, Curtis begins his investigation. Only after he is knocked unconscious and several more murders are committed does he solve the case. Venerable action and western film star Jack Holt portrays Curtis' superior. Former silent and sound screen cowboy Hoot Gibson plays the local sheriff. Pretty Evelyn Ankers doesn't have much to do as the romantic interest. ∎

Flight to Tangier (1953), Par. *Dir.* Charles Marquis Warren; *Sc.* Charles Marquis Warren; *Cast includes:* Joan Fontaine, Jack Palance, Corinne Calvet, Robert Douglas, Marcel Dalio, Jeff Morrow.

A Communist plot to discredit the U.S., a mysterious plane that crashes with no one aboard and a refugee carrying $3 million in negotiable letters of credit make up this confused drama set in picturesque Tangier. The strange array of characters in this web of intrigue includes a U.S. intelligence agent (Joan Fontaine) posing as an American reporter, her partner posing as a freelance pilot, a U.S. war veteran (Jack Palance), a Cold War refugee (Corinne Calvet) who becomes a Soviet agent's mistress so that she can learn about her child trapped behind the Iron Curtain, and a black marketeer (Marcel Dalio) dealing in contraband war matériel.

Because the motivations of many of the principals are never made entirely clear until the final scenes, most of the film appears incoherent as one set of characters pursues the others. The Soviet agent turns on his black market partner after the latter leads the Russian to an abandoned airfield where the war supplies are hidden. "With the papers to prove I'm an American citizen," he explains, "I buy those materials and sell them behind what is referred to as the Iron Curtain. Then I'll have proved the point that the Americans are the warmongers we say they are." The Russian has Dalio killed and, with his minions, continues to pursue Palance and the others in an attempt to get the negotiable papers. Meanwhile, the pursued try to reach a Tangier bank so that the refugee can deposit the $3 million dollars. A final shoot-out in front of the bank results in the deaths of the Russian spies. Palance and Fontaine then return to the U.S. Calvet, who has learned that her child is dead, is killed in the gunfight. The film was originally released in both 3-D and conventional versions. ∎

Fly by Night (1942), Par. *Dir.* Robert Siodmak; *Sc.* Jay Dratler; *Cast includes:* Nancy Kelly, Richard Carlson, Albert Basserman, Martin Kosleck, Walter Kingsford, Nestor Paiva.

An innocent man gets mixed up in a murder and a sinister spy ring in this low-budget World War II Hitchcockian-style drama. Richard Carlson portrays a doctor who gives a seemingly innocuous-looking man a lift in his car. The stranger is an inventor who has escaped from a sanitarium. When the passenger is found murdered, Carlson is arrested for the crime. He escapes and, with the aid of Nancy Kelly, tracks down the actual culprits, a nest of spies trying to steal the victim's "secret weapon." ∎

Flying Blind (1941), Par. *Dir.* Frank McDonald; *Sc.* Maxwell Shane, Richard Murphy; *Cast includes:* Richard Arlen, Jean Parker, Nils Asther, Marie Wilson, Roger Pryor.

Foreign agents try to steal a newly developed transformer for use in fighter aircraft in this low-budget World War II drama, released prior to America's entry into the world conflict. Richard Arlen portrays an air service operator who becomes entangled in the plot. Jean Parker plays his secretary and provides the romantic interest. Eddie Quillan, as his buddy in charge of mechanics, adds some comic relief. Former silent screen star Nils Asther, as a foreign agent, is eventually foiled after a series of exciting incidents.

Arlen and Parker were featured in a series of air action dramas, including *Power Dive* and *Forced Landing*, all released the same year. The latter film concerns political turmoil in a fictitious country where the villainous leadership is usurped by Nils Asther. J. Carrol Naish plays the rebel leader trying to free his land of corrupt forces. ∎

Flying G-Men (1939) serial, Col. *Dir.* Ray Taylor, James W. Horne; *Sc.* Robert E. Kent, Basil Dickey, Sherman Lowe; *Cast includes:* Robert Paige, Richard Fiske, James Craig, Lorna Gray, Sammy McKim.

Aimed chiefly at a juvenile audience, this serial tells of a network of spies who threaten the U.S. with an invasion. A quartet of U.S. Secret Service airmen, led by Robert Paige, help to foil all the plans the sinister enemy agents can muster, including a reign of terror, gun battles and assorted attempts at sabotage. See Serials. ∎

Flying High (1927), Lumas. *Dir.* Charles Hutchison; *Sc.* L. V. Jefferson; *Cast includes:* William Fairbanks, Alice Calhoun, John Wells, Leroy Mason, Cecile Callahan.

A highly respected member of society uses her social contacts and functions as a subterfuge. In reality she spies for her husband who leads a gang of air-mail thieves. To cover his operations, the husband manages an air express business. William Fairbanks, as the hero of this stunt-filled melodrama, portrays a commercial pilot who early in the film has an accidental encounter with the air thieves. Later, he and his assistant are responsible for tracking down the bandits' hide-out and their eventual capture. ■

Flying Saucer, The (1950), Film Classics. *Dir.* Mikel Conrad; *Sc.* Howard Irving Young; *Cast includes:* Mikel Conrad, Pat Garrison, Hantz Von Teuffen, Lester Sharpe, Russell Hicks, Frank Darien.

The U.S. Secret Service drafts a native Alaskan playboy to prevent Russian agents from stealing a flying saucer in this inept drama filmed on location in Alaska. Producer-director Mikel Conrad portrays the hastily recruited government agent. Working with his pretty assistant (Pat Garrison), who also provides some romantic interest, they become enmeshed in several scrapes with the Russian spies before all ends well. A convenient avalanche eliminates the intruders at the proper moment. Russell Hicks portrays the U.S. Secret Service chief who assigns Conrad to the mission. Roy Engel plays the scientist who developed the saucer. ■

Flying Torpedo, The (1916), Triangle. *Dir.* Jack O'Brien, Christy Cabanne; *Sc.* Robert Baker, John Emerson; *Cast includes:* John Emerson, Spotiswoode Aitken, William E. Lawrence, Fred Butler, Raymond Wells, Viola Barry.

A silent fantasy about a foreign invasion of America, the plot centers around the invention of a new weapon, a flying torpedo. An unnamed foreign power sends its spies to steal the model of this powerful destructive force. Armed with the new device, the belligerent country attacks the Pacific coast of the U.S., landing its troops first in California. However, a resourceful American designs a similar weapon, and it is unleashed upon the invaders, driving them out of California.

An advocate of the "preparedness" school of war dramas, the film, according to its studio, received the earnest support of the government. The military provided torpedoes to be exhibited in theater lobbies where they set up recruitment booths. ■

Flying Wild (1941), Mon. *Dir.* William West; *Sc.* Al Martin; *Cast includes:* Leo Gorcey, Bobby Jordan, "Sunshine Sammy" Morrison, Joan Barclay, Dave O'Brien.

Another in the comedy series featuring the Dead End Kids, renamed here the East Side Kids, this entry concerns the comic antics of the gang who are presently employed at a defense plant. They eventually become entangled with an enemy spy ring that is bent on stealing important airplane blueprints. The routine plot results in the usual slapstick mayhem. Joan Barclay provides the romantic interest for Dave O'Brien, who helps the boys uncover the villains. O'Brien had two careers in Hollywood B movies and serials—that of stunt man and leading man. He played in numerous westerns and action dramas when he wasn't doubling for the hero in other films. ■

Follow the Girl (1917), U. *Dir.* L. W. Chaudet; *Sc.* Fred Myton; *Cast includes:* Ruth Stonehouse, Roy Stewart, Jack Dill, Claire Brey, Alfred Allen, Harry Dunkinson.

A World War I drama about a Swedish immigrant maid who becomes entangled with foreign agents plotting against the U.S., the propaganda-oriented film underscores the responsibilities of all citizens to their nation during wartime. Ruth Stonehouse portrays the young Swedish heroine who comes to America in her search for a quiet life. But she is called upon to help her newly adopted country and eventually helps to foil the plans of the enemy agents. Several films of the period dealt with emigrants seeking refuge from strife-torn Europe, including *Fields of Honor*, released the following year. ■

"For the Common Defense" (1942), MGM. *Dir.* Allan Kenward; *Cast includes:* Van Johnson, Douglas Fowley, Jacqueline Dalya, Egon Brecher, Horace McNally.

Part of MGM's "Crime Does Not Pay" series of two-reel shorts, this entry concerns a spy network operating in South America. Its leaders blackmail an American mobster into working for them. Van Johnson soon emerged as one of MGM's major romantic stars. Horace (Steve) McNally became a well-known actor in feature films during the 1950s. See "Crime Does Not Pay." ■

For the Honor of Old Glory or Carrying the Stars and Stripes Into Mexico (1914), World.

A Mexican spy manipulates his way into the good graces of an American colonel and becomes a second lieutenant in the officer's cavalry regiment. The remainder of this silent film, set during the Mexican War, tells how the spy leads the colonel, his family and the regiment into a trap in Mexico. The colonel's pretty daughter is kidnapped, while battles break out between the American troops and Mexican soldiers in this not too realistic story. ■

Forbidden Cargo (1925), FBO. Dir. Tom Buckingham; Sc. Fred Kennedy Myton; Cast includes: Evelyn Brent, Robert Ellis, Boris Karloff.

Robert Ellis portrays a U.S. Secret Service agent stationed in the Bahamas to put a stop to rumrunners operating in the area. He meets Captain Joe (Evelyn Brent), the daughter of a naval captain who has been unjustly cashiered from the service. Determined to help prove her father's innocence, Captain Joe vows to make enough money with her yacht and crew by engaging in smuggling. Meanwhile she falls in love with Ellis. Her jealous first mate (Boris Karloff) learns his true identity and takes him prisoner aboard the fugitive yacht where he is forced to do manual labor.

Following a battle with hijackers in which Captain Joe and Ellis escape, Karloff recaptures the secret service agent and ties him up. Captain Joe, locked in a cabin below, signals a destroyer in the vicinity. She unties Ellis just before an explosion set by Karloff destroys the yacht. The ending includes a scene in which the government absolves Joe's father of all past charges. ■

Forbidden Woman (1927), Pathé. Dir. Paul I. Stein; Sc. Clara Beranger; Cast includes: Jetta Goudal, Ivan Lebedeff, L. Snegoff, Josephine Norman, Victor Varconi, Joseph Schildkraut.

Jetta Goudal, as the daughter of an Arab mother and a French father, acts as spy for her elderly grandfather, a sheik who is trying to resist French conquest in this romantic drama set in Algiers. Assigned to gather military plans from the French, Goudal marries a French colonel (Victor Varconi) as a means of expediting her mission. When her husband journeys to France on a secret military assignment, she follows him and meets a violinist (Joseph Schildkraut) on board ship. They soon fall in love, with neither knowing at the time that he is the colonel's brother. Eventually the officer learns of the illicit romance. Infuriated with his brother, he forces Schildkraut to serve under him in the Foreign Legion. ■

Foreign Agent (1942), Mon. Dir. William Beaudine; Sc. Martin Mooney, John Krafft; Cast includes: John Shelton, Gale Storm, Ivan Lebedeff, Hanz Schumm, William Halligan, George Travell.

Hollywood serves as background for this World War II drama. Nazi spies have a double mission in the film capital. They desire the plans for a special light filter and attempt to persuade citizens to resist the war effort. John Shelton finally uncovers the dual plot. Gale Storm portrays an aspiring actress in this film of life on the home front according to Hollywood. Like several other dramas released during World War II, the film has its share of propaganda, including the song "It's Taps for the Japs." ■

Foreign Correspondent (1940), UA. Dir. Alfred Hitchcock; Sc. Charles Bennett, Joan Harrison; Cast includes: Joel McCrea, Laraine Day, Herbert Marshall, George Sanders, Albert Basserman, Robert Benchley.

Hitchcock's highly suspenseful and exciting drama of political intrigue on the eve of World War II was his second American film. Joel McCrea, as an American reporter sent to Europe in August of 1939 to uncover the truth about the threat of war, becomes entangled in an international spy ring whose members are posing as part of a peace organization. He witnesses the kidnapping of a famous Dutch diplomat and the assassination of the diplomat's double. Several attempts are made on his life as he attempts to expose the leaders of the ring. George Sanders, as a fellow reporter, aids him in the search. Herbert Marshall portrays the mastermind behind the plot, while his daughter (Laraine Day), unaware of her father's ties to Nazi Germany, falls in love with McCrea.

The director has loaded the film with his usual inventive devices and witty style. Mc-

Lobby card with Laraine Day, Joel McCrea and George Sanders working together to unravel a kidnapping plot by enemy agents in Alfred Hitchcock's World War II drama *Foreign Correspondent* (1940).

Crea's pursuit of an assassin through a crowd of umbrella-carrying onlookers is cleverly executed, as is the climactic plane crash of a transatlantic clipper. There is probably more of Hitchcock's humor in this film than in any of his other works. Robert Benchley plays a correspondent who spends half his day rewriting government press releases and the other half drinking. A humorous Latvian who understands no English appears occasionally. There is the running gag of McCrea losing a variety of hats. Much of the dialogue is witty. When McCrea is about to be arrested by Dutch authorities, he says: "I hope the chief of police speaks English." "We all speak English," the officer replies. "That's more than I could say for my country," McCrea quips.

Once war breaks out near the end of the film, the dialogue—much of it written by James Hilton and Robert Benchley—turns serious and patriotic. "This is London," a radio announcer says at the beginning of a worldwide broadcast. "We have as a guest tonight one of the soldiers of the press—one of the little army of historians who are writing history from beside the cannon's mouth." McCrea is about to go on the air, but he is interrupted by an air raid and the lights go out. As bombs rain down on London, he addresses America from the darkened radio studio: "The lights are all out everywhere—except in America. Keep those lights burning. Cover them with steel. Ring them with guns. Build a canopy of battleships and bombing planes around them. Hello, America. Hang on to your lights. They're the only lights left in the world."

This last scene, which intensifies the immediacy of the drama, was hastily added to the film when it became obvious that air attacks over England were forthcoming. In addition, it served as effective propaganda. Few Americans who saw the film realized at the time that the British government had asked the director to stay in Hollywood and continue to turn out propaganda dramas arousing anti-Nazi sentiments. Britain also hoped that such films would prod the U.S. to enter the war. ∎

Foreign Intrigue (1956), UA. *Dir.* Sheldon Reynolds; *Sc.* Sheldon Reynolds; *Cast includes:* Robert Mitchum, Genevieve Page, Ingrid Thulin, Frederick O'Brady, Gene Deckers, Ingrid Tidblad.

The death of a blackmailer leads to a trail of traitors from various countries in this drama set in different European cities. Robert Mitchum, as a press agent for the dead man, becomes curious about his subject's real identity and begins to investigate the victim's background. Meanwhile foreign spies and government agents are also interested in the corpse's identity. It seems the blackmailer was extorting money from well-known Europeans who, during World War II, were working for Hitler and plotting against their own countries. Genevieve Page, as the blackmailer's wife, turns out to be almost as dangerous as her husband. Gene Deckers portrays a government agent seeking the names of those who paid hush money to the dead man. Frederick O'Brady plays a foreign agent who is trying to profit by the situation. Ingrid Thulin provides the romantic interest for Mitchum. ∎

Foreign Legion, The (1928), U. *Dir.* Edward Sloman; *Sc.* Charles Kenyon; *Cast includes:* Norman Kerry, Lewis Stone, Mary Nolan, Craufurd Kent, Walter Perry, June Marlowe.

A weak romantic drama with the legendary French Foreign Legion as background, the film concerns an English army officer who sacrifices his career for a woman who has rejected him. When the officer (Norman Kerry) learns that the woman he loves (Mary Nolan) has married a French spy, he decides to protect her marriage. He accepts responsibility for an attempt to steal some secret plans. In reality, his former sweetheart's husband is the guilty party. The conventional elements of the Foreign Legion genre are present, including marching soldiers, army barracks and desert vistas. Veteran actor Lewis Stone portrays the proverbial avuncular colonel. ∎

Formula, The (1980), MGM. *Dir.* John G. Avildsen; *Sc.* Steve Shagan; *Cast includes:* George C. Scott, Marthe Keller, Marlon Brando, John Van Dreelen, Calvin Jung, John Gielgud.

This botched-up version of Steve Shagan's best-selling novel about international intrigue concerns both the investigation of a murder and the search for a formula for synthetic fuel. The film opens during the last days of World War II. An American major (Robin Clarke) captures a Nazi general (Richard Lynch) who is carrying important documents. The major soon recognizes the value of some of the documents, especially the synthetic fuel formula. The two officers then study the papers as they contemplate their financial future.

The film then shifts to the present where Clarke, now a retired Los Angeles police officer, is found murdered. George C. Scott, an old friend of the victim, is assigned to investigate the killing. Information from the victim's former wife (Beatrice Straight), who is brutally murdered after her talk with the detective, leads Scott to a powerful oil industrialist, played by Marlon Brando. The convoluted plot next takes Scott to Europe and confrontations with several other mysterious figures who have some connection with the murders and the coveted formula, including an enigmatic spy (Marthe Keller) who is assigned by a nebulous organization to befriend him. Several of those who confide in Scott are killed.

A final confrontation with Brando supplies Scott with the motivations behind all the killings and intrigue. "The sole function of any international cartel," Brando explains to the idealistic police officer, "is to insure political harmony. The first obligation of power is to lead. Now that's been the Holy Grail since the Industrial Revolution." Scott, attempting to dispute the tycoon's arrogance, adds: "You trade lives and human dignity for profit." But Brando, who wants to suppress the formula while he drives up the price of oil in America, parries with an inscription on a gold-plated cigarette box: "'Money, not morality, is the principal commerce of civilization.' Thomas Jefferson, 200 years ago."

The film expends much of its energy developing similar conspiracies. John Gielgud, as the German inventor of the fuel, defends himself against Scott's accusations of deception by explaining why none of his plants were bombed by the Allies during the war. "Certain American oil companies," he exclaims, "shared chemical patents with the Third Reich. Americans were in business with the Third Reich then, and the same partnership exists today. There is blood on your hands, too, mister." Early in the film Brando rejects his assistant's suggestion to increase the price of gas 12 cents rather than the more discreet seven cents that Brando settles on. "People will accept the 12 cents now because we can blame it on the Arabs," the man says. "You're missing the point," Brando replies. "We are the Arabs." Both director Avildsen and screenwriter Shagan claimed the final production, edited by the studio, did not represent their individual creative efforts. ∎

Fort Algiers (1953), UA. *Dir.* Lesley Selander; *Sc.* Theodore St. John; *Cast includes:* Yvonne De Carlo, Carlos Thompson, Raymond Burr, Leif Erickson, Anthony Caruso, John Dehner.

The French Foreign Legion faces another Arab insurrection in this action drama. Yvonne De Carlo portrays a French spy masquerading as a café singer. She is assigned to gather information concerning hostile Arab activities. She accomplishes this by developing a friendship with the principal villainous chieftain (Raymond Burr) whose plans include the destruction of strategic oil fields. Burr eventually gets wise to her, but she is rescued by another agent and her true love. Carlos Thompson, as the hero, a former Legionnaire, tries to prove that he was wrongly court-martialed. Exciting action sequences include the obligatory climactic skirmish between the Legion and the Arabs. ∎

49th Man, The (1953), Col. *Dir.* Fred F. Sears; *Sc.* Harry Essex; *Cast includes:* John Ireland, Richard Denning, Suzanne Dalbert, Robert C. Foulk, Touch Connors, Richard Avonde, William R. Klein.

Enemy agents sneak an atom bomb into the U.S. under the cover of a government war game in this far-fetched drama set during the Cold War. The original simulation game is a test to see if U.S. government security agents are capable of tracking down the smuggling of bombs into the nation. John Ireland, as one of the U.S. operatives, uncovers the operation and proves that it was arranged by the Security Investigation Division and navy personnel. But after the success of the experiment, Ireland suspects that real spies have used the situation to bring in an actual atom bomb. He and a fellow agent (Richard Denning) begin investigating and discover the real danger. They drop the captured bomb over a desert testing area where it explodes harmlessly. ∎

Forty Winks (1925), Par. *Dir.* Frank Urson, Paul Iribe; *Sc.* Bertram Millhauser; *Cast includes:* Raymond Griffith, Viola Dana, Theodore Roberts, Cyril Chadwick, Anna May Wong.

A young lieutenant faces a court-martial when spies steal secret military plans in this comedy drama of intrigue. Raymond Griffith, a talented silent screen comedian who specialized in sophisticated roles, portrays Lord Chumley, a seemingly bumbling dolt who in reality is a secret service agent. He traces the stolen papers to one of the conspirators (Anna May Wong) and manages to return them in time to save the youth. Cyril Chadwick portrays the chief villain who arranged the theft. His purpose was to exchange the plans in return for the hand of the lieutenant's sister (Viola Dana), who is engaged to Chumley. The film is based on *Lord Chumley*, a play by David Belasco and Henry C. De Mille. ∎

Four Horsemen of the Apocalypse, The (1962), MGM. *Dir.* Vincente Minnelli; *Sc.* Robert Ardrey, John Gay; *Cast includes:* Glenn Ford, Ingrid Thulin, Charles Boyer, Lee J. Cobb, Paul Lukas, Paul Henreid.

A remake of the popular 1921 silent version of the Ibanez novel, this glossy Technicolor production of a family torn by war and fighting on opposite sides failed critically and at the box office. The story is updated to World War II and offers several imaginative special-effects images of war. But the overall result lacks conviction. Glenn Ford portrays Julio Desnoyers, the role that brought fame to Rudolph Valentino. Ingrid Thulin, whose voice had to be dubbed by Angela Lansbury, plays Marguerite Laurier, Julio's mistress. She is married to a French officer (Paul Henreid) who later joins the Resistance and is killed by the Gestapo. Charles Boyer is featured as Marcelo Desnoyers, Julio's father. Paul Lukas portrays the matriarch of the German branch of the family.

Julio, who has tried to remain neutral and detached from the war, eventually joins the French underground as one of its agents. Able to move freely among Nazi officials in Paris because of his social and financial position, he becomes a valuable asset to the Resistance by providing its leaders with highly classified information. He sacrifices his life for the Allied cause when his superiors assign him to locate a hidden German panzer division somewhere in Normandy. On the pretense of visiting his cousin Heinrich, a German colonel with the camouflaged tank division, he gains access to the area and wires the information to England. Heinrich, however, arrests Julio as a spy. "I . . . envied you once . . . for your independence," the officer confesses, disgusted now with Julio's actions. "No one can be independent, not in your world," Julio replies, resigned to his fate. "Finally, a man's got to take sides, no matter what the reason." The silent version starring Rudolph Valentino has no spy element in the plot. ■

Four Men and a Prayer (1938), TCF. *Dir.* John Ford; *Sc.* Richard Sherman, Sonya Levien, Walter Ferris; *Cast includes:* Loretta Young, Richard Greene, George Sanders, David Niven, C. Aubrey Smith, J. Edward Bromberg.

Four sons are determined to prove the innocence of their father, an English general who has been dishonorably discharged from the service. C. Aubrey Smith, as the patriarch, has been betrayed by underlings and is later murdered by secret agents of an international armaments company. Richard Greene, George Sanders, David Niven and William Henry portray the general's sons who journey to different continents as they seek out clues to clear their father's name and expose those responsible for his murder. Loretta Young portrays the female lead in this tale of international intrigue based on the novel by David Garth. ■

Fourth War, The (1990), New Age Releasing. *Dir.* John Frankenheimer; *Sc.* Stephen Peters, Kenneth Ross; *Cast includes:* Roy Scheider, Jurgen Prochnow, Tim Reid, Lara Harris, Harry Dean Stanton, Dale Dye.

An embittered, alcoholic American career soldier and ex-Vietnam officer who can't come to terms with the silence of guns almost sets off a conflagration between the East and West in this Cold War drama set in 1988 on the West German-Czechoslovak border. Roy Scheider portrays Col. Jack Knowles, who has just been assigned as the new base commander. On his first day at his new assignment, Knowles is forced to simply stand by and watch as a Czech defector is gunned down by the Russians as he tries to cross the border. Frustrated and unable to accept the situation, Knowles can hardly contain

himself. He throws a snowball at the Soviet commander, Colonel Valachev (Jurgen Prochnow), another career officer who had fought in Afghanistan. The Russian returns the snowball with equal vigor. Later, Valachev hovers overhead in a Russian helicopter, which adds fuel to his American counterpart's seething anger.

The remainder of the film concerns a series of covert actions each colonel carries out against the other's command. Following Knowles' solo incursion across the border where he sets a Soviet guard post aflame, Valachev retaliates by destroying Knowles' jeep with a rocket grenade. The potentially deadly games continue until the two antagonists meet in a final hand-to-hand combat—like two anachronistic dinosaurs or over-the-hill knights who have stepped out of the Middle Ages. Harry Dean Stanton, as the U.S. general in charge of operations, acts as the voice of reason. He reprimands Knowles while showing that he understands the psyche of the trigger-happy colonel. The title of the film comes from Albert Einstein, who once said that if a third world war were ever fought with nuclear weapons, the fourth would be fought with stones. The work is based on the novel by Stephen Peters, who collaborated on the screenplay. ■

Fox, The (1921), U. *Dir.* Robert Thornby; *Sc.* Lucien Hubbard; *Cast includes:* Harry Carey, George Nichols, Gertrude Olmsted, Betty Ross Clark, Alan Hale.

Cowboy star Harry Carey, as an undercover agent for the U.S. Secret Service, poses as a hobo to get the goods on a band of outlaws in this routine western drama. Offering some of the usual conventions of the genre, including chases and cavalry action, the film has at least one interesting human interest touch. Carey during his travels rescues a young orphan (Breezy Eason, Jr.) from a cruel animal trainer. He later adopts the boy. Carey allows himself to be jailed so that he can gather information about the outlaw gang operating out of a desert town. He soon rounds up the miscreants and its leader—the president of the local bank. ■

Frantic (1988), WB. *Dir.* Roman Polanski; *Sc.* Roman Polanski, Gerard Brach; *Cast includes:* Harrison Ford, Emmanuelle Seigner, Betty Buckley, John Mahoney, Jimmie Ray Weeks, Yorgo Voyagis.

A luggage mix-up at a Paris airport plunges an American couple into a hellish vortex of international intrigue and murder in this slow-paced drama. Dr. and Mrs. Walker (Harrison Ford and Betty Buckley) are Americans visiting Paris for a physicians' convention where Walker is scheduled to address his fellow physicians. The couple arrive at their hotel where they discover that Mrs. Walker has the wrong piece of luggage. Walker notifies the airline and then takes a shower. Meanwhile his wife answers the telephone and leaves the room. Hours later, when she fails to return, the doctor begins to make inquiries and learns that she was forcibly taken into a car. His encounters with the local police and the U.S. embassy prove helpless, so he decides to investigate on his own.

The remainder of the film concerns his search for his missing wife and his meeting with Michele (Emmanuelle Seigner), the courier who was hired to transport the luggage from the U.S. to France. She helps him unravel part of the mystery. Walker later discovers that the suitcase contains a model of the Statue of Liberty. Inside the model is an electronic triggering device used for setting off nuclear bombs. It seems that Arab agents were expecting the device which had been stolen from the manufacturer. Walker manages to rescue his wife by offering to trade the device for her freedom. A shoot-out occurs between the Arabs and another shadowy group. Michele is mortally wounded in the crossfire and dies in the doctor's arms as his wife looks on in horror. When U.S. embassy security agents ask the physician for the coveted device, he tosses it into a nearby river.

The film is often reminiscent of Hitchcock's screen world where the innocent are suddenly jarred out of their world of order into a chaotic whirlpool of nightmarish events that almost totally engulf them. In addition, director-screenwriter Polanski borrows Hitchcock's plot device of introducing a simple, commonplace incident or object that propels the main character into a world of desperation. In Hitchcock's *North by Northwest*, for example, Cary Grant is innocently mistaken for the enigmatic Mr. Kaplan; Polanski's "inciting force" is the luggage mix-up. Also present is Hitchcock's "MacGuffin," this time in the form of the electronic triggering device. Polanski's main character undergoes similar problems faced by Hitchcock's principals. Walker's frantic search for his wife frequently leads only to frustration—he can't speak French, those he approaches can't help him, and the police represent a tangle of bureaucracy. But unlike Hitchcock, Polanski adopts a more contemporary anti-establishment approach, as demonstrated by the doctor's final response to the U.S. agents' request. ∎

Friendly Enemies (1925), PDC. *Dir.* George Melford; *Sc.* Alfred A. Cohn; *Cast includes:* Joe Weber, Lew Fields, Virginia Brown Faire, Jack Mulhall, Stuart Holmes.

A comedy drama set during World War I, this was the first full-length feature that the famous vaudeville and stage comedians, Weber and Fields, appeared in. They both portray German-Americans. Fields, a loyal patriot of his adopted country, is proud of his son who is in the army and about to be shipped to France to fight against Germany. His friend, Weber, however, remains loyal to the Fatherland and donates money to a German organization which he hopes will bring an early end to the war. He later learns that German spies control the enterprise and that his money was used to sink a troopship of American soldiers. Fortunately, Fields' son was not aboard at the time. The U.S. Secret Service eventually rounds up the enemy agents.

Aside from its humor and love interest, the film, released years after the war, emphasizes the duties and responsibilities of foreign-born Americans and their offspring toward their new homeland. This was a real-life dilemma for many German-American citizens when the original play by Samuel Shipman and Aaron Hoffman first appeared in 1918 during World War I. ∎

Friendly Enemies (1942), UA. *Dir.* Allan Dwan; *Sc.* Adelaide Heilbron; *Cast includes:* Charles Winninger, Charles Ruggles, James Craig, Nancy Kelly, Otto Kruger.

A remake of the 1925 silent comedy drama, this sound version of the Shipman-Hoffman stage play of 1918 has been updated to fit the background of World War II. Unfortunately, the script and comedy material remain in the past. Charles Winninger and Charles Ruggles portray the bickering German-American tycoons who differ in their loyalties to the U.S. and Germany. Winninger, who is sympathetic to Germany, is deceived into contributing to enemy saboteurs and learns too late that he has helped sink an American troop-ship that was transporting his own son. He then joins forces with Ruggles, who plays the fiercely American supporter, to help the secret service capture a German agent. Winninger's son (James Craig), thought to be lost at sea, returns to marry Ruggles' daughter. The film relies heavily on dialect humor for its laughs. ■

From Two to Six (1918), Triangle. *Dir.* Thomas F. Tracey; *Cast includes:* Winifred Allen, Earle Foxe, Forrest Robinson, Robert Fischer, Margaret Greene.

An inventor's daughter is determined to recover the plans for a secret weapon that were stolen from her father in this comedy drama. Following a spy whom she suspects of the theft, the young woman arrives at a hotel room where the chief of the spy ring dwells. She boldly enters and demands the return of the plans. It so happens that a young man has been hiding in the same room and overhears the conversation. In an attempt to escape from his father who is trying to force him into an undesirable marriage, he had entered the spy's quarters through the window of an adjoining room. When he hears the master spy threaten the inventor's daughter, the young

intruder intercedes and rescues her and the plans. The spies are arrested, and a romance blossoms as a result of the incident. The title refers to the time limit placed upon the young man either to marry or lose a hefty inheritance. The daughter accepts his proposal and his fortune is saved. ■

Full of Pep (1919), Metro. *Dir.* Harry L. Franklin; *Sc.* Robert F. Hill; *Cast includes:* Hale Hamilton, Alice Lake, Alice Knowland, Fred Malatesta, Victor Potel.

Hale Hamilton becomes embroiled in a Central American revolution in this satirical comedy set in the fictitious country of Santa Dinero. Agreeing to deliver a large shipment of munitions to the president of the small country who is facing a revolution, our American hero must first go under cover as a patent medicine salesman. His bottles, however, contain whiskey, which he distributes liberally to the soldiers. When the villainous General Lopanzo (Fred Malatesta), leader of the insurrection, gives the signal for the revolution to begin, the army refuses to follow him. The revolt peters out, and the legitimate president regains control of the country. Alice Lake, as a local beauty, plays the female lead. ■

G

Game Chicken, The (1922), Par. *Dir.* Chester Franklin; *Sc.* Fred Myton; *Cast includes:* Bebe Daniels, Pat O'Malley, James Gordon, Martha Mattox, Gertrude Norman.

A U.S. Secret Service agent uncovers a gang of rumrunners operating between Cuba and Massachusetts in this comedy drama. Pat O'Malley, as the investigator, becomes entangled with the strong-headed daughter (Bebe Daniels) of the leader of the smugglers. One of the gang discovers O'Malley's identification card while the agent is investigating a suspicious vessel. The head of the Cuban branch of the gang convinces Daniels that O'Malley has been using her to gain information about her father. She believes him and leads the agent into a trap. O'Malley is tied up and taken aboard a sailing ship, but Daniels has a change of heart and rescues him. The film includes several fights and a last-minute rescue by a navy ship. The couple, of course, resolve their differences. ■

Gas, Oil and Water (1922), FN. *Dir.* Charles Ray; *Sc.* Richard Andres; *Cast includes:* Charles Ray, Otto Hoffman, Charlotte Pierce, Robert Gray, Dick Sutherland.

A U.S. Secret Service agent is assigned to investigate smuggling along the Mexican border in this silent drama. Charles Ray portrays the operative who, as a cover for his inquiries, goes into business as a gas station owner. The flimsy plot includes automobile and motorcycle chases before the culprits are brought to justice. The film never explains what the illegal contraband is. Charlotte Pierce portrays the female lead. Ray was more popular with movie audiences in his sentimental rural dramas. ■

Gay Diplomat, The (1931), RKO. *Dir.* Richard Boleslawski; *Sc.* Doris Anderson; *Cast includes:* Ivan Lebedoff, Genevieve Tobin, Betty Compson, Ilka Chase, Parnell Pratt, Rita La Roy.

Ivan Lebedoff portrays Captain Orloff, a handsome Russian officer, in this World War I romantic spy fable. Women are so overpowered by his charm that they completely confide in him. When the chief of Russian intelligence learns of the officer's romantic talents, he assigns the young officer to Bucharest to track down a female spy who is suspected of penetrating Russian communications in neutral Rumania. When Orloff, at first reluctant to act as a spy, hears that the assignment concerns romancing women, he eagerly accepts. "Many a great soldier has been defeated by a woman," warns the head of Russia's secret police. But Orloff ignores the warning and sets off by train for Bucharest.

Lebedoff first suspects attractive Genevieve Tobin, with whom he falls in love after meeting her aboard the train. Following much inept dialogue and several murders unrelated to the plot, Lebedoff cunningly tricks the actual Rumanian spy into confessing. She turns out to be the wife (Betty Compson) of the chief of Russian agents in Rumania.

The slow-paced plot offers a few moments of interest. The opening sequence consists of exciting cavalry charges at the front where Lebedoff is wounded. The battle scenes are effective but have little to do with ensuing events. There is one lavish set—a ballroom sequence in which Captain Orloff is introduced to Rumanian society and a handful of possible secret agents. Nude statues and statuettes appear in several scenes as preludes to Orloff's several bedroom affairs with women who try to use him for their own ends. Betrayal as well as adultery are treated casually. When a guest at the above-mentioned ball is mysteriously murdered, the chief of the Russian secret police asks the Russian ambassador: "Was he in their secret service or ours?" "Both," the ambassador replies. ■

Geisha Girl (1952), Realart. *Dir.* George Breakston, C. Ray Stahl; *Sc.* C. Ray Stahl; *Cast includes:* Martha Hyer, William Andrews, Archer MacDonald, Kekao Yokoo, Teddy Yakamura, Henry Okawa.

Two American soldiers and an airline hostess stumble upon a nest of Japanese saboteurs in this inept, low-budget drama filmed on location in Japan. William Andrews and Archer MacDonald, as two veterans of the Korean War, are on their way home to the U.S. While in Tokyo, they become entangled with Japanese agents who are using special pills with explosive powers. Martha Hyer, as an American air hostess, joins the Americans in their sleuthing to uncover the conspiracy. Their adventures give the camera a chance to exploit some of the sites and customs of Japan before the local authorities step in and round up the villains. ■

General, The (1927), UA. *Dir.* Buster Keaton, Clyde Bruckman; *Sc.* Al Boasberg, Charles Smith; *Cast includes:* Buster Keaton, Marion Mack, Glen Cavender, Jim Farley, Frederick Vroom, Charles Smith.

Buster Keaton's famous Civil War comedy has a train, *The General*, as his cohero. The plot is based on an actual incident that occurred during the Civil War, known as the Andrews Raid, in which Union soldiers, dressed as civilians, stole *The General*, a rebel locomotive. In Keaton's version, he plays Johnnie Gray, railroad man, who tries to impress his girl (Marion Mack) by enlisting in the army. But those in charge reject him because he is more useful as an engineer. His sweetheart, thinking him a coward, snubs him. However, when he learns that his train has been stolen, he springs into action. Following several hilarious incidents, our Southern hero saves his sweetheart who is held captive by the enemy, foils a Union surprise attack and captures a high-ranking Union officer.

The film has been noted for its authentic backgrounds and its photography. Keaton's superb timing of his sight gags deserves

praise as well, especially in two sequences. In one, an ignited cannon, originally aimed high and situated on a railway car behind Keaton, begins to drop because of the movement of the train until the mouth of the weapon stares him in the face. But the train turns in time and the cannonball barely misses him. The second sequence concerns railroad ties strewn across the tracks before his moving train. He removes all but the last one, which he dislodges by dropping another he is holding on the edge of the first. Both ties fall harmlessly out of harm's way. The marvel of the scene is in Keaton's split-second timing.

Considered by many to be Keaton's best work as well as one of the best films about the Civil War, *The General*, based on William Pittenger's *The Great Locomotive Chase*, contains the longest chase sequence in the history of film comedy. Walt Disney in 1956 used the same source for his film which retained the original title. When asked why the war in his film looked more authentic than it did in *Gone With the Wind*, Keaton replied: "They went to a novel, we went to history." See Andrews' Raid. ■

General Died at Dawn, The (1936), Par. *Dir.* Lewis Milestone; *Sc.* Clifford Odets; *Cast includes:* Gary Cooper, Madeleine Carroll, Akim Tamiroff, Dudley Digges, Porter Hall, William Frawley.

Set in strife-torn China, the drama concerns the conflict between an idealistic agent working for the Chinese and a brutal warlord. Gary Cooper, as the agent, is trying to help the impoverished Chinese people free themselves from the rapacious bandit who is seeking to dominate northern China. Akim Tamiroff portrays the ambitious warlord. He captures a passenger train which carries several suspicious characters, including Cooper whose suitcase contains enough money to supply guns for the bandit's victims. Also aboard are two secret agents of the bandit general, portrayed by a sinister Dudley Digges and a sniveling Porter Hall. Hall's attractive daughter (Madeleine Carroll), on orders from her father, lures Cooper and his money onto the train. Novelist John O'Hara appears briefly as a reporter.

Cooper escapes death at the hands of Tamiroff in a wild, far-fetched climactic sequence. The American soldier of fortune, seeing that the bandit is mortally wounded, plays upon the latter's pride by questioning the loyalty of his troops. The general proves their loyalty by ordering them to line up in two columns, face each other and commit mass suicide as a final gesture of allegiance. The film is based on a novel by Charles G. Booth. ∎

Gentleman of Quality, A (1926), Commonwealth. *Dir.* Wesley Ruggles; *Cast includes:* George Walsh, Ruth Dwyer, Brian Donlevy, Luri di Cardi, Lucian Prival.

American silk smugglers working in collaboration with their Chinese counterparts frustrate attempts of the U.S. Secret Service to crack down on the illegal trade in this lively drama. George Walsh, as a fledgling member of the service, manages to work his way into the gang's confidence and eventually expose them. Ruth Dwyer provides the love interest. Luri di Cardi, as an undercover agent of the secret service, masquerades as a cabaret dancer. Brian Donlevy, who continued on to a fruitful career in sound films, plays the chief villain and is assisted by Lucian Prival in performing the dirty work. ∎

German intelligence: World War I. The intelligence and counterintelligence networks of the Central Powers during World War I were as extensive as those of Great Britain and France. Germany's web of intrigue spread as far as Cuba and Mexico, and its sabotage plots culminated in the shattering Black Tom explosion in New Jersey in 1916.

Before the guns of war fired their first rounds, Germany had set in position one of the most comprehensive spy networks in the world. However, since its military leaders assumed the war would be a relatively short one, Germany concentrated most of its intelligence activities in Europe. When the militarists failed to achieve their quick victory, they realized they would have to stop or slow down military shipments from the Western Hemisphere, particularly the U.S. Dr. Walter von Scheele, a German agent operating in Cuba, was extradited to the U.S. after American intelligence uncovered his operations.

Captain von Papen, the German military attaché, organized dummy corporations to purchase munitions and chemicals used in the production of poison gas, such as chlorine, which would otherwise have been shipped to the Allies. Some of von Papen's corporations paid their employees exorbitant wages with

the aim of inciting resentment and work stoppages at other, legitimate, munitions plants. A number of these dummy enterprises folded without meeting their contractual obligations to provide war materiél to the Allies. The 1918 serial *The Eagle's Eye*, which paints a vicious picture of von Papen, covers some of his espionage activities in the U.S. Munitions-related spy dramas began to appear with some regularity, a few released even before the U.S. entered the conflict. *Arms and the Woman* (1916) depicts German spies operating within the borders of the U.S. and trying to make deals with munitions merchants. In *The Claws of the Hun* (1918) German agents, with the help of a consulting engineer, attempt to steal highly secret papers from an American munitions plant. German spies endeavor to control the production of an American munitions plant in *The Thing We Love* (1918). A U.S. Secret Service agent in *The Sea Flower* (1918) uncovers a plot by German spies to destroy a San Francisco munitions plant.

Von Papen made efforts to recruit agents from the German and Irish ethnic minorities in America. *An Alien Enemy* (1918) concerns a young woman of German heritage who marries an important American involved in military matters. A German agent threatens the couple unless they turn over to him secret documents. *The Price of Applause* (1918) concerns a cowardly and shallow young American of German heritage who, after betraying the U.S., ultimately redeems himself by sacrificing his own life to save an American munitions plant. Perhaps the most striking propaganda drama of this type is *The Prussian Cur* (1918) in which a German saboteur in America visits a town in the West where he tries to convince a German-American to damage an airplane plant. Bristling at the suggestion, the loyal American has the agent arrested. When pro-Germans gather in the street to plan the spy's rescue, white-hooded horsemen ride into town and capture the German sympathizers. The patriotic riders force the Germans to kiss the stars and stripes and then lead them into the jail.

The most daring and subversive move by Germany against the U.S. was exposed in the infamous Zimmermann Telegram. German Foreign Minister Arthur Zimmermann, on January 16, 1917, sent a dispatch to the German minister in Mexico suggesting a German-Mexican military alliance against the

U.S. in which Mexico would regain its lost territories of Texas, New Mexico and Arizona. The British exposure of the telegram infuriated the U.S. and helped to add popular support for Wilson's decision to enter the war on the side of the Allies only a few weeks later. U.S. film studios were quick to exploit the incident and released a handful of spy dramas and comedies which used the Mexican border as background. *The Border Wireless* (1918) shows German agents, in the guise of miners near the Mexican border, operating a secret wireless radio station. In the comedy *I'll Say So* (1918) German spies provoke trouble on the Texas border between Mexican bandits and Americans.

Germany waged a campaign of espionage and sabotage in the U.S. that resulted in a string of conflagrations and explosions at storage depots, in munitions plants and aboard cargo ships. Count von Bernstorff, the German ambassador to the U.S., commanded the Central Powers' espionage network in America. A railroad bridge in Maine was destroyed in 1915. Other plots, aimed at the Welland Canal between Lakes Ontario and Erie and a Canadian Pacific Railway tunnel, were unsuccessful. Hollywood was never far behind the headlines. *The Girl of Today* (1918), set in New York State, concerns a German spy who plots to destroy several munitions factories and New York City's water supply. In *Mrs. Slacker* (1918) German saboteurs plot to destroy a nearby reservoir.

The most devastating act of German sabotage, both psychologically and militarily, was the destruction of the munitions facilities in New Jersey known as Black Tom, on July 30, 1916. Six piers, more than a dozen warehouses and hundreds of freight cars filled with arms and ammunition targeted for the Allies exploded with a terrible blast that shattered windows in lower Manhattan across the New York harbor. After a two-year reign of sabotage, Congress passed the Espionage Act of 1917. Hollywood responded with a string of films that focused on shipyards and harbors as targets of German agents. *Marriages Are Made* (1918) concerns a German spy who plots to mine an American harbor. *The Road to France* (1918) has the American shipbuilding industry in peril as German spies plot its destruction. German agents and sympathizers in *The Yellow Dog* (1918) plot to set fire to an American shipyard, but a local village patriot (Arthur Hoyt) organizes a group of boys

to ferret out the "yellow dogs," or German sympathizers, who are spreading pro-German propaganda throughout the community. The film, which portrays boys spyhunting, was not far from historical truth. Among the various World War I vigilante groups organized by superpatriots was the Boy Spies of America.

American spy films released during the war highlighted German acts of espionage and sabotage occurring outside U.S. borders. Such major directors as D. W. Griffith and screen personalities as Douglas Fairbanks, Mary Pickford and Lillian Gish gave their talents to these propaganda vehicles that invariably placed the German in the most abhorrent position. The enemy is shown committing the most horrible crimes, including lusting after innocent women and bayoneting babies. The German spy, as he carried out his missions, was not above committing these acts, according to some film scripts. German spies steal a small box containing France's secret code in *The Ivory Snuff Box* (1915). *Somewhere in France* (1916) was one of the earliest World War I dramas to feature a female spy. After stealing secret plans from her French lover, Louise Glaum rapidly advances within the ranks of German intelligence.

Occasionally, spy films reflected Germany's widespread intelligence activities in areas other than Europe and the Western Hemisphere. German agents attempt to destroy the sugar plantations of Hawaii in *The Marriage Ring* (1918). In *No Man's Land* (1918) a German agent on a remote Pacific island, using an American wife as his cover, secretly operates a wireless to feed information about Allied shipping to enemy raiders.

Films about German covert activities during the war reached its peak in 1918. More espionage dramas appeared during that year than in any previous year. In *The Crucible of Life* (1918) a gang leader of German descent is in reality a German agent. D. W. Griffith's *The Great Love* (1918), a romantic drama set chiefly in England, has German spies plotting the destruction of a munitions factory. In *His Birthright* (1918) Sessue Hayakawa portrays the illegitimate son of a Japanese mother and American father. Marin Sais, as a German spy, persuades the revengeful Hayakawa to steal important military documents from an American admiral—Hayakawa's father. Jack Mulhall, as an American prisoner of war interned in a German camp in *Flames of*

Chance (1918), discovers that a letter from the States, when held near a candle, contains secret writing. Enemy agents in America, he realizes, are sending messages via this route to Germany.

Films about German spies spilled over into the postwar years. *Bonds of Honor* (1919) concerns a German agent who befriends a young gambler, the son of an important Japanese diplomat. The boy soon mounts up huge debts. To help him raise money, the spy persuades his victim to borrow his father's plans so that they can be photographed. *Love in a Hurry* (1919) concerns a young American's involvement with German agents operating in England. In war films released during the conflict and immediately after, enemy officers as well as their underlings engaged in rape and pillage, burned and bayoneted babies and enslaved the children of captive nations. In all three versions of *Three Faces East* and many other war dramas released after the armistice, the Germans were depicted as suave and sophisticated, often undetectable in manner and dress from the heroes. Hollywood studios by the 1920s were softening their image of the German. In *Mare Nostrum* (1926) a German spy (Alice Terry) gains the love of a Spanish sea captain (Antonio Moreno) who abandons all for her. Eventually she meets her end before a firing squad. George O'Brien, as an English spy in *True Heaven* (1929), falls in love with Lois Moran, a German agent.

By the 1930s the once-feared enemy spy of World War I, capable of unmentionable acts of horror, had been transformed into an attractive gentleman or woman who devoted as much time to romance as to his or her secret mission. Marlene Dietrich, as a German agent in *Dishonored* (1931), traps the infamous spy known as "The Fox," played by Victor McLaglen. But she falls in love with him and is executed. Gilbert Roland plays an Austrian counterspy in *After Tonight* (1933) whose job it is to ensnare enemy spies. Predictably, a Russian agent (Constance Bennett) falls in love with Roland and is arrested. *Stamboul Quest* (1934) is unique in at least two respects. Not only does the drama evoke sympathy for a German spy, it also allows the same German spy to triumph. Myrna Loy portrays a German spy who falls in love with George Brent, an American. Dolores Del Rio, as a German agent in *Lancer Spy* (1937), aids an English double agent (George Sanders) with whom she has fallen in love.

The World War I German spy-as-threat reappears occasionally on screen. However, these films served chiefly as metaphors for contemporary conflicts or vehicles for romantic dramas. *British Intelligence* (1940), released several months after the start of World War II, features Boris Karloff as a master German spy who cleverly installs himself as an employee in the home of a high-ranking British cabinet minister. In *Darling Lili* (1970) Julie Andrews portrays a German spy who falls in love with Allied air squadron leader Rock Hudson.

German efforts at espionage and sabotage, in the U.S. at least, did not change the course of the war or history. Despite several explosions at munitions depots and aboard cargo vessels, German agents were unable to prevent the steady flow of war materials to the Allies. Neither did their anti-British propaganda activities influence America's decision to enter the war. U.S. economic and cultural ties with the Allies and Germany's submarine warfare that claimed American lives took care of that. ∎

German intelligence: World War II.

Germany achieved several initial successes in the secret war of intelligence. Its World War II organization, known as Abwehr, combined its activities with those of the Gestapo. The organization, which dealt in espionage, sabotage and counterespionage, supported vast spy systems in Europe, Asia, North America and Latin America.

One effective intelligence service was Germany's radio network. Uniting special forces of the army, navy and Luftwaffe, the Abwehr was able to attain useful aerial interception and naval detection methods. In the late 1930s, before the war erupted in Europe, the Abwehr set up an elaborate intelligence network in Latin America, especially in Argentina and Brazil. This allowed German agents operating in the U.S. to communicate with other agents in Latin America, a simpler process than transmitting information to Europe or Germany. (*The House on 92nd Street* (1945) includes a scene showing the Abwehr instructing its agents.) Brazil was Germany's major base of operations until 1942, when Allies clamped down on the spies and political events changed. Abwehr headquarters were forced to relocate in Argentina. Many American films released during the war, including, among others, *Nazi Agent* (1941) and *Sherlock Holmes and the Voice of Terror* (1942), showed the German spy's hide-out complete with the radio transmitter and photograph of Hitler on the wall. Swastikas dominated Gestapo and other Nazi headquarters. These images soon became familiar icons to movie audiences and attested to Nazi prewar intelligence preparations and fierce fanaticism.

German intelligence mastered several techniques in the art and science of deception. Early in the war the Germans developed the "microdot" film—a small negative with relatively little grain and almost undetectable. When placed under a microscope the film could reveal the entire text of a document. Since the microdot could be placed anywhere on an envelope, letter, book or periodical, it baffled British intelligence. However, its use was restricted since not all foreign agents had access to the necessary equipment. *Sherlock Holmes in Washington* (1943) describes a similar device; a very important document has been reduced to microfilm and concealed in the cover of a book of matches. *The House on 92nd Street* shows German agents concealing the microdot under a postage stamp.

German intelligence often made use of other methods to mislead its enemies. Radio, troop formations, propaganda and diplomatic officers were all employed in the practice of disinformation. *Appointment in Berlin* (1943) illustrates the Nazis' wide use of broadcasting propaganda. During Germany's Ardennes Offensive Colonel Otto Skorzeny led a troop of English-speaking German soldiers disguised in American uniforms behind Allied lines. There they caused chaos by changing road signs, misdirecting traffic and performing sabotage. These acts of deception have been dramatized in several films, including *The Last Blitzkrieg* (1958), *When Hell Broke Loose* (1958) and *Battle of the Bulge* (1965).

General Reinhard Gehlen operated German military intelligence in Russia during World War II. When he was captured by the U.S. in 1945, he handed over his extensive files and intelligence network which were then utilized by the Western powers. It was only many years later that some Americans first learned about these strange bedfellows and began to question the wisdom of U.S. intelligence for hiring former die-hard Nazis.

Most American spy films produced during the war were either purely propaganda dramas or escapist comedies, both of which relied little on exploring German intelligence techniques. The plots were filled with chases, ended with fist fights or gun battles and presented the usual heroes, heroines and villains—the Gestapo showing up as the most brutal. The films embraced different genres, including the detective *Enemy Agents Meet Ellery Queen*), the western (*Cowboy Commandos*), the musical (*Ship Ahoy*) and the comedy (*Margin for Error*). What these films did suggest were the elaborate and aggressive prewar intelligence preparations on the part of the Axis. This contrasted sharply with American intelligence agencies, which, according to Hollywood, acted only defensively to combat acts of espionage and sabotage.

Nevertheless, some made a serious attempt to expose the extent of German subversion within America's borders while others depicted the widespread Nazi intelligence apparatus in other countries. *Confessions of a Nazi Spy* (1939), one of the first and most important dramas to alert Americans about the threat of German sabotage, stars Edward G. Robinson as an F.B.I. agent who helps to unravel a web of spies in the U.S. *Nazi Agent* (1941) has a network of saboteurs transmitting information about Allied convoys to German U-boats. Alfred Hitchcock's *Saboteur* (1942), featuring Robert Cummings as an innocent worker at a California airplane factory accused of setting fire to the plant, remains one of the best suspenseful films about wartime sabotage. *The House on 92nd Street* (1945), based on actual events, tells the story of how the F.B.I. prevented major military secrets, including the formula for the atomic bomb, from falling into the hands of Nazi agents operating in New York City.

Some dramas revealed the German espionage apparatus at work in foreign lands. *A Yank in Libya* (1942) concerns an American war correspondent who uncovers a Nazi gunsmuggling ring in that country. *Journey Into Fear* (1942) concerns Nazi spies attempting to sabotage Turkey's military build-up. *Background to Danger* (1943) again depicts Nazi and Russian agents operating in Turkey. *Cairo* (1942) has Nazi agents working in Egypt. The drama *Action in Arabia* (1944) has Nazi agents attempting to stir up an Arab revolt and plotting to destroy the Suez Canal. *The Lady Has Plans* (1942) takes place in Lisbon and concerns a Nazi spy ring. Again, Nazi agents in Lisbon pursue a member of the Dutch underground in *The Conspirators* (1944). In the serial *King of the Mounties* (1942) enemy agents of all three Axis powers operating in Canada try to sabotage that nation's production of war matériel.

World War II produced its share of spy films with women as secret agents. Ilona Massey in *International Lady* (1941), for example, plays a dangerous spy who contacts Nazi U-boats and provides them with vital shipping and air force information.

Most other spy films of the period were routine anti-Nazi dramas. *Beasts of Berlin* (1939) shows the brutal methods that the Gestapo employed to gather information. Joel McCrea, as a career diplomat in *Espionage Agent* (1939), discovers that his wife (Brenda Marshall), whom he had recently met overseas, is a former German spy. *They Came to Blow Up America* (1943) tells of eight German saboteurs who are put ashore off Long Island, ultimately caught and brought to trial. Through flashback sequences, the film depicts how the eight were trained for their assignments.

Several used wartime England for their setting. *The Gorilla Man* (1942) has Nazi spies operating in England trying to prevent a commando recently returned from a mission on the continent from delivering military information. In *Counter-Espionage* (1942) the Lone Wolf, played by Warren William, hunts down a Nazi spy network in wartime London while protecting secret military plans.

With the advent of the Cold War and the Soviet Union as the new world threat, post-World War II American dramas about Nazi agents generally softened the role of the German. *Target Unknown* (1951) explores some of the methods used by German intelligence to extract military information from unsuspecting Allied prisoners of war. Gig Young, as a German officer raised in America, poses as an understanding sympathizer in whom captured Americans confide. He even criticizes the brutality of the Gestapo to win the prisoners' confidence. *Five Fingers* (1952), based on actual events, stars James Mason as a valet to the British ambassador. Suave, persuasive and clever, Mason sells secret documents which he has photographed to the Germans. An American-educated German spy, planted in the same barracks with American prisoners of war in *Stalag 17* (1953), surreptitiously passes information to the camp commandant.

For the next several decades American films explored different variations of the spy theme—with mixed results. In *The Enemy General* (1960) Van Johnson, as an O.S.S. agent, is assigned to smuggle a Nazi officer, who in reality is a double agent, out of Europe and escort him safely to England. *Armored Command* (1961) features a female Nazi spy who employs her sexual charms in an attempt to gather information concerning a strategic Allied position. In *Then There Were Three* (1961) a handful of American G.I.s in Italy try to make it back to their lines. However, one of them is actually a Nazi spy assigned to kill an important Italian guerrilla leader. A captured American officer is tricked by the Germans into revealing the actual invasion plans of the Allies in *36 Hours* (1964), set on the eve of the Normandy invasion. ■

Get Going (1943), U. *Dir.* Jean Yarbrough; *Sc.* Warren Wilson; *Cast includes:* Robert Paige, Grace McDonald, Vera Vague, Walter Catlett, Lois Collier.

A World War II comedy drama about wartime Washington with its shortages of available males and housing, the film features Grace McDonald as a newly arrived government worker. She moves in with a group of other young women employed in various government departments. At her typing job she is attracted to Robert Paige and gets his attention by suggesting that she may be in collusion with enemy agents. Paige takes the bait and follows her. They eventually fall in love while McDonald actually uncovers an enemy spy ring. Vera Vague, as one of the heroine's roommates, provides some comedy relief as does character actor Walter Catlett.

The film captures the mood of the capital in the throes of an actual housing shortage during World War II. The condition was made to order for Hollywood writers who exploited it in several light features. *The More the Merrier*, starring Jean Arthur and Joel McCrea and released the same year, was one of the more noteworthy entries of the genre. See Washington, D.C. ■

Getting Even (1986), Goldwyn. *Dir.* Dwight H. Little; *Sc.* M. Phil Senini, Eddie Desmond; *Cast includes:* Edward Albert, Audrey Landers, Joe Don Baker, Rod Pilloud, Billy Streater.

A soldier of fortune and a C.I.A. agent team up to stop a powerful industrialist from blackmailing the city of Dallas with a deadly gas in this suspense thriller. Edward Albert, as Taggar, a superagent, mercenary and soldier of fortune who is called in by the U.S. government for especially difficult assignments, runs his own laboratory. He is called upon to get samples of a new deadly gas being developed by the Soviets at a secret base in Afghanistan. Assisted by his special paramilitary force, Taggar completes the mission and assigns his chemists to develop an antidote for the poison.

A wealthy and ambitious industrialist (Joe Don Baker) secretly sends his underlings to steal the gas cartridges from Taggar's lab and then demands $50 million for their return or he will release the deadly chemical over Dallas. The remainder of the film concerns the efforts of Taggar and a C.I.A. agent (Audrey Landers) to retrieve the cartridges. Following some well-photographed helicopter chases, Baker switches to an airplane and heads for South America. But Taggar blows up the plane, killing Baker. The couple retrieve the cartridges and save Dallas. ■

Ghosts on the Loose (1943), Mon. *Dir.* William Beaudine; *Sc.* Kenneth Higgins; *Cast includes:* Leo Gorcey, Huntz Hall, Bobby Jordan, Bela Lugosi, Ava Gardner, Ric Vallin.

Nazi spies use a supposedly haunted house for their espionage activities in this World War II comedy set in New York City. The East Side Kids, led by Leo Gorcey, innocently enter the house to straighten the place out and become entangled with secret passages, sliding panels and other gimmicks designed to keep intruders away. Huntz Hall, as Gorcey's sidekick, contributes some of the slapstick. Bela Lugosi portrays the leader of the enemy agents. Ava Gardner, as the recent bride of Hall's brother (Ric Vallin), has little to do in this comedy aimed chiefly at a juvenile audience. ■

Girl From Scotland Yard, The (1937), Par. *Dir.* Robert Vignola; *Sc.* Doris Anderson, Dore Schary; *Cast includes:* Karen Morley, Robert Baldwin, Katherine Alexander, Eduardo Ciannelli, Milli Monti, Lloyd Crane.

A string of mysterious explosions and other catastrophes play havoc with England's

Master villain Eduardo Ciannelli is about to sabotage another of England's defense industries in the pre-World War II drama *The Girl From Scotland Yard* (1937).

defense industries in this low-budget drama. Scotland Yard assigns one of its agents (Karen Morley) to investigate these incidents. Romance intrudes temporarily when she meets an American journalist (Robert Baldwin). He joins forces with the attractive secret service agent to help unmask the saboteurs. Eduardo Ciannelli, who specialized in playing evil characters in the 1930s and 1940s, provides the villainy which ends in a dramatic airplane sequence. ■

Girl in the Case (1944), Col. *Dir.* William Berke; *Sc.* Joseph Hoffman, Dorcas Cochran; *Cast includes:* Edmund Lowe, Janis Carter, Robert Williams, Richard Hale, Stanley Clements, Carole Mathews.

A lawyer becomes entangled in a spy plot while innocently aiding a client in this World War II comedy drama. Edmund Lowe, as the attorney whose hobby happens to be picking locks, is hired by a client (Robert Scott) to open a chest. This incident, along with other circumstances, brings Lowe into confrontation with German agent Richard Hale. Janis Carter, as the lawyer's wife, contributes to the comedy that is meant to emulate the witty style of the husband-wife team of MGM's popular "Thin Man" series starring William Powell and Myrna Loy. Stanley Clements portrays Lowe's young assistant. ■

Girl in the Kremlin, The (1957), U. *Dir.* Russell Birdwell; *Sc.* Gene L. Coon, Robert Hill; *Cast includes:* Lex Barker, Zsa Zsa Gabor, Jeffrey Stone, Maurice Manson, William Schallert, Natalia Daryll.

This Cold War drama presents a fanciful

plot that has Stalin alive and well—at least temporarily—and living incognito in Greece. All this is revealed through the efforts of a former officer of the Office of Strategic Services, a professional spy and a pretty Lithuanian refugee who is searching for her twin sister. The frustrated sister (Zsa Zsa Gabor) appeals to the ex-O.S.S. officer (Lex Barker) to help her find her twin who vanished following Stalin's reported death. Jeffrey Stone, as a local spy, joins Barker in the search which takes them to Greece where they learn that Stalin (Maurice Manson) is living under an assumed name and unidentified after some plastic surgery. The former Soviet leader escapes their capture but dies a violent death when his car bursts into flame after careening off a mountain road. William Schallert portrays Stalin's son whose hatred for his father results in Stalin's car crash. See Central Intelligence Agency. ∎

"Girl Nihilist, The" (1908), Kalem. (No other credits.)

This brief silent drama, set in Russia, addresses some of cruelties the peasants suffered under the Czar's regime. A young Russian woman whose impoverished family is threatened by a local tax collector, pleads with him for an extension. She is struck down for her efforts. When she complains to the district governor about the mistreatment she received, he ignores her complaints. The woman happens to be a member of a Nihilist group who draw lots to decide which member will assassinate the governor. The act falls upon the woman. She tosses a bomb at the governor, is caught and, along with her family, is sentenced to Siberia. She manages to escape and make her way to America. ∎

Girl of Today, The (1918), Vitagraph. *Dir.* John Robertson; *Sc.* John Robertson, Harry O. Hoyt; *Cast includes:* Corinne Griffith, Marc MacDermott, Charles A. Stevenson, Ida Darling, Webster Campbell.

A German spy plots to destroy several munitions factories and New York City's water supply in this World War I drama set in New York State. Marc MacDermott, the German agent, poses as a Danish scientist who is in love with an attractive patriot (Corinne Griffith). Webster Campbell, as MacDermott's rival suitor, learns of the spy's plans and goes to his home to challenge him. The German overpowers him, locks him up and forges a note to Griffith saying that he has gone away to avoid the draft. Griffith, however, suspects foul play and places a dictaphone in MacDermott's home. When she discovers the bombing plot, she summons the police who quickly rescue Campbell and foil the spy's plans. The New York State Defense Council cooperated with the production of the film which was shot at various state locales, including Albany and the Erie Canal.

Several plots suggested in the drama were based on actual incidents. Germany's acts of espionage and sabotage included failed plots aimed at the Welland Canal between Lakes Ontario and Erie and a Canadian Pacific Railway tunnel, as well as some which successfully destroyed U.S. defense factories and other military facilities. See German Intelligence: World War I; U.S. Intelligence: World War I. ∎

Girl Philippa, The (1917), Vitagraph. *Dir.* S. Rankin Drew; *Sc.* S. Rankin Drew; *Cast includes:* Anita Stewart, S. Rankin Drew, Frank Morgan, Captain Eyerman, Ned Hay, Stanley Dunn.

A young woman is asked by her guardian, a German agent, to act as a spy in this World War I drama set in the Balkans. Anders Randolf, as the German, assigns his ward Philippa (Anita Stewart), a dancer at a local café, to spy on an Englishman (Frank Morgan). S. Rankin Drew, as a visiting American and friend of Morgan, introduces him to the pretty dancer. Following several suspenseful complications, Morgan manages to protect his country's secret papers from falling into the hands of the German spy. Philippa, meanwhile, has fallen in love with the American. The conclusion of the film reveals that Philippa in reality is a Balkan princess who had been kidnapped when she was only a baby. The drama was adapted from *My Girl Philippa*, a novel by Robert W. Chambers.

The Balkan countries were rarely used as a background in Hollywood films, particularly during World War I, when Germany and France were more topical and familiar to American audiences. The Balkan Wars of 1913–1914 served as background for at least one pre-1920 war drama, Cecile B. DeMille's *The Captive* (1915), with Blanche Sweet and House Peters. ∎

"Girl Spy Before Vicksburg, The" (1911) Kalem. *Dir.* Sidney Olcott.

During the early silent years of the American film industry, dramas and comedies were chiefly one reel, or about ten minutes, in length. Director D. W. Griffith, for example, before creating his classic epic *The Birth of a Nation* in 1915, turned out a cycle of one-reel Civil War dramas in 1911 and 1912, including "His Trust" and "His Trust Fulfilled." In Olcott's "The Girl Spy Before Vicksburg," a silent Civil War drama, the heroine disguises herself as a member of a munitions convoy and destroys the powder wagon. This little film has several other highly implausible incidents.

Aside from the fictional elements of this short film, Vicksburg, Tennessee, was indeed a hub for a particularly active band of Confederate agents. Captain Henry B. Shaw organized and commanded a team of about 50 spies who provided intelligence reports for Confederate generals in the region. Known as Coleman's Scouts—after Shaw's *nom de guerre*—the group constantly engaged in perilous missions which eventually took their toll. Ten were captured, several were hanged—including Sam Davis, the most famous—a few died of wounds and others were court-martialed before Vicksburg finally fell into Union hands. Southern patriots, including several young women, had worked closely with Shaw's spies. Kate Patterson, one such daring belle, placed secret messages in a hollow tree. The brave acts of these local women may well have been the inspiration for the heroine in this and other films which continued to be released well into the sound era. See American Civil War: Intelligence and Covert Actions; *Sam Davis, The Hero of Tennessee* (1915). ∎

Girl Who Knew Too Much, The (1969), Commonwealth. *Dir.* Francis D. Lyon; *Sc.* Charles Wallace; *Cast includes:* Adam West, Nancy Kwan, Robert Alda, Nehemiah Persoff, Patricia Smith, David Brian.

Adam West, better known for his 1960s television role as Batman, portrays a California nightclub owner who aids the C.I.A. in this Cold War drama. It seems that Communist conspirators in the form of Chinese Reds are on the verge of gaining control of a powerful underworld syndicate for the purpose of weakening American trade. Both the C.I.A. and the syndicate force West, a retired agent, to find the murderer of an important underworld gangster. Nancy Kwan, as West's ex-

Adam West is about to get a headache from a member of an underworld syndicate working with Communists in the Cold War drama *The Girl Who Knew Too Much* (1969).

flame and the slain gangster's secretary, is next in line for assassination. West hides her while he goes about unraveling the convoluted plot. Following several other violent deaths, West nears the end of his journey. Patricia Smith, as a Communist spy, has married the recently killed gangster as part of the conspiracy. Allardice, a member of the underworld syndicate, shoots Smith and falls to his death trying to escape. ∎

Doris Day expresses surprise when she discovers she is suspected of spying by C.I.A. agent Eric Fleming and spy Dom De Luise. *The Glass Bottom Boat* (1966).

Glass Bottom Boat, The (1966), MGM. *Dir.* Frank Tashlin; *Sc.* Everett Freeman; *Cast includes:* Doris Day, Rod Taylor, Arthur Godfrey, John McGiver, Paul Lynde, Edward Andrews.

An attractive young widow and public relations employee, suspected by the C.I.A. as a spy, gets mixed up with real enemy agents in this fast-paced comedy. Doris Day, as the widow, works for Rod Taylor, who portrays the head of a space laboratory. Her innocent phone calls made to her home where her pet dog exercises at the sound of the rings bring her under suspicion of C.I.A. agents. She is unaware that a secret formula has been placed in her purse. When she arrives home, a spy tries to gain possession of her purse with the important document. Day escapes through a window, and a wild chase ensues. After C.I.A. agents eventually round up the villains, Day and Taylor get together for a romantic ending. ■

G-Men vs. the Black Dragon (1943) se-
rial, Rep. *Dir.* William Witney; *Sc.* Ronald Davidson, William Lively, Joseph O'Donnell, Joseph Poland; *Cast includes:* Rod Cameron, Roland Got, Constance Worth, Nino Pepitone, Noel Cravat.

U.S. federal agent Rex Bennett takes on Oriental saboteurs bent on disrupting America's war industry in this 15-episode World War II serial. Rod Cameron, as Bennett, battles the sinister Haruchi (Nino Pepitone), a Japanese superspy who has been smuggled into the U.S. by way of a mummy case. After recovering from a state of suspended animation, Haruchi unleashes a series of diabolical schemes against America's war effort. Cameron has his hands full trying to thwart the villain and his army of henchmen. Filled with plenty of action and high explosives in almost each chapter, the serial ends with Haruchi being consumed by flames when his escaping speedboat smashes into an enemy submarine. The serial was converted into a feature-length film for television and retitled *Black Dragon of Manzamar.* See Serials. ■

Gog (1954), UA. *Dir.* Herbert L. Strock; *Sc.*
Tom Taggart, Richard G. Taylor; *Cast includes:* Richard Egan, Constance Dowling, Herbert Marshall, John Wengraf, Phil Van Zandt, Valerie Vernon.

Sabotage plagues the development of America's first space station in this drama that cleverly blends science fiction with international intrigue. When officers of the Office of Scientific Investigation learn of the problem, they assign Richard Egan, one of their top security agents, to investigate the mysterious goings-on at the secret New Mexico under-ground laboratory. Egan soon deduces that Novac, the giant nuclear computer which is running the entire operation, and two robots, are the cause of the problem. It seems that enemy agents somehow have planted a secret device in the computer which they control from a spaceship hovering above the laboratory. A jet plane is assigned to destroy the enemy craft, and the scientists destroy the robots. Herbert Marshall portrays the head of the space project. Constance Dowling portrays the female lead in this interesting but generally slow-paced tale. ■

Gold Racket, The (1937), GN. *Dir.* Louis J.
Gasnier; *Sc.* David Levy; *Cast includes:* Conrad Nagel, Eleanor Hunt, Fuzzy Knight, Frank Milan, Charles Delaney, Karl Hackett.

Federal agents are determined to put an end to an illegal gold-smuggling scheme in this drama. The smugglers are transporting their contraband into the U.S. by way of Mexico. Conrad Nagel, as a federal officer, and his assistant (Eleanor Hunt) are assigned to the case. Hunt goes under cover as an entertainer in a Mexican café where she makes contact with the pilot working for the culprits. Nagel and Hunt, after some slight action and comic relief provided by a local piano player (Fuzzy Knight), manage to unmask the leader and round up the smugglers. ■

Golden Earrings (1947), Par. *Dir.* Mitchell
Leisen; *Sc.* Abraham Polonsky, Frank Butler, Helen Deutch; *Cast includes:* Ray Milland, Marlene Dietrich, Murvyn Vye, Bruce Lester, Dennis Hoey, Quentin Reynolds.

Ray Milland portrays a British spy in this World War II romantic drama adapted from the novel by Yolanda Foldes. The story is unfolded in flashback and told by Milland to journalist Quentin Reynolds (playing himself) aboard an airplane. Operating in Germany with a fellow British agent during the early war years, Milland and his companion are on a secret mission to get the formula for a revolutionary poison gas. But they are captured by the Gestapo. They manage to escape their captors, but Milland's friend is killed. Milland meets Marlene Dietrich as a lone member of an itinerant band of gypsies. She hides him from his pursuers and soon falls in love with him. Taking refuge with a gypsy caravan, he dresses in gypsy garments, darkens his skin and even pierces his ears.

Still determined to complete his original

Lobby card for *Golden Earrings* (1947) with British spy Ray Milland hiding from the Nazis in Marlene Dietrich's gypsy caravan.

mission, he confides to Dietrich that he is a secret agent. The gypsies decide to help him contact the German scientist who, disillusioned with Hitler's New Order, has promised to give the formula to the British. Posing as fortune-tellers, Milland and several gypsies enter the grounds of the scientist's home where the host is entertaining Nazi officers. Milland, still masquerading as a gypsy, offers to tell the scientist's fortune and secretly identifies himself as the British contact. "I believe this is what you wanted," the scientist says, as he hands Milland the formula disguised as money. Milland then bids farewell to his newly made friends and leaves for England. When the war ends, he returns to Dietrich at the place they had first met. The story and characters are chiefly implausible (Dietrich as a Hungarian gypsy cooking fish), but Mitchell Leisen's smooth direction and atmospheric setting make the film worthwhile. The title song became a big hit. See British Intelligence: World War II. ■

Golden Silence (1923), Richard Kipling. *Dir.* Paul Hurst; *Cast includes:* Hedda Nova, Jack Perrin.

A U.S. Secret Service agent, assigned to put an end to mail robberies by an outlaw gang, poses as a drifter in the vicinity of a thriving mining camp. Jack Perrin, as the stranger, learns about an impending frame-up. The head of the gang plans to place the blame for the next holdup on an innocent prospector. The outlaw, posing as a stage line owner for his cover, was rejected as a suitor for the old-timer's daughter. Perrin interferes with the gang's plans, saves the prospector and rounds up the culprits. As a bonus, he wins the affection of the daughter (Hedda Nova). ■

Good Guys Wear Black (1978), Mar Vista. *Dir.* Ted Post; *Sc.* Bruce Cohn, Mark Medoff; *Cast includes:* Chuck Norris, Anne Archer, Lloyd Haynes, James Franciscus, Dana Andrews, Jim Backus.

The former head of a Vietnam commando

rescue team is drawn into a U.S. government conspiracy in this action-oriented drama set after the Vietnam War. Chuck Norris, as a karate expert and instructor, had been abandoned, along with his special small force, on their last mission for the C.I.A. Norris learns that surviving members of his commando unit have recently been murdered. Assisted by a government official, a C.I.A. agent and his lawyer-girlfriend, Norris proceeds to solve the mystery and avenge the fallen members of his unit. The film stresses action, chiefly in the form of Norris' agile karate-fighting techniques, rather than delving into the political ramifications of the corrupt politicos whom he eventually defeats. Anne Archer portrays the canny lawyer. Dana Andrews, as a government official, lends Norris a helping hand. James Franciscus plays the sinister politician who betrayed the unit in Vietnam. See Central Intelligence Agency. ■

Good-bye Kiss, The (1928), FN. *Dir.* Mack Sennett; *Sc.* Mack Sennett, Jefferson Moffitt; *Cast includes:* Johnny Burke, Sally Eilers, Matty Kemp, Wheeler Oakman, Irving Bacon.

Producer-director Mack Sennett's contribution to the parade of World War I comedies that appeared after the conflict features Johnny Burke as an American soldier in France. The war sequences and comic elements in the film switch from a Paris café that undergoes an air raid to the war in the trenches where a doughboy loses his nerve during his first battle. Some heroics blend into the plot when an American soldier, hiding in a spy's automobile, learns about an impending bombing of his unit and saves his buddies at the last moment. Sally Eilers portrays a nurse in this comedy-drama that generally lacked the director's famous ingenuity for evoking laughs. ■

Gorilla Man, The (1942), WB. *Dir.* D. Ross Lederman; *Sc.* Anthony Coldeway; *Cast includes:* John Loder, Ruth Ford, Marian Hall, Richard Fraser, Paul Cavanagh, Lumsden Hare.

Nazi spies operating in England try to prevent a commando recently returned from a mission on the continent from delivering military information in this offbeat World War II drama. John Loder, as the commando officer, returns from his assignment suffering from wounds he received during the raid. Two enemy agents (Paul Cavanagh and John Abbott), operating under cover as English doctors, steer him to their private hospital to keep him from reporting to his superiors with important information. He escapes but is accused of murdering the widow of one of his commandos. Abbott, a psychopathic killer posing as a doctor, committed the horrible crime. Meanwhile, the head of the British military command questions Loder's veracity and judgment. Loder, now labeled the "Gorilla Man" by the press because of his skill at climbing cliffs, is left on his own to hunt down the spy ring and clear his reputation. He discovers that the two phony doctors are using their private hospital to signal the Germans across the English Channel. The film opens with an interesting premise, but the plot bogs down in too many unbelievable incidents and senseless killings by Abbott. See British Intelligence: World War II. ■

Gotcha! (1985), U. *Dir.* Jeff Kanew; *Sc.* Dan Gordon; *Cast includes:* Anthony Edwards, Linda Fiorentino, Alex Rocco, Nick Corri, Marla Adams, Klaus Loewitsch.

An 18-year-old college student who spends his spring break in Paris accompanied by his roommate discovers love and intrigue in this comedy drama. Anthony Edwards, as an obnoxious and immature student who dashes around campus playing war games, wonders why he can't get any dates. His more worldly roommate talks him into going to Paris for a week, promising him seven days of "scoring" with Parisian women. Upon their arrival, Edwards' buddy, posing as a Middle East terrorist, picks up a young woman, leaving Edwards on his own. Edwards relaxes at an outdoor café where an attractive young woman (Linda Fiorentino) joins him at his table and expresses an interest in the young American. After seducing him, she asks him to accompany her to East Berlin where, as a courier, she has to pick up a package.

The remainder of the film concerns Soviet agents following the young couple, chasing Edwards and pursuing him to his home in California. He discovers that the woman he has fallen in love with has placed a roll of film in his shoulder bag. When he reports to the local C.I.A. office to turn over the capsule, he sees Fiorentino in the company of other agents. Disillusioned, he leaves in disgust and arranges a secret meeting with her on his college campus. When they confront each other, he acts coldly as she tries to explain that, as a secret agent for the C.I.A., she was under orders and forced to use him to complete her dangerous mission. Suddenly, Soviet agents, determined to get the roll of film, begin shooting at them. The young couple run to a laboratory where he arms himself with a special tranquilizer gun and a handful of darts and goes after the agents. Relying on his previous experience in the sophomoric campus war games, he manages to neutralize the Soviets who are then rounded up the C.I.A. The young hero then embraces Fiorentino.

Here is another film, although inconsequential, that discredits the C.I.A. by showing some of its agents engaging in unethical, if not illegal, activities. They order one of their fellow agents to place a roll of apparently important film in the shoulder bag of an innocent American student-tourist in East Berlin without his knowledge and later ransack his California apartment for the coveted film. See K.G.B. ■

Gouzenko, Igor. In 1943, when the Western democracies were united with the Soviet Union in fighting for their very existence against Nazi Germany, the defection of Igor Gouzenko, a cipher clerk in the Soviet Embassy in Ottawa, proved both embarrassing and fortuitous. It was embarrassing to those Canadians who believed in Canadian-Soviet cooperation because it revealed that the alliance was built on a foundation of sand. It was fortuitous because Gouzenko revealed some of the extent of Soviet espionage in the U.S., Great Britain and Canada.

Gouzenko had been a lieutenant in the Soviet army and saw action in the battle for Moscow. He had undergone intelligence training, had been "vetted" by the N.K.V.D. for his job and in June of 1943 was placed in the Soviet embassy in Ottawa. Despite the best judgment of the secret police, Gouzenko, in a matter of three months in Ottawa, completely rejected the anti-Western propaganda of his own country and began to appreciate the free, democratic society of Canada. On September 5, 1943, Gouzenko, his wife and child defected to Canada. He had managed to smuggle out of the Soviet embassy original documents, telegraph cables and papers he had been previously instructed to burn.

Despite the volume of documents and, at face value, their extreme significance, Gouzenko had a difficult time in obtaining Canadian protection. He was jostled from one agency to another. Prime Minister Mackenzie King himself was particularly disturbed by the implications of Gouzenko's material. He advised the defector to "return to his embassy."

Gouzenko was able to hide with a neighbor while the Soviet embassy staff went out searching for him. Eventually, Gouzenko and his family received the protection of Commissioner S. T. Wood of the Royal Canadian Mounted Police; Inspector John Leopold was placed in charge of the investigation. Gouzenko's documents were carefully scrutinized and determined to be genuine.

The extent of espionage was devastating. Over 50 Soviet agents' clandestine names were uncovered. Amongst other revelations, the spies were providing the U.S.S.R., an ostensible ally, with information on radar, atomic weapons and electronics research. Gouzenko's documents were so revealing that Prime Minister King personally met with President Truman at the end of September 1943 to discuss the damage; the Canadian Prime Minister then met with Prime Minister Atlee in London.

Scotland Yard determined that the "Alek" mentioned in Soviet documents was in fact Dr. Alan Nunn May, a senior member of the Nuclear Physics Division of the Imperial Chemical industries and a University Reader at Stafford Terrace, Kensington. May matched the clues culled from Gouzenko's documents: he worked in King's College, had recently traveled to Montreal and had easy access to current work being done on atomic energy. Apparently May had been warned, for, although Scotland Yard had him under surveillance for several weeks, he did not do anything suspicious. Eventually May was arrested, confessed to spying for "the sake of humanity," and was sentenced to prison.

Simultaneously, Canadian suspects were arrested and imprisoned. Perhaps the most spectacular was the arrest of the one Communist member of the Canadian House of Commons, Fred Rose. Rose, at the beginning of the war, pushed for Canadian neutrality according to the principles laid down in the Stalin-Hitler Pact. When Hitler attacked Russia, Rose changed his position to conform to the shifting party line. Rose had organized several espionage groups in Canada, according to the documents. He was eventually arrested, found guilty and sentenced to six years in prison.

The most significant result of the Gouzenko defection was to awaken the Western democracies to the extent of Soviet espionage in atomic weapons and advanced technology. Apparently none of the spies were motivated by financial considerations; they were either dedicated Communists or believed that they were serving the greater human cause in transferring technological advances to the Soviet Union.

Two films cover Gouzenko's experiences. In *The Iron Curtain* (1948) Dana Andrews portrays the defector who, at his wife's urging to provide a better life for their child, turns himself over to Canadian authorities. Gene Tierney, as his wife, befriends her Canadian neighbors and falls under the spell of democracy. In *Operation Manhunt* (1954), a highly fictionalized drama of the defector's exploits in Canada, the Soviets assign one of their secret agents to assassinate Gouzenko. Harry Townes portrays Gouzenko, who remains firm in his convictions although he knows he is being hunted. The assassin, played by Jacques Aubuchon, at first stalks his victim diligently but then ends up also defecting. ∎

"Governor's Daughter, The" (1909), Kalem. (No other credits.)

In this silent drama of the American Revolution a minister sides with the Colonists and enlists as a spy. The girl he courts, the governor's daughter, breaks off her engagement to him when she learns of his sympathies. During one of his missions he is discovered and pursued by the British. He asks the governor to hide him and his request is granted. The daughter at first disagrees but allows him to stay. While the British search the house, the officer makes advances toward the girl and the minister saves her. He escapes with the officer's uniform after knocking the soldier unconscious. When the war ends, the minister returns and proposes to his sweetheart. ∎

Graves, Dr. Armgaard Karl. See *Patriotism* (1918). ∎

Gray Parasol, The (1918), Triangle. *Dir.* Lawrence Windom; *Sc.* Charles J. Wilson; *Cast includes:* Claire Anderson, Wellington Cross, Joe Bennett, Ed Brady, William Quinn.

German agents try to obtain a secret formula for an inexpensive coal substitute in this World War I drama. When they learn that a young woman possesses the papers, they pose as representatives of the U.S. government. But just as she is about to hand over the formula, her brother and another man enter and expose the German spies. Claire Anderson portrays the heroine. Joe Bennett, as her brother, at first wants the formula destroyed to help protect the interests of several coal magnates who realize the discovery will affect their profits. Wellington Cross, as the hero, rescues Anderson from a street attack by some ruffians and later helps to prevent the documents from falling into enemy hands. The title refers to Anderson's parasol into whose handle she originally hid the coveted formula. ∎

"Gray Sentinel, The" (1913), Broncho. *Dir.* Burton King; *Cast includes:* Charles Ray, J. Barney Sherry, John Emerson, Fred Mace.

A Southern fisherman volunteers his services as a spy for the Confederates who are attempting to run a Union blockade in this Civil War drama. Eventually, he is shot trying to escape in a small boat. This silent film was one of the first to move the Civil War action from the conventional battlefield to the sea. Charles Ray, who was to emerge within a short time as one of the most popular silent screen stars, portrays the young hero. ∎

Great Day in the Morning (1956), RKO. *Dir.* Jacques Tourneur; *Sc.* Lesser Samuels; *Cast includes:* Virginia Mayo, Robert Stack, Ruth Roman, Alex Nicol, Raymond Burr.

Set in Denver in 1861, the film concerns elements from the North and South attempting to control the gold from Colorado mines for the anticipated Civil War. Robert Stack portrays a Confederate sympathizer who seems more interested in the local women than in the Southern cause. Virginia Mayo, as an Easterner who owns a dress shop in town, falls for Stack. Alex Nicol plays a Union agent sent west on a secret mission. Ruth Roman, as the saloon entertainer, is also interested in Stack, who has won the watering hole in a card game from local bad man Raymond Burr. Action chiefly centers around the two political factions whose emotions continually explode into violence, foreshadowing the tragic war about to descend upon the land. The film is based on the novel by Robert Hardy Andrews. ∎

Great Deception, The (1926), FN. *Dir.* Howard Higgin; *Sc.* Paul Bern; *Cast includes:* Ben Lyon, Aileen Pringle, Basil Rathbone, Sam Hardy, Charlotte Walker.

An Englishman (Ben Lyon) educated in Germany becomes a double agent working for England in this World War I drama. Lyon poses as indifferent to the war so that he can ally himself with Germany. He travels between the two countries giving German headquarters false information while supplying Britain with valuable intelligence. Eventually he is exposed and sentenced to death, but he makes his escape by airplane while saving a young American woman who falls in love with him.

Several years before this film was released, melodramas about World War I spies had become clichés and were mercilessly attacked by contemporary movie critics. *The Great Deception*, with its obvious similarities (including its title) to films like *The Great Impersonation* (1921), was no exception. Despite the critics, similar spy films continued to appear well into the sound era, including *The Counterfeit Traitor* (1962), a well-received World War II drama with William Holden and Lilli Palmer. See British Intelligence: World War I. ■

Great Impersonation, The (1921), Par. *Dir.* George Melford; *Sc.* Monte Katterjohn; *Cast includes:* James Kirkwood, Ann Forrest, Winter Hall, Alan Hale, Truly Shattuck, Fontaine La Rue.

In this drama set just prior to World War I and based on E. Phillips Oppenheim's popular novel, James Kirkwood portrays the dual roles of Sir Dominey and Leopold Von Ragastein. The German secret service sends its agent, who looks very much like Sir Dominey, to replace the Englishman. Ann Forrest portrays the female lead. Two sound versions of the story followed, one in 1935 starring Edmund Lowe, and another in 1942 with Ralph Bellamy in the dual role. ■

Great Impersonation, The (1935), U. *Dir.* Alan Crosland; *Sc.* Frank Wead, Eve Greene; *Cast includes:* Edmund Lowe, Valerie Hobson, Wera Engels, Lumsden Hare, Spring Byington, Frank Reicher.

A remake of the 1921 version of E. Phillips Oppenheim's novel, this adaptation effects a major alteration. Instead of identifying particular countries such as Germany, the film describes the villains as members of an international cartel, merchants of death who foment conflicts around the world so that they can sell their munitions. Edmund Lowe portrays the dual role of Englishman and spy who exposes the sinister ring, including the brains behind the organization (Charles Waldron).

At the time the film was released, newspapers carried stories of a mysterious international personality who amassed great wealth from the sale of weaponry and who lived a luxurious life in Europe, not unlike the infamous arms dealer Sir Basil Zaharoff. Also, several documentaries about World War I released in the 1930s, such as *Dealers in Death* (1934), began condemning the munitions makers and government leaders for making secret deals during the conflict. See Sir Basil Zaharoff. ■

Great Impersonation, The (1942), U. *Dir.* John Rawlins; *Sc.* W. Scott Darling; *Cast includes:* Ralph Bellamy, Evelyn Ankers, Aubrey Mather, Edward Norris, Kaaren Verne, Henry Daniell.

E. Phillips Oppenheim's popular novel is updated to World War II in this third, and probably best, film version. Ralph Bellamy portrays the dual role of an Englishman and a German. Both meet somewhere in Africa before the outbreak of war. The film then concentrates on only one of the men, who assumes an important post in England during the war. But which one? Finally, the audience learns that he is the true Englishman. He is given false plans to turn over to agents in Germany. The film adds a subplot involving Rudolf Hess to the original story. Bellamy dispatches Hess on his notorious journey by plane to Scotland. Evelyn Ankers plays Bellamy's English wife in this suspenseful tale. ■

Great Locomotive Chase, The (1956), Buena Vista. *Dir.* Francis Lyon; *Sc.* Lawrence Edward Watkin; *Cast includes:* Fess Parker, Jeffrey Hunter, Jeff York, John Lupton, Eddie Firestone, Kenneth Tobey.

Based on an actual Civil War incident, this Walt Disney production recounts a Union raid organized by secret agent James J. Andrews to destroy Confederate railroad supply lines. Fess Parker, as Andrews, leads his two dozen troops disguised as civilians into the deep South to destroy rail lines between Atlanta and Chattanooga. Jeffrey Hunter, as a determined Southerner, pursues Andrews and his spies, who have stolen his train. John Lupton portrays William Pittenger, one of the Union agents who later wrote an account of the raid. The film depicts the chase and the capture of Andrews' men.

Andrews and seven of his men were tried and hanged. Six others, including Pittenger, another secret agent, escaped but were soon recaptured. They were later exchanged for Southern prisoners of war in 1863. Secretary of War Edwin Stanton awarded the six men the Medal of Honor. They were the first to receive the newly created commendation. Some of the prisoners later accused Pittenger, who testified against Andrews and the others at their trial, of striking a deal with the Confederates to save his own neck. Pittenger wrote *The Great Locomotive Chase*, an account of the incident, in 1889. Robert Buffum, played by Eddie Firestone, was another Union agent who volunteered to participate in the raid and was captured. He was one of the half-dozen who escaped, was recaptured and later awarded the Medal of Honor. See Andrews' Raid. ■

Great Love, The (1918), Par. *Dir.* D. W. Griffith; *Sc.* D. W. Griffith (listed as Captain Victor Marier), S. E. V. Taylor; *Cast includes:* Lillian Gish, Robert Harron, Henry B. Walthall, Gloria Hope, Maxfield Stanley, George Fawcett.

Director D. W. Griffith's World War I romantic drama about national and personal betrayal is set chiefly in war-torn England where German spies are plotting the destruction of a munitions factory. Lillian Gish, who plays the daughter of a rector, is the love object of a soldier (Robert Harron). But Gish is cajoled into marrying Sir Roger (Henry B. Walthall), a despicable character who recently abandoned a young woman with whom he had had a child. Both were killed in an air raid. Meanwhile, Harron foils a German plot to guide enemy zeppelins to the munitions target. He then kills Sir Roger, a traitor to his country, thereby rescuing Gish from an unsavory marriage. Two years after the film was released, Harron, an established member of Griffith's team of actors, died at age 26, the result of a self-inflicted gunshot wound.

World War I movies made in America almost invariably dealt with only the three major allies—England, France and the U.S.—especially in their choice of principal characters. Belgium was used chiefly as an innocent and helpless symbol of Germany's depravity and aggression. Italy, which seemed inconsequential in Hollywood's view, provided very few heroic characters. In terms of social background, dramas and sophisticated characters, the studios preferred England over France. American movie audiences were already familiar with English types and probably felt comfortable with these settings. The above film is typical in its employment of English society. Griffith used left-over on-location footage from his earlier World War I drama, *Hearts of the World*. See German Intelligence: World War I. ■

Great Shadow, The (1920), Rep. *Dir.* Harley Knoles; *Sc.* Rudolph Berliner; *Cast includes:* Tyrone Power, Donald Hall, Dorothy Bernard, John Rutherford, Louis Stern.

An anti-Bolshevik propaganda film, the drama depicts how Russian agents operate to incite tensions between capital and labor. The focus of the agitators' attentions is an American shipyard where they instigate a major strike by thousands of workers. Labor and management, to thwart off the destructive influence of the insidious foreign agents, soon come to an uneasy agreement. The bosses consent to giving their employees a raise in line with the current cost-of-living increase. At the same time, labor leaders agree to call off any further strikes. Both pledge to work towards a policy that will be mutually advantageous. Tyrone Power portrays the labor leader and father of a young girl. See Labor Unrest; Palmer Raids; Red Scare of 1919–1920. ■

Greatest Power, The (1917), Metro. *Dir.* Edwin Carewe; *Sc.* Albert Shelby; *Cast includes:* Ethel Barrymore, William B. Davidson, Harry Northrup, Frank Currier, William Black, Cecil Owen.

A chemist and his female assistant (Ethel Barrymore) develop a new explosive more powerful than any other currently known. A traitor of German descent plots to steal the formula. This silent story of intrigue, set in the days immediately preceding America's entry into World War I, involves the secret service and a romance. The country may not have been at war with the Central powers at the time of the film's release, but Germans had already appeared in a stream of spy and war dramas as villainous characters capable of all sorts of heinous acts ranging from treachery to rape.

Although a conventional drama in terms of its pivotal gimmick, the proverbial superweapon coveted by the enemy, the film manages to provide an interesting subplot. The young woman prefers that the explosive be turned over to the U.S. while the chemist, a confirmed pacifist, hesitates. It is only when he grows disillusioned with the underhanded machinations of the German spy that he assents to his assistant's suggestion. ■

Guilty of Treason (1950), Eagle Lion. *Dir.* Felix Feist; *Sc.* Emmet Lavery; *Cast includes:* Charles Bickford, Paul Kelly, Bonita Granville, Richard Derr, Roland Winters.

This Cold War drama reenacts the 1949 trial of Josef Cardinal Mindszenty in Communist Hungary. Charles Bickford portrays the cardinal who resists the Communist state's intrusion into the Catholic church's schools. After several conflicts with the totalitarian regime, he is arrested and accused of being an "enemy of the people." He is imprisoned and put on trial. A secret meeting of state bureaucrats, controlled by a Soviet commissar, suggests that Mindszenty's eventual confession was the result of the state's use of hypnosis, psychological torture and drugs.

A romantic subplot involving a young Hungarian (Bonita Granville) and a Russian colonel (Richard Derr) parallels the main story. Granville, a Hungarian patriot and defender of the cardinal, had fought with the French Resistance during World War II. She tries to persuade Derr that he is fighting for the wrong cause—that Soviet Communism is equivalent to Hitler's Nazism. But the colonel, a devoted follower of Stalin's policies, has her arrested. Physically tortured by her Communist guards, she goes to her death rather than confess to false charges concerning the cardinal.

Paul Kelly, as an American correspondent who serves as our guide throughout the drama, arrives in Budapest to report the entire story of the verbal attacks upon the cardinal and his eventual arrest and trial. Early in the film Kelly visits the cardinal at his remote farm. When the cardinal confides to the American that he is resigned to his fate at the hands of the Communists, Kelly asks: "Is there no chance for some compromise?" "What chance is there of an agreement between Christ and the anti-Christ?" the reli-gious leader replies. This mood of pessimism and frustration pervades much of the dialogue and attitudes of ordinary Hungarians. Kelly, surprised that the cardinal's followers and other fair-minded Hungarians have not spoken out in his favor, asks Granville: "What about the underground?" "There is no underground," she explains. "Every day hundreds of people are arrested and never heard of again."

As with other Cold War propaganda films of the period, this entry displays similar shortcomings. It fails to convince because of its stereotyped, one-dimensional characters. The Communist leaders and torturers are all brutal while the few freedom-loving heroes and heroines are overly noble. Also, its didactic speeches and other heavy-handed propaganda elements work against an already strained plot. The film is based partially on *As We See Russia*, a compilation of writings produced by the Overseas Press Club.

Joseph Cardinal Mindzenty represented those elements in the Catholic Church most rigidly opposed to the Communist regime in Hungary. He had been ordained as a priest in 1915, bishop in 1944, primate of Hungary in 1945 and cardinal the following year.

As mentioned in the film, he led the opposition to the Hungarian Communist state's encroachment on the Catholic schools in 1948. He was arrested and convicted of treason in 1949 and sentenced to life in prison; however, he escaped from jail during the Hungarian Revolution in 1956 and sought refuge in the American embassy in Budapest where he remained until 1971. He had repeatedly rejected Vatican entreaties that he leave Hungary and only agreed to leave the American embassy for Austria at the suggestion of U.S. President Nixon.

Jan Masaryk's sudden death in 1948 still remains a mystery. The world may never learn whether he committed suicide or was pushed from his window. Jan Masaryk (1886–1948), the son of Tomas Masaryk, the first President of Czechoslovakia, served as ambassador to Great Britain from 1925 to 1938. During World War II he became the foreign minister of the Czech government-in-exile in London and made regular radio broadcasts to his occupied homeland.

Masaryk was the protege of President Benes and traveled with him to Moscow in 1945. Masaryk was firmly committed to cooperation with the Russians, but he was frustrated by Stalin's rejection of Marshall Plan aid for Czechoslovakia. A non-Communist, Masaryk received an early warning that his life was in danger. On September 11, 1947, he narrowly escaped the threat of a bomb that was mailed to him. Benes convinced Masaryk to remain as foreign minister following the Communist putsch in 1948. But within a few weeks Masaryk was dead. ∎

H

Haldane of the Secret Service (1923), FBO. *Dir.* Harry Houdini; *Cast includes:* Houdini, Gladys Leslie, William Humphrey, Richard Carlyle, Jane Jennings.

The celebrated escape artist Harry Houdini portrays the title character in this drama about a Chinese counterfeit ring. The plot takes Houdini to various European cities, including London and Paris, in his attempt to break up the illegal activities of the oriental cabal. He engages in some of the escape-stunt work for which he was noted at the time of the film's release. The drama offers a climactic battle between Houdini and the villains. Gladys Leslie portrays the heroine in this generally unexciting film.

Harry Houdini, one of the greatest escape artists of all time, was, in all likelihood, born in Budapest, Hungary, in 1874. Like other enterprising young men of that time, he eventually made his way to America, changed his original name of Erich Weiss to Houdini, and underwent a metamorphosis from trapeze artist to magician to escape artist.

Houdini invited members of the audience to bring handcuffs and straitjackets and to personally restrain him in various boxes and prison cells. His later acts included submersion in underwater boxes—from which he invariably escaped. He vigorously exposed a number of crooked mediums who had been unscrupulously exploiting their clients.

Houdini extended his activities into silent films in which he starred (*The Master Mystery* (a 1919 serial); *The Grim Game* (1919); *Terror Island* (1920), etc.) and sometimes produced (*The Soul of Bronze* (1921), *The Man From Beyond* (1922) and *Haldane*).

Priding himself on his physique and fitness, he often permitted guests to strike him in his abdomen. One day he was caught off guard when some visiting adolescents struck him; he suffered severe injuries which caused his death from appendicitis in 1926. See U.S. Secret Service. ■

Hale, Nathan (1755–1776). His parting words—"I only regret that I have but one life to lose for my country" (inspired by a line in Addison's 1713 play *Cato*)—became part of the folklore of the American Revolution. Unfortunately, the American patriot Nathan Hale is remembered today for little more than those last words he uttered before the British hanged him as a spy.

Nathan Hale went to Yale University and was graduated in 1773. After only two years of teaching he joined the Connecticut militia. He fought the British in Boston and then joined the 19th Continental Regiment of the Continental Army. The fictionalized film biography *The Heart of a Hero* (1916), with Robert Warwick and Gail Kane, accurately portrays Hale (Warwick) as a schoolteacher when hostilities erupt in Concord between the British and the colonists. He is seen later volunteering to serve as a spy against the British. Although he accomplishes his mission, he is captured and sentenced to hang.

Hale rose to the rank of captain and then was assigned to New York City in 1776. Lieutenant Colonel Knowlton selected Hale to lead a unit of Rangers. In the meantime, General Howe and his British troops, who were forced out of Boston, arrived in New York City. Howe made his base in Staten Island, launched an attack on Washington's forces in Long Island and beat them. Washington moved the remnants of his troops to Manhattan where they began to dig in. Desperately in need of information about enemy forces and their deployment, he asked Knowlton to find a spy to infiltrate the British lines. Knowlton found only one volunteer, Nathan Hale, for this dangerous mission.

Hale was, from the beginning, an extremely poor choice for a spy. He was tall and didn't even have rudimentary knowledge of espionage techniques. His face was scarred as the result of a previous military incident. To complicate matters further, the purpose of his mission was widely known among Knowlton's Rangers, some of whom may have been British informers. The *piéce de résistance* was the fact that Hale's cousin, Samuel Hale, was the commissioner of prisoners for General Howe and was at that very moment stationed in Staten Island.

Hale moved through Connecticut on September 13–14, 1776, and was transported on a local ship to Long Island. He exchanged his Continental Army uniform for civilian clothes and reconnoitered British positions. While Hale was making his way through British lines in Long Island, the British forces, on the other end, were pushing Washington north, out of Manhattan. Whatever Hale might have learned was, at the time, of minimal value. Hale followed the British and attempted to get through to the American forces. He was captured on September 21 and hanged the next day.

Except for a few silent dramas, Hale has not fared too well as a popular screen subject. The earliest film about the patriot was Edison's 1911 one-reeler titled "The Death of Nathan Hale." This was followed by a 1913 experimental color drama, *Nathan Hale*. By the sound era the patriot's screen image was relegated to that of symbol. In *Joe Smith, American* (1942), a World War II propaganda drama, an aircraft employee (Robert Young) is kidnapped by Nazi spies. He is tortured for hours by his captors who attempt to pry information from him. In his attempts to distract himself from the pain, he focuses his thoughts on special moments with his family and patriotic images, such as those of Nathan Hale. ■

Half Way to Shanghai (1942), U. *Dir.* John Rawlins; *Sc.* Stuart Palmer; *Cast includes:* Kent Taylor, Irene Hervey, George Zucco, J. Edward Bromberg, Henry Stephenson.

Nazi agents attempt to get maps of Chinese defenses and ammunition depots in this World War II drama set in Burma in 1942 before the Japanese invasion. The film chiefly takes place aboard a train bound for Rangoon and offers the usual assortment of diverse passengers. They include, among others, an American engineer (Kent Taylor) returning after spending two years on the Burma Road, a white Russian (Irene Hervey) who has narrowly escaped from Shanghai following the Japanese air raids, and two Nazi spies (George Zucco and Lionel Royce). In addition, J. Edward Bromberg poses as a butterfly collector who is actually a Burmese detective, and Henry Stephenson portrays a retired British officer.

After one murder, another attempted murder and a series of suspicious incidents, the detective uncovers the plot, and the secret plans are saved. The film, a remake of an earlier work titled *Rome Express* (1932), is unremarkable as a drama but offers a few interesting moments. At the beginning, when the Nazi agents board the train at the last minute, the chief conductor asks them what their business is in Shanghai. "Oh," Zucco replies, "I'm a German spy." Later, character actor Willie Fung provides the following prophetic statement in his best Pidgin English: "Japanese people make much problem. They likee pull dragon's tail. One day they be very sorry." See Burma. ■

Ham and Eggs at the Front (1927), WB. *Dir.* Roy Del Ruth; *Sc.* Robert Dillon, James A. Starr; *Cast includes:* Tom Wilson, Karl Dane, Heine Conklin, Myrna Loy, William J. Irving, Noah Young.

A World War I comedy with racist overtones, the film features a white cast made up in blackface. Two pals, played by Tom Wilson and Charlie "Heine" Conklin, go through training together and end up in the trenches where they intercept an enemy message by mistake. Myrna Loy, also in blackface, is sent as a spy to retrieve the information. The script, based on a story by Darryl F. Zanuck, offers the typical barracks and front-line gags, but they are presented entertainingly.

The black stereotypes highlighted in the film (e.g., every player in a poker game has four aces and a razor) may be repugnant to audiences today, but they were generally accepted at the time the film was released. The stage for decades featured minstrel shows and, as late at the 1920s and 1930s, audiences applauded the talents of Al Jolson, Eddie Cantor and other blackface performers. ■

Hammerhead (1968), Col. *Dir.* David Miller; *Sc.* William Bast, Herbert Baker; *Cast includes:* Vince Edwards, Judy Geeson, Beverly Adams, Peter Vaughan, Diana Dors, Michael Bates.

An international criminal, known as Hammerhead, tries to learn the secret plans of the North Atlantic Treaty Organization in this drama that tries too hard to imitate the James Bond films. Vince Edwards portrays a secret agent in ersatz Bond style who is assigned to foil the villain's scheme. Hammerhead, played by Peter Vaughan, collects antique erotica, which gives Edwards the means of infiltrating the villain's inner circle by way of a delivery of coveted artifacts. The film ends conventionally with Edwards upsetting Vaughan's scheme and saving the N.A.T.O. plans. Beverly Adams, who played Dean Martin's secretary in the Matt Helm spy capers, takes time out to appear in this entry. Judy Geeson, as the female lead, falls in love with Edwards in this weak story based on a novel by James Mayo. ∎

"Hand of Uncle Sam, The" (1910), Essanay. *Dir.* Emile Chautard; *Cast includes:* J. Warren Kerrigan.

An early example of gunboat diplomacy, this drama concerns an American in a foreign country who is wrongly accused of spying. J. Warren Kerrigan, as the Yank, is about to face a firing squad when the American consul demands a fair trial. Meanwhile, the Secretary of War sends a torpedo boat to the rescue. In the end the young man is saved and the real traitor is sent to his death. ∎

Hands Up (1926), Par. *Dir.* Clarence Badger; *Sc.* Monte Brice, Lloyd Corrigan; *Cast includes:* Raymond Griffith, Marion Nixon, Virginia Lee Corbin, Mack Swain, Montagu Love.

Silent screen comic Raymond Griffith, whose genius and originality have been almost forgotten today, portrays a Southern spy in this Civil War farce. He is assigned to stop a much-needed gold shipment from reaching President Lincoln. Meanwhile, Lincoln has sent a Union officer to make sure the shipment gets through. Probably one of Griffith's best comedies, the film offers several good visual gags, an Indian attack on a stagecoach and a wild chase in a western mining town where Union soldiers pursue the elusive Griffith. Suddenly peace is declared and the hunt

for Griffith ends. Meanwhile, two daughters of a mine owner fall in love with Griffith, who, inspired by the Mormons, rides off with the sisters in a stagecoach headed for Salt Lake City. The film, based on a story by Reginald Morris, takes liberties with its portrayals of historical figures, including Lincoln, Allan Pinkerton (who created the first U.S. spy service) and Brigham Young. See Allan Pinkerton. ∎

Hangmen Also Die (1943), UA. *Dir.* Fritz Lang; *Sc.* John Wexley; *Cast includes:* Brian Donlevy, Walter Brennan, Anna Lee, Gene Lockhart, Dennis O'Keefe.

One of the strongest indictments against the Nazi regime to come out of wartime Hollywood, this World War II propaganda drama is a fictionalized account of the assassination of the Nazi executioner, Reinhard Heydrich, known by his victims as the Hangman. Brian Donlevy plays the Czech doctor whom the Prague underground assigns to kill Heydrich. After the assassination, Donlevy, wounded in the attack, seeks temporary refuge in the home of a professor (Walter Brennan) and his daughter (Anna Lee). When her father, along with hundreds of other Czech citizens, is taken as hostage, the daughter plans to turn Donlevy over to the Nazis. But she relents, realizing that he represents the free spirit of the people. Donlevy escapes while the underground frames a local quisling (Gene Lockhart) for the killing.

The script is based on a story by Fritz Lang and Bertholt Brecht; however, Brecht claimed that little of his material was used. Although the drama is based on actual incidents, it loses some credibility as a result of the stereotyped, heavy-handed treatment of the Germans. Several other dramas about Heydrich appeared during the war years. See Reinhard Heydrich. ∎

Hard Contract (1969), TCF. *Dir.* S. Lee Pogostin; *Sc.* S. Lee Pogostin; *Cast includes:* James Coburn, Lee Remick, Lilli Palmer, Burgess Meredith, Patrick McGee, Sterling Hayden.

James Coburn portrays an emotionless international assassin without moral or political convictions until he falls in love in this ambiguous drama set chiefly in Spain and Belgium. A professional killer who works alone, he asks few questions concerning his intended victims. Coburn accepts a "hard contract" to annihilate three Europeans. Burgess Meredith, as the shadowy person who hires Coburn, theorizes about murder and believes "there's no such thing as crime anymore." Lee Remick, as the female lead who forces Coburn to have self-doubts, portrays the rich leader of a group of jet-setters. She falls in love with Coburn although she is aware of his icy indifference toward others. Patrick McGee, as one of Remick's entourage and a convicted Nazi, conveys a pathetic figure. Lilli Palmer, as another member of the group, portrays a superficial woman who makes a play for Burgess when he appears on the scene.

The film was one of the earliest dramas to reflect the cynicism that followed in the wake of the U-2 spy plane shot down over the Soviet Union and the involvement of U.S. intelligence in the abortive invasion of Cuba. Politics and morality, these incidents inferred, are not necessarily inextricably bound to one another. Coburn's character revealed this shifting attitude that soon pervaded such diverse spy dramas as *Executive Action* (1973), *Three Days of the Condor* (1975) and *The Formula* (1980). ∎

Headin' for God's Country (1943), Rep. *Dir.* William Morgan; *Sc.* Elizabeth Meehan, Houston Branch; *Cast includes:* William Lundigan, Virginia Dale, Harry Davenport, Harry Shannon, Addison Richards, J. Frank Hamilton.

An enemy agent leads a Japanese assault on a small Alaskan village in this World War II drama that takes place immediately following Japan's attack on Pearl Harbor. Harry Shannon, as the agent working with the Japanese, steals a tube from the only radio receiver in the community and contacts the small force of Japanese. William Lundigan, as a stranger in the community who has been mistreated as a vagrant, leads the defense of the villagers against the raiding party which is eventually annihilated. Virginia Dale, as the local radio operator, falls in love with Lundigan. Harry Davenport portrays the local newspaper publisher. ∎

Heart of a Hero, The (1916), World. *Dir.* Emile Chautard; *Sc.* Frances Marion; *Cast includes:* Robert Warwick, Gail Kane, Alec Francis, George McQuarrie, Clifford Gray, Henry West.

A fictionalized biographical drama of Nathan Hale's role in the American Revolution, the film is set just prior to and during the rebellion. Hale (Robert Warwick) is a schoolteacher when hostilities erupt in Concord between the British and the colonists. He organizes a company of volunteers to join the Minutemen. Gail Kane portrays a young woman with whom Hale falls in love. When he volunteers to serve as a spy against the British, she pleads with him not to go. Her appeals are futile. He accomplishes his mission but is captured and sentenced to hang.

Released during World War I but one year before America's entry into the conflict, the film anticipates the numerous patriotic dramas that were to appear within the next two years. Besides having all the right propaganda elements—heroism, duty and self-sacrifice, the film starred Robert Warwick, a stalwart and earnest actor who was popular on the stage before he entered films. The work was adapted from the 1899 play *Nathan Hale* by Clyde Fitch. See Nathan Hale. ∎

Heart of Lincoln, The (1915), Gold Seal. *Dir.* Francis Ford; *Sc.* W. W. Young; *Cast includes:* Francis Ford, Grace Cunard, Ella Hall, William Quinn.

This Civil War drama opens before the hostilities with a Southern colonel and his daughter Betty visiting a Northern colonel in Washington. At a party which Lincoln attends, he is attracted to Betty's charms. Later in the evening the two colonels get into an argument, and Betty's father leaves for home, taking her with him. War breaks out and the two officers meet once again, this time in battle. Betty's mother falls ill and sends a message to her husband. But the home is occupied by Union troops and the Southern colonel must don a Union uniform to pass the guards. He is captured and sentenced to death as a spy. Betty calls on the President who intervenes on the colonel's behalf.

Francis Ford, John Ford's mentor and older brother, directed and acted in several historical films during the early silent period, including *The Invaders* (1912), *When Lincoln Paid* (1913) and *Washington at Valley Forge* (1914). Some of these films featured his wife, Grace Cunard. He portrayed George A. Custer in "Custer's Last Raid" (1912). During the 1920s he directed westerns and action dramas. ∎

Heart Trouble (1929), FN. *Dir.* Harry Langdon; *Sc.* Earle Rodney, Clarence Hennecke; *Cast includes:* Harry Langdon, Doris Dawson, Lionel Belmore, Madge Hunt, Bud Jamieson, Mark Hamilton.

Harry Langdon portrays Harry Van Housen, a German-American who tries desperately to enlist in the U.S. Army in this silent comedy set during World War I. His main reason is to prove his patriotism to his sweetheart (Doris Dawson). But Harry is rejected on numerous grounds—he is several inches too short, underweight, flatfooted and nearsighted. He also has a bad case of dandruff. But fate provides the opportunity for Harry to prove that he is a true American. He accidentally stumbles across a hidden base where spies are supplying German submarines. Unknown to him, Harry has helped rescue an American officer and is the cause of the destruction of the base and the capture of the enemy agents. His town turns out to honor its local hero, but Harry is too occupied with wooing his sweetheart to notice. ▪

Held by the Enemy (1920), Par. *Dir.* Donald Crisp; *Sc.* Beulah Marie Dix; *Cast includes:* Lewis Stone, Jack Holt, Agnes Ayres, Wanda Hawley, Josephine Crowell, Lillian Leighton.

A Civil War drama based on William Gillette's play, the film stars Lewis Stone as a captain in the Confederate army while Jack Holt portrays a Union colonel. The captain, betrothed to a Southern belle, returns as a spy to his city that is now occupied by Union troops. He is eventually captured and tried as a spy. Several suspenseful battle sequences help to expand the original stage version.

Lewis Stone had a long and distinguished career with MGM, gaining popularity during the 1930s and 1940s as Judge Hardy, Mickey Rooney's unruffled father in the "Andy Hardy" films. Jack Holt starred in numerous action and adventure dramas during the next two decades and continued in films as a character actor into the 1940s. Director Donald Crisp, who had worked as an actor for D. W. Griffith before World War I, eventually gave up directing to emerge as one of the screen's great character actors during the silent and sound periods. Gillette's play has been considered by some critics as the first significant drama of the Civil War. ▪

Hell's Bloody Devils (1970), Independent-International. *Dir.* Al Adamson; *Sc.* Jerry Evans; *Cast includes:* Broderick Crawford, Scott Brady, Kent Taylor, Keith Andes, John Carradine, Erin O'Donnell.

Undercover agents infiltrate a neo-Nazi organization operating in the U.S. and linked to the Las Vegas Mafia in this violent action drama. John Gabriel, as Adams, an F.B.I. agent who has been accepted by the underworld, has been assigned to investigate the Mafia's ties with a neo-Nazi movement. Meanwhile, Vicki Volante, as an Israeli agent, has become the mistress of the Nazi leader (Kent Taylor) in the hope that he will lead her to her parents' murderer. Taylor has joined forces with the Mafia in his plan to distribute counterfeit money. His "soldiers" consist of a group of California motorcyclists known as the Bloody Devils. The F.B.I. agent, as a liaison among the groups, meets the Israeli agent and begins to fall for her. Taylor soon uncovers her real identity and kills her. Gabriel, along with other agents, then annihilates Taylor's minions while Taylor and his fanatic daughter (Erin O'Donnell) perish in a helicopter filled with explosives. ▪

Her Country First (1918), Par. *Dir.* James Young; *Sc.* Edith Kennedy; *Cast includes:* Vivian Martin, John Cossart, Florence Oberle, Brydine Zuber, J. Parks-Jones, Larry Steers.

Vivian Martin portrays a patriotic young woman who is anxious to do her share for the war effort in this World War I drama. She organizes a girls' aviation auxiliary, and the group trains on a farmer's property. The farmer is a veteran and promises to teach them military tactics. Later, when some German spies invade her home, she and the girls spring into action and help capture the enemy agents. The film, adapted from a novel by Mary Roberts Rinehart, famous for her mystery stories, not only exemplifies the patriotic spirit of the period. It was one of many features released during the conflict to draw the female population into the war effort by paying tribute to the role of women on the home front. ▪

Her Debt of Honor (1918), Fox. *Dir.* O. A. C. Lund; *Sc.* Eva Unsell; *Cast includes:* Eric Mayne, Irving Cummings, Peggy Hyland, Frank Goldsmith, Hazel Adams.

Peggy Hyland portrays the wife of a U.S. Senator who is in charge of troop movements to the European front in this World War I drama. A German agent (Frank Schiller) has an affair with the unsuspecting wife so that he can gain the vital information for his own country. Irving Cummings, who plays the husband, eventually switched to directing films. The romantic plot is a familiar one and was used often during World War I with other major and minor actresses playing the vulnerable wife, including Gloria Swanson, who made three such films within a two-year period. One of the unique qualities of this entry is its attractive visual compositions. ■

Her Man o' War (1926), PDC. *Dir.* Frank Urson; *Sc.* Charles Logue; *Cast includes:* William Boyd, Jimmie Adams, Jetta Goudal, Robert Edeson, Frank Reicher.

Two American soldiers (William Boyd and Jimmie Adams) volunteer to act as deserters in this World War I drama. Their mission is to find a route behind enemy lines to a big gun that is preventing an Allied attack. The men are accepted by the Germans and assigned to work on farms near where the gun is installed. But Boyd's real mission is exposed, and he is sentenced to face a firing squad. A local farm girl who has fallen in love with him contacts the American troops and he is saved. Boyd, whose screen popularity declined with the advent of the sound era, began a new career in a western series as Hopalong Cassidy, which was to bring him new acclaim during the next three decades. ■

Heydrich, Reinhard (1904–1942). Appointed second in command to Himmler in the Gestapo and the S.S., Heydrich was better known to his victims as "Heydrich the Hangman" for his atrocities in Nazi-occupied countries during World War II, especially in Czechoslovakia. His assassination by Czech agents in 1942 so angered the Nazis that more than 5,000 people were summarily executed and the village of Lidice destroyed. The Nazi reign of terror failed to break the spirit of the Czech people and only further fueled the determination of the Allied nations to crush the Axis powers.

His infamous activities have been described in a handful of films, chiefly World War II propaganda dramas. In *Hangmen Also Die* (1943), a fictionalized account of the assassination of Heydrich, Brian Donlevy plays the Czech doctor whom the Prague underground assigns to kill the Hangman. *Hitler's*

Hangman, released the same year, recounts the story of Czechoslovakian resistance to Nazi oppression, the assassination of Heydrich (John Carradine) and the Nazi reprisals which led to the destruction of the village of Lidice. *One Inch From Victory* (1944), chiefly a World War II documentary about the battle of Russia, also covers Reinhard Heydrich's funeral and Hitler's attendance at his burial in Berlin. *Operation Daybreak* (1976) is another reenactment of the assassination of Heydrich by Czech freedom fighters parachuted into Czechoslovakia by the British and the resultant destruction of Lidice by the Germans.

The eventual tragedy that befell Sergeants Josef Gabcik and Jan Kubis, the two Czech agents dropped by parachute on May 27, 1942, to assassinate the "butcher of Prague," is told in detail in Callum MacDonald's book *The Killing of Reinhard Heydrich.* As Gabcik, in charge of the assassination team, was about to fire his gun, it jammed. Kubis threw the bomb that killed Heydrich. The two sergeants were later betrayed by some partisans. Trapped in a Prague church, they took their own lives with their remaining bullets rather than fall into the hands of the Gestapo. ■

Hidden Code, The (1920), Pioneer. *Dir.* Richard Le Strange; *Cast includes:* Grace Davison, Ralph Osborne, Richard Le Strange.

Another drama about World War I with the Germans as the antagonists, the film centers on a secret formula for a high explosive. The inventor, ever fearful of the secret falling into the wrong hands, is in a dilemma as to where to hide it. He decides to tattoo a portion of it on his daughter's shoulder and, through a special process, makes it invisible. The remainder of the film is taken up with international spies in pursuit of the "hidden code." The tattoo ploy was used more than twenty years later in the World War II comedy drama *The Lady Has Plans* (1942), with Paulette Goddard being mistaken for a spy who has been temporarily tattooed with secret plans. ■

Hidden Enemy, The (1940), Mon. *Dir.* Howard Bretherton; *Sc.* C. B. Williams, Marian Orth; *Cast includes:* Warren Hull, Kay Linaker, William Von Brinken, George Cleveland, William Castello, Fern Emmett.

A World War II drama, the film concerns an experimental metal that is three times lighter than aluminum and at the same time much stronger than steel. International spies as well as other characters would like to obtain the secret of this valuable formula. George Cleveland portrays the American inventor while Warren Hull plays his son, a newspaper reporter who is soon entangled in the plot to steal to his father's discovery. The "hidden enemy" of the title seems to suggest Russian and Italian agents although these countries are never mentioned directly. ■

High Velocity (1977), First Asian. *Dir.* Remi Kramer; *Sc.* Remi Kramer, Michael J. Parsons; *Cast includes:* Ben Gazzara, Britt Ekland, Paul Winfield, Keenan Wynn, Alejandro Rey, Victoria Racimo.

Intrigue, treachery and violence make up the ingredients of this superficial drama about the rescue of an international corporation executive kidnapped by an Asian guerrilla force. Ben Gazzara and Paul Winfield portray pals, both Vietnam veterans, who hire out to rescue the captive. Gazzara's motivation, besides the money, is his romantic interest in the victim's attractive wife, played by Britt Ekland. Alejandro Rey, as a crafty Asian official, buys the services of the two American adventurers. Keenan Wynn, as Ekland's secret lover, is a corrupt businessman who exploits others. In the end, the two heroes are betrayed by Rey. Although the film makes a half-hearted attempt to deal with the problem of American corporate leaders bribing local authorities—and the much larger issues of politics and morality that began to infiltrate spy dramas by the late 1960s—much of the film concentrates on the action concerning the rescue. ■

Highest Trump, The (1919), Vitagraph. *Dir.* James Young; *Sc.* H. H. Van Loan, Earle Williams; *Cast includes:* Earle Williams, Grace Darmond, Robert Byrem, John Cossar, C. H. Geldart, Robert Bolder.

Earle Williams plays a dual role in this World War I spy drama. When his twin brother, a German agent, is killed, Williams replaces him and is accepted as a German spy. In reality, he is working for the U.S. government. Grace Darmond, as Williams' sweetheart, believes he has turned traitor. One of the earliest war films to focus on the use of airplanes in combat, it contains numerous aerial scenes. The ploy of twins or look-alikes fighting on opposite sides was already familiar to audiences and appeared on screen

in several postwar films, including three versions of *The Great Impersonation*, based on E. Phillips Oppenheim's popular novel. In addition, the World War II drama *Nazi Agent* (1942) features Conrad Veidt in a similar role as that of Williams, in which Veidt, a loyal American who owns a small bookstore, impersonates his brother, a fanatical Nazi officer. ■

Hillbilly Blitzkrieg (1942), Mon. *Dir.* Ray Mack; *Sc.* R. S. Harris; *Cast includes:* Bud Duncan, Cliff Nazarro, Edgar Kennedy, Doris Linden, Lucien Littlefield, Alan Baldwin.

Based on the Snuffy Smith and Barney Google comic strip characters created by Billy De Beck, this World War II comedy concerns the protection of a government rocket invention in the backwoods of Tennessee. Comic character actor Edgar Kennedy portrays a sergeant and Bud Duncan plays Private Snuffy Smith. Both are assigned to guard the secret weapon which interests the U.S. government. Meanwhile, spies are plotting to steal the plans and destroy the site. Alan Baldwin and Doris Linden provide a slight romantic subplot. The most interesting part of this comedy is the title. ■

Hillbillys in a Haunted House (1967), Woolner Bros. *Dir.* Jean Yarbrough; *Sc.* Duke Yelton; *Cast includes:* Ferlin Husky, Joi Lansing, Don Bowman, John Carradine, Lon Chaney, Jr., Basil Rathbone.

Two country singers and their manager get involved with enemy agents who are trying to steal atomic secrets from the U.S. in this comedy reminiscent of the 1940s. Ferlin Husky and Joi Lansing, as the entertainers, and Don Bowman as their manager, all on their way to Nashville, wind up in the middle of a shootout between police and foreign spies. The three travelers stop in an abandoned town to quiet the manager's nerves. A sudden storm quickly drives the trio into a deserted mansion that soon appears to be haunted. In reality, the house is being used as a cover for an espionage gang headed by Madame Wong (Linda Ho). When the spies steal atomic documents from a nearby base, an agent from M.O.T.H.E.R. (Master Organization to Halt Enemy Resistance) follows them back to the mansion. The singers and the agent join forces, with the help of a real ghost, to capture the ring. ■

Hillcrest Mystery, The (1918), Pathé. *Dir.* George Fitzmaurice; *Sc.* Ouida Bergere; *Cast includes:* Irene Castle, J. H. Gilmour, Ralph Kelland, Wyndham Standing.

Murder and espionage are blended into a tale that results only in a routine drama. When the owner of a shipyard is murdered after he turns the company over to the government, his secretary becomes the chief suspect. However, when the mystery is unraveled, the real culprit is uncovered. He is one of the owners who has been operating as a German agent and trying to keep the company out of government control. The famed dancer, Irene Castle, portrays the daughter of the murdered man. ∎

Hills of Missing Men (1922), Pathé. *Dir.* J. P. McGowan; *Sc.* J. P. McGowan; *Cast includes:* J. P. McGowan, Jean Perry, James Wang, Charles Brindley, Helen Holmes.

A U.S. Secret Service agent poses as an outlaw to help round up a secret army trying to gain control of lower California in this western drama. J. P. McGowan, as the government operative, masquerades as The Dragon, the alleged leader of a gang of outlaws. Jean Perry, as Crando, a crazed visionary who dreams of creating his own empire, has been assembling an army of fugitives to help him carry out his plans. When he hears that The Dragon is on the run from the law, he signs him up as well. This gives the agent the opportunity to uncover the entire plot. With the help of the U.S. Cavalry, McGowan corrals the mercenary troops, thereby shattering Perry's grandiose dream. Helen Holmes provides the romantic interest. ∎

Hindenburg, The (1975), U. *Dir.* Robert Wise; *Sc.* Nelson Gidding; *Cast includes:* George C. Scott, Anne Bancroft, William Atherton, Roy Thinnes, Gig Young, Burgess Meredith.

The fatal 1937 Atlantic crossing of the lighter-than-air zeppelin the *Hindenburg* is explored in this disaster drama. The film purports that a German saboteur, one of the crewmen, planted the timing device so that it would detonate after the airship landed in Lakehurst, New Jersey, and all the passengers had embarked. However, bad weather prevented the flight from arriving on schedule and the resultant disaster ensued. The film attempts to differentiate between full-blown Nazis and anti-Hitler Germans, leaving the impression that Hitler was supported by only a few fanatical followers. Another issue raised was why the ship used the more volatile hydrogen rather than helium, a safer gas. (Harold Ickes, one of President Roosevelt's cabinet members, refused to sell helium to Hitler.)

George C. Scott, as a colonel in the German air force, has recently completed a tour of duty in the Spanish Civil War—an assignment he looks back upon with regret and disgust. "I wasn't proud after last week," he confides to a fellow passenger. "Guernica—a little Basque village—a few hundred peasants. We dropped 3,000 bombs on her." He is appointed security officer aboard the *Hindenburg* after authorities receive threats that a time bomb will be placed somewhere on the airship. Scott reluctantly accepts the assignment although he considers it demeaning. In addition, he believes the ship, which he calls a "flying dinosaur," is obsolete and should be grounded. However, his superior describes it as a "symbol of German power." The *Hindenburg* serves as an ironic metaphor for Nazi Germany's vanity—powerful but volatile—a hollow ship journeying forth to its futile destiny, doomed to perish in flames.

William Atherton portrays the young German saboteur. A former member of the Hitler youth movement, he has grown disillusioned with Germany's oppressive and belligerent policies. He has joined a small resistance group and volunteered to blow up the airship with himself on board. "This ship is the Nazis' greatest propaganda weapon," he explains his motives to Scott, who eventually unmasks Atherton as the saboteur. "It will prove there is a resistance. Decent Germans will get the courage to join us."

Other passengers add some slight interest to the plot. Anne Bancroft, as a kooky German countess. Roy Thinnes, as a Gestapo officer assigned to help Scott, frowns upon Scott's more quiet and subtle methods of investigation during the journey. Thinnes prefers a more direct and brutal approach to uncovering the saboteur. Charles Durning, as the no-nonsense captain of the ship, is a devout Nazi. Burgess Meredith, Rene Auberjoinois and Robert Clary supply some strained comedy relief.

The 804-foot long *Hindenburg*, built in 1936, burst into flames on May 6, 1937, while making its first scheduled Lakehurst, New Jersey, landing for that year. The airship was destroyed, taking 36 lives. The passengers were the first fatalities in commercial airship history. Although atmospheric electricity is mainly given for the cause of the disaster, sabotage has never been completely ruled out. ■

His Birthright (1918), Mutual. *Dir.* William Worthington; *Sc.* Frances Guihan; *Cast includes:* Sessue Hayakawa, Marin Sais, Howard Davies, Mary Anderson, Tsuru Aoki.

German spies steal important government documents from a rear admiral of the U.S. Navy in this drama set during World War I. The plot, however, increases in complexity. The officer (Howard Davies), who had been stationed at a Japanese port many years earlier, had fathered an illegitimate son, the result of an affair with a young Japanese woman. Sessue Hayakawa, as the son, was raised in Japan by an old man. When he learns the truth, the son journeys to the U.S. to avenge his mother who had committed suicide.

Hayakawa meets a beautiful woman (Marin Sais) who persuades him to steal some important military documents from the admiral. After he turns over the papers to her, he learns that she never cared for him. He further discovers that she is the leader of a group of German spies. A fist fight ensues with several of the agents, and he recovers the documents. The police and his father enter in time to round up the spies. The admiral confesses that he loved the young man's mother and brings his son to his home. Hayakawa, in turn, enlists in the U.S. Army. See Japanese War Scare of 1907. ■

His Daughter Pays (1918), Piedmont. *Dir.* Paul Trinchera; *Cast includes:* Gertrude McCoy, Pauline Curley, Charles Graham, Henry Sedley, Barry Whitcomb, Johnny Walker.

A daughter suffers a series of degradations as the result of her father's debts in this drama set in France and based on Frederick H. James' play *La Baccarat.* Charles Graham, as the father of two daughters, has accumulated large debts. He consents to sell government secrets to a spy network but fails to deliver the papers. The head of the spy ring then kidnaps the man's older daughter (Gertrude McCoy) and coerces her to dance at his café. The captive's sister (Pauline Curly), in an effort to help McCoy and salvage her own engagement, begins to investigate those who

frequent the café. The father finally confides the whole seedy tale to the police who then save the daughter. Her sister is now free to marry her fiancé. ■

His Majesty, the American (1919), UA. *Dir.* Joseph Henaberry; *Sc.* Joseph Henaberry, Douglas Fairbanks (listed as Elton Banks); *Cast includes:* Douglas Fairbanks, Marjorie Daw, Frank Campeau, Sam Sothern, Jay Dwiggins.

Conspirators plot the overthrow of a small European country in this romantic comedy drama starring Douglas Fairbanks. The acrobatic Fairbanks portrays a New York *bon vivant* who receives large sums from an unidentified source to journey to the mythical kingdom. He arrives in the nick of time to foil the band of plotters from usurping the rightful dynasty which includes Fairbanks as the heir to the throne. Marjorie Daw, as a local countess, provides the romance in this rather lavish production well suited to the energetic talents of the star. ■

Hiss, Alger. See *The Trials of Alger Hiss* (1980). ■

Hitler—Dead or Alive (1942), Ben Judell. *Dir.* Nick Grinde; *Sc.* Sam Neuman, Karl Brown; *Cast includes:* Ward Bond, Dorothy Tree, Warren Hymer, Paul Fix, Bob Watson, Russell Hicks.

In 1942, newspapers carried an unusual item. An American businessman offered a $1 million reward for the capture of Hitler, dead or alive. This implausible film is based on that premise. A wealthy scientist, attempting to avenge his brother who was murdered by the Nazis, (Russell Hicks) places the offer in a local newspaper. Three former jailbirds, played comically by Ward Bond, Warren Hymer and Paul Fix, accept the contract. At first the scientist is unconvinced that the trio, led by Ward Bond, are capable of carrying out the unusual assignment. "The guy is nothing but a mobster," Bond confidently explains, referring to Hitler. "He can be had—just like any other big shot."

The three ex-gangsters journey to Canada where they enlist in the Royal Canadian Air Force as paratroopers. They arrive in England for their training and, during one practice flight, force the pilot, another American, to take them to Germany. The four men then bail out over enemy territory and make their way to Berlin, explaining whenever they are stopped that they have a personal message for Hitler. A suspicious German officer locks them up in a concentration camp until he can learn more about their mission.

Meanwhile, the officer's mistress (Dorothy Tree), who is actually an underground leader known as "Rosebud," plots to free the four Americans. With her help and disguised as musicians, they are admitted to a private party for Hitler. Following a gun battle, Bond takes the Nazi leader hostage and orders the American pilot to return to England. Bond, after his two pals are killed, takes his captive to an underground hide-out where he shaves off Hitler's mustache. A German patrol follows and captures Bond, two anti-Nazi Germans and Hitler, who fails to convince his officers that he is their leader. All are shot by the Nazis, including Hitler.

Released during the war, the script has its share of propaganda. Before Bond is shot by a firing squad, the camera moves in for a close-up as he exclaims: "War against men is one thing. But when it comes to butchering kids, there ain't a guy in the world . . . who would stop fighting for one minute until this rotten breed of Nazis is wiped clear off the face of the earth." The film, told in flashback, returns in the last scene to the scientist who is recounting the story to two reporters. "We must never rest until all the Nazi warlords and the things they represent are scraped off the face of the earth," he concludes, repeating Bond's sentiments. "We owe that much to humanity—not least to the honest Germans . . . who have been working and dying in secret for world freedom. . . . We must shatter the mail fist forever." Because of the preposterous plot and broadly painted characterizations of the principal characters, it is sometimes difficult to tell the intentions of the work—whether it is satire or drama. Bob Watson, who portrays the Nazi dictator, impersonated Hitler throughout the war years in several films. ∎

Holt of the Secret Service (1942) serial, Col. *Dir.* James W. Horne; *Sc.* Basil Dickey, George Plympton, Wyndham Gittens; *Cast includes:* Jack Holt, Evelyn Brent, Montague Shaw, Tristam Coffin, John Ward, Ted Adams.

A master counterfeiting ring threatens the stability of the U.S. economy in this 12-chapter serial. Veteran action player Jack Holt

portrays the title character—a daring, two-fisted special government agent assigned to smash the gang. As a ploy to help him in his goal, he masquerades as a criminal type to gain the confidence of the counterfeiters. At one point he is frustrated by local police who are not aware that Holt is working under cover as a government agent. But his superiors soon take care of the matter. The role of his resourceful and aggressive assistant, played by Evelyn Brent, breaks with the familiar tradition of the serial. Whereas the heroine usually portrays a more passive character, in this serial she is highly visible and initiates much of the action—a heroine who must have appeared quite disconcerting to many fans of the genre. ∎

Holy Terror, The (1937), TCF. *Dir.* James Tinling; *Sc.* Lou Breslow, John Patrick; *Cast includes:* Jane Withers, Anthony Martin, Leah Ray, Joan Davis, El Brendel, Joe Lewis.

Secret agents attempt to steal the plans for a new secret airplane at a U.S. Navy aviation base in this slapstick comedy featuring an array of comics. Jane Withers, a precocious and prankish youngster, frolics around the base and nettles some of the top brass, particularly the earnest base commander, played by Andrew Tombes. Two romances flourish in this loosely plotted film. Leah Ray, as the singing owner of a local café-restaurant frequented by the sailors stationed at the base, falls in love with one of the seamen (Anthony Martin). The second romance, a comical one, concerns comics El Brendel and Joan Davis. ∎

Honeybaby, Honeybaby (1974), Kelly-Jordan. *Dir.* Michael Schultz; *Sc.* Brian Phelan; *Cast includes:* Diana Sands, Calvin Lockhart, Seth Allen, J. Eric Bell, Brian Phelan, Bricktop.

An American interpreter who wins a vacation to the Middle East instead finds herself embroiled in regional murder and intrigue in this comedy drama. Diana Sands portrays the American heroine whose vacation turns into a nightmare when she gets mixed up with the corpse of a deposed African leader. Calvin Lockhart, as an adventurer who is hired to dispatch the body, becomes romantically involved with Sands. J. Eric Bell portrays Sands' young brother who joins her on her journey. This was Sands' last screen appearance. She died of cancer in 1973 shortly after completing the film. ∎

U.S. undercover agent Gene Barry finds himself in a tough spot when Communist agents get the drop on him. *Hong Kong Confidential* (1958).

Hong Kong Confidential (1958), UA. Dir. Edward L. Cahn; Sc. Orville H. Hampton; *Cast includes:* Gene Barry, Beverly Tyler, Allison Hayes, Noel Drayton, Edward Kemmer, Michael Pate.

Communist agents kidnap the young son of an Arab potentate and intend to blame the West for the crime in this Cold War drama involving British and U.S. agents. Gene Barry, as an American undercover agent posing as a nightclub singer in Hong Kong, is assigned by his superiors to rescue the victim who is being held captive somewhere in the vicinity. Before he is able to accomplish his mission, he becomes romantically involved with Beverly Tyler. Allison Hayes portrays a spy working for the Communists, who plan to kill their victim and Barry, thereby linking the West to the kidnapping. ■

Hopscotch (1980), Avco. Dir. Ronald Neame; Sc. Brian Garfield, Bryan Forbes; *Cast includes:* Walter Matthau, Glenda Jackson, Ned Beatty, Sam Waterston, Herbert Lom, David Matthau.

A disgruntled C.I.A. agent who has been relegated to a dreary filing job decides to expose the espionage game and unmask its chief players in this entertaining comedy. Walter Matthau portrays the experienced agent whose unorthodox methods cause his overly rigid superior to remove him from field operations. The embittered Matthau goes into hiding where he plans to write a book to humiliate both the C.I.A. and foreign agents, but this also leads to unforeseen problems for Matthau, who now becomes the quarry of several assassins who prefer to end his literary career. The remainder of the comedy deals with Matthau's eluding his pursuers, including his C.I.A. superior's minions. Matthau maneuvers events in such a way that all his pursuers follow him to his former chief's new home which they proceed to destroy in their attempt to capture their elusive prey.

Glenda Jackson, as a former agent and widow, joins Matthau in his escapade. Ned Beatty portrays the up-tight, obnoxious C.I.A. chief who precipitated the problem. Herbert Lom, as a Russian agent and one-time companion of Matthau, joins in the hunt to protect his own cover. Sam Waterston, as the pursued's former buddy, is put in charge of the search since he knows Matthau's techniques the best. The film is based on the novel by Brian Garfield. See Central Intelligence Agency. ■

Hot and Deadly (1984), Arista. Dir. Elliot Hong; Sc. Larry Stamper; Cast includes: Max Thayer, Shawn Hoskins, Randy Anderson, Lenard Miller, Bud Cramer.

A recent C.I.A. recruit quickly becomes disillusioned with the agency, especially its cold-blooded tactics, in this weak chase drama. Max Thayer portrays the young man who is persuaded by his friend to join the U.S. intelligence organization. He is assigned to bring in the author (Lenard Miller), an ex-C.I.A. agent, of a not-yet-published manuscript exposing the agency's covert activities. Thayer is stunned, then disgusted, when his partner (Bud Cramer) callously murders an innocent bystander. Shawn Hoskins, as the author's sister, becomes Cramer's next target. But Thayer decides to protect her. He foils the agency's attempts on her life and goes into hiding with Hoskins. The couple find time to fall in love with each other. They attempt to get the manuscript published while their enemies continue in hot pursuit. When the author is finally caught by the agents, Thayer tries to rescue him. See Central Intelligence Agency. ■

Hotel Berlin (1945), WB. Dir. Peter Godfrey, Jack Gage; Sc. Jo Pagano, Alvah Bessie; Cast includes: Helmut Dantine, Andrea King, Raymond Massey, Faye Emerson, Peter Lorre, George Coulouris, Henry Daniell.

A World War II melodrama set in 1945 during the final days of the Nazi regime, the film, inordinately steeped in propaganda, is an adaptation of the novel Berlin Hotel by Vicki Baum, who also wrote Grand Hotel. The once elegant hotel, a metaphor for the decline of Nazi Germany, has been damaged by periodic Allied air raids. Elevators don't work, the general structure requires additional support and guests are herded below into shelters at regular intervals. A sense of impending defeat permeates the atmosphere of the hotel.

Helmut Dantine, as an underground leader, has escaped from a concentration camp and seeks shelter in the hotel where some of his conspirators are employed. Meanwhile, in another room, Nazi officers plan their escape to the U.S. where they intend to prepare for World War III. "This time we shall be anti-Nazis," one explains, "poor refugees who have escaped from Germany. . . . Americans forgive and forget easily. But we must spread rumors and create dissension and distrust." Andrea King, who portrays a successful stage actress, at first helps Dantine to elude the Gestapo but eventually informs on him to protect her own future. Her lover (Raymond Massey), a high-ranking German officer involved in an assassination plot against Hitler, is given 24 hours to "do the honorable thing." An unrepentant Nazi to the end, he says to a fellow officer: "We have lost this war. Tell those who come after us they must prepare better for the next one. We must never lose again." Peter Lorre portrays a German Nobel prizewinner and professor who has been brainwashed to cooperate with the Third Reich but ultimately returns to the underground to help turn out anti-Nazi propaganda. Steven Geray, as the chief hotel clerk, adds some comic relief, particularly when he is drafted. A pathetic figure in his new uniform, he looks at a portrait of Hitler hanging over the hotel desk and remarks: "I'd like to see him hung in a different way."

The film ends with Allied bombers again raiding Berlin as a message scrolls up the screen: "Our purpose is not to destroy the German people—but we are determined to disband all German armed forces . . . bring all war criminals to just and swift punishment—wipe out the Nazi Party and Nazi laws from the life of the German people—Germany must never again disturb the peace of the World." The signatures of Winston Churchill, Franklin Roosevelt and J. Stalin appear at the bottom. See Nazi Subversion: Post-World War II. ■

Hotel Imperial (1927), Par. Dir. Mauritz Stiller; Sc. Jules Furthman; Cast includes: Pola Negri, James Hall, George Seigmann, Max Davidson, Michael Vavitch, Otto Fries.

Pola Negri portrays a hotel chambermaid in this World War I drama adapted from the play by Lajos Biro. The hotel is nestled in a border town that is alternately occupied by Austro-Hungarian and Russian troops. She hides an Austrian soldier (James Hall) in the hotel during a Russian advance into Galicia. The Russians occupy the village, and their general (George Seigmann) makes the hotel his headquarters. He quickly takes a liking to

Negri, but she falls in love with Hall. When a Russian spy appears with information about the Austrian army, Hall kills him and makes his way to his own troops. The Austrians attack and drive the Russians back. Hall returns to his love and marries her while his commander, grateful for both their brave deeds, gives Hall leave for a honeymoon.

The film presents a unique background in comparison to other World War I films by concentrating on the Austrian-Russian conflict and setting the story along the Austro-Hungarian border. This was one of the earliest war dramas to sympathetically portray a hero of the Central powers.

Historically, Russia did overrun Galicia in 1914 and occupied the eastern section for about a year. After the war, the Ukrainians declared the area an independent state, but Poland soon claimed Galicia as part of its territory, putting an end to the short-lived independent nation. ■

Hotel Imperial (1939), Par. *Dir.* Robert Florey; *Sc.* Gilbert Gabriel, Robert Thoeren; *Cast includes:* Isa Miranda, Ray Milland, Reginald Owen, Gene Lockhart, J. Carrol Naish.

A weak remake of the 1927 film of the same title starring Pola Negri, this version of the World War I drama introduces the European personality Isa Miranda to American audiences. The international star portrays a young woman seeking revenge for the death of her sister. She works as a chambermaid at the Hotel Imperial, the same position and hotel where her sister was employed. The town has changed hands several times in the course of the war between the Austrians and Russians. Ray Milland plays an Austrian officer she finds hiding in a room. They soon fall in love. Milland manages to escape while the town is in the hands of the Russians and makes it back to his lines in time to save his army from defeat. When the Austrians retake the town, he resumes his romance with the young chambermaid who has solved the death of her sister. Reginald Owen plays a buffoonish Russian general.

Billy Wilder's suspenseful World War II drama, *Five Graves to Cairo* (1943), starring Franchot Tone as an English officer hiding from the Germans who have occupied an Egyptian hotel and Anne Baxter as a chambermaid who falls in love with him, has borrowed much of its material from these earlier versions of Lajos Biro's play. ■

Hour Before the Dawn, The (1944), Par. *Dir.* Frank Tuttle; *Sc.* Michael Hogan, Lesser Samuels; *Cast includes:* Franchot Tone, Veronica Lake, Binnie Barnes, John Sutton, Henry Stephenson, Philip Merivale.

Franchot Tone portrays a conscientious objector in this colorless World War II drama set in England. Tone is excused from further military service because of his farm work. Veronica Lake, as a Nazi agent, marries Tone as a cover for her clandestine activities. She attempts to get him involved in her espionage work with her fellow spies. Following a German air raid aimed at a nearby airfield, he sheds his pacifist views, kills his wife and enlists in the Royal Air Force. The script, based on W. Somerset Maugham's novel of the same name, was updated and given a World War II background. See British Intelligence: World War II. ■

House of a Thousand Candles, The (1936), Rep. *Dir.* Arthur Lubin; *Sc.* H. W. Hanemann, Endre Boehm; *Cast includes:* Phillips Holmes, Mae Clarke, Irving Pichel, Rosita Moreno, Fred Walton, Mischa Auer.

Phillips Holmes portrays an English diplomatic courier whose journey from London to Geneva is hampered by several potentially hazardous incidents in this drama of international intrigue. It seems that a mysterious spy ring is trying to prevent him from delivering a secret code message. Irving Pichel, as the chief villain, uses quite a few devilish tricks in his attempt to foil Holmes' mission, including the lure of a sultry dancer. Mae Clarke portrays the hero's American sweetheart who accompanies him and, at times, contributes to his problems. Rosita Moreno, as the dancer, later changed her name to Rita Moreno and in 1961 won an Academy Award as best supporting actress for *West Side Story*. The film was adapted from the novel by Meredith Nicholson. ■

House on 92nd Street, The (1945), TCF. *Dir.* Henry Hathaway; *Sc.* Charles G. Booth, Barre Lyndon, John Monks, Jr.; *Cast includes:* William Eythe, Lloyd Nolan, Signe Hasso, Gene Lockhart, Leo G. Carroll, Lydia St. Claire.

This World War II spy drama is considered by many as a landmark film for its cinematic techniques and documentary style. A young German-American student (William Eythe) informs the F.B.I. about his apprehensions

William Eythe (standing), working under cover for the F.B.I., joins members of a Nazi spy ring in *The House on 92nd Street* (1945).

concerning fellow Germans who have approached him to become a spy. A special Bureau inspector (Lloyd Nolan) takes charge of the case and uses the young man to gain further information about a suspected network of Nazi agents operating in the heart of New York City. Working as a double agent for the Bureau, Eythe infiltrates the network. The F.B.I. keeps track of Eythe and the enemy agents' activities by using a variety of techniques, including movie cameras behind special mirrors and screen radio transmissions. One of the more suspenseful elements concerns the mysterious and elusive Mr. Christopher (Signe Hasso), the head of the spy ring, who is not unmasked until the end.

What made this film, with its otherwise familiar plot, significant was its style. Producer Louis de Rochemont, who had already received acclaim for his successful "March of Time" documentaries, used a similar semi-documentary approach—the story was based on F.B.I. files and the film was shot on actual locations in New York. An off-screen narrator (Reed Hadley) acts as a "bridge" between

scenes or events, keeping the audience informed. Detailed intelligence and counter-intelligence methods were revealed (microdot films under postage stamps, customs inspections, hidden cameras) for added authenticity. The film avoided the typical propaganda and concentrated instead on the professional work of the F.B.I., which prevented major military secrets, including the formula for the atomic bomb, from falling into enemy hands. See Federal Bureau of Investigation; German Intelligence: World War II; U.S. Intelligence: World War II. ■

House Un-American Activities Committee. Representative John McCormack, Democrat of Massachusetts, served as chairman of the House Committee to Investigate Nazi and Other Propaganda during the years 1934–1935. This committee was the precursor of the House Un-American Activities Committee (H.U.A.C.) and, in many respects, served as a model for the latter. Representative Samuel Dickstein, Democrat of New York, was the vice-chairman of the earlier committee; in that capacity Dickstein took to the floor of the House where he made strong anti-German speeches and read numerous names of citizens whom he accused of being Nazis. When McCormack left and to prevent Dickstein from being seated as chairman, the House disbanded the entire committee.

In 1938 the House Un-American Activities Committee was formed to replace McCormack's committee. A majority of the new committee was composed of Republicans and conservative Democrats opposed to Roosevelt and the New Deal. Martin Dies, Democrat of Texas, was chosen chairman and the committee was given an initial appropriation of $25,000. Under Dies, targets of the investigation shifted from Nazis to the C.I.O. (a leading radical labor union of the period), the Civil Liberties Union, the International Negro Congress and the W.P.A. (Works Progress Administration).

No effort was made to establish the credibility of witnesses prior to testifying before the committee. The press and photographers were treated to scenes of witnesses, spectators and committee members shouting at each other. Roosevelt attacked the Dies Committee, as it had become known, for its blatant appeal for news headlines and its disregard of the truth. The committee's first report maintained that Communists held key positions in the Roosevelt Administration and that they were subverting government policy by failing to enforce the deportation laws. The report also condemned the American Communist Party for being a branch of the Soviet government and, in a sop to the anti-Nazis, similarly censured the German-American Bund for operating as a subsidiary of Nazi Germany. Roosevelt opposed continuing the committee. A compromise was agreed upon with funding set at $100,000, and the committee's life was extended for one rather than the usual two years. A six-one majority opposed to Roosevelt was reduced to four-three with the departure of two conservatives and their replacement by two liberal Democrats—Jerry Voorhis and Joseph Casey.

The new session of the House Un-American Activities Committee turned from scrutinizing government agencies and labor unions to investigating the American Communist Party and its members. Despite numerous appeals from members of the House, Dies refused to investigate the Ku Klux Klan and Father Coughlin, the neo-Fascist and anti-Semitic priest from Chicago who regularly broadcast his views over his radio programs.

Among the witnesses called before the committee were William Z. Foster, the former head of the American Communist Party; Earl Browder, former general secretary of the party; Robert Pitcoff, former director of Amtorg, the Soviet trading organization; and Walter Krivitsky, former head of Soviet intelligence in Western Europe.

Without offering proof of guilt of any sort, Dies continued to discredit individuals hauled before the committee. During one hearing, Chairman Dies read the mailing list of the American League for Peace and Democracy and claimed that these individuals were cooperating with the Third International. At various times Dies claimed that the Catholic Church had been "penetrated" by Communists, Jews were Soviet agents, and that Shirley Temple and Humphrey Bogart were under suspicion of being part of the Communist conspiracy.

In a poll taken in 1941, 57 percent of the respondents supported a $1 million budget for the House Un-American Activities Committee while only 11 percent opposed the budget and 32 percent offered no opinion.

Martin Dies and H.U.A.C. have a sporadic history on the American screen. In *Murder in the Air* (1940), a grade B World War II action drama, a U.S. government agent (Ronald Reagan) goes under cover as a spy and joins a dangerous gang of saboteurs. Propaganda elements extend to a sequence concerning a fictitious "Rice Committee," apparently based on the real-life Dies hearings of the period. The Cold War drama *I Was a Communist for the FBI* (1951) was made chiefly to assuage the House Un-American Activities Committee, which was busily engaged in investigating Communist influence in Hollywood. The film is based on the true story of Matt Cvetic, who posed as a Communist for nine years. Frank Lovejoy, as the double agent, exposes various Communist plots before H.U.A.C. *Big Jim McLain* (1952) stars John Wayne who, as a special investigator for the House Un-American Activities Committee, hunts down Communist subversives in Hawaii. *Man on a String* (1960), with Ernest Borgnine, is based on Hollywood producer Boris Morros' biography *Ten Years a Counterspy*. Morros, who was caught spying for the Soviets, was never charged with espionage. He testified before the House Un-American Activities Committee as a friendly witness.

For such varied reasons as wartime patriotism or Cold War propaganda, Hollywood dramas that dealt even slightly with H.U.A.C. were all complimentary of the committee's work. It was not until 1980 that American audiences saw another side to H.U.A.C. The documentary *The Trials of Alger Hiss* (1980) interviews a range of public figures, including Robert Stipling, investigator of the House Un-American Activities Committee, jurors and witnesses, F.B.I. agents and Hiss himself. Finally, *Blockade* (1938), a superficial and innocuous drama of the Spanish Civil War (1936–1938) starring Henry Fonda, stirred a series of controversies before and during its release. The film was to haunt for several years some of those who participated in its production. One decade later, for example, it was used against screenwriter John Howard Lawson when he was brought before the House Un-American Activities Committee investigating Communist influence in Hollywood. ■

Human Duplicators, The (1965), Crest. *Dir.* Hugo Grimaldi; *Sc.* Arthur C. Pierce; *Cast includes:* George Nader, Barbara Nichols, George Macready, Dolores Faith, Richard Kiel, Hugh Beaumont.

A U.S. government agent discovers a scheme concocted by alien creatures to gain control of Earth by duplicating humans as androids in this modest science-fiction drama. A scientist from a remote galaxy arrives on Earth and starts a laboratory to produce androids—human-like robots implanted with an electrical brain. George Nader, as the special agent, suspects that humans are being replaced by these creatures and swings into action. Following the usual setbacks, he eventually saves the planet.

Barbara Nichols portrays a fellow agent who is working incognito. Venerable screen villain George Macready, as an American scientist, succumbs as one of the alien's victims who is duplicated. Dolores Faith portrays Macready's blind daughter with whom the alien-scientist (Richard Kiel) falls in love. ■

Human Factor, The (1975), Bryanston. *Dir.* Edward Dmytryk; *Sc.* Tom Hunter, Peter Powell; *Cast includes:* George Kennedy, John

Mills, Raf Vallone, Arthur Franz, Rita Tushingham, Frank Avianca.

A government employee working in Europe with N.A.T.O. seeks revenge upon terrorists who have killed his family in this weak drama that advocates vigilantism. George Kennedy portrays the grieving husband and father whose low-echelon war-planning position with North Atlantic Treaty Organization forces in Italy hardly makes him a worthy target of the terrorists. However, he goes on a rampage of revenge in Charles Bronson style. Barry Sullivan portrays an embittered U.S. embassy official. Frank Avianca plays the leader of the terrorists. John Mills, as Kennedy's confidant, has a minor role. The film concentrates more on violence than on motivation. ■

Hun Within, The (1918), Artcraft. *Dir.* Chester Withey; *Sc.* Granville Warwick (D. W. Griffith); *Cast includes:* George Fawcett, Dorothy Gish, Charles Gerrard, Douglas MacLean, Bert Sutch, Max Davidson.

A domestic drama of World War I, the film centers on an American family of German descent. The father sends his son to Germany to study, but when World War I breaks out the boy joins the German army. His sweetheart back home (Dorothy Gish) breaks off her engagement to him and his father disowns him. When he returns as a German spy, he shoots his father during an altercation, wounding the old man. Meanwhile, the spy ring has planted a time bomb in a troopship headed for France. An agent in the U.S. Secret Service, a new beau of Gish's, helps to prevent the ship's destruction and assists in the roundup of the spy network. D. W. Griffith supervised the production of the film and wrote the screenplay under a pseudonym. ■

Huns Within Our Gates (1918), Arrow. *Sc.* Marie Genores, Jesse J. Goldburg; *Cast includes:* Derwent Hall Caine, Valda Valkyrien, Harry Robinson, Robin Townley, Bessie Wharton.

A German spy causes problems for an American inventor of an experimental airplane engine in this World War I drama. Derwent Hall Caine, as the inventor, requires cash to finish developing his revolutionary engine. He rejects an offer from a German agent who wants to buy his invention. The foreigner, still desiring the new engine for his government, assigns a seductive countess

(Bessie Wharton) to persuade Caine. When this plan fails, the spy decides to blow up the inventor's laboratory. However, the family dog removes the bomb and places it near where the spy is concealed. The German is killed by the explosion which tears a gap in the ground to reveal Caine's family's lost fortune. ■

Hunt for Red October, The (1990), Par.

Dir. John McTiernan; *Sc.* Larry Ferguson, Donald Stewart; *Cast includes:* Sean Connery, Alec Baldwin, Scott Glenn, James Earl Jones, Sam Neill, Joss Ackland.

A Soviet submarine commander and his officers decide to defect in this Cold War thriller based on Tom Clancy's best-selling novel. The film makes clear in a screen caption that the story takes place in 1984, before Gorbachev assumed power. "It's time for change," says Capt. Marko Ramius (Sean Connery), "time to take a desperate chance for peace." But the Soviet skipper's decision is no simple matter, for it triggers harrowing incidents involving ballistic missile nuclear subs, killer submarines and high-tech decoys as the East and West confront each other for an Armageddon-like final showdown. At stake is the question of human survival.

Depressed since his wife's death and haunted by fears of a terrible and devastating war between the major powers, Ramius decides to take matters into his own hands. After he kills one of his officers, he heads his high-powered top-secret underwater vessel, *Red October*, into a U.S. port as a sign of peace. But he is shadowed by both a Soviet fleet, which is puzzled by Connery's actions and at one point tries to torpedo *Red October*, and American nuclear-equipped submarines, whose officers are suspicious of its purpose. Meanwhile, on board the submarine is a Soviet saboteur. The renegade captain has another problem—an atomic meltdown has begun aboard his vessel.

The film conjures up reminiscences of earlier Cold War dramas whose plots often brought Washington and Moscow to the brink. The incident in the present work signals concern in major capitals around the world while the film shifts from Washington to London and to Moscow. The Pentagon in desperation calls upon Ryan (Alec Baldwin), a gutsy C.I.A. operative who trusts the Soviet captain. Ryan had met Ramius previously and believes he can learn the truth behind the captain's erratic behavior. The agent makes a perilous attempt to board suspicious sub.

The suspenseful thriller suggests that just such a confrontation might have shaken the Soviet political and military leaders into altering its basic national and international policies that resulted in glasnost. "There will be hell to pay in Moscow when the dust settles from all this," Ramius is warned. "Perhaps some good will come of it," he responds quietly.

Although the climax of Clancy's novel has the skipper ram his vessel into a Soviet attack submarine which has been closing in on *Red October*, the film changed this. Instead, the pursuing vessel is destroyed by its own captain's incompetence. "I felt it would be difficult for people to sympathize with the Russian captain if he killed 100 innocent countrymen like that," director John McTiernan explained in a *New York Times* interview (February 25, 1990).

Clancy's novel is based on an actual incident that occurred in November 1975 when a Soviet anti-submarine ship tried to defect to Sweden. Capt. Valery Sablin, a deputy commander, directed an attempted mutiny aboard the *Storozhevoy* after he sequestered the commander and other loyal officers and tricked the crew into submission. He then steered the ship into the Baltic Sea toward Sweden, but his vessel was intercepted and forced to return to the Soviet Union where Sablin was tried, convicted and sentenced to face a firing squad. *Izvestia*, the official Soviet newspaper, acknowledged this incident in February 1990 before the release of the film. ■

Hunting of the Hawk, The (1917), Pathé.

Dir. George Fitzmaurice; *Sc.* George B. Seitz; *Cast includes:* William Courtenay, Marguerite Snow, Robert Clugston.

The head of the U.S. Secret Service poses as a gentleman of leisure as a ploy to catch The Hawk, an international jewel thief, in this contrived drama. William Courtenay, as the agent, makes the acquaintance of a social secretary (Marguerite Snow) while they are both returning from Europe. She is the wife of The Hawk, whom she innocently married thinking he was respectable. Courtenay is attracted to the young woman who works for a wealthy family. Once in the States, he is invited to a social function at her employers' estate. The Hawk, masquerading as a detective, has also been invited. He plans to steal a valuable necklace. The thief is killed by one of his cronies, and Courtenay reveals his true identity. ■

Hurricane's Gal (1922), FN. *Dir.* Allen Holubar; *Sc.* Allen Holubar; *Cast includes:* Dorothy Phillips, Robert Ellis, Wallace Beery, James O. Barrows, Gertrude Astor.

A U.S. Secret Service agent stows away on the *Tahiti Belle*, a three-masted schooner whose owner is suspected of smuggling in this action-packed drama. Robert Ellis, as the government agent, is discovered by members of the crew. He undergoes some rough treatment by the first mate (Wallace Beery), all the while keeping his true identity hidden. Lola (Dorothy Phillips), the owner of the vessel and daughter of the late Hurricane, a notorious smuggler, is aboard and is soon won over by the agent's charms. When the *Tahiti Belle*, with its illegal cargo, reaches San Francisco, revenue officers of an official ship board her and a fight breaks out. Ellis reveals his identity and joins the officers while Lola and her first mate escape during the fracas.

Bent on revenge, Lola decides to kidnap Ellis' fiancée (Gertrude Astor). She and Beery take their captive aboard another schooner and sail out to sea. When Ellis learns of this, he assigns a navy destroyer to pursue the vessel while he takes off in a seaplane. Meanwhile, aboard the fugitive ship Beery ties up both women and heads for an uncharted isle in the South Seas. When Ellis' plane approaches, Beery orders his crew to shoot it down with anti-aircraft guns. Ellis, now in the water, is saved in time by the U.S. warship that closes in on the schooner. Another fight erupts when sailors of the U.S. Navy board the vessel. Ellis and his fiancée are reunited. ■

I

I Deal in Danger (1966), TCF. *Dir.* Walter Grauman; *Sc.* Larry Cohen; *Cast includes:* Robert Goulet, Christine Carere, Horst Frank, Donald Harron, Werner Peters, Eva Pflug.

Robert Goulet portrays a double agent who infiltrates the Nazis by posing as an American traitor in this drama set during World War II. Compiled from the first three episodes of *Blue Light*, a television espionage series, the film concerns Goulet's mission to locate and destroy an experimental super-submarine the Germans hope to use to defeat the U.S. Christine Carere portrays another Allied secret agent. Horst Frank, as the chief of Nazi security, fails to prevent Goulet from blowing up the underground installation. Donald Harron plays a British agent. ■

I Dood It (1943), MGM. *Dir.* Vincente Minnelli; *Sc.* Sig Herzig, Fred Saidy; *Cast includes:* Red Skelton, Eleanor Powell, Richard Ainley, Patricia Dane, Sam Levene, Thurston Hall.

Chiefly a musical designed to showcase the talents of such performers as Lena Horne, Hazel Scott, Bob Eberly and Jimmy Dorsey and his orchestra, the film offers a slight plot involving spies. This allows comedy star Red Skelton to engage in his entertaining antics. The comic portrays a tailor's assistant who becomes infatuated with a stage star (Eleanor Powell) from a distance. He then becomes entangled in a marriage that leads to his involvement with the enemy agents. The script was an adaptation of Buster Keaton's silent film *Spite Marriage* (1929). The MGM-Skelton-Keaton affiliation recurred with the Civil War spy comedy *A Southern Yankee* (1948), with Skelton playing a Union spy assigned to penetrate Confederate lines and Keaton supplying some of the ideas for the visual gags. ■

I Escaped From the Gestapo (1943), Mon. *Dir.* Harold Young; *Sc.* Henry Blankfort, Wallace Sullivan; *Cast includes:* Dean Jagger, John Carradine, Mary Brian, Bill Henry, Sidney Blackmer, Ian Keith.

A minor World War II drama, the film concerns Nazi activities in the U.S. Gestapo agents, to realize one of their subversive schemes in America, help an expert counterfeiter (Dean Jagger) escape from prison. When he learns of their plans to create havoc in domestic and Allied financial markets, he goes along with the spies long enough to effect their capture. John Carradine plays the head of the enemy agents. The title was later changed to *No Escape*. Jagger and Carradine, two popular and talented character players during the 1930s and 1940s, deserved better. ■

I Married a Communist (1949), RKO. *Dir.* Robert Stevenson; *Sc.* Charles Grayson, Robert H. Andrews; *Cast includes:* Laraine Day, Robert Ryan, John Agar, Thomas Gomez, Janis Carter, Richard Rober.

Looking suspiciously like a conventional gangster movie, this Cold War drama stars Robert Ryan as an ex-Communist who is threatened by his former party bosses. Ryan, who is married to Laraine Day, has advanced to the vice-presidency of a shipping firm and is an expert on labor relations. The Communists, led by Thomas Gomez, want him to foment labor trouble, reminding him that no one "quits" the party. Meanwhile, his wife's brother is lured on by Janis Carter into joining the party. When he is killed by some of Gomez' henchmen, Ryan avenges his death by way of an old-fashioned shoot-out. The film is also listed as *Woman on Pier 13*. See Cold War; Labor Unrest; Soviet Spies in the U.S. ■

I Married a Spy (1938), GN. *Dir.* Edmond Greville; *Sc.* Basil Mason, Hugh Perceval, Edmond Greville; *Cast includes:* Neil Hamilton, Brigitte Horney, Ivor Barnard, Charles Carson, Gyles Isham, Frederick Lloyd.

A young woman, an escapee from a German concentration camp, is conscripted as a spy into the French secret service in this World War I drama reportedly based on actual incidents. Faced with a bleak future as a refugee of war-torn Europe, the woman resigns herself to the role of spy laid out for her by a French agent (Ivor Barnard). Brigitte Horney portrays the German-born heroine who has been raised in France. An arranged marriage to a French citizen (Neil Hamilton) saves her from being deported from Switzerland. However, a romance blooms between the couple who decide to remain together when the war ends. But the conclusion of the plot suggests a more pessimistic future for the spy.

The drama, made on the eve of World War II, follows the trend of most other similar films of the period by remaining chiefly uncommitted in its political or national sympathies, concentrating instead on the adversities and dangers the heroine continually faces. Neither the French nor the German espionage network appears more skilled or humane than its adversary. ■

I Want to Forget (1918), Fox. *Dir.* James Kirkwood; *Sc.* James Kirkwood; *Cast includes:* Evelyn Nesbit, Russell Thaw, Henry Clive, Alphonz Ethley, William R. Dunn.

World War I affects the lives of a young couple in this romantic drama. Evelyn Nesbit portrays Varda, a carefree soul who has led a rather promiscuous life before she met John (Henry Clive). The couple fall deeply in love and marry. Varda is regenerated by her new life. When war erupts, John enters the service as a lieutenant. Varda, determined to do her bit, joins the secret service. Assigned to secure valuable papers from a suspected German spy who is one of her admirers, she applies her unique womanly charms to that end.

Actress Evelyn Nesbit was the woman in the sensational Stanford White murder at Madison Square Garden in 1906. The 1981 film *Ragtime*, based on E. L. Doctorow's semi-fictitious novel, touches upon some of the characters involved. ■

I Was a Communist for the FBI (1951), WB. *Dir.* Gordon Douglas; *Sc.* Crane Wilbur; *Cast includes:* Frank Lovejoy, Dorothy Hart, Philip Carey, James Millican, Richard Webb, Konstantin Shayne.

Based on the article "I Passed As a Communist for the FBI," which recounted the actual experiences of Matt Cvetic, this didactic drama tells the story of how he posed as a member of the Communist party for nine years, all the while gathering information for the Federal Bureau of Investigation. Made during the Cold War, the film emphasizes how the Communists infiltrate industry and education and how they cause dissension between Americans by exploiting strikes and racism. Frank Lovejoy, as Cvetic, joins the Pittsburgh cell. He eventually testifies before the House Un-American Activities Committee, exposing the various Communist plots. Dorothy Hart portrays a Communist teacher who eventually reforms. The director concentrates the suspense around Cvetic, who on several occasions comes very close to being exposed as a double agent.

Perhaps more revealing than its anti-Communist theme to perceptive audiences was the film's denigrating stereotypes of blacks, workers and other groups and its obsequious approval of the excesses of H.U.A.C. See Cold War; Federal Bureau of Investigation; House Un-American Activities Committee. ■

I Was an American Spy (1951), Mon. *Dir.* Lesley Selander; *Sc.* Sam Roeca; *Cast includes:* Ann Dvorak, Gene Evans, Douglas Kennedy, Richard Loo, Leon Lontoc, Philip Ahn.

Ann Dvorak plays the title role in this drama about the actual experiences of Claire Phillips during World War II. The film opens with the fall of Manila to the Japanese. After Mrs. Phillips' husband is killed during the Bataan death march, she joins a band of guerrillas led by Gene Evans. She then masquerades as an Italian national and operates a Manila nightclub where she obtains bits of useful information which she gives to Evans. She is finally exposed and imprisoned, but Evans and his small force rescue her before she is executed. The film is based on both a novel, *Manila Espionage*, by Claire Phillips and Myron B. Goldsmith and a Reader's Digest article. Mrs. Phillips received the Freedom Medal for her espionage activities. See U.S. Intelligence: World War II. ■

Frank Lovejoy (r.), posing as a traitor so that he can infiltrate the Communists, accepts a beating from a former friend who thinks Lovejoy has betrayed his country. *I Was a Communist for the FBI* (1951).

Ice Station Zebra (1968), MGM. *Dir.* John Sturges; *Sc.* Douglas Heyes; *Cast includes:* Rock Hudson, Ernest Borgnine, Patrick McGoohan, Jim Brown, Tony Bill, Lloyd Nolan.

American and British agents at the North Pole clash with Russian troops in this Cold War action drama based on the novel by Alistair MacLean. Rock Hudson stars as a nuclear submarine commander who is assigned to retrieve a space capsule that landed on the North Pole. Ernest Borgnine portrays a Russian defector who accompanies the secret mission. Jim Brown, as a U.S. Marine Corps captain, represents the military arm of the group. Brown's marine force eventually battles it out with the Russians who want to retrieve highly strategic film aboard the capsule. The coveted film is destroyed with neither side winning. To cover up the incident which has almost triggered World War III, with its nuclear ramifications, the superpowers release news reports announcing that the Russians and English-Americans have joined forces in a peaceful mission.

Although the specific plot and characters are fictitious, the film is reminiscent of an actual incident which occurred in the spring of 1954 that almost brought the two major world powers to the brink of war. U.S. intelligence, bent on picking up Soviet military transmissions, installed several monitoring stations on ice islands near the North Pole. One of these islands, filled with highly technical monitoring equipment and operators, suddenly began drifting toward Soviet territory. The U.S. Air Force dispatched a rescue plane, but it crashed. Soviet planes made several passes over the island while the American officer in charge ordered his men to prepare for an attack. Meanwhile, they thought they detected a squadron of bombers flying toward North America. The U.S. air defense system received the alarm and went into action—only to discover that their potential adversary was a formation of migrating ducks. A helicopter eventually rescued the men and equipment from the island. The incident inspired novelist MacLean. See Cold War. ■

U.S. nuclear submarine commander Rock Hudson (r.) creates a tense moment when he and operations officer Ted Hartley suddenly awaken British secret agent Patrick McGoohan in *Ice Station Zebra* (1968).

I'll Say So (1918), Fox. *Dir.* Raoul Walsh; *Sc.* Ralph Spence; *Cast includes:* George Walsh, Regina Quinn, William Bailey, James Black, Ed Kelsey.

George Walsh portrays a navy reject in this World War I comedy. Since his flat feet prevent him from fighting for his country, he seeks other means to keep himself active. He gets entangled with some German spies who provoke trouble on the Texas border between Mexican bandits and Americans. He outwits them with his nimble acrobatics in the style of Douglas Fairbanks. Walsh, who had starred in several war-related features during this period, was the brother of director Raoul Walsh. See German Intelligence: World War I.

Comedies about World War I, such as this one and those starring Mary Pickford, Douglas Fairbanks and other popular movie personalities, were virtually relegated to homefront locales. Evidently, the war itself was considered too serious a matter to be treated lightly. It remained for Charlie Chaplin, with his highly popular *Shoulder Arms* (1918), a satire about the average doughboy's life in the trenches, to break from this convention. ∎

Illegal Entry (1949), U. *Dir.* Frederick De Cordova; *Sc.* Joel Malone; *Cast includes:* Howard Duff, Marta Toren, George Brent, Gar Moore, Tom Tully, Paul Stewart.

An undercover agent is assigned to investigate the operations of a gang dealing in smuggling illegal aliens into the U.S. in this drama. George Brent, as the chief of the Department of Immigration and Naturalization, appoints Howard Duff to infiltrate the gang. Following the usual plot manipulations employed by this type of tale, Duff eventually unmasks the leader and helps to capture the gang. Marta Toren, as a reluctant member of the smugglers, provides the romantic angle for Duff, who rescues her from their sinister clutches. ∎

In Again—Out Again (1917), Artcraft. *Dir.* John Emerson; *Sc.* Anita Loos; *Cast includes:* Douglas Fairbanks, Arline Pretty, Walter

Special agent James Coburn cautiously enjoys the company of members of a secret women's organization plotting to take control of the world. *In Like Flint* (1967).

Walker, Arnold Lucy, Helen Greene, Homer Hunt.

Acrobatic Douglas Fairbanks portrays a brash young man whose stand on preparedness results in his pacifist sweetheart jilting him in this World War I comedy. He swears off females, but after being arrested for drunkenness the night before, he is attracted to the pretty daughter of his jailer. The remainder of the plot concerns his romance with his latest love interest and his attempts to stay in jail so that he can be near her. The film contains anti-pacifist sentiments in its derogatory images of those opposed to the war in Europe. Scenes suggest that they are surreptitiously involved in dealing in war matériel with the Germans. Fairbanks himself rebukes them for endangering America. "Your puny, pussyfooting policies are pulling the punch out of preparedness!" he exclaims. ■

In Enemy Country (1968), U. Dir. Harry Keller; *Sc.* Edward Anhalt; *Cast includes:* Tony Franciosa, Anjanette Comer, Guy

Stockwell, Tom Bell, Paul Hubschmid, Patric Knowles.

Allied forces, after suffering heavy losses at sea from a new type of torpedo invented by the Germans, assign secret agents to learn more about the weapon and where it is manufactured in this World War II action drama. A French intelligence officer (Tony Franciosa) assists Allied agents to infiltrate the plant where the torpedoes are made. An American air force officer (Guy Stockwell) accompanies the special force. Tom Bell plays a British explosives expert. Anjanette Comer, as a French spy, also provides the feminine interest. Paul Hubschmid portrays a Nazi intelligence officer. Aided by the French underground, the team manages to appropriate one of the highly secret torpedoes which some of the members of the special force take back to England. Allied bombers, meanwhile, destroy the factory in this predictable tale. ■

In Like Flint (1967), TCF. Dir. Gordon Douglas; *Sc.* Hal Fimberg; *Cast includes:* James

Coburn, Lee J. Cobb, Jean Hale, Andrew Duggan, Anna Lee, Hanna Landy.

The success of the British-made James Bond spy films, with their light approach to sex, suspense and intrigue, led to an outpouring of American efforts to duplicate the style, including this pale imitation. James Coburn, as the titular special agent, is assigned to foil the attempts of a secret organization of women bent on taking control of the world in this spoof of the spy genre. Anna Lee, as part of a trio of sexy females directing the scheme, is in cahoots with some male villains who have replaced the President of the U.S. with an actor look-alike (Andrew Duggan). Our urbane hero, between his romantic pursuits, allots some time to put an end to the feminine plot. Lee J. Cobb, as Flint's bewildered superior, adds to the comedy, particularly in one bit in which he dresses in drag. ■

"In Old Kentucky" (1909), Biograph. *Dir.* D. W. Griffith; *Sc.* Stanner Taylor; *Cast includes:* Henry B. Walthall, Kate Bruce, Owen Moore, Verner Clarges, Mary Pickford.

In this silent Civil War drama two brothers fight on opposite sides of the conflict. The younger brother who has joined the Confederate cause is sent with dispatches through the Union lines and is captured by his own brother. He escapes and hides in his mother's home. The pursuing brother follows him and begins to search each room. When the Union son comes to his mother's bedroom where the fugitive is concealed, the mother threatens to shoot herself if he continues the search. He leaves quietly. The film shifts to the end of the war when the older brother, now an officer, returns home, as does the younger boy who has been wounded. They shake hands in reconciliation.

Griffith directed eleven one- and two-reel dramas which used the Civil War as background during his tenure with the Biograph studio. The reconciliation scene, a highlight and poignant moment in the film, anticipated a similar scene in the director's 1915 masterpiece, *The Birth of a Nation.* ■

In Pursuit of Polly (1918), Par. *Dir.* Chester Withey; *Sc.* Eve Unsell; *Cast includes:* Billie Burke, Thomas Meighan, Frank Losee, A. J. Herbert, William Davidson.

Billie Burke plays an ingenue pursued by three suitors in this World War I spy comedy. She becomes embroiled in a German plot, is captured and is about to be electrocuted by the spies. The hero, a secret service agent played by Thomas Meighan, suspects our heroine of being a German spy when she signs a hotel register using a false name. Her only intent was to elude her suitors. Meighan arrives in time to shoot the German agent who is about to pull the fatal switch. Billie Burke had a successful career on Broadway and in silent films and continued as a popular character actress in the sound era playing feather-brained women. ■

In the Diplomatic Service (1916), Metro. *Dir.* Francis X. Bushman; *Sc.* Francis X. Bushman; *Cast includes:* Francis X. Bushman, Beverly Bayne, Helen Dunbar, Henri Bergman, William Davidson.

This drama, set chiefly in Washington, concerns a secret service agent's attempts to prevent military secrets from falling into the hands of foreign spies. When the U.S. Secret Service learns that certain highly classified information has been mysteriously leaked to foreign nations, the agency assigns Dick Stansbury (Francis X. Bushman) to the case. His uncle is chief of the diplomatic corps. Aside from unraveling the mystery, Bushman finds time to romance a rich heiress (Beverly Bayne) who is loosely involved in the case. ■

In the Fall of '64 (1914), U. *Dir.* Francis Ford; *Sc.* Grace Cunard; *Cast includes:* Francis Ford, Grace Cunard.

Director-actor Francis Ford portrays a Confederate captain arrested for spying behind Union lines in this Civil War two-reel drama. Grace Cunard plays Ford's sweetheart, a Southern belle whose estate is captured by Northern troops. When Ford is captured, she poses as a slow-witted boy to gain access to Union quarters where Ford is being held. She manages to extinguish a candle, allowing her lover to escape in the ensuing darkness. She later steals the enemy's battle plans and crosses into Confederate territory. The information permits Ford and his troops to score a victory over the Union.

The melodramatics of the plot are no doubt fictitious, but a similar incident actually occurred during the conflict in Nashville. Ann Patterson, daughter of a Southern physician whose family members were all spies for the Confederacy, helped free Thomas Joplin after his capture by Union troops. Joplin was a guerrilla spy in Coleman's Scouts, a force of about 50 agents operating in Tennessee. ■

Inside the Lines (1918), World. *Dir.* David M. Hartford; *Sc.* Monte M. Katterjohn; *Cast includes:* Lewis Stone, Marguerite Clayton, George Field, Arthur Allardt, David M. Hartford, Joseph Singleton.

Lewis Stone portrays an English officer in this drama with a World War I background. It seems that the Germans have plans to blow up Gibraltar and cripple a large part of the English navy anchored there. Marguerite Clayton plays a young Englishwoman whom Stone suspects of spying for Germany. In a short time Stone goes into action to foil the plot, after which he learns that the woman he has fallen in love with is actually an English agent. The two stars repeated the same roles they had in Earl Derr Biggers' original stage play upon which the film is based. A sound remake appeared in 1930. The plot of the male and female spies playing cat and mouse was to become a familiar Hollywood staple during the next several decades. See British Intelligence: World War I. ■

Inside the Lines (1930), RKO. *Dir.* Roy J. Pomeroy; *Sc.* Ewart Adamson, John Farrow; *Cast includes:* Betty Compson, Ralph Forbes, Montagu Love, Mischa Auer, Ivan Simpson.

Adapted from a 1915 stage play by Earl Derr Biggers (who also created the famous Honolulu detective Charlie Chan), this World War I spy drama about attempts to destroy the British fleet was a remake of a 1918 silent screen version of the play. This time around Ralph Forbes portrays the English agent who saves Gibraltar from German plots, and Betty Compson poses as a German spy. Each suspects the other of working as a secret agent. By the end of the film Forbes learns the truth that the spy whom he has fallen for is actually working for the British. Mischa Auer portrays a villainous Hindu. ■

International Crime (1938), GN. *Dir.* Charles Lamont; *Sc.* Jack Natteford; *Cast includes:* Rod LaRocque, Astrid Allwyn, Thomas Jackson, Oscar O'Shea, William von Brinken, William Frawley.

Foreign agents attempt to foil the underwriting of a large bond transaction in this partially suspenseful drama based on "The Fox Hound," a story by Maxwell Grant. Rod LaRocque, as a nationally famous radio and newspaper crime reporter, suspects foul play and eventually exposes the underhanded manipulations after a financier is murdered. Astrid Allwyn, as a fellow reporter who at times frustrates LaRocque's sleuthing, provides the romantic element. William von Brinken portrays the head of the foreign cartel. William Frawley, as a former convict, and Lew Hearn, as a local cabby, supply some comic relief. ■

International Lady (1941), UA. *Dir.* Tim Whelan; *Sc.* Howard Estabrook; *Cast includes:* George Brent, Ilona Massey, Basil Rathbone, Gene Lockhart, George Zucco.

A dangerous international spy poses a threat to Allied shipping in this World War II cautionary drama about the enemy within. Ilona Massey portrays the spy whose method of contacting Nazi U-boats and providing them with vital shipping and air force information is quite unusual. She uses tonal phrasings and musical notes in her songs during her radio broadcasts. George Brent, as an F.B.I. agent who woos Massey, combines forces with Basil Rathbone, as a member of Scotland Yard, to track down the spy network. The film blends the spy elements of the story with action sequences in the air and on the sea in this suspenseful drama. ■

International Settlement (1938), TCF. *Dir.* Eugene Forde; *Sc.* Lou Breslow, John Patrick; *Cast includes:* Dolores Del Rio, George Sanders, June Lang, Dick Baldwin, Ruth Terry, John Carradine.

The drama mixes newsreel footage of the Sino-Japanese War with the plot of gunrunners and hijackers in strife-torn China. An American adventurer (George Sanders) poses as a smuggler so that a shipment of illegal contraband can be freed, but he ends up getting captured by hijackers. The Japanese bombing of Shanghai saves him from his captors. The gunrunners are busy shipping arms and ammunition to China although the film takes no side concerning political issues. Dolores Del Rio appears as the heroine of this action feature. ■

Intrigue, The (1916), Par. *Dir.* Frank Lloyd; *Sc.* Julia Crawford Ivers; *Cast includes:* Dustin Farnum, Lenore Ulrich, Cecil Van Auker, Howard Davies, Herbert Standing, Florence Vidor.

Foreign agents attempt to murder an American inventor of a long-range X-ray gun in this mystery drama. The agents, who represent a fictitious principality, fear that even if they purchase the secret weapon, the inventor may still reveal its secret to other nations. Meanwhile, the inventor falls in love with a Red Cross nurse, played by Lenore Ulrich. In reality she is a wealthy countess whose humanitarian calling has led her to give service to others. Circumstances allow her to save the inventor's life. Believing that she is a poor refugee, he proposes marriage. She asks him to destroy his weapon before it brings death and destruction to mankind and then reveals her true status.

Released before America's entry into World War I, the film was one of a handful that suggested pacifist views. However, Germany's announced submarine warfare against neutral ships, reports of German atrocities in Belgium and a host of preparedness films soon drowned out pacifist voices in America and on screen. ∎

Invasion U.S.A. (1985), Cannon. *Dir.* Joseph Zito; *Sc.* James Bruner, Chuck Norris; *Cast includes:* Chuck Norris, Richard Lynch, Melissa Prophet, Alexander Zale, Alex Colon, Eddie Jones.

A crazed Russian agent leads a small military force in an assault on Florida in this action drama. Rostov, the Soviet spy (Richard Lynch), fears only one man who may interfere with the success of his invasion—Matt Hunter, a U.S. intelligence superagent. So he assigns some of his top underlings to annihilate Hunter. Chuck Norris, as the agent, is currently retired and living with his wife in Florida's Everglades. His former chief asks Hunter to return to duty, suspecting Rostov, Hunter's old nemesis, is somewhere in the U.S. plotting subversive activities. "The Company really needs you this time," the visitor pleads. "This one is something special." But the contented Norris rejects the request. When Rostov's henchmen blow up his house and murder an old Indian friend, Hunter swings into action.

Meanwhile the terrorists have divided into small bands and begun attacking military targets and spreading panic throughout the state. Hunter, in an effort to capture Rostov, the brains behind the invasion, sets up a trap. Hunter allows himself to be taken by the police, thereby inviting his adversary to try once again to kill him. The two men confront each other in an abandoned building and engage in a fight to the death. At the same time, U.S. Army troops wipe out Rostov's army of terrorists. Melissa Prophet portrays a courageous reporter who questions Hunter's methods in this drama filled with repetitious slaughter, wrecked cars and demolished real estate. ∎

Invisible Agent (1942), U. *Dir.* Edwin L. Marin; *Sc.* Curtis Siodmak; *Cast includes:* Ilona Massey, Jon Hall, Peter Lorre, Sir Cedric Hardwicke, J. Edward Bromberg, Albert Basserman.

A World War II espionage drama, the plot concerns the attempt of Nazi agents to obtain a secret formula that makes people invisible when it is injected into the body. Jon Hall, as the hero and grandson of the inventor of the serum, escapes from the enemy spies, volunteers his services to the government and parachutes into Germany to cause havoc among Nazi and Japanese leaders as an invisible agent. He manages to capture plans for an air attack on New York City. Ilona Massey portrays a counterspy for the Allies. Peter Lorre plays a sadistic Japanese while Sir Cedric Hardwicke also contributes to the mayhem. An implausible but entertaining yarn drawn from James Whale's *The Invisible Man* (1933), in turn based on H. G. Wells' novel, it captures some of the magic of the original. ∎

Invisible Enemy (1938), Rep. *Dir.* John H. Auer; *Sc.* Albert J. Cohen, Alex Gottlieb, Norman Burnstine; *Cast includes:* Alan Marshal, Tala Birell, Mady Corell, C. Henry Gordon, Herbert Mundin, Gerald Oliver Smith.

A secret agent foils a plot by a master criminal against international oil companies in this drama of intrigue. Alan Marshal, as the hero, romances the wife of the villain (C. Henry Gordon) in a ploy to gain information about Gordon's plans. Hired by a group of pacifist tycoons, Marshal undergoes several narrow escapes before he puts an end to Gordon's operations. Released before World War II, the film anticipates the importance of oil to the war effort. The drama is also interesting in its presentation of the tycoons as sympathetic characters—a view that was to change drastically in a series of cynical films that were to appear during the following decades. For instance, *Executive Action* (1973) suggests that some industrialists plotted the assassination of President Kennedy, while, more directly, *The Formula* (1980) dealt with a conspiracy by oil billionaires to raise the price of oil while suppressing a formula for synthetic fuel. ∎

Iron Curtain, The (1948), TCF. *Dir.* William A. Wellman; *Sc.* Milton Krims; *Cast includes:* Dana Andrews, Gene Tierney, June Havoc, Berry Kroeger, Edna Best, Stefan Schnabel.

This drama of a Russian clerk who blows the whistle on a Soviet spy network operating in Canada marked the beginning of Hollywood's cycle of Cold War films. Dana Andrews plays the sincere and idealistic underling who, at his wife's urging to provide a better life for their child, turns himself and several important documents over to Canadian authorities. Gene Tierney portrays his wife who befriends her Canadian neighbors and falls under the spell of democracy and a life without fear. The plot and characters have the familiar trappings of the conventional espionage thriller, including the stereotypical villains who bully and threaten and a female agent (June Havoc) who tries to seduce Andrews.

Gouzenko, who is assigned to the Soviet embassy code room, arrives from Russia in 1943. He is a patriotic and dutiful Soviet servant who remains aloof of his Canadian neighbors and refuses to listen to anti-Soviet remarks from a discontent fellow Russian (Eduard Franz), who is eventually ordered home. His wife arrives shortly after and announces that she is pregnant. It is concern for the future of their son that the couple have second thoughts about returning to Russia. After the war, Gouzenko believes that his country, who has been stealing military and atomic secrets from the Canadians and Americans, may be leading the world down the road to another conflict. He steals a number of important documents that prove the Soviet embassy has installed a large-scale network of spies in Canada, reaching into the scientific community and the House of Commons.

The drama, which follows the semi-documentary style of *The House on 92nd Street* (1945), uses voice-overs in which a narrator introduces important incidents and personal-

ities, newsreel excerpts and location shooting for external scenes. When the film was released, several governments, including The Netherlands, considered it too controversial and banned it from their countries, labeling it offensive. A sequel, *Operation Manhunt*, was released in 1954, in which Gouzenko appears in the epilogue.

The film is based on the memoirs of Igor Gouzenko and the famous Canadian spy case of 1946. Gouzenko, a Russian code clerk and member of the Russian embassy staff in Ottawa, named a host of Soviet spies operating on Canadian soil. His testimony, as well as a series of files he sneaked out of his embassy, led to the arrests of a member of the Canadian parliament, a noted scientist and several others. See Defection; Igor Gouzenko. ∎

Ivory Snuff Box, The (1915), World. *Dir.* Maurice Tourneur; *Sc.* E. M. Ingleton; *Cast includes:* Holbrook Bliss, Alma Belwin, Norman Trevor, Robert Cummings.

German spies steal an ivory snuff box containing France's secret code in this World War I drama based on the novel by Frederic Arnold Kummer. Holbrook Bliss, as an American detective working for the French secret police, is assigned to retrieve the box which was taken from the French Ambassador in England. The only problem is that Bliss, just married to a fellow American (Alma Belwin), is set to go on his honeymoon. Instead, he rushes to England to recover the vital code. His wife follows, seeking to help. Bliss asks her to journey to Brussels and investigate a sanitarium run by a suspected German spy.

The remainder of the film deals with various dangers and setbacks the couple face before they resolve the mystery. At one point Bliss is tortured by the head of the sanitarium to make him reveal where he has hidden the box that he now has in his possession. His wife, who is forced to witness the torture, tells the doctor the location. But it is too late. Bliss has cleverly changed the numbers of the code, rendering it useless. The detective finally turns the authentic code over to the proper authorities, and he and his wife resume the honeymoon. ∎

J

Jaguar Lives! (1979), AI. *Dir.* Ernest Pintoff; *Sc.* Yabo Yabolonsky; *Cast includes:* Joe Lewis, Christopher Lee, Donald Pleasence, Barbara Bach, Capucine, Joseph Wiseman.

Joe Lewis, a former undefeated world heavyweight karate champion, portrays Jonathan Cross, informally known as Jaguar, the nemesis of international criminals, in this routine action drama which uses various countries for its locales. Jaguar's latest assignment is to journey around the world and smash multiple drug-smuggling operations. Aiming particularly at the masterminds behind each ring, our hero must first use his karate expertise to break through small armies of underlings. All these skirmishes tend to become repetitious. Some of Jaguar's adversaries include John Huston, Christopher Lee and Donald Pleasence. ■

Japanese war scare of 1907. Japan's 1905 victory in the Russo-Japanese War made that nation a viable threat to U.S. naval power. Japan's aggressive moves toward territorial expansion in the Far East were looked upon by the U.S. as a threat to American possessions in the Pacific, including the Philippines. Unconfirmed stories that Japan had leased from Mexico ports on the Pacific coast of Baja California further exacerbated tensions. U.S. agents were sent to investigate the eastern coast of Mexico. Japan added more fuel to the heated friction in 1911 by sending its fleet to visit Mexico. One admiral, Yashiro, publicly announced a possible military alliance between Japan and Mexico against the U.S. Washington responded by sending navy officers to Japan to learn the language and formulating war plans in the event of a Japanese-American conflict. President Theodore Roosevelt, continually informed of Jap-

anese activities, displayed American naval power by ordering the U.S. "Great White Fleet" to sail around the world. The Office of Naval Intelligence in 1912 finalized War Plan Orange, a blueprint for a full-scale war with Japan. However, World War I turned America's attentions from Japan to a new and more imminent danger—Germany.

Within a few years the Japanese war scare had moved from the front page into movie theaters. The American film industry, quick to exploit current events, produced a string of espionage and war dramas in which the Japanese were chiefly portrayed unfavorably. *The Clue* (1915), with Blanche Sweet and Sessue Hayakawa, concerned a mysterious map desired by the Japanese but in the possession of two Russians emigrés. (Hayakawa, a popular Japanese silent screen star, brought more than an exotic element to his films; his restrained acting style contrasted sharply with the exaggerated stage gestures of many of his contemporaries.) In *Yankee Pluck* (1917), set before America's entry into World War I, Japanese agents attempt to steal plans for an anti-submarine device.

Serials as well as dramas depicted the Japanese as abhorrent and evil. The anti-Japanese serial *Patria* (1916), with the famous Broadway personality Irene Castle, matinee idol Milton Sills and Warner Oland, depicted the Japanese so repulsively that President Wilson was prompted to send a note to those responsible, complaining that the film was "extremely unfair to the Japanese. . . ." The serial, financed by newspaper tycoon William Randolph Hearst, capitalized on contemporary reports about a secret alliance between Mexico and Japan to invade the U.S. This may not have been as far-fetched as it appears. Sidney F. Mashbir, an Arizona National Guard captain, was assigned to observe Japanese military activity in northern Mexico. He informed his superiors that Japanese troops had landed from a warship, but Washington never followed up on the information. *Pearl of the Army* (1916) starred the silent serial queen Pearl White as the intrepid lass who prevents Oriental agents from sabotaging the Panama Canal. *The Secret of the Submarine* (1916), a 14-chapter serial, had Japanese agents planning to steal a device which allows a submarine to remain submerged indefinitely.

Some World War I dramas pictured the Japanese, who entered the war on the side of the Allies, in a favorable light. For example, in *The Secret Game* (1917), with Sessue Hayakawa, Jack Holt, Florence Vidor and Raymond Hatton, Hayakawa portrays a Japanese secret agent on the trail of spies in Los Angeles who are leaking information to the Germans. Japanese warships act as convoys to American transports on their way to Russia. In *His Birthright* (1918), also with Sessue Hayakawa, he portrays the illegitimate son of a Japanese mother and American father. Marin Sais, as a German spy, persuades Hayakawa, bent on revenge, to steal important military documents from an American admiral— Hayakawa's father. When he discovers that Sais is working for the Germans, he recovers the documents from the spies, comes to terms with his father and enlists in the U.S. Army.

Post-World War I dramas reverted to the adverse image of the Japanese and were in conflict with national and international efforts, in progress at the time, toward establishing a lasting peace. Negotiations, critics charged, might be hampered by suggestions in these dramas of Japanese duplicity. For example, in *Who's Your Servant?* (1920), set in post-World War I Washington, a Japanese spy plots to steal secret plans from a U.S. Navy officer. In *The Pride of Palomar* (1922), which takes place after World War I, Japanese secret agents plot to gain possession of a tract of California land for a native colony. Several inflammatory scenes were blatantly anti-Japanese. At one point Okada (Warner Oland), a Japanese agent frustrated in his attempts to possess the land in question, exclaims: "You won't sell me the land now, but someday I'll come with a Japanese army and take your damned ranch!" He ends his ranting by scraping a match across George Washington's face appearing on a nearby marble statue.

Pre-World War II sound films placed Japanese characters in more sympathetic roles. *Marie Galante* (1934) had a secret agent of Japan joining forces with those of the U.S. and England to prevent the destruction of the Panama Canal. Peter Lorre portrayed Mr. Moto, a Japanese sleuth in a series of detective dramas throughout the 1930s, in which he occasionally assisted U.S. and British agents. However, this accord in Japanese treatment on the screen came to a sudden halt with Japan's sneak attack on Pearl Harbor. ∎

Jedburgh operations. General Eisenhower, prior to the Normandy invasion in 1944, brought the Office of Strategic Services into his grand strategy. Men of the O.S.S. were to be dropped behind German lines and link up with the French Resistance. Together, the O.S.S. and the Resistance would harass the Germans from the rear by performing such missions as destroying bridges, blowing up rail lines and ambushing convoys.

The American agents trained in Jedburgh, Scotland, and thus the name of the operations. Eventually, three-man groups were parachuted behind enemy lines. Each Jedburgh team comprised a radio operator and two officers, and efforts were made to include a Frenchman, an American and a British national in each crew. About 90 Jedburgh teams conducted operations in German-occupied France and Scandinavia. They organized the undercover work of various Resistance groups composed of between 30 to 50 members each. Their general assignment was to contact Resistance fighters, distribute supplies, provide communications and, when possible, coordinate guerrilla actions.

Dropped in France, Belgium and Holland on and after D-Day, the teams were of enormous help to the main Allied armies. They changed enemy road signs, destroyed fuel dumps, damaged drawbridges and placed hidden mines on major roads. Because Jedburgh volunteers wore uniforms, they were considered soldiers, not undercover agents or saboteurs. In *Captain Carey, U.S.A.* (1950), for example, Alan Ladd and a fellow O.S.S. agent, operating behind enemy lines in Italy during the war, are appropriately attired in uniform. Therefore, when Ladd is wounded and captured, he is sent to a prisoner-of-war camp instead of to a firing squad. However,

Arab terrorists, vying for control of the population, gun down a rival leader in the streets of Jerusalem. *The Jerusalem File* (1972).

in most Hollywood films dealing with O.S.S. operations, agents are shown in civilian attire.

For such a potentially dramatic subject, it seems surprising that only a handful of dramas have appeared portraying the work of these teams. The moviegoing public's awareness of such missions evolves not from the number of these films but from the overall impact of the relatively few that were produced. No doubt such major screen personalities as Alan Ladd, James Cagney and Gary Cooper contributed to this image. In *O.S.S.* (1946), starring Alan Ladd, four agents are sent into Nazi-occupied France to blow up an otherwise inaccessible railway tunnel. Geraldine Fitzgerald, as the female member of the team, is treated with hostility by one of the agents (Alan Ladd). When the leader of the operation is captured by the Gestapo, Ladd assumes command. Fitzgerald eventually proves her value, to the satisfaction of Ladd, who ends up falling in love with her. James Cagney, as an O.S.S. chief in *13 Rue Madeleine* (1946), parachutes into France after he learns that one of his teams has a double

agent in its midst. Richard Conte, as the Nazi spy who has secretly trained with the O.S.S. under Cagney, captures him and has him tortured to learn the location of the forthcoming Allied invasion. In *Cloak and Dagger* (1946) Gary Cooper portrays an American scientist whom the O.S.S. conscripts near the end of World War II to journey to Europe to learn the extent of Nazi experiments with atomic energy.

Other dramas about similar Jedburgh missions appeared occasionally decades after World War II. In *The Enemy General* (1960), for example, Van Johnson, as an American agent in the O.S.S., is assigned to smuggle a Nazi officer out of Europe and escort him safely to England. *A Face in the Rain* (1963) concerns an American agent who has parachuted behind enemy lines into Italy and is forced to spend most of his time fleeing from the pursuing Nazis. ■

Jerusalem File, The (1972), MGM. *Dir.* John Flynn; *Sc.* Troy Kennedy Martin; *Cast includes:* Bruce Davison, Nicol Williamson,

Daria Halprin, Donald Pleasence, Ian Hendry, Koya Yair Rubin.

A naive, idealistic American archaeology student studying in Israel mingles into regional politics in this turbulent drama shot on location. A joint U.S.-Israeli production, the film is set after the Six-Day Arab-Israeli War. Rival terrorist groups are vying for control of the Palestinian population. One particularly violent faction has been gunning down important members of another, more popular group.

Bruce Davison, as the American student, meets with a former Yale classmate (Zeev Revah) who is now an Arab terrorist leader and wanted by the Shin Bet, Israel's intelligence agency responsible for internal security. Davison explains that he is about to leave Israel and return to the U.S. As they are sitting outside an Arab shop and bidding farewell to each other, rival terrorists in a passing car fire upon the two friends. Revah, although wounded, escapes while Davison is hurt and rushed to a hospital. Major Samuels (Donald Pleasence), an Israeli security police chief, questions the student about his Arab friends, especially Revah, but Davison refuses to give any information. His professor (Nicol Williamson) gets him released from the hospital, and they leave on an expedition in the desert.

Williamson's mistress (Daria Halprin) and several student activists secretly persuade Davison to arrange with Revah a meeting between Arab terrorists and Israeli students where they can discuss some of their differences. The professor, who suspects what his students are planning, warns Davison not to go through with the arrangements. Nevertheless, the American contacts an Arab storekeeper who is a double agent. But the agent is killed by the rival terrorist faction.

Later, the Arab terrorist contacts his friend, Davison, and sets up the student meeting. The Israeli students, explaining that the rendezvous concerns only Israelis, request that the American stay behind. In an attempt to stop the potentially perilous gathering, the professor notifies the major. The warning comes too late. The two suspicious groups of young people move cautiously toward each other at a remote location in the desert. They slowly introduce themselves and begin to shake hands. The barriers of hostility between the Arab guerrillas and Israeli students quickly collapse as they talk and laugh. But the atmosphere of new-found camaraderie is suddenly shattered by the crackling sound of gunfire. The rival terrorists, who have learned of the meeting, ambush and wipe out the small party. ■

Jet Pilot (1957), U. *Dir.* Josef von Sternberg; *Sc.* Jules Furthman; *Cast includes:* John Wayne, Janet Leigh, Jay C. Flippen, Paul Fix, Richard Rober.

Janet Leigh portrays a Russian jet pilot who defects to the West and falls in love with an American colonel, played by John Wayne, in this implausible Cold War drama. Leigh is unconvincing as a Soviet pilot who shoots down her fellow countrymen and machineguns ground troops while making her escape. Wayne, in charge of an Alaskan air force base, is assigned to gather information from her. They fly to Washington where they fall in love and marry. Then the army learns that she is actually a spy. Army intelligence arranges for Wayne to pose as a defector and for the couple to escape to Russia. But when Wayne undergoes tough scrutiny at the hands of the Communists, Leigh arranges for their escape back to the United States.

Although the film was completed in 1950, producer Howard Hughes, who could not resist tampering with it, did not release it until 1957. In his desire to turn out another airplane classic in the style of *Hell's Angels,* he kept replacing directors, reshooting sequences and updating the jet planes. But the original script was hopelessly flawed before all the changes were made. Hughes' other dream was to turn Janet Leigh into another national sex symbol as he did with Jean Harlow in *Hell's Angels* in the early 1930s. Leigh appears in one scene in a thinly clad negligee and in another with only a bath towel, but audiences remained unimpressed. See Defection. ■

Jewels of Brandenburg (1947), TCF. *Dir.* Eugene Forde; *Sc.* Irving Cummings, Jr., Robert G. North, Irving Elman; *Cast includes:* Richard Travis, Micheline Cheirel, Leonard Strong, Carol Thurston, Lewis Russell, Louis Mercier.

A U.S. agent is assigned to retrieve stolen jewels which are in the hands of a group of Nazis in this familiar drama set in Lisbon at the close of World War II. Richard Travis, as the agent, goes under cover posing as a smuggler so that he can gain the gang's confidence.

Leonard Strong, as the villainous Nazi leader who, working as a double agent, was able to obtain the jewels, accepts Travis into the fold. Following several fights, Travis recovers the cache from its hiding place and puts an end to the Nazi's career. Micheline Cheirel portrays Strong's voluptuous wife. See Nazi Subversion: Post-World War II. ■

Joan of Ozark (1942), Rep. *Dir.* Joseph Santley; *Sc.* Robert Harari, Eve Greene, Jack Townley; *Cast includes:* Judy Canova, Joe E. Brown, Eddie Foy, Jr., Jerome Cowan, Alexander Granach, Anne Jeffreys.

Hillbilly comedienne Judy Canova gets entangled with Nazi agents in this low-brow World War II comedy. When Judy, in her native Ozarks, accidentally shoots down a pigeon, she notices that it was carrying a message from enemy agents. After turning over the evidence to the F.B.I., she becomes a local heroine. Meanwhile the chief of the spy network (Jerome Cowan) who runs a New York nightclub to mask his espionage activities, wants to put Judy out of the way—permanently. He sends Joe E. Brown, as a booking agent, to the Ozarks to sign up Judy for a nightclub act. To convince her to return with him to New York, he tells her he is a secret government agent. When she insists on becoming a fellow agent, he agrees. The remainder of the farce takes place in Cowan's club and includes several musical numbers, including "Lady From Lockheed." ■

Joan of Paris (1942), RKO. *Dir.* Robert Stevenson; *Sc.* Charles Bennett, Ellis St. Joseph; *Cast includes:* Michele Morgan, Paul Henreid, Thomas Mitchell, Laird Cregar, May Robson.

This World War II drama shows how the French underground helped downed British fliers to escape capture by the Nazis and eventually maneuver their way back to England. Paul Henreid, as a French patriot and flier, helps four fellow Royal Air Force airmen by contacting British intelligence, all the while placing his own life in danger. Michele Morgan, as a young French barmaid inspired by her patron saint Joan of Arc, diverts the Nazis while the five escape. She later pays with her life for helping the Allied fliers. Thomas Mitchell portrays a priest who harbors the men temporarily. May Robson plays a British agent. A romance develops between Henreid

and Morgan, but it does not dilute the dramatic action.

Americans largely unfamiliar with the perilous but strategic role of the French underground, especially those members of the Paris unit, received a fairly unromanticized picture of their efforts in this film. The participation of the priest in Resistance operations is based on actual incidents. During the war a Bordeaux priest organized a network of agents that included nuns and other priests. Through their contacts with British Secret Intelligence Service (S.I.S.) agents, they provided the Allies with much invaluable information about German troops. ■

Joan of Plattsburg (1918), MGM. *Dir.* George Loane Tucker, William Humphrey; *Sc.* George Loane Tucker; *Cast includes:* Mabel Normand, Robert Elliott, William Fredericks, Joseph Smiley, Edward Elkas, John Webb Dillion.

Mabel Normand portrays an orphan who fantasizes that she is a modern Joan of Arc in this light spy film set during World War I. A captain, played by Robert Elliott, stationed at a nearby military training camp, gives her a book about the life of Joan of Arc, which she takes to a basement room of the orphanage and reads. She then overhears a plot by enemy agents concerning the sale of government documents. The young orphan manages to foil the efforts of the spies and win the captain's love. The film is based on a play by Porter Emerson Browne. ■

Joe Smith, American (1942), MGM. *Dir.* Jack Chertok; *Sc.* Allen Rivkin; *Cast includes:* Robert Young, Marsha Hunt, Harvey Stephens, Darryl Hickman, Jonathan Hale.

Robert Young portrays an aircraft employee who is kidnapped by Nazi spies after he is assigned to work on a secret project in this World War II propaganda drama. Carefully screened by F.B.I. agents, Young is accepted for the job. "The U.S. Army secret bombsight," he is told, "is the one secret in the world this country has that no other country could get. This may mean the difference between defeat and victory. . . . No one is to know what you are doing." A simple family man, Young, in the title role, is followed one night as he leaves the plant. Several men force his car off the road, knock him unconscious and take him to their hide-out. When he awakens, his captors torture him for hours to pry from him information about the bombsight. In his attempts to distract himself from the pain, he focuses his thoughts on special moments with his family and patriotic images, such as those of Nathan Hale. Hours later, after failing to learn anything from Young, the enemy agents blindfold him and take him for a ride. Young, waiting for a chance to escape, realizes that he has to determine where he has been held prisoner so that he can lead the police back to the hide-out. He begins to count the number of stairs, memorize the sounds he hears and make mental notes about the various turns the car is making. When the driver stops for a light, Young escapes from the car. The spies, afraid others may see them, decide to drive away rather than go after Young. Later, he aids government agents and the police in locating the spies by cleverly retracing his blindfolded journey.

Aside from the taut script and the suspenseful plot, the film provides an overabundance of patriotic symbols. The camera closes in on a picture of the American flag on a notebook as Young drives his young son to school. He then watches as his son joins his teacher and other students in the "Pledge of Allegiance" when the flag is raised. Later, during his capture, he sees a similar notebook with the flag on the cover. In addition, the wartime drama seems to suggest that no matter how mundane the job of the factory worker may appear, he, too, is a hero. To make certain no one misses the point, the film begins with a foreword which states: "This is a story about a man who defended his country. His name is Joe Smith. He is an American." The drama ends with Young explaining to his family and friends: "Nobody's a hero in this country. All of us guys are the same. We've got homes, wives and kids. . . . We don't like anyone pushing us around." ∎

Johnny Allegro (1949), Col. Dir. Ted Tetzlaff; Sc. Karen DeWolf, Guy Endore; Cast includes: George Raft, Nina Foch, George Macready, Will Geer, Gloria Henry, Ivan Triesault.

George Raft portrays a former gangster who volunteers to help the U.S. government smash a counterfeiting ring operating on an island off the coast of Florida in this unexceptional drama. Raft masquerades as a cop-killer, wins the confidence of the gang leader's wife and is soon accepted as one of the members. George Macready, as the sophisticated head of an international gang, is being paid by foreign powers to deluge the U.S. with bogus bills, thereby throwing the nation's economy into turmoil. Nina Foch, as his wife, falls in love with Raft and implies that she would like to leave the racket. When Raft's cover is exposed, Macready stalks him with a bow and arrow. Raft is rescued at the last minute as federal agents swoop down on the counterfeiters. ∎

Johnny Stool Pigeon (1949), U. Dir. William Castle; Sc. Robert L. Richards; Cast includes: Howard Duff, Shelley Winters, Dan Duryea, Anthony Curtis, John McIntyre, Gar Moore.

A U.S. federal agent enlists the aid of a convict to help him crack a drug-smuggling operation in this crime drama. Howard Duff, as the agent, effects criminal Dan Duryea's release from prison, and both men go under cover. Duryea then guides Duff to the gang who accepts Duff as a member. Following the pattern of similar dramas, the gang leader's moll, played by Shelley Winters, falls for Duff and helps him in his investigation. Anthony (Tony) Curtis, as one of the smugglers, discovers Duff's true identity, but it is too late. Duryea saves the agent's life. Other agents close in on the gang members and put an end to their operations. Barry Kelley portrays the leader of the smugglers. Duff appeared in a similar film the same year titled *Illegal Entry*, which dealt with smuggling aliens into the U.S. ∎

Jordan, Thomas. See *The Bright Shawl* (1923). ∎

Journey Into Fear (1942), RKO. Dir. Norman Foster; Sc. Orson Welles, Joseph Cotten; Cast includes: Joseph Cotten, Dolores Del Rio, Ruth Warwick, Agnes Moorehead, Jack Durant, Everett Sloane.

Based on Eric Ambler's World War II spy novel, the film presents a murky but nevertheless absorbing drama about Nazi agents trying to cripple Turkey's military capacity. Joseph Cotten portrays an American naval ordnance engineer who has been helping Turkey update its weaponry. Sought after by Nazi spies, he becomes a target for their hired assassin. In a Turkish nightclub a magician, mistaken for Cotten, is shot to death. Cotten falls into Nazi hands while aboard a sleazy freighter. The Nazi agent who has been assigned to dispose of Cotten corners him in a cabin. "If you should die before you get back to America," the agent explains, "someone else will be sent to take your place. But your work will be delayed. That is all we're interested in." Cotten, confused by and unaware of his role as pawn in this real-life game of international intrigue, undergoes a series of dangerous encounters, including his capture in which he is hurried off the ship to a waiting automobile. He cleverly escapes his captors in a suspenseful street scene, finally turns on his pursuers and annihilates the top Nazi assassin.

The other passengers aboard the strange Balkan vessel afford an interesting array of characters, including, among others, a mercenary Eurasian dancer (Dolores Del Rio), her gigolo stage partner, an ancient Greek sea captain, a pompous German archaeologist and a Greek widow. Orson Welles, who began directing this atmospheric film but was soon taken off the project, portrays Colonel Saki, the head of the Turkish secret police on the trail of the German spies. Everett Sloane is simultaneously offensive and obsequious as a Turkish businessman who propels Cotten into some of his nightmarish experiences.

The film offers many rewarding moments in several areas. The dark photography and various camera angles capture the mood, intrigues and conflicts. Especially effective are the sequences in a Turkish nightclub where a magician is murdered, aboard the vessel where Cotten faces danger and his narrow escape from his captors holding him prisoner in their car. The dramatic and suspenseful climax, with Cotten confronting his assassin on the ledge of a building at night, reflects the talented contributions of Welles, the director. An unsuccessful Canadian remake of the film appeared in 1975. ∎

Journey to Freedom (1957), Rep. *Dir.* Robert C. Dertano; *Sc.* Herbert F. Niccolls; *Cast includes:* Jacques Scott, Genevieve Aumont, George Graham, Morgan Lane, Jean Ann Lewis, Peter E. Besbas.

An anti-Communist who has brought down upon himself the wrath of Soviet agents is pursued halfway across the world, from the Iron Curtain to the U.S., in this little Cold War drama. Jacques Scott portrays the hunted, an advocate of the "Voice of Freedom." Forced to leave Bulgaria in a hurry be-

cause of his anti-Red activities, he journeys to America, only to find his life in constant danger. Genevieve Aumont, as a nurse who helps him to recover from a car accident, falls in love with him and thereby is caught up in Scott's efforts to elude the Soviet agents who are determined to eliminate him. ∎

Judith (1966), Par. *Dir.* Daniel Mann; *Sc.* John Michael Hayes; *Cast includes:* Sophia Loren, Peter Finch, Jack Hawkins, Hans Verner, Zharira Charifai, Shaga Friedman.

An American-produced film with a chiefly British cast, the drama concerns the search of a Jewish ex-wife for her Nazi war-criminal husband against the backdrop of Israel's War of Independence. Sophia Loren, as a woman who was betrayed by her husband and sent to Dachau, joins forces with the Haganah, the Jewish underground, which also seeks her husband, but for other reasons. Loren wants revenge, but the Israelis want her husband, a former tank expert now employed by the Arabs, for his military knowledge of an impending battle.

Peter Finch, as a kibbutz leader and member of the underground, helps her to find her former husband who eventually is killed. Jack Hawkins, as a British major, is sympathetic to the Israeli cause and assists Finch and Loren. Suspenseful sequences include the smuggling of a boatload of Jewish refugees into the territory and battles between the Israelis and Arabs, especially the Syrians. ∎

Jungle Heat (1957), UA. *Dir.* Howard W. Koch; *Sc.* Jameson Brewer; *Cast includes:* Lex Barker, Mari Blanchard, Glenn Langan, James Westerfield, Rhodes Reason, Miyoko Sisaki.

Enemy agents on a Hawaiian island pose problems for local authorities in this bland drama set just before Japan's attack on Pearl Harbor. James Westerfield, as a local plantation owner, in reality is a spy for the Japanese. Lex Barker portrays a local doctor who sides with the native workers and their labor problems. Glenn Langan, as a company agent assigned to quell the labor unrest, journeys to the island with his pretty wife (Mari Blanchard). Langan soon falls under the influence of the sinister Westerfield who is seeking to incite the workers. Barker now has to contend with Westerfield's conspiracy and Langan's inept and callous handling of the natives. A climactic battle ensues between the

National Guard and Westerfield's agents in which Langan perishes. ∎

Junior Army (1942), Col. *Dir.* Lew Landers; *Sc.* Paul Gangelin; *Cast includes:* Freddie Bartholomew, Billy Halop, Bobby Jordan, Huntz Hall, Boyd Davis.

Former "Dead End" kid Billy Halop portrays a youth from the wrong side of the tracks who has problems at an elite military academy in this World War II juvenile drama. Halop, a drifter, becomes friends with a young English refugee (Freddie Bartholomew) living on his uncle's farm. The uncle, thinking the academy will help Halop, sends him, along with the nephew, to the school. But Halop has troubles and is expelled. He returns to his former gang which is involved with a Nazi spy. Halop's sense of loyalty prevails, and he effects the capture of a group of saboteurs in this minor tale. ∎

Junior G-Men of the Air (1942) serial, U. *Dir.* Ray Taylor, Lew Collins; *Sc.* Paul Huston, Griffin Jay, George Plympton; *Cast includes:* Billy Halop, Gene Reynolds, Lionel Atwill, Frank Albertson, Kathryn Adams, Huntz Hall.

The popular Dead End Kids team up with the Little Tough Guys to battle a gang of enemy agents in this World War II serial intended for juveniles. Billy Halop leads the two groups of young mischief-makers to take an interest in flying while they use their own unorthodox methods to foil a spy ring's efforts at sabotage. The boys also join the State Patrol and the Junior G-men organizations. The chapters provide plenty of low-comedy humor and action, including numerous chases, fist fights and airplane stunts. See Serials. ∎

K

Kaiser's Finish, The (1918), WB. *Dir.* John Joseph Harvey, Clifford B. Saum; *Sc.* John Joseph Harvey; *Cast includes:* Earl Schenck, Claire Whitney, Percy Standing, Louis Dean, John Sunderland, Fred G. Hearn.

Earl Schenck portrays the Kaiser's illegitimate son who was raised in the U.S. in this patriotic World War I drama. Schenck, who can easily be mistaken for the Kaiser, turns secret agent and journeys to Germany to assassinate the Crown Prince and his son. The film cleverly blends its scenes with actual newsreel inserts of the Kaiser inspecting the front lines. At times, it is difficult to discern which portions are fictitious and which are real.

The film added fuel to America's hatred of the Kaiser, a feeling brought about four years earlier by Germany's show of militancy as reflected by a series of international confrontations. One particular scene suggests that he be lynched in Times Square. This was one of Warner Brothers' first entries into the burgeoning film industry and helped launch the studio into its eventual success. ■

Kaiser's Shadow, The (1918), Par. *Dir.* R. William Neill; *Sc.* J. G. Hawks; *Cast includes:* Thurston Hall, Dorothy Dalton, Edward Cecil, Otto Hoffman, Charles French.

A World War I drama, the film centers around secret plans for a new type of rifle invented by an American. This leads to much intrigue on the part of the Germans whose spies set out to steal the plans. Thurston Hall, as an American secret service agent, poses as a German spy. Dorothy Dalton, as a French agent, also masquerades as a German spy. Both are trying to uncover the identity of the leader of an espionage network in this inventive but unbelievable plot that derived from a magazine serial. The dual-spy device would become a Hollywood staple, especially during the next two decades. The film, supervised by silent screen pioneer Thomas Ince, was adapted from a magazine serial by Octavus Roy Cohen. ■

"Keep 'Em Sailing" (1942), MGM. *Dir.* Basil Wrangell; *Cast includes:* Jim Davis, Lou Smith, Byron Foulger, Ian Wolfe.

Another in MGM's "Crime Does Not Pay" series, this two-reel World War II short deals with an F.B.I. agent who operates undercover to delve into the causes of several acts of sabotage plaguing the American shipping industry. See "Crime Does Not Pay." ■

Key to Yesterday, The (1914), Alliance. *Dir.* J. Francis Dillon; *Sc.* Robert A. Dillon; *Cast includes:* Carlyle Blackwell, Edna Mayo, Gypsy Abbott, George Brunton, J. Francis Dillon.

Carlyle Blackwell portrays a dual role in this convoluted drama based on the 1910 novel by Charles Neville Buck and set in several countries. Blackwell is first seen as a spy in Mexico during that country's revolution. He is captured but manages to escape. Later, an artist is seen in his studio suffering from a loss of memory. His only clue to his past is a key to his Paris apartment. When clean shaven, he resembles the escaped spy. This adds further problems for him. Eventually he finds the right lock and, upon seeing some familiar faces, he regains his memory. He learns that his wife has died. He returns to the U.S. where he had earlier fallen in love with a young woman he had met when he lost his memory. ■

K.G.B. "When Westerners think of the K.G.B.," a Russian citizen once confided to a foreign correspondent, "they think of spies. When we think of the K.G.B., we think of our neighbors." British intelligence had described the K.G.B. as "the biggest spy machine for the gathering of secret information which the world has ever seen." Understanding the K.G.B. means having to know Russian history, for the secret police structure is a product of that past as well as a determining force in contemporary Soviet life.

The despotic autocrat, Ivan the Terrible, who ruled Russia from 1547 through 1584, consistently confronted the landed aristocracy and earned their opprobrium. Consequently, he was fearful of assassination and organized the first secret police of Russia, the Oprichnika. Three czars had been assassinated in the last century and a half prior to the execution of Czar Nicholas II during the Revolution.

Nicholas I crushed the Decembrist Revolution in 1823, executed its leaders and, for the first time in Russian history, used exile to Siberia as a punitive tool for the remaining conspirators. Nicholas imposed a police state and heavy censorship of all publications. His special creation, the Third Section, enforced his decrees. This secret police force was empowered to exile any Russian for any reason within a few hours' notice; there was no appeal. The last Romanov Czar, Nicholas II, was a committed reactionary who organized a new police force, the Okhrana, which placed its agents within the revolutionary movement—inside as well as outside Russia. The Okhrana employed thousands of career bureaucrats who, at times, created nonexistent conspiracies on paper to advance their own careers and, at other times, used agents provocateurs to initiate violence.

Several early silent dramas dramatize the abuses of the Russian secret police, including *Threads of Destiny* (1914). Romanoff, the lascivious head of czarist Russia's secret police, tries to ruin a defenseless young woman to satisfy his own lust.

The original Russian revolutionaries dismantled the dreaded Okhrana. To combat counterrevolutionaries at home and abroad, the opposing White Army and interfering foreign spies, Lenin turned to Felix Dzershinsky, a Polish aristocrat who had joined the Socialist Revolutionary Party and then switched to the Bolsheviks. Dzershinsky re-

introduced terror as a state weapon and organized the Cheka as Lenin's tool.

The Soviet Secret Police used various acronyms. However, until Gorbachev, its authority constantly grew and it began to take over the powers of the Communist party and the State. Unlike Western intelligence agencies which have separate and distinct organizations for domestic and international operations, the K.G.B. combines both functions. The First Chief Directorate is concerned with operations outside the Soviet Union while the Second Chief Directorate handles all counterintelligence at home.

The N.K.V.D. and the M.G.B., as the Secret Police were known in the 1930s, used kidnapping and murder as normal routines. Trotsky's execution in Mexico City in 1940 by a Soviet agent, however, caused such revulsion amongst international Communists that the N.K.V.D. shelved its high-profile, violent operations.

Stalin appointed Lavrenti Beria, a fellow Georgian, as chief of the N.K.V.D. in 1938. Beria was the longest-lived Soviet secret police chief and directed the organization until his death in 1953. Beria was the antithesis of Stalin. Whereas the former was urbane and educated, the latter was a boor and a misanthrope. Nevertheless, they were equally sadistic and determined. Beria scoured the regular police ranks and university students for the most promising agents. He distrusted the foreign, intellectual Communists and used them solely as "moles." Once foreign spies such as the Englishmen Philby, Burgess and Maclean were uncovered and "came in from the cold" to Moscow, they were never assigned any useful work. Recruits to the N.K.V.D., especially those to be dispatched to the English-speaking countries, were trained for years in the language and customs of the country of their destination.

Perhaps the most serious damage the K.G.B. inflicted upon the West was in atomic espionage. Several American spy films reflect this concern over atomic secrets. *Walk a Crooked Mile* (1948), for instance, depicts Soviet agents bent on stealing America's atomic information. The following year *Project X*, a low-budget drama, has Soviet spies once again trying to get their hands on the same atomic secrets. This time they are done in by one of their own party members who cooperates with U.S. government investigators. In *Walk East on Beacon* (1952) George Murphy, as an F.B.I. chief, foils a Soviet plan to steal scientific information from a refugee scientist who is threatened with the death of his son.

The defection in 1954 of Igor Gouzenko, a cipher clerk in the Soviet embassy in Ottawa, revealed some of this damage. Dr. Allan Nunn May, a leading British physicist, had transferred data to the U.S.S.R. Dr. Klaus Fuchs, a British national who had fled Nazi Germany, was another conspirator, and Bruno Pontecorvo, a pupil of Enrico Fermi, served as a Soviet agent inside the American atomic establishment. Gouzenko's defection has been dramatized in *The Iron Curtain* (1948).

There is evidence that Stalin, in his last year, was planning to liquidate Beria, whom he had begun to view as a personal threat. Fortunately for the K.G.B. chief, Stalin died suddenly in 1953, perhaps with a little help from Beria. The surviving Central Committee members moved immediately to prevent Beria from consolidating his authority. The evidence is unclear whether one of the members of the Central Committee shot and killed him during a meeting or a trial was held in camera and he was sentenced to be executed.

The deaths of Stalin and Beria sealed the most violent phase of the K.G.B.'s history. Henceforth the cost of political opposition within the ruling elite was reduced from execution to demotion in rank. Krushchev continued this "liberalization" of the secret police; his policies earned him the enmity of that organization which contributed to his removal in 1964.

Leonid Brezhnev viewed Yuri Andropov as an ally on the Central Committee in planning Krushchev's ouster. Brezhnev had already improved his standing with the armed forces in supporting their military budget and, with the appointment of Andropov as K.G.B. chief in 1967, First Secretary Brezhnev consolidated his authority. Despite Brezhnev's sponsorship, Andropov began to investigate the corruption under the First Secretary and, eventually, came to oppose him.

Yuri Andropov, the chairman of the Supreme Soviet in the U.S.S.R. and the secretary-general of the Communist Party in the years 1982–1984, moved into office with a policy of reforms which, in some respects, anticipated those of Mikhail Gorbachev today. However, Andropov's reforms were limited to reducing the corruption which ran rampant during the Brezhnev era, increasing produc-

tion efficiency and diminishing the role of centralized planning in the economy. Andropov's reforms were intended to strengthen the strong, monolithic Communist state while Gorbachev, on the other hand, has given strong support to a more open and pluralistic society.

Andropov rose through the ranks of the Communist Youth League, served in the Party's Central Committee in Moscow in 1951, and was appointed Ambassador to Hungary and personally supervised the suppression of the Hungarian Revolt in 1956 prior to being elected to the Secretariat of the Central Committee in 1962. In 1973 he was elected to the Politburo and, in the same year, became chairman of the K.G.B. From his power base in that organization Andropov was able to consolidate his authority so that in November 1982, at the death of Leonid Brezhnev, he was chosen secretary-general of the Communist Party. Personal illness prevented him from continuing his reform plans and, in February 1984, he died of kidney failure.

Gorbachev's apparently sincere effort to restructure the Soviet Union presents new challenges for the K.G.B. It must now learn to live with and not simply arrest political dissidents, religious elements and labor and ethnic groupings. There is even talk among the members of the new Supreme Soviet to restrict K.G.B. activities to foreign espionage and domestic counterespionage.

However, the K.G.B. presently employs 250,000 persons. Stanislav Levchenko, a defector and former K.G.B. agent, in his book *On the Wrong Side*, claims that adding outside informants to the above number would bring the total to one million employees busily engaged in spying on everyone else. The lesser-known G.R.U., the chief intelligence arm of the Soviet military, concentrates chiefly on foreign spying through its own military attachés and operates its own assassination squads. The two agencies are hostile rivals and exchange information only when forced to.

The ruthlessness of K.G.B. activities in American films depends on the fragile relations between the East and West at the time of the feature's release. During the Cold War, for example, Soviet agents tended to be callous and brutal, fanatics who were willing to kill to achieve their goals. Their main target concerned the atom bomb, already mentioned above. The Soviet spy, as a dangerous international archvillain, often played on the public's worst fears. In the drama *Panic in the City* (1968) a fanatical Soviet agent, going off on his own, threatens Los Angeles with an atomic bomb. George Segal in *Russian Roulette* (1975) portrays the Canadian Mountie who prevents a group of maverick K.G.B. agents from carrying out a plot to assassinate Soviet Premier Kosygin during his 1970 trip to Vancouver, B.C. *The Soldier* (1982) concerns Soviet agents, posing as terrorists, threatening to blow up half the world's supply of Middle East crude oil unless the Israelis pull out of the West Bank. In *Invasion U.S.A.* (1985) a crazed Russian agent leads a small military force in an assault on Florida. The perils extended to spy comedies as well. The Soviets in *The Nasty Rabbit* (1965), a weak spy spoof, plot to release a deadly bacteria in the U.S.

Once the paranoia of the Cold War relented, films began to soften their image of K.G.B. agents, resulting in relatively more realistic characters. In *Scorpio* (1973) Paul Scofield, as an aging, philosophical K.G.B. agent operating in Europe, befriends Burt Lancaster, portraying a C.I.A. agent on the run. Some of Lancaster's superiors believe he is a double agent for the East. Sometimes Soviet agents are even helpful. For instance, in *Telefon* (1977) a hard-line Communist fanatic (Donald Pleasence), who is against a U.S.-Soviet move toward detente, tries to instigate a war between the two world powers. Charles Bronson, as a K.G.B. agent, is assigned to stop him. When, in *Little Nikita* (1988), a renegade Soviet agent, named "Scuba" by the F.B.I., begins murdering fellow agents in an attempt to blackmail the U.S.S.R., a top Soviet agent arrives from Moscow to bring in the killer.

However, some recent films have reverted to the more menacing portrayals of the K.G.B. *Avalanche Express* (1979) shows the C.I.A. using a high-ranking Soviet defector to ensnare a dangerous Soviet agent. *Gotcha!* (1985), a minor comedy drama about an American college student on vacation in Europe who gets mixed up in an espionage plot, has K.G.B. agents trailing him from the Continent to his home in California. Kevin Costner, in *No Way Out* (1987), portrays a Soviet agent who has infiltrated U.S. intelligence. When he escapes from the Pentagon and is picked up by the K.G.B. which tries to force him to return to the Soviet Union, he refuses and leaves. Two agents, about to shoot him,

are stopped by their chief, who remarks: "He'll be back. Where else can he go?"

Recent allegations by ex-K.G.B. agents suggest that some film plots about the agency's range and intensity of activities may not have been so far-fetched. For example, Major Victor Ivanovich Sheymov, a former cipher specialist with the K.G.B., said at a news conference on March 2, 1990, that the K.G.B. was involved in the 1981 assassination attempt by a Turkish gunman on Pope John Paul. Sheymov, who had defected in 1980 and is now an American citizen, also charged that "two sources" in the U.S. State Department supplied the Soviet Union with information on various political issues. See Harold "Kim" Philby; Soviet Spies in the U.S. ∎

Kidnapping of the President, The (1980), Crown. *Dir.* George Menduluk; *Sc.* Richard Murphy; *Cast includes:* William Shatner, Hal Holbrook, Van Johnson, Ava Gardner, Miguel Fernandes, Cindy Girling.

An international terrorist group kidnaps the American President while he is visiting Canada and demands a large ransom in this joint U.S.-Canadian production. Miguel Fernandes, as a crazed and sinister terrorist leader, handcuffs himself to the President who is mingling with Toronto crowds. Fernandes then warns security guards and police that he is strapped with dynamite. He locks the President in a van that is wired to explosives and connected with sensors and demands $100 million and two airplanes from the U.S. government in exchange for his hostage.

William Shatner, as a secret service chief, bears the burden of trying to free the President while negotiating with the terrorist. He is also in conflict with the arrogant C.I.A. chief who demands that his agency handle the crisis. Hal Holbrook, as President Adam Scott, remains cool and insists that the ransom not be paid. Van Johnson portrays the Vice-President who must make the final, awesome decision of whether or not to pay the terrorists. Stationed in the White House, he speaks to Shatner on the telephone about the situation and ends by asking his advice. "It's my belief," Shatner replies hesitantly, "that the presidency never dies." Ava Gardner, as Johnson's opportunistic wife, makes him aware of the political ramifications of either decision.

Shatner earlier had received some vague

information concerning the presidential trip and tried to warn Holbrook of the possibilities of a plot against him. "The secret service," Holbrook reminds Shatner, "was designed for the President, not the President for the secret service." After the kidnapping, Shatner tracks down the young woman who is Fernandes' accomplice and discovers her in the crowd. She is holding the detonator for the van. After his men capture her, he convinces her that Fernandes had brutally murdered her sister. The remainder of the drama shows how Shatner foils Fernandes' escape and effects Holbrook's rescue from the van. The film was adapted from the novel by Charles Templeton. See Central Intelligence Agency; U.S. Secret Service. ■

Killer Elite, The (1975), UA. *Dir.* Sam Peckinpah; *Sc.* Marc Norman, Stirling Silliphant; *Cast includes:* James Caan, Robert Duvall, Arthur Hill, Bo Hopkins, Mako, Burt Young, Gig Young.

Deception, betrayal, greed and revenge are only some of the elements that make up the tangled web of intrigue of this convoluted drama. James Caan portrays a mercenary working for a private security company headed by Gig Young and Arthur Hill. The firm takes on all types of contracts, from assassination to protection, with 11 percent of its gross provided by the Central Intelligence Agency. Robert Duvall, as Caan's buddy and coworker, switches sides and kills a client he and Caan are supposed to protect. Duvall intentionally wounds his pal in the arm and knee to put him out of commission. The remainder of the film concerns Caan's efforts to seek revenge.

After a slow and painful recuperation, Caan is assigned to protect an Asian politician. He is anxious to take the job when he learns that Duvall is part of the assassination team. He hires a former pal (Burt Young) as his driver and an expert gunman (Bo Hopkins) as his backup. Young, now retired from the security agency, views all these undercover machinations as a political sham. "There's not one power system that cares about its civilians," he says. But he goes along with Caan out of friendship. Arthur Hill, as Caan's employer, disapprovingly remarks about Caan's choices: "One's retired, the other's crazy." More interested in revenge than in guarding his subject, Caan sets up the

Asian as bait. When Duvall makes his move late one night, Caan kills him.

The final showdown occurs amid the dead storage hulls of the Pacific Reserve Fleet, a symbol perhaps of the anachronisms men like Caan and Duvall have become. Caan and his team appear with the Asian politician and his entourage who are ready to leave for home. Caan discovers that Hill, his own employer, has sold out, hired Duvall and used Caan. "Everybody pays you, don't they," he asks in disgust, "our side, their side?" "They all want the same thing," Hill rationalizes his own actions, "to be in power." Caan then shoots him, disabling him in a similar manner that Duvall had earlier shot Caan.

Much of the dialogue reflects the political and anti-establishment cynicism that had infiltrated the spy genre of the 1970s. A C.I.A. agent, in contracting the private company to protect the Asian, explains his agency's expediency: "We don't want Chong killed in the U.S. Right now we can't afford the publicity." Assassinations and killings are described in a detached tone and circuitous terms. "There's someone on the Asian team," Hill discloses to Caan, "we want you to tag for us. He's shopping for the oriental." Near the end of the film Burt Young tries to enlighten Caan about the type of work both are involved in. "I know the rationale—self defense, God and country, another assignment in the national interest. Damn it, you're so busy doing their dirty work, you don't know who the bad guys are." The film is based on the novel by Robert Rostand. See Central Intelligence Agency. ■

Kim (1950), MGM. *Dir.* Victor Saville; *Sc.* Leon Gordon, Helen Deutsch, Richard Schayer; *Cast includes:* Errol Flynn, Dean Stockwell, Paul Lukas, Robert Douglas, Thomas Gomez, Cecil Kellaway.

Based on Rudyard Kipling's novel, the film tells about a young orphan boy's adventures in late-nineteenth-century British-ruled India during a period of "turmoil and bloodshed." Dean Stockwell portrays Kim, the son of Irish parents. Kim's mother died when he was born, and his father, a sergeant in an Irish regiment, died several years later. The boy was left in the care of a half-caste woman. Raised in the streets of India, Kim became knowledgeable in the customs of the land. Later, trained by British agents in the art of espionage, known as "the great game," and masquerading as a street waif, Kim helps British intelligence unmask a villainous czarist plot to promote Russian interests in India by fermenting military uprisings. "Russian influence," announces the head of the British secret service (Robert Douglas), "once again advances like a tide across Asia. . . ."

Errol Flynn, sporting a red beard and native attire, portrays Mahbub Ali, a horse merchant, who in reality is a British intelligence agent. Using Kim to deliver a message to Douglas, he eventually introduces the boy to the methods of the secret service. He employs Kim, disguised as a native, as one of his messengers. They both become entangled in the plot which ends with Kim's helping the British. Paul Lukas plays an elderly lama whom Kim, the street urchin, takes a liking to. The lama is seeking a sacred river, and Kim, encouraged by Flynn, joins him on his journey. As they travel together, the old man imparts his wisdom to the young lad. He later leaves a sum of money for Kim's education.

The film captures much of the sweep and spectacle of Kipling's novel and cleverly blends location footage with studio shots. A narrator occasionally helps to bridge the plot elements. For example, when Flynn gives the boy a strategic document pinpointing the five locations of the impending attack, a voice-over explains: "Although he did not understand the meaning of the five holes in the parchment, for him it was the beginning of 'the great game.'" The story unfolds at a leisurely pace but has spurts of action, including an attempt by spies on Flynn's life. Kim, however, discovers the plot and warns Flynn in time. The conspiracy concerning Russian spies was not an afterthought or conciliatory move by the studio in response to the Cold War; it is part of the original work. ∎

King of the Cowboys (1943), Rep. Dir. Joseph Kane; Sc. Olive Cooper, J. Benton Cheney; Cast includes: Roy Rogers, Smiley Burnette, Bob Nolan, Peggy Moran, Gerald Mohr, Dorothea Kent.

Following a series of acts of sabotage, a governor assigns one of his special agents to investigate the explosions in this updated, World War II western. Roy Rogers portrays a rodeo headliner appointed to work under cover as the special investigator. The saboteurs are suspected of working out of a tent show. Rogers joins the show and, after several fist fights and some flying bullets, eventually unmasks the entire setup, including a phony mystic act that is sending coded messages to a collaborator in the audience. The head of the spy operations turns out to be the governor's aide. This was one of several westerns released during World War II to conjure up a plot involving contemporary spies. ∎

King of the Kongo, The (1929), Mascot. Dir. Richard Thorpe; Cast includes: Jacqueline Logan, Walter Miller, Richard Tucker, Boris Karloff, Larry Steers, Harry Todd, Richard Neill.

U.S. Secret Service agent Walter Miller travels to Africa to find his brother, another agent who has mysteriously disappeared, in this ten-chapter serial. Jacqueline Logan portrays another American searching for a lost family member—her father. Miller meets her and observes that she possesses a gold trinket, similar to one that he has, and concludes that these are clues to a possible buried treasure in the vicinity of a jungle temple. Ivory thieves, however, control the temple. The title refers to a giant gorilla who is a continual menace to Miller and Logan. The serial was shot in three versions—silent, sound-on-disc and sound-on-film. Boris Karloff, who portrays a suspicious character throughout the serial, is not part of the gang. Karloff had appeared earlier in the same year in another Mascot serial, *The Fatal Warning*. In fact, he first appeared in serials in 1921, a Kosmik Film release titled *The Hope Diamond Mystery*. ∎

King of the Mounties (1942) serial, Rep. Dir. William Witney; Sc. Taylor Caven, Ronald Davidson, William Lively, Joseph O'Donnell, Joseph Poland; Cast includes: Allan Lane, Gilbert Emery, Russell Hicks, Peggy Drake, George Irving, Abner Biberman.

A 12-episode World War II serial, the plot has Allan Lane portraying Sergeant King of the Royal Mounted. He is confronted with enemy agents of all three Axis powers as he protects the production of war matériel necessary to win the war. The sets include a miniature volcano used as a hide-out for the villains who enter by means of a "bat plane." The last chapter ends with a struggle between King and the enemy, the latter finally being destroyed when some bombs are dislodged and set off a spectacular explosion in the once-dormant volcano. Of course the hero escapes in the nick of time. See Serials. ∎

King of the Royal Mounted (1940) serial, Rep. *Dir.* John English, William Witney; *Sc.* Franklyn Adreon, Norman Hall, Joseph Poland, Barney Sareckey, Sol Shor; *Cast includes:* Allan Lane, Robert Strange, Robert Kellard, Tom Merrit, Lita Conway, Herbert Rawlinson.

Canada's Sergeant King fights a nest of Nazi espionage agents in this exciting 12-chapter World War II serial. Allan Lane, as the Mountie, foils the plans of alien spies who want to get their hands on large quantities of a rare compound. The substance, known as Compound X, is capable of curing infantile paralysis. When enemy agents discover that its magnetic properties can be transformed to make their mines more effective against British warships, they plot to obtain as much as possible and ship it back to Berlin. However, they find the stalwart King a formidable barrier to their scheme. Republic released a sequel, *King of the Mounties*, two years later, also starring Allan Lane as the indomitable sergeant. See Serials. ∎

King of the Texas Rangers (1941) serial, Rep. *Dir.* John English, William Witney; *Sc.* Ronald Davidson, Norman Hall, William Lively, Joseph O'Donnell, Joseph Poland; *Cast includes:* "Slingin' Sammy" Baugh, Neil Hamilton, Pauline Moore, Duncan Renaldo, Charles Trowbridge, Herbert Rawlinson.

An unidentified foreign power is bent on destroying America's essential industries in this 12-episode World War II serial. The archvillain, known only as His Excellency, operates from a dirigible located high above Texas where he directs his secret agents to create havoc in that state's oil fields, dams and tunnels. His chief minion on the ground is played by Neil Hamilton, who loyally carries out his leader's biddings. Meanwhile, "Slingin' Sammy" Baugh, a famous football player of the 1930s, portrays the hero who vows to bring an end to the saboteurs who have killed his father, a Texas Ranger. The acts of sabotage allow for some novel special effects produced by the studio's creative Howard Lydecker. Among these include the destruction of the enemies and their dirigible consumed in a burst of flames. Directors John English and William Witney, two deans of the serial genre, set their action in America's Southwest after tackling Canada's wilderness the previous year in *King of the Royal Mounted*. ∎

King's Game, The (1916), Pathé. *Dir.* Ashley Miller; *Cast includes:* Pearl White, Sheldon Lewis, George Probert, Nora Moore, George Parks.

A complicated drama involving a Russian army officer who escapes to America with his daughter, a group of Nihilist assassins and an archduke, the plot concerns an assassination attempt on a Russian archduke during a parade. U.S. Secret Service agents manage to capture the chief assassin who happens to resemble the intended victim. So they substitute him for the missing archduke by tying him down in the carriage. Meanwhile the real archduke is mistaken by the Nihilists for their leader. However, all works out satisfactorily somehow. The archduke is rescued, the terrorists are rounded up and the officer and his daughter are exonerated from any wrongdoing. The film is based on the 1910 novel by George Brackett Seitz. ∎

Knock on Wood (1954), Par. *Dir.* Norman Panama, Melvin Frank; *Sc.* Norman Panama, Melvin Frank; *Cast includes:* Danny Kaye, Mai Zetterling, Torin Thatcher, David Burns, Leon Askin, Abner Biberman.

Danny Kaye, as a ventriloquist who is not getting along with his dummies, gets entangled with two rival spy rings who are seeking the blueprints of a secret weapon in this madcap comedy. On the advice of his manager, Kaye visits a psychiatrist (Mai Zetterling), carrying with him his dummies who are answering him back. Meanwhile, one group of spies hides the papers for the weapon in the dummies' heads, unknown to Kaye. The remainder of the film deals with his escaping the clutches of both gangs, avoiding getting killed and eluding the police who are also after him. Chases abound, one of which leads Kaye to join a Russian ballet troupe on stage. However, all turns out well for Kaye, who cures his pretty psychiatrist of her hang-ups while he overcomes his. Torin Thatcher portrays the chief spy in this romp that cleverly blends musical numbers with its comedy routines. ∎

Korean War: intelligence and covert actions. By the time the guns fell silent and a truce was arranged in July 1953, the Korean conflict (1950–1953) raised the U.S. defense budget from $14 billion in 1949 to $44 billion in 1953, cost the lives of 54,000 Americans, left another 103,000 wounded, set back domestic reforms and forced President Truman into retirement.

Although the North Koreans had been moving troops and armor to their side of the border along the 38th parallel for almost a year prior to invading South Korea on June 25, 1950, the U.S. had ignored all the signs. In later testimony before a Senate committee, Director Hillenkoetter of the C.I.A. maintained that a week before the invasion his people had warned the President and the Secretaries of Defense and State of an impending invasion. The two secretaries, in testimony before the same Senate committee, denied receiving any such warnings.

General Ridgeway, who was to replace General Douglas MacArthur as Supreme Commander of the U.S. forces in Korea, indicated in his memoirs that, six days prior to the invasion, a C.I.A. Korean analysis group did warn of extensive North Korean troop movements and the transfer of civilians from the North Korean side of the border. Army intelligence in Tokyo hadn't been alarmed at the report and forwarded it, together with other data, to Washington.

General MacArthur had stonewalled C.I.A. intelligence efforts in the Far East. The general preferred to use his own army intelligence staff, headed by General Charles Willoughby, to develop analyses. Given these conditions, North Korean actions in restricting radio traffic to normal broadcasting probably explains American unpreparedness for the invasion.

Although the U.S. had been surprised by the initial North Korean invasion, the C.I.A. did warn President Truman of probable Chinese intervention to protect their electric plants on the Yalu River and their border areas should non-Korean troops approach the Chinese frontier. The Joint Chiefs of Staff ordered MacArthur not to send non-Korean troops north, close to the Chinese border, but MacArthur ignored their command. On November 25, 1950, the Chinese threw 200,000 troops into the wedge between the two advancing columns of U.N. and American troops and forced them back below the 38th parallel.

The new director of the C.I.A., General Walter Bedell Smith, compelled MacArthur to accept additional "Company" stations in Japan. Hans Tofte was the station chief at Atsugi Naval Air station north of Tokyo. He worked with air force intelligence in establishing an escape route for American pilots shot down behind enemy lines. MacArthur tolerated the joint C.I.A.-air force operation because it was limited to guerrilla actions and the escape route and did not cross over to army intelligence.

In one of these covert operations, ethnic Koreans were sent behind enemy lines to disrupt Communist supply lines from Manchuria. Another action, named Paper, involved rearming the disorganized remnants of the Chinese Nationalist Army in Burma and sending them in disruptive forays into China proper. General Li Mi led the largest private Nationalist army, consisting of 14,000 men. In 1951 General Li Mi's troops invaded Yunan Province in China to a depth of 60 miles before it was halted by the Communists and sent reeling back to Burma. Several other invasion attempts were similarly unsuccessful.

Operation Tropic was yet one more fanciful but rather limited guerrilla action against mainland China. The C.I.A. in 1951 recruited ethnic Chinese in Hong Kong and sent them to Japan for training in covert actions. The following year the agency dropped a number of these operatives into Communist China in the hope of stimulating an anti-Communist uprising among people unaffiliated with the Nationalist Party of Chiang Kai-shek. This effort, too, resulted in failure.

The most successful intelligence operation of the war was in photoreconnaissance. General George Goddard initiated the work of interpreting aerial color photographs. The U.S. Air Force was able to determine changes in the color of grass where men and vehicles had passed a short while earlier. A wide-angle lens enabled the air force to obtain a full-horizon picture of enemy installations, and techniques were developed which differentiated between vegetation and camouflage. Almost half the intelligence data was obtained from aerial reconnaissance. One result of the war was the increased role which the military and defense contractors were to play in American society.

The Korean police action, as the conflict was labeled at the time, initiated more than 50 war dramas from American studios. But, unlike America's involvement in other wars, the Korean conflict generated relatively few spy films. One of the earliest appeared in 1951. A minor drama, *Tokyo File 212* concerns Communist spies operating in Tokyo.

U.S. Army intelligence sends in one of their top agents to investigate.

The Communist treatment of U.S. prisoners became a heated issue both during and after the war and launched a series of dramas that tried to come to grips with the subject. Some tried to whitewash the problem while other films, even more inept, blended exaggerated flights of fancy with stereotyped villains reminiscent of the propaganda films of World War II. *The Bamboo Prison* (1954), for example, suggests that some American prisoners held by the Communists and who turned collaborator were actually agents working for the U.S. Government. *Prisoner of War* (1954) has American intelligence officers dropping a volunteer (Ronald Reagan) into North Korea to check on a series of stories emanating from behind enemy lines about the brutal treatment of captured soldiers. He joins a detachment of American prisoners and witnesses first-hand a variety of atrocities executed by a Russian colonel (Oscar Homolka) and others.

The war also brought in its wake another phenomenon—brainwashing, as practiced by the Communists upon prisoners of war. Once again, Hollywood responded, this time with more imaginative dramas like *The Manchurian Candidate* (1962), which recounts the collective nightmare of a group of former prisoners of war. Frank Sinatra and Laurence Harvey portray army buddies who, along with other captives, have been brainwashed during their internment in a North Korean prison camp. Harvey has been programmed to carry out a series of assassinations in the U.S. In *The Destructors* (1968) John Ericson portrays a Korean War hero who has temporarily turned traitor as a result of Communist brainwashing. ■

Kremlin Letter, The (1970), TCF. *Dir.* John Huston; *Sc.* John Huston, Gladys Hill; *Cast includes:* Bibi Anderson, Richard Boone, Max von Sydow, Orson Welles, Nigel Green, Dean Jagger.

A spurious letter detailing an alliance between the U.S. and the Soviet Union in the event of trouble with China becomes the focus of a desperate search before it reaches the hands of the Chinese in this Cold War espionage drama. Richard Boone, as a Russian official interested in retrieving the document, uses karate to kill a woman informer. Max von Sydow, another power-wielding Russian, plays a role in the drama, as does Bibi Anderson as his prostitute-wife. Patrick O'Neal, a former U.S. naval officer, is assigned by his government to get the letter back. Other actors offer fascinating interpretations. George Sanders, for example, is an agent who is also a drag queen. Nigel Green portrays a delightful procurer-spy, exhibiting the right amount of sleaziness. The film, based on the novel by Noel Behn, is saturated with duplicitous spying and counterspying, drugs, torture, lesbianiam, as well as convoluted incidents. ■

Kultur (1918), Fox. *Dir.* Edward J. Le Saint; *Sc.* Fred Myton; *Cast includes:* Gladys Brockwell, William Scott, Georgia Woodthorpe, Willard Louis, Charles Clary, William Burress.

A fictitious reenactment of the events leading up to World War I provides the background for this tragic love story. Early scenes show the Kaiser plotting for war. Meanwhile, his emissary, Baron von Zeller, is sent to convince the Crown Prince's father, Franz Josef, to cooperate. Rene, a French intelligence officer, is assigned to Vienna and told to gain the confidence of a countess, played by Gladys Brockwell, who is close to Franz Josef. They soon fall in love with each other. Archduke Ferdinand, suspicious of Brockwell's influence, orders her to leave Vienna. A fanatic is then dispatched to assassinate the archduke at Sarajevo. When the assassin is captured, von Zeller orders him to say he is a Serbian. "We shall have no difficulty in proving Serbia responsible for the crime," the Baron remarks. He then orders the countess to betray the Frenchman, whom he is suspicious of. Instead, she helps her lover to escape with plans of Germany's invasion. When von Zeller and a handful of soldiers enter her apartment, she admits to assisting the spy and is immediately shot. ■

L

Labor unrest. Early American films about labor, especially the silent melodramas, contrasted sharply with novels, plays and poems about American workers. The latter often championed the cause of the labor movement, condemning the degrading working conditions and pitiful lives of the working class. By the 1930s the literary genre known as proletarian literature, with its emphasis on the struggle between workers and employers, reached its peak. This struggle has never been a major theme in American films; instead, when studios did show the plight of the working class, they often exploited the subject matter for dramatic or propaganda purposes while skirting the real social and economic issues such as poverty, housing, working conditions, unionism. Laborers, these dramas implied, were a generally contented group of hard-working, patriotic Americans who were occasionally misled by either a few troublemakers or outside agitators with ulterior motives.

Several early dramas dealt with espionage and sabotage plots by German agents during World War I. In *The Road to France* (1918), for instance, the hero breaks up a German plot to foment a strike at a shipyard. In *The Spirit of '17* (1918), a group of twelve-year-old boys, hungry for excitement and adventure, uncover a plot by German spies to stir up dissent among miners.

The post-World War I years and the rise of the Red Scare introduced new screen villains bent on inciting labor trouble. *Safe for Democracy* (1919) attacks members of the International Workers of the World, a radical union of the period, equating them with foreign agents determined to subvert war production. *Dangerous Hours* (1920), an anti-Bolshevik propaganda film set during the post-World War I years, concerns Russian agents sent to the U.S. to foment industrial unrest. Lloyd Hughes portrays an unsuspecting American who is duped by Communist agitators. *The Great Shadow* (1920), an anti-Bolshevik propaganda drama, depicts how Russian agents operate to ignite tensions between capital and labor. The focus of the agitators' attentions is an American shipyard where they instigate a major strike by thousands of workers.

Following World War II, the Cold War years reintroduced the Communist threat to the American economy. In *I Married a Communist* (1949), which lapses into an old-fashioned gangster melodrama, Robert Ryan, as an ex-Communist, is warned by his former party bosses that no one "quits" the party. They want him to foment labor trouble.

Other films of intrigue depicted labor unrest in various parts of the globe. *Jungle Heat* (1957), set just before Japan's attack on Pearl Harbor, features Glenn Langan as a plantation company agent assigned to quell labor unrest. He soon falls under the influence of a sinister Japanese spy who is seeking to incite the workers. A climactic battle ensues between the National Guard and the spy's henchmen. In more recent times several films have accused the C.I.A. of interfering in strikes and unions in foreign countries. The documentary *On Company Business* (1980) strongly suggests that the C.I.A. interjected itself into labor strikes in Europe. In *The Falcon and the Snowman* (1985), based on actual incidents, a U.S. security clerk (Timothy Hutton) accidentally stumbles across messages that implicate the C.I.A. in infiltrating an Australian union to break an impending strike. See also Palmer Raids; Red Scare of 1919–1920. ■

Ladies of Washington (1944), TCF. *Dir.* Louis King; *Sc.* Wanda Tuchock; *Cast includes:* Trudy Marshall, Ronald Graham, Anthony Quinn, Sheila Ryan.

Trudy Marshall, portraying a government worker, shares her living quarters with a friend who has recently arrived in crowded wartime Washington in this World War II drama. Sheila Ryan, as the newcomer to the capital, becomes romantically involved with Anthony Quinn, who turns out to be a foreign agent. His only interest in Ryan is to get information about someone she knows. All eventually is set right at the conclusion. The capital served as background for several wartime dramas and comedies, ranging from *Sherlock Holmes in Washington* to *The More the Merrier*, both released in 1943. The latter earned Charles Coburn an Academy Award. ■

Lady Has Plans, The (1942), Par. *Dir.* Sidney Lanfield; *Sc.* Harry Tugend; *Cast includes:* Paulette Goddard, Ray Milland, Roland Young, Albert Dekker, Margaret Hayes, Cecil Kellaway.

A World War II comedy-drama concerning espionage in Lisbon, the film features Ray Milland as a correspondent and Paulette Goddard as his assistant. Together, they help British intelligence by uncovering a Nazi espionage ring led by Albert Dekker at a nearby seaport. The plot hinges on Goddard's being mistaken for a spy who has been temporarily tattooed with secret plans. Nazi and British agents attempt to undress her in an effort to pry upon the supposed plans. Milland and Goddard supply some good-natured humor as well as romance in this implausible but entertaining tale. The clever use of the tattoo appeared in an earlier film, *The Hidden Code* (1920), about a scientist who tattoos a portion of a secret formula on his daughter's shoulder. ■

Lafayette, We Come! (1918), Affiliated. *Dir.* Leonce Perret; *Sc.* Leonce Perret; *Cast includes:* E. K. Lincoln, Dolores Cassinelli, Emmet C. King, Ethel Winthrop, Ernest Maupain, Valentine Petit Perret.

A World War I drama, the film concerns an American youth (E. K. Lincoln) who, while studying music in France before the war, meets a young Frenchwoman (Dolores Cassinelli). He returns to America, joins the army and is sent to France where he is wounded in battle. He later renews his acquaintance with the young woman whom he discovers has dealings with German spies. But all ends well when he learns that in reality she is an American double agent. The title refers to the remark, "Lafayette, we are here!," allegedly made by one of General Pershing's aides at the tomb of Lafayette following the arrival in France of the first American Expeditionary Forces. ■

Lancer Spy (1937), TCF. *Dir.* Gregory Ratoff; *Sc.* Philip Dunne; *Cast includes:* Dolores Del Rio, George Sanders, Joseph Schildkraut, Virginia Field, Sig Rumann, Lionel Atwill.

George Sanders plays a dual role in this World War I drama. He is a German officer captured by the British and sent to England where a British look-alike (also Sanders) studies the German's every move so that he may emulate him. Finally, an escape is arranged and the English surrogate makes it to Berlin where he is to learn the latest military strategy of the enemy. Dolores Del Rio, as a German agent, aids the Englishman with whom she has fallen in love. The film was the last of the decade's dramas to take place during World War I. See British Intelligence: World War I. ■

Lansdale, Edward. See *The Quiet American* (1958). ■

Lassiter (1984), WB. *Dir.* Roger Young; *Sc.* David Taylor; *Cast includes:* Tom Selleck, Jane Seymour, Lauren Hutton, Bob Hoskins, Joe Regalbuto, Ed Lauter.

A London jewel thief in the early 1930s is forced to help local authorities by stealing $10 million in diamonds from the Nazis in this purely escapist drama. Tom Selleck, as the thief Lassiter, is given the choice of going to prison or helping the police and the F.B.I. in preventing Nazi agents from exporting the diamonds out of London. Naturally, he opts for the latter. Lauren Hutton, as a depraved German spy, is assigned as the dispatcher of the loot. Jane Seymour portrays Lassiter's girlfriend who helps him in his mission. Bob Hoskins, as the inimical officer in charge of the case, makes Lassiter's job more difficult. Despite several picturesque settings and some action sequences in which Lassiter attempts to get his hands on the diamonds, the film remains dull. ■

Nazi officer Van Johnson (2nd from r.) plans to pose as an American soldier and lead a group of similarly disguised Germans behind Allied lines in *The Last Blitzkrieg* (1958).

Last Blitzkrieg, The (1958), Col. *Dir.* Arthur Dreifuss; *Sc.* Lou Morheim; *Cast includes:* Van Johnson, Kerwin Mathews, Dick York, Larry Storch, Lise Bourdin.

Van Johnson portrays a German lieutenant in this World War II drama about a squad of Nazi soldiers who infiltrate behind the lines posing as American soldiers. The men are singled out because of their expertise in speaking English. Their mission is to link up with American units and demoralize the Allies and cause confusion. Johnson slowly turns against the Nazi regime and is especially repulsed by their sadistic tendencies as exemplified by one of his own soldiers (Kerwin Mathews). The Americans eventually learn of his masquerade and make him a prisoner. In the final scenes he goes to his death helping his enemies by annihilating a group of German soldiers.

This is one of the handful of war films made after the conflict in which a German is both the main character and a sympathetic figure. The infiltration of English-speaking German soldiers behind Allied lines had some limited success, especially during the Battle of the Bulge. See German Intelligence: World War II. ∎

Last Embrace (1979), UA. *Dir.* Jonathan Demme; *Sc.* David Shaber; *Cast includes:* Roy Scheider, Janet Margolin, John Glover, Sam Levene, Charles Napier, Christopher Walken, Jacqueline Brooks.

A U.S. government agent, forced out of his job because of a nervous breakdown resulting from the murder of his wife by unknown assassins, becomes the target of the same killers in this tense drama. Roy Scheider, as an operative for an unnamed secret U.S. government agency, journeys with his wife to Mexico to meet a contact. Instead he is met with a hail of bullets which claims his wife. He soon discovers that the bullets were meant for him. Other attempts on his life follow. At one point, while he is standing on a railroad platform, someone almost succeeds in shoving him in front of an oncoming train. He then receives a cryptic note mysteriously signed "Avenger of Blood."

Janet Margolin, as a graduate student who allegedly comes to his aid, in reality has been responsible for a series of revenge murders. It seems her grandmother was forced into prostitution by a ring of New York Jewish criminals during the turn of the century. Linking Scheider's family with the old mob, Margolin plots his death as well. The film, a homage to Hitchcock in many respects, was adapted from Murray Teigh Bloom's novel *The Thirteenth Man*. ∎

Last Escape, The (1970), UA. *Dir.* Walter Grauman; *Sc.* Herman Hoffman; *Cast includes:* Stuart Whitman, John Collin, Pinkas Braun, Martin Jarvis, Gunther Neutze, Margit Saad.

Another World War II secret-mission action drama set behind enemy lines, the plot concerns the efforts of an O.S.S. agent and a handful of British soldiers to escort German rocket scientists and their families out of German territory. It is 1945 and, as Hitler's Third Reich is being pulverized by the Allies, both the combined British-American forces and Soviets want the leading German rocket scientists. The latter have sent out an advanced unit to capture the scientists.

Stuart Whitman, as a tough O.S.S. officer assigned to bring out top scientist von Heinken and his assistants, has to battle a green English lieutenant, pursuing German troops and a determined trio of Soviet tanks. Martin Jarvis, as the inexperienced lieutenant, insists on commanding his small unit over the protesting and domineering American. Near the end of the film, he sacrifices his life to buy time for his men, Whitman and the civilians, to cross over to the American sector. Margit Saad portrays a German widow who has become a Gestapo officer's mistress to protect her young son from being sent to a German youth camp. She falls in love with Whitman although she earlier berates him when he plans to leave the civilians behind. "Thank God I could still feel," she says. "For you it's too late. Inside you are dead."

When the escaping group finally reach their last checkpoint, Whitman learns that the operation has been canceled. "Political considerations," a British soldier explains. "The Allied branch in London made a deal. This side of the river, including the scientists, belongs to the Russians." But Whitman announces that he did not hear the new orders and, defying his superiors, proceeds with his charges to the U.S. sector and safety. ■

Last of the Lone Wolf (1930), Col. Dir. Richard Boleslawsky; Sc. John T. Neville; Cast includes: Bert Lytell, Patsy Ruth Miller, Lucien Prival, Otto Matieson, Alfred Hickman, Maryland Morne.

Bert Lytell portrays the title character in this romantic drama about a much-coveted ring and a mythical European kingdom. It seems the king of this principality, who has given a ring to his queen, suspects that she has given it to her secret lover, a military attaché. The king requests that she wear the ring at an upcoming social affair. Lytell, as the private sleuth known as the Lone Wolf, becomes enmeshed in the intrigue when he is captured and offered his release only if he cracks the safe of the attaché and returns the ring to the prime minister. Meanwhile a pretty countess (Patsy Ruth Miller) is on a similar mission but is working for the queen. Lytell joins forces with her, secures the ring and helps to return it to the queen in time. The incident has been borrowed from Dumas' novel The Three Musketeers. The film is based on the novel by Louis Joseph Vance. ■

Last of the Secret Agents?, The (1966), Par. Dir. Norman Abbott; Sc. Mel Tolkin; Cast includes: Marty Allen, Steve Rossi, John Williams, Nancy Sinatra, Lou Jacobi, Carmen.

Marty Allen and Steve Rossi, a popular comedy team of the 1960s, portray American tourists in France who unknowingly become entangled in an international art-smuggling scheme in this weak spoof of the spy genre. Theo Marcuse portrays the sinister head of the smuggling ring, known as T.H.E.M. Meanwhile, G.G.I. (Good Guys, Inc.) recruits the two tourists as special agents to investigate the art thieves. Marty and Steve are issued a piece of high-tech equipment, called The Umbrella, although it has been rejected by

James Bond and Derek Flint. As entertainers at Marcuse's lavish estate, they discover that he intends to steal the Venus di Milo. They transmit the information to their superiors who assign the pair to remain with the thieves until they can be rounded up. After Marty and Steve undergo several madcap misadventures, the gang is caught and the Americans return home to a heroes' welcome. The film ends with the Statue of Liberty about to be stolen. ■

Last Outpost, The (1935), Par. Dir. Louis Gasnier, Charles Barton; Sc. Philip MacDonald; Cast includes: Cary Grant, Claude Rains, Gertrude Michael, Kathleen Burke, Colin Tapley.

Cary Grant and Claude Rains, as two British officers assigned to the Middle East during World War I, soon become principal players in a romantic triangle involving Rains' wife. They assist each other during battle but are in love with the same woman. Grant falls in love with his nurse while he is recuperating from a previous battle. He later learns that she is the wife of a British intelligence officer (Rains) who has saved Grant's life. Rains returns to his wife after a three-year absence, but her love for him has vanished. Several effective action sequences include native uprisings, a realistic and brutal retreat of hordes of natives fleeing from a savage Kurdish attack and a rousing, climactic last-minute rescue of a beleaguered Sudanese outpost. The film was adapted from The Drum, a novel by F. Britten Austin. ■

Last Train From Bombay (1952), Col. Dir. Fred F. Sears; Sc. Robert Yale Libott; Cast includes: Jon Hall, Christine Larson, Lisa Ferraday, Douglas R. Kennedy, Michael Fox, Donna Martell.

An American diplomat in strife-torn India gets drawn into a plot by conspirators to foment a civil war by assassinating a young prince in this post-World War II drama. Jon Hall, as the diplomat who has recently arrived in India, encounters a former army pal (Douglas R. Kennedy). Kennedy confides to Hall that he is a member of a ring that plans to blow up a train carrying a popular prince, thereby plunging the already politically troubled country into open warfare. Later, Kennedy is killed and Hall is the key suspect. He decides to hunt down the leader of the conspiracy, prevent the train wreck and establish his innocence. Before he accomplishes all this, he becomes romantically involved with Christine Larson and receives some help from a bar girl (Lisa Ferraday). ■

Latin America. German military intelligence became interested in Latin America as early as the mid-1930s. The continent was close to American shipping routes. Large communities of German immigrants were already established in several Latin American countries. German agents based in the U.S. found it easier to transmit messages to fellow agents in Latin America—who would then send the information on to Berlin—than to transmit directly to Germany.

About the same time, German intelligence in Latin America began to interest the U.S. Adolf A. Berle (1895–1971), a U.S. diplomat and intelligence officer, became assistant secretary of state for Latin American Affairs in 1938. During World War II he helped the F.B.I.'s Special Intelligence Service carry out counterintelligence operations against German agents. He worked out an agreement with Argentina's President Juan Perón to keep Germany from using that country as a base for espionage. Axis activities were further curtailed in the region by an anti-Axis agreement, which Berle helped to formulate, involving 20 Latin American countries.

F.B.I. agents worked either under cover as attachés of U.S. embassies or as members of private companies. The agency's purpose was to foil German operations in Argentina, Chile, Brazil and Mexico. It even foiled a pro-German coup in Bolivia against the pro-British government. By the end of World War II, the F.B.I. had helped to apprehend more than 400 Axis agents and close down two dozen secret radio transmitters.

In espionage and war dramas Latin America generally comes off unfavorably. It is often depicted as a base for espionage agents, saboteurs and propagandists, and, during and after World War II, as a refuge for escaped Nazi war criminals. As early as the silent period, the American film industry used the region as background for various plots. In *A Royal American* (1927), for instance, a member of the U.S. Coast Guard masquerades as a waterfront roustabout in this sea melodrama about arms and munitions smuggling to South America.

By World War II Latin America gained a reputation as a place where assassination, revolution and general intrigue ran rampant. In *The Falcon's Brother* (1942), a low-budget detective drama, German agents concoct an assassination plot against a Latin American diplomat in an attempt to cool relations between the intended victim's country and the U.S. In *Notorious* (1946), with Ingrid Bergman, Cary Grant and Claude Rains, the daughter (Ingrid Bergman) of a convicted Nazi spy assists U.S. intelligence to expose a network of Nazis operating in post-World War II Brazil.

Postwar Latin American dramas offered few changes. The post-World War II drama *Cornered* (1945), starring Dick Powell, concerned high-ranking Nazis who had escaped prosecution by the Allies and had settled in Argentina where they were busy planning the next war. In *The Bribe* (1949), with Robert Taylor and Ava Gardner, a U.S. federal officer is assigned to spy on a war-surplus racket operated from a Latin American island.

More recent films of intrigue have dealt with familiar themes in addition to the influence of the C.I.A. and drug traffic. In *The Boys From Brazil* (1978) Gregory Peck portrayed the infamous Josef Mengele, the cold-blooded concentration-camp doctor during World War II who performed genetic experiments on Jewish inmates and eventually was responsible for the deaths of thousands. Having taken refuge somewhere in South America, he is busy on another bizarre experiment. In *Love and Money* (1982) a bank employee, enchanted by a young married woman, becomes the dupe in an assassination plot against a South American dictator. *Commando* (1985) had Arnold Schwarzenegger foil a plot to assassinate the current democratic president of a fictitious Latin American country so that a dictator can return.

World War II documentaries occasionally focused on South America. "For the Common Defense" (1942), for example, tells about a South American spy network's link to American gangsters. South America came under scrutiny in several entries of the prestigious "The March of Time" series. "The Argentine Question" (1942) discusses Argentina's controversial ties with the Axis powers and her questionable neutrality. "South American Front" (1944) analyzes the different alignments of Argentina and its Fascist sympathies and democratic Brazil. The documentary made for general distribution in movie theaters has fallen out of favor in more recent times. However, *On Company Business* (1980) explores the C.I.A.'s interference in various European strikes and covert operations in other parts of the globe, particularly Latin America. ■

Laughing at Danger (1924), FBO. *Dir.* James W. Horne; *Sc.* Frank Howard Clark; *Cast includes:* Richard Talmadge, Eva Novak, Joe Girard, Joe Harrington, Stanhope Wheatcraft.

The U.S. Navy comes under threat of destruction in this action drama. Conspirators from an unnamed country steal a newly developed "death ray" device from its inventor. They plan to direct it toward America's Pacific fleet, but they are foiled by the acrobatic antics of Richard Talmadge, who portrays the hero. Talmadge's father is in the process of helping the inventor sell his new weapon to the U.S. government. The father, meanwhile, seeing his son in a depressed state as a result of romantic complications, tries to persuade the young man to return to his old self.

Talmadge soon becomes enmeshed in a real situation with the group of conspirators. All the while he thinks the plot is a gag arranged by his father. He also wins the affection of the scientist's pretty daughter (Eva Novak) after he saves the fleet. The government, it seems, is not interested in the invention and wires a navy captain to destroy the weapon before it falls into the wrong hands. Talmadge's stunt work, which includes leaping from rooftops, driving cars at breakneck speed and riding a horse through city streets, dominates the film. ■

Laughing at Death (1929), FBO. *Dir.* Wallace Fox; *Sc.* Frank Howard Clark; *Cast includes:* Bob Steele, M. Joyce, Hector V. Sorna, Ellan Ludlow, Lou Schmidt.

Bob Steele, better known for his cowboy roles, plays a dual role in this silent drama of intrigue. The plot concerns a prince of a fictitious European country who is on a secret mission to the U.S. Steele, an American stoker on a vessel, happens to resemble the prince, whose life is in danger. The prime minister, who is the prince's traveling companion, notices the similarity between the stoker and the royal emissary and suggests that the two young men exchange places. The stoker agrees, realizing the dangers involved. He survives several attempts on his life and indulges in some acrobatics and fist fights before the journey is completed and the prince arrives safely at his destination. ■

Law Unto Herself, A (1918), Hodkinson. *Dir.* Wallace Worsley; *Sc.* Jack Cunningham; *Cast includes:* Louise Glaum, Joseph F. Dowling, S. A. DeGrasse, Edward Coxen, Irene Rich.

Louise Glaum portrays the daughter of a wealthy French vineyard owner. When her young French lover is killed, she resigns herself to marriage with a German suitor (S. A. DeGrasse). The German had murdered the Frenchman and placed the blame on local peasants. A son is born to the couple. When World War I erupts, the husband, who pretends to be a French citizen but in reality is a German spy, journeys to Berlin. German troops invade France and ravish the village in which the wife and son live. The boy, now old enough to serve his country, dons a uniform. His mother tells him that he is the son of her first husband, whom she had married secretly. When the German returns, the son has him arrested as a spy and traitor. ■

Le Queux, William Tufnell (1864–?). Amateur spy, world traveler, war correspondent and novelist, Le Queux played a major role in the birth of England's Secret Intelligence Service (S.I.S.) and that nation's pre-World War I anti-German hysteria. Born in London of a French father and an English mother, he developed a paranoid suspicion and hatred of Germany. He was convinced that thousands of German spies had already been planted throughout Britain. He continually lectured and wrote articles in the early 1900s about the Kaiser's plans to invade Britain, although all his charges remained unsubstantiated. Colonel James Edmonds, who headed a small, under-funded counter-intelligence agency at the time, used many of the fanciful stories conjured up by Le Queux to persuade a 1909 subcommittee to establish an independent secret service bureau. The S.I.S. became the world's first governmental intelligence agency staffed by civilians and empowered in peace and war to filch other countries' secrets while guarding its own.

Le Queux believed that a gigantic German spy network covered all of Britain, which was under the peril of imminent invasion. His novels, *The Invasion of 1910* (1906) and *Spies of the Kaiser: Plotting the Downfall of England*, which soon followed, whipped up the English citizenry to a frenzy. The latter, which first appeared in a weekly periodical as a series of accounts "based on serious facts," undoubtedly served as plots for a series of spy films produced in the U.S. during World War I. *Patriotism* (1918) concerns spies operating along the coast of Scotland and sending signals to German submarines. In *The Great Love* (1918) German spies plot the destruction of an English munitions factory. *The Man Who Wouldn't Tell* (1918) concerns a nest of German spies and members of the British secret service who are on the enemy agents' trail. Although these dramas dealt with the English alarmist's works in a general way, other spy films, such as the 1917 serial *Who Is Number One?*, borrowed from his array of imaginative secret weapons, such as super submarines and the newly developed military airplane.

Le Queux's obsession with the German threat of an army of spies inhabiting pre-World War I England and his repeated warnings about an impending invasion contrasted sharply with actual events, which were less than overwhelming. Between 1914 and 1918 only 30 German spies were arrested in England. After the war, the general consensus, including assessments by military and intelligence officers, was that German espionage in England accomplished very little. However, Britain's S.I.S. soon set the pattern for permanent governmental intelligence agencies established by other countries. ∎

Leap to Fame (1918), World. *Dir.* Carlyle Blackwell; *Sc.* Raymond Schrock; *Cast includes:* Carlyle Blackwell, Evelyn Greeley, Muriel Ostriche, Alec B. Francis, Frank Beamish.

German secret agents try to steal the plans of an important secret weapon in this World War I drama. Carlyle Blackwell portrays a New York cub reporter who ultimately foils the spies' plot to appropriate the invention which the American military is depending upon to help win the war. Earlier in the story Blackwell's father had cast him off for wasting his time in college. After he rescues the valuable documents as well as the scientist's pretty daughter, his father forgives him. ∎

Legion of Terror (1936), Col. *Dir.* C. C. Coleman, Jr.; *Sc.* Bert Granet; *Cast includes:* Bruce Cabot, Marguerite Churchill, Crawford Weaver, Ward Bond, Charles Wilson, John Hamilton.

A secret terrorist organization, known as the Legion of Terror, threatens a local community and the national fabric of democracy in this drama based loosely on the activities of Detroit's infamous Black Legion. Once the gang members use the U.S. mail for their criminal acts (sending bombs to Congressmen), the U.S. Postal Service becomes interested in their activities. Two government agents, portrayed by Bruce Cabot and Crawford Weaver, are assigned to investigate the Legion. Charles Wilson plays the sinister leader of the organization. Marguerite Churchill, as the sister of one of the gang's victims, is captured, along with Weaver, by the Legion and sentenced for execution. But Cabot and the state police effect a last-minute rescue. ∎

Legion of the Condemned (1928), Par. *Dir.* William Wellman; *Sc.* John Monk Saunders, Jean de Limur; *Cast includes:* Gary Cooper, Fay Wray, Barry Norton, Lane Chandler, Francis MacDonald.

A silent World War I aviation drama turned out by the same director as *Wings*, released a year earlier, the film concerns a group of American airmen in the Lafayette Escadrille who continually volunteer for suicide missions because of some personal incident in their past lives. Gary Cooper, one of the fliers, was in love with an attractive young woman (Fay Wray) whom he had seen at a gathering with a German officer. Disillusioned, he joined the other members of the Legion. What he didn't know was that she was a French spy ordered to develop a friendship with the German. He volunteers for the next assignment— dropping a spy behind enemy lines. The spy turns out to be the young woman he is trying to forget. She explains all and the mission proceeds, with Cooper scheduled to return for her at a specific time. She is caught and used as bait to capture the pilot. When he comes for her he is seized as well. His fellow pilots attack, drop bombs and rescue both the hero and heroine.

Wellman, the director, utilized some of the footage of his previous air epic. The story, however, is different, if weaker. Cooper's motivation for joining the "legion of the condemned" seems silly, as do the reasons given by his fellow pilots. Coscreenwriter Jean de Limur, a former member of the Escadrille, had been credited with shooting down seven enemy aircraft during the war. ■

Lest We Forget (1918), Metro. *Dir.* Leonce Perret; *Sc.* Leonce Perret; *Cast includes:* Hamilton Revelle, Rita Jolivet, L. Rogers Lytton, Kate Blancke, Emil Roe.

A large-scale production based on the sinking of the *Lusitania* and its aftermath, the unabashedly propagandistic drama pleads for revenge. The fictitious plot concerns an opera singer who survives the ordeal of the sinking, an American millionaire who enlists in the French army and a German baron who turns out to be a spy. The film stars Rita Jolivet, one of the actual survivors of the sinking. Scenes include the salon of the vessel with the passengers dressed in evening clothes, the inside of a submarine with a view of a torpedo speeding toward the ill-fated ship, people rushing to the decks, others jumping overboard, children swimming helplessly. The film later shows scenes in the trenches where an American (Hamilton Revelle) joins a Canadian unit fighting against the Germans so that he can avenge the one he loves.

Released during World War I, the production contains an abundance of patriotic elements, including much flagwaving. A doughboy, for instance, salutes the flag while he is in the trenches; another fatally wounded soldier embraces Old Glory in his arms. Concluding with a cry for revenge, the drama evokes images of the Statue of Liberty and the spirit of Edith Cavell, the English nurse who was executed by the Germans. The propaganda element was so persuasive that during one of Rita Jolivet's appearances in Connecticut, she was able to raise more than $250,000 in sales of Liberty Bonds. After the armistice, the German consul in Geneva, Switzerland, objected so strongly to the film being shown there that several scenes had to be cut from the production.

The British luxury liner *Lusitania* was sunk without warning by a German submarine, the U-20, in May 1915, with the loss of 1,198 lives, 128 of whom were American citizens. The German attack was part of an all-out submarine war designed to force Britain out of the conflict by cutting her vital supply lines. Although the German embassy, through notices in American newspapers on the day the ship sailed, had warned prospective passengers to stay off the vessel because it was a potential target once it reached the war zone, the incident became a rallying cry against German barbarity and probably turned many Americans, who were still neutral, against the Central powers. The sinking resulted in controversy which continued for many years after the war ended. The Germans charged that the vessel was a "floating arsenal," carrying war matériel to England. Colin Simpson, in his exhaustive book, *Lusitania*, substantiates this claim and suggests that the British intentionally sacrificed the ship to accelerate America's entry into the war. ■

Life's Greatest Problem. See *Safe for Democracy* (1918). ■

Lifting Shadows (1920), Pathé. *Dir.* Leonce Perret; *Sc.* Leonce Perret; *Cast includes:* Emmy Wehlen, Stuart Holmes, Wyndham Standing, Julia S. Gordon, F. French.

International intrigue threatens the life of a political refugee in this drama set in post-World War I America. Emmy Wehlen portrays the young woman who comes to the U.S. after her father, a Russian revolutionary, is killed by one of his own bombs that goes off accidentally. She soon enters into an unfortunate marriage. When her husband (Stuart Holmes), a drug addict, one night begins to attack her, she is forced to shoot him. Defended by a sympathetic attorney (Wyndham Standing) who has fallen in love with her, she faces further difficulties when Russian revolutionary agents, known only as members of the "Ring of Death," appear and want her father's documents. A detective hired by the lawyer to protect his sweetheart kills an agent who has broken into her home. Before he dies, he confesses that he killed her husband. This frees the young lovers to get married. ■

Light of Victory, The (1919), Bluebird/Universal. *Dir.* William Wolbert; *Sc.* Waldemar Young; *Cast includes:* Monroe Salisbury, Bob Edmond, Fred Wilson, Fred Kelsey, Andrew Robson, Betty Compson.

A young alcoholic officer in the U.S. Navy (Monroe Salisbury) is entrusted with important documents in this World War I drama. He goes into a sleazy bar, gets drunk and loses the papers to German spies. His fellow officers find him and return him for a court-martial. The officers, his former friends, suggest that he take his own life. When he refuses, they abandon him on a Pacific island. He soon finds employment with the Germans, supplying information to those aboard an enemy submarine. The sub then plans to sink Salisbury's ship, the U.S.S. *Victory*. The exiled lieutenant manages to warn those on board, and the ship sinks the German submarine. He then struggles with a German officer and is mortally wounded. The young American's repentance—a final salute to his country's colors before he dies—comes too late. He is honored posthumously aboard his old ship. ∎

Lincoln Conspiracy, The (1977), Sunn. *Dir.* James L. Conway; *Sc.* Jonathan Cobbler; *Cast includes:* Bradford Dillman, Robert Middleton, John Anderson, John Dehner, Whit Bissell, James Green.

In an apparent attempt to exploit the public's fascination in assassinations and their related conspiracies, this piece of fiction suggests that John Wilkes Booth was not trapped in the burning barn; it was another who was eventually buried. Booth, according to the questionable script, survived and probably escaped to Canada. The film, which advertised that the real facts had been covered up for more than 100 years, discounts the numerous books and articles written about the assassination and the resultant events, and proceeds along its own unsubstantiated lines. Other distortions in the film concern Doctor Mudd, who had until recently been unjustly associated with the conspiracy. New findings have completely exonerated him, but the drama fails to mention this.

John Anderson, as Lincoln, adds some authenticity to the generally weak script. Robert Middleton portrays Edwin M. Stanton, the Secretary of War who carries on a vendetta against the South and abhors the President's humanitarianism. John Dehner, as a colonel in the special national detective force, portrays one of the chief villains. The film was adapted from the book by David Balsiger and Charles F. Sellier, Jr.

The actual assassin, John Wilkes Booth, an actor and a fervent Southern sympathizer, shot Lincoln at Ford's Theater in Washington on April 14, 1865, in front of a full theater audience. Lincoln's murder brought the entire Union government to a standstill. Fortunately for the United States, but unfortunately for his own position in history, Stanton was the highest federal official with sufficient foresight to conduct an investigation into the assassination and to impose martial law in Washington to prevent the complete breakdown of law and order. Stanton then organized a search for Booth and eight of his co-conspirators. On April 26, federal soldiers tracked Booth and two cohorts to a tobacco farm in Port Royal; in the ensuing battle the troops set fire to the barn and shot Booth to death as he emerged with gun in hand.

A flourishing industry sprang up following the murder of President Abraham Lincoln. The favorite villain in this tragedy was Lincoln's Secretary of War, Edwin M. Stanton. According to the conspiracy theory, Stanton violently opposed Lincoln's plans for reconstruction of the South. Whereas Lincoln was supposed to advocate leniency, Stanton reflected the views of radical Republicans who wanted to severely chasten the South. Accordingly, Stanton arranged for Lincoln to be protected by an incompetent bodyguard on the night of the assassination, thus permitting Booth clear access to the President. Stanton was then supposed to have allowed Booth to escape Washington and then to have arranged for the latter's murder.

Stanton's complicity was never proven; rather, the facts tend to point in the opposite direction. Stanton had been James Buchanan's attorney general; he had been critical of Lincoln at the beginning of the war but, due to his loyalty to the Union and his organizing abilities, Lincoln selected him as war secretary. As the months and years passed, Lincoln and Stanton developed a close, personal relationship. Finally, their views on reconstruction of the South were similar: Lincoln had rather harsh opinions on the subject as did Stanton himself.

Undoubtedly secret conspiracies have determined numerous historical events and have encouraged the "conspiracy theory of history," which automatically looks for a secret cause of events while disregarding the obvious. In our own time we have witnessed the proliferation of conspiracy theories surrounding the assassination of President John F. Kennedy. ∎

Lisbon. Portugal's capital and a chief international port, the city has served as background for several tales of intrigue. During World War II, especially, the city became an espionage capital. British Secret Intelligence

Service agents debriefed central Europeans who escaped from German labor forces. Czechoslovakia's government-in-exile operated an agency in Lisbon where military intelligence about Germany was fed to the Allies. American films contrived complex plots laced with sensational incidents and peopled with agents and double agents and shadowy characters whose loyalties could be bought cheaply.

Hollywood's romanticized vision of Lisbon included comedies and dramas and extended to World War II plots released after the conflict. In *One Night in Lisbon* (1941), a romantic comedy, an American pilot (Fred MacMurray) ferrying planes across the Atlantic to England falls in love with a conservative young Englishwoman (Madeleine Carroll). A whirlwind romance takes the couple to Lisbon where their love affair hits a snag when he believes that she is being used as a decoy for enemy agents. *The Lady Has Plans* (1942), a World War II comedy drama concerning espionage in Lisbon, features Ray Milland as a correspondent and Paulette Goddard as his assistant. Together, they help British intelligence by uncovering a Nazi espionage ring led by Albert Dekker. *Storm Over Lisbon* (1944), a routine wartime drama of intrigue, features Vera Hruba Ralston as a seductive nightclub dancer. An unscrupulous Nazi sympathizer (Erich von Stroheim) who owns the club and trades in lives and military information, tries to prevent American correspondent Richard Arlen from leaving for the States with highly secret documents.

Postwar films continued to utilize Lisbon as a city of intrigue. In *Jewels of Brandenburg* (1947), a drama set in Lisbon at the close of World War II, Richard Travis, as a U.S. agent, is assigned to retrieve stolen jewels which are in the hands of a group of Nazis. *The Secret Door* (1964), another World War II drama made after the war, involves two convicted safecrackers (Robert Hutton and Peter Allenby) who are released from prison for the purpose of breaking into a safe in the Japanese embassy in Lisbon and photographing vital documents.

Lisbon also served as background for themes other than those about World War II. Ray Milland returned to the picturesque city in *Lisbon* (1956), a drama about an American smuggler hired to rescue a prisoner from behind the Iron Curtain. In the comedy *A Man Could Get Killed* (1966), James Garner, as an American executive on a business trip to Lisbon, is mistaken for a British secret agent and reluctantly becomes enmeshed in a web of intrigue.

Perhaps Paul Henreid best sums up Lisbon's widely held image as a city cloaked in mystery in *The Conspirators* (1944), a drama about Nazi and anti-Nazi agents operating in the city, when he addresses an attractive secret agent (Hedy Lamarr). Trying to escape from an assassin who has killed her contact, she seeks refuge at Henreid's table in a café. "I'm told Lisbon is a strange city," he says nonchalantly, "a city of echoes and shadows. A hundred eyes watch your every move." ■

Lisbon (1956), Rep. *Dir.* Ray Milland; *Sc.* John Tucker Battle; *Cast includes:* Ray Milland, Maureen O'Hara, Claude Rains, Yvonne Furneaux, Francis Lederer, Percy Marmont.

An American smuggler is hired to rescue a prisoner from behind the Iron Curtain in this tale of intrigue shot on location. Captain Evans (Ray Milland), the American, entertains himself by using his boat for various smuggling activities. The young wife of the captive (Maureen O'Hara) wants him rescued for her own ulterior motives—his money, which she can only get when he is dead. She hires Mauros, a sadistic international mercenary (Claude Rains) to handle that end of her scheme. Mauros agrees to help her and hires Milland and his boat for the mission. O'Hara accompanies the American and, during some romancing, reveals her true intentions to him. Milland, who has some scruples, is turned off by O'Hara's greed and renews his romantic interest in Yvonne Furneaux, who is one of Rains' playmates. He wrecks the plot of the pair of conspirators and disappears with his new-found love. ■

Little Drummer Girl, The (1984), WB. *Dir.* George Roy Hill; *Sc.* Loring Mandel; *Cast includes:* Diane Keaton, Yorgo Voyagis, Klaus Kinski, Sami Frey, Michael Christofer, David Suchet.

A pro-Palestinian American actress working in London is persuaded by the Israelis to help them track down a dangerous terrorist in this drama shot at numerous locations and based on the best-selling thriller by John Le Carré. After Michel, the Palestinian terrorist's brother, kills a top Israeli official, an elite Israeli intelligence unit decides to exploit the talents of the American actress (Diane

Keaton) in their plan to wipe out the band of terrorists. The Israeli chief of operations (Klaus Kinski) arranges for one of his agents (Yorgo Voyagis) to become romantically involved with Keaton. She falls for the agent and is taken to the Israeli's hide-out where she at first resents being kidnapped. "I'm pro-Palestinian!" she insists. "Leave the Arabs alone. Why don't you give the Arabs back the land you stole from them?" "Where would you have us go," Kinski asks quietly, "back to the ghettos?" Finally, convinced that Voyagis loves her, she agrees to help the Israelis for his sake.

She allows Palestinians to contact her and volunteers to work for them. They take her to Beirut where she undergoes rugged training in the nearby hills and learns about explosives. To test her loyalty, they assign her to deliver a bomb to an Israeli professor about to lecture at a hall in Frankfurt, Germany. But the Israeli agents substitute a harmless bomb to give her cover and arrange for local radio stations to announce that the speaker and many guests were killed. She returns to the head Palestinian terrorist, Khalil (Sami Frey), who at first believes the mission was a success. But he soon grows suspicious and learns that she has betrayed him. "You believe in nothing," he says scornfully when she admits that she is spying because she has fallen in love with an Israeli. The Israeli agents, who have followed her, break into the Palestinian stronghold and annihilate all those present, including Khalil, their main objective. Keaton, who is splattered with Khalil's blood, goes into a state of shock and is taken to an Israeli hospital to recuperate.

In the final scenes, she is seen back on the London stage where Voyagis comes to visit her and tell her that he loves her. "I'm dead," she says, "you killed me, remember? I'm dead." The last shot shows them walking down a street with the Israeli holding her close to comfort her.

Some of the dialogue is pointed and at times ironic. In one scene the chief Israeli agent, who is about to use Keaton as a double agent, brings in Khalil's captured brother. "You get your girls to do your work for you," he says in disgust to his prisoner. These themes about the hidden tolls the Middle East violence takes on decent human beings and how both sides of the conflict have their extremists are lost in the muddled plot and implausible events. The Palestinians are as dedicated to their cause as the Israelis are to theirs. Both groups are resented by other nations who are grudgingly forced to help the Israelis prevent terrorist bombings. In an early scene, after an Israeli official and his family have been killed, a German official says apologetically to Israeli agents: "After all, between Germans and Jews today, we are normalized." After the agents leave the room, the German remarks to his assistant: "It's not our fault. They have problems with the Arabs. They have problems with everyone—always." See Mossad. ∎

Little Miss Rebellion (1920), Par. *Dir.* George Fawcett; *Sc.* Wells Hastings; *Cast includes:* Dorothy Gish, Ralph Graves, George Siegmann, William Riley Hatch, Marie Burke.

Bolshevik agents pursue the ex-princess of a European country to New York in this romantic drama. Dorothy Gish portrays the former royal figure whose principality has been overthrown during a revolution. Escaping with the crown jewels and a faithful servant, she journeys to the U.S. for safety. Rebel forces at home order her assassination and want the valuable jewels returned. The alien agents track her down to her humble apartment and, during their search, take her prisoner when she returns and tie up her personal bodyguard. They then proceed to pressure her into revealing the whereabouts of the jewels. A former U.S. serviceman (Ralph Graves), who had met her while he had been stationed overseas, learns her address and arrives at her apartment in time to rescue her. Following his victorious battle with the culprits, the police burst in and march off with the Bolsheviks in custody.

The plot concerning royal jewels may have been inspired by several stories circulating in Europe during and after World War I about the sale of czarist diamonds. One such tale suggested that Russia's imperial jewels had been sold to finance the pro-labor newspaper, the *Daily Herald*, in England, then in the midst of its own "Red scare." See Red Scare of 1919–1920. ∎

Little Nikita (1988), Col. *Dir.* Richard Benjamin; *Sc.* John Hill, Bo Goldman; *Cast includes:* Sidney Poitier, River Phoenix, Richard Jenkins, Carolina Kava, Richard Bradford, Loretta Devine.

The film presents an interesting thesis with

a tale about a bright American teenager who suddenly discovers that his parents are Soviet agents "planted" in the U.S. 20 years earlier for future subversion. However, contrived theatrics sabotage the original idea which gets lost in an extended climactic chase and last-minute rescue. River Phoenix portrays Jeff, the son of the Grants, ostensibly a hard-working couple, loving parents and patriotic Americans. They participate in local parades, the P.T.A. and other conventional activities. When Jeff applies to the Air Force Academy, an F.B.I. agent (Sidney Poitier), making a routine investigation of his parents, discovers that the Grants' identities don't check out. He develops a rapport with Jeff and finally confides to him the truth about the boy's parents.

Meanwhile, a renegade Soviet agent, named "Scuba" by the F.B.I., is murdering fellow agents stationed in the U.S. in an attempt to blackmail the U.S.S.R. He demands $200,000 or he will continue to kill off other agents. A top Soviet spy, arriving in Mexico City at the Russian embassy, has been assigned to bring in the renegade. He crosses the border into the U.S. to begin his hunt. Poitier, whose partner had been murdered by Scuba 20 years earlier, also wants the agent. The film ends with a trade-off arranged by Poitier. Scuba is turned over to the Soviet agent, and Jeff, who was destined to return to Russia, is released to his parents who decide to stay in the U.S.

The drama has one interesting cynical note early in the plot. The recently arrived Soviet spy is warned by members of his embassy to operate covertly. "What we fear most," they remind him, "is the American media." "I remember," the agent retorts, "when we used to fear the C.I.A." "Everything changes," they explain, watching a television broadcast of President Reagan and Soviet President Gorbachev shaking hands. The spy, older and perhaps wiser than the others, watching the same screen image, smiles and says, "Nothing changes." The idea of Soviet spies as "sleepers" may have been based on the real-life experiences of Karl F. Koecher. See K.G.B.; Soviet Spies in the U.S. ■

Little Patriot, A (1917), Pathé. *Dir.* William Bertram; *Sc.* Lela Leibrand; *Cast includes:* Baby Marie Osborne, Herbert Standing, Marian Warner, Jack Connolly, Frank Lanning.

A World War I comedy about a group of youngsters instilled with the patriotic spirit of the times, the story centers on little Baby Marie, who is strongly influenced by stories of Joan of Arc. She persuades her unemployed father to enlist in army. Later, she saves her grandfather from a bomb planted by spies whom she helps to capture.

Always seeking new approaches to familiar themes, American film studios readily employed children to aid the patriotic cause in dramas and comedies concerning the home front during World War I. Movie producer William Fox, for example, presented the popular Lee twins in two comedies, *Smiles* and *Doing Their Bit*. The girls went after slackers and also helped in capturing spies. But perhaps *A Little Patriot* went too far in its patriotism when the title character encourages her pals to spit on those children whose fathers were slackers. ■

Little Tokyo, U.S.A. (1942), TCF. *Dir.* Otto Brower; *Sc.* George Bricker; *Cast includes:* Preston Foster, Brenda Joyce, Harold Huber, Don Douglas, June Duprez, George F. Stone.

The Japanese-American quarter of Los Angeles known as "Little Tokyo" provides the background of this drama that takes place just prior to the Japanese attack on Pearl Harbor. Preston Foster, as a police officer on duty in this section, uncovers an espionage network with the assistance of a radio news reporter (Brenda Joyce).

The Japanese-Americans had enough problems resulting from their evacuation to internment camps during the war and a general national hostility toward them as a minority group without this low-budget film attributing fictitious acts of betrayal to these otherwise loyal Americans. According to the F.B.I. and other government sources, not one act of espionage or sabotage was ever committed during the war by any Japanese-American. ■

Little Wildcat (1922), Vitagraph. *Dir.* David David; *Sc.* Bradley J. Smollen; *Cast includes:* Alice Calhoun, Ramsey Wallace, Herbert Fortier, Oliver Hardy, Adele Farrington, Arthur Hoyt.

A girl of the slums is saved from a life of crime by a social reformer in this drama set against a World War I background. Alice Calhoun portrays the title character, a slum child in trouble with the law. The local judge's friend, a social theorist who believes that girls like Alice are victims of their environment, decides to experiment with her. He removes her from a police line-up and raises her as a member of the upper social class. During World War I she serves as a Red Cross nurse and a spy for the Allies. While behind German lines, she discovers that the judge, now a major, has been captured. She helps him to escape. When he returns to the States, he relates the events to his friend who informs him that the young woman was the same one whom the judge had released in the friend's custody. Ramsey Wallace plays the judge. Oliver Hardy, several years before his successful teaming with Stan Laurel, appears in a small role as "Bull" Mulligan. ■

Little Yank, The (1917), Triangle. *Dir.* George Siegmann; *Sc.* Roy Summerville; *Cast includes:* Dorothy Gish, Frank Bennett, A. D. Sears, Robert Burns, Fred Turner.

A romantic plot dominates this Civil War tale that includes several battles and the employment of spies. Dorothy Gish portrays the daughter of a family of Union sympathizers residing within Southern lines. Johnnie, a Confederate soldier, gives her permission to pass as she heads for a Union position carrying hospital supplies. When her brother, a Union soldier, is captured, the young Confederate again allows her to pass to visit her brother. Dorothy and Johnnie grow fond of each other. A major, who is a Union spy and Dorothy's former beau, is jealous of Johnnie and arranges for his capture. He then charges the prisoner with spying. Dorothy enters the major's tent and distracts him while Johnnie escapes. After the war, the young lovers reunite. General Grant is portrayed in one humorous sequence in which he temporarily halts hostilities so that a soldier can cross no-man's land. ■

Littlest Scout, The (1919), Independent Sales. *Dir.* Paula Blackston; *Cast includes:* Charles Stuart Blackton, Paula Blackton, William Bittner, Violet Blackton, Wellington Prater, Stephen Carr.

Chiefly a tale about children, the World War I plot also includes a romance between a widow who lost her husband in the war and a pacifist who is converted by the widow. When German spies kidnap two children—the widow's seven-year-old daughter and the pacifist's little boy—the girl's little brother reports to the Boy Scouts. They tell the proper authorities and lead them to where

the spies are. The Germans are caught and an enemy submarine is then sunk. Producer J. Stuart Blackton, who shot the script at his Oyster Bay, Long Island, estate, made the film a family affair. His wife played the widow and their real-life children portrayed the widow's little boy and girl. ■

Lody, Carl Hans. See *Patriotism* (1918). ■

London Blackout Murders (1942), Rep. *Dir.* George Sherman; *Sc.* Curt Siodmak; *Cast includes:* John Abbott, Mary McLeod, Lloyd Corrigan, Lester Matthews, Anita Bolster, Louis Horell.

An unusual drama in which a murderer stalks about London killing members of a spy ring, the film features John Abbott in the role of the sympathetic criminal-hero who plies his trade during blackouts. Having murdered his wife following World War I, Abbott, a former surgeon, turns into a psychopath with a murder complex. Mary McLeod, as Abbott's neighbor, has lost both parents in an air raid. Lloyd Corrigan plays a Scotland Yard inspector who is on Abbott's trail. ■

Lone Wolf, The (1924), AE. *Dir.* S.E.V. Taylor; *Sc.* S. E. V. Taylor; *Cast includes:* Dorothy Dalton, Jack Holt, Wilton Lackaye, Tyrone Power, Charlotte Walker.

The Lone Wolf, a popular fictional Robin Hood character created by Louis Joseph Vance, teams up with Lucy Shannon, a U.S. Secret Service agent, in this familiar drama of intrigue. The plot centers on some coveted secret papers that contain military plans of the U.S. Early in the film the Lone Wolf (Jack Holt) is unaware that Shannon (Dorothy Dalton) is working under cover. A notorious underworld figure, the Lone Wolf holds the police and criminals at bay while he unravels the plot. When all is resolved, he reforms under the influence of the heroine. The story is replete with car chases, secret messages, hidden passageways and a climactic airplane crash. The Lone Wolf became a popular series character in silent and sound films and was played by various actors. See Detectives and Spies. ■

Lone Wolf Spy Hunt, The (1939), Col. *Dir.* Peter Godfrey; *Sc.* Jonathan Latimer; *Cast includes:* Warren William, Ida Lupino, Rita Hayworth, Virginia Weidler, Ralph Morgan, Tom Dugan.

Enemy agents seek to steal secret U.S. plans in this routine drama set in pre-World War II Washington. To get their hands on these anti-aircraft secrets, the spies kidnap the Lone Wolf, whose expertise at opening safes is well known to them. However, only some of the papers are taken from the War Department safe. Warren William, as the suave title character, then turns the tables on the agents. He captures the gang, turns the group over to the proper authorities and retrieves the important plans. Ida Lupino, as William's leading lady, also at times frustrates his attempts at solving the case. The film was adapted from Louis Joseph Vance's novel *The Lone Wolfe's Daughter*. See Detectives and Spies. ∎

Lord Haw-Haw. Few American films refer to the infamous turncoat, Lord Haw-Haw, the British male counterpart to America's Tokyo Rose. Born William Joyce in New York City in 1906, the product of an Irish father and a British mother, he moved to England and attended London University where he graduated with honors. He was a member of the British Fascist movement during the 1930s and, in 1939, moved to Germany.

It was in Hitler's Third Reich, working for the German Ministry of Propaganda, that Joyce achieved his notoriety as a radio broadcaster for Joseph Goebbels. The broadcasts, beamed at Great Britain, where Joyce became known as "Lord Haw-Haw," were aimed at undermining the British war effort. His ironic style of delivery, coupled with inaccurate news, brought him large audiences in Britain which, from the German point of view, was attracted to him for the worst of reasons— they found him amusing.

The comedy drama *Passport to Destiny* (1944), about English charwoman Elsa Lanchester's determination to assassinate Hitler, accurately depicts the Nazis' disenchantment with the English traitor, portrayed by Gavin Muir. When his Nazi superiors begin to treat him with suspicion, he realizes his life is in danger. "I really felt the New Order was good for the English," he confides to Lanchester, trying to rationalize his actions.

Following the war, Joyce was arrested in Germany and tried for treason. His defense claimed immunity on grounds of his being an American national. His claim was dismissed when authorities discovered that, during the period of his broadcasts, he held a valid British passport. His sentence of death was upheld by the Court of Appeals and the House of Lords, and he was executed in 1946.

Two other World War II spy dramas have fictional characters whose traitorous activities resemble those of Lord Haw-Haw. However, they are actually working under cover for the Allies. In *Appointment in Berlin* (1943) George Sanders flees to Germany, gains the trust of the Nazis and secretly broadcasts military information to England under the guise of pro-Nazi propaganda. *We've Never Been Licked* (1943) has Richard Quine posing as an American who is sympathetic to the Japanese cause. He returns to Japan, where he had lived for a number of years before the war, and broadcasts Japanese propaganda to the U.S. and elsewhere. Quine, however, secretly sends military information to American intelligence. ∎

Losers, The (1970), Fanfare. *Dir.* Jack Starrett; *Sc.* Alan Caillou; *Cast includes:* William Smith, Bernie Hamilton, Adam Roarke, Daniel Kemp, Houston Savage, Gene Cornelius.

The U.S. government hires a motley gang of motorcyclists to rescue a C.I.A. agent whom the North Vietnamese are holding captive in Cambodia in this implausible Vietnam War action drama. Made during the student protests against the Vietnam War and an atmosphere of general social unrest in America, the film manages to squeeze in some sophomoric anti-American commentary. U.S. soldiers are seen indiscriminately killing innocent villagers as well as enemy soldiers; American military officers are portrayed as callous and reckless; the captured agent seems unmoved when informed of the heavy toll in lives his rescue has meant. William Smith plays the head of the motorcycle group. Bernie Hamilton portrays an army captain. Director Jack Starrett plays the captured agent in this weak tale that was shot in the Philippines. ∎

Love and Money (1982), Par. *Dir.* James Toback; *Sc.* James Toback; *Cast includes:* Ray Sharkey, Ornella Muti, Klaus Kinski, Armand Assante, King Vidor, Susan Heldfond.

A bank employee, enchanted by a young married woman, becomes the dupe in an assassination plot against a South American dictator in this romantic drama. Ray Sharkey, as the fall guy in the plot, lives a simple, insulated existence with his despondent grandfather, played by former film director King Vidor. Sharkey has an ongoing romance with Susan Heldfond, a local librarian. But when he meets Ornella Muti, as the pretty wife of an international tycoon, he immediately falls in love with her and submits to her will. Muti's sinister husband (Klaus Kinski) hatches a plot that ensnares the innocent Sharkey. He journeys to a fictitious South American country to help Kinski negotiate with the present Castro-like dictator whom Sharkey knows from his early college years. Although Sharkey responds virtuously in his dealings with the dictator and the attempted assassination, he ends up as the chump. When he arrives home he learns that his librarian girlfriend is gone and that his own life has been left in disarray. The film music was written by Aaron Copland. See Latin America. ■

Love and the Law (1919), Edgar Lewis Productions. *Dir.* Edgar Lewis; *Sc.* William H. Osborne; *Cast includes:* Ruth Roland, Glenn White, Josephine Hill, Arnold Storer, Paul Ker, W. T. Clark.

A World War I drama about espionage on the home front, the film features Glenn White as the hero who foils the plot of enemy saboteurs. White portrays a New York City policeman who accidentally discovers that foreign agents plan to blow up a military troop train. Ruth Roland, more famous for her serials, provides the romantic interest. Several war dramas of the period concentrated on spies lurking about American defense plants, mines and coastlines bent on creating havoc with the nation's production and transportation of military supplies. These domestic films were obviously cheaper to produce than combat dramas which required larger casts and special effects. ■

Love in a Hurry (1919), World. *Dir.* Dell Henderson; *Sc.* Wallace C. Clifton; *Cast includes:* Carlyle Blackwell, Evelyn Greeley, Isabel O'Madigan, George MacQuarrie, William Bechtel.

An implausible but entertaining spy tale set during World War I, the plot concerns a young American's involvement with German agents operating in England. Carlyle Blackwell portrays the Yank who has been rebuked by his wealthy father for living a dissolute life. The son, determined to make his own way in life, journeys to England as a muleteer aboard a tramp steamer. He visits the estate of his mother's relatives and is suspected of being a German spy. Actually, he is collaborating with U.S. Secret Service officers who are trying to track down a group of enemy agents. Evelyn Greeley, as Lady Templar, falls in love with the rambunctious American and helps him in pursuing the spies. Director Dell Henderson, a member of D. W. Griffith's troupe, was one of the first directors to be supervised by Griffith. See German Intelligence: World War I. ■

Love Light, The (1921), UA. *Dir.* Frances Marion; *Sc.* Frances Marion; *Cast includes:* Mary Pickford, Fred Thomson, Evelyn Dumo, Edward Phillips, Albert Prisco, Raymond Bloomer.

Mary Pickford, "America's Sweetheart," portrays a young Italian lighthouse keeper who lives in a small fishing village in this World War I romantic drama. Her two brothers have been lost in the war. One day she discovers a man washed up on the shore. He poses as an American sailor, but in reality he is a German spy. Pickford falls in love with him and they marry. When she learns the truth, that he was sent to transmit messages about Allied shipping to the Germans, she rejects him. She hides him from the authorities until she discovers that it was his signal to a German submarine that led to her brother's death. She then reveals his whereabouts, and he is killed. Later, she finds contentment and love with a former beau who has lost his sight in the war. Fred Thomson, a former army chaplain in real life and who was later to become a popular screen cowboy, plays the German spy. Edward Phillips portrays the blind lover. ■

Love Thief, The (1916), Fox. *Dir.* Richard Stanton; *Sc.* Ben Cohn; *Cast includes:* Alan Hale, Frances Burnham, Gretchen Hartman, Edwin Cecil, Willard Louis.

The drama, inspired by contemporary incidents along the Mexican border, involves American border troops, a romance between an officer and his California sweetheart, and U.S. Secret Service agents who are trying to prevent Mexican guerrillas from buying American arms. Alan Hale portrays a cavalry captain who is ordered to patrol the border. He leaves behind his fiancée (Frances Burnham). Gretchen Hartman and Edwin Cecil, as two guerrilla agents from below the border, seek to buy weapons for their army from Burnham's guardian. When the U.S. Secret Service learns of this, the arms dealer and his ward escape to Mexico where they are captured by the guerrillas and sentenced to death. The captain and the American troops ride to the rescue.

During this unstable period in Mexico, the U.S. at first recognized the forces of Pancho Villa as the legitimate representatives of the people. But by 1915 President Wilson rejected Villa and recognized Carranza, another revolutionary leader and Villa's major adversary. Angered with Wilson's reversal and in a desperate ploy to defeat his enemy, Villa attacked Columbus, New Mexico, killing several American citizens. He hoped the U.S. would be drawn into armed conflict against Carranza's forces. Instead, President Wilson sent an expeditionary force under General Pershing into Mexico to hunt down Villa. But the punitive expedition failed. One of the unexpected results of the incident was the large amount of newsreel footage shot by the numerous cameramen assigned by film companies to cover the action. Much of the resultant footage ended up in documentaries, feature films and serials of the period. ■

Lucille Love, the Girl of Mystery (1914)

serial, U. *Dir.* Francis Ford; *Sc.* Grace Cunard; *Cast includes:* Francis Ford, Grace Cunard, Harry Schumm, Ernest Shields.

An early silent serial concerning the machinations of a not-too-sinister international spy, the plot allowed for the conventional chases, fights and rescues as well as for a variety of locales. The story begins with the archvillain's theft of military plans from an army lieutenant stationed in the Philippines. Lucille Love, the heroine (Grace Cunard) and sweetheart of the officer, is determined to retrieve the papers. Her attempts involve her in a series of near disasters, including a plane crash, a shipwreck on a South Seas island and capture in China and Mexico. She ultimately recovers the plans in San Francisco.

The employment of spies as a chief element in serials has long been a mainstay of the genre. When the serial *The Adventures of Kathlyn* (1913), produced by Selig's studio, became a huge commercial success, Carl Laemmle, the head of Universal, sought to emulate that success with a serial of his own. He made his request known to Isadore Bern-

stein, Universal's West Coast manager in the early days of that studio's history. Bernstein suggested the subject matter for the intended serial to screenwriter Grace Cunard and director Francis Ford. The couple had been successful in turning out several action dramas in which they also appeared as the leads. "A serial is going to have to cover a lot of ground," Bernstein explained. "A spy background will let us go anywhere and do just about anything." *Lucille Love* became Universal's first serial. See Philippines; Serials. ■

Luck and Pluck (1919), Fox. *Dir.* Edward Dillon; *Sc.* Adrian Johnson; *Cast includes:* George Walsh, Virginia Lee, Joe Smiley, George Fisher, Corinne Uzzell, George Halpin.

George Walsh portrays an acrobatic burglar who gives up his life of crime after he captures a German spy ring in this World War I drama. He meets and falls in love with Virginia Lee, a pretty young woman he rescues from the clutches of enemy agents. He eventually rounds up the gang and turns them over to the proper authorities. Walsh gives a poor man's imitation of the then popular Douglas Fairbanks. He performs some exciting stunting as he scales walls and trees in his evasions of the police and in several rousing fight scenes with the spies. Director Edward Dillon had been an actor with D. W. Griffith's troupe. ■

Lucky Jordan (1942), Par. *Dir.* Frank Tuttle; *Sc.* Darrell Ware, Karl Tunberg; *Cast includes:* Alan Ladd, Helen Walker, Sheldon Leonard, Mabel Paige, Marie McDonald, Lloyd Corrigan.

A small-time racketeer is drafted into the army after failing to buy his way out and soon turns patriotic in this offbeat World War II drama. Alan Ladd, as the gang leader, rebels against authority when he is drafted. After escaping from his army camp, he learns that his former mob, now controlled by Sheldon Leonard, has thrown in with Nazi agents. Ladd suddenly reforms and saves certain pilfered army tank plans from falling into enemy hands. Helen Walker portrays a newspaper reporter whom Ladd kidnaps when she follows him in an attempt to convince him to report back to his outfit. The film is dotted with some snappy dialogue which is used to enhance character and add some humor. In one scene, for example, Ladd's sergeant rebukes him for shoveling dirt on his foot. "Sorry," Ladd snarls," I thought it was your face." Earlier in the film Ladd rebukes his lawyer for not making the right connections to get him back to civilian life. "You can't fix Washington," his attorney (Lloyd Corrigan) explains. "For one thing, you can't find out who's in charge." ■

Lure of the Islands (1942), Mon. *Dir.* Jean Yarbrough; *Sc.* Edmond Kelso, George Bricker, Scott Littleton; *Cast includes:* Margie Hart, Robert Lowery, Guinn Williams, Ivan Lebedeff, Warren Hymer.

Federal agents investigate enemy spies on a remote island in this low-budget World War II drama. Robert Lowery portrays the hero who foils the plot of Ivan Lebedeff, the master spy of a Nazi network. Character actors Guinn "Big Boy" Williams and Warren Hymer provide the lowbrow comedy. Margie Hart plays a native islander attired voluptuously in a tight-fitting sarong. Hart had been a successful stripper before she entered films.

The plot and the dialogue should have been better, considering that the film boasted three screenwriters. The level of the one-liners may best be represented in a scene near the conclusion. "Pick your man and fire at will," agent Lowery orders. "Which one is Will?" Williams retorts. ■

M

Madam Who? (1918), W. W. Hodkinson. *Dir.* Reginald Barker; *Sc.* Monte M. Katterjohn; *Cast includes:* Bessie Barriscale, Edward Coxen, Howard Hickman, Joseph J. Dowling, David M. Hartford, Fanny Midgley.

A young Confederate, willing to sacrifice her life for the South, engages in the dangerous act of espionage in this Civil War drama. Bessie Barriscale portrays the brave Southerner who, when accused of being a traitor, determines to find the real spies. She succeeds in her mission after cleverly outmaneuvering several Union officers. In one particularly dramatic scene, she battles a drunken villain (Howard Hickman). Although chiefly a spy tale, the film provides a few battle scenes near the conclusion. See American Civil War: Intelligence and Covert Actions. ■

Madame Spy (1918), Universal. *Dir.* Douglas Gerrard; *Sc.* Harvey Gates; *Cast includes:* Jack Mulhall, Wadsworth Harris, George Gebhart, Jean Hersholt, Donna Drew, Claire Du Brey.

Jack Mulhall portrays an admiral's son in this World War I comedy drama involving female impersonation. Mulhall, to the disappointment of his father, has failed the naval academy test. One day he happens to notice his father's butler giving a German diplomat classified information pertaining to the placement of mines in a harbor. He overhears them mention that the German will turn over the document to a female spy who will arrive shortly. Mulhall, with a trusted friend, finds the woman, a German baroness, exiting from a ship and takes her prisoner. Then, to redeem himself in his father's eyes, he decides to impersonate her. Dressed as the spy, he retrieves the important plans. However, the baroness escapes, but Mulhall recaptures her and effects the roundup of the entire nest of spies. The admiral is overjoyed when he learns of his son's actions. ■

Madame Spy (1934), U. *Dir.* Karl Freund; *Sc.* William Hurlburt; *Cast includes:* Fay Wray, Nils Asther, Edward Arnold, John Miljan, David Torrence, Douglas Walton, Oscar Apfel.

A World War I drama set in Austria and Russia, the film tells an implausible story about a Russian spy (Fay Wray) who weds the chief of the Austrian diplomatic service (Nils Asther) and spies on him. Two experienced Austrian agents (John Miljan, Edward Arnold) in his charge pursue a mysterious spy known only as B-24, who in reality is Asther's wife. Noah Beery portrays a Russian general with an eye for the women. Several war scenes are interspersed among the tame spying incidents. The film is a remake of a German feature, *Unter Falsche Flaggen* (1932). ■

Madame Spy (1942), U. *Dir.* Roy William Neill; *Sc.* Lynn Riggs, Clarence Upson Young; *Cast includes:* Constance Bennett, Don Porter, John Litel, Ed Brophy, John Eldredge, Edmund MacDonald.

Constance Bennett plays an American counter-espionage agent in this routine World War II drama. She is married to a war correspondent (Don Porter). While he is away gathering timely stories, she becomes involved with the head of a Nazi spy ring in New York. Her husband returns and gets mixed up in the intrigue until the spies are captured and Bennett reveals that she is a double agent. John Litel plays the lead spy in this weak plot. ■

Make Your Own Bed (1944), WB. *Dir.* Peter Godfrey; *Sc.* Francis Swann, Edmund Joseph, Richard Weil; *Cast includes:* Jack Carson, Jane Wyman, Alan Hale, Irene Manning, George Tobias, Robert Shayne.

A slow-witted detective and his fiancée, tricked into working as butler and maid, stumble upon a spy plot in this fast-paced World War II farce. Wealthy suburban dweller Alan Hale, faced with a servant shortage, cajoles Jack Carson, a gullible private detective, into posing as a butler at a special function. He convinces the sleuth that German spies will be attending the affair. Jane Wyman, as Carson's gal, goes along as a maid. After a string of slapstick incidents and some strained light dialogue, the inept private eye discovers that a real spy plot is unfolding. Carson ends up foiling the attempts of German agents as they try to get secret war plans from the host. The film is based on a play by Harvey J. O'Higgins and Harriet Ford. ∎

Malaya (1949), MGM. *Dir.* Richard Thorpe; *Sc.* Frank Fenton; *Cast includes:* Spencer Tracy, James Stewart, Valentina Cortesa, Sydney Greenstreet, John Hodiak, Lionel Barrymore.

The U.S. government, desperate for rubber during the early part of World War II, hires two adventurers to smuggle tons of it out of Japanese-held Malaya. A convicted smuggler (Spencer Tracy) and an unscrupulous and cynical journalist (James Stewart) renew an old friendship and set out to buy the rubber hidden from the Japanese by various plantation growers. Stewart's reasons for taking on the dangerous task are more noble than Tracy's. "He got stopped at Wake Island," Stewart explains, referring to his dead brother. "I thought I'd take it the rest of the way." Tracy, at the beginning, accepts the assignment as a way of getting out of prison.

They arrive in Malaya posing as two shipwrecked Irish sailors and contact Tracy's acquaintance, the "Dutchman," a café owner (Sydney Greenstreet) who arranges the details. After transporting most of the rubber to a hidden American cargo ship, Tracy and Greenstreet suggest they stop. Stewart, however, decides to make one more haul although they all suspect the Japanese are lying in ambush. He is killed while taking his boats up the river. Tracy then takes over the transport of the last shipment as if paying a debt to his dead pal. He also kills the Japanese officer

in charge of the ambush. The drama is based on an actual incident during the war.

The dialogue is well above average for this type of adventure film, with Greenstreet getting most of the good lines. When the Japanese officer enters his café, the Dutchman warns the two Americans: "You'd better let me do the talking. The only thing that stands between you and eternity is my vocabulary." Near the end of the film, Tracy announces to the Dutchman that his former partner was a fool for taking too many chances. "He's dead for something," Greenstreet replies. "When I'm dead it will be for nothing, just as it will be for you. . . . He believed in something." ∎

Malone (1987), Orion. *Dir.* Harley Cokliss; *Sc.* Christopher Frank; *Cast includes:* Burt Reynolds, Cliff Robertson, Kenneth McMillan, Cynthia Gibb, Scott Wilson, Lauren Hutton.

A superpatriotic organization plots a military takeover of the U.S. in this absurd action drama based on the novel *Shotgun* by William Wingate. A power-crazed industrialist (Cliff Robertson), trying to impose his own brand of patriotism on the country, is forcing people off their land somewhere in Oregon as part of his scheme. "Ours is an American cause," Robertson reminds his small fanatical army of secret agents at a meeting. "We are determined to set this country right."

Burt Reynolds, as an ex-C.I.A. agent-assassin and Shane-like loner who has grown weary of killing, ends up siding with the oppressed local citizens. Instead of galloping through the area on horseback, he stops at a gas station to have his revered 1969 Mustang repaired. He immediately makes a hit with the owner's daughter (Cynthia Gibb) who is younger than his car. Whenever some of Robertson's hired bullies show up, Reynolds dispenses with them by applying a few well-directed karate chops or by means of a more deadly weapon. Robertson, who later meets with Reynolds and is impressed by the brash young man, wants the ex-C.I.A. agent to join his organization. When Reynolds turns him down, Robertson hires gunmen from the East to dispose of Reynolds.

As in a host of other similar dramas, the film denigrates the C.I.A. In this case, however, the script offers no reason for this negative attack upon the agency. Early in the film Malone confides to his partner (Lauren Hutton) that he is resigning from the C.I.A. "Nobody just walks away," she replies forebodingly. Later, the C.I.A. chief, for apparently no plausible reason, assigns Hutton to assassinate Reynolds. But she has second thoughts about killing her former partner. When Robertson's agents murder her, Reynolds vows revenge. The remainder of the film resorts to an orgy of violence as Reynolds single-handedly disposes of a horde of killers and Robertson and rides off into the sunset. ∎

Man at Large (1941), TCF. *Dir.* Eugene Forde; *Sc.* John Larkin; *Cast includes:* Marjorie Weaver, George Reeves, Richard Derr, Steve Geray, Milton Parsons, Elisha Cook, Jr.

An escaped German flier from a Canadian prisoner-of-war camp becomes the object of a search by a reporter and an F.B.I. agent in this low-budget World War II drama. Marjorie Weaver portrays the journalist while George Reeves, as the federal agent, poses as a competing journalist. They both pursue the German and eventually become entangled with a murderous spy ring. The film employs a familiar spy genre convention—the agent posing as a dentist—also used in such films as *The Man Who Knew Too Much* (1956) and *Marathon Man* (1976). Reeves was to repeat his role as a newspaperman years later when he starred as Clark Kent/Superman in the popular television series. ∎

Man Beneath, The (1919), Mutual. *Dir.* William Worthington; *Sc.* L. V. Jefferson; *Cast includes:* Sessue Hayakawa, Helen Jerome Eddy, Pauline Curley, Jack Gilbert, Fontaine La Rue.

International spies threaten the life of an Englishman in this drama set both in England and India. Sessue Hayakawa portrays a Hindu scientist educated in England. His former school friend (Jack Gilbert) gets involved with an international crime ring and seeks Hayakawa's help. The scientist, now practicing in his native land, extricates his friend from his complications. The film provides a racial subplot concerning Hayakawa. He falls in love with a young Englishwoman who rejects him. Admitting that she loves him, she feels she cannot marry him because of their different races. The film is based on the 1910 novel *Only a Nigger* by Edmund Mitchell. ∎

Man Called Dagger, A (1967), MGM. *Dir.* Richard Rush; *Sc.* James Peatman, Robert S. Weekley; *Cast includes:* Terry Moore, Jan Murray, Paul Mantee, Sue Ane Langdon, Eileen O'Neill, Maureen Arthur.

Ex-Nazis, stationed in Los Angeles, plot to take over the world by controlling its national leaders in this inept drama which tries to imitate the success of the James Bond type of spy films that proliferated in the 1960s. Paul Mantee, as Dagger, a superagent whose political interests remain ambivalent, trails a former Nazi scientist to America. The suspect plans to link up with an ex-S.S. colonel and concentration camp commandant (Jan Murray) who has concocted the above scheme. Murray intends to kidnap the world leaders and place miniature radio receivers in their teeth from which Murray will then control their actions.

The emotionless Dagger, equipped with an array of superweapons, overcomes the conventional obstacles and eventually puts an end to the mad dream of conquest. Murray ends up dangling on a meat hook. Terry Moore has little to do as the major feminine interest in a chiefly unbelievable plot. See Nazi Subversion: Post-World War II. ∎

Man Called Flintstone, The (1966), Col. *Dir.* Joseph Barbera, William Hanna; *Sc.* Harvey Bullock, R. S. Allen; *Cast includes:* (voices) Alan Reed, Sr., Mel Blanc, Jean Vanderpyl, Gerry Johnson, Don Messick, Janet Waldo.

An animated spy spoof based on the popular "Flintstones" television series, the plot concerns Fred Flintstone's impersonation of a famous master spy. When Rock Slag, the superspy, is put out of commission by the evil Green Goose's underlings, Fred is recruited to take Slag's place. An exact lookalike, Fred poses as a tourist and, with his family and his neighboring family, goes to Paris for a supposed vacation. Tanya, the alluring accomplice of Green Goose, leads Fred into a trap. The real superspy shows up in time to rescue Fred and capture the entire spy network. The culprits are transported into outer space while the two families return home. ∎

Man Could Get Killed, A (1966), U. *Dir.* Ronald Neame, Cliff Owen; *Sc.* Richard Breen, T. E. B. Clarke; *Cast includes:* James

Garner, Melina Mercouri, Sandra Dee, Tony Franciosa, Robert Coote, Roland Culver.

An American executive on a business trip to Lisbon is mistaken for a British secret agent and reluctantly becomes enmeshed in a web of intrigue in this familiar but entertaining comedy. James Garner, as the supposed agent who has been murdered, is persuaded by the dead man's girlfriend and a self-serving con artist masquerading as a diamond smuggler to continue the agent's search for a cache of stolen diamonds. This leads Garner into further difficulties when other assorted agents and smugglers begin to pursue the same objective. Following some slapstick chases and Garner's repeated denials about his being a secret agent, he manages to retrieve the diamonds.

Melina Mercouri, as the attractive woman interested in Garner and a share in the loot, provides half the romantic interest. Sandra Dee, as an American tourist, provides the other half for Tony Franciosa who portrays the bogus smuggler. Roland Culver, as an English physician, is secretly mixed up in the diamond-smuggling racket. Robert Coote plays an official of the British embassy. The film was adapted from David Esdaile Walker's novel *Diamonds for Danger*. ■

Man From Brodney's The (1923), Vitagraph. *Dir.* David Smith; *Sc.* C. Graham Baker; *Cast includes:* J. Walter Kerrigan, Alice Calhoun, Wanda Hawley, Pat O'Malley, Miss Du Pont, Kathleen Key.

A romantic drama laid on a fictitious island, the film centers on political intrigue as well as action. A discontented native stirs up the inhabitants against the white owners of the land. He leads a native attack on the whites who barricade themselves in a house. Finally, an American destroyer, firing rounds of shells and dispatching troops, comes to the aid of the besieged whites. The curious plot concerns two partners who own the island, one has a son and the other a daughter. Their will says that their heirs can only take over if they marry each other; otherwise, the island becomes the property of the natives. ■

Man From Button Willow, The (1965), United Screen Artists. *Dir.* David Detiege; *Sc.* David Detiege; *Cast includes:* (voices only) Dale Robertson, Edgar Buchanan, Howard Keel, Herschel Bernardi, Ross Martin, Barbara Jean Wong.

Allegedly about the U.S. government's first undercover agent, this animated western, set in 1869, tells of the exploits of Justine Eagle. With Dale Robertson supplying his voice, Eagle, a farmer who lives near the town of Button Willow, is sometimes recruited by the government to protect its interests. He defends the local landowners against an unscrupulous financier who represents land speculators seeking to cash in on the encroaching transcontinental railroad. Our stalwart hero eventually saves the life of a U.S. senator who is kidnapped and taken aboard a schooner in the San Francisco Bay. Eagle, with the help of another prisoner, overpowers the crew and turns the schooner around. Much of the film concerns Eagle's Chinese ward and her experiences with her various creature friends, including, among others, her horse, dog and carrier pigeon—all evidently designed to satisfy a juvenile audience. ■

Man From Downing Street, The (1922), Vitagraph. *Dir.* Edward Jose; *Sc.* Bradley J. Smollen; *Cast includes:* Earle Williams, Charles Hill Mailes, Boris Karloff, Betty Ross Clarke, Kathryn Adams.

The British secret service is interested in learning who is responsible for instigating a revolt in India in this drama of intrigue. Earle Williams, as a British agent, is assigned to the case to uncover the traitor who has also gained access to a secret code. Posing as a local native, Williams journeys to the military post in Delhi and is faced with a host of suspects. They include several officers, their wives and daughters and a local dancer. At one point in the plot a lieutenant, about to reveal information to the secret agent, is shot by an unknown assailant. Williams eventually sets up a trap which exposes the commander of the post as the guilty party. The dancing girl, to Williams' surprise, turns out to be another British agent who is also working on the case. It is she who has seen the commander fire the fatal shot. ■

Man From Headquarters (1928), Rayart. *Dir.* Duke Worne; *Sc.* Arthur Hoerl; *Cast includes:* Cornelius Keefe, Edith Roberts, Charles West, Lloyd Whitlock, Ludwig Lowry.

A drama of intrigue set in a fictitious European country, the film concerns the assassination of a duke and the search for an important document. The unfortunate duke, believed to be carrying secret papers, is killed aboard a train. The killers, however, are only partially successful in their mission; they find half the document. Cornelius Keefe, as a member of the U.S. Secret Service, who has been assigned to the area, arrives after the crime has been committed and retrieves the other half. Edith Roberts, a member of the conspiracy, is dispatched to get the missing papers from the American. Keefe and Roberts soon fall in love, but Keefe retains his resolve to track down the murderers and recover the stolen document. He faces death several times before his mission is accomplished. ∎

"Man From U.N.C.L.E., The" A popular television spy series of the mid-1960s that inspired several feature-length films. The writers no doubt were influenced by Alfred Hitchcock's 1959 witty comedy-thriller *North by Northwest* and the highly successful James Bond features imported from Great Britain and based on Ian Fleming's novels. Robert Vaughn portrayed Napoleon Solo (whose name was created by Fleming), an especially gifted secret agent who worked for U.N.C.L.E., an intelligence organization dedicated to fight international crime and terrorism. David McCallum, as the blond Russian agent Ilya Kuryakin, played Solo's able partner. Leo G. Carroll, who had appeared in Hitchcock's film as a C.I.A. chief, enacted Mr. Waverly, Solo's droll superior.

Vaughn and McCallum brought a new type of hero to the spy genre—one who depended more on his intellect than on physical prowess. Each episode focused on adventure, tongue-in-cheek dialogue and incidents, and technological gadgetry. U.N.C.L.E.'s chief adversary was T.H.R.U.S.H. (Technological Hierarchy for Revenge, Undermining and Subjugation of Humanity). Vaughn, in a television interview years later, described it as "an organization that represented evil incarnate throughout the world."

The initial entries did not immediately catch on with television audiences. But college students soon discovered the show and female viewers succumbed to McCallum's charm. These two factors were chiefly responsible for turning the series into a hit. At its peak, "The Man From U.N.C.L.E.," with its catchy theme music by Jerry Goldsmith, appeared in more than 60 countries and generated thousands of fan-mail letters each

week. In 1968, after 134 entries and several successful years, the series left prime time. The T.V. show also spawned several feature films, including *To Trap a Spy* (1966), *One of Our Spies Is Missing* (1966), *One Spy Too Many* (1966) and *The Spy With My Face* (1966). The films, however, never achieved the commercial success or popularity of the larger-budgeted James Bond entries. ∎

Man Hunt (1941), TCF. *Dir.* Fritz Lang; *Sc.* Dudley Nichols; *Cast includes:* Walter Pidgeon, Joan Bennett, George Sanders, John Carradine, Roddy McDowall.

A suspenseful and far-fetched tale about an attempt to assassinate Hitler, the film stars Walter Pidgeon as a British big-game hunter whose expertise in the hunt brings him into direct confrontation with the Gestapo. He decides to enter Germany surreptitiously and gain access to Hitler's private lair to prove to himself that he could knock off the dictator if he wanted to. Just as he gets the Nazi leader in his sights, he is captured by guards. The Gestapo torture Pidgeon, demanding that he sign a confession that he was sent by the British government. He manages to escape and eventually reach England where, ironically, he is now the one who is stalked by Nazi agents. Director Fritz Lang's suspenseful film ends with Pidgeon's decision to return to Germany, this time to finish off his prey. The film was remade as a British television production in 1976 starring Peter O'Toole and titled *Rogue Male*, the original title of Geoffrey Household's novel. ∎

Man on a String (1960), Col. *Dir.* Andre De Toth; *Sc.* John Kafka, Virginia Shaler; *Cast includes:* Ernest Borgnine, Kerwin Mathews, Colleen Dewhurst, Alexander Scourby, Glenn Corbett, Vladimir Sokoloff.

The Central Intelligence Agency convinces a Russian-born American citizen who has been caught helping Soviet agents in the U.S. for ten years, to turn counterspy in this suspenseful Cold War drama shot in several European locales. Ernest Borgnine, as a successful Hollywood producer turned traitor, agrees to collaborate with Soviet spies in the U.S. on the condition that they allow his father to join him. Once his father arrives in Hollywood, Borgnine begins introducing the espionage agents to important Americans. However, Borgnine has been under constant surveillance by U.S. intelligence and by his own assistant, an undercover agent.

Borgnine agrees to spy on the Russians for the C.I.A. and journeys to West Berlin, reportedly to make a film. Actually, he is assigned to gather information about East Berlin. Fellow agents, suspicious of Borgnine, have him ordered to Moscow, where he proves his loyalty by testifying against a former friend. He then gains access to a list of Soviet spies destined for the U.S. But the Russians discover that he is a counterspy. A climactic gun battle ensues in a West Berlin hotel, and Borgnine escapes. He turns over the vital names to U.S. authorities, and the enemy agents are rounded up. The film is based on Boris Morros' biography *Ten Years a Counterspy.*

Some controversy arose from the screen version of Morros' story. Several critics attacked the film for not bringing out the damage which resulted from Morros' subversive activities while working for the Soviets. Others objected to the false theatrics injected into the plot, Morros' exaggerated contributions to U.S. security and the distorted spy-training program in Moscow.

Boris Morros, born in St. Petersburg in imperial Russia in 1895, escaped to Turkey during the Russian Revolution. Here he produced a show called *Flying Bats* and repeated its success in New York City. Adolph Zukor, the head of Paramount Pictures, discovered Morros and persuaded him to move to Hollywood. The Russian prodigy was intelligent enough to read the signs of the times, and he eschewed classical Russian music for modern American jazz. He was appointed director of music at Paramount in 1928.

Several years later Morros received a phone call from the Soviet Embassy asking to provide a false reference as a talent scout for Edward Herbert, a man unknown to him. He learned that Herbert was to be sent to Germany, presumably as an espionage agent, and agreed to complete the reference. When Morros' mother died in 1939, he appealed to the Soviet Embassy to permit his aging father to emigrate to the U.S. This request was almost immediately followed by a visit from Vassili Zubulin, the Second Secretary of the Soviet Embassy in Washington. Zubulin agreed to help, providing Morros reciprocated in the form of signing ten new false recommendations for "talent scouts." Morros once again capitulated and signed the affidavits. Follow-

ing a number of delays, his father emigrated to the U.S. in 1943.

Morros' career advanced to full producer at Paramount. He then branched out into independent music and movie productions. It was at this point, in 1943, after his father had been in the U.S. for two months, that Morros was approached once again by Zubulin, who proposed expanding Morros' business and using it as a "front," presumably for espionage activities. After much consideration, Morros, for his own reasons, felt compelled to accept Zubulin's offer. His businesses became a "front" for Communist espionage. Morros and the people who worked as his agents were to provide the Soviet Union with information ranging from personal lives of leading American politicians to national defense to names of secret American agents abroad.

The Hollywood producer was introduced to Jack Soble, Zubulin's superior, and Jane and George Zlatovski, who were providing U.S. Army information to the Russians. Zlatovski had been commissioned as a lieutenant in the American Army's Counter-Intelligence Corps while Jane had worked for the Office of Strategic Services (O.S.S.) during World War II. They were now both working for the Russians. Apparently deeply troubled about his role in assisting the Soviet espionage network, Morros in 1947 turned himself in to the F.B.I. To his astonishment, he learned that the Bureau already had a file on him. Morros then agreed to become a counterspy.

Lavrenti Beria, the head of the K.G.B., moved Morros to Vienna where the latter went into movie production and began to import Soviet films. While in Vienna, Morros, under instructions from the F.B.I., deliberately began to feed misinformation to the Soviets via George Zlatovski.

When Beria was killed in 1953, his successor, General Serov, warned of Morros' possible duplicity, had the producer carefully watched. In 1956 Morros was apparently marked for liquidation. It was at this point that the F.B.I. decided to arrest Morros' contacts, charging them with espionage. Apparently the only government witness against them was Morros. A grand jury soon issued several indictments which led to long prison terms for many of Morros' fellow agents. Morros was never charged and went on to testify before the House Un-American

Activities Committee. See Soviet Spies in the U.S. ■

Man on a Tightrope (1953). TCF. *Dir.* Elia Kazan; *Sc.* Robert E. Sherwood; *Cast includes:* Fredric March, Terry Moore, Gloria Grahame, Cameron Mitchell, Adolphe Menjou.

A Czechoslovakian circus owner, fed up with Communist bureaucracy and oppression, plots to smuggle his entire enterprise across the Eastern border in this Cold War drama. Fredric March portrays the owner, a peaceful and reticent small-time entrepreneur, who is almost overwhelmed by excessive bureaucratic red tape and is under suspicion by officials. Gloria Grahame, as his cheating wife, loses respect for her weak husband until he organizes the daring escape plan. Terry Moore plays his pretty daughter who has an affair with a migrant hand who is really an American soldier trapped behind the Iron Curtain by an unusual string of events. Adolphe Menjou plays an incompetent state propaganda minister who misjudges the moral character of March. Director Kazan has captured the futility and fear that some Eastern bloc citizens have to face in their daily dealings with their own government. The film, based on the story "International Incident" by Neil Patterson, has the "look" of location work done in Eastern Europe. ■

Man on the Box, The (1925), WB. *Dir.* Charles Riesner; *Sc.* Charles A. Logue; *Cast includes:* Sydney Chaplin, David Butler, Alice Calhoun, Kathleen Calhoun, Theodore Lorch.

Sydney Chaplin, as a rich man's son, becomes entangled in a romantic triangle and an international plot in this farcical comedy. He decides to financially back an airplane invention in which the U.S. government is interested. A representative of a foreign power, who would like to get his hands on the invention, sends one of his spies to steal the plans from the inventor's home. Meanwhile, the inventor (Theodore Lorch) suspects Chaplin of being more interested in his wife (Kathleen Calhoun) than his apparatus. One of the highlights of the film occurs when the suspicious husband returns to find Sydney in the wife's bedroom. The innocent Sydney had been summoned to search for the intruder.

The plot, based on the novel and play by Harold MacGrath and an earlier film version, provides the silent comic, Charlie's brother, with many opportunities to demonstrate his talents, including dressing in drag. He had scored a hit in a similar role in *Charley's Aunt*, released several months earlier. ■

Man Who Knew Too Much, The (1956), Par. *Dir.* Alfred Hitchcock; *Sc.* John Michael Hayes, Angus McPhail; *Cast includes:* James Stewart, Doris Day, Brenda de Banzie, Bernard Miles, Ralph Truman, Daniel Gelin.

An American family becomes entangled in an assassination plot in this suspenseful tale set in colorful Marakesh and then in London. James Stewart, as an American doctor traveling with his wife (Doris Day) and their young son, meets a mysterious stranger who later is mortally wounded in a local marketplace. The man stumbles toward Stewart and whispers to the doctor details of an impending assassination attempt in London before he dies. The couple's son is then kidnapped to prevent Stewart from telling the police what he has learned. Stewart and Day, who learn that the stranger was a British agent, then journey to London in the hope of finding their son.

The trail leads the emotionally distressed parents to Albert Hall, where the killing of a foreign head of state is to occur during a concert performance in his honor. When Day sees the assassin about to fire his pistol, she screams in horror. The gunman fails to kill his victim and falls to his own death. The statesman, who received only a superficial wound, later thanks the Americans for saving his life. Stewart and Day, who believe their son is being held hostage at a foreign minister's embassy, ask him for an invitation for that evening. As planned in advance, Day, who is recognized as a popular American entertainer, sings "Whatever Will Be," hoping that her son will hear her. Stewart hears the boy's whistling and rescues him.

The film, a remake of a Hitchcock thriller of the same title made in England in 1934, presents essentially the same plot but makes several changes designed to update the material and appeal to American audiences. The opening was altered from Switzerland to the more strange and intriguing Morocco. The sequence in Albert Hall remains similar, including the original music of Arthur Benjamin, but the overall tone is treated more lightly. Finally, Doris Day's character was changed to that of a Broadway entertainer so that her singing could play a significant role in her child's rescue. ∎

Man Who Won, The (1919), Vitagraph. *Dir.* Paul Scardon; *Sc.* Edward J. Montague; *Cast includes:* Harry T. Morey, Betty Blythe, Maurice Costello, Bernard Siegel, Robert Gaillard.

The drama, set during World War I, blends a spy plot involving a German agent with a mystery tale. Harry T. Morey, as an adventurer who discovers platinum in Siberia, takes it to Oregon and hides it for government purposes. His Malay crew, however, mutinies and the American is forced to kill them. Betty Blythe, who portrays a vacationer, finds Morey severely wounded and helps him. They later meet but do not recognize each other. Famed stage actor Maurice Costello, as Blythe's villainous fiancé, masquerades as a U.S. Secret Service agent. In reality a German spy, he hopes to discover the location of the hidden platinum. A fight ensues between the two rivals and ends with Morey throwing the spy off a cliff. Blythe appears with a bona fide government agent. The film is based on Cyrus Townsend Brady's 1919 novel. ∎

Man Who Wouldn't Tell, The (1918), Vitagraph. *Dir.* James Young; *Sc.* Bess Meredyth; *Cast includes:* Earle Williams, Grace Darmond.

A World War I drama in an English setting, the film concerns a nest of German spies and members of the British secret service who are on the enemy agents' trail. See British Intelligence: World War I. ∎

Man With One Red Shoe, The (1985), TCF. *Dir.* Stan Dragoti; *Sc.* Robert Klane; *Cast includes:* Tom Hanks, Dabney Coleman, Lori Singer, Charles Durning, Jim Belushi, Carrie Fisher, Ed Hermann.

A spoof of the spy genre, this zany comedy aims its barbs chiefly at the incompetent chiefs of the C.I.A. and its competing intelligence agency, both of which are filled with blundering operatives. When a C.I.A. agent in Morocco allows himself to be set up and arrested as a smuggler, the resultant headlines cause a furor with a U.S. Senate investigating committee. Its members decide to look into C.I.A. activities and request that Ross (Charles Durning), its chief, report for questioning in 72 hours. Ross, to discredit his rival, Cooper (Dabney Coleman), sets a trap for him. Ross assigns his assistant (Ed Hermann) to select anyone arriving at the Washington airport as a supposed contact so that Cooper will expend his resources investigating an innocent person. Hermann dutifully proceeds to the airport and, intrigued by a young man (Tom Hanks) stepping off a plane and wearing one red shoe, selects him as the target.

The remainder of the comedy concerns Cooper's desperate attempts to learn what Hanks knows about the upcoming investigation. This results in a chain of mishaps that befall Hanks, who is an eccentric musician, and Ross' and Cooper's minions. When Hanks makes an innocent appointment with a dentist, Cooper, who has been tapping Hanks' telephone, thinks the musician has microfilm concealed in a tooth. He orders his men to take over the dentist's office and extract all of Hanks' teeth until they find the film. When Hanks decides to leave the office without having any work done, another agent, who has been following him, enters and has his teeth pulled out by other overzealous agents.

The frustrated Cooper next assigns his sexiest agent (Lori Singer) to invite the musician to her apartment and seduce him in an attempt to get Hanks to reveal his alleged connection with the C.I.A. Instead, when the lovemaking begins, Singer gets her hair caught in Hanks' pants zipper. Fascinated by Hanks' erratic behavior, Singer begins to fall in love with him as Cooper and other agents observe all behind a two-way mirror. Following this fiasco, the exasperated Cooper orders Hanks' assassination. However, all the attempts fail as agents of both teams eliminate each other.

U.S. intelligence chiefs and their operatives are attacked mercilessly. "Why don't we just kill him?" a gun-happy agent early in the film suggests, referring to Hanks. "No," Cooper replies, reminding the impatient man about the Senate inquiry. Later, when Ross is finished exploiting Hanks, he orders the musician's assassination. The sensitive and idealist Hermann asks the C.I.A. chief: "Wouldn't it bother you to send an innocent man to his grave?" "Are you serious?" Ross replies. "We're talking about my career." The film ends with Cooper carried off as the crazed head of a conspiracy, Ross replaced by Hermann, and Hanks and Singer continuing their romance. The comedy is a remake of a

1972 French film titled *The Tall Blond Man with One Black Shoe.* ∎

Man Without a Country, The (1925), Fox.

Dir. Rowland V. Lee; *Sc.* Robert N. Lee; *Cast includes:* Edward Hearn, Pauline Starke, Lucy Beaumont, Richard Tucker, Earl Metcalfe, Wilfred Lucas.

The second screen version, also silent, of Edward Everett Hale's tale is more accurate to its original source than the 1917 screen adaptation that used World War I as a framework for the tragic story of Philip Nolan. The later film covers Lieutenant Nolan's naive belief in Aaron Burr's plot against the U.S. government. Nolan (Edward Hearn) is indicted for conspiracy and at the trial utters the words that were to seal his fate: "Damn the United States. I hope that I may never hear of the United States again." He is then given his unusual sentence—to remain at sea for the rest of his life, never to set foot on American soil and never to hear the name of the United States mentioned.

The film covers the incident in which Nolan distinguishes himself in a naval battle with another vessel. Action sequences include Decatur's battle at Algiers and a sea fight with a pirate ship. In the written work he dies alone after fifty years of exile, a forgotten man aboard an American ship. In this film, however, a former sweetheart (Pauline Starke), after several futile appeals to various Presidents, gains a pardon for Nolan from Abraham Lincoln (George Billings). The news reaches Nolan just before his death. As the vessel reaches port, his old flame also dies and the spirits of the two lovers unite as the woman, now transformed by death to her former youth, places an American flag over Nolan's shoulders.

Although the Nolan character is fictitious, the Burr trial was real. Aaron Burr, who served as third Vice-President of the U.S. under Jefferson, later conspired with his friend General James Wilkinson to invade Mexico and set up an independent empire styled after that of Napoleon's. The traitorous American general was actually in the pay of Spain. The two conspirators hoped to incite several western states to secede from the U.S. and join their Mexican venture. But Wilkinson, disturbed by Burr's lack of discretion about the plot, betrayed his friend to President Jefferson. He was arrested and tried before Chief Justice John Marshall in Virginia. However, because Burr was stopped before he had a chance to commit any treasonable act, he was acquitted. ∎

Manchurian Candidate, The (1962), UA.

Dir. John Frankenheimer; *Sc.* George Axelrod, John Frankenheimer; *Cast includes:* Frank Sinatra, Laurence Harvey, Janet Leigh, Angela Lansbury, Henry Silva, James Gregory.

Set during and after the Korean War and based on Richard Condon's novel of political assassination and Cold War paranoia, the film recounts the collective nightmare of a group of former prisoners of war. Frank Sinatra and Laurence Harvey portray army buddies who, along with other captives, have been brainwashed during their internment in a North Korean prison camp. Harvey has been programmed to carry out the assassination of a presidential candidate. When they return to the U.S., Harvey settles in with his mother (Angela Lansbury) and stepfather (James Gregory), a right-wing Senator who is a hired agent of the Soviet Union. The Senator hopes by the assassination to win the office, thereby bestowing upon him "powers that will make martial law seem like anarchy." Harvey's scheming mother, meanwhile, is part of the conspiracy. Sinatra begins to untangle the Chinese Communist plot involving Harvey, who outwardly is an acknowledged war hero. Sinatra stops Harvey at the last moment during a convention at Madison Square Garden.

Frankenheimer's perceptive direction and his and Axelrod's literate screenplay heighten the tension. One especially highly effective scene shows a group of half-sleeping G.I.s seated at a women's club lecture on flowers at a New Jersey hotel. As the camera pans around the hall, the speaker is now transformed into a Chinese expert in mind control. He directs Harvey, one of the G.I.s, to shoot another soldier. Several of Frankenheimer's visual techniques, some of which were quite disorienting for audiences in the 1960s, were unique for their time.

A disturbing drama in many respects, the film had been out of circulation for many years until its rerelease in 1988, when it stirred new interest. It had been pulled from distribution because of a financial dispute between Sinatra and United Artists, the releasing company, and not the result of any conspiracy speculation. The film originally generated mixed reviews and did poorly at the box office. Years later its director was to comment: "It went from failure to classic without ever passing through success."

Its original release anticipated the series of traumatic assassinations which the nation was soon to experience. A plot that had once seemed highly improbable was later seen in a new light. Scenes such as those in the prison camp involving brainwashing of American prisoners that originally appeared as far-fetched had a more chilling effect years later. The possibilities of a single individual, perhaps in the employ or under the influence of a foreign power, killing a national leader and plunging an entire country into political turmoil, unfortunately moved from the realm of fiction to tragic reality with the deaths of President John F. Kennedy, Senator Robert Kennedy and civil rights leader Martin Luther King. In addition, the themes of political corruption and betrayal poignantly dissected an ailing nation before it was fashionable to do so. See Brainwashing. ∎

Mandrake the Magician (1939) serial, Col. *Dir.* Sam Nelson, Norman Deming; *Sc.* Basil Dickey, Joseph F. Poland, Ned Dandy; *Cast includes:* Warren Hull, Doris Weston, Al Kikume, Rex Downing, Edward Earle, Forbes Murray.

A master villain heads a host of secret agents in his efforts to gain possession of a secret invention in this 12-chapter serial based on a popular comic strip created by Lee Falk and Phil Davis. Warren Hull as the title character, a master magician and detective, foils the gang's plans at every turn as he defends the inventor against the theft of his apparatus. Doris Weston, as the inventor's daughter, provides the romantic interest for the magician. Edward Earle portrays the elusive Wasp, the chief culprit who poses as a friend of the inventor's family. ∎

Marathon Man (1976), Par. *Dir.* John Schlesinger; *Sc.* William Goldman; *Cast includes:* Dustin Hoffman, Laurence Olivier, Roy Scheider, William DeVane, Marthe Keller, Fritz Weaver.

A Columbia University graduate student suddenly gets caught up in a maze of international intrigue in this convoluted drama set in the 1970s and based on William Goldman's novel. Dustin Hoffman, as the restless student who lives in New York and enjoys

running, soon finds himself the target of kidnappers who question and torture him for information he doesn't possess. Because his brother had been a member of a nebulous secret government agency, Hoffman is suspected of receiving information from his mortally wounded brother.

His brother (Roy Scheider) secretly works as a courier for the "division," a covert government group that does the C.I.A.'s dirty work. He has kept his work a secret from Hoffman, telling his brother that he is in the oil business in Washington. While on the trail of a Nazi war criminal, Scheider is stabbed and mortally wounded. He stumbles back to his brother's apartment before he dies or has a chance to name his assassin.

Scheider's killer, an elderly Nazi (Laurence Olivier), headed an experimental unit at the Auschwitz concentration camp during World War II. Described as the "wealthiest and most wanted Nazi left alive and hiding out somewhere in Uruguay," Olivier is forced to come to New York City to pick up his cache of diamonds that have been stored for years in a safety deposit box. After killing Scheider, whom he thinks has set a trap for him, he goes after Hoffman, whom he suspects knows about the alleged trap.

William DeVane plays a fellow intelligence agent ostensibly working with Scheider. In reality, he is collaborating with the Nazi. When DeVane realizes that Scheider wants Olivier captured, he plots against Scheider and, later, against Hoffman. In an attempt to find out what Hoffman knows, he explains that Olivier, to protect his own safety, has been cooperating with the "division" by informing on other Nazi war criminals from time to time.

Although the drama remains murky for most of the film, it has some terrifying scenes. These include an attempted strangulation of Scheider by an assassin, Olivier's torturing of Hoffman by drilling into the nerves of his teeth and Hoffman's recapture by his torturers after he thinks he has been rescued by DeVane. Also, betrayal is everywhere, touching all the main characters. DeVane betrays Scheider, Hoffman and Olivier. Marthe Keller, as an innocent-looking Columbia student, is actually in the employ of Olivier to spy on Hoffman.

The film reflects the cynicism toward secret government agencies that dominated many spy movies of the 1970s. DeVane describes the paranoia and competition between the two major U.S. intelligence branches. "When the gap gets too large between what the F.B.I. can handle effectively and what the C.I.A. doesn't want to deal with, that's when we (the "division") come in." Later, he orders Olivier to leave the country. "You're uncontrollable," he points out to the former Nazi. "What you offer us is valuable, but you're not worth the chaos you cause us." The screenplay then underscores the similarities between men like DeVane and Olivier. "I'm just doing my job," he says. "I believe in my country." Olivier stares at the agent in contempt and says, "So did we all." ∎

Mare Nostrum (1926), MGM. *Dir.* Rex Ingram; *Sc.* Willis Goldbeck; *Cast includes:* Alice Terry, Antonio Moreno, Michael Brantford, Fernand Mailly, Hughie Mack.

Based on a novel by Blasco Ibanez, the World War I drama concerns a German spy (Alice Terry) who gains the love of a Spanish sea captain (Antonio Moreno). He abandons all for her. Eventually she meets her end before a firing squad. Her lover dies in a sea battle with a German submarine but manages to get off a final shot from a deck gun which sinks the U-boat. The film, made chiefly in Spain and Italy, includes several effective scenes of submarine warfare that are not too flattering for Germany.

Why MGM would release this type of propaganda film eight years after World War I is not clear. As for Ibanez turning out this material, the motivation is even more obscure, since Spain remained neutral during the war. ∎

Margin for Error (1943), TCF. *Dir.* Otto Preminger; *Sc.* Lillie Hayward; *Cast includes:* Joan Bennett, Milton Berle, Otto Preminger, Carl Esmond, Howard Freeman, Ed McNamara.

Jewish policemen guard a German consulate in New York City in this World War II comedy. Milton Berle plays one of the officers who investigate suspicious events inside the closed doors of the Nazi headquarters, including the murder of a consul (Otto Preminger). Joan Bennett portrays his wife who is forced to stay with the consul to protect her family in German-occupied Europe. She is accused of shooting him. Another suspect is charged with stabbing the consul. To add to the confusion, officials discover that Prem-

Otto Preminger (l.) portrays a German consul stationed in New York City who is found murdered in the World War II comedy *Margin for Error* (1943).

inger had taken poison. The film, based on Clare Booth's Broadway play, is a disappointment as comedy or drama, despite its original idea of having Jewish cops protecting Nazi officials. ∎

Marie Galante (1934), Fox. *Dir.* Henry King; *Sc.* Reginald Berkeley; *Cast includes:* Spencer Tracy, Ketti Gallian, Ned Sparks, Helen Morgan, Siegfried Rumann, Arthur Byron.

Secret service agents from the U.S., England and France are assigned to prevent a saboteur from blowing up the Panama Canal in this drama of intrigue. Since the government agents are working independently, each becomes a suspect in the eyes of the others. Meanwhile Siegfried Rumann, as the villain, almost succeeds in his sinister plot of destruction until he is foiled by Spencer Tracy, who portrays the American agent. French actress Ketti Gallian, as an innocent young Frenchwoman, is shanghaied and abandoned in the Canal Zone where she works in local dives to raise enough money to return to France. She soon becomes enmeshed in Rumann's plot but is saved in time by Tracy, who falls for her. Singer Helen Morgan, as a café entertainer, provides a few songs. Ned Sparks and Stepin Fetchit handle the comic relief. The film was remade in 1940 as *Charlie Chan in Panama*, a World War II mystery-spy drama. ∎

Marines Come Through, The (1943), Astor. *Dir.* Louis Gasnier; *Sc.* D. S. Leslie; *Cast includes:* Wallace Ford, Toby Wing, Grant Withers, Sheila Lynch, Michael Doyle, Don Lanning.

Nazi agents plot to steal the latest model of a secret bombsight in this weak World War II drama. The film features Wallace Ford as the U.S. Marine hero who eventually outwits the enemy spies. Toby Wing provides the romance. The slow-paced film offers few action sequences. ■

Marriage Ring, The (1918), Par. *Dir.* Fred Niblo; *Sc.* R. Cecil Smith; *Cast includes:* Enid Bennett, Robert McKim, Jack Holt, Maude George, Charles K. French, Lydia Knott.

German agents attempt to destroy the sugar plantations of Hawaii in this routine World War I drama distinguished only by its picturesque setting. Enid Bennett portrays the wife of a brutal, alcoholic husband (Robert McKim). He is in league with German spies. When he tries to burn a plantation, he sets himself on fire and plunges off a cliff to his death. Jack Holt plays a plantation owner. Despite its unusual setting for a spy tale, the film exemplifies the genre of the period in its use of propaganda to depict the Germans as vicious and contemptible. ■

Marriages Are Made (1918), Fox. *Dir.* Carl Harbaugh; *Sc.* Raymond L. Schrock; *Cast includes:* Peggy Hyland, Edwin Stanley, George Clarke, Al Lee, Dan Mason, Ellen Cassidy.

A German spy plots to mine an American harbor in this World War I comedy drama. William H. Boyd, as a saboteur who owns a houseboat, invites some innocent guests aboard, including an attractive young woman (Peggy Hyland). Her family wants her to marry an effete playboy (Al Lee), one of the spy's guests. However, she loves another, a man (Edwin Stanley) who has rescued her from drowning. Stanley swims to the houseboat and finds the bombs to be used in mining the port. After a scuffle, the spy forces Hyland into his speedboat and takes off to set the mines. Stanley swims to the shore, places himself on a low bridge and yanks his sweetheart from the speedboat which then hits one of the mines and explodes, killing the spy. See German Intelligence: World War I. ■

Mask of Dimitrios, The (1944), WB. *Dir.* Jean Negulesco; *Sc.* Frank Gruber; *Cast includes:* Peter Lorre, Sydney Greenstreet, Zachary Scott, Faye Emerson, Victor Francen, Eduardo Ciannelli.

Peter Lorre and Sydney Greenstreet brighten this dark tale of murder, espionage and assassination set in pre-World War II Europe. Lorre, a Dutch writer of detective novels, becomes intrigued with the unscrupulous life of Dimitrios (Zachary Scott), an international thief whose body is found washed ashore on a beach in Istanbul. Through a series of interviews with some of Scott's victims whose stories are told in flashbacks, Lorre learns the details of the thief's lurid misdeeds. These include an assassination attempt on the life of a Bulgarian premier, a scheme that results in the theft of a map detailing Yugoslavia's minefields and countless betrayals of some of his collaborators.

Greenstreet, as a convicted smuggler who was betrayed by Scott, discovers that the body found on the shore was not that of Dimitrios but one of his victims. When he learns that Dimitrios is alive and well and living in Paris, Greenstreet, accompanied by Lorre, plans to blackmail his enemy. In a final act of betrayal and greed, the two adversaries kill each other, leaving Lorre to piece together the loose ends of a story he considers fascinating.

Though the film, adapted from Eric Ambler's novel, gets bogged down in too many flashbacks and never defines the motivations behind the malevolence of Dimitrios, its somber atmosphere, exotic settings and colorful characters offer some compensations. A debonair employer of spies (Victor Francen) pays Dimitrios handsomely for copies of the minefield map only to be robbed by him in the end. A minor government clerk (Steven Geray) with a sexually repressed wife is tricked by Dimitrios into stealing the map; the guilt-ridden man eventually takes his own life. A young woman of questionable morals (Faye Emerson) falls for Dimitrios' charms and discovers too late that he has only been using her. Greenstreet, however, towers over the others as a vivid and interesting character consumed by greed and revenge. He finds some solace in quoting aphorisms. "There's not enough kindness in the world," he repeatedly apprises Lorre. He describes a book as "a lovely thing—a garden stocked with beautiful flowers, a magic carpet on which to fly away to unknown climes." He mouths this as he holds a gun on Lorre. ■

Masked Marvel, The (1943) serial, Rep. *Dir.* Spencer Bennet; *Sc.* Royal K. Cole, Ronald Davidson, Basil Dickey, Albert Duffy,

Grant Nelson, George Plympton, Joseph Poland; *Cast includes:* William Forrest, Louise Currie, Johnny Arthur, Rod Bacon, Richard Clarke.

The stalwart and mysterious Masked Marvel battles a Japanese espionage network trying to cripple America's war production in this 12-episode World War II serial. William Forrest, as one of four insurance investigators, slips in and out of his disguise as the masked hero who eventually tracks down the diabolical Sakima (Johnny Arthur), head of the enemy agents. The final showdown between hero and villain is a classic, even for this genre. "Your bullets are all gone," announces Sakima after Forrest empties his weapon during a furious gun battle, "but I have one left." As he moves in to discharge his weapon, the Masked Marvel shoots the master spy. "Did it not occur to your Oriental mind," the masked man retorts, "that I might reload?" The serial was later reedited into a feature-length film for television and retitled *Sakima and the Masked Marvel*. See Serials. ∎

Master Race, The (1944), RKO. *Dir.* Herbert J. Biberman; *Sc.* Herbert J. Biberman; *Cast includes:* George Coulouris, Stanley Ridges, Osa Massen, Carl Esmond, Nancy Gates, Morris Carnovsky.

Nazi leaders begin their strategy for the next war as Allied armies push toward Berlin in this World War II cautionary drama. George Coulouris portrays a high Nazi official and advocate of German supremacy who orders his military staff to go underground and cause turmoil among the liberated nations of Europe until the Nazis are strong enough to rise again. He journeys to an American-occupied Belgian village where he poses as a patriot. He soon starts to spread dissension and unrest among the villagers before he is exposed. A quotation from another war movie, *Till We Meet Again*, released the same year and in which a character prophetically states: "One is never through with the Germans," may well be the theme of this film. See Nazi Subversion: Post-World War II. ∎

Mata Hari (1876–1917). When Greta Garbo affirms in *Mata Hari* (1932): "I am Mata Hari—I am my own master," she was giving an accurate account of the most famous spy of World War I. The name "Mata Hari" is synonymous with the archetypical female espionage agent. Although she was the daughter of a burgher, born in the Netherlands in 1876, she preferred to masquerade as the child of an Indian dancer. Mata Hari further embellished her legend by claiming to have been raised in a Brahman temple presided over by Shiva, the god of evil.

In reality, she was born Margaretha Geertruida Zelle who, at age 18, married a 40-year-old Scottish officer. She moved with her husband, Campbell MacLeod, to Indonesia where he served with the Dutch army. It was probably during this period in her life (1897–1902) that she began to cultivate her Indian alter-ego.

The MacLeods returned to the Netherlands in 1903 whereupon Margaretha obtained a divorce and quickly moved to Paris. There she developed her erotic/religious dancing repertoire. Beginning with vaudeville, Mata Hari, as she was now known, ascended to private performances for individual members of the political and military elites of the Western European community.

The German high command soon discovered her usefulness and trained her as an espionage agent. Mata Hari continued her close, personal contacts with numerous English, French and Russian army officers and transferred her information to her German superior. During World War I Mata Hari, as a citizen of the neutral country of the Netherlands, was able to travel freely between France and Germany. Although the French and Italian secret services suspected her of being a German agent and had compiled a thick dossier on her, they were reluctant to arrest her because of her important connections. Nevertheless, both secret services waited patiently and, in February 1917, they acted; they intercepted a secret German telegram to Mata Hari in Madrid ordering her to return to Paris. French intelligence now felt it had a strong case and arrested her. Incredibly, she was carrying a German check for 15,000 pesetas.

Mata Hari was tried for espionage and shot in October 1917. At the time of her trial there was speculation that her work for the Germans led to the deaths of approximately 60,000 Allied soldiers. Other accounts play down her value as a spy, concluding that she achieved very little in the way of useful military information. Major-General Gemp, who had been with German intelligence during World War I, wrote in 1929 that Mata Hari contributed nothing in her role as spy.

Lobby card showing Greta Garbo, as the infamous German spy Mata Hari, standing trial in a French court where she is convicted of espionage and sentenced to death in the World War I drama *Mata Hari* (1932).

Several highly fictional film biographies, discussed below, recount her espionage and romantic exploits. Although both Greta Garbo and Sylvia Kristel depict the notorious spy as a sympathetic character—caught up in world events not of her making—Garbo offers a more worldly and complex portrayal. Both films highly romanticize the spy's life. In the World War I drama *Stamboul Quest* (1934) Myrna Loy, as a German spy, is depicted as having caused the demise of Mata Hari. ∎

Mata Hari (1932), MGM. Dir. George Fitzmaurice; *Sc.* Benjamin Glazer, Leo Birinski, Doris Anderson, Gilbert Emery; *Cast includes*: Greta Garbo, Ramon Navarro, Lionel Barrymore, Lewis Stone, Henry Gordon, Karen Morley.

Greta Garbo portrays the title character, the notorious World War I German spy who gained a reputation for sleeping with her victims, in this romantic drama set in Paris. The film opens with several ominous hints of foreshadowing. A foreword appears on the screen: "In 1917, war-ridden France dealt summarily with traitors and spies," followed by firing squads disposing of some of France's enemies. Observing the executions are a Russian general (Lionel Barrymore) and the head of the French secret service (C. Henry Gordon) who suspects the exotic dancer Mata Hari of being a German spy. Barrymore scoffs at his companion's suspicions and changes the conversation to the war: "Some dance and some die." "And some do both," the intelligence officer adds.

The remainder of the film focuses on Garbo and her romantic intrigues with Barrymore, whom she soon neglects for a young Russian lieutenant (Ramon Navarro). Garbo's superior (Lewis Stone), the ruthless leader of a spy ring, orders her to obtain secret papers from Navarro. More foreshadowing occurs when Stone, referring to Carlotta, another of his spies, says, "A spy in love is a tool that has outlived its usefulness." As she leaves to carry out her assignment, death crosses her path in the form of the body of Carlotta, carried by two of Stone's henchmen.

Garbo completes her mission but unexpectedly falls in love with the young Russian. She is forced to kill Barrymore when, in a jealous rage, he threatens to denounce her young lover as a traitor. She escapes and reports to Stone, where she learns that Navarro has been wounded. Stone warns her not to see Navarro again. "You can't frighten me," she exclaims. "I'm Mata Hari and my own master." When she leaves, Stone remarks to another agent, "The only way to resign from our profession is to die."

When she discovers that Navarro has lost his sight, Garbo feels that she is partly responsible. She is tried as a German agent and sentenced to face a firing squad. Remorseful over her actions, she lets the blind Russian believe that she is in a hospital preparing for an operation instead of a prison cell awaiting a firing squad. Although the film is based on true incidents, it is very similar to *Dishonored*, another World War I drama released the previous year, in which Marlene Dietrich, as a notorious spy, also places love before duty at the cost of her own life. In both cases the female star dominates the familiar plot. ■

Mata Hari (1985), Cannon. *Dir.* Curtis Harrington; *Sc.* Joel Ziskin; *Cast includes:* Sylvia Kristel, Christopher Cazenove.

Another version of the legendary spy, the film opens in Paris in the spring of 1914 before World War I. Two close friends, one a Frenchman and the other a German officer, meet the beautiful dancer, Mata Hari (Sylvia Kristel), in a museum and both fall in love with her. When war breaks out, the German returns to Berlin and Mata Hari travels by train to Berlin to appear on stage. She is framed for a murder that occurs in one of the railway cars and is forced to spy for Germany. When she returns to Paris, she is arrested as a spy and volunteers her services as a double agent for the French. She becomes involved in a plot to blow up a cathedral filled with important members of the military but disconnects the charge in time. Caught in the act of dismantling the bomb, she is associated with the spies and sentenced to death by a French firing squad. At her trial she admits that whatever she has done, she did for love. A few battle scenes are included, but the bulk of the work focuses on her affairs with different men, including the two friends she met in the museum. ■

May Blossom (1915), Par. *Dir.* Allan Dwan; *Cast includes:* Gertrude Morgan, Russell Bassett, Marshall Neilan, Donald Crisp, Gertrude Robinson.

A conventional romantic drama with a Civil War background, the film concerns May Blossom (Gertrude Morgan), the pretty daughter of a lighthouse keeper, who marries a young man, Richard Ashford, against her father's wishes. The father had another potential husband in mind, Steve Harland, a young fisherman. Ashford is arrested by Union troops as a spy. Harland witnesses the scene but does not tell May, who thinks he has drowned. Harland and May marry. One year later Ashford returns and, when he discovers that May is married, he enlists in the army and dies in battle. The film was adapted from David Belasco's 1884 play. ■

Meet Boston Blackie (1941), Col. *Dir.* Robert Florey; *Sc.* Jay Dratler; *Cast includes:* Chester Morris, Rochelle Hudson, Richard Lane, Charles Wagenheim, Constance Worth, Jack O'Malley.

Chester Morris portrays the reputed safecracker Boston Blackie, a Robin Hood type of character who has been known to work on both sides of the law, in this low-budget drama about a series of murders and a group of spies. When he comes under suspicion by the police, Blackie decides to investigate the murders to clear himself. With the aid of female lead Rochelle Hudson, he not only solves the killings but uncovers a nest of spies.

The title character is based on the fictional creation of Jack Boyle. Blackie first appeared on screen in the World War I drama *The Silk-Lined Burglar* (1919) with Sam De Grasse as the safecracker. Lionel Barrymore portrayed Boston Blackie in *A Face in the Fog* (1922). See Detectives and Spies. ■

Men of the Sky (1931), FN. *Dir.* Alfred E. Green; *Sc.* Otto Harbach, Jerome Kern; *Cast includes:* Irene Delroy, Jack Whiting, Bramwell Fletcher, John St. Polis, Frank McHugh, Edwin Maxwell.

Irene Delroy, as a French spy in this World War I musical drama, falls in love with an American flier (Jack Whiting) during her activities as an undercover agent. But her happiness is short-lived. She, her father (John St. Polis) who countenanced her becoming a spy, and the American are captured and shot by the enemy. One unique note about the film is the father's patriotic prophecy that his daughter was destined to serve France in this capacity. Similar to dozens of other works in the spy genre, the plot calls for few action or war sequences. Screenwriters Jerome Kern and Otto Harbach wrote the songs which include, among others, "Every Little While," "Boys March" and "You Ought to See Sweet Marguerite." ■

Mengele, Josef. In *The Boys From Brazil* (1978) a character describes his adversary as one "who killed 2 1/2 million people, experimented with children—Jewish and non-Jewish—using twins, mostly, injecting blue dyes into their eyes to make them acceptable Aryans, amputating limbs and organs from thousands without anesthetics. . . ." This grotesque description sounds like something lifted from a 1930s grade B horror movie replete with the proverbial mad scientist. Unfortunately for his victims, it is an accurate account of the activities of Josef Mengele, known as the "Angel of Death" to the inmates at Auschwitz. He has come to personify the contemporary scientist-as-madman.

Mengele had studied philosophy and, in the 1920s, was shaped by the radical ideas of Aryan racial superiority as spelled out by Alfred Rosenberg. He received his medical training at the University of Frankfurt, became a Nazi and, upon graduation, joined the research staff of the Institute for Hereditary Biology and Racial Hygiene. He served on the Eastern front and, in 1943, was appointed by Himmler as the principal medical doctor at Auschwitz. Not bound by any orders or conventions and left free by Himmler and Hitler to pursue his racial experiments, Mengele conducted scientific tests on his Jewish prisoners. He usually injected his subjects with viruses and bacteria-carrying diseases. His most infamous experiments involved twins, one of whom was injected with deadly bacteria while the other was the control.

The "Angel of Death" escaped capture at the end of the war, working as a farmhand in Bavaria for four years and then escaping in 1949 through Italy to South America. He moved freely through Brazil, Uruguay and Paraguay, where rumors circulated that he enjoyed an especially close relationship with the President of Paraguay, General Stroessner. Other stories occasionally surfaced that

Mengele continued his medical experiments while living in South America.

He renewed his friendship with an old Nazi, Wolfgang Gerhard, also living in South America. Reports of Mengele's death and interment under Gerhard's name precipitated an international team of forensic experts to journey to Brazil where the investigators determined that the "Angel of Death" had succumbed to a stroke while swimming in 1979.

Few American films, especially spy dramas, have alluded to Mengele and his horrible experiments. Perhaps studio moguls concluded that these subjects were too grisly or too real for audiences who usually came in from the cold expecting a lighter form of entertainment. Or perhaps, as happened immediately after World War I, the public wanted to forget the more horrifying aspects of World War II. Although several explicit documentaries focused on the horrors of the conflict, the handful of dramas that reached the screen did not appear until many years after the war. *The Boys From Brazil*, albeit a flawed drama, presented the most accurate screen portrayal of Mengele (Gregory Peck). The proud, arrogant doctor, still the unrepentant Nazi devoted to his experiments, is seen in his South American jungle laboratory, hiding from the democratic nations seeking to bring him to justice. He is busily obsessed with trying to create a clone of Hitler. In *Marathon Man* (1976), a convoluted drama about international intrigue set in the 1970s, Laurence Olivier plays "The White Angel," a sinister Mengele-like escaped Nazi war criminal who is wanted by several governments for his brutal experiments in Hitler's concentration camps. One haunting scene occurs on the streets of New York where some of his victims, even after 25 years, recognize him as their torturer and try to stop him. See Latin America; Nazi Subversion: Post-World War II. ■

Message of the Mouse, The (1917), Vitagraph. *Dir.* J. Stuart Blackton; *Sc.* Edward J. Montague; *Cast includes:* Anita Stewart, Franklyn Hanna, L. Rogers Lytton, Julia Swayne Gordon, Rudolph Cameron, Robert Gaillard.

A young woman accidentally discovers a secret plot by foreign agents to subvert American defense interests in this little drama set during World War I. Anita Stewart, as the heroine, is about to toss a sheet of paper into a fireplace when she discovers that the heat of the flames has brought out some latent writing. The U.S. Secret Service then takes over and rounds up the spies. Rudolph Cameron portrays a young American agent who falls in love with Stewart. The mouse referred to in the title acts as the inciting force in the plot. The creature playfully carries the encoded paper into the heroine's room. ■

Slovenly Wallace Beery (l.) is assigned to help John Boles, as Lieutenant Andrew Rowan, deliver President McKinley's message to a Cuban general during the Spanish-American War. *A Message to Garcia* (1936).

Message to Garcia, A (1916), K-E-S-E. *Dir.* Richard Ridgely; *Cast includes:* Mabel Trunnelle, Robert Conness, Herbert Prior, Robert Kegereis, Bradley Sutton, Charles Sutton.

Adapted from Elbert Hubbard's popular 1899 essay of the same name, this early silent drama tells about American Lieutenant Rowan's efforts to deliver President McKinley's message of U.S. support to Cuba's insurgent leader Emanuel Garcia. Rowan (Robert Conness) journeys to Cuba where he meets a young woman (Mabel Trunnelle) who sympathizes with the revolution against Spain. She volunteers to help him reach Garcia. When they are halted by Spanish troops, Rowan's pretty guide fires upon the soldiers to give him a chance to escape. The Spaniards kill Trunnelle but fail to prevent the American from accomplishing his mission. Like its remake 20 years later, the film fictionalizes much of Rowan's account. See Andrew S. Rowan. ■

Message to Garcia, A (1936), TCF. *Dir.* George Marshall; *Sc.* Gene Fowler, W. P. Lipscomb; *Cast includes:* Wallace Beery, Barbara

Stanwyck, John Boles, Alan Hale, Herbert Mundin.

A fictional rendition of the experiences of Lieutenant Andrew Rowan in Cuba during the Spanish-American War, the film is based on his book and Elbert Hubbard's popular essay. The drama, which opens after the U.S.S. *Maine* blows up in Havana Harbor, recounts Rowan's assignment to convey President McKinley's message to General Garcia, the leader of the insurgents in Cuba. In essence, the message ensures U.S. support for the revolution against Spain. John Boles, as Rowan, endures a variety of dangers and tortures as he relentlessly journeys through jungle and shark-infested areas. He is captured at one point and tortured by another spy (Alan Hale). Wallace Beery portrays a slovenly, amoral sergeant who reluctantly assists Boles. Barbara Stanwyck seems miscast as the daughter of a Cuban patriot in this disappointing tale. See Andrew S. Rowan. ■

Michael Strogoff (1910), Edison. *Dir.* J. Searle Dawley; *Sc.* J. Searle Dawley; *Cast includes:* Mary Fuller, Charles Ogle.

This silent version of Jules Verne's 1876 novel about a dedicated Russian courier during the Russo-Turkish War (1877–1878) is the earliest known adaptation. It was made at Thomas A. Edison's New York studio. Little is known about the production values although the two leading players became popular screen actors within a few short years. Other film versions of Verne's story were to follow, including *The Soldier and the Lady* (1937). ■

Michael Strogoff (1914), Alco. *Dir.* Lloyd B. Carleton; *Sc.* Benjamin Kotlowsky; *Cast includes:* Jacob J. Adler, Daniel Makarenko, Eleanor Barry, Rosetta Brice, Ormi Hawley, Lloyd B. Carleton.

Based on Jules Verne's novel about a loyal and determined Russian courier during Russia's conflicts with the Tartars (Russo-Turkish War of 1877–1878), the drama features the popular Yiddish stage actor Jacob Adler in the title role. Adler plays Czar Alexander II's personal messenger who is entrusted with secret plans that will defeat the belligerent Tartars in an impending attack. Strogoff begins his assignment disguised as a trader. He meets Nadia (Ormi Hawley), a young woman who is journeying to Siberia where her politically exiled father lives.

Strogoff goes through a series of harrowing experiences, including being blinded by the enemy, before he delivers the important message to the Czar's brother, the Grand Duke, of an imminent Tartar rebellion. The Tartars are severely beaten, and Strogoff marries Nadia, who helped him complete his mission.

The novel underwent many film adaptations during the next two decades, including two silent versions, one French and the other German, as well as a 1937 American sound remake, *The Soldier and the Lady* starring Anton Walbrook, followed by another foreign adaptation in 1960 with Curt Jurgens. ■

Midas Run (1969), Cin. Dir. Alf Kjellin; Sc. James Buchanan, Ronald Austin; *Cast includes:* Richard Crenna, Anne Heywood, Fred Astaire, Ralph Richardson, Cesar Romero, Adolfo Celi.

A disgruntled British secret service agent plots to steal a large shipment of gold bullion in this caper-drama dominated by greed and betrayal. Fred Astaire, as the agent who thinks he has been unfairly passed over for knighthood, organizes the complex heist. He persuades his American crony (Richard Crenna), a war-games and military buff, to join him. Other members of the conspiracy include Astaire's female partner (Anne Heywood), an ex-Italian general and a former Luftwaffe pilot.

However, each member of the gang has his or her own plan for stealing the gold from the others. Even Astaire has an ulterior motive for initiating the heist. He intends to solve the crime, arrest the general who is wanted by the law and thus make himself a hero in the eyes of his superiors. The film ends happily for most of the principals, with Astaire being knighted and Crenna winning Heywood. ■

Midnight Angel (1941). See *Pacific Blackout* (1942). ■

Midnight Taxi (1937), TCF. Dir. Eugene Forde; Sc. Lou Breslow, John Patrick; *Cast includes:* Brian Donlevy, Frances Drake, Alan Dinehart, Sig Rumann, Gilbert Roland, Harold Huber.

Brian Donlevy portrays a U.S. government agent who is assigned to smash a counterfeiting ring in this moderately budgeted, suspenseful drama. He poses as a taxi driver to gain the confidence of the gang. The counterfeiters, to their eventual regret, soon take

Cab driver Harold Huber, a member of a counterfeit gang, points out a problem to his boss in *Midnight Taxi* (1937).

Donlevy into their confidence. They discuss their operations quite openly in his cab. Francis Drake, as a member of the gang, attracts Donlevy's interest. ■

Million Dollar Mystery (1914) serial, Thanhouser. Dir. Howard Hansell; Sc. Lloyd B. Lonegan; *Cast includes:* Albert Norton, Florence La Badie, Sidney Bracey, Marguerite Snow, James Cruze.

An early silent serial, the plot concerns a secret society of Russian millionaires, foreign spies and a heroine who as a child had been left on the doorstep of a private school. Stanley Hargraves (Albert Norton), a member of the society which calls itself the Black Hundred, places his young daughter on the doorstep of a school and leaves a note promising to reward the headmistress for caring for the child. Years later, Hargrave is recognized by two spies who follow him home. He escapes his pursuers with a balloonist friend whom he signals from his roof. Meanwhile, his daughter has grown into an attractive young woman (Florence La Badie) who is asked to come to Hargrave's home. The serial continues with convoluted plot twists and the appearance of other characters. A woman spy is sent to the home to gain the daughter's confidence; attempts are made to kidnap the young woman; a young reporter who is investigating the strange circumstances grows fond of La Badie. James Cruze, who portrays the hero-reporter, became a major Hollywood director of silent and sound films. ■

"Miniature, The" (1910), Edison. (No other credits.)

A short historical drama concerning a conspiracy to kill Andrew Jackson who is a presidential candidate, the film takes many liberties with actual events. Jackson's enemies plot to embroil him into a duel by spreading stories about his wife. When he is informed of this, he accepts the challenge and meets his opponent for a pistol duel. The man fires first, causing Jackson to stagger slightly. Then the candidate returns the volley and kills his opponent. It seems that Jackson was wearing a breastplate which saved his life. The title refers to a miniature portrait of Jackson's wife which he takes with him and places next to his heart. ∎

Ministry of Fear (1944), Par. *Dir.* Fritz Lang; *Sc.* Seton I. Miller; *Cast includes:* Ray Milland, Marjorie Reynolds, Carl Esmond, Hillary Brooke, Dan Duryea, Alan Napier, Percy Waram.

Based on a novel by Graham Greene, this World War II drama set in England stars Ray Milland as Stephen Neale, who has recently been released from an asylum. He had been wrongfully confined for several years for the mercy killing of his wife who was suffering from an incurable illness and who had taken her own life. On his way to London, Neale stops at a local carnival while waiting for his train to arrive. He innocently gets involved with a network of spies when he wins a cake at a raffle. He eventually discovers that a capsule of microfilm has been embedded in the cake. The spies have been transmitting military secrets to Germany.

The agents are using a seemingly worthy organization, "Mothers of the Free Nations," run by an Austrian refugee, as their front. Neale, by investigating this group, becomes involved in a mysterious séance and a murder before he eventually exposes the entire gang. He falls in love with the leader's sister (Marjorie Reynolds) who is not a member of the spy ring. She voices the fears and anxieties of the victims of Nazism when she learns that the enemy has infiltrated the charity organization. "They're Nazis, I know it," she says to her brother. "The same as they were in Austria. It's the way they work—all around you—knowing about everybody and everything. They're here in London."

Fritz Lang, a German expatriate-director known for his expressionistic films in his native country, incorporates several elements of this style in *Ministry of Fear.* There are close-ups of dark clocks, high-angle shots of men-

acing iron doors and sound effects that hint at danger for Neale. Lang is also known for his *film noir* work in the U.S. Intrigue, paranoia and deception dominate the film. Many of the scenes take place at night or in dimly lit rooms. Characters often are not what they seem to be—an innocent blind man turns out to be an assassin; an affable and elderly bookseller transports bombs in suitcases; a fashionable tailor sews capsules of microfilm into the shoulders of suits. The hero becomes a helpless victim. Neale, at one point, echoes one of the essential characteristics of *film noir* when he says: "I wonder if you know what it means to stand all alone in a dark corner." ∎

Miss Jackie of the Army (1917), Mutual. *Dir.* Lloyd Ingraham; *Sc.* Chester Blinn Clapp; *Cast includes:* Marguerita Fischer, Jack Mower, L. C. Shumway, Hal Clements.

Miss Jackie, the daughter of an army colonel, is in love with her father's aide, Lieutenant Adair. One night she hears someone in her father's parlor. Thinking it is her officer, she investigates. But the intruder is a spy. She learns that he is involved in a plot to blow up a train carrying military officers. There are some earlier scenes in which Miss Jackie organizes several of her female acquaintances into an unofficial young women's military auxiliary until her father puts an end to the project. This was the second in a series of "Miss Jackie" films, the first being *Miss Jackie of the Navy* (1916). ∎

Miss V From Moscow (1942), PRC. *Dir.* Albert Herman; *Sc.* Arthur St. Claire, Sherman Lowe; *Cast includes:* Lola Lane, Noel Madison, Howard Banks, Paul Weigel, John Wosper, Anna Demetrio.

A Russian agent (Lola Lane) is sent to Nazi-occupied Paris to pose as a German spy whom she happens to resemble. Her mission in this World War II drama is to learn the whereabouts of enemy submarines that have been preying upon Allied supply ships. Working closely with the French underground, she is able to deceive the German high command long enough to gather the vital information and, with the help of an American agent, escape to Russia. The drama, a variation of the frequently filmed Oppenheim novel *The Great Impersonation,* relies at times too heavily on stock footage for its action sequences. This is especially evident in the shots of a convoy of American merchant ships engaged in a deadly battle on its way to Russia. ∎

Modern Youth (1926), Sun. *Dir.* Jack Nelson; *Cast includes:* Gene Corrado, Olive Kirby, Rhea Mitchell, Alma Rayford, Joseph Girard.

An agent of the U.S. Secret Service becomes involved in the intrigue of a fictitious Central American republic in this inept drama. Gene Corrado, as an ex-French army captain who has seen action in World War I, yearns to travel, relax and put the violence behind him. However, he soon discovers that the leisurely life is not for him. He volunteers to work for the U.S. as a special agent. Assigned to the mythical republic of Centralia, he soon uncovers a plot to overthrow the current president. Corrado also effects the rescue of the heroine who is held captive by the plotters. ∎

Mollycoddle, The (1920), UA. *Dir.* Victor Fleming; *Sc.* Tom Garaghty, Douglas Fairbanks; *Cast includes:* Douglas Fairbanks, Ruth Renick, Betty Boulton, Wallace Beery, George Stewart.

A better-than-average Douglas Fairbanks vehicle, this comedy adventure features the acrobatic star as a foppish character who is transformed into a hero by the Arizona desert and his affection for the heroine. Fairbanks portrays a pampered gentleman who is mistaken for a U.S. Secret Service agent by a smuggler (Wallace Beery). This mistaken identity helps to save our hero's life. In reality, the heroine (Ruth Renick) is the spy assigned to get evidence against the smuggling operation. Beery later holds Renick prisoner. Fairbanks sheds his "mollycoddle" image with his resourceful and daring rescue of his loved one and the capture of the chief villain. ∎

Moon Pilot (1962), Buena Vista. *Dir.* James Neilson; *Sc.* Maurice Tombragel; *Cast includes:* Tom Tryon, Brian Keith, Edmond O'Brien, Dany Saval, Bob Sweeney, Kent Smith.

A U.S. government security agent suspects a shapely visitor from another planet of being a spy in this Walt Disney production which spoofs the country's obsession with the space race. Tom Tryon, as a reluctant astronaut, is given a three-day pass before his journey to the moon and is commanded not to reveal his mission. Dany Saval, as the attractive space alien, becomes romantically involved with Tryon. Edmond O'Brien portrays a frazzled security agent who follows Tryon to make certain he does not divulge any information. Brian Keith, as a pompous U.S. Air Force general, adds to the comedy of this witty tale. ∎

Morgan, John Hunt (1825–1864). A Confederate general, he became famous for his raids during the Civil War. Operating chiefly behind Union lines, he and his raiders captured a Northern Garrison in Huntsville, Alabama, in 1862. He was rapidly promoted to brigadier general. He was captured by the Union on one of his forays later that year but managed to escape. Morgan, in his zeal to gain military intelligence about the enemy, had often penetrated Union lines disguised as a farmer, Northern officer or drover. Transferred to a different command, he was killed in action in Greenville, Tennessee.

His daring exploits into enemy territory made exciting screen material. *The Chest of Fortune*, released in 1914 by Kalem, was the first to appear. It portrayed Morgan and his raiders as cold-blooded murderers who butcher a Northern officer and his family. Other action melodramas include *Morgan's Raiders* (1918), *The Little Shepherd of Kingdom Come* (1920) and *Morgan's Last Raid* (1929) although the figure of Morgan was never the main character. ∎

Morgan's Last Raid (1929), MGM. *Dir.* Nick Grinde; *Sc.* Bradley King, Harry Braxton; *Cast includes:* Tim McCoy, Dorothy Sebastian, Wheeler Oakman, Allan Garcia, Hank Mann.

Tim McCoy portrays a Southern captain who decides not to take up arms against Tennessee, his home state, when it secedes from the Union. Dorothy Sebastian, as the young woman he loves, accuses him of being a traitor. Later, he joins John Morgan and his raiders, a unit of the Confederates. During one of their raids, McCoy rescues Sebastian who, of course, forgives him. The film was one of four westerns McCoy made for MGM before he moved on to other studios where he became a popular cowboy star. ∎

Morgan's Raiders (1918), Bluebird. *Dir.* Wilfred Lucas; *Sc.* Bess Meredyth; *Cast includes:* Violet Mersereau, Edward Burns, Barbara Gilroy, Frank Holland.

In this Civil War drama a young Southern belle falls in love with a Union captain. With the outbreak of the war the girl's father joins John Morgan and his Confederate raiders. When a messenger is shot and killed, Morgan asks for a volunteer to take the dead soldier's place. The girl volunteers and, dressed in men's clothing, carries the message across Union lines. Later in the film she is captured and eventually rescued by Morgan's raiders. At the end of the drama she is reunited with her lover from the North. ■

Moritori (1965), TCF. *Dir.* Bernhard Wicki; *Sc.* Daniel Taradash; *Cast includes:* Marlon Brando, Yul Brynner, Janet Margolin, Trevor Howard, Wally Cox, William Redfield.

This World War II drama, based on the novel by Werne Joerg Luedecke, concerns a German freighter that is carrying vital crude rubber. The Nazis desperately need the cargo which the British prefer to capture before the captain can destroy it. British intelligence agents blackmail a German Jew (Marlon Brando) into working for them. He is forced into accepting the assignment as an alternative to being returned to the Nazis. His job is to disconnect any fuses designed to blow up the valuable rubber in the event that there is any danger of the ship's being captured. The German captain (Yul Brynner) suspects that Brando is a Gestapo agent placed on board the ship to spy on him. Brynner, who is apolitical, has grown disillusioned with the Nazis, especially after his son is killed in battle. Janet Margolin plays a Jewish refugee-prisoner placed aboard the freighter after she has been used sexually by Nazi officers in a concentration camp.

Like so many internationally financed films with a World War II background released after the conflict, the drama blurs the line between hero and villain. Only several years earlier, it would have been unthinkable to place the British in the role of blackmailer and tormentor of a lone Jewish refugee trying to escape the horrors of Nazism. The conflict between the Allies and Nazis is relegated to a minor role. The film tampers with World War II history and events, turning military leaders into objects of derision and Germans into innocent, misguided or disillusioned pawns of

their leaders. One of the German officers aboard the ship, for example, joins Brando and several crew members—political prisoners—in an aborted takeover of the vessel. Brynner displays compassion for the prisoners placed in his charge. "All wars are idiotic," Brando says to Margolin, expressing his own bitterness and isolation as he tries to stay alive. "I don't care who wins." ■

Morros, Boris. See *Man on a String* (1960). ■

Mosby, John Singleton (1833–1916). A Virginia lawyer and Confederate partisan leader during the American Civil War, he led his Mosby's Raiders against Union cavalry, supply trains and communications. Appointed by Gen. J. E. B. Stuart as a reconnaissance officer, Mosby continually supplied military intelligence to Southern generals, including information that led directly to Gen. Thomas "Stonewall" Jackson's victory in 1862 at Cedar Mountain. His most notable achievement was the capture of Union General Edwin Stoughton behind Union lines at Fairfax Courthouse in 1863. The daring leader, who had at one time won the sincere admiration of his chief enemy, General Grant, later served as U.S. consul in Hong Kong from 1878 to 1885. He also served with the Justice Department from 1904 to 1910 as an assistant attorney.

His wartime exploits appeared on film as early as 1909 in "The Old Soldier's Story." In 1910 77-year-old Mosby played himself in "All's Fair in Love and War." The plot concerned his daughter's activities as a Confederate spy although she was allegedly wed to a Union officer at the time. The film was remade in 1913 as "The Pride of the South," a Broncho release with Joseph King in the role of Mosby. ■

Mossad. The name "Mossad"—the agency responsible for gathering and analyzing information and retaliating against Israel's enemies—is used as a general term to cover Israeli intelligence. Actually, there are several Israeli intelligence agencies; Mossad is but one of them. The Shin Bet is responsible for internal security. Military Intelligence is another agency. At times, these organizations, like bureaucracies in other countries, have not coordinated their actions and have been at odds with each other; for the most part, however, they have pooled their resources for the common goal.

These security agencies share a common birth that goes back to the days before the birth of the modern-day State of Israel. The common denominator of all three organizations was the Hagannah, the Jewish underground army in the days of the British mandate over Palestine. Sherut Yediot, later known as Shai, was the intelligence unit of the Hagannah. Its agents penetrated into the British military and civilian organization and various Arab institutions as well as competing Jewish organizations. The Palmach was the elite military section of the Hagannah which was rushed throughout the country to meet any emergency. The organization responsible for purchasing arms anywhere in the world was known as Rekesh while Mossad le-Aliyah Bet was established for smuggling immigrants illegally into Palestine. Some of Rekesh's activities are dramatized in Otto Preminger's *Exodus* (1960), a fictionalized history of Israel's War of Independence. The latter organization's operations are touched upon both in *Exodus* and in George Sherman's *Sword in the Desert* (1949), about Jewish refugees from Europe being smuggled into Palestine.

In 1948 there were a number of Jewish groups in Palestine fighting the British and the Arabs. The Hagannah was the official military arm of the Jewish agency; it was largely composed of Socialists and some Communists who wanted to ease the British out of Palestine; Ben Gurion was its chief. Menachem Begin led the conservative Irgun Zevai Leumi which resorted to terrorist attacks on British troops while the Stern gang was on the far right. Even as the British army was leaving Palestine and the Arab armies began their invasion, the three organizations were engaged in an internecine jockeying for power. Again, this is illustrated in *Exodus*.

The "Lavon Affair," a major intelligence scandal in Israel in the early 1950s, has never been fully explained. Contrary to a major tenet of Israeli intelligence not to involve Jews resident in foreign countries as agents, a number of Egyptian Jews were recruited. They bombed several British and American properties in Egypt, hoping to deceive these countries into believing that Arab extremists were responsible. The Egyptian conspirators were caught; two were sentenced to death, two given life imprisonment and the others

sentenced from three to 15 years. An immediate investigation was launched in Israel. Pinchas Lavon, the Minister of Defense, denied ever approving the operation. The investigating panel, however, rejected his assertions and fixed responsibility on Lavon.

Attaining Krushchev's secret 1956 speech attacking Stalin was a more successful operation of Israeli intelligence. The British S.I.S. and the American C.I.A. learned of Krushchev's speech and were offering vast sums of money throughout Eastern Europe for a copy. The Mossad had but one "mole" inside the vast Soviet government apparatus who was to be activated only in cases of dire emergency. Isser Harel, the chief of Mossad, decided to use the "mole" at this time. The secret operative obtained an unauthorized copy of Krushchev's speech from a member of an Eastern European embassy who mailed it back home through his diplomatic pouch. The copy cost the Mossad a nominal $5,000. Isser Harel personally flew the text to James Angleton, a C.I.A. official, in Washington. The C.I.A., in exchange for this plum, agreed to share data on the Arab world with the Israelis. Essentially, the agreement moved the C.I.A. from the Arab side to a pro-Israeli position.

President Nasser of Egypt, on July 21, 1962, announced the launching of Egyptian-made rockets. The Mossad soon discovered that German scientists had developed these rockets for the Egyptians and were also engaged in the manufacture of a low-grade atomic bomb. The Israelis began a campaign of intimidation against these scientists, both in Europe and in Egypt. Letter bombs killed several men while direct assassination eliminated others. Eventually the remaining Germans got the message and abandoned Egypt as well as the rocket and atomic bomb projects.

The Six-Day War in 1967 owed its success to the espionage efforts of a number of intelligence operatives. Elie Cohen was an Egyptian Jew who had emigrated to Israel. The Mossad decided to infiltrate Cohen into Syria. He first moved into the Syrian community in Argentina, where he posed as a wealthy Syrian businessman. He then was able to successfully transfer to Syria where he infiltrated the top level of the Ba'ath Party. Cohen was shown Syrian fortifications along the Golan Heights facing Israel. His suggestion to a Syrian commander of planting trees in order to provide shade for soldiers guarding army positions was accepted; the trees were later used by the Israeli Air Force as markers in pinpoint bombing of the Syrian positions. Cohen was caught and hanged in 1965 by the Syrians.

A mysterious telephone call to the Israeli embassy in Paris in 1964 opened one of the most profitable episodes in the history of Israeli military intelligence. A Christian squadron leader, Munir Redfa, whose family was being financially ruined by the Moslem government and who saw the bleak future for all Christians in Iraq, offered to fly a MIG 21 out of the country in exchange for the evacuation of his family and 500,000 British pounds. Israeli intelligence quickly agreed. On August 15, 1966, Redfa flew his plane to Turkey where he was met by American Phantoms and escorted to Israel; his large family was simultaneously moved through Kurdistan into Turkey. Israel provided the C.I.A. with full access to the Soviet's most advanced fighter aircraft, and an amazing intelligence coup was scored.

Israeli intelligence integrated the technical knowledge gained by an analysis of the MIG 21 into its defense system in in the Six-Day War. Israeli agents had been previously disbursed as laborers to various Egyptian airfields. These operatives discovered two weak links in the Egyptian air defense system: Egyptian radar faced Israel in the north but did not cover hostile aircraft approaching from the Mediterranean; also, there was a hiatus in personnel coverage between 7:30 and 7:45 a.m. The night crews' shift had ended and they were tired; the day crews were just about finished eating breakfast and were starting to wander over to their aircraft. At precisely 7:30 a.m. on June 5, 1967, the Israeli Air Force swept in from the Mediterranean and, in three hours, destroyed 16 Egyptian airfields with all aircraft on the ground. In addition, the Israelis simultaneously wrecked the Jordanian and Syrian air forces as well.

To rub salt in Egyptian wounds, the Mossad taped a telephone conversation on a supposedly top-security line between President Nasser and King Hussein of Jordan in which the Egyptian suggested blaming the Israeli victory on American pilots. The Mossad subsequently released the tapes.

Numerous books have been written about the Israeli raid on the Entebbe Airport in Uganda, the bombing of the Iraqi nuclear plant at Osirik and the Mossad response to the P.L.O. murders of Israeli athletes at Munich. However, only a few American films mention the Mossad.

Plots involving agents of the Mossad focus on intrigue, terrorism and action, sometimes adding flair and suspense to a weak plot. In the comedy *The Nasty Rabbit* (1965) about a Soviet plot to release a deadly bacteria in the U.S., secret agents from Israel, Japan, Mexico and Germany pursue Mischa Terr as the chief Soviet spy. Cliff Gorman portrays an Israeli secret agent in *Rosebud* (1975), a bland drama about five rich young girls held captive by P.L.O. terrorists. In *Black Sunday* (1977) Robert Shaw, as an Israeli agent, accidentally discovers part of a terrorist plan to carry out a mass slaughter of the Super Bowl stadium audience. He links up with F.B.I. agents to prevent the impending disaster. Diane Keaton in *The Little Drummer Girl* (1984) portrays a pro-Palestinian English actress who is persuaded by the Mossad to act as an Israeli spy.

As with women spies in other American films, female members of the Mossad are often minor characters. In *Hell's Bloody Devils* (1970), an inane drama about a group of neo-Nazis, Vicki Volante, as an Israeli agent, has become the mistress of the Nazi leader (Kent Taylor) in the hope that he will lead her to her parents' murderer. Alberta Watson, as an Israeli secret agent in *The Soldier* (1982), provides some romantic interest for hero Ken Wahl. The bland plot concerns Soviet agents, posing as terrorists, threatening to blow up half the world's supply of Middle East crude oil unless the Israelis pull out of the West Bank.

Occasionally Americans are portrayed as naive dabblers in the intrigues of the Middle East while the Israelis are depicted as the more knowledgeable. *Death Before Dishonor* (1987), for example, concerns a gung-ho U.S. Marine sergeant battling an extremist Arab terrorist group operating in the Middle East. Following a succession of blunders on his part, Mossad agents invite him to join them in a raid on the terrorist headquarters. The film also provides an opportunity for a Mossad leader to interject a wry comment. "These rebels," the leader enlightens the American sergeant, "are not a rag-tag army. What the Russians didn't give them, you probably sold them." ∎

Mothers of Men (1920), Rep. *Dir.* Edward Jose; *Sc.* Henry Warner, De Witte Kaplan; *Cast includes:* Claire Whitney, Lumsden Hare, Gaston Glass, Martha Mansfield, Hal Reid, Mrs. Hal Reid.

Of French and Austrian heritage, a young woman (Claire Whitney) is raised in Vienna where she is seduced by an Austrian officer in this World War I drama. She moves to France and stays with relatives. After the war breaks out, she discovers that the officer is a guest in her relative's home. When he threatens to expose her unless she steals military plans for him, she kills him. All ends happily when she marries a young Frenchman. ■

Mr. Billings Spends His Dime (1923), Par. *Dir.* Wesley Ruggles; *Sc.* A. S. LeVine; *Cast includes:* Walter Hiers, Jacqueline Logan, George Fawcett, Robert McKim, Patricia Palmer.

Conspirators seeking to gain control of a Central American country make the error of hiring an incompetent American as their spy in this comedy of intrigue. Walter Hiers portrays a daydreaming American who falls in love with the daughter of the president of a small Central American country. Hiers has seen her picture but once and can only dream about meeting her. Circumstances afford him the opportunity to visit that foreign land. He meets the conspirators (George Fawcett and Robert McKim) aboard a steamer and agrees to act as their agent. Unknowingly, he manages to foil the traitors' plans to oust the president and take over the republic. His accidental heroic acts win for him the affection of the president's daughter (Jacqueline Logan). ■

Mr. Dynamite (1941), U. *Dir.* John Rawlins; *Sc.* Stanley Crea Rubin; *Cast includes:* Lloyd Nolan, Irene Hervey, J. Carrol Naish, Robert Armstrong, Ann Gillis, Frank Gaby.

Spies plan to blow up a munitions plant in this drama set before America's entry into World War II. Lloyd Nolan, as a famous baseball pitcher visiting a New York amusement park, meets Irene Hervey, who is employed at a concession. He suddenly becomes entangled in a murder. Helping the girl to escape from the police, he learns that she is a British agent. The man who was killed had given her information about a sabotage plot involving a munitions factory. The couple then start out to expose the spy network while at the same time eluding the police. They receive some

help from teenager Ann Gillis. The enemy agents had been using a ventriloquist act to send their messages. The film was adapted from Dashiell Hammett's story "On the Make." ■

Mr. Grex of Monte Carlo (1915), Par. *Dir.* Frank Reicher; *Sc.* Marion Fairfax; *Cast includes:* Theodore Roberts, Dorothy Davenport, Carlyle Blackwell, James Neill, Horace B. Carpenter, Frank Elliott.

A member of the British secret service and an American visitor to Monte Carlo join forces to foil a Russian diplomat's plot to cause political problems for England in this drama of intrigue and impersonation. Theodore Roberts, as the Russian Grand Duke Augustus Peter and diplomat for his country, poses as Mr. Grex, a typical gambler. His purpose is to negotiate a secret treaty which will link France and Germany to Russia, thereby isolating England. He plans to sign the papers with his conspirators in Monte Carlo. Carlyle Blackwell, as a wealthy American and friend of the British secret agent (Frank Elliott), is attracted to Feodora (Dorothy Davenport), the conspiring Russian diplomat's daughter. Elliott, to divert attention from himself, directs the conspirators' suspicions toward the American. Then the two friends prevent the treaty from being signed. The film ends with Blackwell abducting Feodora aboard his yacht and marrying her in international waters.

The film is based on the 1915 novel by E. Phillips Oppenheim, who gained greater recognition for his popular spy novel *The Great Impersonation*, which underwent three screen adaptations in as many decades. ■

Mr. Logan, U.S.A. (1918), Victory. *Dir.* Lynn Reynolds; *Sc.* Lynn Reynolds; *Cast includes:* Tom Mix, Kathleen Connors, Dick La Reno, Val Paul, Charles Le Moyne, Jack W. Dill.

Tom Mix stars as the title character, a government agent assigned to investigate turmoil at a tungsten mine, in this World War I drama. He discovers that German agents have gained control of key positions in the running of the mines and have manipulated the workers into calling a strike. Since tungsten is important to the war effort, Mix ends the strike and rounds up the enemy conspirators with lightning speed, although he is blocked by several obstacles before he can accomplish

Lobby card for *Mr. Moto Takes a Chance* (1938), with Peter Lorre as Mr. Moto, Robert Kent, Rochelle Hudson and J. Edward Bromberg joining forces to prevent a fanatic from fomenting a holy war against white people.

these feats. Our hero performs some of his usual stunting as he rides his horse up and down staircases, uses his lasso with expertise and chases after an automobile in which the chief villain has taken flight with the heroine. Kathleen Connors portrays the daughter of a mine foreman. See U.S. Intelligence: World War I. ■

Mr. Moto Takes a Chance (1938), TCF. *Dir.* Norman Foster; *Sc.* Lou Breslow, John Patrick; *Cast includes:* Peter Lorre, Rochelle Hudson, Robert Kent, J. Edward Bromberg, Chick Chandler, George Regas.

The Japanese detective Mr. Moto joins forces with a secret agent to foil the plans of a fanatical priest somewhere in Southeast Asia. The demented holy man intends to kill all white people in the region. Peter Lorre portrays the international sleuth who poses as an archaeologist in an effort to uncover the priest's operations. He eventually discovers a secret cave where the priest has stored his ammunition. Rochelle Hudson portrays the

special agent assigned to the same case. George Regas plays the chief villain. Robert Kent provides the romance for Hudson while Chick Chandler supplies some comic relief in this otherwise bland drama. ■

Mr. Moto's Last Warning (1939), TCF. *Dir.* Norman Foster; *Sc.* Philip MacDonald, Norman Foster; *Cast includes:* Peter Lorre, Ricardo Cortez, Virginia Field, John Carradine, George Sanders, Joan Carol.

An international spy ring plots to disrupt British and French influence in the Middle East in this suspenseful drama set in preWorld War II Egypt. Peter Lorre, as the famous Japanese detective Mr. Moto, is employed by the International Police to uncover the conspiracy. He masquerades as a shopkeeper while he investigates the activities of the spies. After narrowly escaping death several times, he manages to prevent the villains from carrying out their plans. Ricardo Cortez, as head of the spy network, plots to destroy the French Fleet as it sails toward Port Said—

until Lorre intervenes. John Carradine portrays a secret service agent. The film is one of the better entries in this detective series. ■

Mrs. Pollifax—Spy (1971), UA. *Dir.* Leslie Martinson; *Sc.* C. A. McKnight; *Cast includes:* Rosalind Russell, Darren McGavin, Nehemiah Persoff, Harry Gould, Albert Paulsen, John Beck.

Rosalind Russell, as a widow who volunteers to serve as a spy for her country, soon finds herself a captive of Communist agents in this anemic spy spoof. The film begins with Russell's sauntering into C.I.A. quarters to offer her services. "I have no ties and am expendable and am ready to die for my country," she announces matter-of-factly. Initially treated as an eccentric, she is then chosen by some bureaucrat as a possible undercover agent to pose as a traveler. She is assigned to Mexico where she is to secure some microfilm also coveted by Chinese Communists.

Her first assignment, however, does not go smoothly. She and another C.I.A agent (Darren McGavin) are kidnapped and taken to Albania where her fellow agent is tortured. The resolute neophyte spy, meanwhile, remains optimistic regardless of their hopeless predicament. Applying her feminine qualities, Russell charms her captors into freeing her and McGavin. The film has a few chase sequences, but it chiefly remains a rather static tale with little comedy.

Although the plot is pure fiction, there is some plausibility to the method in which Mrs. Pollifax is hired. Called "walk-ins" in intelligence parlance, these volunteers on occasion are accepted by espionage agencies like the C.I.A. However, walk-ins who receive preferred treatment are those from other countries who have information of value. Ironically, one valuable walk-in during World War II, Dr. Fritz Kolbe, a German foreign ministry official, was rejected by British intelligence as a possible double agent. Kolbe, a professed anti-Nazi, was determined to turn over his large stack of copies of secret documents and telegrams to the British. He handed them to the Americans, instead, and soon proved to be one of the most useful secret agents ever to fall into the hands of American intelligence. One of the most important cases of a walk-in involved Igor Gouzenko, an agent working as a cipher clerk in the Soviet embassy in Canada in 1945. He eventually exposed an entire Soviet spy network operating in Canada. See Igor Gouzenko. ■

Mrs. Slacker (1918), Pathé. *Dir.* Hobart Henley; *Sc.* Agnes Johnston; *Cast includes:* Gladys Hulette, Creighton Hale, Paul Clerget, Walter Hiers.

A minor World War I drama, the film concerns a cowardly young man who rushes into marriage with his fiancée, a local laundress, to keep out of the draft once the U.S. enters the war. When the wife (Gladys Hulette) learns of her husband's real reason for the hasty marriage, she insists that she will not be known as "Mrs. Slacker." She is determined to set an example for her spineless husband (Creighton Hale). An opportunity presents itself when German agents plot to destroy a nearby reservoir. When she foils their plans, her embarrassed husband enlists in the army.

This was just another of numerous patriotic films of the period that helped to encourage enlistments and singled out the "slackers" as cowards. The plot to sabotage the reservoir was not too far-fetched; German spies planned and carried out several similar acts of sabotage in the U.S. during the war. See German Intelligence: World War I. ■

Murder in the Air (1940), WB. *Dir.* Lewis Seiler; *Sc.* Raymond Schrock; *Cast includes:* Ronald Reagan, John Litel, Lya Lys, James Stephenson, Eddie Foy, Jr., Robert Warwick.

A U.S. government agent goes under cover as a spy and joins a dangerous gang of saboteurs in this routine World War II drama. Ronald Reagan portrays "Brass" Bancroft, the heroic agent who puts his life on the line so that he can expose the sinister group. The plot concerns a newly developed secret weapon known as an inertia projector, a device capable of destroying planes in the air. The saboteurs destroy a navy blimp before they are finally rounded up. James Stephenson plays the leader of the culprits. Eddie Foy, Jr., as Reagan's comic sidekick, acts as his sole contact with other agents. Lya Lys, as another espionage agent, provides the feminine interest. John Litel portrays the F.B.I. chief. This was the last in the "Brass" Bancroft series with Ronald Reagan.

Made before America's entry into World War II, and adapted from "Uncle Sam Awakens," a story by Raymond Schrock, the film includes a treatise on the clever tactics used by spies. These propaganda elements extend to a fictitious sequence concerning a "Rice Committee," apparently based on the real-life Dies hearings. Martin Dies, the chairman of the House Un-American Activities Committee (H.U.A.C.), early on discovered the public relations value of investigating Hollywood stars and writers. Dies was thoroughly anti-Communist as well as anti-New Deal. He used the Communist menace in an attempt to discredit President Franklin Roosevelt's social policies, interchanging the terms "New Dealers" and "Communists." See "Brass" Bancroft; House Un-American Activities Committee. ∎

Murder in the Fleet (1935), MGM. *Dir.* Edward Sedgwick; *Sc.* Frank Wead, Joe Sherman; *Cast includes:* Robert Taylor, Jean Parker, Ted Healy, Una Merkel, Nat Pendleton, Jean Hersholt.

The U.S. Navy is threatened with the destruction of one of its cruisers in this comedy drama that includes murder and sabotage. Robert Taylor, as a navy lieutenant, is assigned to assemble a newly developed fire gear that will prove valuable in wartime. The apparatus is designed to aim and fire the guns by electricity. The navy has only 24 hours to install and test the equipment or it will be sold to another nation. It is under this pressure that Taylor must uncover the saboteur, save the ship and see that the gear remains under U.S. control.

Meanwhile the saboteur has caused the delay of the gear by having it shipped elsewhere and precipitated mishaps aboard the cruiser, including the murders of the company's electrical engineer and a sailor. Taylor finally tracks him down in the powder magazine of the ship where he is planning to blow up the warship. The crazed man, played by Jean Hersholt, claims that the company stole the invention from him. Taylor subdues Hersholt after a fierce struggle. Ted Healy, Una Merkel and Nat Pendleton provide the slapstick comedy. Healy and Pendleton, rival lovers, engage in banter fresh from vaudeville. "I had four girls chasing me down the street—" Healy boasts to other sailors. "What did you do," interrupts Pendleton, "steal a pocketbook?" ∎

Murder on the Waterfront (1943), WB. *Dir.* B. Reeves Eason; *Sc.* Robert E. Kent; *Cast includes:* Warren Douglas, Joan Winfield,

John Loder, Ruth Ford, Bill Crago, Bill Kennedy.

A secret U.S. Navy thermostat forms the core of this inept World War II drama involving murder, revenge and a musical revue for seamen about to sail. A company of entertainers arrives at a waterfront naval base. Among them are a suspicious-looking magician-knife thrower, his female assistant and a young woman married to one of the sailors. Meanwhile, an inventor has arrived to check on his secret thermostats—a new development that will permit the ship's guns to operate under extreme temperatures. During a show for the sailors the inventor is mysteriously murdered, and the magician becomes the prime suspect. For some unexplained reason, the murderer turns out to be a navy officer whom a U.S. Navy intelligence agent has suspected. Some critics, pointing out several incongruities and other shortcomings in the plot, have marked this 1943 adaptation of the play *Without Warning* by Ralph Spencer Zink, as one of the worst films ever made. Boris Karloff appeared in the original 1938 version of this humorless film titled *Invisible Menace*, which was set in an army camp instead of a naval installation. ∎

Murder Over New York (1940), TCF. *Dir.* Harry Lachman; *Sc.* Lester Ziffren; *Cast includes:* Sidney Toler, Marjorie Weaver, Robert Lowery, Ricardo Cortez, Donald MacBride, Melville Cooper.

Sidney Toler portrays Charlie Chan, the internationally famous Hawaiian detective, who once again digresses from unmasking the conventional-type criminals to uncover a spy ring in this routine drama. It seems the spies are determined to sabotage U.S. bombers designated for Britain. A British secret service agent (Frederick Worlock) arrives to investigate matters but he is soon murdered by the enemy agents. The usual variety of suspects come under the sleuth's scrutiny until he unravels the mystery and identifies the murderer and head of the spy ring. ∎

Murderers' Row (1966), Col. *Dir.* Henry Levin; *Sc.* Herbert Baker; *Cast includes:* Dean Martin, Ann-Margret, Karl Malden, Camilla Sparv, James Gregory, Beverly Adams.

In this sequel to *The Silencers*, released earlier the same year, Dean Martin again portrays Matt Helm, a laid-back secret agent who works under cover as a photographer. This time around he journeys to the French Riviera to foil supervillain Karl Malden, who plans to destroy Washington with a powerful beam. Camilla Sparv, as a dangerous villain, is only one of the obstacles Helm has to overcome before he saves the capital. Ann-Margaret contributes to the mayhem by wearing a miniskirt containing a high explosive. Beverly Adams appears as Helm's secretary, Lovey Kravezit. The comedy-drama, based on Donald Hamilton's novel, not only pokes fun at the genre but tosses a few barbs in the direction of the French. Another American attempt to imitate the popular James Bond series (even to the point of using double entendres in the characters' names), the film lacks the originality and wit of the English films. ■

My Country First (1916), Unity. *Dir.* Tom Terriss; *Sc.* Tom Terriss; *Cast includes:* Tom Terriss, Helene Ziegfeld, John Hopkins, Alfred Heming, Joseph Baker, Joseph Sterling.

German agents attempt to steal the formula for a newly discovered high explosive in this typical World War I drama. Tom Terriss portrays the chemist while Alfred Vosburgh, whose make-up invokes the image of the Kaiser, plays the German secret agent. Although the U.S. was still neutral when the film was released, espionage and war dramas, which chiefly reflected the sympathies of their audiences, did little to hide which side of the European conflict they favored. This entry was only one of many that presented an unfavorable view of the Germans. Earlier films, such as *The Fall of a Nation*, came under fire by both film critics and Washington politicos for its anti-German sentiments. Released after a German submarine sank the *Lusitania* (May 7, 1915) with the loss of more than 1,000 lives, of which 128 were Americans, *My Country First* came and went without comment. ■

My Favorite Blonde (1942), Par. *Dir.* Sidney Lanfield; *Sc.* Don Hartman, Frank Butler; *Cast includes:* Bob Hope, Madeleine Carroll, Gale Sondergaard, George Zucco, Victor Varconi.

Bob Hope, as a small-time vaudevillian, gets mixed up with a beautiful British agent, Nazi spies and a squadron of bombers in this fast-paced spy comedy. Madeleine Carroll portrays the British agent who arrives, along with Nazi spies, in New York aboard a Swed-

ish freighter. In an attempt to elude her enemies, she seeks refuge in Hope's dressing room at a vaudeville theater. He performs an act with a seal that gets a higher salary than Hope. Carroll confides that she is a British agent. "Too late, sister," Hope quips. "I've already got an agent." However, she persuades him to assist her. They make their way to California by truck, taxi and trains, all the while pursued and shot at by enemy agents who are planning to destroy a squadron of American bombers. Our hero and heroine arrive in time to warn the flight commander of the impending danger.

Carroll played the female lead in the British spy drama *The 39 Steps*, with Robert Donat, as the innocent, caught up in a sinister assassination plot. In the comedy with Bob Hope, she practically parodies her earlier role. The film concentrates more on the comic elements than on the nature of spying or espionage, centering on a cross-country chase and Hope's one-liners. The basic premise of an unwilling hero and a desperate heroine served as one of the comedian's screen staples. ■

My Favorite Brunette (1947), Par. *Dir.* Elliott Nugent; *Sc.* Edmund Beloin, Jack Rose; *Cast includes:* Bob Hope, Dorothy Lamour, Peter Lorre, Lon Chaney, John Hoyt, Charles Dingle.

Gags and comic situations abound as Bob Hope becomes entangled in a spy plot involving land deeds and valuable ore deposits in this spy comedy. The film opens with Hope in prison on Death Row. When he learns that no word has arrived from the governor for a stay of execution, Hope says: "No word, eh? Well, I'll know who to vote for next time." The warden allows him to tell his story to the press, and the remainder of the film unfolds in flashback. He begins by telling the reporters that he had the best racket in San Francisco. "Was it legitimate?" someone asks. "Better than legitimate," Hope replies. "It was profitable." He is a baby photographer with a yen to be a private detective like his next door neighbor. While in his friend's office, Dorothy Lamour enters and, thinking Hope is a detective, hires him to help her find her missing father. As he blunders his way through the plot details, he uncovers the ring of spies and wins Lamour's love.

Hope made this comedy during his peak period at Paramount. The following year he would make *The Paleface*, considered by many critics to be his best film. Hope's comedy depends to a large extent on his one-liners, and they are numerous. "I feel as though someone is watching me," Lamour says while they are alone. "Yeah," Hope quips, "that's me." She desperately confesses to Hope that she's in trouble, while showing him a photograph. "What's the wheelchair for?" Hope asks. "My husband is an invalid," she explains. "He hasn't been out of that chair in seven years." "You're in trouble," he agrees. A government agent confides to him that a foreign country is after the rare ore known as kryolite. "Kryolite, huh?" Hope ponders. "Well, we can't let them get it. What's kryolite?" "Kryolite is an ore containing kriptobar," the man explains. "Kriptobar," Hope echoes. "Well, we can't let them get that. What's kriptobar?" He repeats his customary role of a coward who struggles to help an attractive heroine. As in several of his features, guest stars appear in cameo roles for laughs. In this film Alan Ladd shows up in the beginning as a private eye while Bing Crosby enters for a funny bit at the end as Hope's disappointed executioner. ∎

Bandleader Kay Kyser, working under cover for army intelligence, is questioned by enemy agents in *My Favorite Spy* (1942).

My Favorite Spy (1942), RKO. *Dir.* Tay Garnett; *Sc.* Sig Herzig, William Bowers; *Cast includes:* Kay Kyser, Ellen Drew, Jane Wyman, Robert Armstrong, William Demarest.

Bandleader Kay Kyser portrays himself in this bland World War II spy comedy produced by former silent screen comic Harold Lloyd. After mistakenly being inducted into

the service as a lieutenant on his wedding day, he is assigned by army intelligence the task of hunting down espionage agents. After several assassination attempts on his life fail, he manages to capture the spies who have taken him to an abandoned theater.

Ellen Drew, as Kyser's perplexed wife, is not let in on her husband's undercover work. She walks in and out of his life several times. Jane Wyman portrays a government agent who is assigned to work with the inept Kyser in his hunt. Robert Armstrong plays a Nazi agent who works at the same nightclub as Kyser and manages to place codes into the musical arrangements that reveal troop convoy movements to the enemy. Veteran comic character actor William Demarest plays a police officer frustrated by Kyser's antics.

The sight gags, one-liners and general comedy material are weak—even for a B film. For example, when an intelligence officer informs Kyser that agents X-10, 11 and 12 have been murdered, the bandleader asks: "Who's X-13?" "That's you," comes the reply. Unfortunately, Kyser gets to lead his band in only two numbers. ∎

My Favorite Spy (1951), Par. *Dir.* Norman Z. McLeod; *Sc.* Edmund Hartmann, Jack Sher, Edmund Beloin, Louis Breslow, Hal Kanter; *Cast includes:* Bob Hope, Hedy Lamarr, Francis L. Sullivan, John Archer, Iris Adrian, Arnold Moss.

Bob Hope portrays a spy for the U.S. government in this comedy. At first mistaken for a notorious international agent, Hope, a vaudeville performer, is arrested by government agents. They find him in an alley moving his name on a poster from the bottom to the top. "Put your hands up higher!" the G-men order. "I can't," Hope counters, "they're attached to my wrists." When they capture the real spy, the agents have trouble persuading Hope to impersonate the prisoner. "What are you, a sniveling coward, a yellow belly . . .?" a G-man fires at Hope. "I'm in there somewhere," he replies.

Hope's mission, after he reluctantly accepts, is to transport one million dollars in his money belt to Tangier where he is to pick up microfilm of secret plans for a pilotless airplane. Hedy Lamarr, portraying another agent, meets him at the airport. As expected, Hope becomes embroiled in a series of comic misadventures, including chases and escapes and a romance with Lamarr. Francis L. Sullivan plays a chief spy who has employed the lovely Lamarr and desperately covets the plans for his own profit. ■

My Official Wife (1914), Vitaphone. *Dir.* James Young; *Sc.* Marguerite Bertsch; *Cast includes:* Clara Kimball Young, Harry T. Morey, Rose E. Tapley, Mary Anderson, Earle Williams.

Clara Kimball Young portrays a Nihilist who enters Russia posing as the wife of an American in this drama adapted from Richard Henry Savage's 1891 novel. Her purpose is to assassinate the Czar. Arthur Lennox (Harry T. Morey), her alleged American husband, meets her accidentally in St. Petersburg and covers for her until he learns her secret mission. He stops her from committing the murder after falling in love with her. When his real wife arrives, Lennox leaves the Nihilist. Meanwhile the chief of the Russian secret police (L. Rogers Lytton) is in hot pursuit. With the aid of Sacha, a young aristocrat (Earle Williams), Young escapes on a yacht. ■

My Son John (1952), Par. *Dir.* Leo McCarey; *Sc.* Myles Connolly, Leo McCarey, John Lee Mahin; *Cast includes:* Helen Hayes, Robert Walker, Van Heflin, Dean Jagger, Frank McHugh, Richard Jaeckel.

A mother becomes distraught when she suspects one of her sons of being a Communist in this Cold War drama. Helen Hayes portrays the American mother whose two other sons are on their way to fight in Korea. She is upset when her third boy, played by Robert Walker, misses their departure. She soon learns that he is under investigation by the F.B.I. and that he carries a key to an apartment of a young woman who has been taken into custody as a spy. Throughout the film Walker has revealed signs that disturb his mother. He objects to his father's literal interpretation of the Bible, for example. The film ends with Walker's confession which he had recorded before his murder. His words are repeated at a college commencement program. Dean Jagger plays Walker's patriotic father. This was Robert Walker's last film; the actor died soon after the film was made.

The film stirred up its share of controversy soon after its release. Some critics argued that, in director Leo McCarey's zeal to expose the evils of Communism, he seems to be endorsing religious conformity, anti-intellectualism and guilt by association. See Cold War. ■

Mysterious Lady, The (1928), MGM. *Dir.* Fred Niblo; *Sc.* Bess Meredyth; *Cast includes:* Greta Garbo, Conrad Nagel, Gustav von Seyffertitz, Edward Connelly, Richard Alexander.

Greta Garbo portrays a Russian spy who falls in love with an Austrian officer in this familiar romantic plot set in Austria before World War I. Conrad Nagel, as the officer, falls for Garbo, unaware that she is a spy. When his uncle, the head of the Austrian secret service, informs him of this fact, he rebukes her. Garbo steals Austrian military plans and leaves for Warsaw. Nagel, who is held responsible for the theft, is imprisoned. His uncle, however, has him released so that he can follow her and recover the documents.

When he locates her, she tries to prove her love for him by promising to return the stolen plans. However, they are now in the hands of a Russian general (Gustav von Seyffertitz). She is forced to kill the Russian when he learns of her true objective. Garbo and Nagel, in a suspenseful sequence, escape across the border to safety. The film was adapted from the novel *War in the Dark* by Ludwig Wolff. ■

Mysterious Mr. Moto (1938), TCF. *Dir.* Norman Foster; *Sc.* Philip MacDonald, Norman Foster; *Cast includes:* Peter Lorre, Mary Maguire, Henry Wilcoxon, Erik Rhodes, Harold Huber, Leon Ames.

Peter Lorre portrays the title character, an international detective, who is on the trail of a gang of international spies and assassins, in this low-budget but suspenseful drama set chiefly in London. The Japanese detective masquerades as a criminal and is temporarily imprisoned on Devil's Island where he befriends one of the gang members. They both escape and return to London to join the remainder of the spies. Eventually the gang discovers Lorre's real identity, and his life is threatened. But he foils their attempts to kill him and helps Scotland Yard to capture the whole network. Writer John P. Marquand created the fictional character of Mr. Moto, a popular sleuth during the 1930s who fell into disfavor when the Japanese attacked Pearl Harbor on December 7, 1941. ■

Mystery Plane (1939), Mon. *Dir.* George Waggner; *Sc.* Paul Schofield, Joseph West; *Cast includes:* John Trent, Milburn Stone, Marjorie Reynolds, Jason Robards, Peter George Lynn.

Based on Hal Forrest's popular newspaper

comic strip, "Tailspin Tommy," this drama concerns international agents who are interested in an innovative airplane bombing device. John Trent portrays Tailspin Tommy while Milburn Stone plays Skeeter, his sidekick. They are both airplane buffs who have invented the new bombing apparatus. Spies kidnap the pair and Tailspin's sweetheart, played by Marjorie Reynolds. The captives escape by plane and engage their pursuers in a dogfight as the police on the ground close in on the gang of spies in this low-budget film. ■

Mystery Sea Raider (1940), Par. *Dir.* Edward Dmytryk; *Sc.* Edward E. Paramore; *Cast includes:* Carole Landis, Henry Wilcoxon, Onslow Stevens, Kathleen Howard, Wallace Rairdon, Sven-Hugo Borg.

German agents hijack an American freighter and convert it to a raider in this conventional drama that flounders during most of its voyage. Onslow Stevens, as a Nazi secret service agent who is actually a captain in the German navy, takes control of the vessel from her American skipper, played by Henry Wilcoxon. Carole Landis, as a passenger tricked by Stevens' posing as an importer, provides the romance for Wilcoxon. Onslow and his German crew use the innocent-looking freighter to lure unsuspecting ships to their demise. Eventually the intervention of one of His Majesty's cruisers brings a deserving end to the German raider's preying upon British shipping. ■

Mystery Ship (1941), Col. *Dir.* Lew Landers; *Sc.* David Silverstein, Houston Branch; *Cast includes:* Paul Kelly, Lola Lane, Larry Parks, Trevor Bardette, Cy Kendall, Roger Imhof.

Two U.S. Secret Service agents accompany a shipload of hardened criminals and alien agents marked for deportation to an unknown destination in this action drama. Larry Parks and Paul Kelly portray the G-men assigned to the task. They who soon face a riot aboard the ship which eventually falls into the hands of the criminals. Kelly shrewdly manages to regain control of the situation. Lola Lane, as a news reporter and stowaway, provides the romantic interest for Kelly. ■

Mystery Submarine (1950), UI. *Dir.* Douglas Sirk; *Sc.* George W. George, George F. Slavin; *Cast includes:* Macdonald Carey,

Marta Toren, Robert Douglas, Carl Esmond, Ludwig Donath, Fred Nurney.

A renegade German submarine remains active after World War II in this drama. Its sinister captain (Robert Douglas) uses his undersea vessel for nefarious activities, such as snatching a German scientist living peacefully in the U.S. and turning him over to an undisclosed organization. As the captain sails off to meet a tanker, his U-boat is sighted by the U.S. Navy. A series of depth charges brings the submarine to the end of its journey.

Director Douglas Sirk left repressive Nazi Germany in 1937 and eventually found his way to Hollywood where his past achievements in the German theater as producer and director and his directorial work in German films were ignored. An under-appreciated film director, he was forced by Hollywood studios to work chiefly with low-budget material. However, he managed to transcend this obstacle by adding visual wit and style to his films. ■

Mystery Woman (1935), Fox. *Dir.* Eugene Forde; *Sc.* Philip MacDonald; *Cast includes:* Mona Barrie, Gilbert Roland, John Halliday, Rod LaRocque, Mischa Auer, William Faversham.

The wife of a French officer who has been convicted of treason seeks to clear his name in this drama of international intrigue and mystery set chiefly aboard a liner. Mona Barrie, as the loyal wife, must retrieve an important document to prove that her spouse (Rod LaRocque) was the victim of a conspiracy. Suspecting that a well-known personage (John Halliday) possesses the paper, she sails aboard a liner where he and a group of wealthy socialites are passengers. Gilbert Roland, as another mysterious passenger, is also searching for the document. Roland and Barrie eventually become friends and together achieve their goal. Roland, however, is shot, but Barrie manages to escape and effect the release of her husband. ■

Mystic Faces (1918), Triangle. *Dir.* E. Mason Hopper; *Sc.* E. Magnus Ingleton; *Cast includes:* Jack Abbe, Martha Taka, Larry Steers, Clara Morris, W. H. Bainbridge.

An unusual film for the period, the drama takes place during World War I in San Francisco's Chinatown. The plot includes an abundance of melodrama, including German spies, gunplay and kidnapping. Jack Abbe portrays a Japanese delivery boy who daydreams of a more romantic life than has been allotted to him. He soon becomes entangled with the German agents. Martha Take provides the romantic interest, and a clever dog supplies some of the comic relief. ■

N

Nasty Rabbit, The (1965), Fairway-International. *Dir.* James Landis; *Sc.* Arch Hall, Sr., Jim Critchfield; *Cast includes:* Mischa Terr, Arch Hall, Jr., Melissa Morgan, William Watters, Little Jack Little, Ray Vegas.

The Soviets plot to release a deadly bacteria in the U.S. in this weak spoof. Mischa Terr portrays a Soviet agent who is assigned to journey to the U.S. with a rabbit carrying a vial filled with bacteria. His mission is to release the creature somewhere in the Continental Divide where the bacteria will eventually kill millions of Americans. Meanwhile, secret agents from Israel, Japan, Mexico and Germany pursue Terr who, masquerading as a cowboy, temporarily rents a room at a local dude ranch. The ranch owner, an undercover F.B.I. agent, links up with an entertainer (Arch Hall, Jr.) to foil the Russian agent's plot. The film, also known as *Spies A-Go-Go*, tries unsuccessfully to blend farcical situations with serious Cold War themes while simultaneously spoofing spy thrillers. See K.G.B. ■

Nation's Peril, The (1915), Lubin. *Dir.* George Terwilliger; *Sc.* George Terwilliger, Harry Chandlee; *Cast includes:* Ormi Hawley, William H. Turner, Earle Metcalfe, Eleanor Barry, Arthur Matthews, Herbert Fortier.

A war drama extolling preparedness, the film tells of a young army lieutenant who invents an aerial torpedo. He is in love with an admiral's granddaughter who objects to his invention on the grounds that it will take human life. A spy, interested in stealing the plans for the torpedo, gains her trust by pretending to be interested in her antiwar beliefs. A group of spies captures an American coastal town, but the U.S. Navy shells the area and retakes the town. The pacifist heroine realizes she was wrong and becomes a staunch supporter of preparedness.

Released during World War I, the film is an early example of the industry's growing attack on pacifism. Using the familiar literary tool of ridicule, the writers reduced the heroine, played by Ormi Hawley, to a capricious, scatterbrained embodiment of pacifism. ■

Navy Blues (1937), Rep. *Dir.* Ralph Staub; *Sc.* Gordon Kahn, Eric Taylor; *Cast includes:* Richard Purcell, Mary Brian, Warren Hymer, Joseph Sawyer, Edward Woods, Horace MacMahon.

Members of a spy ring set out to assassinate a visiting diplomat in this low-budget drama. In the foreground of the plot is a bragging, swaggering sailor, played by Richard Purcell, who makes a wager with his buddies that he can date a certain attractive librarian (Mary Brian). When his pose as an Annapolis candidate fails, he confides to her that he is really a naval intelligence officer—another desperate ploy on his part. By this time he becomes involved with a group of secret agents bent on murdering a diplomat. The sailor and the librarian are kidnapped by the gang of spies, but the navy soon rescues them. The assassination plot is foiled as romance flourishes. Warren Hymer and Joseph Sawyer provide some comic relief. ■

Navy Secrets (1939), Mon. *Dir.* Howard Bretherton; *Sc.* Harvey Gates; *Cast includes:* Fay Wray, Grant Withers, Dewey Robinson, William von Brincken, Craig Reynolds, George Sorrell.

When U.S. Navy officials discover that several military secrets have been stolen, they assign two different agents to uncover the plot. It seems that foreign spies representing an unnamed country are at the bottom of the theft. Fay Wray, as a special intelligence officer for the navy, poses as a foreign agent while Grant Withers attempts to smash the spy ring in his own way. Each doesn't know the other is working for the U.S. Navy on the same case. However, they finally discover this fact and join forces to bring the culprits to justice in this weak drama. ■

An enemy agent signaling to his accomplices is about to be surprised by Eleanor Hunt and Jack Doyle aboard a vessel controlled by a foreign power in *Navy Spy* (1937).

Navy Spy (1937), GN. *Dir.* Crane Wilbur; *Sc.* Crane Wilbur; *Cast includes:* Conrad Nagel, Eleanor Hunt, Judith Allen, Jack Doyle, Phil Dunham, Don Barclay.

Conrad Nagel plays a U.S. Navy lieutenant who is kidnapped by foreign agents in this action drama. Nagel possesses a secret formula that is coveted by a foreign power. The remainder of the film consists of the Federal Bureau of Investigation's attempts to secure his release and capture the spy ring. A navy boat ultimately rescues Nagel in a thrilling climax. Eleanor Hunt provides the romantic interest in this B feature which occasionally employs stock footage of naval vessels. ■

Nazi Agent (1942), MGM. *Dir.* Jules Dassin; *Sc.* Paul Gangelin, John Meehan, Jr.; *Cast includes:* Conrad Veidt, Ann Ayars, Dorothy Tree, Frank Reicher, Sidney Blackmer.

Conrad Veidt plays a dual role in this routine drama about Nazi saboteurs operating in the U.S. before the nation enters World War II. Otto, a proud American citizen, runs a

bookshop and collects stamps. Hugo, his identical twin brother, is a member of the German consulate and part of a network of saboteurs. Hugo forces his peaceful brother to allow the shop to be used as a front for the spies' messages. Later, Otto kills his brother in self-defense and assumes the loyal German's identity. This gives him an opportunity to work his way into the nest of spies who are responsible for attacks on Allied convoys and other acts of sabotage. Otto secretly calls in tips to the police about the spies' activities, including their scheme to have a vessel blown up at the Panama Canal. He eventually exposes the entire operation to the F.B.I. but at the cost of his own life. When his consulate secretary (Martin Kosleck) threatens an innocent woman's family living in Europe, Otto volunteers to return with him to Germany as a confessed traitor in exchange for the family's safety. The ironic last scene at the pier is especially effective. Otto, still impersonating his brother, boards the vessel for Germany as outraged Americans jeer him.

The film is remarkably free of propaganda speeches until the last few scenes. "I hope you don't think," Kosleck reminds Otto before leaving the U.S., "that anything you have done will put an end to our work here." "No, I don't," Otto replies. "But I'm only one—one of 130 million Americans who together with all the good people of the world are rising to crush you and everything you stand for once and for all." The bulk of propaganda utterances did not enter World War II dramas until after America entered the war. The film, whose original title was *Salute to Courage*, strains plausibility in several scenes. ■

Nazi Spy Ring. See *The Dawn Express* (1942). ■

Nazi subversion: post-World War II. In *Till the End of Time*, a half-forgotten World War II film released in 1944, a minor character remarks: "One is never through with the Germans." These words were soon to have a prophetic ring. Before the war drew to a close, German intelligence, reading the handwriting on the wall, began preparing for postwar Nazi subversive activities. The funds for such operations were to come from the sale of art treasures stolen from the four corners of Europe by the Germans, including jewels, gold and silver. The counter-espionage branch of America's Office of Strategic Services, known as X-2, uncovered the plot and organized its Art Looting Investigating Unit to retrieve these items and foil the postwar plans of these Nazis.

Hollywood, in its unique, uncanny way, was quick to turn out dramas about unrepentant Nazis planning for the next onslaught as early as 1944. During the next few decades dozens of plots centered around schemes by former Nazis to steal gold and jewels, restore their former glory and spread fear and hatred among the peoples of the world. A few were earnest attempts to expose the flight of war criminals, some were simple entertainments and others were undisguised propaganda films.

Some of the earlier films were cautionary dramas, warning the victors and victims of Nazism that their struggle against totalitarianism would not end with the armistice. In *The Master Race* (1944), for instance, Nazi leaders begin their strategy for the next war as Allied armies push toward Berlin. George Coulouris portrays a high Nazi official and advocate of German supremacy who orders his military staff to go underground and cause turmoil among the liberated nations of Europe until the Nazis are strong enough to rise again. Nazi officers in *Hotel Berlin* (1945), released during the last months of the war, plan their escape to the U.S. where they intend to prepare for World War III. "This time we shall be anti-Nazis," one explains, "poor refugees who have escaped from Germany. . . . Americans forgive and forget easily. But we must spread rumors and create dissension and distrust."

South America became the favorite exotic sanctuary of former Nazi officers—both in fact and in films. *Cornered* (1945), released just months after the war, reflected the fears of many as stories filtered out of Europe about Nazi war criminals eluding the net of justice. Its tone is almost paranoid. The plot concerns high-ranking Nazis who have escaped prosecution by the Allies and have settled in Argentina where they are busy planning the next war. "They do not consider themselves defeated," explains the leader of a group dedicated to exposing the Nazi conspirators. "We must destroy not only the individuals but their friends, their very means of existence, wherever they start to entrench themselves. . . ." *Notorious* (1946), Hitchcock's suspenseful drama starring Cary Grant and Ingrid Bergman, is played more for sus-

pense than as a warning against a possible rebirth of Nazism. The plot concerns a network of Nazis, operating in post-World War II Brazil, which arouses the interest of U.S. intelligence.

Some former Nazis preferred to hide in the shadows of Europe, surrounded by more familiar languages and culture. In *Jewels of Brandenburg* (1947) a U.S. agent is assigned to retrieve stolen jewels which are in the hands of a group of Nazis in Lisbon at the close of World War II. The drama *Berlin Express* (1948) focuses on a group of Nazis who continue to create mayhem in strife-torn postwar Germany. A secret plot hatched in 1947 in post-World War II Germany to resurrect the Nazi party provides the basis of *The Devil Makes Three* (1952). The neo-Nazis, who are shipping looted gold across the border to help finance their new secret army, are waiting for the occupation to end before they rise up. The names of former Nazi collaborators during World War II become the subject of *The Salzburg Connection* (1972), set in contemporary Austria. When neo-Nazis murder an ex-British agent who has found a suspicious list of names in a chest at the bottom of a lake, others become interested in the incident. *Brass Target* (1978), a fictionalized version of General Patton's death at the hands of assassins, concerns a contrived plot about the theft of Nazi Germany's gold.

The U.S. provided another relatively safe haven. An escaped Nazi war criminal, wanted by the Allied War Crimes Commission, goes under cover in a small New England town in Orson Welles' *The Stranger* (1946). Edward G. Robinson, as a U.S. government agent, tracks down the mass murderer, played by Welles. "I'll stay hidden until the day that we strike again," the unrepentant Welles confides to a former Nazi friend. In *Step by Step* (1946), a minor drama with Lawrence Tierney and Anne Jeffreys, Nazis who have taken refuge in the U.S. attempt to restore their party to its former glory. In *Close-Up* (1948) a gang of ex-Nazis operating under cover in New York tries to destroy newsreel clips which prove damaging evidence against one of its members. Ex-Nazis, stationed in Los Angeles, plot to take over the world by controlling its national leaders in the drama *A Man Called Dagger* (1967).

The Cold War provided Hollywood with an opportunity to align former Nazi officers with the Communist cause. *The Whip Hand* (1951) has some of Hitler's most loyal followers now joining the Communists in secret experiments in germ warfare in the Wisconsin mountains. *Night People* (1954) in part concerns neo-Nazis working in league with the Communists against the West.

Some Hollywood plots bordered on the fantastic. Nazi scientists experiment with atomic energy for the purpose of blowing up major cities in the post-World War II drama *Rendezvous 24* (1946). Although the war has ended, a group of former Nazi scientists working in a remote area of the Harz Mountains plans to wipe out New York City and Paris from their laboratory using a remote control device. *They Saved Hitler's Brain* (1963) concerns an international conspiracy of neo-Nazis. Led by the preserved brain of Hitler, the group plots to conquer the world in this inane low-budget drama. A group of Nazis, operating from its base in a fictitious South American country, obtains a deadly gas formula powerful enough to fell entire armies. Gregory Peck in *The Boys From Brazil* (1978) portrays the infamous Josef Mengele, the cold-blooded World War II concentration-camp doctor, who is now busily working on a bizarre experiment somewhere in South America. The mad doctor has successfully turned out "little Hitlers" from the dictator's tissue.

Several comedies, which exploited the themes of ex-Nazis and wartime treasure, seemed to trivialize the war. *A Night in Casablanca* (1946), for example, brings the Marx Brothers into conflict with Nazi conspirators who are lurking around the Hotel Casablanca in search of a cache of hidden wartime loot.

The bulk of these films about unrepentant Nazis hiding in the bowels of remote lands or unimportant villages, with their grandiose dreams of returning to power, are pure fiction. Some are laughable while others remain dramatically poignant. All occur in another place, another time, thereby distancing us from these themes. Nevertheless, they cannot erase the words of Heinrich Himmler, one of the architects of the Third Reich: "True wars, wars between races, are merciless and fought to the last man, until one side or the other is eliminated without a trace." ∎

Neal of the Navy (1915) serial, Pathé. *Dir.* W. M. Harvey; *Sc.* Douglas Bronston; *Cast includes:* Lillian Lorraine, William Courtleigh,

Jr., William Conklin, Bruce Smith, Helen Lackaye, E. J. Brady.

A 14-part serial about the exploits of a heroic sailor and an 18-year-old orphan, the sprawling story extends over 14 years and covers a variety of locations. William Courtleigh, Jr., as the title character, and Lillian Lorraine, as the orphan, find themselves in weekly difficulties, including their escape from smugglers and conspirators, a search for a stolen map and lost island, their involvement in a mutiny and a battle between revolutionaries and American sailors. More often than not, the U.S. Navy comes to the couple's rescue in the nick of time. E. J. Brady portrays the chief villain. See Serials. ∎

Never Let Me Go (1953), MGM. *Dir.* Delmer Daves; *Sc.* Ronald Millar; *Cast includes:* Clark Gable, Gene Tierney, Bernard Miles, Richard Haydn, Theodore Bikel.

An American journalist attempts to smuggle his Russian wife out of the Soviet Union in this implausible Cold War drama. Clark Gable portrays the newspaperman who marries a Russian ballerina, played by Gene Tierney. Expelled from Russia, he is forced to leave his wife behind. Meanwhile, his wife is not permitted to leave the country. After exhausting all diplomatic channels in Washington and elsewhere, he links up with an Englishman (Richard Haydn) who is in the same predicament. They travel to the Baltic by boat where they effect the escape of their wives.

A product of the Cold War, the script is filled with anti-Communist propaganda. "The Russian bear," a Soviet official remarks, "is the only animal that can eat its honey and have it." Gable provides the following voice-over during a parade celebrating the end of World War II: "That was the last time the flags of the free nations were marched across Red Square in Moscow." Agents of the N.K.V.D. appear ominously from time to time, striking fear in the hearts of innocent people. Frustrated with his failure to get a visa for his Russian wife, Gable vents his anger at a high Soviet bureaucrat, who personifies Russian belligerency. "I wouldn't ask," Gable exclaims, "what madness— what neurotic fear—is driving you to interpret the humblest needs of the human heart as an affair of state. I won't even ask what demon's driving you to take the good will of the world and deliberately strangle it overnight. You know what I see? The Union of Soviet Socialist Republics' riding headlong down the road marked 'This way to the jungle' via man's inhumanity to man." The film, a British co-production, is based on the novel *Came the Dawn* by Roger Bax. ■

Never Say Never Again (1983), WB. *Dir.* Irvin Kershner; *Sc.* Lorenzo Semple, Jr.; *Cast includes:* Sean Connery, Klaus Maria Brandauer, Max von Sydow, Barbara Carrera, Kim Basinger, Bernie Casey.

An unacknowledged remake of *Thunderball* (1965), this James Bond adventure of intrigue and romance has the diabolical international crime syndicate S.P.E.C.T.R.E. blackmailing the world governments under threat of detonating two nuclear warheads which its underlings have stolen from the U.S. military. Sean Connery, who returns to the role of the superspy 007 after a 12-year absence, portrays a retired James Bond who is currently engaged in teaching. However, the perilous global situation propels him back into action. The light satirical tone of previous Bond escapades has been retained and is exemplified by the British secret service's special weapons expert's wry comment. "Now that you're on the case," "Q" (Alec McGowan) says to Bond, "I hope we're going to have some gratuitous sex and violence." The heavy reliance on technology that dominated some of the later entries has been curbed in favor of plot machinations and romance.

Filmed chiefly in the Bahamas and the French Riviera, the yarn offers the traditional villains and action sequences, including a car-motorcycle chase and an underwater fight. Klaus Maria Brandauer, as Bond's chief adversary, portrays a rich, delightful villain. Barbara Carrera, as Fatima Blush, a self-centered secret agent whom Brandauer assigns to assassinate Bond, provides some of the romantic interest, along with Kim Basinger, who plays Brandauer's mistress. Max von Sydow, as Blofeld, the head of S.P.E.C.T.R.E., has a minor role. Bernie Casey portrays a C.I.A. agent.

The film was the first American production in the Bond series. Other entries starring Sean Connery, considered by many as the definitive Bond, include *Dr. No* (1962), *From Russia With Love* (1963), *Goldfinger* (1964), *Thunderball* (1965), *You Only Live Twice* (1967), *Diamonds Are Forever* (1971). Roger Moore and Timothy Dalton have continued

in Connery's tradition of portraying Bond as a sexy, sophisticated agent. See James Bond. ■

New Lives for Old (1925), Par. *Dir.* Clarence Badger; *Sc.* Adelaide Heilbron; *Cast includes:* Betty Compson, Wallace MacDonald, Theodore Kosloff, Sheldon Lewis, Jack Joyce, Margaret Sneddon.

Betty Compson stars as a Parisian café dancer who falls in love with an American officer in this World War I drama. When he is sent to the front lines, she volunteers to serve as a spy. She is assigned to have an affair with an officer who is ultimately convicted as a traitor. When the war ends, her American lover returns and takes her back to the U.S. The spy, who escaped from French captivity, appears and shows interest in the American's sister. Betty exposes him at the risk of her own reputation, but conveniently a French official arrives and straightens matters out between Betty and her American family. ■

Next Man, The (1976), AA. *Dir.* Richard C. Sarafian; *Sc.* Mort Fine, Alan Trustman, David M. Wolf, Richard C. Sarafian; *Cast includes:* Sean Connery, Cornelia Sharpe, Albert Paulsen, Adolfo Celi, Marco St. John, Ted Beniades.

A Saudi Arabian diplomat becomes the target of Arab terrorists when he proposes making peace with Israel in exchange for technological development in this drama about the strife-torn Middle East. Sean Connery, as the conciliatory diplomat, is assigned by the leaders of his country to present their controversial proposal before the United Nations. In direct contradiction to the fervent anti-Israeli policy of other Arab countries, Connery's proposal arouses an immediate reaction from a group of terrorists. They dispatch several international agents to assassinate the visionary minister.

Cornelia Sharpe, as one of the hired assassins is efficient at her job. The opening scenes show her seducing a middle-aged victim, then drugging him and finally ruthlessly asphyxiating him in a hotel room. She calmly gathers up her things, changes her hair color and leaves for the Austrian Alps to meet her contact aboard a train. He innocently offers her his newspaper in which a picture of Connery—her next victim—is circled. She cleverly arranges to make his acquaintance in New York. Connery is soon lured by her charm and beauty and they quickly become lovers. She later is ordered to kill him and carries out her assignment.

The film, chiefly concerned with political assassination, escapes its social and political responsibilities by suggesting a general tone of cynicism and corruption and not specifying the rotten forces at work. Connery, as the newly appointed Saudi Arabian minister of state, is given several controversial speeches which he presents at the U.N. "We will enter into partnership with any country for the research and development of new sources of energy," he boldly announces. "I call for a direct dialogue with Israel so we can create a Palestinian state with men of good will—from a conference table and not from the debris of exploded villages and human life." Later, at a private meeting with a Palestinian leader, he is asked how the Palestinian problem should be handled. "Accept the responsibilities for the Palestinians," he replies. "We shoveled their youths onto those garbage dumps where they either rot or, in their despair, become terrorists and try to blow up the world."

Connery's speeches antagonize Western and Soviet-bloc leaders as well of those of the Middle East. A fellow Middle East U.N. delegate equates Connery with Santa Claus. While Connery and Sharpe are on a weekend tryst in the Bahamas, a team of unidentified assassins is sent to murder him. But they fail and the couple return to New York. His close confidant, friend and fellow countryman finally turns against him and orders Sharpe to fire the fatal shot. Marco St. John portrays the chief of U.S. security. Charles Cioffi, as a crafty Syrian U.N. delegate, engages in several debates with the controversial Connery. ∎

Nick Carter, Master Detective (1939), MGM. *Dir.* Jacques Tourneur; *Sc.* Bertram Millhauser; *Cast includes:* Walter Pidgeon, Rita Johnson, Henry Hull, Stanley Ridges, Donald Meek.

MGM purchased the rights to all the Nick Carter stories, updated the material from its pre-World War I background to the World War II period and featured dapper Walter Pidgeon as the master sleuth in this low-budget series.

The undistinguished first entry deals with spies stealing copies of blueprints from an airplane factory. Carter is called in to unravel the mystery. "With all our precautions," the plant chief explains to the detective, "plans do get out." "They've got a better organization than you have," Carter concludes. He discovers that Stanley Ridges, as the plant doctor, has been smuggling microfilm of the secret plans to his network of spies by concealing the film in bandages of workers who were feigning accidents. Henry Hull portrays an inventor of a revolutionary airplane coveted by the enemy agents. Comic character actor Donald Meek volunteers his services as the detective's assistant. Rita Johnson, as an airline stewardess, plays the female lead.

This detective series differed from others in that Carter was usually engaged in tracking down enemy agents and saboteurs rather than run-of-the-mill criminals and murderers. For example, in *Phantom Raiders* (1940), the second entry, saboteurs are busy attacking ships in the Panama Canal region before Carter puts a stop to their activities. The third and final entry, *Sky Murder*, also released in 1940, again concerned foreign spies. See Detectives and Spies. ∎

Night in Casablanca, A (1946), UA. *Dir.* Archie Mayo; *Sc.* Joseph Fields, Roland Kibbee; *Cast includes:* Groucho Marx, Harpo Marx, Chico Marx, Lisette Verea, Charles Drake, Lois Collier, Dan Seymour.

Nazi conspirators lurk around the Hotel Casablanca in search of a cache of hidden wartime loot in this post-World War II comedy. The intrigue results in several hotel managers being murdered. To the eventual regret of the villains, the Marx Brothers soon become entangled in the clandestine machinations. Enter Groucho as the next manager who temporarily falls under the enchantment of *femme fatale* Lisette Verea. Chico runs a camel-renting service and is assisted by Harpo, who chances upon the coveted loot.

Slapstick, one-liners and chases contribute to the zany Marx Brothers antics in this broad comedy which ends with the capture of the Nazi plotters. An early scene has Harpo leaning against a building. A policeman moves Harpo along, suggesting facetiously that he cannot linger around holding up a building. When Harpo leaves, the structure comes crashing down. Groucho proves that he has lost little of his sharpness in delivering his funny retorts in this late entry to the brothers' comedy series. "I'm Beatrice Rheiner," a seductive guest announces, "I stop at the hotel." "I'm Ronald Cornblow," Groucho returns, "I stop at nothing." Sig Ruman once again appears as Groucho's foil. Charles Drake and Lois Collier provide the slight romantic subplot. ∎

Night People (1954), TCF. *Dir.* Nunnally Johnson; *Sc.* Nunnally Johnson; *Cast includes:* Gregory Peck, Broderick Crawford, Anita Bjork, Rita Gam, Walter Abel, Buddy Ebsen.

The kidnapping of a G.I. in Berlin by East German Communists sets off a chain of dramatic events in this Cold War drama set in postwar Germany. Gregory Peck, as an American colonel, engages in a battle of wits with the captors as he maneuvers to rescue the young soldier (Ted Avery). The Communists, some of whom are former Nazis, want to trade the American for a German couple who were involved in a wartime plot against Hitler. However, Peck has other problems. Broderick Crawford, as the captive's wealthy and politically influential father, appears on the scene and demands quick action. Anita Bjork, as Peck's former lover and liaison with the Eastern bloc, is in reality a double agent working for the Communists. Meanwhile, a U.S. State Department officer warns Peck not to create an incident that would exacerbate international tensions.

Peck berates the G.I.'s father for interfering in the investigation and trying to throw his weight around. "If there's anything that burns me," the colonel exclaims, "it's an amateur trying to tell a professional how to do his job." He then tries to explain to Crawford the type of adversary they are dealing with. "These are cannibals," he explains, "headhunting, bloodthirsty cannibals who are out to eat us up." After U.S. intelligence informs him about Bjork's real identity, Peck devises a plan to use her to get the G.I. back. He arranges through her an exchange with the Communists but at the last moment substitutes the double agent, whom he has knocked unconscious, for the innocent German couple the Communists want.

The intelligent screenplay quietly brings out the East-West tensions of the early days of the Cold War and the delicate balance U.S. military and civilian personnel were forced to maintain in dealing with the Communists. The film also suggests that unrepentant Nazis are working in league with the Communists against the West. See Cold War; Nazi Subversion: Post-World War II. ∎

Night Plane From Chungking (1943), Par. *Dir.* Ralph Murphy; *Sc.* Earl Felton, Theodore Reaves, Lester Cole; *Cast includes:* Robert Preston, Ellen Drew, Stephen Geray, Sen Yung, Soo Yong, Otto Kruger.

The Sino-Japanese War provides the background for this routine drama dotted with gunplay and patriotic speeches. When a passenger plane en route to India from Chungking lands at a secret air base, an American pilot (Robert Preston) working for the Chinese army takes over the controls of the ship. But Japanese fighters force the aircraft down, and the passengers are captured. On board are a corrupt businessman (Otto Kruger), a Nazi agent disguised as a priest and a Chinese woman on a special mission. Ellen Drew provides the romantic interest in this weak remake of the 1932 film *Shanghai Express* starring Marlene Dietrich. ∎

Nighthawks (1981), U. *Dir.* Bruce Malmuth; *Sc.* David Shaber; *Cast includes:* Sylvester Stallone, Billy Dee Williams, Rutger Hauer, Nigel Davenport, Persis Khambatta, Lindsay Wagner.

Sylvester Stallone takes Rambo out of the Asian jungle and has him stalk the mean streets and other environs of New York City in this highly implausible but entertaining action drama. Stallone, as a New York policeman who works in the decoy division together with his partner (Billy Dee Williams), is assigned to a newly created special counter-terrorist unit. Unhappy about being taken off the streets to sit in a classroom, Stallone clashes with the Interpol agent-instructor (Nigel Davenport). When Wulfgar (Rutger Hauer), an international terrorist, blows up a building in Wall Street, Stallone forgets his personal grievances. Wulfgar is the threat the instructor has been preparing special unit for.

A ruthless and cunning killer, Wulfgar has come to New York to boost his reputation worldwide as an effective terrorist-for-hire. His last act of terror and destruction—the blowing up of a London department store with the resultant the deaths of innocent women and children—did not sit well with those who have hired him in the past. Branded a pariah in Europe and hunted by law enforcement agencies, he sets out for New York to prove he is the best in his field. He justifies his acts by claiming he is a "liberator" who represents "oppressed victims who have nothing."

The remainder of the plot concerns Stallone's efforts to track down Wulfgar. This takes the pair into the bowels of the city's subway, through back alleys, onto the overhead Roosevelt Island tram and to a local museum. The elusive terrorist manages several escapes, each leaving a trail of victims in its wake. Stallone puts an end to Wulfgar's bloody career when the terrorist, seeking revenge, breaks into the home of Stallone's girlfriend. Wielding a knife and ready to pounce, Wulfgar is surprised to find his victim is Stallone, dressed as the victim.

The film offers some insight into the lengths necessary to combat urban terrorism. The Interpol representative, training the special unit in how to kill a terrorist, evokes a hostile response from Stallone. "I didn't join the force to kill people," the police officer says. "For God's sake, man," the instructor exclaims, "to combat violence, you need greater violence!" But the script fails to identify the nature and source of Wulfgar's affiliations (perhaps hoping for a larger international market). "Wulfgar has just struck a blow against British colonialism," the terrorist announces over the telephone after his London bombing. "Be warned that I have a long arm, and I am prepared to fight my enemies wherever they may be." Such anachronistic vagueness adds little to the character's credibility. The drama, in effect, is just another violent cops-and-robbers tale. ■

Nightmare (1942), U. *Dir.* Tim Whelan; *Sc.* Dwight Taylor; *Cast includes:* Diana Barrymore, Brian Donlevy, Henry Daniell, Eustace Wyatt, Arthur Shields, Gavin Muir.

An American gambler, down on his luck in London, gets entangled in murder and Nazi intrigue in this slow-paced World War II drama. Brian Donlevy, as the impoverished Yank, breaks into the home of Diana Barrymore to get something to eat. Instead, he stumbles upon a murder. Barrymore pays him to remove the body, but later it turns up again. They escape from the police and journey in a stolen car to her family's estate in Scotland. Gavin Muir, as her cousin, resides there. At first, Muir is unknown to the pair, who are beginning to fall for each other. He is actually a Nazi spy whose agent-cronies are being parachuted into the area. Following an action-filled fight involving Donlevy and the unwelcome visitors, the spies are captured. The film was adapted from the story "Escape" by Philip MacDonald. See British Intelligence: World War II. ■

No Man's Land (1918), MGM. *Dir.* Will S. Davis; *Sc.* A. S. LeVino; *Cast includes:* Bert Lytell, Anna Q. Nilsson, Charles Arling, Eugene Pallette, Mollie McConnell, Edward Alexander.

Bert Lytell portrays the hero of this weak World War I drama based on Louis Joseph Vance's 1910 novel. He is unjustly imprisoned for a murder he did not commit. Meanwhile, the young woman he loves (Anna Q. Nilsson) marries another (Charles Arling) who takes her to a remote Pacific island. She discovers that her husband is a German agent who is using a wireless to feed information about Allied shipping to enemy raiders. Lytell is pardoned, sails to the island and rescues his true love. The traitorous husband is killed. ■

No Time for Flowers (1952), RKO. *Dir.* Don Siegel; *Sc.* Laslo Vadnay, Hans Wilhelm; *Cast includes:* Viveca Lindfors, Paul Christian, Ludwig Stossel, Adrienne Gessner, Peter Preses, Manfred Inger.

A government secretary in Communist Czechoslovakia undergoes a secret loyalty test before she can be considered for a job in the U.S. in this offbeat drama shot in Europe. Viveca Lindfors portrays the worker about to be promoted. Red officials, however, fear that Western materialism may corrupt the candidate, so they set up an experiment, unknown to her, to test her resistance. They assign Paul Christian to masquerade as an agent who has recently returned from America to wine and dine Lindfors. She is told to report everything to the local police chief (Peter Preses). Not surprisingly, the couple fall in love and take off across the border for the West.

At times the film seems to border on satire, particularly in the stereotyped portrayals of some of the bureaucratic officials. In fact, this approach may have enhanced the story which otherwise remains ambiguous in its tone. ■

No Way Out (1987), Orion. *Dir.* Roger Donaldson; *Sc.* Robert Garland; *Cast includes:* Kevin Costner, Gene Hackman, Sean Young, Will Patton, Howard Duff, George Dzunoza.

A U.S. Navy security officer investigating a murder finds himself the chief suspect in this convoluted drama about espionage, political intrigue and fiery sex. Kevin Costner portrays the navy career officer whose act of bravery and influence in Washington get him assigned as an aide to the Secretary of Defense (Gene Hackman). During a previous visit to the capital, Costner met the attractive Sean Young, whom he now becomes emotionally involved with. When he suspects that she has another lover, she admits that it is Hackman, his boss. Hackman, during an unscheduled visit to her apartment, sees a figure leaving and, in a fit of anger, has a violent argument with Young, which results in her accidental death.

Hackman returns, distraught, to his civilian aide (Will Patton), an ambitious and devious underling who enjoys wielding power. Patton decides to cover up Hackman's involvement in the young woman's death by blaming it on an imaginary Soviet agent known only as Uri. Both Hackman and Patton assign Costner to investigate the death. However, a handful of clues and witnesses lead to Costner himself. He tries to slow down the investigation until he figures a way out of the dilemma. He asks his friend (George Dzunoza), a computer expert at the Pentagon, where the remainder of the drama chiefly unfolds, to help him.

Dzunoza at first agrees but later becomes suspicious of his friend's state of mind. He arranges a secret meeting with Patton, who cold-bloodedly kills Dzunoza and sends two henchmen after Costner. Meanwhile, security guards escort two witnesses through every room of the Pentagon. They had seen Costner with Young. In a suspenseful and emotional climax Costner confronts Hackman, threatens him with exposure based on new evidence that links the Secretary with Young and tells him about Patton's involvement. Patton then commits suicide. Costner escapes from the Pentagon and is picked up by Soviet agents, a completely surprising twist of events. It seems that he is actually the Russian agent who has infiltrated U.S. intelligence. When his cohorts try to force him to return to the Soviet Union, he refuses and leaves. Two agents are about to shoot him, but their chief stops them, saying: "He'll be back. Where else can he go?"

The film is based on the novel *The Big Clock* by Kenneth Fearing. An earlier film version under the original title appeared in 1948 with Ray Milland and Charles Laughton. A straight crime drama, it contained nothing about spies or government intrigue. See K.G.B.; Soviet Spies in the U.S. ∎

Normandy invasion. See Operation Overlord. ∎

North by Northwest (1959), MGM. *Dir.* Alfred Hitchcock; *Sc.* Ernest Lehman; *Cast includes:* Cary Grant, Eva Marie Saint, James Mason, Jessie Royce Landis, Leo G. Carroll, Philip Ober.

Alfred Hitchcock's witty and suspenseful drama about a smug Madison Avenue executive whose life is threatened by enemy agents who mistake him for a U.S. intelligence agent has invoked many lengthy discussions by film historians and critics. The director has once again selected Cary Grant (*Suspicion, Notorious, To Catch a Thief*) to portray Thornhill, an innocent caught up in a web of intrigue, and placed him in commonplace but deceptively menacing surroundings. Unidentified enemy agents mistake Grant for a C.I.A. agent when he signals a hotel employee who has been paging a Mr. George Kaplan. Assuming Grant is Kaplan, the agents make several attempts on his life. Ironically, the alleged agent does not exist; he has been created by the C.I.A. to divert the enemy's attention from the real spy who has infiltrated their circle.

The cat-and-mouse game allows Hitchcock to take his cameras to such familiar sites as New York's Plaza Hotel, Grand Central Station, the United Nations and Mount Rushmore National Monument—all popular, crowded locales which give the illusion of security and safety. But in Hitchcock's world, national monuments often turn to milieus of impending disaster where one may be murdered—and often is. In a suspenseful sequence on Mount Rushmore, for example, Grant and Saint almost fall to their deaths as they try to elude the villains. One of the most chilling—and most written about—sequences occurs on a desolate prairie where Grant is sent. Standing alone at a crossroad, Grant notices an apparently harmless crop-dusting airplane in the distance slowly flying toward him. He soon realizes that the pilot is after him. He starts to run to evade the plane, barely escaping with his life. The plane eventually crashes into a truck.

Hitchcock portrays U.S. intelligence agencies in a rather unfavorable light. Leo G. Carroll, as the unemotional chief of a U.S. intelligence unit, has little sympathy for Grant, who is mistaken for the nonexistent agent. Addressing a meeting composed of his top aides, he decides to let Grant continue as a target of the spy network to protect his own undercover agent. Another C.I.A. member at the conference muses, "Goodbye, Mr. Thornhill, wherever you are." Later, Grant, who barely manages to stay alive, meets Carroll and remarks: "I don't like the games you play."

James Mason portrays the menacing leader of the spies who is planning to flee the U.S. with valuable microfilm hidden in a statuette. Eva Marie Saint, as the undercover U.S. agent who is Mason's mistress, falls in love with Grant. Jessie Royce Landis, as Grant's featherbrained mother, adds to the comedy relief. In one particular scene, she and Grant are being followed by two assassins in a crowded elevator. "Are you gentlemen trying to kill my son?" she announces loudly. This is one of Hitchcock's more delightful works. ∎

North of Shanghai (1939), Col. *Dir.* D. Ross Lederman; *Sc.* Maurice Rapf, Harold Buchman; *Cast includes:* James Craig, Betty Furness, Keye Luke, Morgan Conway, Russell Hicks.

The Sino-Japanese War furnishes the background for this minor drama concerning a newsreel cameraman, played by James Craig, and a reporter, portrayed by Betty Furness. Assigned to cover the war by different employers, the two leads join forces to uncover a spy ring that is being directed by the head of the Shanghai office of Furness's newspaper. The film includes several sequences of the bombing of Chinese cities and the war in general in this low-budget production. ∎

Northern Pursuit (1943), WB. *Dir.* Raoul Walsh; *Sc.* Frank Gruber, Alvah Bessie; *Cast includes:* Errol Flynn, Julie Bishop, Helmut Dantine, John Ridgely, Gene Lockhart, Tom Tully.

A Nazi submarine deposits several saboteurs on the shores of northern Canada in this World War II drama. Helmut Dantine, as the leading enemy agent, is captured by two members of the Royal Canadian Mounted Police (Errol Flynn and John Ridgely) but manages to escape from a prisoner-of-war camp. He is determined to succeed in his original mission of sabotage.

Flynn quits the force and poses as a Nazi sympathizer in an attempt to prevent the saboteur and his underlings from accomplishing their purpose. Julie Bishop, as Flynn's sweetheart, is taken hostage by the spies who distrust the ex-Mountie. After Flynn leads the agents to their objective—an abandoned mine containing crates of airplane parts—Dantine boastfully reveals his target: "One of the most vital waterways connecting the U.S. and Canada. A main artery of all war supplies going to England. Eight bombs placed with scientific precision will destroy the canal and the locks and block shipping for months. I will drop those bombs with precision." The Germans spend the next few days assembling the bomber. Each night they lock Flynn in a room, intending to kill him before they leave. But Flynn foils their plan at the last moment by boarding the plane disguised as a crew member whom he has overpowered only moments earlier. He shoots the other Germans and bails out before the plane crashes. Gene Lockhart plays a Nazi agent in this action drama that makes ample use of the wintry wastelands of Canada's Northwest.

In the last scene Flynn adds a private joke as he embraces Julie Bishop. The actor in real life had been charged with statutory rape. "I've known many girls," Flynn confides to Bishop, "but you—you're the only one I've ever loved." He then turns to the camera, smiles, and adds: "What am I saying?" The film is based on "Five Thousand Trojan Horses," a story by Leslie T. White. ∎

Northwest Conspiracy (1864). The most ambitious plot on the part of the South during the American Civil War was known as the Northwest Conspiracy. The scheme involved both the Knights of the Golden Circle, a Southern subversive group, and the Copperheads, Southern sympathizers residing in the North. The idea was to encourage, with the help of the Sons of Liberty, as the Knights were now known, the defection from the Union of several Western states which would then establish a Northwest Confederacy sympathetic to the South. The plan never reached fruition, thanks to the penetration of the Sons of Liberty by Union agents. The Union army had been privy to a number of plans of the Sons of Liberty, for it had placed one of its agents into an Indiana branch. Felix Stidger rose to become secretary of the Knights in Indiana. He reported to General Carrington, the leader of the Union army in Indianapolis.

A handful of spy dramas dealt with Southern espionage in the West. In *The Copperhead* (1920), for example, Lionel Barrymore portrays a Union agent whom President Lincoln has secretly assigned to infiltrate the Copperheads. *Operator 13* (1934) depicts a Union colonel explaining the conspiracy to Marion Davies, who portrays a Northern spy assigned to expose its leader. "The Sons of Liberty," the officer says, "is a military and secret organization formed in the North by Southern sympathizers. This is a well-knit organization having over half-a-million members. They plan to seize Ohio, Indiana, Illinois, Kentucky and Missouri and proclaim a new nation to be known as the Northwest Confederacy." ■

Notorious (1946), RKO. *Dir.* Alfred Hitchcock; *Sc.* Ben Hecht; *Cast includes:* Cary Grant, Ingrid Bergman, Claude Rains, Louis Calhern, Leopoldine Konstantin, Reinhold Schunzel.

The daughter of a convicted Nazi spy assists U.S. intelligence to expose a network of Nazis operating in post-World War II Brazil in this suspenseful drama. Ingrid Bergman, as the daughter who falls in love with her intelligence agent contact (Cary Grant), at first hesitates to go through with her assignment because of her feelings for him. But she accepts when he leaves the decision up to her. She renews her relationship with one of the leaders of Brazil's Nazi spy ring (Claude Rains). When he grows suspicious of her meeting with Grant, he tests her love by proposing marriage. Once again she waits for Grant to comment on the proposal, but when he remains silent she decides to go through with the marriage.

Bergman, who never hears Grant protecting her honor and reputation, thinks he is uncaring. However, before she enters the American embassy with her story about the proposal, Grant, who is otherwise distant, cynical and professional, has an altercation with one of the officials who refers to Bergman as a "woman of that sort." "She may be risking her life," Grant reminds the man, "but when it comes to being a lady, she doesn't hold a candle to your wife, sir, sitting in Washington playing bridge with three other ladies of honor and virtue." The focus of the investigation concerns uranium ore deposits. Hitchcock expertly handles the suspense elements. The film has been singled out for several of its distinct attributes. Its sensual love scenes are some of the strongest ever shown on the commercial screen up to that time. The direction and cinematography, especially the now-famous long crane shot from the top of a staircase to the close-up of a significant key in Bergman's palm, have retained their power to grip an audience. Perhaps most important is the film's ambiguous morality. Grant, as the hero, propels Bergman into the arms of the villain and then rejects her. To some degree, the audience feels more compassion for Rains, whose greater love for Bergman is requited only with betrayal. In one understated scene, when Rains discovers Bergman's real identity, he enters the bedroom of his mother, who is already suspicious of Bergman's intentions. "Mother," Rains announces quietly, "I'm married to an American agent." See Latin America; Nazi Subversion: Post-World War II. ■

Now We're in the Air (1927), Par. *Dir.* Frank Strayer; *Sc.* Tom J. Geraghty; *Cast includes:* Wallace Beery, Raymond Hatton, Louise Brooks, Russell Simpson, Emile Chautard, Malcolm Waite.

Wallace Beery and Raymond Hatton portray a pair of dimwitted airmen in this comedy set during World War I. A runaway circus balloon takes them into enemy territory. When they return to their own lines, they are picked up as spies and barely escape execution. The pair indulge chiefly in slapstick as they embark on a series of misadventures. The plot concerns their efforts to get the inheritance of an elderly Scotsman. To help them gain acceptance by the rich man, they wear kilts. Louise Brooks provides the female lead in this raucous and crude comedy. This was the last of a three-part series of war comedies that Beery and Hatton starred in as a team. The other entries were *Behind the Front* and *We're in the Navy Now*, both released the previous year. ■

Nude Bomb, The (1980), U. *Dir.* Clive Donner; *Sc.* Arne Sultan, Bill Dana, Leonard B. Stern; *Cast includes:* Don Adams, Sylvia Kristel, Rhonda Fleming, Dana Elcar, Pamela Hensley, Andrea Howard.

Don Adams returns as Maxwell Smart, the inept U.S. secret agent with the notorious shoe telephone, in this weak comedy based on "Get Smart," the once-popular television series. In this misadventure Smart is assigned to foil a plot concerning the launching of missiles which will lead to the nudity of the world's population. Andrea Howard, as Smart's fellow agent, provides some laughs and romantic moments. However, fans of the television series will miss Barbara Feldon, who portrayed the original Agent 99. The film generally fails to capture the loony spirit and pungent satire that contributed to the success of the weekly T.V. show. ∎

Nurse Edith Cavell (1939), RKO. *Dir.* Herbert Wilcox; *Sc.* Michael Hogan; *Cast includes:* Anna Neagle, Edna May Oliver, George Sanders, May Robson, ZaSu Pitts, H. B. Warner.

An antiwar drama that appeared too late (war was declared only days after its opening in New York), the film highlights the historical events in the remarkable life of the title character. Anna Neagle plays Edith Cavell, whose noble sacrifices include helping German as well as Allied soldiers during World War I. Remaining in German-occupied Belgium, she aids prisoners of war to escape across the border. She is finally captured by the enemy and executed.

The film attacks the German military hierarchy rather than the rank-and-file occupation troops. "Leniency will only be mistaken for weakness," the German officer in charge of the Belgian city's occupation states to his subordinates as he calls for the death of the English nurse. The American ambassador's secretary pleads with the officer for Cavell's life, describing her sentence as a "crime against humanity." But the German refuses to revoke the decision. The American concludes that the defendant is a victim of the German war machine. In contrast, a German soldier selected as part of the firing squad refuses to carry out the assignment and is arrested for disobeying orders. The film is based on the novel *Dawn* by Capt. Reginald Berkeley.

English director Herbert Wilcox had already made a silent version in 1928 of Nurse Cavell's war experiences, a film that also stressed antiwar sentiments. This later adaptation did not meet with great box-office success, but it contributed to RKO's image as a studio capable of turning out prestigious features. An early American silent version of Cavell's life was produced in 1918 titled *The Woman the Germans Shot*. ∎

O

Office of Strategic Services (O.S.S.). The United States, upon entry into World War II, lacked an effective international secret service agency. President Franklin D. Roosevelt created the O.S.S. on July 13, 1942, modeled upon the British secret service known as the Special Operations Executive or S.O.E. Roosevelt appointed his friend and confidant, Col. William "Wild Bill" Donovan, as its director. Donovan had studied the operations of the S.O.E. Intelligence operations within the U.S. and in Latin America were to remain in the province of the F.B.I.

The O.S.S., because of its unorthodox methods of operation and personnel, encountered resistance from a good number of high-ranking military leaders, including General Douglas MacArthur, who refused to allow it to operate in his theater of war in the Pacific. Colonel Benjamin Dickson, of the First Army fighting in Europe, banned the O.S.S. from his area of operations. William Casey, in his history of the O.S.S. titled *The Secret War Against Hitler*, points out that spies were necessary in the region of the Ardennes since German forces maintained radio silence, and Colonel Dickson's belligerence put the Allied forces at a disadvantage when Hitler suddenly unleashed his all-out offensive in the winter of 1944–1945. On the other hand, O.S.S. relations with some of General Eisenhower's key officers were slightly better. They welcomed O.S.S. operations behind German lines. Stewart Alsop and Thomas Braden, who later became well-known columnists, were two such members of the O.S.S. who took part in these covert and perilous activities.

O.S.S. functions fell into three areas—propaganda, the gathering and analyzing of information in areas where American forces might become involved, and secret intelligence. The last category received the most glamorized publicity, particularly in such World War II dramas as *O.S.S.*, starring Alan Ladd as a representative agent operating in France, and *13 Rue Madeleine*, starring James Cagney who assigned himself to France as an O.S.S. agent. Both films were released in 1946. The O.S.S. infiltrated operatives into enemy territory to promote sabotage, organize guerrilla resistance and conduct campaigns against enemy forces. All three of these operations were depicted in the two films. Some its biggest successes included aiding in the capture of Corsica, coordinating guerrilla attacks in Burma that resulted in 15,000 Japanese casualties (killed and wounded) and a massive infiltration of agents into the lowlands and France to coordinate guerrilla groups in preparation for the invasion of western Europe.

The counterespionage arm of the O.S.S., known as X-2, was responsible for capturing enemy agents, penetrating enemy intelligence and spreading disinformation, among other tasks. One of these—converting captured Germans to double agents—was dramatized in *Decision Before Dawn* (1951). Oskar Werner, as a captured Luftwaffe medic disillusioned with Hitler, acts as a secret agent for the Americans. He volunteers to locate the position of a Panzer division endangering an Allied advance.

Allen Dulles, who later became head of the Central Intelligence Agency, was in charge of one of the most successful bureaus of the O.S.S., located in Bern, in neutral Switzerland. Dulles and his agents penetrated Germany's Gestapo (secret police), Foreign Office and military. Through his contacts, Dulles effected the surrender of all German troops in Italy a week before the end of the war in Europe. The O.S.S. went out of existence after the war.

Most films about O.S.S. members seem to involve former agents. These heroes have been converted into screen icons endowed with the now-mythical qualities of O.S.S. operatives—courage, loyalty and toughness. Hollywood has tossed these shadow warriors into a variety of intrigues. In *Sofia* (1948), a far-fetched drama about a small group of Americans conducting undercover activities behind the Iron Curtain, Gene Raymond portrays a tough ex-O.S.S. agent who is a major part of an operation that helps key scientists escape to the U.S. Alan Ladd, as a former O.S.S. agent in *Captain Carey, U.S.A.* (1950), returns to Italy after World War II to unmask a traitor responsible for several deaths. Lex Barker, as a former O.S.S. officer in *The Girl in the Kremlin* (1957), helps Zsa Zsa Gabor find her twin who vanished following Stalin's reported death. In *Brass Target* (1978), a fictionalized version of General Patton's death at the hands of assassins, John Cassavetes portrays a veteran of the O.S.S. who helps in the investigation.

Sometimes a film may use an ex-agent to comment on the changing, often blurred, face of the enemy. John Houseman in *Three Days of the Condor* (1975) portrays an embittered C.I.A. chief who is disillusioned with the present political and economic stagnation of the U.S. A former O.S.S. agent during World War II who misses the "clarity" of that conflict, he takes part in a secret conspiracy he thinks will restore the role of the U.S. as a world power. See William J. "Wild Bill" Donovan. ∎

On Company Business (1980), Dratch. *Dir.* Allan Francovich; *Sc.* Allan Francovich.

Using chiefly interviews and stock newsreel footage, this documentary explores some of the abuses of the Central Intelligence Agency since its founding in the early Cold War years. The film strongly suggests that the C.I.A. interjected itself into labor strikes in Europe and the Bay of Pigs fiasco. Those interviewed state that the agency took part in the attempt to assassinate Castro. The C.I.A.'s covert actions in Latin America also come under scrutiny, particularly in Argentina, Brazil, Chile and Uruguay. Eyewitnesses describe in detail examples of torture and terror

employed by C.I.A.-backed local police and state militia.

Other areas in which the C.I.A. played a vital role include Angola and Chile, the latter resulting in a reprimand of the agency at U.S. Senate hearings. One outgrowth of the Watergate Hearings in 1975 was an 18-month investigation by Congress which verged on indicting C.I.A. director Richard Helms. The documentary uses film clips and data from the investigation to underscore damaging revelations about the agency as reported by several of its former agents. Abuses by intelligence agencies and its arrogant directors, the film hints, are not only counter-productive but leave in their wake dishonor and contempt for the democratic process. See Central Intelligence Agency; Labor Unrest; Latin America. ∎

On Dangerous Ground (1917), World. *Dir.* Robert Thornby; *Sc.* Burton E. Stevenson; *Cast includes:* Carlyle Blackwell, Gail Kane, William Bally, Stanhope Wheatcroft, Frank Leigh, Florence Ashbrook.

An early World War I drama set in Germany, the film pits agents representing both sides of the conflict against each other. The production was one of a series of propaganda films to show the Germans as a ruthless foe. One sequence focuses on the Germans as they torture a French maiden (Gail Kane) who had helped a young American escape from German-controlled France. The film was released several months before America's entry into the war and no doubt contributed to the surge of anti-German feeling that prevailed at the time. The film is based on the 1915 novel *Little Comrade: A Tale of the Great War* by Burton E. Stevenson. ∎

On the Border (1930), WB. *Dir.* William McGann; *Sc.* Lillian Hayward; *Cast includes:* John Litel, Armida, Philo McCullough, Bruce Covington, Walter Miller, Rin-Tin-Tin.

The smuggling of Chinese across the Mexican border provides the basis of this routine drama. John Litel, as a U.S. border patrol agent, goes under cover as a drifter to smoke out the gang of smugglers. He is aided by the famous canine Rin-Tin-Tin. Philo McCullough portrays the head villain who is finally brought to justice by Litel. Armida, as the daughter of a ranch owner, gets a chance to sing a few songs. ∎

On the Double (1961), Par. *Dir.* Melville Shavelson; *Sc.* Jack Rose, Melville Shavelson; *Cast includes:* Danny Kaye, Dana Wynter, Wilfrid Hyde-White, Margaret Rutherford, Diana Dors.

A G.I. (Danny Kaye) stationed in England during World War II is called upon to double for a British general whom he happens to resemble. The action takes place on the eve of the Normandy invasion in which the general plays a strategic role. To keep him out of harm's way, British intelligence conjures up the plan involving the American. Kaye becomes entangled with the general's chauffeur (Diana Dors) who turns out to be a German spy and with the general's wife (Dana Wynter). At one point he is kidnapped and taken to Germany where he has a series of further misadventures. During the course of the farce, which probably was written specifically for Kaye, he impersonates Marlene Dietrich and Hitler. ∎

On the Jump (1918), Fox. *Dir.* Raoul Walsh; *Sc.* Ralph Spence; *Cast includes:* George Walsh, Frances Burnham, James Marcus, Henry Clive, Ralph Faulkner.

Released only a few days before the signing of the armistice, this World War I propaganda film had already become dated by the time it reached the theaters. George Walsh portrays a resourceful salesman of Liberty bonds whose unusual techniques get him involved with a banker whose sympathies lie with the Germans. Walsh also becomes embroiled with some spies in this fast-paced but inconsequential action drama. The Liberty Drive had virtually ended when the film was released. ∎

Once Upon a Honeymoon (1942), RKO. *Dir.* Leo McCarey; *Sc.* Sheridan Gibney; *Cast includes:* Ginger Rogers, Cary Grant, Walter Slezak, Albert Dekker, Albert Basserman.

A World War II comedy drama, the film is an odd combination of events, blending the devastation of Czechoslovakia, Poland and France with the frivolous desires of a young burlesque entertainer from Brooklyn looking for a titled husband. Ginger Rogers portrays an American dancer and husband hunter. Cary Grant plays an American reporter with whom she ends up. But before this happy conclusion comes about, the misguided Rogers marries Austrian nobleman Walter Slezak, unaware that he is a Nazi agent. Grant, who knows the truth about the bridegroom, hounds the cou-

ple on their honeymoon through war-torn Europe and finally to France. He eventually convinces her to leave her husband who has helped to bring about the fall of Austria, Czechoslovakia, Poland and other countries. Albert Dekker, as an American agent, poses as a French photographer who is spying on the Germans. "No income tax!" he quips to Rogers about his complex situation which results in a triple salary.

Dekker convinces Rogers to return to her husband and learn what the Germans have planned for the U.S. Grant, meanwhile, agrees to work for Slezak as a radio commentator. Instead of praising the Nazis in his broadcasts to the U.S., Grant uses American idioms and expressions which result in discrediting Hitler and his cohorts. When Rogers delivers a key secret Nazi code to Dekker, he tells her that her job is finished. The American agent is killed by the Gestapo. Rogers and Grant then board a ship for the U.S.

The film is a curious mixture of comedy and drama that more often clashes with each other than blends. Some of the incidents are quite funny, as are the lines. Grant, looking out of a hotel window, witnesses the arrival of Nazis troops. "Hitler is here!" he announces excitedly to Rogers. "I can't see him now," she replies. "I'm dressing." Later, Grant jokingly comments on Rogers' intellectual capacity. "If a gnat dove into your pool of knowledge, he would have broken his neck."

Mingled with these light moments are others of national and personal tragedy. There are scenes of destruction as each nation crumbles from the betrayal of quislings and the armed aggression of Germany. A concentration camp filled with Jewish refugees rounded up by the Gestapo reverberates with the wailing songs of its inhabitants. Rogers exchanges passports with her hotel maid, a Polish Jew with two children. "Go someplace where it's safe," Rogers suggests. The maid stares blankly at Rogers. "Where?" the distraught woman replies, smiling nervously. This is perhaps the most poignant moment in the film.

Several critics, who seemed more aware than those who produced this inane work of the plight of European countries being overrun by Nazi Germany, singled out the film as tasteless and unfunny. This is particularly noticeable in a Nazi concentration camp sequence involving Rogers and Grant. Another comedy film of the same period also attacked for bad taste was Ernst Lubitsch's *To Be or Not to Be* (1942) starring Jack Benny. ▪

One Chance in a Million (1927), Lumas. *Dir.* Noel Mason Smith; *Sc.* L. V. Jefferson; *Cast includes:* William Fairbanks, Viora Daniels, Charles K. French, Henry Herbert, Eddie Borden.

Acrobatic performer William Fairbanks, who had completed another action drama, *Flying High*, several months earlier, portrays the hero in this silent film about jewel thieves. This time around, the obligatory chase and action sequences involve cars instead of airplanes. Fairbanks, as an undercover agent for the U.S. Secret Service, falls under suspicion as a possible suspect in the jewel thefts until he reveals his true identity and exposes the leader of the culprits. Viora Daniels provides the romantic interest in this fast-paced tale whose chief attributes are its fist fights and car chases rather than dialogue and characterization. ▪

One Night in Lisbon (1941), Par. *Dir.* Edward H. Griffith; *Sc.* Virginia Van Upp; *Cast includes:* Madeleine Carroll, Fred MacMurray, Patricia Morison, Edmund Gwenn, Billie Burke, John Loder.

An American pilot (Fred MacMurray) ferrying planes across the Atlantic to England falls in love with a conservative young Englishwoman (Madeleine Carroll) in this World War II romantic comedy. After meeting Carroll in a London air raid shelter, MacMurray woos her in a whirlwind romance that takes the couple to Lisbon. The affair then hits a snag when he believes that she is being used as a decoy for enemy agents. John Loder, as a navy officer who wants to marry Carroll, presents a further complication for the aggressive MacMurray. Billie Burke, as a dizzy socialite, adds to the confusion. Based on the play *There's Always Juliet* by John Van Druten, the film fails in its attempt to mix screwball comedy and romance with wartime events. The latter takes a back seat through the entire production. ▪

One of Our Spies Is Missing (1966), MGM. *Dir.* E. Darrell Hallenbeck; *Sc.* Howard Rodman; *Cast includes:* Robert Vaughn, David McCallum, Leo G. Carroll, Maurice Evans, Vera Miles, Ann Elder, Bernard Fox.

Another theatrical release deriving from edited entries in "The Man From U.N.C.L.E."

television series, this routine drama focuses on a formula for reversing the aging process of humans. Robert Vaughn, as Napoleon Solo, and David McCallum, as Illya Kuryakin, two of U.N.C.L.E.'s most overworked agents, are assigned to investigate the disappearance of a professor who has been working in the field of genetics. Their superior (Leo G. Carroll) suspects the scientist has developed an electronic process that peels away years from a person's life.

Two opposing forces are also interested in the professor's discovery—a power-hungry woman (Vera Miles) who has built up a hatred for men, and an agent (Bernard Fox) from T.H.R.U.S.H., an international organization dedicated to promoting world chaos and evil. Miles early in the film gains the lead by kidnapping the professor and having him restore the youth of a former powerful British statesmen (Maurice Evans)—now a sickly old man. "In a world controlled by men," Miles cackles, "I have found a way to control the controllers." Fox, meanwhile, has his own plans. He sends out his henchmen to kidnap the professor and then blackmails Miles to influence the statesman to do T.H.R.U.S.H.'s bidding.

Vaughn and McCallum thus far have blundered their way through the plot without success, including being drugged, knocked unconscious and captured several times. In addition, they have allowed their foes to escape and failed to rescue the scientist. Undaunted, they bounce back with spirit after each setback until they finally succeed in gaining possession of the coveted formula. By this time, the professor, fearing that evil forces may wrest the secret from him by torture, has committed suicide, and Miles sacrifices her life to save the elder statesman who regrets that he has been exploited politically. Evans, the venerable stage and screen actor, is always worth watching and listening to as he adds dignity to such lines as "Time is the enemy. It wounds you with its days." See "The Man From U.N.C.L.E." ▪

One Spy Too Many (1966), MGM. *Dir.* Joseph Sargent; *Sc.* Dean Hargrove; *Cast includes:* Robert Vaughn, David McCallum, Rip Torn, Dorothy Provine, Yvonne Craig.

Robert Vaughn and David McCallum, as two international espionage agents, trail a dangerous fanatic who has delusions about controlling the world in this conventional tale. The film is drawn from two episodes of the popular television series *The Man From U.N.C.L.E.* Rip Torn portrays the master villain who has stolen a supply of "will gas" from the U.S. Army Biological Warfare Division and escaped to Greece. The two agents, accompanied by Torn's wife (Dorothy Provine) who wants a divorce from him, journey to Greece but are soon captured by Torn and abandoned in a Greek temple. Barely escaping with their lives, Vaughn and McCallum follow their prey to the U.S. and, after an exciting battle, end the fanatic's career and save the globe from the nerve gas. See "The Man From U.N.C.L.E." ■

Only the Brave (1930), Par. *Dir.* Frank Tuttle; *Sc.* Edward E. Paramore, Jr.; *Cast includes:* Gary Cooper, Mary Brian, Phillips Holmes, James Neill, Morgan Farley, Gay Oliver.

A Union captain (Gary Cooper) in this Civil War drama volunteers to act as a spy on a secret mission certain to bring about his death. He asks for the assignment after seeing the woman he loves in the arms of another man. His task is to purposely get caught with important papers designed to mislead the Southern generals. He makes his way into enemy territory and reaches the house where members of the Confederate general staff are billeted. He is captured but manages to survive. When the war ends he marries a Southerner whom he met during his mission. Near the end of the film, Generals Grant and Lee are shown signing the historic armistice. Four years later Cooper switched sides in a similar story. He plays a Confederate agent in *Operator 13* (1934) and uncovers a pretty Union spy (Marion Davies) with whom he falls in love. ■

Operation CIA (1965), AA. *Dir.* Christian Nyby; *Sc.* Bill S. Ballinger, Peer J. Oppenheimer; *Cast includes:* Burt Reynolds, Kieu Chinh, Danielle Aubry, John Hoyt, Cyril Collick.

A C.I.A. agent (Burt Reynolds) in this drama of intrigue is sent to Saigon during the Vietnam War to investigate the murder of a fellow agent. Masquerading as a professor of agriculture, he meets his contact (Kieu Chinh) who tells Reynolds of a plot to assassinate the U.S. ambassador. Reynolds is kidnapped by the terrorists involved in the plot

but escapes in time to prevent the murder. Danielle Aubry plays a French spy who, in reality, is a double agent working with the terrorists. Except for some of the scenes that were shot in Saigon, the film, also listed as *Last Message From Saigon*, is of routine interest. See Central Intelligence Agency; Vietnam War: Intelligence and Covert Actions. ■

Operation Crossbow (1965), MGM. *Dir.* Michael Anderson; *Sc.* Richard Imrie, Derry Quinn, Ray Rigby; *Cast includes:* Sophia Loren, George Peppard, Trevor Howard, John Mills, Tom Courtenay, Paul Henreid.

Allied forces decide to send three specially trained agents, masquerading as pro-German technicians, behind enemy lines to seek out, infiltrate and help destroy a secret missile base in this tense and action-filled World War II drama. British intelligence, suspecting Germany of having long-range rockets, requests that the Royal Air Force bomb the sites. The raids slow down enemy progress in rocket weaponry, but the British soon learn that the Germans have built an underground factory impregnable to aerial attacks.

George Peppard, as an American officer, Tom Courtenay, as a Dutch patriot, and Jeremy Kemp, an English officer, make up the special team. They parachute into Holland and, with false identity papers of dead men, plan to enter Germany. However, they face several setbacks. The man Courtenay is impersonating is wanted for murder by the Dutch police who do not know he has been killed in an air raid. Courtenay is arrested, recognized by a Gestapo officer as a British agent and tortured. Refusing to admit he is a spy, he is placed before a firing squad and shot. Peppard has his own problems when the wife (Sophia Loren) of the man he is impersonating suddenly appears in his hotel room. Peppard innocently reassures her she will not be harmed if she promises not to expose him. When he leaves for the German rocket base, a member of the Dutch underground (Lilli Palmer) kills Loren.

Kemp and Peppard get jobs in the underground site and manage to illuminate the missile stronghold for a squadron of Allied bombers. The base is destroyed, but the two agents lose their lives in carrying out their mission. The film ends with Prime Minister Winston Churchill praising those who planned the operation and the bombing crews. "Let us clear the rubble and lay the bricks," he adds. "Let us do so in the firm conviction that we are building for the future; that never again shall we have to embark upon such a conflict that we have recently endured. I solemnly believe that the price of such a folly would be far more than mankind could afford to pay."

The actual Operation Crossbow concerned Allied attacks against the launching sites of Germany's V-1 flying bombs and V-2 rockets, the so-called vengeance weapons that caused havoc over London and took a terrible toll in lives—more than 6,000 before the last rocket fell on England in March 1945. The major launching pads were in Holland and France. Allied bombing raids were not entirely effective in destroying all the launch sites, some of which were difficult to locate. ■

Operation Daybreak (1976), WB. *Dir.* Lewis Gilbert; *Sc.* Ronald Harwood; *Cast includes:* Timothy Bottoms, Karel Curda, Joss Ackland, Nicola Pagett, Anthony Andrews, Anton Diffring.

This World War II drama reenacts the assassination of Nazi officer Reinhard Heydrich, also known as "Heydrich the Hangman" by Czech freedom fighters, and the resultant destruction of Lidice by the Germans. A special group of Czech agents is parachuted by the British into Czechoslovakia for the purpose of killing the brutal Nazi administrator. Following the assassination, the Germans retaliate by destroying the town of Lidice and murdering most of its citizens. The Germans, aided by an informer, capture the members of the special force and execute them. (The two real-life assassins committed suicide rather than surrender to the Gestapo.) Timothy Bottoms portrays one of the assassins. Anton Diffring impersonates Heydrich. Nicola Pagett provides the romantic interest for Bottoms in this tale based on facts. The film was adapted from the novel *Seven Men at Daybreak* by Alan Burgess. Fritz Lang's *Hangmen Also Die* (1943) dealt with the same subject. See Reinhard Heydrich. ■

Operation Manhunt (1954), UA. *Dir.* Jack Alexander; *Sc.* Paul Monash; *Cast includes:* Harry Townes, Irja Jensen, Jacques Aubuchon, Robert Goudier, Albert Miller, Caren Shaffer.

The Soviets assign one of their secret agents to assassinate a former Russian code clerk who has exposed a Communist spy network operating in Canada in this drama based on the experiences of Igor Gouzenko. Shot chiefly in a semi-documentary style on location in Canada, the film uses many Canadians in its cast. Harry Townes portrays Gouzenko, who remains firm in his convictions although he knows he is being hunted. The assassin, played by Jacques Aubuchon, at first stalks his victim diligently but then ends up also defecting. Irja Jensen, as the ex-code clerk's wife, has only a small role. Westbrook Van Voorhees serves as narrator, and the real Gouzenko appears briefly in an epilogue.

Although the plot is highly fictional, there is some credence in the attempt on Gouzenko's life. He had not only done irreparable damage to the Soviet spy network in the Western Hemisphere but helped to smash a spy ring that was stealing atomic secrets from the U.S. and Britain. He also helped to expose to other nations the Soviet Union's master plan of worldwide espionage through its embassies. For these reasons he was kept incognito until his death in 1982. The K.G.B. marked him for assassination. See Igor Gouzenko. ■

Operation Nordpol. Perhaps the greatest setback suffered by British intelligence during World War II was the German penetration and control of Britain's Netherlands operation. The Germans, after capturing a Dutch radio operator working for the British S.O.E. (Special Operations Executive), forced him to transmit their messages. The S.O.E. operator in London, failing to recognize a predetermined warning signal sent by his Dutch counterpart, assumed that further broadcasts were legitimate. Therefore, the Germans were able to entrap a string of Allied agents who quickly fell into Gestapo hands. The bewildered captives, like their fellow Dutch operative, were soon persuaded to broadcast under German control. The immediate success of Operation Nordpol, as it was named by Berlin, encouraged the Germans to increase the number of Dutch transmitters aimed at London. The S.O.E., believing it was supplying its agents and members of the Dutch underground, began to parachute large quantities of food, ammunition, currency and other items to the enemy.

The debacle was compounded when two S.O.E. agents who had escaped from the Germans returned to England and told about the enemy takeover of the Dutch operation. S.O.E. officers rejected the escapees' charges, labeled them double agents working for the Germans and quickly imprisoned them. Eventually other witnesses confirmed what was happening in the Netherlands, forcing the S.O.E. to reassess the entire operation. By the time the Germans shut down Operation Nordpol in 1944, more than 100 men and women paid with their lives for the disaster. In September, alone, of that year, the Germans sentenced to death more than 40 S.O.E. agents.

Several American films about World War II deal with events in the Netherlands, but none allude to the notorious Nordpol affair. In *First Comes Courage* (1943) a British commando (Brian Aherne) sent to Norway is captured by the Germans. *The Conspirators* (1944), an intrigue-filled drama set in Lisbon, has Paul Henreid as a Dutch guerrilla leader hunted by Nazis for his sabotage activities. Meanwhile, another agent about to return to Holland on a secret mission is killed. The drama *Betrayed* (1956) concerns treason within the Dutch underground. A guerrilla leader (Victor Mature) causes the deaths of his fellow resistance fighters when he learns that the underground has condemned his mother for collaborating with the Germans. Seeking revenge upon the Dutch citizenry, he secretly informs German intelligence about future raids by the resistance. These representative dramas reveal the perils of intelligence work and armed resistance but never mention how British intelligence was duped by the Germans. ∎

Operation Overlord. The Germans, lulled by bad weather and a successful Allied plan of deception known as Ultra, had been largely caught off guard that early morning of June 6, 1944. At 6:30 A.M., as darkness lifted, an armada of 5,000 ships began to disperse the first waves of 154,000 Allied troops onto the beaches of Normandy, France. The greatest amphibious assault in history, by a combined force of Americans, British and Canadians, sought to penetrate Hitler's "Atlantic Wall," a string of in-depth fortifications facing the English Channel. The date of the Normandy invasion had been dubbed "D-Day," and the entire undertaking was called "Operation Overlord."

The Nazi high command delayed bringing armored units and reserves into Normandy. It had been tricked by false documents, double agents and other ruses into believing that the

main landings would come at Calais, further north and east, at the shortest crossing point on the English Channel. Lord Boothby, in a July 1973 article in *Books and Bookmen*, writes that a "remarkable coup was the feeding to the Germans, in the Second World War, of an entirely false Allied Order of Battle at the time of the Normandy invasion."

The Allies further impeded German movement by coordinating guerrilla activities of the French Resistance. As a result, the Allies were able to consolidate their grip at the invasion sites in several days of fighting. Hitler, incidentally, had intuitively suspected Normandy would be the main landing site, but he was not able to convince his generals to deploy their troops and defenses accordingly.

Some World War II historians believe that the well-kept secret of the time and place of the Normandy invasion on June 6, 1944, was highly exaggerated—that, in fact, Berlin was generally aware of Allied strategy. They point out that Germany held their main war games in Normandy during 1943–1944. Also, German spies reported that more than 20 French Resistance groups were assigned to organize sabotage activities in the spring of 1944 between Normandy and Paris. In addition, a string of air strikes by Britain's Royal Air Force, which continually pounded the various routes between the coast of Normandy and Paris, did not go unnoticed by Germany's high command.

Several spy dramas used Operation Overlord as background for their plots. They all assumed that the Germans did not know the exact date and location of the invasion. In *13 Rue Madeleine* (1946) James Cagney, as an O.S.S. officer, discovers that a Nazi agent (Richard Conte) has penetrated one of his special assault teams operating behind enemy lines. Cagney decides to follow the group into German-held territory. Conte captures Cagney and has him tortured to learn the exact location of the forthcoming Allied invasion. In *Count Five and Die* (1958) British and U.S. intelligence forces devise a plan to baffle the Germans about the actual location of the Allied invasion. Annamarie Duringer, as a double agent working for the Nazis, is killed before she can spoil the elaborate scheme to deceive the Nazi military defense forces. Perhaps the most elaborate plot about the secret of the Allied invasion appeared in the suspenseful drama *36 Hours*. James Garner portrays a captured American officer who is tricked by the Germans into revealing the actual invasion plans of the Allies. Garner is drugged and made to believe that he has been suffering from amnesia for six years. He discovers the Nazi scheme after he mentions Normandy but proceeds to confuse the landing place in the minds of his captors. See German Intelligence: World War II. ■

Operation Secret (1952), WB. *Dir.* Lewis Seiler; *Sc.* James R. Webb, Harold Medford; *Cast includes:* Cornel Wilde, Steve Cochran, Phyllis Thaxter, Karl Malden, Paul Picerni, Lester Matthews.

A World War II drama unfolded through flashbacks, the film involves the French underground and a traitor. The story opens at a trial concerning a murder during the war. As former members of the underground and others connected with the crime testify, the chief suspect seems to be Cornel Wilde, an American agent believed killed in an airplane crash during the conflict. He suddenly appears in the courtroom and gives evidence that proves the real murderer was a Communist spy masquerading as a French patriot (Steve Cochran). Action sequences include Wilde's wartime exploits in capturing Nazi films of a jet airplane and his suspenseful escape from behind enemy lines. Phyllis Thaxter portrays a member of the underground. The film is based on *The Life of Peter Ortiz*, by Lt. Colonel Ortiz, a World War II marine hero. ■

Operator 13 (1934), MGM *Dir.* Richard Boleslawsky; *Sc.* Harvey Thew, Zelda Sears, Eve Greene; *Cast includes:* Marion Davies, Gary Cooper, Jean Parker, Katharine Alexander, Ted Healy.

Except for a few songs interspersed by the Mills Brothers, including "Sleepy Head," this routine Civil War drama offers few surprises. A Union actress (Marion Davies) volunteers to work for detective Allan Pinkerton as a secret agent for the North. She journeys South, impersonating a young black servant to Pauline Cushman (Katharine Alexander), another Union spy. While passing information to the North, Davies meets Gary Cooper, who plays a Confederate spy. Cushman's real identity is discovered and she is arrested. Davies helps her to escape, and both spies return to Pinkerton in the North to await further duties.

The second half of the drama concerns Davies' second foray into the South to spy on Cooper, whom Union officers suspect of organizing a conspiracy in the North. A Union colonel explains the details to Davies. "The Sons of Liberty," he says, "is a military and secret organization formed in the North by Southern sympathizers. This is a well-knit organization having over half-a-million members. They plan to seize Ohio, Indiana, Illinois, Kentucky and Missouri and proclaim a new nation to be known as the Northwest Confederacy." The obligatory love affair follows when Cooper meets Davies but does not recognize her as the black servant he had encountered earlier. When Cooper discovers her real identity, he pursues and captures her and plans to bring her back for a court-martial.

Davies, sensing his hatred for her, reminds him that he, too, is a spy. "Yes, I am," he replies. But I'm a man—a soldier. I'm not a woman who lets people befriend her because she is a woman and then stabs them in the back." George Brent in *Stamboul Quest*, released the same year as *Operator 13*, also objects to nations using women as secret agents. Brent rebukes German spy Myrna Loy, whom he loves, and wants her to give up her espionage work. "I know what war is," he reassures her. "You go out and fight. You shoot and get shot. That's what war is. You don't use women as weapons." *Virginia City* (1940), another Civil War drama, also comments on the role of women spies—this time from the spy's point of view. Confederate officer Randolph Scott orders fellow undercover agent Miriam Hopkins to lead Union spy Errol Flynn into a trap because he may endanger their entire plan. "So I must lead him quietly and unsuspectingly to his death," Hopkins muses caustically, "because I am a woman. That's only something a woman can do." However, Davies saves Cooper's life when Union troops suddenly appear. The war continues as the two lovers continue to serve their respective causes. Following Lee's surrender, the lovers find each other and vow to put the war behind them.

Ted Healy, who introduced the Three Stooges comedy team to the stage and ultimately to the screen, plays a trouper in a medicine show who in reality is working for the Union secret service. This was the second Civil War drama for Cooper, who displayed a sense of impartiality concerning the war; in

Only the Brave (1930) he played a Union spy who operated behind Confederate lines. After completing the film, which was adapted from the novel by Robert W. Chambers, Marion Davies left MGM to work for Paramount. Only a few moments in the film bear any resemblance to real events. Pauline Cushman was an actual spy for the Union, and the Sons of Liberty and their Northwest Confederacy plot was a real threat to the Union until it was uncovered by Northern secret agents. See American Civil War: Intelligence and Covert Actions; Pauline Cushman. ∎

Orient Express (1934), Fox. *Dir.* Paul Martin; *Sc.* Paul Martin, Carl Hovey, William Counselman, Oscar Levant; *Cast includes:* Heather Angel, Norman Foster, Ralph Morgan, Herbert Mundin, Una O'Connor, Irene Ware.

Intrigue aboard the famous Orient Express journeying from France to Turkey provides the background for this suspenseful and atmospheric drama about a revolutionary traveling incognito. Ralph Morgan, as the fanatic, has his life threatened aboard the train as other passengers play various related roles. Heather Angel portrays a dancer; Norman Foster a businessman; Roy D'Arcy an assassin; and Dorothy Burgess a journalist. Morgan is returning to an unnamed Balkan country to foment an uprising. Opposing forces are determined to prevent him from reaching his destination in this Grand Hotel-style tale. Herbert Mundin and Una O'Connor provide some comic relief. ∎

O.S.S. See Office of Strategic Services. ∎

O.S.S. (1946), Par. *Dir.* Irving Pichel; *Sc.* Richard Maibaum; *Cast includes:* Alan Ladd, Geraldine Fitzgerald, Patric Knowles, Richard Benedict, Richard Webb, Don Beddoe.

Four agents of the American Office of Strategic Services are sent into Nazi-occupied France to blow up an otherwise inaccessible railway tunnel in this World War II drama. Geraldine Fitzgerald, as the female member of the team, is treated with hostility by one of the agents (Alan Ladd). The leader of the operation is captured by the Gestapo, and Ladd assumes command. When Fitzgerald proves her value to the mission, Ladd not only changes his attitude but falls in love with her. After they accomplish their objective, they are asked to remain in France to gather information for the approaching Allied invasion. Following this, Fitzgerald is captured by the Gestapo as she and Ladd are about to make their escape. Ladd regretfully is forced to abandon her so that the vital information can be turned over to Allied headquarters. Although the film includes the typical heroics of a Ladd drama of this period—parachute drops behind enemy lines, derring-do escapes and plenty of action—the final capture of Fitzgerald adds a note of realism to the drama. See Jedburgh Operations; Office of Strategic Services. ∎

Osterman Weekend, The (1983), TCF. *Dir.* Sam Peckinpah; *Sc.* Alan Sharp, Ian Masters; *Cast includes:* Rutger Hauer, John Hurt, Craig T. Nelson, Dennis Hopper, Chris Sarandon, Meg Foster.

The C.I.A. convinces an influential television interview host to spy on his friends who are suspected of being Soviet agents in this convoluted drama about the invasion of privacy. A C.I.A. agent (John Hurt), acting under orders, persuades Rutger Hauer, as the talk show personality, that some of his friends may be secret agents conspiring with the Soviet Union. Hauer permits the agent to wire his home with an array of sophisticated cameras and other eavesdropping equipment in preparation for his weekend guests. Meg Foster and Christopher Starr, as Hauer's wife and son, remain for the fateful weekend, although Hauer tries to get them to leave. The social event deteriorates when the guests suspect that they are being spied upon. Hurt and his fellow agents then begin to manipulate the fate of each guest. The film ends with Hauer forced but determined to defend his home against violators.

Burt Lancaster, who has a cameo role as a C.I.A. chief, assigns Hurt to the case. Lancaster sees himself as a possible candidate for the presidency. Chris Sarandon portrays a fiery entrepreneur. Cassie Yates, as his wife, is not averse to expressing her sexual frustrations. Dennis Hopper portrays a doctor who is burdened with a drug-addicted wife (Helen Shaver). The film was adapted from a novel by Robert Ludlum. See Central Intelligence Agency. ∎

Our Man Flint (1966), TCF. *Dir.* Daniel Mann; *Sc.* Hal Fimberg, Ben Starr; *Cast includes:* James Coburn, Lee J. Cobb, Gila Golan, Edward Mulhare, Benson Fong, Shelby Grant.

James Coburn, as superspy Derek Flint, foils the ambitious plans of three mad scientists who try to control the world by manipulating the weather in this action-packed spoof of the espionage genre. The Zonal Organization on World Intelligence Espionage (Z.O.W.I.E.) chooses Flint, a loner, to find the sinister trio and end their diabolical plot. Surrounded equally by buxom semi-clad women and special advanced weaponry, Flint journeys to France to fulfill his mission. Using physical prowess, consisting chiefly of karate, and a handy little cigarette lighter which serves multiple functions, he battles his way through tremendous obstacles before he ends the world threat.

His nemesis is Galaxy, a secret organization bent on world domination and whose chief agent is the seductive Gila Golan. Her underlings include Edward Mulhare as a sophisticated but deadly Englishman and Michael St. Clair as an assassin whose misfortune it is to cross Flint's path. Lee J. Cobb, as the superagent's flustered superior, frowns upon Flint's unorthodox methods. Benson Fong, Rhys Williams and Peter Brocco portray the scientists. ■

Outrageous Fortune (1987), Buena Vista. *Dir.* Arthur Hiller; *Sc.* Leslie Dixon; *Cast includes:* Shelley Long, Bette Midler, Peter Coyote, Robert Prosky, John Schuck, George Carlin.

Two women discover that their lover, supposedly killed in an explosion, was a double agent working for the Soviets in this adventure-chase comedy with a "lady and the tramp" theme. Shelley Long portrays a straight-laced struggling New York actress who never seems to get a break. She has already exhausted more than $30,000 of her parents' money for acting lessons. Bette Midler plays another aspiring actress with a more earthy background, her latest role being in a porno epic titled *Ninja Vixens*. She adorns one of her ears with an earring she has lifted "off a Christmas tree at Saks." With her brashness and big mouth, two of her greatest attributes, she manages to force her way on an airline ("There's a kidney in Kansas City that ain't gettin' any fresher! she exclaims). The two thespians discover that they both have been in love with the same man (Peter Coyote) when they appear at the morgue to identify his body. However, they conclude that the corpse is not that of their lover.

The two jilted women join forces to track down Coyote so that he can choose between them. During their misadventures, which includes a clever comic bit in which they rob a drug dealer with a toy gun, they learn that Coyote was using them to deliver secret information to their acting teacher (Robert Prosky), in reality his Soviet contact. They finally locate Coyote after fending off a host of spies and save the North American continent in this offbeat, zany and occasionally hilarious farce. The title of this buddy movie with a feminine twist comes from a soliloquy by Hamlet, whom Long, as a notoriously bad actress, dreams someday of playing. ■

Outsider, The (1980), Par. *Dir.* Tony Luraschi; *Sc.* Tony Luraschi; *Cast includes:* Craig Wasson, Sterling Hayden, Patricia Quinn, Niall Toibin, Elizabeth Begley, T. P. McKenna.

A young Irish-American, raised on the stories of Ireland's struggles against Britain, decides to join the Irish Republican Army in this contemporary drama about the problems in Northern Ireland. Craig Wasson portrays the green American who wants to fight for Irish nationalism. Sterling Hayden, as the grandfather, has regaled Wasson with the glories of the past. However, Wasson is soon disillusioned by the conflict. Members of the I.R.A. have their own use for the recruit. They intend to have him killed by a British bullet so that they can more readily raise funds in America for their cause. The British, meanwhile, plan to frame Wasson so that the identity of one of their own informants is not uncovered. Wasson returns to the States in disgust.

The film, shot chiefly in Dublin, captures the tragedy of the conflict without sensationalizing it. Children are seen preparing incendiary bombs; British troops gun down children fleeing from an explosion and torture I.R.A. sympathizers; young Irish lads who have spent a lifetime steeped in violence turn into callous killers. The film was adapted from the novel *The Heritage of Michael Flaherty* by Colin Leinster. ■

Over Secret Wires (1915), Kay-Bee. *Cast includes:* Thomas Chatterton, Harvey Clark.

Enemy agents contact German submarines off the Pacific coast in this World War I drama. Thomas Chatterton, as a U.S. Secret Service agent, uncovers a plot involving German spies who are signaling their U-boats about American shipping off the coast of Oregon. Submarine warfare, which provided a relatively new and fascinating element to war dramas of the period, was considered a serious threat to the overall war effort. See U.S. Secret Service. ■

Over the Top (1918), Vitagraph. *Dir.* Wilfred North; *Sc.* Robert Gordon Anderson; *Cast includes:* Arthur Guy Empey, Lois Meredith, James Morrison, Arthur Donaldson, Julia Swayne, Mary Maurice.

Based on the World War I book of the same name by Arthur Guy Empey, the film digresses at times from the original story. Sergeant Owen, the main character, is shown receiving decorations for his bravery on the Mexican border. Later, while in London, he enlists in the British army and is sent to the front lines in France during World War I. The film includes a plot involving a German spy who later becomes a general in the German army. There is also a suspenseful escape by airplane to the American lines by Owen and a young American woman who has been held captive by the general.

The principal character, Owen, was played by Empey himself. In the film another character, called "Folly," supposedly was fashioned after Senator Robert Marion La Follette. Folly is seen dealing with the German spy. In real life La Follette (1855–1925), who had served as congressman, governor of Wisconsin and U.S. senator, had been highly criticized for his outspoken opposition to America's entry into World War I and was censured in the Senate. However, he was never directly indicted for treason or any other war crime. ■

P

Pacific Blackout (1942), Par. *Dir.* Ralph Murphy; *Sc.* Lester Cole; *Cast includes:* Robert Preston, Martha O'Driscoll, Philip Merivale, Eva Gabor, Louis Jean Heydt, Thurston Hall.

Robert Preston portrays a fugitive who has escaped from the law during a practice blackout in this World War II drama. Wrongly accused of murder, he is determined to find the real killer before the police arrest him. Meanwhile, saboteurs are planning to blow up an ammunition factory under cover of the blackout. Martha O'Driscoll provides the romantic interest in this suspenseful and entertaining low-budget film. Its basic plot about an innocent man on the run and his attempts to extricate himself owes much to Alfred Hitchcock. The film had been previously reviewed by some critics in December 1941 under its original title, *Midnight Angel*, but was held back from its release until early in 1942. ■

Pacific Rendezvous (1942), MGM. *Dir.* George Sidney; *Sc.* Harry Kurnitz; *Cast includes:* Lee Bowman, Jean Rogers, Mona Maris, Carl Esmond, Paul Cavanagh, Blanche Yurka.

A young U.S. Navy lieutenant manages to capture a Nazi spy ring in Washington, D.C.— in spite of the bewildering title of this inept drama. Lee Bowman plays the stalwart officer who is hampered by his fiancée, portrayed by Jean Rogers. Mona Maris and Carl Esmond portray two of the enemy agents. The film is a remake of the World War I drama *Rendezvous* (1935), which in turn was adapted from the novel *The Blonde Countess* by Herbert Osborn Yardley. ■

Palmer raids. Attorney General A. Mitchell Palmer dreaded the possible rise of anarchy, sedition or even revolution when the American Communist and Communist Labor parties emerged in the wake of World War I and the Russian Revolution. An outbreak of strikes in 1919 brought fear to industrialists, politicians and the general public, many of whom accused radicals, aliens and Communists of fomenting the unrest. By June, bombs went off in eight major American cities. Other bombs were mailed to the homes of such notable dignitaries as John D. Rockefeller, Seattle's Mayor Hansen and the Postmaster General. Palmer's home was damaged by a similar explosive.

The Attorney General met with J. Edgar Hoover in June and requested that he organize an anti-radical branch of the Department of Justice. In November Palmer organized raids against radicals in a dozen cities, resulting in hundreds of arrests and several deportations. By December of 1919 deportations grew to hundreds, many of whom had no criminal records and were not affiliated with any Communist organization. Mass arrests increased to 4,000 on one night alone (January 2, 1920) and extended across the nation to 33 cities.

By the end of 1920 the fear of Bolshevism subsided in the U.S. and Europe, and many of those arrested were released. Americans ignored Palmer's warnings of imminent revolution. The callous treatment of dissenters during this period revealed the most extensive assault on civil liberties in the country's history.

Palmer's report to Congress on American radicals shows his total inability to understand the fundamental liberties of Americans under the Bill of Rights. "If there be any doubt of the general character of the active leaders and agitators amongst these avowed revolutionists," he stated in part, "a visit to the Department of Justice and an examination of their photographs would dispel it. Out of the sly and craft eyes of many of them leap cupidity, cruelty, insanity, and crime; from the lopsided faces, sloping brows, and mis-shapen features may be recognized the un-mistakable criminal type." Palmer's punitive attitudes no doubt helped to incite the public against the rights of dissenters.

Several films of the period refer to enemy aliens, Bolsheviks and plotters determined to agitate workers, assassinate political and in-dustrial leaders and generally cause turmoil. Virtually all the releases were blatantly anti-labor and portrayed workers as dupes of rad-icals deliberately instigating trouble. No film showed any sympathy for a dissenter. The films most likely reflected the mood of the country and the attitudes of studio bosses.

The Bomb Throwers (1915) ironically an-ticipates some of the turbulence the country was to face during the next few years. Com-munists seek revenge after one of their mem-bers, a dangerous terrorist, is jailed through the efforts of a district attorney. The Reds convince Tony, a poor Italian immigrant wid-ower, that the D.A. was responsible for his wife's death. They then persuade him to place a bomb under the home of their victim. *The Volcano* (1919), a controversial propa-ganda drama about a Communist conspiracy, shows a Communist leader plotting to assas-sinate several dignitaries, including, among others, New York Governor Alfred E. Smith and Attorney General A. Mitchell Palmer. In *The Undercurrent* (1919) Russian agents spread dissent and propaganda among Amer-icans in the hope of eventually bringing about a world revolution. *The Great Shadow* (1920) depicts how Russian agents operate to incite tensions between capital and labor. Their target is an American shipyard where they instigate a major strike by thousands of workers. See also Labor Unrest; Red Scare of 1919–1920. ∎

Panama Canal. This strategically impor-tant waterway linking the Atlantic and Pa-cific oceans has been the subject of several Hollywood spy films. Within this genre the Panama Canal has been the target of various foreign agents who were bent on stealing plans of its structure or destroying its locks.

One of the earliest dramas to focus on the Panama Canal was the serial *Pearl of the Army* (1916). Silent serial queen Pearl White portrays an intrepid lass who prevents Ori-ental agents from sabotaging the Canal. *The Silent Command* (1923), a spy story involv-ing the mining of the Canal, centers on secret agents trying to steal an American navy offic-er's (Edmund Lowe) plans for the mine fields.

With the advent of World War II, the num-ber of dramas about the Canal increased in proportion to its strategic significance. The films, most of which were low-budget entries, explored the determination of Axis spies to halt or at least slow down the transport of vital Allied war supplies. The plots were chiefly fictitious, but the dangers at the time seemed real to American audiences. In *Panama Patrol* (1939), for instance, Leon Ames portrays an army major who captures a spy ring operating in the Canal Zone. In *Phantom Raiders* (1940) saboteurs were busy attacking ships in the region before master detective Nick Carter (Walter Pidgeon) puts a stop to their activities. In *Charlie Chan in Panama*, released the same year, the Hawaiian sleuth, working with U.S. intelligence, snuffs out a plot to blow up a portion of the Canal. *The Phantom Submarine* (1941), a weak drama about a mysterious sub lurking in the waters off the Canal, features Anita Louise as a secret agent who is assigned by the U.S. Navy to learn the vessel's where-abouts and its mission. Humphrey Bogart in *Across the Pacific* (1942) portrays an Ameri-can agent posing as a court-martialed army officer trying to prevent Sydney Greenstreet from bombing the Canal. *Betrayal From the East* (1945), with Lee Tracy and Nancy Kelly, concerns Japanese agents seeking a blueprint of the Panama Canal defenses. Thanks to Hol-lywood and the American armed forces, the Panama Canal survived World War II intact. ∎

Panama Patrol (1939), GN. *Dir.* Charles La-mont; *Sc.* Arthur Hoerl; *Cast includes:* Leon Ames, Charlotte Wynters, Weldon Heyburn, Adrienne Ames, Abner Biberman.

Leon Ames portrays an army major who captures a spy ring operating in the Panama Canal in this conventional World War II drama. Charlotte Wynters plays his aide and fiancée. Abner Biberman has the unpleasant task of impersonating an Oriental responsible for the espionage in this low-budget yarn. Ames and Wynters had teamed up one year earlier in *Cipher Bureau*, another drama in which they played similar roles. See Panama Canal. ■

Panic in the City (1968), Commonwealth. *Dir.* Eddie Davis; *Sc.* Eddie Davis, Charles E. Savage; *Cast includes:* Howard Duff, Linda Cristal, Stephen McNally, Nehemiah Persoff, Anne Jeffries, Oscar Beregi.

A fanatic Soviet spy, going off on his own, threatens Los Angeles with an atomic bomb in this low-budget drama. Howard Duff, as a U.S. government agent, is assigned to locate the renegade spy who has assembled the destructive bomb. Linda Cristal, as a radiologist, helps Duff in his investigation. Nehemiah Persoff portrays the crazed Soviet. Anne Jeffries plays his collaborator. Suggestions for evacuating the city arise but are never carried forth as Persoff threatens to detonate the bomb. Duff manages to save Los Angeles by disposing of the triggered atomic bomb in a scene that defies credibility. ■

Parallax View, The (1974), Par. *Dir.* Alan J. Pakula; *Sc.* David Giler, Lorenzo Semple, Jr.; *Cast includes:* Warren Beatty, Hume Cronyn, William Daniels, Paula Prentiss, Kelly Thorsden.

Warren Beatty portrays a small-time cynical reporter who goes under cover to investigate the assassination of a senator in this suspenseful thriller based on Loren Singer's novel. The murder was followed by an official investigation and the following conclusion: "The committee wishes to emphasize that there is no evidence of any wider conspiracy." Although the deaths of several witnesses are attributed to accidental or natural causes, Beatty suspects otherwise. "Somebody is systematically knocking off witnesses to that assassination," he says to his managing editor (Hume Cronyn) who is himself murdered shortly afterward.

Beatty learns about a shadowy organization called the Parallax Corporation and, assuming a pseudonym, applies for a job. He is soon contacted by one of its representatives. "If you qualify," the stranger announces, "we are prepared to offer you the most lucrative and rewarding work of your life." Beatty agrees to undergo a series of written and psychological tests. He discovers that whoever is behind Parallax "is in the business of recruiting assassins." Following one of the members, he comes upon a plot to assassinate George Hammond (Jim Davis), another sena-

tor, at a rally rehearsal. Hammond is killed and Beatty is suspected. As the police close in, he tries to escape through an open door near the roof and is shot dead by one of the members of Parallax. The film ends with another committee report which concludes: "There is no evidence of a conspiracy in the assassination of George Hammond."

One of the highlights of the film is the sequence involving the psychological test that Beatty takes. A series of flashing screen images invokes strong emotions of family, home and country—all contrived to measure the candidate's antisocial and psychotic tendencies. These are valuable assets to the organization's search for individuals who show low self-esteem but desire the material symbols of success—likely subjects for future assassins. The slick, suspenseful drama, with its themes of political cynicism, paranoia and conspiracy, is reminiscent of John Frankenheimer's *The Manchurian Candidate* (1962). ■

Paris Calling (1941), U. *Dir.* Edwin L. Marin; *Sc.* Benjamin Glazer, Charles S. Kaufman; *Cast includes:* Elisabeth Bergner, Randolph Scott, Basil Rathbone, Gale Sondergaard, Lee J. Cobb.

A World War II drama set in Paris immediately after the Nazi occupation of France, the film concerns the heroic efforts of the French underground in resisting the invaders. Elisabeth Bergner portrays a wealthy Frenchwoman who volunteers to work with the French underground after her mother is killed by Nazi planes as the pair try to leave Paris. Bergner is forced to kill her ex-lover (Basil Rathbone) when he turns traitor. An American flier (Randolph Scott) with the Royal Air Force is hunted by the Germans. The film depicts how underground members disrupt the German war machine. ■

Paris Playboys (1954), AA. *Dir.* William Beaudine; *Sc.* Elwood Ullman, Edward Bernds; *Cast includes:* Leo Gorcey, Huntz Hall, Bernard Gorcey, Veola Venn, Steven Geray, John Wengraf.

Another entry in the lowbrow Bowery Boys comedy series, this excursion takes them to Paris where they ply their comic antics as they get mixed up with a network of spies. Huntz Hall, as Leo Gorcey's stooge, plays a dual role; he is also a look-alike for a French scientist engaged in developing a new rocket fuel. Enemy agents attempt to steal the formula but are frustrated by Hall's odd behavior. The real scientist eventually returns. Veteran character actor Steven Geray portrays the chief spy. Diminutive Bernard Gorcey, one of the Bowery Boys, does a sprightly impersonation of Toulouse-Lautrec, probably the highlight of this strained comedy. ■

Paris Underground (1945), UA. *Dir.* Gregory Ratoff; *Sc.* Boris Ingster, Gertrude Purcell; *Cast includes:* Constance Bennett, Gracie Fields, Kurt Kreuger, Charles Andre, Leslie Vincent, Richard Ryen.

This World War II drama concerns two women, an American and an Englishwoman, and their activities in the French underground. Constance Bennett portrays the American wife of a Frenchman in the foreign office, and Gracie Fields plays the owner of a book shop in Paris. The two women join forces and help more than 250 Allied airmen escape from occupied France. Their adventures include a suspenseful pursuit by the Gestapo, their killing of a member of the Gestapo and their capture and ultimate rescue by allied troops who arrive just in time to save their lives. The film, which was Gracie Fields' last screen appearance, was based on the the the novel by Etta Shiber. The author, who in real life helped Allied pilots to escape from the Nazis, recounted many of her experiences in the book. ■

Passage to Marseilles (1944), WB. *Dir.* Michael Curtiz; *Sc.* Casey Robinson, Jack Moffitt; *Cast includes:* Humphrey Bogart, Michele Morgan, Claude Rains, Philip Dorn, Sydney Greenstreet, Peter Lorre.

The antagonisms between the Free French and those who were soon to back Marshall Petain's Vichy government are played out aboard a French freighter in this World War II drama. The ship rescues a group of men in a small boat. They soon admit they are escaped prisoners from Devil's Island who want to fight for France against the Nazis. The ship then continues on its course back to France. When the captain (Victor Francen) learns from the ship's wireless that France has surrendered, he tearfully reads the news to his passengers, labeling the capitulation "The blackest day in French history." He clandestinely decides to deliver his vessel and cargo to a British port rather than turn them over to his country's conquerors.

However, trouble erupts when one of the passengers (Sydney Greenstreet), a French major who sides with Petain and has voiced his loathing for the Republic, initiates a plot to take over the ship. He stirs up a handful of mutineers and a battle rages aboard the decks. Humphrey Bogart portrays a former journalist who opposed the pacifists and those who appeased Hitler. He was falsely imprisoned in an attempt to silence him. Bogart leads his fellow ex-convicts in the fight against the mutineers. The forces of Free France triumph but suffer several casualties.

The film succeeds in its symbolic intents of having the ship represent an embattled France, with its intrigues and conflicting forces of treachery and patriotism, and a downed German plane reflecting the defeat of totalitarianism. But the well-meaning drama suffers from several shortcomings. The plot is told in a series of complex flashbacks by Claude Rains, as a French liaison officer, to an American reporter who is writing a feature story on the Free French. This technique only serves to slow down the pace. In addition, a disturbing scene shows Bogart machine-gunning the defenseless crew of the downed German plane. The film, based on the novel by Charles Nordhoff and James Norman Hall, includes several patriotic speeches, some condemning isolationism and pacifism, others extolling the virtues of a free France and her allies. See Vichy France. ■

Passport to Adventure. See *Passport to Destiny* (1944). ■

Passport to Alcatraz (1940), Col. *Dir.* Lewis D. Collins; *Sc.* Albert DeMond; *Cast includes:* Jack Holt, Noah Beery, Jr., Cecilia Callejo, Maxie Rosenbloom, C. Henry Gordon, Guy Usher.

Enemy agents plot to destroy America's munitions factories in this standard drama set before the nation's entry into World War II. Jack Holt, as a special government agent assigned to apprehend the gang of saboteurs, poses as one of the gang and soon brings an end to the culprits' schemes. Noah Beery, Jr. portrays the square-jawed detective's assistant and shares the romantic subplot with Cecilia Callejo. The perennial screen villain, C. Henry Gordon, plays Holt's antagonist. The film is also known as *Passport to Hell*. ■

Passport to Destiny (1944), RKO. *Dir.* Ray McCarey; *Sc.* Val Burton, Murial Roy Boulton; *Cast includes:* Elsa Lanchester, Gordon Oliver, Lenore Aubert, Lionel Royce, Fritz Feld, Joseph Vitale.

A London charwoman travels to Germany to assassinate Hitler in this inept World War II comedy-drama. Believing that her late husband's snake-eye charm will protect her from harm, widow Ella Muggins (Elsa Lanchester) journeys to Nazi Germany by stowing away on a French ship, carrying her pail and brush all the way. She manages to get hired as a cleaning woman in the Nazi chancellery by masquerading as a mute but is eventually arrested. However, an officer in the underground (Gordon Oliver) whom she had earlier befriended rescues her during a British bombing raid on German headquarters. He steals a German plane and flies her, along with his sweetheart, to safety. When they arrive in England, the charwoman is treated as a heroine. An interesting sidelight occurs in the scene in which Lanchester refers to a picture of her late husband—a photograph of Charles Laughton, her real-life husband.

The usual period propaganda permeates the plot—the Nazi officers are overly ruthless; good Germans work heroically within the underground to resist Hitler; outsiders who have joined the Nazi cause are betrayed by those they believed in, as exemplified by Lord Haw-Haw (Gavin Muir). Originally a British subject, he turned traitor by volunteering to broadcast Nazi ideology to the English people. When his position is threatened, he seeks to escape. "I really felt," he confides to Lanchester, "the New Order was good for the English." Lanchester finally gains admittance to Hitler's office while he is away. She fantasizes what she will say to him before she kills him. "Things are going to be different, Mr. Hitler, when you're gone," she rehearses, pointing a Luger at his empty chair. "People are going to smile again; little children are going to play in the streets again; and all over the world the lights will go on and there'll be laughter and happiness again. . . ." The film was originally released as *Passport to Adventure.* See Lord Haw-Haw. ■

Passport to Hell, A (1932), Fox. *Dir.* Frank Lloyd; *Sc.* Leo Gordon, Bradley King; *Cast includes:* Elissa Landi, Paul Lukas, Warner Oland, Alexander Kirkland, Donald Crisp.

Elissa Landi stars in this drama with a World War I background. Driven out of England because of a scandal, she ends up in a British colony where once again she meets with hard luck. She is blamed for the suicide of a British official and sent into German territory. When World War I breaks out, she marries a German commandant's son to avoid being imprisoned as an English subject. Her father-in-law sends the couple to a northern province where the groom, after selling military secrets to a British agent to raise money for his wife, kills himself. Meanwhile Landi has an affair with another officer. She burns her husband's suicide note to protect his honor and leaves for parts unknown, hoping that the postwar period will reunite her with her lover. The film reveals little of the war in Europe. ■

Passport to Suez (1943), Col. *Dir.* Andre De Toth; *Sc.* John Stone; *Cast includes:* Warren William, Ann Savage, Eric Blore, Sheldon Leonard, Lloyd Bridges.

An entry in the popular Lone Wolf detective series, this World War II drama has Warren William, as the suave sleuth, playing a double agent. He joins a Nazi spy ring in Egypt in an effort to retrieve stolen plans concerning the Suez Canal. The film provides several twists to the plot and adds various agents to the complications. Comic character actors Eric Blore, as William's butler, and Sheldon Leonard add some comic relief to this low-budget, often implausible film. See Detectives and Spies. ■

Pastorius Project. See *They Came to Blow Up America* (1943). ■

Pathfinder, The (1952), Col. *Dir.* Sidney Salkow; *Sc.* Robert E. Kent; *Cast includes:* George Montgomery, Helena Carter, Jay Silverheels, Walter Kingsford, Rodd Redwing, Stephen Bekassy.

Adapted from James Fenimore Cooper's novel set during the French and Indian War, this drama features George Montgomery as the title character. A British scout, he is assigned to spy upon a French fort. Helena Carter accompanies him as his interpreter, masquerading as a French girl. They learn that the French plan to control the Great Lakes, but they are caught when Carter's former suitor, a British traitor, exposes her.

British troops come to the rescue as the couple are about to face a firing squad. ∎

Patria (1916) serial, Cosmopolitan. *Dir.* Theodore Wharton, Leo Wharton, Jacques Jaccard; *Cast includes:* Irene Castle, Milton Sills, Warner Oland, Dorothy Green, Floyd Buckley, Marie Walcamp.

A serial overflowing with foreign intrigue and international agents challenging the U.S. Secret Service, the film created almost as much interest off the screen as it did in theaters. An actual incident precipitated *Patria*, with its anti-Japanese and anti-Mexican overtones. William Randolph Hearst, the influential publisher, owned a large ranch in Mexico. He became enraged when the Mexican bandit-general Pancho Villa raided his property and distributed his 60,000 head of cattle to the peons. Hearst ordered his editors to lash out against Mexico, claiming it had a secret alliance with Japan to invade the U.S. He also financed the serial *Patria*, which echoed this threat. Dancer Irene Castle, portraying an American heiress, provides secret funds designed to prepare America against an enemy attack. The film depicts the Japanese so repulsively that President Wilson was prompted to send a note to those responsible, complaining that the film was "extremely unfair to the Japanese. . . ." See Japanese War Scare of 1907; Serials. ∎

Patriot and the Spy, The (1915), Mutual. *Dir.* Frank L. Gereghty, M. N. Litson; *Cast includes:* Alphonse Ethier, James Cruze, Marguerite Snow.

When a local villager in an unnamed European country marries a pretty girl, another suitor harbors feelings of jealousy and revenge in this World War I drama. At first, the remote village seems out of danger of the war, but the conflict soon spreads. The husband (James Cruze), hurt by a speeding car while rescuing one of his children, is unable to serve in the army. Later, his former rival (Alphonse Ethier), now a spy and traitor, tricks the hero, desperately seeking a way to serve his country, into blowing up a bridge. The husband is captured by the invading troops but escapes in time to find his wife (Marguerite Snow) being threatened by the spy. A fight ensues with predictable results. The war, like the country, goes unnamed in this silent drama, but the Continental setting, characters' names, battle sequences and weaponry mark it as World War I. James Cruze became a popular film director. ∎

Patriotism (1918), W. W. Hodkinson. *Dir.* Raymond B. West; *Sc.* Julian Louis Lamothe; *Cast includes:* Bessie Barriscale, Charles Gunn, Herschel Mayall, Arthur Allardt, Joseph J. Dowling, Mary Jane Irving.

Allied officials during World War I suspect a spy, operating along the coast of Scotland, has been sending signals to German submarines in this drama. Bessie Barriscale, as a young Scot, has converted her seacoast home into a hospital for wounded soldiers. Two local villagers (Herschel Mayall, Arthur Allardt) both love Bessie. But she has fallen for a young American doughboy (Charles Gunn). Several Allied officers appear in the village to investigate possible acts of espionage. During an air raid one of the officers is nearly killed. The two Scot suitors, jealous of the American, accuse the Yank. Barriscale begins to investigate on her own, with the aid of a Belgian orphan, and learns that Mayall, who owns a nearby estate, who has been sending messages to German submarines. The American then leaves for duty at the front as his sweetheart sees him off.

The plot about spies operating in Scotland may have been based loosely on the exploits of two secret agents with entirely different personalities. Dr. Armgaard Karl Graves was an eccentric character who dallied in freelance spying in Edinburgh and Glasgow. However, local Scotsmen knew of his activities and considered them harmless. Nevertheless, Graves was sentenced to 18 months' imprisonment in 1912. He was released after several months and emigrated to the U.S. where he had his memoirs published on the eve of World War I. The book, which soon became a best-seller, tells about his highly imaginative experiences as a spy during the Boer War, his adventures in the Balkans and his meeting with the Kaiser.

Carl Hans Lody, a German patriot and lieutenant in the German Naval Reserve, posed as an American tourist. He was finally captured in Edinburgh sending letters and telegrams to his German contacts in other countries. The English court tried him in October 1914, found him guilty of espionage and sentenced him to death by firing squad. See British Intelligence: World War I. ∎

Paws of the Bear (1917), Triangle. *Dir.* Reginald Barker; *Sc.* J. G. Hawks; *Cast includes:* William Desmond, Clara Williams, Robert McKim, Wallace Worsley, Charles French.

Set during Germany's invasion of Belgium in World War I, this romantic drama concerns a young Russian woman (Clara Williams) and an American citizen (William Desmond). She decides to take a shot from the window of an inn at a German officer and kills him. Desmond, who is staying at the same inn, is arrested along with the Russian. Both are sentenced to face a firing squad. Fortunately for the two, an Allied airplane bombs the area, and the Germans retreat. The couple part only to meet again some time later. He is carrying secret documents back to the U.S. while Williams, as a Russian agent, is assigned to stop the papers from reaching their destination. However, all turns out well for the couple who eventually marry. ■

Paying the Price (1916), World. *Dir.* Frank Crane; *Sc.* Gardner Hunting; *Cast includes:* Gail Kane, George Relph, Gladden James, Lydia Knott, George Mageroni.

A drama involving a secret formula for a high explosive, the film concerns foreign agents bent on stealing the prized formula. The action moves from Washington, D.C., to an American torpedo boat. The film contains several spectacular sequences showing the effectiveness of torpedoes. ■

Pearl Harbor. Although the U.S. Navy had been concerned with the military threat posed by Japan ever since the Russo-Japanese War of 1904, the Japanese attack on Pearl Harbor on Sunday morning, December 7, 1941, is considered by many as the worst intelligence failure in America's history.

When the attack ended, a large part of America's military power in the Pacific had been wiped out. Two battleships had been sunk. Six others were temporarily put out of action. Two destroyers and a target ship were also gone, as were 261 out of a total of 481 planes, most caught on the ground in neat, closely spaced rows. At least 3,226 American military personnel died in the attack and another 1,272 were wounded. The Japanese lost 29 planes, five midget submarines and about 100 men.

In 1940 William Friedman, a cryptologist and director of the Army's Signal Intelligence Service, broke Code Purple, the secret Japanese communications code. Despite this impressive intelligence coup, neither the navy nor the army predicted the Japanese attack on Pearl Harbor. Code breakers gathered evidence concerning Japan's plan to bomb both America's naval fleet docked at Pearl Harbor and the surrounding air bases, but the report remained entombed in Washington, D.C.

Few films deal directly with Japanese or U.S. intelligence involving the attack. Some touch upon the historical aspects of the incident while others use it as a springboard for character motivation. *Remember Pearl Harbor* (1942), an action drama that takes place on the eve of Pearl Harbor, is about two soldier-pals stationed in the Philippines. One gets mixed up with a group of spies working for the Japanese. He realizes the error of his ways and quickly redeems himself. He not only exposes an espionage network but crashes an airplane into a Japanese troopship. In *Two Yanks in Trinidad* (1942) two rival gangsters who have joined the army hear that the Japanese have attacked Pearl Harbor. They decide to put aside their differences and join forces to foil a plot by a Nazi spy involved in transporting oil to the Axis. The attack motivates shipyard workers in *Fighting Coast Guard* (1951) who, angered by the bombing, enlist in the military. Many low-budget action dramas such as *Submarine Raider* (1942) used Japan's strike on Pearl Harbor as plot background.

Blood on the Sun (1945), about a tough American newspaper editor in pre-World War II Japan who discovers a Japanese plot for world conquest, mentions the infamous Tanaka Memorial. This was an actual Japanese document stolen in 1927 which included, among other proposed Japanese military ventures, a plot to bomb America's naval base at Pearl Harbor. The plan was so outlandish at the time that no one treated it seriously. *Tora! Tora! Tora!* (1970), which recreates the attack on Pearl Harbor, points out that while the Japanese were unified on the purpose of their sneak attack, many of the American leaders were unprepared and uncertain of Japan's intentions. E. G. Marshall, as an Army Intelligence officer, continually tries to warn his superiors about Japan's goals, but he is ignored. ■

Pearl of the Army (1916) serial, Pathé. *Dir.* Edward José; *Cast includes:* Pearl White, Ralph Killard, Marie Wayne, Floyd Buckley, Theodore Freibus, W. T. Carleton.

Pearl White, the queen of silent serials, once again undergoes a string of perilous adventures before she subdued a host of oriental spies determined to destroy the Panama Canal in this popular serial. Although not identified as such in this serial, the Japanese often served as villain in silent films, ever since the Japanese war scare of 1907. The work was advertised as "the serial with a purpose."

Pearl White starred in the most famous of all serials, *The Perils of Pauline*, released in 1914 and composed of 20 episodes, each making up a complete story. Her success in this medium gave rise to many imitators, including, among others, Ruth Roland, Helen Holmes, Eileen Sedgwick, Grace Cunard and Arline Pretty. See Serials. ■

Penalty, The (1920), Goldwyn. *Dir.* Wallace Worsley; *Sc.* Charles Kenyon, Philip Lonergan; *Cast includes:* Lon Chaney, Claire Adams, Kenneth Harlan, Charles Clary, Ethel Grey Terry.

Ethel Grey Terry portrays a U.S. Secret Service agent assigned to investigate a master criminal operating in San Francisco. Lon Chaney, as Blizzard, the subject of the investigation, has had his legs amputated accidentally while still a youth. Also suffering from a contusion at the base of the skill, Blizzard uses his innate intelligence for evil purposes, including revenge upon the doctor who operated on him and society in general. He has emerged as the master criminal of that city's underworld. His ultimate plan is to arouse the numerous foreign workers to attack the entire city.

The secret service agent, in awe of the madman's superior intelligence, falls in love with him despite the revelations about his destructive aims. The strange couple soon marry, leading to suspicion on the part of other underworld figures. His henchmen, sensing a transformation in their leader's original villainy, decide to kill him. The film is based on the novel by Gouverneur Morris. ■

Phantom Creeps, The (1939) serial, U. *Dir.* Ford Beebe, Saul A. Goodkind; *Sc.* George Plympton, Basil Dickey, Mildred Barish; *Cast includes:* Bela Lugosi, Robert Kent, Regis Toomey, Dorothy Arnold, Edward Van Sloan, Eddie Acuff.

Clashes among foreign agents, a mad scientist and members of the U.S. Secret Service form the basis of this 12-chapter serial that depends chiefly on the conventional trappings of this genre. Bela Lugosi, as the scientist Dr. Zorka, also portrays the chief villain who invents a device that produces suspended animation and a belt that renders its owner invisible. Bent on controlling the world, he uses his inventions to help him gain his nefarious goals. Other devices Lugosi utilizes include a deadly mechanical spider and a giant-sized robot that appears occasionally to threaten both hero and heroine.

Foreign spies want to get their hands on the crazed scientist's inventions, especially Edward Van Sloan, who portrays the chief of an international spy ring. He operates from an office called International Foreign Language, which he uses as a front for his subversive activities. Robert Kent, as a U.S. government agent, and Regis Toomey, as his loyal assistant, foil the plans of Lugosi and the spies, but not before the mad scientist knocks them unconscious several times, sabotages their plane, sends them in their car careening over a cliff and endangers their lives in other ways. Dorothy Arnold, as a snooping reporter in search of a scoop, becomes embroiled in much of the intrigue. ■

Phantom Plainsman, The (1942), Rep. *Dir.* John English; *Sc.* Robert Yost, Barry Shipman; *Cast includes:* Bob Steele, Tom Tyler, Rufe Davis, Robert O. Davis, Lois Collier, Charles Miller.

Set before America's entry into World War II, this entry in the "Three Mesquiteers" western series deals with a plot by Nazi agents to purchase horses for Germany. Bob Steele, Tom Tyler and Rufe Davis, as the "Mesquiteers," stumble across the plot while working as wranglers at a local ranch. The ranch owner, a confirmed pacifist, refuses to sell horses for military use to any government. Although he is informed by the hero-trio of the intentions of the Nazi buyers, the owner faces a new dilemma. The Germans tell him that his son, visiting Germany, has been jailed and will not be released until the horses are sold. However, the fighting trio soon resolve the situation. Rufe Davis and Vince Barnett, as the local sheriff, provide some comedy relief.

Lobby card for *Phantom Raiders* (1940) with Walter Pidgeon (2nd from r.), as sleuth Nick Carter looking on as Nat Pendleton manhandles Donald Meek.

This was another in a group of updated westerns that were designed to take advantage of current events. *Texas to Bataan*, featuring the Range Busters and released by Republic at about the same time, had a similar plot involving spies. ∎

Phantom Raiders (1940), MGM. *Dir.* Jacques Tourneur; *Sc.* William R. Lipman; *Cast includes:* Walter Pidgeon, Donald Meek, Joseph Schildkraut, Florence Rice, Nat Pendleton.

When English ships carrying Allied war matériel mysteriously disappear in the Panama Canal Zone, master sleuth Nick Carter is assigned to solve the problem in this World War II drama. Walter Pidgeon repeats his role as the dapper detective in this second entry in the series. Donald Meek also is aboard as his assistant and comic relief. Joseph Schildkraut, as head of the spy ring, supplies enough villainy to sustain the suspense and excitement in this moderately budgeted tale. Unfortunately, only one more film, *Sky Murder*, also released in 1940, was scheduled for

the series before the studio canceled it. Pidgeon, however, was destined for bigger things, including the role of Greer Garson's husband in *Mrs. Miniver* (1942). See Panama Canal. ∎

Phantom Submarine, The (1941), Col. *Dir.* Charles Barton; *Sc.* Joseph Krumgold; *Cast includes:* Anita Louise, Bruce Bennett, Oscar O'Shea, John Tyrell, Pedro de Cordoba.

A weak drama about a mysterious submarine lurking in the waters off the Panama Canal, the film stars Anita Louise who is assigned by the U.S. Navy to learn its whereabouts and its mission. With the help of a deep sea diver (Bruce Bennett), they discover that the undersea vessel plans to place mines targeted for American ships. This low-budget film provides little in the way of action or suspense. See Panama Canal. ∎

Philby, Harold "Kim." The infamous trio of Soviet moles in British intelligence, Burgess, Maclean and Philby, have come to represent the betrayal of the West by some of its most privileged sons. All three spies-to-be attended Cambridge University in the 1930s and were drawn to Communism as the best hope for defeating Nazism.

Harold Philby joined the Communist Party as an undergraduate at Cambridge and, at that early date, began working for Soviet intelligence. He soon began to write for a British newspaper syndicate and, as part of his cover, favored conservative causes. He was soon sent to cover the Spanish Civil War and reported favorably on the Phalangist forces. Franco was so impressed by the young British correspondent that he awarded him the Red Cross of Military Merit.

The *London Times* soon dispatched Philby to France to cover the opening battles of World War II. It was here in the capacity of foreign correspondent that British intelligence recruited Philby and gave him the opportunity to become a double agent. He received rapid promotions within the Secret Intelligence Service, thanks undoubtedly to the old-boy network of Cambridge graduates, and, in 1944, was made head of the Russian desk at British intelligence.

Following the end of the war, Philby was dispatched to Washington and promoted to liaison officer between the S.I.S. and American intelligence agencies. He worked in close cooperation with Allen Dulles and James Angleton. It was through his C.I.A. connection that Philby learned of S.I.S. suspicions of Donald Maclean, another Soviet mole. Philby called on his close friend Guy Burgess, who was another Soviet agent and the Second Secretary of the British embassy in Washington, to warn Maclean. Both Burgess and Maclean managed to defect together to the Soviet Union on May 25, 1951.

Despite the fact that suspicion soon fell upon Philby, he was simply recalled to London where he continued to function, albeit in a lower capacity, within British intelligence. Apparently, upper-class members of the S.I.S. felt more bound to protect the reputation of the agency and a member of their class than they felt obliged to protect the country. Eventually Philby, still a member of the S.I.S., was assigned to Lebanon where he defected to Moscow in 1963.

Another Cambridge man, Anthony Blunt, was discovered to be a fourth Russian mole and, in 1962, the Russian intelligence agent and defector Anatoli Golitsin, suggested that there was an additional fifth spy in S.I.S. The "fifth mole theory" has been a matter of dispute ever since, with some analysts maintaining that Golitsin introduced his thesis as disinformation, while others suspect Sir Roger Hollis, Deputy Director of MI5, the British counterintelligence agency, or his deputy directors, Guy Liddell and Graham Mitchell.

No American films have dealt directly with the exploits of Philby—an obvious embarrassment both to British and American intelligence agencies. To take advantage of the headlines, and several books that came in the wake of the exposures, some studios touched upon the topic in highly fictionalized versions. In *Dead to the World* (1962), for instance, a U.S. State Department employee is charged with betraying his country when officials discover that secrets have been transmitted to the Communists. *Subterfuge* (1969), a British-U.S. coproduction, features an American C.I.A. agent (Gene Barry) who is assigned to ferret out a British double agent operating in England. ■

Philippines. Several silent and sound films used the Philippines for their background. Some were purely fictitious plots while others concerned covert operations based on actual events. The earliest record of U.S. intelligence interest in this region occurred after the Spanish-American War (1898). The Military Information Division, established in 1885, had gathered almost no information about the Philippines before or during the war. The American military governor of the islands, Gen. Elwell S. Otis, stationed in Manila, set up a bureau in 1899 to maintain files on Filipino insurgents, recruit Filipino undercover agents and establish communications with all the U.S. Army posts throughout the islands.

Lucille Love, the Girl of Mystery (1914), an early silent serial, concerns the machinations of a not-too-sinister international spy. The archvillain steals military plans from an army lieutenant stationed in the Philippines. Lucille Love (Grace Cunard), the heroine and sweetheart of the officer, is determined to retrieve the papers. *Across the Pacific* (1926), a drama set in the Philippines following the Spanish-American War, concerned a group of rebel islanders who are on the verge of overthrowing the democratic regime. The U.S. government assigns one of its agents (Monte Blue) to uncover the leader.

By World War II U.S. intelligence had an

array of maps and other information available to effectively direct paramilitary operations against the Japanese who controlled the Philippines for several of the war years. Jack Hawkins, for example, a U.S. Marine assigned to the Allied Intelligence Bureau, led a force of Filipino guerrillas on covert missions against the Japanese. Several World War II dramas, including *Back to Bataan* (1945) and *American Guerrilla in the Philippines* (1950), are reminiscent of Hawkins' exploits with the guerrilla war against the Japanese. In the former, John Wayne portrayed an American colonel who stays behind after the fall of Bataan to help organize native resistance against the Japanese invaders. In the latter, Tyrone Power played a navy officer who spies on the Japanese for the U.S. and helps the natives fight against the enemy troops.

Other World War II films set in the Philippines relied more on fiction. *Remember Pearl Harbor* (1942), an action drama that took place on the eve of Pearl Harbor, was about two soldier-pals stationed in the Philippines. One gets mixed up with a group of spies working for the Japanese. He realizes the error of his ways and quickly redeems himself. He not only exposes an espionage network but crashes an airplane into a Japanese troopship. In *Ambush Bay* (1966), with Hugh O'Brian and Mickey Rooney, a Japanese-American secret agent sacrifices her own life to help the success of the Allied invasion of the Philippines. ∎

Phillips, Claire. See *I Was an American Spy* (1951). ∎

Pickup on South Street (1953), TCF. Dir. Samuel Fuller; *Sc.* Samuel Fuller; *Cast includes:* Richard Widmark, Jean Peters, Thelma Ritter, Murvyn Vye, Richard Kiley, Milburn Stone.

A small-time pickpocket accidentally comes in possession of films of a secret formula coveted by Communist spies in this little drama. Richard Widmark, as the thief prowling the subways for his prey, snatches the wallet of Jean Peters, who is unaware that she is carrying military secrets. Meanwhile, federal agents have been following Peters, suspecting her of working with a Communist spy ring. Her boy friend-employer (Richard Kiley) requests that she track down Widmark and recover the wallet.

The remainder of the film deals with the Communists' attempts to get the film and Widmark's moral redemption when a colorful street vendor (Thelma Ritter) is murdered by the gang. At first he is willing to negotiate for the contents of the wallet, but the death of his street crony propels Widmark to go after spies. A blossoming romance between Widmark and Peters also serves to stir up his latent patriotism.

Director Sam Fuller's gutsy and lyrical images, focus on otherwise commonplace objects and subjects and iconoclastic approach to filmmaking had made him a controversial and influential force in post–World War II films. Perhaps critic Andrew Sarris described him best when he called Fuller "an authentic American primitive." ∎

Pidgin Island (1916), Metro. Dir. Fred J. Balshofer; *Sc.* Fred J. Balshofer, Richard V. Spencer; *Cast includes:* Harold Lockwood, May Allison, Doc Pomeroy Cannon, Lester Cuneo, Fred Wilson, Lillian Hayward.

A U.S. Secret Service agent goes on vacation after solving a tough case in New York's Chinatown in this drama based on the 1914 novel by Harold MacGrath. On Pidgin Island, in Lake Ontario, the agent (Harry Lockwood) meets a mysterious young woman (May Allison) who also happens to be a member of the secret service. Lockwood soon discovers that a gang of smugglers is operating nearby. It turns out that the head of the gang is the father of the young woman with whom Lockwood has fallen in love. She agrees to marry him if he will not press charges against the old man who promises to halt his activities. ∎

Pigeon That Took Rome, The (1962), Par. Dir. Melville Shavelson; *Sc.* Melville Shavelson; *Cast includes:* Charlton Heston, Elsa Martinelli, Harry Guardino, Debbie Price, Brian Donlevy.

An American officer during World War II is assigned to undercover work in Nazi-occupied Rome with unexpected results in this comedy. Charlton Heston portrays the Yank who communicates his strategic information about German activity by carrier pigeons—until an Italian family consumes the birds during an Easter feast. The bewildered Heston is then given German pigeons as a replacement. He proceeds to send out erroneous reports to disrupt the enemy who intercept his communications. Eventually, the Allies take Rome with little difficulty. Elsa

Martinelli provides the romantic interest while Harry Guardino plays Heston's assistant. The film was adapted from *The Easter Dinner* by Donald Downes.

Gen. William J. Donovan's O.S.S. initiated several actual undercover operations in Italy during World War II. In January 1944, Donovan selected Peter Tompkins, an intelligence officer fluent in Italian, to gather intelligence and organize sabotage operations among the partisans in Rome in preparation for Allied landings at Anzio. Following several setbacks, including the discovery of his clandestine radio station by German agents and the arrest of partisans collaborating with him, he remained in Rome and persuaded the superior officers of the Italian army to thwart the acts of sabotage by the retreating Germans. The Allies finally liberated Rome on June 4. To his dismay, he later learned that none of his intelligence reports transmitted to the O.S.S. had been acted upon. In other words, he concluded that his covert mission, fraught with so much danger, had generally been a waste of time. Tompkins wrote about his World War II exploits in *A Spy in Rome*, published in 1962. ■

Disgruntled photographer James Garner and his model Eva Renzi become prisoners of drifter George Kennedy in the satirical comedy *The Pink Jungle* (1968).

Pink Jungle, The (1968), U. *Dir.* Delbert Mann; *Sc.* Charles Williams; *Cast includes:* James Garner, Eva Renzi, George Kennedy, Nigel Green, Michael Ansara, George Rose.

An American photographer who decides to take some photographs for a lipstick advertisement in a South American jungle is mistaken for a C.I.A. agent in this satirical tale which blends comedy with adventure. James

Garner portrays the camera bug who raises the suspicions of the local police of an unidentified country. He becomes further involved in intrigues when he innocently buys a map of a hidden diamond mine. He and Eva Renzi, as his model, take off for the mine and are joined by an unscrupulous drifter (George Kennedy) who forces his presence upon them. Adventures and misadventures follow as plots and counterplots unfold in this zany story. Fabrizio Mioni, as a local colonel who has been relegated to a lower rank, hopes that by proving Garner to be a secret agent he can be reinstated to his former position. Nigel Green portrays a prospector who abandons the trio in a desert. The film is based on the novel *Smoke Water* by Alan Williams. ■

Pinkerton, Allan (1819–1884). The famous detective founded the Pinkerton National Detective Agency in 1850. Primarily involved in solving railroad crimes, the agency uncovered an assassination plot against President-elect Lincoln in 1861. During the Civil War Pinkerton gathered information about the South for the Union. His spy service was the first use of secret intelligence in the U.S.

Two Civil War films portray him busy at his work of employing agents. In *Hands Up* (1926), a silent comedy, Raymond Griffith portrays a Southern spy assigned to prevent a gold shipment from reaching President Lincoln. Meanwhile, Pinkerton sends a Union spy to make certain the shipment gets through. In *Operator 13* (1934) Pinkerton solicits the services of a Union woman (Marion Davies) to spy on the South. ■

Pirates of the Sky (1927), Pathé. *Dir.* Charles Andrews; *Sc.* Elaine Wilmont; *Cast includes:* Charles Hutchison, Wanda Hawley, Craufurd Kent, Jimmie Aubrey, Ben Walker.

The U.S. Secret Service, frustrated by a gang of clever air- mail thieves, calls on the services of a master criminologist to help break the case. Charles Hutchison, as the amateur detective, is a wealthy bachelor renowned for his peculiar sleuthing methods and his acrobatics. After some daredevil stunts, including changing planes while in the air, Hutchison solves the case and helps round up the air pirates. Craufurd Kent portrays the sophisticated leader of the gang. Jimmie Aubrey, as a secret agent and Hutchison's assistant, supplies some comic relief. Wanda Hawley provides the romantic interest. *Flying High*, an independently produced film with a similar plot and starring William Fairbanks, another acrobatic performer, was released several months earlier. ∎

Poe, Anthony. C.I.A. intelligence officer. See *Apolcalypse Now* (1979). ∎

Port of New York (1949), EL. *Dir.* Laslo Benedek; *Sc.* Eugene Ling; *Cast includes:* Scott Brady, Richard Rober, K. T. Stevens, Yul Brynner, Arthur Blake, Lynn Carter.

Two U.S. government agents are assigned to smash a drug-smuggling ring operating out of the New York area in this far-fetched drama lensed chiefly on location for authenticity. Scott Brady and Richard Rober, as the agents, have little to go on. Through leg work, interrogations and informers, they begin to learn about the operations of a gang, led by Yul Brynner. They decide to go under cover and join the smugglers so that they can gain hard evidence. However, the gang discovers Brady's real identity and he is killed. Rober is left to his own devices and soon, following a climactic shoot-out aboard a yacht, brings an end to Brynner and his drug operations. Brynner, in his film debut, portrays a sinister smuggler-leader whose cold-blooded methods include making his drug exchanges off shore and then murdering his contacts to prevent them from informing. ∎

Port Said (1948), Col. *Dir.* Reginald LeBorg; *Sc.* Brenda Weisberg; *Cast includes:* Gloria Henry, William Bishop, Steven Geray, Edgar Barrier, Richard Hale, Ian MacDonald.

A father, accompanied by his daughter, seeks out those responsible for the death of his wife in Italy during World War II in this routine postwar drama. They journey to the Egyptian port to find several pro-Fascist relatives. Edgar Barrier plays the father while Gloria Henry portrays a dual role. She enacts Barrier's daughter as well as a villainous cousin. William Bishop plays the hero who becomes involved in the plot when his friend is murdered. He unravels the intrigue and exposes the unscrupulous members of the family. ∎

Powder Town (1942), RKO. *Dir.* Rowland V. Lee; *Sc.* David Boehm; *Cast includes:* Victor McLaglen, Edmond O'Brien, June Havoc, Dorothy Lovett, Eddie Foy, Jr.

Edmond O'Brien portrays an eccentric scientist who works for a huge munitions cor-

poration in this inept World War II drama. The company is filled with secret agents, including a high-ranking officer, who are trying to steal the scientist's new formula for an explosive that can annihilate an entire army. Victor McLaglen plays a bodyguard hired by the company to protect O'Brien. June Havoc, as a dancer, provides the romantic interest while Eddie Foy, Jr. contributes some comic relief. The film was adapted from the novel by Max Brand. ∎

President Vanishes, The (1934), Par. *Dir.* William Wellman; *Sc.* Carey Wilson, Cedric Worth, Lynn Starling; *Cast includes:* Arthur Byron, Janet Beecher, Paul Kelly, Peggy Conklin, Rosalind Russell, Sidney Blackmer.

This blatant propaganda film, with its simplistic solutions to national and international problems, nevertheless provides some intriguing moments. As the U.S. is being drawn into a European military conflict and a martial Congress is about to vote on a declaration of war, the President suddenly disappears. The nation's interests suddenly turn from thoughts of war to the President's kidnapping. Meanwhile militant groups, including those who would profit by war, and a Fascist organization known as the Gray Shirts, jockey for power.

Arthur Byron, as the pacifist President Stanley, has arranged his own disappearance to prevent the nation's entry into war and expose those jingoistic forces who would lead the nation down this destructive path. He contrives events so that he is found by U.S. Secret Service agents bound and gagged in the headquarters of the Gray Shirts. His ploy allows him to persuade the citizenry to reject the war hysteria and instead follow his peaceful course.

Paul Kelly portrays a sympathetic secret service member. Peggy Conklin, as Kelly's sweetheart, provides the romantic interest. Edward Ellis, as Lincoln Lee, heads the neo-Fascist group. Andy Devine and Irene Franklin contribute to the comic relief. The film is based on an anonymous novel. ∎

President's Analyst, The (1967), Par. *Dir.* Theodore J. Flicker; *Sc.* Theodore J. Flicker; *Cast includes:* James Coburn, Godfrey Cambridge, Severn Darden, Joan Delaney, Pat Harrington, Barry Maguire.

James Coburn portrays a psychiatrist who is chosen to act as the U.S. President's per-

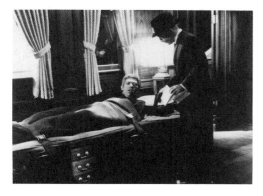

Psychiatrist James Coburn falls into the hands of enemy agents in the spy spoof *The President's Analyst* (1967).

sonal analyst in this satirical film which aims its barbs as several institutions, including, among others, the F.B.I, the C.I.A., liberals, conservatives and hippies. Some agencies are lightly disguised (F.B.R., C.E.A.). Coburn himself becomes the target of both inept domestic and foreign agents. The villains end up killing each other off as they attempt to assassinate the psychiatrist while he is having an affair with hippie Jill Banner in a field of flowers—a swipe at the often-used romantic setting of 1960s youth-oriented films. William Daniels, as a liberal, is part of a family that indulges in firearms and karate. Joan Delaney, as a secret agent, poses as Coburn's mistress. The chief culprit behind much of the intrigue, Coburn soon discovers, is the telephone company. See Central Intelligence Agency. ■

Price of Applause, The (1918), Triangle. *Dir.* Thomas Heffron; *Sc.* Doris Schroeder; *Cast includes:* Jack Livingston, Claire Anderson, Joe King, Walt Whitman.

A cowardly and shallow young American of German heritage ultimately redeems himself in this complex drama set during World War I. Jack Livingston portrays Karl, a German sympathizer before the U.S. enters the conflict. Saying and doing anything that will attract attention from his artistic acquaintances, he announces that he intends to enlist in the French army after news of the sinking of the *Lusitania* appears. This time he is compelled to carry out his offer when a friend decides to join him. Once in the trenches, Karl is stricken with fear. In no man's land he exchanges uniforms with a dead German soldier and is taken prisoner, hoping to spend

the remainder of the war in relative safety. He later escapes to America where he meets a fellow German prisoner who has also escaped. He leads Karl to a nest of spies who plan to blow up a munitions plant. Karl realizes the mess he has made of his life and, after denouncing the German cause, sets off the explosive. All in the room are killed. ■

Price of Malice, The (1916), Metro. *Dir.* O. A. C. Lund; *Cast includes:* Hamilton Revelle, Barbara Tenant, William Davidson, Helen Dunbar, William Calhoun.

This was an unusual drama to have been released while Britain was in the midst of World War I, since it deals with jealousy and duplicity on the part of an English captain at the War Office. The U.S. generally favored the Allied cause while invariably treating the Germans as the aggressors as early as 1914 when the first rounds were fired. Virtually all other American war dramas released before America's entry in the conflict in 1917 were pro-British.

William Davidson, as the captain who is temporarily left in charge of the War Office, is extremely jealous of a secret service agent (Hamilton Revelle) favored by Colonel Brendon, Davidson's superior. The captain decides to frame the innocent agent by accusing him of stealing a secret document. Revelle, suspecting the captain of removing the paper, dons a disguise and joins Davidson's yachting party where he retrieves the stolen document. Back at the War Office, Revelle reveals the entire conspiracy to the colonel who quickly dismisses Davidson from his post. ■

Pride of Palomar, The (1922), Par. *Dir.* Frank Borzage; *Sc.* Grant Carpenter, John Lynch; *Cast includes:* Forrest Stanley, Marjorie Daw, Tote Du Crow, James Barrow, Joseph Dowling, Warner Oland.

Japanese secret agents plot to gain possession of a tract of California land for a native colony in this blatantly anti-Japanese drama set in the post-World War I period. An Eastern tycoon decides to foreclose on the property and sell it to the Japanese. The owner of the land dies before the transaction goes through. His son (Forrest Stanley) returns from France in time to try to stop the sale. The remainder of the film concerns his efforts to raise enough money to pay off the mortgage, thereby preventing the Japanese from gaining possession of the coveted property. Meanwhile Okada (Warner Oland), the chief of the foreign agents, orders his underlings to stop Stanley's progress. Marjorie Daw, as the rich man's daughter, helps Stanley in his efforts.

The film, based on Peter B. Kyne's novel, presents several anti-Japanese scenes. At one point Okada, frustrated in his attempts to possess the land in question, exclaims: "You won't sell me the land now, but someday I'll come with a Japanese army and take your damned ranch!" He ends his ranting by scraping a match across George Washington's face appearing on a nearby marble statue. See Japanese War Scare of 1907. ■

Pride of the Army (1942), Mon. *Dir.* S. Roy Luby; *Sc.* Jay Vlahos; *Cast includes:* Billy Lee, Addison Richards, Kay Linaker, Bradley Page, Herbert Rawlinson, Bryant Washburn.

The training of dogs for military purposes is the subject of this minor World War II drama. The plot concerns little Billy Lee who donates his dog for the defense of a war plant. His father, an alcoholic as the result of war wounds, works at the plant. When saboteurs attempt to destroy the factory, Billy's dog discovers the plot while his father sacrifices his life to save the plant. The film is sometimes listed under its alternate title, *War Dogs.*

The film is based on the actual recruitment of canines during the war. Under the auspices of Dogs for Defense, Inc. and the Quartermaster General of the U.S. Army, 50,000 dogs were recruited and trained for defense and war duties. ■

Prisoner of Japan (1942), PRC. *Dir.* Arthur Ripley; *Sc.* Robert Chapin; *Cast includes:* Alan Baxter, Gertrude Michael, Ernest Dorian, Corinna Mura, Tommy Seidel, Billy Roya.

Japanese agents operating from a Pacific island threaten American warships in this low-budget World War II drama. Using a hidden radio station, the spy ring is responsible for the sinking of a battleship. Eventually, our hero and heroine, played by Alan Baxter and Gertrude Michael, who are prisoners on the island, manage to contact a second warship. The action sequences are stock shots in this routine drama. ■

Prisoner of War (1954), MGM. *Dir.* Andrew Marton; *Sc.* Allen Rivkin; *Cast includes:* Ronald Reagan, Steve Forrest, Dewey Martin, Oscar Homolka, Robert Horton, Paul Stewart.

The treatment of prisoners of war by the North Koreans forms the background of this Korean War drama. To check on a series of stories emanating from behind enemy lines about the brutal treatment of captured soldiers, American forces decide to drop a volunteer officer into North Korea. Ronald Reagan, as Captain Sloane, a World War II hero now fighting in South Korea, is asked to make the sacrifice. "We know the North Koreans are paying no attention to the Geneva Convention," Major Halle (Henry Morgan in his pre-"M*A*S*H" days) explains. "We need proof, and we need it documented."

Reagan quickly agrees to accept the assignment and parachutes behind enemy lines. He soon joins a detachment of American prisoners who are being force-marched in the dead of winter to a remote prison camp. Of some 700 captives, a Korean officer reports, only slightly more than 200 have survived the brutal trek. Once at the compound, Reagan witnesses first-hand a variety of atrocities executed by a Russian colonel (Oscar Homolka) and others. Homolka has been assigned by Moscow to help the North Koreans indoctrinate the prisoners in Communist ideology. The men are subjected to beatings and torture and, on occasion, are killed. Dewey Martin portrays a collaborator while Steve Forrest, as another American soldier, continuously resists his captors.

The film, based on actual interviews of former prisoners and documented evidence of the atrocities of the Communists, opens with the words of Dr. Charles W. Mayo, U.S. delegate to the U.N., printed on the screen: "Such testimony as this seems to teach that the spirit of man can run deep—far beyond the reach of Communist tortures." But the weak script, which tries to develop this theme, lacks credibility. One problem is the weak dialogue that predominates. "We feed better food to our pigs back home," says an American prisoner of war. Caricatures instead of villains don't help the film either; they work against the basic theme. Homolka, dressed at times as though he were in the Russian Tea Room, condemns Russian cigarettes while praising American tobacco. His Soviet aide and yes-man, eager to please, keeps interjecting with "Yes, indeed," until Homolka is forced to rebuke him. "At least wait till I finish my sentence." See Brain-washing; Korean War. ■

Private Snuffy Smith (1942), Mon. *Dir.* Edward Cline; *Sc.* Billy De Beck; *Cast includes:* Bud Duncan, Edgar Kennedy, Sarah Padden, Doris Linden, J. Farrell MacDonald.

Cartoonist Billy De Beck's popular comic strip, "Snuffy Smith," is transformed into a routine service comedy in this low-budget film. Silent screen comedian Bud Duncan portrays the dwarfish, bulbous-nosed title character. Snuffy, a hillbilly who joins the army, is hounded by comic character actor Edgar Kennedy, who portrays his sergeant. The simple plot concerns some spies whom Snuffy and company eventually get tangled up with in this minor comedy also known as *Snuffy Smith, Yardbird.* ■

Prize, The (1963), MGM. *Dir.* Mark Robson; *Sc.* Ernest Lehman; *Cast includes:* Paul Newman, Edward G. Robinson, Elke Sommer, Diane Baker, Micheline Presle, Gerard Oury.

Communist agents plot to kidnap a Nobel Prize candidate in this oddly blended Cold War comedy drama adapted from Irving Wallace's novel and set in Sweden during the week in which Nobel prizewinners are selected. The victim of the plot (Edward G. Robinson) is an American citizen and physicist who emigrated from Germany after World War II. When he refuses to cooperate with Soviet agents sent to Stockholm to persuade him to reject the Nobel Prize, denounce American imperialism and defect to East Germany, they kidnap him and replace him with a double.

Another American Nobel Prize candidate (Paul Newman), a boorish, self-pitying, burnt-out writer, accidentally stumbles upon the Soviet scheme when he notices a slight change in the bogus physicist's appearance and attitude toward him. Newman confides in the missing scientist's niece (Diane Baker) who thinks his suspicions are completely unfounded. Unknown to the writer, she has been forced to take part in the conspiracy to save the life of her father whom she believes is being held captive behind the Iron Curtain. Newman investigates further and, although his life is threatened several times, no one will believe his story. Undaunted, Newman continues on his own to rescue the physicist and Elke Sommer, who portrays a Swedish aide assigned by her government to help the

writer during his stay in Stockholm. Sommer had been taken hostage to prevent Newman from further interference. Newman gets the physicist back to Awards night in time to receive his prize and expose his double.

The well-paced film offers many treats. There are some witty moments, including one sequence in which Newman escapes his pursuers by intruding upon a meeting of nudists. Plenty of suspense occurs as the writer ventures forth alone to find the real physicist. Playful sexual encounters between Newman and female characters add charm to the production. Although it tried to bring some semblance of dignity to the Nobel Prize procedure ("Once again, man bestows immortality upon his fellow man," announces the committee chairman), the film came under fire from several quarters, including criticism from Swedish citizens. They attacked the drama's improprieties concerning their country's sexual morals and its ignoble treatment of the awards process. ■

Project X (1949), Film Classics. *Dir.* Edward J. Montagne; *Sc.* Gene Hurley; *Cast includes:* Keith Andes, Rita Colton, Jack Lord, Kit Russell, Joyce Quinlan, Harry Clark.

A network of Communist agents plans to steal atomic secrets in this low-budget drama. A former member of the party volunteers to help U.S. Government investigators capture the spies. Rita Colton provides the romantic interest. The film contains a weak plot and little action. See Cold War; Soviet Spies in the U.S. ■

Project X (1968), Par. *Dir.* William Castle; *Sc.* Edmund Morris; *Cast includes:* Christopher George, Greta Baldwin, Henry Jones, Monte Markham, Harold Gould, Phillip E. Pine.

A weak, low-budget science fiction drama set in the year 2118, the story concerns this not-so-brave futuristic world and its scientists who try to restore the unconscious memory of a figure from the past (circa 1968). Their subject had been a U.S. government agent who uncovered a Sino-Asian scheme to annihilate the Western powers. The scientists, seeking a secret germ warfare formula, provide him with a new personality—that of a 1968 bank robber. They call their experiment Project X and consider it, according to one scientist, "the single most important project in the world today; it may determine

Lobby card for the Sherlock Holmes World War II spy thriller *Pursuit to Algiers* (1945).

whether or not the western world survives.'' Christopher George portrays the experimental subject-hero. Greta Baldwin provides the romantic interest in this dull tale. ∎

Protocol (1984), WB. *Dir.* Herbert Ross; *Sc.* Buck Henry; *Cast includes:* Goldie Hawn, Chris Sarandon, Richard Romanus, Andre Gregory, Gail Strickland, Cliff De Young.

Goldie Hawn portrays an ingenuous cocktail waitress thrust into the milieu of Washington diplomacy and Middle East chaos in this light comedy. When she accidentally foils a plot to assassinate a visiting Emir (Richard Romanus), she becomes an instant celebrity. Meanwhile, some members of the White House staff scheme to have Hawn delivered to the Emir, who secretly desires her, as another member of his harem in exchange for a strategic military base in his land. The slightly dizzy Hawn soon catches on that she is being manipulated and gives a didactic speech about how government officials have the responsibility of working for the citizens. Gail Strickland, as the chief villain, conspires against Hawn, hatching the plot to have

Hawn join the Emir's harem. Chris Sarandon, as a government worker, provides some romantic interest for Hawn. The comedy consists chiefly of slapstick, one-liners and some satiric barbs aimed mostly at the press, television and politics. ∎

Prussian Cur, The (1918), Fox. *Dir.* Raoul Walsh; *Sc.* Raoul Walsh; *Cast includes:* Miriam Cooper, James Marcus, Patrick O'Malley, Lenora Stewart, Sidney Mason, Walter McEwen.

An anti-German propaganda film made during World War I, the drama concerns a German spy bent on initiating acts of sabotage in America. He visits a town in the West where he tries to convince a German-American to damage an airplane plant. Bristling at the suggestion, the loyal American has the agent arrested. When pro-Germans gather in the street to plan the spy's rescue, white-hooded horsemen ride into town and capture the German sympathizers. The patriotic riders force the Germans to kiss the stars and stripes and then lead them into the jail. The climactic scene resembles that of the Ku Klux

Klan coming to the rescue of a Southern town in D. W. Griffith's *The Birth of a Nation* (1915). At least one reviewer criticized the film for advocating mob violence as the means to a just end. ∎

Pursuit to Algiers (1945), U. *Dir.* Roy William Neill; *Sc.* Leonard Lee; *Cast includes:* Basil Rathbone, Nigel Bruce, Marjorie Riordan, Martin Koslek, John Abbott.

Another of the updated Sherlock Holmes entries of the 1940s, this World War II drama lacks the atmosphere of the earlier films which adhere to the time period created by A. Conan Doyle. The film involves a plot against a young king's life by an unnamed enemy although there are hints that this foe represents totalitarian forces. Emissaries of a mythical country appeal to Holmes to help safeguard their king's journey from England to Algiers. "For the sake not only of our country," one of the men pleads, "but for liberty and good government everywhere, we implore you to undertake this mission." Holmes, not only the master detective but a strong supporter of universal freedom in these updated melodramas, replies: "In the interest of democratic government, I shall do my utmost." He accompanies the king, who travels incognito aboard a vessel. Holmes protects him from several attempts on his life. The amiable Dr. Watson contributes to the comic relief as Holmes exposes the assassins and successfully completes his mission.

The plot raises an interesting question. The representatives who entreat Holmes to safeguard their king's journey suggest that their nation is a democracy, but they never explain how their homeland could be democratic and have a king. Holmes, who extols the virtues of liberty in the film, never questions this paradox. See Detectives and Spies. ∎

Q

Quebec (1951), Par. *Dir.* George Templeton; *Sc.* Alan Le May; *Cast includes:* John Barrymore, Jr., Corinne Calvet, Barbara Rush, Patric Knowles, John Hoyt, Arnold Moss.

French Canadian conspirators plot to overthrow British rule in Quebec in this historical drama set in 1837. Corinne Calvet, as the estranged wife of the brutal Colonel Durossac and the lover of the rebel leader, is the secret head of the conspiracy, known only as "Lafleur" to both friend and foe. As the charming and beautiful hostess Madame Stephanie Durossac, she sponsors parties in her luxurious Quebec home while plotting with fellow conspirators for the overthrow of British rule, especially that of Colonel Durossac, military commander of Quebec. Patric Knowles, as the backwoods rebel leader Charles Douglas and Madame Durossac's secret lover and coconspirator for 18 years, has raised their illegitimate son (John Barrymore, Jr.). Barrymore, who believes his mother is dead, is invited to stay in Quebec with Madame Durossac, whom he meets for the first time and immediately senses a close bond. At this point the conspirators agree that the time has come for open rebellion, including the capture of the strongly fortified citadel guarding Quebec.

The remainder of the drama deals with the failed rebellion. Knowles is killed, shot in the back by the treacherous colonel. Barrymore is captured and faces a similar fate. Calvet goes before her husband to plead for the boy's life. Durossac finally agrees to allow the boy to walk out of the prison unharmed. Calvet, however, suspects foul play and disguises herself as her son that evening. As she walks toward the gate, she is shot down, mistaken for her son. Later, a sympathetic priest gains the boy's release, and he leaves the strife-torn city with his mother's ward (Barbara Rush), finally realizing that Lafleur was his mother.

Most of the political discussion has been left to Father Antoine, played by John Hoyt, a friend to the conspirators but not part of the rebellion. A strong believer in the English government, he condemns the conspiracy. "You are only postponing Canada's great days," he warns young Barrymore. "Good things must grow," he explains. "Believe me, the liberties you seek will grow best within the government we have." When the youth, confused by the priest's words, mentions the struggle and sacrifices of Calvet and his father, the priest replies: "They are like all rebel leaders. They mistake their own bitterness and frustration and hatred for devotion to a cause." ∎

Quicksands (1923), Selznick. *Dir.* Jack Conway; *Sc.* Howard Hawks; *Cast includes:* Helene Chadwick, Richard Dix, Alan Hale, Noah Beery, J. Farrell McDonald.

A U.S. Customs agent is sent across the border into Mexico to investigate drug-smuggling into the States in this western drama. Richard Dix, as the secret agent, arrives at a canteen where he notices a young Mexican woman who resembles his fiancée, the daughter of his boss, the head of customs. Upon his return, he discovers certain evidence that proves that his sweetheart and the Mexican are the same person. Concluding that she is part of the smuggling operation, he decides to resign from his post. Then he hears that his chief is being held captive by the gang and that the daughter has been using the masquerade only to help her father. He returns across the border to rescue the father but is captured by the smugglers. The U.S.

Cavalry then comes to their rescue. Helene Chadwick portrays the daughter. ■

Quiet American, The (1958), UA. *Dir.* Joseph L. Mankiewicz; *Sc.* Joseph L. Mankiewicz; *Cast includes:* Audie Murphy, Michael Redgrave, Claude Dauphin, Giorgia Moll, Bruce Cabot.

An American in Vietnam in 1952 during the French Indo-China War clashes ideologically with an English correspondent in this talky drama based on Graham Greene's novel. Greene's attack on the U.S. and its botched foreign policy has been diluted by having Audie Murphy portray a private American citizen instead of an official who believes there is an alternative between Communism and French colonialism in that part of the world. Michael Redgrave, as a cynical writer who loses his objectivity, becomes an agent of the Communists who use him as a dupe and ultimately double-cross him. He is partially responsible for Murphy's death by informing the Communist guerrillas that Murphy is

American Audie Murphy, searching for an alternative between Communism and colonialism in French Indo-China, explains his theory to cynical Communist agent Michael Redgrave in *The Quiet American* (1958).

dealing in explosives. Giorgia Moll, as Redgrave's mistress, falls in love with the American who proposes to her. Limited action sequences concern guerrilla activities against the French forces.

Tony Martin, as a U.S. agent hired to track down a missing shipment of army rifles, questions post commander Ron Randell and Peggie Castle, whose soldier-brother was killed in action. *Quincannon, Frontier Scout* (1956).

In the biography *Edward Lansdale: The Unquiet American* by Cecil B. Currey, the author suggests that his subject was the model for Greene's main character, as played by Murphy in the film version. Lansdale, who died in 1987, was a U.S. Air Force general, a famous agent and a dedicated political crusader who, some believe, "created" South Vietnam. A C.I.A. operative in the Philippines, he achieved success in helping Ramón Magsaysay win that country's presidency. The C.I.A., hoping for similar results, then assigned him to Vietnam. He began to make inroads in gaining the confidence of the people through both overt and covert actions, but he also made enemies among American military and government officials. Differences emerged over the eventual role of the U.S. Lansdale firmly believed that the war must be fought chiefly by the Vietnamese. After a two-year stint at the Pentagon, he was reassigned by President Johnson in 1965 to Vietnam. But for Lansdale—and the U.S.—it was too late. America had already plunged its military forces headlong into the ominous whirlpool of the Vietnam War. See Vietnam War: Intelligence and Covert Actions. ■

Quiet Please, Murder (1942), TCF. *Dir.* John Larkin; *Sc.* John Larkin; *Cast includes:* George Sanders, Gail Patrick, Richard Denning, Lynne Roberts, Sidney Blackmer, Kurt Katch.

An unusual drama blending mystery, murder and Nazi spies, the film stars George Sanders as a book forger who steals valuable editions from a library, copies them and sells the counterfeits as originals. Nazi agents somehow are intertwined into the plot when a German art collector, played by Sidney Blackmer, ships the books to Berlin. Richard Denning portrays a detective on the trail of Sanders while Gail Patrick, as his accomplice, develops a romantic interest in the detective. Limited settings (chiefly the library) betray this low-budget but interesting little film. ■

Quincannon, Frontier Scout (1956), UA. *Dir.* Lesley Selander; *Sc.* John C. Higgins, Don Martin; *Cast includes:* Tony Martin, Peggie Castle, John Bromfield, John Smith, Ron Randell.

Tony Martin portrays the title character, an ex-army captain, in this routine action drama. Having earlier served under General Custer and witnessing a particularly coldblooded Indian massacre executed by the general, he resigned from the military. When a secret shipment of repeating rifles en route to an army outpost disappears, Quincannon is hired to investigate the incident. Following a series of skirmishes with Indians, he exposes the post commander (Ron Randell) as the traitor who sold the rifles to the hostiles. Peggie Castle portrays the attractive sister of a soldier killed in battle. ■

R

Radar Patrol vs. Sky King (1950) serial, Rep. *Dir.* Fred Brannon; *Sc.* Royal K. Cole; *Cast includes:* Kirk Alyn, Jean Dean, Anthony Warde, George J. Lewis, Eve Whitney, John Merton.

An especially cunning and effective saboteur frustrates the efforts of U.S. military intelligence for most of the 12 chapters in this routine serial. Known only as Baroda, this sinister villain sends out his teams of saboteurs to unleash a reign of destruction upon the landscape. Kirk Alyn, as the U.S. government agent who is assigned to bring Baroda to his just end, undergoes the conventional fights and faces the familiar cliff-hanging perils of the genre. Since economy superseded production values in the serials of the post-World War II years, the studio used an inordinate amount of stock footage in this entry. Perennial screen villain George Lewis is present and up to his old, old tricks. ∎

Raid on Rommel (1971), U. *Dir.* Henry Hathaway; *Sc.* Richard Bluel; *Cast includes:* Richard Burton, John Colicos, Clinton Greyn, Danielle De Metz, Wolfgang Preiss.

Richard Burton portrays a British intelligence officer in this action drama set in North Africa during World War II. A British plan to infiltrate German lines and knock out the enemy's guns at Tobruk before the British fleet arrives hinges upon a specially trained commando unit that has been captured by the Germans. Burton allows himself to be taken prisoner so that he can free the group. But he learns too late that the men have been transferred to another base. Interned chiefly with a group of medics, he decides to enlist their aid in accomplishing the mission. The film then proceeds with a series of suspenseful escapes and skirmishes with the enemy as the newly formed assault team goes about destroying strategic targets as well as crippling Rommel's tanks by igniting his fuel supply. Some of the spectacular action sequences used in the film *Tobruk* (1966) have been cleverly intercut into this present work. ∎

Raiders of the Lost Ark (1981), Par. *Dir.* Steven Spielberg; *Sc.* Lawrence Kasdan; *Cast includes:* Harrison Ford, Karen Allen, Wolf Kahler, Paul Freeman, Ronald Lacey, John Rhys-Davies.

A light-hearted adventure yarn in the spirit of the old serials, director Steven Spielberg's action-packed, incredulous drama set in 1936 concerns an adventurous American archaeologist who foils a Nazi attempt to possess a hidden chest allegedly containing magical powers. Indiana Jones (Harrison Ford), the stalwart hero assigned by U.S. intelligence to gain possession of the Lost Ark of the Covenant, which Hitler, who believes in the occult, covets. The Nazi leader is counting on the prize as a psychological boon to his plans for world domination. Ford manages to end up with the coveted Ark, which has changed hands several times between the American and Nazis agents. Karen Allen, as the heroine, shares many of the dangers with Ford. Paul Freeman, as a rival archaeologist, is in league with the Nazi agents. Ronald Lacey plays the chief Nazi agent and Ford's archenemy.

Intentionally fashioned after the old 1930s serials, the film offers almost non-stop action as Ford, the archetypal serial hero, eludes all dangers in his path, including poisoned darts and dangerous tarantulas. For example, in the opening sequence, one of the highlights of the film, Ford is in a South American tomb where he finds a sack of treasure. Suddenly a huge boulder is released and comes hurtling towards him and his guide. He uses his whip as a rope and allows his companion to swing across a bottomless pit to safety. The guide then asks Ford to toss him the treasure sack. Ford mechanically does so, only to see the guide loosen the whip and escape, thereby leaving Ford to face the impending danger. However, he beats the boulder to the mouth of the cave and leaps to safety. Other narrow escapes and hair-raising chases take place in the mountains of Nepal, in the streets of Cairo, on the desert sands of Egypt (where Ford has a frenetic ride in a truck) and on a remote island. In all these remote places Ford is hounded by Nazi agents bent on eliminating him.

The well-produced and lively escapist film, which cost $20 million to produce and generated more than $200 million in box-office receipts, sparkles with a host of spectacular special effects. Two sequels, *Indiana Jones and the Temple of Doom* and *Indiana Jones and the Last Crusade*, appeared in 1984 and 1989, respectively. ▪

"Railroad Raiders of '62" (1911), Kalem. *Cast includes:* Sidney Olcott.

An early silent historical drama, this short film deals with an actual event that occurred during the Civil War. A troop of about two dozen Union soldiers, dressed as civilians, penetrates behind enemy lines and steals "The General," a Confederate train. The leader of the raid was an officer named Andrews. The incident became the basis of Buster Keaton's silent comedy *The General* (1927) and a Walt Disney feature titled *The Great Locomotive Chase* (1956). Kalem, a studio known more for its one-reel westerns, also turned out a series of historical dramas during this period. See also Andrews Raid. ▪

"Ransomed, or a Prisoner of War" (1910), Vitagraph. *Cast includes:* Clara Kimball Young, Leo Delaney.

A short silent drama set during the Civil War, the story concerns a Confederate soldier who crosses Union lines to visit his son who is celebrating his sixth birthday. As the father makes his way back to his own lines, he is captured and sentenced to death as a spy. His little son intervenes by appealing to the Union general and saves his father's life. The simple little domestic drama has no battle scenes. ▪

Raw Deal (1986), De Laurentis. *Dir.* John Irvin; *Sc.* Gary M. DeVore, Norman Wexler; *Cast includes:* Arnold Schwarzenegger, Kathryn Harrold, Sam Wanamaker, Paul Shenar, Robert Davi, Ed Lauter.

A former F.B.I. agent, dismissed for roughing up a suspect, is coaxed to unofficially help his former chief in exposing a leak in the agency in this routine action-oriented drama. Arnold Schwarzenegger, as the ex-F.B.I. agent now relegated to sheriff of a small North Carolina town, is anxious to return to his former job. Darren McGavin, as the F.B.I. chief whose son was killed by a Chicago gang leader (Sam Wanamaker) along with a key witness prepared to testify against Wanamaker, asks the former agent to work his way into the mob. Schwarzenegger agrees and soon wins the confidence of Wanamaker by tangling with the leader's rival. Hired as Wanamaker's bodyguard, the undercover agent helps his boss wipe out the rival gang. When he discovers the next target is the F.B.I. chief, the agent turns his guns on Wanamaker and his gang. Among the victims is a corrupt district attorney who is partially responsible for Schwarzenegger's dismissal. The former agent returns to his wife and is soon rehired by the F.B.I. One of the few poignant moments in an otherwise violent film occurs when Schwarzenegger helps his chief recover from bullet wounds, the result of a gun battle with the gang leader. ▪

Rebel City (1953), AA. *Dir.* Thomas Carr; *Sc.* Sydney Theil; *Cast includes:* Wild Bill Elliott, Marjorie Lord, Robert Kent, Keith Richards, Stanford Jolley, Denver Pyle.

Southern sympathizers stir up trouble in Kansas in this low-budget Civil War drama. A gambler (Wild Bill Elliott) journeys to a small Kansas town to find out who murdered his father, the former owner of the local freight line. He decides to investigate the death on his own after the local Union colonel, burdened with Copperhead problems, fails to help him. Ultimately he unmasks a Union captain (Robert Kent) who was responsible for the murder and heads the local troublemakers in this routine tale. See American Civil War: Intelligence and Covert Actions; Copperheads. ▪

Reckoning Day, The (1918), Triangle. *Dir.* Harry Clements; *Sc.* Bob Hill; *Cast includes:* Belle Bennett, Jack Richardson, J. Barney Sherry, Tom Buckingham, Lenore Fair.

This complex drama, set during World War I, involves German spies, a U.S. senator, a gang of thieves and a murder. Belle Bennett portrays a lawyer assigned by her district attorney to uncover some denizens of the underworld who are in the employ of German agents. Jack Richardson, as the gang leader, loves Lola (Lenore Fair), who is working for the spies. When he overhears her plotting with the enemies of this country, his patriotic spirit is aroused and he kills her. Tom Buckingham, as the young son of a senator (J. Barney Sherry), also loves Lola and is eventually accused of murdering her. Bennett finally traps the spies, criminals and the murderer, thereby exonerating the senator's son. ∎

Recoil, The (1917), Pathé. *Dir.* George Fitzmaurice; *Sc.* Anthony P. Kelly; *Cast includes:* William Courtenay, Lillian Greuse, Frank Belcher, Cora Mills Adams, William Raymond.

A U.S. Secret Service agent breaks up an international spy ring, thus preventing the outbreak of war, in this complex drama. William Courtenay, as the agent, faces a series of obstacles including romantic complications while on a special mission. Unable to reveal anything to the woman he loves (Lillian Greuse), he leaves mysteriously with a fellow agent to carry out his assignment. However, the spy they are following manages to trap the two men in a cellar somewhere in the country. Here they remain prisoners under guard for several weeks.

His sweetheart, meanwhile, receives news that Courtenay is dead, so she agrees to marry another suitor. Eventually the two agents escape and return to the pursuit of the spy. They learn that he is about to sail for Europe and that he is carrying information that will drag the U.S. into a war. Courtenay boards the ship in time. His former sweetheart's husband, in the meantime, has been killed. When the ship docks in London, Courtenay effects the arrest of the spy and his cronies. He then returns to New York where he renews his romance with the widow. ∎

Red Barry (1938) serial, U. *Dir.* Ford Beebe, Alan James; *Sc.* Norman S. Hall, Ray Trampe; *Cast includes:* Larry Crabbe, Frances Robinson, Edna Sedgwick, Syril Delevanti, Frank Lackteen, Wade Boteler.

A resourceful detective and a reporter battle against an international plot involving a conflict between Asians and Russians over a large munitions deal in this 13-episode serial. Larry "Buster" Crabbe, who gained popularity as the title character in the highly successful Flash Gordon serial, portrays Red Barry, an aggressive detective whose unorthodox ideas nettle his chief. Frances Robinson, as the reporter who has a crush on Barry, faces several dangerous moments as she helps him track down the foreign agents and some missing bonds worth $2 million. Edna Sedgwick, as an entertainer, in reality is a spy for Soviet agents. Frank Lackteen portrays one of the chief villains Barry continually has to confront. Wade Boteler, as Barry's superior, frowns upon the publicity his underling gets as a result of Robinson's stories. See Serials. ∎

Red Dragon, The (1945), Mon. *Dir.* Phil Rosen; *Sc.* George Callahan; *Cast includes:* Sidney Toler, Fortunio Bonavona, Benson Fong, Robert E. Keane, Willie Best, Carol Hughes.

A weak entry in the popular Charlie Chan detective series, this slight drama, set in Mexico City, concerns attempts by enemy agents to steal secret plans for the atomic bomb. Sidney Toler, as the Hawaiian sleuth, finally solves the mystery after several inexplicable killings occur. The murderer, Chan deduces, has been using a remote-control apparatus to commit his crimes. Incidentally, the detective protects the atomic secrets from falling into the wrong hands. Benson Fong, as one of Chan's sons, and Willie Best (who alternated with Mantan Moreland as the sleuth's chauffeur), provide some comedy relief. Fortunio Bonavona portrays a local police inspector who joins Chan in his search for the head villain. ∎

Red Menace, The (1949), Rep. *Dir.* R. G. Springsteen; *Sc.* Albert DeMond, Gerald Geraghty; *Cast includes:* Robert Rockwell, Hanne Axman, Shepard Menken, Betty Lou Gerson, Barbara Fuller, Lester Luther.

A cautionary tale about the evils of Communism, this low-budget Cold War film depicts the Communist party as an organization composed of villainous types ready to betray its own members if that serves its cause. A disgruntled, disillusioned veteran, played by

Robert Rockwell, becomes the target of the party which offers him alcohol and sex as inducements to join the cause. He accepts, naively thinking that the Communists can change the social ills of America. The film points out other types who fall prey to the party's promises. They include a young black student, a young woman whose indigent background has led her to distrust the capitalistic system and a refugee whose father was a strong Communist supporter. As these members grow suspicious of the party and seek to leave, they are intimidated by the leaders in this chiefly implausible yarn. See Cold War; Soviet Spies in the U.S. ■

Red Scare of 1919–1920. The advent of the Communist Revolution in Russia in 1917 stirred up an international wave of fear in Western capitalist countries. To the general public in the U.S., anarchists and Communists were linked together as violent, anti-American bomb tossers.

A number of bombs were thrown during the course of some fierce strikes in the post-World War I years. As a result, public opinion was ready to support anti-Red legislation. Attorney General A. Mitchell Palmer led a national drive to incarcerate Communist radicals. During the course of the campaign, Palmer's Washington home was bombed. Eventually about 6,000 suspected Red agitators were arrested. Of these, 250 were deported to Russia.

Various states joined the anti-Red crusade. Legislation was passed to prohibit the use of violence as a political weapon. After a bomb was thrown in Wall Street in 1920 that killed 38 people and wounded hundreds more, additional anti-Red pressure was brought to bear in state legislatures and the federal government. Members of the International Workers of the World were prosecuted solely because they belonged to that radical union.

The American film industry used the Red Scare for various plots ranging from drama to comedy. Although most of these films were based on fiction, they reinforced in the moviegoer his or her own conceptions of the Communists. Labor unrest was a popular film theme. *Dangerous Hours* (1920), an anti-Bolshevik propaganda film set during the post-World War I years, concerns Russian agents sent to the U.S. to foment industrial unrest. Lloyd Hughes portrays an unsuspecting American who is duped by Communist agitators. *The Great Shadow* (1920) depicts how Russian agents operate to incite tensions between capital and labor. The focus of the agitators' attentions is an American shipyard where they instigate a major strike by thousands of workers. In *The Right to Happiness* (1919) Dorothy Phillips portrays a Russian spy who is sent to the U.S. to stir up industrial unrest.

Films also exploited the themes of general disorder and violence. *The Volcano* (1919), a controversial propaganda drama about a Communist conspiracy, dealt with bomb plots, Red agitators and a New York schoolteacher-heroine who becomes embroiled with the conspirators. The Communist leader plots to assassinate Governor Alfred E. Smith, Attorney General Alexander Palmer and others. In *The Undercurrent* (1919) Russian agents spread dissent and propaganda among Americans in the hope of eventually bringing about a world revolution. In *Little Miss Rebellion* (1920), with Dorothy Gish and Ralph Graves, Bolshevik agents pursue an ex-princess of a European country to New York. Dorothy Gish portrays the former royal figure whose principality has been overthrown during a revolution.

The Red Scare managed to penetrate several popular genres usually devoid of political controversy. First it affected the silent comedy. *The Amazing Impostor* (1919), a comedy starring Mary Miles Minter, has two Bolshevik agents trying to steal important documents. In *Bullin' the Bullsheviki* (1919), another comedy, a young American woman journeys to Russia to wipe out Bolshevism. In one scene the heroine reports to the battlefield and sends an ultimatum to the Communist leader that he and his followers take a bath and seek employment. Next, it touched the detective genre. Lionel Barrymore, as Boston Blackie in *A Face in the Fog* (1922), becomes entangled in an international plot to restore the monarchy in Bolshevik Russia.

American film studios were quick to exploit the Russian Revolution as a screen topic. D. W. Griffith's *Orphans of the Storm* (1921), a historical drama about the French Revolution, no doubt was one of the earliest and set the generally anti-revolutionary tone for those films to follow. Griffith used his opening titles to warn his audiences against "Bolshevism." See also Labor Unrest; Palmer Raids. ■

Red Snow (1952), Col. *Dir.* Boris L. Petroff, Harry S. Franklin; *Sc.* Tom Hubbard, Orville Hampton; *Cast includes:* Guy Madison, Ray Mala, Carole Mathews, Gloria Saunders, Robert Peyton, Philip Ahn.

The Cold War reaches into vast, cold regions where Alaska almost meets Siberia in this drama about Soviet mischief among the Eskimos. A U.S. major is flown to a remote American outpost to investigate strange lights emanating from Siberia, the disappearance of Eskimos who have been lured to the Soviet side of the Bering Strait and mysterious Soviet flights over Alaskan territory. He assigns three Eskimo scouts to return to their tribes to make intelligence reports about any infiltration by Siberian Eskimos. Guy Madison, as a lieutenant with the Alaskan Air Rescue Service, makes several flights in the area and helps to rescue stranded Eskimos on ice islands.

Meanwhile, Soviet agents have been preparing to release a small but powerful bomb to test its effectiveness. They send up two planes, one to drop the experimental weapon and the other to photograph the results. The Soviet pilot realizes that he will be killed by the explosion and opts to land his plane at the nearest American base. His copilot, however, overpowers him, but the plane crashes. One of the Eskimo scouts (Ray Mala) finds the secret weapon and delivers it to the American base. Philip Ahn, as a Siberian Eskimo and Soviet spy, infiltrates Mala's northern Alaskan tribe and is caught trying to kill a wounded Eskimo who has escaped from the Soviets. Much of the film is composed of stock footage, including scenes of Eskimo life and rituals, most of which are skillfully blended into the drama. ■

Redhead and the Cowboy, The (1950), Par. *Dir.* Leslie Fenton; *Sc.* Jonathan Latimer, Liam O'Brien; *Cast includes:* Glenn Ford, Edmond O'Brien, Rhonda Fleming, Alan Reed, Morris Ankrum, Edith Evanson.

Union and Confederate spy activities during the closing days of the Civil War dominate the plot of this entertaining little western drama. Rhonda Fleming, as the titled redhead, portrays the Southern spy assigned to deliver a message to a Confederate leader about to attack a gold train. Glenn Ford, as a cowboy accused of murder who needs Fleming as a witness to help clear him of the charges, follows her on her mission. Edmond O'Brien portrays the undercover Union spy

determined to round up a nest of Confederate agents and their leader while saving the Union gold shipment. He joins Fleming and Ford, hoping they they will eventually lead him to the rebel leader. Another conflict arises when a disgraced officer (Alan Reed) decides to keep the gold for himself and take off with Fleming. ■

Robert Cummings, posing as one of Robespierre's followers, tries to prove that the fanatical revolutionary has plans to make himself dictator of France. Arnold Moss has other plans for Cummings. *Reign of Terror* (1949).

Reign of Terror (1949), EL. *Dir.* Anthony Mann; *Sc.* Philip Yordan, Aeneas MacKenzie; *Cast includes:* Robert Cummings, Arlene Dahl, Richard Hart, Arnold Moss, Richard Basehart.

The search for a valuable diary forms the plot of this offbeat drama set during the French Revolution. When several idealistic revolutionaries learn that Robespierre (Richard Basehart) plans to make himself dictator, they enlist the aid of a loyal companion (Robert Cummings) to pose as one of Robespierre's followers. His mission is to locate a small black book that lists the names of those destined for the guillotine. He manages to obtain the book and expose the contents, thereby foiling the intended dictator's plans. Although it includes little in the way of historical fact, the film presents an array of historical figures—Saint Just (Jess Barker), Barras (Richard Hart) and Fouché (Arnold Moss). The film is significant for its *film noir* elements (intense atmosphere, low-key lighting, dark settings). It has appeared on television under its alternate title, *The Black Book.*

Many historians consider Maximilien

Robespierre (1758–1794) an enigmatic revolutionary. Sometimes called "The Incorruptible" because of his idealism and extreme regard for virtue, he nevertheless suggested the formation of the infamous Committee of Public Safety which charted the way for the Reign of Terror. Unable to control the beast he had created, he eventually became one of its many victims after serving it for the last four of his 36 years. An acknowledged intellectual who commanded the applause of senates, he was unable to survive in one of France's most ruthless and sanguinary epochs which he helped to bring about. ∎

Remember Pearl Harbor (1942), Rep. *Dir.* Joseph Santley; *Sc.* Malcolm Stuart Boylan, Isabel Dawn; *Cast includes:* Donald Barry, Alan Curtis, Fay McKenzie, Sig Ruman, Ian Keith, Rhys Williams.

An action drama that takes place on the eve of Pearl Harbor, the film features Donald Barry and Alan Curtis as two soldier-pals stationed in the Philippines. Barry is a roughneck and troublemaker while Curtis is the more serious-minded of the pair. When news of Japan's attack on Pearl Harbor reaches Barry, who has become mixed up with a group of enemy agents working for the Japanese, he realizes the error of his ways and quickly redeems himself. Not only does he expose an espionage network, but he crashes an airplane, kamikaze-style, into a Japanese troopship. Other battle sequences include land engagements between Americans and Japanese forces in the Philippines. Fay McKenzie provides the romance in this low-budget film that was one of the earliest to appear following the attack on Pearl Harbor. See Pearl Harbor; Philippines. ∎

Rendezvous (1935), MGM. *Dir.* William K. Howard; *Sc.* P. J. Wolfson, George Oppenheimer; *Cast includes:* William Powell, Rosalind Russell, Binnie Barnes, Lionel Atwill, Cesar Romero.

William Powell stars in this comedy drama set in Washington during World War I. A dapper newspaper puzzle editor, he resigns to join the army. Rosalind Russell, as a young woman who falls for him, pulls a few strings in Washington and has him assigned to the intelligence department where her influential uncle is in charge. Powell is disappointed at not going overseas with his unit but soon set-

tles into his new post. After several ineffectual attempts and some gross blundering by the intelligence agency, Powell manages to capture the German spies, led by Cesar Romero and Binnie Barnes. His work finished, he hopes to go to France to join his unit. But once again he is plucked away to return to the intelligence agency. This was Rosalind Russell's first leading role. The film has been singled out as the first American espionage film to introduce a large dose of wit.

Although the drama has a weak plot, it describes in detail the extent of German espionage during the war. Secret agents are seen operating in Washington, California and Mexico, where U.S. secrets about troopships and convoys are transmitted to German submarines. According to the script, the spies seem more adept and professional at the art of espionage than their American counterparts. The opening foreword, appearing on the screen, pays tribute to secret agents: "Behind every strategic move in war, a secret army toils ceaselessly. On the accuracy of their dangerous work depends the launching of battles, the sinking of ships and the destinies of thousands of soldiers on land and sea."

The film is based on *The Blonde Countess*, a novel by Herbert Osborn Yardley (1889–1959), a writer and cryptologist. Yardley, an obscure code clerk in the State Department before World War I, proved to his superiors that all their codes may be broken—which he did in his spare time as a prank. When the U.S. entered the war, Yardley was promoted to captain and put in command of MI-8, the newly formed code section of the Military Intelligence Division. The section soon created new codes, broke foreign ciphers and developed new chemical formulas for invisible writing. In 1919 Yardley broke Japan's diplomatic code. This helped U.S. negotiators during a multi-national armaments conference, since they knew in advance the limits and compromises Japan had set for itself. Yardley later turned to writing for a living. ∎

Rendezvous 24 (1946), TCF. *Dir.* James Tinling; *Sc.* Aubrey Wisberg; *Cast includes:* William Gargan, Pat O'Moore, David Leonard, Maria Palmer, Kurt Katch, Herman Bing.

Nazi scientists experiment with atomic energy for the purpose of blowing up major cities in this post-World War II drama. Although the war has ended, a group of unconverted Nazi scientists working in a remote area of the Harz Mountains plans to wipe out New York City and Paris from their laboratory using a remote control device. Fortunately, the U.S. sends one of its top agents (William Gargan) to foil the plot in time to save the first target, the City of Lights. He is assisted by a British agent (Pat O'Moore). Maria Palmer portrays an attractive German agent in this routine story. See Nazi Subversion: Post-World War II. ∎

Renegades (1930), Fox. *Dir.* Victor Fleming; *Sc.* Jules Furthman; *Cast includes:* Warner Baxter, Myrna Loy, Noah Beery, Gregory Gaye, George Cooper.

The French Foreign Legion is the background of this drama. Four recalcitrant Legionnaires, led by Warner Baxter, break away from the ranks and temporarily join forces with the enemy. When the friends learn about an attack on their fellow soldiers, they return to aid the Legion. All die in the final battle. Myrna Loy, who often played the *femme fatale* in the late 1920s, portrays a spy in this film and is the cause for much of the conflict. One of the four Legionnaires manages to shoot her before he dies. The film, adapted from *Le Renegat*, a novel by Andre Armady, features a native attack across the desert sands. ∎

Retaliator, The (1987), Trans World. *Dir.* Allan Holzman; *Sc.* Robert Short; *Cast includes:* Robert Ginty, Sandahl Bergman, Alex Courtney, Paul Walker, Louise Claire Clark, Peter Bromilow.

A covert U.S. experimental scientific agency transforms a Middle East female terrorist into a robot killing-machine in this far-fetched drama that mixes intrigue with science fiction. Robert Ginty, as a free-lance secret operative with his own band of mercenaries, is rehired by the Central Intelligence Agency to rescue two American schoolchildren held hostage in Beirut by a group of Middle East terrorists. Hassim, who leads the group, is an old adversary of Ginty's. With the help of an Arab collaborator, the small American force infiltrates the terrorist headquarters, annihilates most of the group and rescues the two prisoners. Ginty, meanwhile, captures Hassim's terrorist-girlfriend (Sandahl Bergman), who is critically wounded during the raid.

Back in Los Angeles, Dr. Brock (James Booth) claims the patient, who is declared "brain dead" following an unsuccessful operation to save her. Brock, who heads the secret scientific laboratory sponsored by the C.I.A., performs several experimental operations on the terrorist, among which includes replacing her frontal lobe with microcircuitry. Brock and his group of surgeon-scientists end up creating a cyborg—programmed to kill terrorists. She is returned to Beirut where she enters Hassim's old hideaway. In a violent attack, she wipes out the entire outfit, including her former lover. All her movements are transmitted via television to C.I.A. headquarters.

However, something goes amiss. The killing machine recalls through memory images her past associations with her former allies as well as pictures of those who have turned her against them. She now seeks vengeance upon the latter. Realizing the subject is out of control, the C.I.A. chief once again calls upon Ginty, one of her intended victims, to destroy the cyborg, who has already assassinated several members of the department. In another blood bath at a secret military base, Ginty finally destroys the creature. ∎

Reunion in France (1942), MGM. *Dir.* Jules Dassin; *Sc.* Jan Lustig, Marvin Borowsky, Marc Connelly; *Cast includes:* Joan Crawford, John Wayne, Philip Dorn, Reginald Owen, Albert Basserman, John Carradine.

A rich French socialite (Joan Crawford) is unconcerned about world events or even the fall of her country to the Nazi invaders in this unconvincing World War II drama. Her conscience is finally awakened when she discovers that her fiancé (Philip Dorn) is involved with the occupiers. She assists a downed American pilot (John Wayne), a volunteer in the Royal Air Force, who is being pursued by the Germans. Although she becomes emotionally involved with Wayne, she decides to return to Dorn, whom she learns is manufacturing defective weapons for the Germans while he is assembling a guerrilla army for the overthrow of the invaders.

The major weakness in this drama is the absence of any mention of the French Resistance fighters of the period—men and women who daily faced death and torture. They were not members of the French aristocracy or participants in the active Parisian social life that the principals shared in the film. Most of the major scenes take place in expensive nightclubs, luxurious homes or exclusive shops.

As with similar films produced in Hollywood during the war years, including *Casablanca*, *Reunion* stresses that duty to one's country and self-sacrifice take precedence over matters of the heart and personal happiness. American audiences, who saw their loved ones march off to war, not only understood but expected this personal sacrifice. When Wayne and other downed R.A.F. airmen take off for England after a harrowing escape, Crawford returns to her husband in Paris. In the last scene they both look up and see a British airplane spelling out across the skies the word "COURAGE" for the French to see. Dorn explains that the plane appears every morning and the Germans don't bother to shoot at the pilot since he doesn't drop any bombs. "If the Nazis only knew how dangerous he is to them—if they only knew France!" ■

Revenge of the Pink Panther (1978), UA. *Dir.* Blake Edwards; *Sc.* Frank Waldman, Ron Clark, Blake Edwards; *Cast includes:* Peter Sellers, Herbert Lom, Dyan Cannon, Robert Webber, Burk Kwouk, Paul Stewart.

The indomitable Inspector Clouseau once again becomes embroiled in events which almost overwhelm him, but his indefatigable spirit—and a lot of luck—pull him through in this erratic comedy. Peter Sellers repeats his role as Clouseau in this new entry which finds him in pursuit of an international drug operation. Robert Webber, as a tycoon and head of the smuggling ring, is Sellers' chief opponent. Dyan Cannon portrays Webber's abandoned mistress. Several members of the series return in their familiar roles, including Herbert Lom as Sellers' exasperated superior and Burk Kwouk as Cato, Sellers' faithful but zany houseboy. ■

Revenge of the Zombies (1943), Mon. *Dir.* Steve Sekely; *Sc.* Edmund Kelso, Van Norcross; *Cast includes:* John Carradine, Robert Lowery, Gale Storm, Veda Ann Borg, Mantan Moreland, Mauritz Hugo.

A mad scientist, who also happens to be a Nazi agent operating in the bayou country of the U.S., turns out a small army of zombies to perform acts of sabotage in this weird, inane World War II drama. John Carradine portrays the crazed German doctor. Collaborating with him is the local sheriff who is actually an undercover agent. Veda Ann Borg, as the spy's wife who controls the life-in-death creatures, is murdered. Her death results in the zombies turning on Carradine. Robert Lowery and Gale Storm, in the roles of hero and heroine, have little to do in this inept plot that attempts to blend horror with intrigue. ■

Revere, Paul. See American Revolution: Intelligence and Covert Actions. ■

Revolutionary War. See American Revolution. ■

Ride a Violent Mile (1957), TCF. *Dir.* Charles Marquis Warren; *Sc.* Eric Norden; *Cast includes:* John Agar, Penny Edwards, John Pickard, Richard Shannon, Charles Gray, Bing Russell.

According to this poorly conceived Civil War drama that takes place in the West, the Confederacy, faced with a blockade, tries to gain access to Mexican ports by trading beef to its southern neighbor. Rebel agents infiltrate a western town where they intend to carry out their mission. Penny Edwards, as a Union spy assigned to investigate Confederate activities in the area, poses as a dancer in a western saloon. John Agar portrays a drifter attracted to Edwards and ends up protecting her from Southern agents who discover her true identity. Meanwhile, the U.S. marshal (John Pickard), a sadistic lawman, happens to be the leader of the Southern spy ring. ■

Right to Happiness, The (1919), U. *Dir.* Allen Holubar; *Sc.* Olga Linck Scholl; *Cast includes:* Dorothy Phillips, William Stowell, Stanhope Wheatcroft, Robert Anderson, Henry Barrows.

Dorothy Phillips portrays a Russian spy who is sent to the U.S. to stir up industrial unrest in this anti-Bolshevik drama. Raised as a revolutionary by a Russian peasant family, in reality she is the lost daughter of an American millionaire. During the turmoil of a pogrom years earlier, the American, residing near Petrograd at the time, was able to save only one of his daughters, thinking the other had perished in a fire. Phillips arrives in the States and begins instigating the workers of her own father's factory. She is ultimately killed by a gunshot while protecting her sister from a frenzied mob. See Red Scare of 1919–1920. ■

Riley of the Rainbow Division (1928), Anchor. *Dir.* Robert Ray; *Sc.* Arthur Hoerl; *Cast includes:* Creighton Hale, Al Alt, Pauline Garon, Joan Standing.

Creighton Hale and Al Alt portray two army buddies who find themselves in the guardhouse on their wedding day in this silent comedy set on a military base during World War I. Pauline Garon and Joan Standing, as the two sweethearts of the unfortunate doughboys, masquerade as soldiers and enter the army grounds. Aside from the typical comic antics that result from the girls' disguises, the film winds up with the capture of enemy agents who have infiltrated the army camp. ■

Rio Rita (1942), MGM. *Dir.* R. Sylvan Simon; *Sc.* Richard Connell, Gladys Lehman; *Cast includes:* Bud Abbott, Lou Costello, Kathryn Grayson, John Carroll, Patricia Dane, Tom Conway.

MGM borrowed the popular comedy team Abbott and Costello, who were at their peak at this time, from Universal to star them in this musical based on a Broadway show which was made into a hit film in 1929. The plot was updated to thrust the comedy team into an intrigue concerning Nazi spies operating from a hotel on the Texas border and transmitting secret messages to their cohorts. Along with secret codes, mysterious radio broadcasts and other acts of espionage, the film provides several songs and a romance between Kathryn Grayson and John Carroll. Tom Conway, who would soon be featured in his own detective series as the Falcon, portrays the chief Nazi agent. Bud and Lou join Carroll in breaking up the activities of the enemy agents. ■

Rip Roaring Riley (1935), Puritan. *Dir.* Elmer Clifton; *Sc.* H. K. Gordon; *Cast includes:* Lloyd Hughes, Grant Withers, John Cowell, Marion Burns, Eddie Gribbon, Kit Guard.

International spies attempt to steal the formula for a newly developed poison gas in this routine drama set chiefly upon an island. Lloyd Hughes, as a U.S. government agent, is assigned to ferret out the villains. John Cowell portrays the professor who is conducting the secret experiments on the remote island. He is accompanied by his daughter (Marion Burns) who also provides the romantic interest for Hughes. Grant Withers and Paul Ellis,

as the lurking spies, are finally done in by the same poison gas they were seeking to steal. For additional dramatic effect, the film includes a rousing finalé replete with U.S. Marines. ■

Road Through the Dark, The (1918), Select. *Dir.* Edmund Mortimer; *Sc.* Kathryn Stuart; *Cast includes:* Clara Kimball Young, Jack Holt, Henry Woodward, Eleanor Fair, Bobby Connolly.

Clara Kimball Young portrays a young French patriot who saves her village and its people in this World War I drama. She elects to become the mistress of a German aristocrat to protect the village from being destroyed and her neighbors from being slaughtered by the advancing German army. Meanwhile, for the remainder of the war, she acts as a spy for the Allies, gathering information about enemy troops and strategy. Some critics, disturbed by the heroine's loss of innocence, questioned the moral tone of the film. ■

Road to France, The (1918), World. *Dir.* Dell Henderson; *Sc.* Harry Hoyt; *Cast includes:* Carlyle Blackwell, Evelyn Greeley, Jack Drumier, Muriel Ostriche, Jane Sterling.

The American shipbuilding industry serves as background and target of German spies in the World War I drama. Carlyle Blackwell portrays a young man with a drinking problem which makes him a social outcast. Rejected by the draft because of a past football injury, he seeks work in a local shipyard. He manages to foil a plot by German spies who are trying to hamper the war effort by inciting a general strike. Evelyn Greeley, as the daughter of the shipyard owner who had known him earlier, provides the romantic interest. See Labor Unrest. ■

Roar of the Press (1941), Mon. *Dir.* Phil Rosen; *Sc.* Albert Duffy; *Cast includes:* Wallace Ford, Jean Parker, Jed Prouty, Suzanne Kaaren, Harlan Tucker, Robert Frazer.

An apparent suicide followed by a puzzling murder leads an inquisitive police reporter into a network of espionage agents in this World War II drama. Wallace Ford, as the ace reporter, temporarily abandons his newly wed wife (Jean Parker) to follow up on clues so that his daily gets the scoop on the two deaths. As he gets closer to the truth about the crimes, the secret agents kidnap Ford and his wife. Ford's cronies, local gangsters, come to his rescue in this incredulous tale about city newspaper life. Jed Prouty portrays the city editor. ∎

Robinson Crusoe of Clipper Island

(1937) serial, Rep. *Dir.* Mark V. Wright, Ray Taylor; *Sc.* Maurice Geraghty, Barry Shipman, John Rathmell; *Cast includes:* Mala, Mamo Clark, Herbert Rawlinson, William Newell, John Ward, Selmer Jackson.

A 14-episode serial, the plot of this juvenile cliff-hanger concerns sabotage on a remote island. Mala, who gained prominence in the documentary *Eskimo*, portrays a Polynesian-born F.B.I. agent whom his superiors assign to investigate an unidentified dirigible that has crashed on a remote Pacific island. Before he resolves the mystery, he has to fight off hostile islanders and an international spy ring. He is assisted by his companions Rex, a clever horse, and Buck, an equally smart dog. Mamo Clark, who attracted attention in her native role in *Mutiny on the Bounty*, provides the romantic interest. The serial is visually interesting although much of the scenic footage derives from stock shots. See Serials. ∎

Rogue's March

(1952), MGM. *Dir.* Allan Davis; *Sc.* Leon Gordon; *Cast includes:* Peter Lawford, Richard Greene, Janice Rule, Leo G. Carroll, John Abbott.

Russia stirs up trouble in 19th-century India as a British soldier, branded a traitor, tries to prove his worth in this routine adventure drama. Peter Lawford portrays the young Englishman accused of being a turncoat. He enlists in the service to prove to his father that the charges are false. Once in India he performs honorably as well as heroically, saving his entire regiment. The highlight of this minor film that tries to mirror such past adventure dramas as *Lives of a Bengal Lancer* (1935) and *Gunga Din* (1939) is its battle sequences between the British troops and the dissident tribes. The natives are stirred up by the Russian representatives of the Czar who seeks a foothold on the continent. John Abbott plays a Russian spy working within the British War Office. Janice Rule provides the slight romantic interest. ∎

Rogues' Regiment

(1948), UI. *Dir.* Robert Florey; *Sc.* Robert Buckner; *Cast includes:* Dick Powell, Marta Toren, Vincent Price, Stephen McNally, Edgar Barrier, Henry Rowland.

Stephen McNally, as an escaped Nazi war criminal, gets the drop on fellow German Vincent Price in *Rogues' Regiment* (1948).

An American army officer is assigned to hunt down a ruthless Nazi war criminal who has escaped justice at the Nuremberg trials in this post-World War II drama. Dick Powell, in another of his tough, post-World War II dramas, portrays the clever and relentless American who pursues the Nazi to Saigon. Stephen McNally portrays the hunted, now in civilian clothes and ready to lose his identity as a common soldier in the Foreign Legion engaged in battling the Vietnamese insurrectionists. Powell eventually discovers his identity and brings him to justice. Although released several years after World War II, the film depicts the Germans in a negative light and includes a didactic narration of Nazi brutality and other crimes.

When McNally, as Martin Bruner, goes to his death at the end of the drama, the narrator announces: "The last steps of Martin Bruner upon that scaffold are a warning to the world that such men must not march again. There is no other road to justice and mankind's dream for a lasting peace." Vincent Price plays a German passing himself off as a Dutch businessman. Marta Toren is engaged as a French spy working as a café singer.

Perhaps more interesting is the subplot of the French colonial war in Indo-China. Early in the film a French colonel aboard a train bound for Saigon shows his frustration with the war. Unable or unwilling to accept the natives' struggle for self-determination, he blames the military conflict on those who are selling arms to the guerrillas while viewing the political struggle as that between communism and democracy. "The people of French Indo-China are fighting only because they are tired of French injustice and misrule," a fellow passenger replies to the officer's simple explanation of the conflict. "No," the colonel insists, "there are only two marching songs in the world today— the 'Internationale,' which may be theirs, and 'La Marseillaise,' which will always be ours!" He then leaves the compartment. ■

Romance of the Air, A (1918), Crest. Dir. Franklin B. Coates, Harry Revier; Sc. Franklin B. Coates; Cast includes: Bert Hall, Edith Day, Florence Billing, Stuart Holmes, Herbert Standing, Brian Darley.

Based on Lieutenant Bert Hall's 1918 book In the Air, the film recounts his experiences in the Lafayette Escadrille during World War I. Hall, a flier with the famous air group, is shot down over Germany during an air battle. He dons a fallen enemy's uniform and convalesces in a German hospital. He meets his American sweetheart in Germany who has been trapped there since the beginning of the war. Together with a female German spy who poses as an Allied sympathizer, they fly to freedom. When they reach France, he is charged with betraying the French as a result of the German spy's actions. His girlfriend, however, finds proof of his innocence, and he is saved at the last moment from a firing squad.

Hall received several medals from the French, including the Croix de Guerre. He and Major William Thaw (portrayed by Herbert Standing in the film) allegedly were the only survivors of the original group of Americans who joined the celebrated Escadrille. The love story was added to the film version of the book. It was one of the few air war movies made by an American company during or immediately after the war. Another was The Zeppelin's Last Raid (1917). Interest in this genre did not develop until William Wellman's epic Wings appeared in 1927. ■

Romanoff and Juliet (1961), UI. Dir. Peter Ustinov; Sc. Peter Ustinov; Cast includes: Peter Ustinov, Sandra Dee, John Gavin, Akim Tamiroff, Alix Talton, Rick von Nutter.

The U.S. and the Soviet Union desperately employ spying, bribery and wiretapping to influence the United Nations vote of the president of a small country in this comedy adapted from Ustinov's 1957 stage play. When a U.N. debate becomes deadlocked, the vote of an obscure, tiny country called Concordia becomes important. Its president (Pe-

ter Ustinov), who holds the important deciding vote, does not grasp the subject matter of the debate. He abstains and leaves for home. The two world powers send their ambassadors and secret agents scurrying to Concordia to win his vote and promise him all kinds of economic aid. Ustinov, meanwhile, cleverly arranges a romance between the Soviet ambassador's son (John Gavin) and the U.S. ambassador's daughter (Sandra Dee). During a national holiday the couple are covertly married in historical costumes. The parents, shocked and outraged, soon see the humor in the event and accept the marriage. Ustinov achieves his personal goal of remaining neutral. ■

Rosebud (1975), UA. Dir. Otto Preminger; Sc. Erik Lee Preminger; Cast includes: Peter O'Toole, Richard Attenborough, Cliff Gorman, Claude Dauphin, John V. Lindsay, Peter Lawford.

A C.I.A. agent helps to rescue five rich young girls held captive by P.L.O. terrorists in this colorless drama based on the novel by Joan Hemingway and Paul Bonnecarrere. Peter O'Toole, as the agent who has been working under cover as an international correspondent for a weekly magazine, is assigned to the kidnapping. Richard Attenborough, as a shadowy figure who is pro-Arab, exploits the Palestine Liberation Organization in his fanatical anti-Israeli efforts. Cliff Gorman portrays an Israeli secret agent. Claude Dauphin, John V. Lindsay (former mayor of New York City) and Peter Lawford play some of the fathers whose daughters are held for ransom aboard the terrorists' yacht. The film ends with the Israelis' capture of the P.L.O. terrorists and Attenborough, followed by some propagandizing by both sides of the conflict. See Central Intelligence Agency; Mossad. ■

Rosenberg, Julius and Ethel See Daniel (1983). ■

Rowan, Andrew S. (1857–1943). Born in what is now West Virginia, Andrew Rowan became a career military officer specializing in cartography. He made a secret survey for the U.S. Army of the Canadian Pacific Railroad and its environs in 1890. Apparently, some devious Washington bureaucrats in the military were making contingency plans for

annexing sections of Canada in the event of a future conflict.

Rowan reported to the map section of the Adjutant General's Office while working in Chile, Central America and Cuba. His secret mission in Cuba was to develop military intelligence, including accurate maps, in preparation for the Spanish-American War. He left Jamaica with a group of Cuban revolutionaries and landed with them in Cuba on April 24, 1898, two days after the outbreak of war. Rowan met Cuban guerrilla leader General Garcia, who furnished him with maps and military intelligence; this highly sensitive material was sent back to the U.S. War Department and eventually used by American forces when they landed in Cuba in June of 1898.

Rowan's journey became world famous when Elbert Hubbard, editor of *The Philistine*, a monthly magazine, wrote in the March 1899 issue about the lieutenant's experience, using it as a symbolic sermon. He embellished the incident to underline how one determined individual views his task and accomplishes it. The essay became so popular that the issue sold out immediately, reprints by the millions were circulated during World War I, and the article was translated into more than a dozen languages. Meanwhile, Rowan resigned from the army after serving in the Philippines in 1909 and wrote a book about his actual experiences, which were chiefly ignored or altered in two screen versions. Hubbard, who had helped to make Rowan an international celebrity, died on the *Lusitania* on May 7, 1915.

Thomas Edison's film studio produced the silent drama *A Message to Garcia* in 1916, the first film version of the essay. Actress Mabel Trunnelle, as the heroine who sacrificed her life to help Rowan complete his mission, was the only notable performer in the drama. She had almost as large and sympathetic a role as Robert Conness, who portrayed the American lieutenant. In 1936 Twentieth Century-Fox released its sound adaptation of Hubbard's essay and Rowan's book. Once again the actor who played Rowan (John Boles) took a back seat. The popular screen personality Wallace Beery, as Rowan's slovenly assistant, received top billing, followed by Barbara Stanwyck, who portrays the daughter of a Cuban patriot. However, the film provides sufficient action and the winning personality of Beery. ∎

Royal African Rifles, The (1953), AA. *Dir.* Lesley Selander; *Sc.* Dan Ullman; *Cast includes:* Louis Hayward, Veronica Hurst, Michael Pate, Steven Geray, Angela Greene.

Louis Hayward stars as a British navy officer in this World War I drama set in East Africa. He is on the trail of a shipment of rifles and machine guns stolen from his ship, weapons sorely needed by British colonial troops but destined for a hostile tribe. The Germans, who are behind the scheme, hope to tie up British troops with a native uprising. Fortunately, Hayward, with the help of an African corporal, foils the plot before the arms are widely distributed. He also finds time to woo the daughter of the chief gunrunner. The major battle between the insurgents and the loyal British natives occurs in the final sequence of this weak film. ∎

Royal American, A (1927), Rayart. *Dir.* Harry J. Brown; *Sc.* George W. Pyper; *Cast includes:* Reed Howes, Nita Martan, Bill Franey, David Kirby, J. P. McGowan.

Acrobatic performer Reed Howes, as a member of the U.S. Coast Guard, masquerades as a waterfront roustabout in this stunt-oriented sea melodrama about munitions smuggling to South America. After brawling with some rough sailors, Howes is shanghaied aboard the *Hawk*, helmed by a savage captain. Before he is able to signal to a Coast Guard vessel, Howes becomes involved in several chases and fist fights aboard the ship carrying the contraband cargo to South America. He eventually places the captain under arrest. The film never discusses the purposes of the cargo, to which country it is being shipped or for what cause. The chase and thrills dominate this fast-moving tale. See Latin America. ∎

Rush to Judgment (1967), Impact Films. *Dir.* Emile de Antonio; *Sc.* Mark Lane.

Based on Mark Lane's nonfiction bestseller *Rush to Judgment*, this documentary tries to establish through witnesses and interviews a conspiracy theory concerning the Kennedy assassination. Lane's commentary and narration goes against the findings of the official Warren Commission which concluded that Lee Harvey Oswald was the lone assassin. Using chiefly visual materials and interviews with witnesses who were on the scene, Lane focuses on the possibility that several alleged shots fired from a grassy knoll, rather than those fired from the Dallas book depository window, killed the President. He points out that Oswald was not a crack shot, according to a fellow marine. Lane reminds his audience of missing and trimmed photographs, of one such picture showing a figure closely resembling Oswald in the crowd at the time of the assassination, and of Jack Ruby's close ties with the Dallas police. Although not fully convincing, the film continues to raise important questions that have never been fully answered satisfactorily. ∎

Russian Roulette (1975), Avco. *Dir.* Lou Lombardo; *Sc.* Tom Ardies, Stanley Mann, Arnold Margolin; *Cast includes:* George Segal, Cristina Raines, Bo Brundin, Denholm Elliott, Gordon Jackson, Peter Donat.

A suspended Canadian law officer foils an attempt on Soviet Premier Alexei Kosygin's life during his 1970 trip to Vancouver, B.C., in this suspenseful drama filmed in Vancouver. George Segal portrays the officer who prevents a group of maverick K.G.B. agents from carrying out their assassination plot. Opposed to Kosygin's proposed offers to the West concerning arms reduction and a relaxation of the Cold War tensions, the hawkish renegades plot to kill him by using a captured and drugged C.I.A. agent.

The film provides a more interesting array of characters than are usually found in similar spy-assassination dramas. Segal, as the officer in hot water with his department, soon finds himself being manipulated by the Canadian secret service and eventually captured by the K.G.B. Denholm Elliott, as a shabbily clothed, arrogant Canadian chief agent, inveigles Segal into entering a web of intrigue from which he barely escapes. When Segal expresses his anger after playing the dupe, Elliott laughs it off, replying: "There's nothing that boosts the spirit like a little der-ring-do." Richard Romanus portrays a smooth-talking, nattily dressed Detroit "hit man" who is hired by the K.G.B. to kidnap the C.I.A. agent and Segal. Forced out on a trestle ledge over a river at gunpoint by Segal, the hoodlum evades the officer's probing questions about who hired him. "What's the matter with you," he protests. "You know how guys like me work. I'm a businessman. I get an assignment, I follow through, I make a delivery. I don't know to whom." His nervousness causes him to fall to his death.

The entire plot is fictitious but the various location shooting in Canada, especially in the vicinity of Vancouver, give the production an authentic look. The film was adapted from Tom Ardies' novel *Kosygin is Coming*. See K.G.B.

S

Sabotage (1939), Rep. *Dir.* Harold Young; *Sc.* Lionel Houser, Alice Altschuler; *Cast includes:* Arleen Whelan, Gordon Oliver, Charles Grapewin, Lucien Littlefield, Paul Guilfoyle.

A routine drama about espionage at an American airplane factory, the film tells how a father hunts down the spies who are responsible for his son's false imprisonment. Charles Grapewin plays the determined father, a watchman at the factory, who enlists the aid of his fellow World War I veterans to help round up the nest of spies. Gordon Oliver portrays the framed son while Arleen Whelan adds the romantic interest in this low-budget film. The names of the enemy agents hint that they are of German origin although the plot never states their background. ∎

Sabotage Squad (1942), Col. *Dir.* Lew Landers; *Sc.* Bernice Petkere, Wallace Sullivan, David Silverstein; *Cast includes:* Bruce Bennett, Kay Harris, Edward Norris, Sidney Blackmer, Don Beddoe, John Tyrrell.

A mild World War II drama about Nazi saboteurs blowing up American war plants, the film centers on a young bookie, played by Edward Norris, who is rejected from military service when he tries to enlist. He eventually finds a way to serve his country, but his brave act costs him his life. He blows himself up together with the leader of a Nazi spy ring in a truck targeted to destroy an airplane factory. Kay Harris plays the romantic lead in this low-budget melodrama. ∎

Saboteur (1942), U. *Dir.* Alfred Hitchcock; *Sc.* Peter Viertel, Joan Harrison, Dorothy Parker; *Cast includes:* Priscilla Lane, Robert Cummings, Norman Lloyd, Otto Kruger, Alan Baxter, Alma Kruger.

In this World War II suspense thriller by Alfred Hitchcock, an innocent worker (Robert Cummings) at a California airplane factory is accused of causing a fire that has destroyed the plant. He eludes the police and, to clear his name, pursues Frank Fry (Norman Lloyd), the real saboteur, across the continent. He is joined in the chase by pretty Priscilla Lane, who at first distrusts him but then believes his almost incredible story. Cummings finally confronts his prey in the exciting climax at the Statue of Liberty.

The saboteurs, led by the suave Otto Kruger who continually mocks the idealism of Cummings, plot to blow up a ship launching attended by thousands at the Brooklyn Navy Yard. In contrast to the saboteurs, Hitchcock introduces several colorful minor characters who are compassionate and understanding and who help Cummings on his journey. A truck driver assists him by diverting the police. Members of a traveling circus vote to hide him. A blind man takes Cummings into his cabin and "sees" innate innocence and goodness in the young man.

This is unmistakably a Hitchcock film. As in his other works made both in his native England and in the U.S., he uses national monuments (the Statue of Liberty) and commonplace environments to illustrate that these places, accepted symbols of tranquillity and relative safety, are not always exempt from the external world of violence (a shoot-out at Radio City Music Hall). He makes good use of humorous characters (the circus freaks). He emphasizes suspenseful scenes through specific close-ups (Fry's finger stretching to press a button that will detonate a bomb, and the seam of his jacket splitting open while he dangles from the top of the Statue of Liberty).

Released only a few months after America's entry into World War II, this film was a timely story about the possible dangers on the home front. A few patriotic speeches occur occasionally. One circus entertainer extols the virtues of the democratic process; Priscilla reads aloud a portion of Emma Lazarus' poem inscribed on the base of the Statue of Liberty. *Variety*, in its review of April 29, 1942, noted the following in the sequence involving Miss Liberty: "Incidentally, one of the sightseer-extras is a Negro, a genuinely realistic touch." See German Intelligence: World War II. ■

Sacrifice (1917), Par. *Dir.* Frank Reicher; *Sc.* Beatrice de Mille, Leighton Osmun; *Cast includes:* Margaret Illington, Jack Holt, Winter Hall, Noah Beery.

An unexceptional tale of intrigue and spying during a fictitious Balkan war, the drama casts former stage actress Margaret Illington in a dual role. She portrays both Vesta, the illegitimate daughter of a warlord, and Mary, her half-sister, the legitimate daughter. Vesta is a spy who steals strategic military plans from a neighboring country. At the border she persuades her sister, Mary, to exchange passports. Mary is then arrested as a spy and sentenced to face a firing squad. Vesta delivers the vital information to the proper sources and returns to take her place before the firing squad. Mary is reunited with her beau (Jack Holt), a captain in her country's army. ■

Sad Sack, The (1957), Par. *Dir.* George Marshall; *Sc.* Edmund Beloin, Nate Monaster; *Cast includes:* Jerry Lewis, David Wayne, Phyllis Kirk, Peter Lorre, Gene Evans, Mary Treen.

Jerry Lewis stars at the title character in this zany service comedy. The misfit soldier seeks help from an army psychiatrist, played by Phyllis Kirk. He also becomes involved with a group of villainous conspirators in Morocco and entangled in a WAC barracks. David Wayne, as a corporal, befriends Lewis and romances Kirk. Peter Lorre portrays a suspicious Moroccan. The title character is based on George Baker's cartoon strip. ■

Safe for Democracy (1918), FN. *Dir.* J. Stuart Blackton; *Sc.* Anthony Paul Kelly; *Cast includes:* Mitchell Lewis, Ruby de Remer, Gus Alexander, Ida Darling, Helen Ferguson.

A patriotic drama with World War I as the background, the film describes a variety of slackers—Americans shirking their duty either as soldiers or workers in war-related jobs. It also presents a story filled with intrigue as members of the International Workers of the World, a radical union of the period, initiate a bomb plot. J. Stuart Blackton, who produced the work, interjects newsreel footage between the fictional scenes. This adds a note of authenticity. In the end, the men realize their responsibilities to the war effort and join the fight.

The theme of the film was suggested by a remark made by a military leader at the time. "Work or fight!" General Crowder demanded of the citizenry. Blackton's attack on members of the I.W.W., whose leaders he equates with alien agents, casts the drama more in the form of an anti-union tract than as a patriotic tale. The film was retitled *Life's Greatest Problem*. See Anarchists in the U.S.; Labor Unrest. ■

Safecracker, The (1958), MGM. *Dir.* Ray Milland; *Sc.* Paul Monash; *Cast includes:* Ray Milland, Barry Jones, Jeanette Sterke, Victor Maddern, Ernest Clark.

This World War II drama stars Ray Milland as a convicted master safecracker imprisoned in England when the war erupts. British intelligence has Milland released for an important secret mission. A complete list of German spies operating in England is locked in a vault in a Belgian chateau. Milland's task is to obtain the list, photograph it and put it back without the enemy's awareness. Milland is trained in commando tactics, is parachuted into Belgium with a commando unit and carries out his mission. Ernest Clark portrays the English officer in charge of the secret operation while Jeanette Sterke plays a Belgian resistance fighter's daughter. The suspenseful film, which was made in England, is composed of two separate stories—Milland's prewar life as a safecracker and the war sequence. ■

Salamander, The (1981), Associated Film. *Dir.* Peter Zinner; *Sc.* Robert Katz; *Cast includes:* Franco Nero, Anthony Quinn, Martin

Balsam, Sybil Danning, Christopher Lee, Cleavon Little.

An Italian counter-intelligence officer discovers a plot involving a Fascist coup d'etat during his investigation of a slain army general in this lifeless Italian political drama, a joint U.S.-British-Italian production. Franco Nero, as the cynical investigator who attempts to expose the conspiracy, carries the burden of narrating most of the tale. He also romances Sybil Danning, who portrays a cold-blooded spy. Anthony Quinn, as a World War II partisan fighter, is a dedicated hunter of war criminals and prosperous businessman. He devotes his life to seeking justice. Quinn is likened to the salamander, a creature with remarkable survival capabilities. Eli Wallach portrays the conspiring general behind the Fascist plot. Christopher Lee plays Nero's treacherous superior. The film was adapted from Morris L. West's novel. ■

Salome, Where She Danced (1945), U. *Dir.* Charles Lamont; *Sc.* Laurence Stallings; *Cast includes:* Yvonne De Carlo, Rod Cameron, David Bruce, Walter Slezak, Albert Dekker, Marjorie Rambeau.

A sprawling drama that perhaps covers too much ground, the film begins with the American Civil War, shifts to the court intrigues of Europe and concludes in a bustling, young San Francisco. Yvonne De Carlo, in her first starring role, portrays an exotic European dancer who, caught spying for Austria against Prussia, is forced to flee the continent for the U.S. Rod Cameron, as an American journalist for a weekly paper, meets De Carlo in Berlin where he is on assignment after covering the American Civil War. He persuades her to spy for him and in behalf of her Austrian prince. Cameron wants her to gather information from an arrogant Prussian military official, played by Albert Dekker, concerning Bismarck's plans to attack Austria. She succeeds in her mission, but Austria loses the war. Dekker finds a letter on the dead Austrian prince which implicates De Carlo as a spy working for Austria. When he tries to arrest her, Cameron knocks him unconscious and helps De Carlo and her music teacher (J. Edward Romberg) to escape.

The trio then journey to San Francisco where Cameron, who has fallen in love with her, intends to make her a star. Before they reach their destination, they are forced to stop in a western town where De Carlo gives a special performance to raise money for their travels. Here she meets a bandit (David Bruce) who reminds her of the slain Austrian prince. He accompanies the party to San Francisco where they meet a wealthy Russian (Walter Slezak) and a Chinese philosopher (Abner Biberman) who has the best lines in the far-fetched drama. De Carlo learns that the vindictive Prussian officer has followed her to San Francisco. "Conspiring in their intrigue," the oriental sage says to Cameron, "she has incurred the highest penalty. Revenge in conceit is without mercy. And the blood of this girl is the only thing that will restore the honor of the count." However, Bruce ends Dekker's threat in a fencing duel in which the Prussian is killed. ■

Salute to Courage (1942). See *Nazi Agent* (1942). ■

Salvation Joan (1916), Vitagraph. *Dir.* Wilfrid North; *Cast includes:* Edna May, Harry T. Morey, Dorothy Kelly, Donald Hall, Bobby Connelly, L. Rogers Lytton.

Edna May, as the title character, gets mixed up with an international spy in this early drama set in England. Bored with her rich friends and shallow social position, Salvation Joan decides to work in the London slums as a member of the Salvation Army. Engaged to Philip Ralston (L. Rogers Lytton), who is secretly in the employ of a foreign government, she suspects he is up to no good and dissolves the relationship. She then meets a slum derelict (Harry T. Morey) whom she tries to reform after sensing that he has finer qualities. In reality he is a British secret agent whose slum contacts feed him vital information. Ralston, meanwhile, who is paid to gather political secrets, plots to steal vital documents from a major political figure. He hires some local thugs, including the undercover agent, to carry out the theft. Needless to say, Morey foils the scheme, helps to round up the gang and wins Joan's affections after he reveals his true identity. Ralston is shot trying to avoid capture. ■

Salzburg Connection, The (1972), TCF. *Dir.* Lee H. Katzin; *Sc.* Oscar Millard; *Cast includes:* Barry Newman, Anna Karina, Klaus-Maria Brandauer, Karen Jensen, Joe Moross, Whit Bissell.

The names of former Nazi collaborators during World War II become the subject of this weak espionage drama set in contemporary Austria. When neo-Nazis murder an ex-British agent who has found a suspicious list of names in a chest at the bottom of a lake, others become interested in the incident. A U.S. secret agent (Joe Moross), in an effort to protect collaborators or their descendants from potential blackmail, tries to prevent the list of names from falling into the wrong hands. Barry Newman portrays an American lawyer vacationing in Salzburg who becomes entangled in the intrigue. Anna Karina, as the dead agent's widow, knows the contents of the sealed chest and becomes a target of the spies. The film was based on Helen MacInnes' popular novel. See Nazi Subversion: Post-World War II. ■

Sam Davis, The Hero of Tennessee (1915), Connor. *Sc.* Lillian Nicholson Shearon.

Sam Davis, a Confederate soldier who enlisted when the Civil War erupted, becomes involved with rebel spies, is caught carrying their military secrets to his own lines and is hanged by Union troops in this drama based on actual incidents. A female spy working for the South attracts the attention of a Union captain who is tricked by her into sketching out the plans for an upcoming battle. The pretty spy takes the plans and turns them over to a fellow spy who, masquerading as a doctor, has penetrated Union lines. He, in turn, hands them to Sam Davis and tells him to deliver them to the Southern military staff. Davis rides off with the important map but is captured by Northern troops who then sentence him to hang. Davis goes to his death a Southern hero.

The real Samuel Davis (1844–1863) was a product of Rutherford County, Tennessee, where he had the misfortune to get caught up in the torrents of the Civil War. Tennessee had seceded from the Union, and Davis, an uneducated farmer, joined the state's infantry. He participated in the Battle of Stones River at the end of 1862 and the Battle of Chickamauga in September 1863, both under the leadership of General Bragg.

In the fall of 1863 Davis was sent as a scout to reconnoiter Union positions in Tennessee and Alabama. He was soon assigned as a full-time spy for Captain Henry Shaw, who ran the intelligence service for General Bragg. Davis was sent back through Union lines on several other occasions. In November 1863,

Shaw and Davis set off for Pulaski, Tennessee, which was within Union lines. They split up and Davis continued north where he joined Confederate agents who provided him with plans of Union fortifications in Tennessee. After meeting with these agents, Davis was stopped by two men in Confederate Army uniforms who were actually working for the Union counterintelligence unit of General Naron. Upon producing Confederate Army identification, Davis was seized; his secret documents were discovered and he was delivered to General Naron.

Davis was given the choice of execution or revealing his Confederate contacts; the Southern agent steadfastly refused to name his coconspirators whereupon he was court-martialed and hanged on November 27, 1863. ■

Samson (1914), U. *Dir.* Lorimer Johnston; *Sc.* Lorimer Johnston, G. P. Hamilton; *Cast includes:* J. Warren Kerrigan, Kathleen Kerrigan, George Periolat, Lule Warrenton, Edith Bostwick, Harold Lloyd, Hal Roach.

Delilah probably represents the earliest prototype of the female spy. The bride of Samson and daughter of a Philistine, she is forced by the Philistines to trick her husband into revealing the secret of a riddle to her. Threatened with death, she reluctantly agrees. Samson, however, learns of her betrayal and casts her out. Later, when he is more rational, he attempts to reconcile their differences only to learn that she has been promised to someone else. Samson burns down her home. The flames kill both Delilah and her father. The remainder of the film follows the biblical tale. Samson is portrayed by J. Warren Kerrigan. Kathleen Kerrigan, his sister, plays Delilah. Harold Lloyd and Hal Roach have minor roles as Egyptians.

David Lewis, a British journalist whose 1976 book explores the use of sex in espionage, writes: "In the tenth century, B.C., the first recorded sex spy, Delilah, used her charms to destroy the Jewish hero Samson." ■

Samurai (1945), Cavalcade. *Dir.* Raymond Cannon; *Sc.* Raymond Cannon; *Cast includes:* Paul Fung, Luke Chan, David Chow, Barbara Woodell, Fred C. Bond.

A low-budget World War II propaganda drama, the film blends newsreel footage with staged sequences of atrocities to bring out its anti-Japanese theme. David Chow portrays a Japanese youth who is raised in the U.S. He turns traitor, joins the Japanese secret service and takes part in a scheme involving the Japanese invasion of California. The film was released after the war had ended and therefore lost much of its impact. ■

Santiago (1956), WB. *Dir.* Gordon Douglas; *Sc.* Martin Rackin, John Twist; *Cast includes:* Alan Ladd, Rossana Podesta, Lloyd Nolan, Chill Wills, Paul Fix, L. Q. Jones.

A pretty Cuban agent persuades a mercenary American gunrunner to get involved in Cuba's struggle for independence against Spain in this slow-paced drama set on the eve of the Spanish-American War. The film opens in Tampa, Florida, the "jumping-off place for contraband shipments to Cuba," where gunrunner Alan Ladd delivers rifles and gunpowder to Cuban agents. They thank him, thinking he believes in their cause. "You are part of Cuba's war for freedom," one agent states. Ladd, who just wants to get paid, replies, "I don't care which side wins."

Forced to transport his shipment to Cuba to receive his money, he journeys by riverboat where he meets and falls in love with a Cuban revolutionary (Rossana Podesta). At first she is repulsed by his lack of commitment. But after she recites a string of patriotic lines ("Fighting men will always bleed to make freedom a reality") she convinces him to join the good fight. Lloyd Nolan, as a competitor-smuggler, at first brawls with Ladd and then links up with him to fight the Spanish. Chill Wills, as captain of the vessel that Ladd uses to run the Spanish blockade, sacrifices his life by blowing himself up with his vessel to delay the Spanish fleet from overtaking the cargo of guns. The film is based on the novel *The Great Courage* by Martin Rackin, who also wrote the screenplay. ■

Satan Bug, The (1965), UA. *Dir.* John Sturges; *Sc.* James Clavell, Edward Anhalt; *Cast includes:* George Maharis, Richard Basehart, Anne Francis, Dana Andrews, Edward Asner, Frank Sutton.

An ex-army intelligence officer is brought back to active duty to track down a lethal virus capable of killing the inhabitants of an entire city in this suspenseful drama. The potent liquid, known as the "Satan Bug" and developed in a secret U.S. laboratory as part of the country's experiments in bacteriological warfare, has been stolen by a crazed millionaire (Richard Basehart). An antiwar extremist, he threatens to unleash its destructive power in Los Angeles if the research installation is not closed down. George Maharis, as the government agent, along with fellow operatives, has the difficult assignment of finding Basehart and the flask. Dana Andrews portrays the general who is leading the investigation. Anne Francis plays his pretty daughter. Edward Asner and Frank Sutton portray Basehart's underlings in this film adapted from a novel by Ian Stuart (Alistair MacLean). ■

Savage Drums (1951), Lippert. *Dir.* William Berke; *Sc.* Fenton Earnshaw; *Cast includes:* Sabu, Lita Baron, H. B. Warner, Sid Melton, Steven Geray, Bob Easton.

Communist agents conspire to control a small but strategic Pacific island in this low-budget drama set during the Cold War. Sabu, as a native of the island who has gained some reputation as a boxer in the U.S., is recalled home when the king, his brother, is killed. H. B. Warner, as Sabu's elderly adviser, also is murdered by the plotters when he tries to help Sabu, who has become the new king. Sabu discovers that Steven Geray, a Communist spy, is in collusion with Sabu's cousin (Paul Marion). The young king must also contend with the villainous machinations of Margia Dean, as the female lead in the drama, before he manages to marshal his subjects to rise up against an imminent invading force. A climactic battle, with Sabu effectively manning a machine gun, highlights the action. Some ineffective comedy relief is provided by Sid Melton and Bob Easton, who portray Sabu's American pals. ■

Savage Mutiny (1953), Col. *Dir.* Spencer G. Bennet; *Sc.* Sol Shor; *Cast includes:* Johnny Weissmuller, Angela Stevens, Lester Matthews, Nelson Leigh, Charles Stevens, Paul Marion.

Enemy agents plot to create an international incident which would be detrimental to the U.S. and Britain in this Cold War drama. The two Western nations are in the process of moving natives off a West African island which will be used for testing an atom bomb. Conspirators scheme to keep the locals from leaving so their deaths will reflect upon the Western countries. Johnny Weissmuller, as Jungle Jim, is assigned the difficult job of getting the natives to leave. Once he accomplishes this, the spies then use an airplane to spray the natives with radioactive dust. Angela Stevens portrays a local doctor in this weak entry in the Jungle Jim series based on Alex Raymond's comic strip character. ■

"Saved by Wireless" (1915), Keystone. *Dir.* Walter Wright; *Sc.* Mack Sennett; *Cast includes:* Mack Swain, Chester Conklin, Andrew Anderson, Nick Cogley, Ora Carew, Harry McCoy.

An early two-reel silent comedy that satirizes the spy genre, the film pokes fun at several conventions employed by these films, such as bomb throwing and chases. Various transportation devices are used, including airplanes, boats and motorcycles, all adding to the comedy. The famed comic performer Mack Swain portrays the chief spy who is helped by his assistant (Chester Conklin). They, in turn, are aided by a butler (Andrew Anderson). Nick Cogley plays the minister of war. ■

Sawdust Doll, The (1919), Pathé. *Dir.* William Bertram; *Sc.* Agnes C. Johnston; *Cast includes:* Baby Marie Osborne, Jack Connolly, Clare Du Brey, William Quinn.

A little girl saves a troop train of American soldiers in this World War I drama. Baby Marie Osborne, as the daughter of a village blacksmith (Jack Connolly), discovers that a local druggist is a German spy. William Quinn, as the saboteur, plans to wreck a trainload of soldiers, among whom is Baby Marie's father who has recently enlisted. She informs her stepmother, and both rush off to try to stop the train. Clare Du Brey, as the stepmother, has married the child's father for her own security and cares little for Baby Marie. Her secret lover is the druggist. Once the blacksmith enlists, thinking his daughter is in safe hands, Du Brey plans to run off with the druggist—until she learns the truth that he is a spy. The child uses her sawdust doll as a torch and successfully halts the oncoming train. ■

Scarlet Clue, The (1945), Mon. *Dir.* Phil Rosen; *Sc.* George Callahan; *Cast includes:* Sidney Toler, Benson Fong, Mantan Moreland, Helen Devereaux, Robert Homans, Virginia Brissac.

Another entry in the popular Charlie Chan detective series, this little drama, set during World War II, deals with an attempt on the part of spies to steal secret radar plans from the U.S. government. Sidney Toler, as the Hawaiian sleuth, enters the case, which includes a couple of murders. Benson Fong, as one of Chan's sons, and Mantan Moreland, who portrays the sleuth's chauffeur, contribute some comedy relief in this tale that has more suspense than usual. ■

Scarlet Coat, The (1955), MGM. *Dir.* John Sturges; *Sc.* Karl Tunberg; *Cast includes:* Cornel Wilde, Michael Wilding, George Sanders, Anne Francis, Robert Douglas, John McIntire.

A colonial major poses as a spy for the British in an effort to uncover an actual traitor who turns out to be Benedict Arnold in this historical drama of the American Revolution. Cornel Wilde portrays the major, a patriot who masquerades as the traitor so that he may infiltrate the British military staff. Michael Wilding, as Major John André, a British officer, develops a fondness for his adversary, the American spy. George Sanders, as a doctor working for the British, fails to convince the officers that Wilde actually is working for the Continental Army. Robert Douglas plays Benedict Arnold. John McIntire portrays General Howe. Anne Francis plays the female lead. The film offers little on the armed conflict of the period, concentrating, instead, on characterization and intrigue. See John André; Benedict Arnold; Defection; American Revolution: Intelligence and Covert Actions. ■

Scarlet Lady, The (1928), Col. *Dir.* Alan Crosland; *Sc.* Bess Meredyth; *Cast includes:* Lya De Putti, Don Alvarado, Warner Oland, John Peters, Otto Matiesen.

Lya De Putti portrays a Communist spy in this drama about the Russian Revolution. As the mistress of a Red leader, she is used to betray members of the royalty. Don Alvarado, as one of her potential victims, learns of her assignment the morning after she has stayed with him and sends her away. Later, when he is captured and about to be assassinated, the Communist leader gives the gun to De Putti, expecting her to kill the prisoner. Instead, she shoots the leader and escapes with Alvarado.

Unlike the handful of films of the Russian Revolution, such as *The Red Dance*, also released in 1928, that tried to explain the reasons for the uprising or depicted heroes and villains on both sides, this work turns all the

Communists into revengeful miscreants while portraying the nobility as honorable and maligned victims. ■

Scarlet Oath, The (1916), World. Dir.
Frank Powell, Travers Vale; Sc. Gardner Hunting; Cast includes: Gail Kane, Philip Hahn, Carleton Macey, Lillian Paige, Alan Hale, Boris Korlin.

A Russian nihilist and his daughter Olga, after years of exile in the U.S., return to Russia to seek revenge. Philip Hahn, as the vindictive father, and Gail Kane as his obedient daughter, plot to kill the man (Montagu Love) who murdered the nihilist's wife years ago. However, Love's agents slay Hahn before he has a chance to act. Olga, in turn, kills Love and plans to escape to America. Olga has a twin sister, Nina, whom the father, desperate for money, had turned over to a rich Russian couple before he escaped to the U.S. Nina has an American fiancé (Alan Hale). Olga, now forced to leave Russia, poses as her twin sister. She journeys safely to the U.S. but is followed by Russian spies who kill her. Hale mistakenly thinks his fiancée has been murdered until Nina appears to explain matters. ■

Scorpio (1973), UA. Dir. Michael Winner;
Sc. David W. Rintels, Gerald Wilson; Cast includes: Burt Lancaster, Alain Delon, Paul Scofield, John Colicos, Gayle Hunnicutt, J. D. Cannon.

Intrigue and betrayal within the C.I.A. dominate this spy drama set in several locales, including Washington, D.C., and Vienna, during the Cold War. Burt Lancaster portrays an aging C.I.A. agent whom some of the bureau chiefs believe is a double agent for the East. They want him assassinated. To get Lancaster's young assistant (Alain Delon) to do the job, the agents frame him for possession of drugs and threaten him with a 30-year sentence and as an accomplice to an earlier assassination. At first Delon refuses to turn on his partner-friend, but when his requests for money and other considerations are met, he agrees to carry out the assignment. He asks why the agency wants Lancaster executed. "He's a double agent," the chief replies. "He sold to the opposition, and he has a lot more to sell." The remainder of this cynical drama consists of Delon's hunting his prey and Lancaster's wily attempts at escape.

Lancaster over the years has gained the trust of many informers and other agents. He seeks temporary refuge in Vienna with his counterpart, a Soviet agent (Paul Scofield), who calls his friend "one of Donovan's last adventurers," a reference to Col. William Donovan, the head of the Office of Strategic Services during World War II. The Russian invites the American to relocate in Moscow, hinting that perhaps the American is or has been a double agent. Lancaster insists that he is not a traitor—that he just wants "out." The Russian suggests the intricacies of international intrigue when Lancaster asks him where he obtained certain information. "I buy from a Bulgarian who works for the Chinese," the Soviet agent replies.

The film also hints at the changes that have taken place in the new breed of spies. "Have you noticed," Scofield muses, "that we are being replaced by young men with blank stupid faces . . . and a dedication to nothing more than efficiency? Keepers of machines, pushers of buttons, hardware men with highly complex toys and, except for language, not an iota of difference between the American model and the Soviet model."

The final scenes drive home the expendability of these agents. Delon ultimately catches up with his former partner in a deserted garage and shoots him in cold blood. "There is no good and no bad," Lancaster says, lying on the ground mortally wounded. He compares the job of espionage to a deadly game. "The object is not to win or not to lose. And the only role is to stay in the game." When Delon leaves the garage, he himself is gunned down by another agent on orders from above.

The C.I.A. chief (John Colicos) seems more sinister and brutal than suspected double agent Lancaster or Soviet spy Scofield. Colicos thinks little about framing Delon, imperiling the lives of his own agents or killing Lancaster's wife. The C.I.A. itself, according to the film, engages in wholesale criminality. In these respects, the film follows the trend of spy dramas of the period which cast suspicions upon various C.I.A. activities and depicted C.I.A. leaders as despicable and treacherous paranoid characters obsessed with their own power. It was not unreasonable, therefore, for audiences by that time to accept this characterization. By the time the film was released, the public had already become aware of a string of abuses by the C.I.A.

and F.B.I. See Central Intelligence Agency; K.G.B. ■

Scotland Yard (1930), Fox. *Dir.* William K. Howard; *Sc.* Garrett Fort; *Cast includes:* Edmund Lowe, Joan Bennett, Lumsden Hare, Barbara Leonard, Donald Crisp.

Edmund Lowe portrays a Raffles-type character in this formula World War I drama based on the play by Denison Clift. To evade the law, which is hot on his trail, Lowe joins the British army and is sent to the trenches in France where he is wounded in the face by shrapnel. About to have his face restored, he shows a French plastic surgeon a picture of Sir John Lasher, an English nobleman who has died in the war. Lowe returns to England and assumes his new identity, which fools the friends and relatives of the late Sir John, including his estranged wife (Joan Bennett) with whom Lowe falls in love. Meanwhile, a Scotland Yard inspector and friend of Bennett's family suspects Lowe. But the former criminal's redemption as a result of his war experiences and his new-found love result in his going straight. The film ends with the inspector bowing out of the picture. ■

Sea Devils (1953), RKO. *Dir.* Raoul Walsh; *Sc.* Borden Chase; *Cast includes:* Yvonne De Carlo, Rock Hudson, Maxwell Reed, Denis O'Dea, Michael Goodliffe, Bryan Forbes.

An attractive British spy encounters unexpected problems in this costume drama set in 1800 during the Napoleonic Wars and based on Victor Hugo's novel *The Toilers of the Sea.* Yvonne De Carlo, as the spy, is assigned to gain information about the location of the French fleet and other military matters. She has been chosen because she closely resembles a French countess who has been caught spying and is currently imprisoned in the Tower of London.

Rock Hudson, as a smuggler, volunteers to take her to the coast of France in his small sailboat. Unable to reveal her real purpose, she tells him she is trying to rescue her imprisoned brother from the French. During the voyage, he falls in love with her. When he is mistakenly told that she is a French spy, he kidnaps her and returns her to the Channel Islands and the local magistrate, who is actually her superior. He secretly releases her so that she can continue to carry out her mission.

Later, when the French discover her real identity and imprison her, the magistrate strikes a deal with Hudson, now languishing in jail for brawling, to rescue her. Once again he sets out for France, finds her and helps her escape with the plans for a French invasion. The film gets bogged down in too many weary trips back and forth across the English Channel. In addition, a steady flow of clichés undermines both the few action sequences and the personal conflict in which De Carlo is torn between her duty to her country and her love for Hudson. ■

Sea Flower, The (1918), Bluebird. *Dir.* Colin Campbell; *Sc.* H. Tipton Stock; *Cast includes:* Juanita Hansen, Alfred Whitman, Fred Huntley, Eugenie Besserer, Frederick Starr, George Pearce.

A U.S. Secret Service agent uncovers a plot by German spies to destroy a San Francisco munitions plant in this World War I drama. Alfred Whitman, as the secret agent, poses as a sailor to investigate a schooner owner (Frederick Starr) who has been hired by a German spy (George Pearce). The vessel, Whitman soon learns, is on its way to the South Seas with contraband weapons aboard meant for German sea raiders. The American agent also discovers that Starr, Pearce and their network of spies plan to blow up a major munitions factory in San Francisco. Starr suspects Whitman's real identity and throws the agent overboard. Whitman manages to swim to an island, board a steamer for the States and foil the plot. Juanita Hansen portrays the pretty daughter of a beachcomber whom Whitman meets on the island and falls in love with. The film was adapted from the short story by George Charles Hull. See U.S. Intelligence: World War I. ■

Sealed Cargo (1951), RKO. *Dir.* Alfred Werker; *Sc.* Dale Van Every, Oliver H. P. Garrett, Roy Huggins; *Cast includes:* Dana Andrews, Carla Balenda, Claude Rains, Philip Dorn, Onslow Stevens, Skip Homeier.

A fishing-boat captain (Dana Andrews) discovers a wolf pack of Nazi submarines off the coast of Newfoundland in this tense World War II drama. While rescuing an innocent-looking vessel, he learns that it is a supply ship for German U-boats. The cargo consists of torpedoes and mines, cleverly hidden in secret compartment in the hold of the ship. Andrews enlists the aid of other local fishermen in a plan to outwit the spies and destroy the square-rigger where it will not harm the village. Claude Rains portrays the sophisticated German captain of the supply ship. Carla Balenda plays an innocent caught up in the Nazi plot when she is taken hostage by the Germans. ∎

"Sealed Instructions" (1909), Selig.

A U.S. government worker is handed a sealed packet of instructions that immediately become the target of a spy. The employee is trailed to his home where the agent attempts to steal the information. Little is revealed about the contents of the package in this vague melodrama. ∎

Sealed Verdict (1948), Par. Dir. Lewis Allen; Sc. Jonathan Latimer; Cast includes: Ray Milland, Florence Marly, Broderick Crawford, John Hoyt, John Ridgely.

A U.S. Army prosecutor of Nazi war criminals falls in love with the ex-mistress of one of the defendants in this romantic drama set in post-World War II Germany. The prosecutor (Ray Milland) learns that the Nazi (John Hoyt) may take his own life before the sentence is carried out, and thus become a martyr to other unrepentant Nazis. Milland prevents the attempted suicide by dislodging a poisonous vial from a scar in the defendant's cheek. Florence Marly portrays the heroine suspected of being a Nazi sympathizer who in reality is a patriot gathering evidence against Hoyt. The film was adapted from the novel by Lionel Shapiro. ∎

Seas Beneath, The (1931), Fox. Dir. John Ford; Sc. Dudley Nichols; Cast includes: George O'Brien, Marion Lessing, Mona Maris, Walter C. Kelly, Walter McGrail.

A World War I sea drama, the plot concerns a U.S. Navy "mystery" ship, disguised as an innocent schooner, that lures German submarines into a trap. The vessel is accompanied by a U.S. sub. George O'Brien portrays an American captain who must train the crew to act like merchant seamen when a U-boat appears and drill the concealed gun crew to act quickly when the enemy undersea vessel surfaces.

O'Brien and his crew go ashore in a foreign port where his ship picks up some cargo. It is here that German spies, particularly women, pry secrets about cargoes and destinations from unwary sailors. O'Brien falls in love with a German agent (Marion Lessing). Less-

ing's brother is the commander of the infamous U-172, a German submarine, and her true lover is an officer aboard her brother's vessel.

Ensign Costello (Walter C. Kelly), one of O'Brien's young and inexperienced officers, falls for a Spanish entertainer (Mona Maris), who is also a German spy. She lures him to her room above the waterfront café and drugs him. Her cohorts enter and learn from his papers that he is an American officer in the U.S. Navy. That same night, after crew members make a futile attempt to locate the missing officer, the ship sails without him. Meanwhile, German submarine officers make plans to intercept the ship.

Once at sea, O'Brien prepares the schooner for its fatal meeting with the enemy. The U-boat cautiously studies the vessel, surfaces and fires several rounds at her. O'Brien's concealed gun crew, together with a U.S. submarine, eventually sink the U-boat. O'Brien watches as the spy, her brother and her fiancé, rescued from the water, are taken away as prisoners of war.

The first half of Ford's rambling film offers little in the way of action. Instead, he explores the camaraderie among the sailors, engages in some humorous situations and presents a ritualistic burial at sea. The American seamen seem naive while on leave in a foreign port—easy prey for several female spies who have little trouble obtaining information from them. On the other hand, the German officers, posing as civilians in the same port, appear sophisticated and organized in espionage work. ∎

Seats of the Mighty, The (1914), World. Dir. T. Hayes Hunter; Cast includes: Lionel Barrymore, A. P. Jackson, Clinton Preston, Millicent Evans, Glen White, Lois Meredith.

A Virginian captain, after facing several dangers during the French and Indian War, manages to escape and turn over military documents to General Wolfe in this historical drama based on Sir Gilbert Parker's novel. Glen White, as the captain, is captured by French troops and sent to Canada where he is interrogated by Doltaire (Lionel Barrymore) concerning the whereabouts of important documents. The prisoner, who is in love with the daughter (Millicent Evans) of Canada's governor, incurs the wrath of Doltaire who secretly wants the young woman for himself. He fabricates a story that his prisoner is a spy, then approaches his secret love to break off with the captain if she wants to save his life. Instead, she arranges to rescue her true love, and they both escape to British lines where the captain gives the strategic papers to General Wolfe. The British attack Quebec and capture the city. Doltaire is killed in the fight. ∎

Secret Agent of Japan (1942), TCF. *Dir.* Irving Pichel; *Sc.* John Larkin; *Cast includes:* Preston Foster, Lynn Bari, Noel Madison, Sen Young, Janis Carter.

Espionage forms the core of this World War II drama set in an international settlement in Shanghai. Preston Foster portrays an American soldier of fortune and café owner. Lynn Bari plays a British agent on the trail of spies working for the Japanese. An unsurprising romance develops between the hero and heroine as the intrigue mounts. Noel Madison plays the master spy. Released in April 1942, the film, with its plot about competing British and Japanese agents, was rushed into theaters to exploit its wartime theme and was one of the earliest spy dramas to appear after Japan's attack on Pearl Harbor. ∎

Secret Agent X-9 (1945) serial, U. *Dir.* Lew Collins, Ray Taylor; *Sc.* Patricia Harper, Joseph O'Donnell; *Cast includes:* Lloyd Bridges, Jan Wiley, Keye Luke, Victoria Horne, Samuel S. Hinds, Cy Kendall.

Lloyd Bridges portrays the title character in this 12-chapter World War II serial about Nazi secret agents trying to destroy America's war industries. Jan Wiley provides the object of the villains' interest until Bridges bursts upon the scene to rescue her in the nick of time. This Universal production does not match up to the World War II Republic serials which offered better sets and more action. Bridges, who was not a serial regular, played in several low-budget westerns and major productions before becoming a television star in his own series. See Serials. ∎

Secret Code (1918), Triangle. *Dir.* Albert Parker; *Sc.* Catherine Carr; *Cast includes:* Barney Sherry, Gloria Swanson, Rhy Alexander, Leslie Stewart, Joe King, Dorothy Wallace.

In this World War I drama, Gloria Swanson portrays the wife of a senator who is almost compromised by her indiscreet actions. Because of the nature of his work, the senator is forced temporarily to neglect her when the U.S. declares war on Germany. Much younger than her husband (Barney Sherry), Swanson seeks diversion and becomes romantically involved with a member of the Russian embassy. Another woman (Rhy Alexander), a German spy posing as a patriot, gains the confidence of the senator so that she can have access to government secrets. She suggests to the husband that his wife is supplying the Germans with military and diplomatic secrets by way of her Russian lover. The senator, therefore, wrongly suspects his wife of being an agent in the employ of the enemy. However, a secret service agent uncovers the German spy network and proves to the senator that his wife is innocent—that is, of spying. ∎

Secret Code, The (1942) serial, Col. *Dir.* Spencer Bennet; *Sc.* Robert Beche, Leighton Brill, Basil Dickey; *Cast includes:* Paul Kelly, Anne Nagel, Clancy Cooper, Alex Callam, Trevor Bardette, Robert O. Davis.

The mysterious Black Commando, a masked hero, struggles against the evil forces of the Axis powers in this 15-episode World War II serial. Paul Kelly, as the masked defender of America's military secrets, thwarts the enemy agents' plans to steal a secret formula for the production of synthetic rubber. The serial offered at least one unique feature. At the end of each week's chapter, it presented a short lecture and presentation to those in the audience on how to solve codes. The versatile Kelly, who displayed a strong face and tough appearance, portrayed a variety of heroes and villains in a string of action features during the 1930s and 1940s. ∎

Secret Command (1944), Col. *Dir.* Ed Sutherland; *Sc.* Roy Chanslor; *Cast includes:* Pat O'Brien, Carole Landis, Chester Morris, Ruth Warrick, Barton MacLane, Tom Tully.

Nazi saboteurs threaten an American shipyard in this World War II espionage drama. Pat O'Brien portrays a U.S. Navy intelligence officer who goes under cover as a worker at the yard to investigate attempts at sabotage. To allay any possible suspicions, the navy provides O'Brien with a ready-made family— a wife and two children. He eventually helps to round up the spy ring, thereby preventing the destruction of an aircraft carrier about to be launched. Carole Landis plays the bogus wife to whom O'Brien proposes at the end of the film. Chester Morris, as the undercover agent's brother, is suspicious of O'Brien's new-found family. ■

Secret Door, The (1964), AA. *Dir.* Gilbert L. Kay; *Sc.* Charles Martin; *Cast includes:* Robert Hutton, Sandra Dorne, Peter Illing, Peter Allenby, George Pastell, Shirley Lawrence.

Greed and lust lead to betrayal and death in this World War II drama filmed in Europe. Two convicted safecrackers (Robert Hutton and Peter Allenby) volunteer to assist U.S. Naval Intelligence after Japan's attack on Pearl Harbor. They are released from prison for the purpose of breaking into the Japanese embassy in Lisbon and photographing certain vital documents. They arrive in Lisbon and meet their contacts, a dealer (Peter Illing) in stolen papers and a Russian (Sandra Dorne). Allenby learns that the coveted papers are worth $1 million. He and Hutton accomplish their mission, but Brentano, who hopes to sell the photographs and win Dorne, betrays his American partner. The dealer, who is actually the Russian's husband, kills Brentano. The couple then die in a car accident while U.S. intelligence gets the film it wanted. Hutton is caught and taken prisoner aboard a Japanese vessel. When the ship is sunk, Hutton is rescued and pardoned. ■

Secret Enemies (1942), WB. *Dir.* Ben Stoloff; *Sc.* Raymond L. Schrock; *Cast includes:* Craig Stevens, Faye Emerson, John Ridgely, Charles Lang, Robert Warwick.

F.B.I. agents close in on a Nazi spy network operating out of a New York hotel in this World War II drama. Craig Stevens portrays an attorney who eventually joins the F.B.I. when his friend is killed by the German agents operating in the U.S. John Ridgely, as another F.B.I. agent, suspects Stevens has been too friendly with a group of suspicious Germans, particularly a refugee doctor. The doctor is being blackmailed by the head of the spy ring (Robert Warwick). "Once a German, always a German," Warwick insists. At first, the elderly doctor refuses. "My loyalty," he replies, "belongs to the country that took me in when I had nothing and gave me a chance to live and work like a free man." But then Warwick threatens to put the man's ailing wife, who is still in Germany, into a concentration camp.

The F.B.I. tracks the enemy to a New York hotel. Most of the spies are eventually rounded up, but the leaders elude the federal agents. Ridgely and Stevens pursue them to a rural hideaway where they, too, are captured following a noisy gun battle. The doctor, during the din of the gunfight, uses a wireless to notify authorities about a German U-boat waiting off shore. He is then killed by another spy. Faye Emerson plays a *femme fatale*, secretly married to Warwick, who almost fools Stevens. However, he arrests her in the last scene. Stevens later went on to television fame as detective Peter Gunn. ■

Secret Game, The (1917), Par. *Dir.* William C. DeMille; *Sc.* Marion Fairfax; *Cast includes:* Sessue Hayakawa, Jack Holt, Florence Vidor, Raymond Hatton, Mayne Kelso, Charles Ogle.

In this World War I spy story Sessue Hayakawa portrays a secret agent on the trail of spies in Los Angeles who are leaking information to the Germans. Japanese warships are acting as convoys to American transport ships on their way to Russia, and the Germans want the exact route of the convoy. Hayakawa helps to transport Americans by way of Siberia to the Russian front. He falls in love with a white woman but commits suicide, thereby permitting her to return to her true (white) hero. See Japanese War Scare of 1907. ■

Secret Invasion, The (1964), UA. *Dir.* Roger Corman; *Sc.* R. Wright Campbell; *Cast includes:* Stewart Granger, Raf Vallone, Mickey Rooney, Edd Byrnes, Henry Silva, Mia Massini.

A British officer leads a handful of volunteer convicts on a special assignment in Nazi-occupied Yugoslavia in this World War II action drama. Stewart Granger has the thankless task of supervising this motley crew of experts whose mission is to rescue an Italian general held prisoner in a Nazi stronghold. The general is needed to lead his troops against the Germans and perhaps help to end the war sooner. Raf Vallone portrays a former gang leader; Mickey Rooney, a dynamite expert; and Henry Silva, a sharpshooter. They portray some of the criminals who, if successful during the mission, are promised a pardon.

The small force links up with two partisans (Peter Coe and Mia Massini). After they succeed in their mission, they learn that they have only rescued the prisoner's double whom the Nazis have substituted after the real general died. Silva, dressed in a German uniform, forces the bogus general to address the Italian troops anyway and encourage them to battle the Nazis. When the impersonator instead begins to entreat the soldier to remain loyal, Silva shoots him. The killing angers the troops and incites them against the Germans. The mission is accomplished. The film, which ends tragically with only one member of the special force surviving, provides plenty of action. The plot device of using prisoners for a dangerous mission anticipates the more popular World War II action drama, *The Dirty Dozen* (1967). ■

Secret Kingdom, The (1916) serial, Vitagraph. *Dir.* Theodore Marston, Charles Brabin; *Cast includes:* Charles Richman, Dorothy Kelly, Arline Pretty, Joseph Kilgour, Ned Finley, Charles Wellesley.

International intrigue and treachery dominate this early serial about a murdered king, a usurper to the throne and the search for the dead ruler's son who escaped the clutches of the villainous prime minister. Charles Richman portrays the sought-after prince who knows nothing of his past and is now living in relative safety in the U.S. Madame Savatz (Dorothy Kelly) and her husband, secret agents of the usurper, have been sent to America to find and kill the prince. The serial is made up of 15 chapters, with the action set in various locations, including America's Southwest and Chicago. ■

Secret of the Submarine, The (1916) serial, American. *Dir.* George Sargent; *Cast includes:* Juanita Hansen, Tom Chatterton, William Tedmarsh, Lamar Johnstone, Hylda Hollis, George Clancy.

Juanita Hansen portrays the harassed heroine in this early silent 14-chapter serial. Set during World War I, the plot has Japanese agents planning to steal a device which allows a submarine to remain submerged indefinitely. The coveted invention draws oxygen from sea water. Hansen and her boy friend, played by Tom Chatterton, go through numerous adventures and engage the spies in many battles before they emerge the victors. See Japanese War Scare of 1907; Serials. ■

Secret Orders (1926), FBO. *Dir.* Chet Withey; *Sc.* J. Grubb Alexander; *Cast includes:* Harold Goodwin, Robert Frazer, Evelyn Brent, John Gough, Marjorie Bonner.

Evelyn Brent portrays a telegrapher who joins the U.S. Secret Service in his World War I drama. Her life is complicated by earlier events. She had married a criminal who was posing as a salesman (Harold Goodwin). When she discovered the truth about him, she informed the police. Later, she falls in love with her superior, thinking that her husband is dead. The spy plot concerns enemy agents and their attempts to learn about troop sailings. By the end of the film, her husband is killed, leaving her free to marry her boss. ■

Secret Service, U.S. See U.S. Secret Service. ■

Secret Service (1919), Par. *Dir.* Hugh Ford; *Sc.* Beulah Marie Dix; *Cast includes:* Robert Warwick, Wanda Hawley, Theodore Roberts, Edythe Chapman, Raymond Hatton, Guy Oliver.

Based on William Gillette's famous 1896 Civil War spy play, this silent film drama features Robert Warwick as the Union secret service agent who is assigned the task of helping to bring about the fall of Richmond. Dressed as a Confederate, the Union captain, a skilled telegrapher, infiltrates enemy lines. During the course of the mission he saves the life of a Southern officer who introduces Warwick to his sister (Wanda Hawley). The secret agent soon falls in love with the attractive young Confederate woman. Meanwhile Hawley's former suitor (Irving Cummings), who is suspicious of his new rival, traps Warwick. The Union spy is arrested and sentenced to death. However, Union troops capture Richmond in time to save Warwick's life. The couple are then reunited. Guy Oliver portrays the role of an elderly black. Playwright Gillette portrayed the role of the Union officer on stage. This film marked Robert Warwick's return to the screen following his military service in the Great War. ■

Secret Service (1931), RKO. *Dir.* J. Walter Ruben; *Sc.* Gerrit J. Lloyd, Bernard Schubert; *Cast includes:* Richard Dix, Shirley Grey, William Post, Jr., Fred Warren.

A sound version of William Gillette's Civil War play, the film stars Richard Dix as a Union captain who journeys into Confederate territory to gather information. Dressed in the enemy's uniform, he comes across a wounded son of the South. He carries the boy home and is invited to stay with the family. He then becomes romantically involved with the boy's sister (Shirley Grey). His love for her results in his being torn between his duty to the North and his devotion to Grey. She finds it difficult to believe that he is a spy when she sees him caught and taken away. ■

Secret Service in Darkest Africa (1943) serial, Rep. *Dir.* Spencer Bennet; *Sc.* Royal K. Cole, Ronald Davidson, Basil Dickey, Albert Duffy, Joseph O'Donnell, Joseph Poland; *Cast includes:* Rod Cameron, Joan Marsh, Duncan Renaldo, Lionel Royce.

Rod Cameron portrays a U.S. Secret Service agent who battles Nazi enemy agents in this 15-episode World War II serial. Set in wartime Africa, with Republic Studio's back lot substituting for the real thing, Cameron is up against the ruthless Baron von Rommler, a master Nazi villain, as well as belligerent Arabs. The baron, with Lionel Royce portraying a dual role, has taken the place of his double, a local sultan friendly to the Allied cause. This creates further complications for the American agent who finally unmasks the bogus sultan. The serial was recycled years later into a feature-length film for television titled *The Baron's African War*. Cameron portrayed another federal agent in the serial *G-Men vs. the Black Dragon*, released the same year, in which he struggled against Japanese spies in the U.S. ■

Secret Service of the Air (1939), WB. *Dir.* Noel Smith; *Sc.* Raymond Schrock; *Cast includes:* Ronald Reagan, John Litel, Ila Rhodes, James Stephenson, Eddie Foy, Jr.

The U.S. Secret Service goes after a gang of smugglers who are flying in illegal aliens from Mexico in this routine drama. Newly recruited into the air wing of the U.S. Secret Service, Ronald Reagan volunteers to go undercover to get evidence against the culprits. According to a plan arranged by his bureau chief (John Litel), Reagan, who has been flying for a private airline, is discredited at a trial linking him with a ring of counterfeiters and then placed in a jail cell with a suspected member of the smuggling gang. Reagan makes contact with the leader (James Stephenson) who soon discovers the pilot's real identity. Following a few setbacks, Reagan helps to round up the gang. Ila Rhodes provides the slight romantic interest. See "Brass" Bancroft. ■

Secret War of Harry Frigg, The (1968), U. *Dir.* Jack Smight; *Sc.* Peter Stone, Frank Tarloff; *Cast includes:* Paul Newman, Sylvia Koscina, Tom Bosley, Andrew Duggan, John Williams, James Gregory.

Paul Newman portrays a slow-witted G.I. assigned to rescue a handful of Allied generals held captive by the Germans and Italians in this World War II comedy. James Gregory, as the American general who devises the scheme, has Newman masquerade as a general so that the five officers he is to free will follow their rescuer's orders. Tom Bosley and Andrew Duggan play two of the incarcerated generals who have to contend with Newman's incompetent hijinks. Sylvia Koscina is the only woman in the cast of this weak comedy. ■

Secret Ways, The (1961), UI. *Dir.* Phil Karlson; *Sc.* Jean Hazlewood; *Cast includes:* Richard Widmark, Sonja Ziemann, Charles Regnier, Walter Rilla, Howard Vernon, Senta Berger.

An American soldier of fortune accepts the difficult assignment of rescuing a famous scholar from behind the Iron Curtain in this inept Cold War drama made in Europe. Richard Widmark, as the adventurous American who is hired by an international anti-Communist organization, journeys to Hungary where he begins his mission to pluck the brilliant professor (Walter Rilla) from the Reds.

To help him locate Rilla, he calls upon the professor's daughter (Sonja Ziemann). Hungarian freedom fighters escort Widmark to Rilla's hidden laboratory. However, Communist agents discover the whereabouts of the secret lab and capture the couple, who are then imprisoned and tortured. Following several clashes with the secret police and a few chases, Widmark finally accomplishes his mission in this bland story. Howard Vernon portrays a sadistic Red colonel in charge of capturing Rilla. The film is based on Alistair MacLean's novel. ■

Secrets of Scotland Yard (1944), Rep. *Dir.* George Blair; *Sc.* Denison Clift; *Cast includes:* Edgar Barrier, Stephanie Bachelor, C. Aubrey Smith, Lionel Atwill.

This World War II film explores some of

the methods employed by Scotland Yard to break enemy codes and shows the dangers employees face. Edgar Barrier portrays a dual role in this drama. When his twin brother is killed by Nazi agents, he takes the dead man's place. The code-solving agency loses two of its members before the spy network is rounded up, including one traitor within the bureau. Lionel Atwill plays an enemy agent. Stephanie Bachelor enacts the female lead. The film is based on the novel *Room 40, O.B.* by Denison Clift. See British Intelligence: World War II. ◾

Secrets of the Underground (1943), Rep. *Dir.* William Morgan; *Sc.* Robert Tasker, Geoffrey Homes; *Cast includes:* John Hubbard, Virginia Grey, Lloyd Corrigan, Robin Raymond.

Nazi agents use a posh gown shop for their undercover work in this anemic World War II drama. They spread panic on the home front by passing counterfeit war stamps. Virginia Grey plays a curious reporter who eventually uncovers the network of spies. She is helped by her boyfriend, John Hubbard, who is also the district attorney in this low-budget film. Pudgy, innocent-looking Lloyd Corrigan portrays the chief spy. ◾

Security Risk (1954), AA. *Dir.* Harold Schuster; *Sc.* Jo Pagano, John Rich, Frank McDonald; *Cast includes:* John Ireland, Dorothy Malone, Keith Larsen, John Craven, Joe Bassett.

The F.B.I. clashes with the Communists in this unexceptional Cold War drama. John Ireland, as a federal agent on vacation, becomes involved in the murder of an atomic scientist. Keith Larsen plays the victim's assistant and murderer who wants the dead man's atomic secrets for the Communists. Dolores Donlon plays a witness to the murder who steals the coveted papers and tries to sell them to the enemy agents. Larsen is forced to shoot her as well. Ireland, in turn, kills Larsen and captures the rest of the spy network. See Cold War. ◾

Seeing Red (1983), Heartland. *Dir.* James Klein, Julia Reichert.

A documentary exploring the history of American Communists over the last five decades, the film relies chiefly on interviews and stock newsreel footage. It presents the human side of those Americans who sought

through Communism the answers to many of their country's ills. Longshoremen, professors and union organizers are only some of the party members interviewed. Among the more well known is folk singer Pete Seeger. For the most part, they are likable, eloquent and quite persuasive, and help to remove the image of Communists as diabolical plotters or revolutionary radicals bent on overthrowing the government. Although such famous persons as Herbert Hoover, Harry S. Truman, Ronald Reagan and Richard M. Nixon are seen in film clips, only the interviewers, former and present party members, are permitted to expound their convictions. The film points out that the Communist Party suffered its severest blow when, in the 1960s, the enormity of Stalin's purges came to light. Party membership shrank from one million to a few hundred thousand. The documentary has been attacked for ignoring the undemocratic framework of the party and its direct links to Moscow. ◾

Semi-documentary spy films. Dramas based upon true stories, shot on location, using many of the original participants and/or non-professional players, and often containing social overtones are known as semi-documentary films. Several spy dramas have some or all of these characteristics. *The Caillaux Case* (1918), one of the earliest attempts at this realistic style, was based on an actual sensational contemporary French trial involving spies and traitors. Set during World War I, it presented the incidents and courtroom scenes in semi-documentary style.

The semi-documentary as we know it today did not reach the screen until 1945, with the release of *The House on 92nd Street*. Produced by Louis de Rochemont, who had earlier turned out semi-documentary shorts as part of a series called "The March of Time," the film was a dramatic recounting of an actual espionage case from F.B.I. files. It was shot at the locations where the incidents took place, including New York City and Washington, D.C. *Close-Up* (1948), although based on a fictitious plot about Nazi agents, was shot in New York City for authenticity and was one of the first of many post-World War II films to use location shooting there. The following year *Alaska Patrol*, an otherwise low-budget espionage tale, added some interesting effects by using a documentary-like approach. *Customs Agent* (1950), a drama about a gang of drug smugglers and its Chinese-American connection, was enhanced slightly by its semi-documentary style. Two films in 1952, *The Atomic City*, a Cold War drama shot at the Los Alamos nuclear plant, and *Walk East on Beacon*, photographed in the Boston area and based on a magazine article by F.B.I. director J. Edgar Hoover, were clearly enhanced by adding semi-documentary elements. *Operation Manhunt* (1954), about a Soviet attempt to assassinate a code clerk who has defected, was based on the experiences of Igor Gouzenko, was shot chiefly on location in Canada, and used many Canadians in its cast. The real Gouzenko appears briefly in an epilogue. *Executive Action* (1973) used semi-documentary characteristics to dramatize its interpretation of the Kennedy assassination, suggesting the President's death was the result of a conspiracy on the part of a group of ruthless businessmen.

The semi-documentary approach can help promote propaganda during "hot" and "cold" wars; add another dimension of authenticity to a routine film; or support social and political dramas. Other genres, besides the spy drama, have used it effectively. For example, Elia Kazan's incisive *On the Waterfront* (1954), starring Marlon Brando, was a powerful indictment of corruption and the conspiracy of silence on the docks of New York, where it was shot. ■

Serials. The movie serial, at one time one of Hollywood's most reliable staples, witnessed its last chapter in 1956, another victim of television's encroachment. But before its demise, the serial, designed to bring audiences back to the theaters week after week, poured forth hundreds of titles and encompassed many genres, including westerns, detective stories, mysteries, and spy and war dramas. The serials with either World War I or II as background were concerned with such usual conventions as superweapons, secret formulas and spies. The heroes ranged from men of action to more vulnerable but steadfast women and children. When the final, long-awaited twelfth or fifteenth chapter finally appeared on screen, all breathed a sigh of relief. America was once again safe from peril, the spies were under lock and key and the secret weapon was in the hands of the government to be used effectively against its menacing enemies.

Different military branches flashed across the screen during the World War I period. *Neal of the Navy* (1915) featured William Courtleigh and Lillian Lorraine in 14 exciting chapters. *Pearl of the Army* (1916) starred the silent serial queen Pearl White as the intrepid lass who prevents oriental agents from sabotaging the Panama Canal.

Germany posed the largest threat to the U.S., according to the serials. In *Wolves of Kultur* (1918) Charles Hutchison and Leah Baird track down the German designer of a new and powerful torpedo. Jane Vance, as the title character in *A Daughter of Uncle Sam* (1918), bravely battles German agents for 12 chapters. *The Eagle's Eye* (1918), an epic serial in 20 chapters, added a touch of paranoia to the threat of enemy agents by suggesting that hundreds of German spies were running rampant across America. The nation's youth were given a chance to serve their country in *Boy Scouts to the Rescue* (1918). They ferret out a nest of German agents.

Japan won second place as the next largest threat to the country's security. Besides *Pearl of the Army*, mentioned earlier, *The Secret of the Submarine* (1916), a 14-chapter serial, has Japanese agents planning to steal an apparatus which can increase the effectiveness of a submarine.

An actual incident precipitated *Patria* (1916), an anti-Japanese and anti-Mexican serial which was financed by William Randolph Hearst. The influential publisher, who owned a large ranch in Mexico, was enraged when Pancho Villa raided his property and distributed his 60,000 head of cattle to the peons. Hearst ordered his editors to lash out against Mexico, claiming it had a secret alliance with Japan to invade the U.S. The serial *Patria* echoed this threat. Dancer Irene Castle, as an American heiress, provides secret funds designed to prepare America against an enemy attack. It depicts the Japanese so repulsively that President Wilson was prompted to send a note to those responsible, complaining that the film was "extremely unfair to the Japanese. . . ."

Following the Armistice, our heroes and heroines kept busy battling power-crazed master villains (*Drums of Fu Manchu*), tracking down gangs of kidnappers (*The Clutching Hand*), taming the wilderness (*Custer's Last Stand*), hunting for lost treasure (*The New Adventures of Tarzan*), braving the perils of the jungle (*Darkest Africa*), protecting the skies from airborne criminals (*Mystery*

Squadron) and traveling in space to save our planet (*Flash Gordon*). All these exploits, although not spy-related, proved valuable training for the next world conflict in which America's serial heroes, battling numerous attempts at espionage and sabotage, stemmed the tide of totalitarianism on our shores and elsewhere.

In Republic's *Robinson Crusoe of Clipper Island* (1937), directed by Mark V. Wright and Ray Taylor, the U.S. sends its Polynesian operative (Mala) to a remote island to investigate a string of sabotage acts committed by an international spy ring. In Universal's *Red Barry* (1938), directed by Ford Beebe and Alan James, Larry "Buster" Crabbe, as the titular sleuth, and reporter Frances Robinson battle an international plot involving a conflict between Asians and Russians over a large munitions deal. Columbia's *Flying G-Men* (1939), directed by Ray Taylor and James W. Horne, has Robert Paige leading a squad of government pilots against a network of spies attacking the country's defense systems.

Once again the enemies chiefly were imported from Germany and Japan. (Italy, the third Axis power, was virtually nonexistent in World War II serials.) Masks often hid the identities of villains as well as heroes, both of whom fought relentlessly to gain control of superweapons, secret formulas and other vital information. The masked *Spy Smasher* (1942), starring Kane Richmond, fights against a Nazi leader called the Mask. In *King of the Mounties*, released the same year, Allan "Rocky" Lane battles the enemy in Canada's backwoods. Don Terry, as the intrepid seaman Don Winslow, clashes with the Germans in two serials, *Don Winslow of the Navy* (1942) and *Don Winslow of the Coast Guard* (1943). It took both to subdue the dangerous Scorpion (not to be confused with Tom Tyler's archrival of the same name in *The Adventures of Captain Marvel*), who is bent on crippling America's defenses. The fun-loving juvenile delinquents, better known as the Dead End Kids or the Little Tough Guys, turn patriotic when they collide with enemy agents in *Junior G-Men of the Air* (1942) and *Adventures of the Flying Cadets* (1943). Ruth Roman, as the *Jungle Queen* (1945), helps to quell a tribal revolt, incited by Nazi agents, against the Allies. Lloyd Bridges as *Secret Agent X-9* (1945) does his share for the war effort by rounding up a gang of Nazi saboteurs.

While German agents were being bested by these stalwart defenders of the American way, Japanese spies faced the same fate. Rod Cameron in *G-Men vs. the Black Dragon* (1943) pursues Haruchi, a nefarious figure who ultimately is killed in a ball of flame when his speedboat smashes into a Japanese submarine. Another nasty Oriental agent, Sakima, meets a violent death at the hands of William Forrest as *The Masked Marvel* (1943). The famous comic-book hero, The Batman, in a 1943 serial of the same name, takes on Dr. Saka (J. Carrol Naish), another wicked Japanese agent whose diabolical inventions almost end the masked hero's career.

Fist fights and chases were the mainstay of the serials. (Budgets did not permit battle sequences of the war. When establishing shots were required, e.g., the U.S. Navy fleet in the *Don Winslow* serials, stock footage was used.) With all their frenetic action, serials hardly had time for messages or preaching. But the opposing wartime ideologies were clearly embodied in the principal characters. Since the heroes emerged from the country's popular culture, e.g., the comics, radio and pulp fiction, and the villains were so plainly identifiable, the propaganda and patriotic elements were never far off. ∎

Seven Days in May (1964), Par. *Dir.* John Frankenheimer; *Sc.* Rod Serling; *Cast includes*: Burt Lancaster, Kirk Douglas, Fredric March, Ava Gardner, Edmond O'Brien, Martin Balsam.

Based on Fletcher Knebel and Charles W. Bailey's 1962 novel, the film concerns a chilling military conspiracy designed to overthrow the U.S. government. Gen. James M. Scott (Burt Lancaster)—a superpatriotic member of the joint chiefs of staff—strongly opposes a recently signed nuclear pact with the Soviet Union. Conspiring with other top military leaders, he plans to seize control of the executive branch within seven days in May.

Hints of the conspiracy are revealed when a colonel (Kirk Douglas), a loyal aide to General Scott, suspects a plot against the President. He informs the President about a secret air force base somewhere in Texas. In addition, an admiral, a disillusioned member of the conspiracy, is willing to sign a confession exposing the coup attempt. General Scott is asked to resign, but he refuses and threatens to take his case to the people. The President, armed with enough evidence against the plotters, appears on television, exposes the coup and asks for the instigators' resignations.

Jordan Lyman (Fredric March), the idealistic and insightful President, summarizes the conditions that have caused the now aborted conspiracy. "The enemy is an age," he explains, "a nuclear age. Out of this comes a sickness. And every now and then we look for a man in red, white and blue. For some of us it was a Senator McCarthy. For others a General Walker. And now a General Scott." Edmond O'Brien as a Southern senator, Martin Balsam as Lyman's aide, and George Macready as Secretary of the Interior are all loyal to the President and help him uncover the plot. Ava Gardner portrays a Washington hostess.

During the 1960s the military-industrial became a popular film target (Stanley Kubrick's 1964 satire *Dr. Strangelove*, etc.), and the political thriller *Seven Days in May* remains one of the most powerful. As expected, the Pentagon offered little assistance to the production, but President Kennedy's White House staff, especially Press Secretary Pierre Salinger, proved cooperative. ∎

Seven Graves for Grogan (1979). See *A Time to Die* (1983). ∎

Seven Miles From Alcatraz (1942), RKO. *Dir.* Edward Dmytryk; *Sc.* Joseph Krumgold; *Cast includes:* James Craig, Bonita Granville, Frank Jenks, Cliff Edwards, George Cleveland, Erford Gage.

Two escaped convicts from Alcatraz stumble upon a network of Nazi agents operating in San Francisco in this fast-paced World War II drama. James Craig and Frank Jenks, as the two escapees, make their break during a blackout and a heavy fog. The tide carries them to a lighthouse occupied by an old sea captain, his daughter, a helper and a radio operator (Erford Gage). Craig and Jenks discover that Gage is a Nazi agent transmitting coded signals to his accomplices in San Francisco. They further learn that an enemy sub is waiting for secret documents from these spies. Jenks kills the radio operator who tries to stop the convicts from taking the launch. The leaders of the spy ring show up by motorboat when Gage fails to meet them. Following an unconvincing fight with Craig and Jenks, the spies are captured with the help of

the U.S. Navy. Planes are then sent to sink the U-boat. The two convicts are returned to Alcatraz with a promise of early release. Bonita Granville portrays the lighthouse keeper's daughter.

The prison-break and spy plots are burdened down with plenty of wartime propaganda. Craig is first seen on screen in his Alcatraz cell telling other convicts he doesn't care who wins the war. Later, at the lighthouse, all its inhabitants voice their concern about the war except Craig. The old seaman (George Cleveland) then berates Craig as an anachronism, virtually equating him with the enemy. "You've no place here, on the outside. We've got a job to do and you're not part of it. You're simply a bad mistake. And what we're doing is erasing you and everyone like you and starting over again." Craig, for a moment, is startled by these remarks. "What did this country ever give me?" he fires back. "A chance," the captain replies. Even Craig's buddy feels the call of patriotism when the Nazi agents appear. "We're hoodlums," Jenks acknowledges, "but we're American hoodlums." Of course, by the end of the film, Craig hides the Nazi agents' maps and papers of San Francisco intended for the submarine and refuses to turn them over even as he is being beaten. ∎

Seventh Cross, The (1944), MGM. *Dir.* Fred Zinnemann; *Sc.* Helen Deutsch; *Cast includes:* Spencer Tracy, Signe Hasso, Hume Cronyn, Jessica Tandy, Agnes Moorehead.

This somber, realistic drama explores the disintegration of human values in pre-World War II Germany. It also suggests that not all Germans were ardent Nazis. George Heisler (Spencer Tracy), an anti-Nazi whom the Gestapo has arrested and beaten, is a prisoner in a Nazi concentration camp. He and six other inmates manage to escape. The commandant orders seven trees stripped bare and crosses mounted on them for the seven escapees. He vows to hang them to the crosses after they are captured and tortured. Six of the men eventually are killed or caught, but Heisler, as the seventh, eludes the Gestapo who pursues him relentlessly. As a result of his defiance and will to remain free, the seventh cross, an ironic symbol of Nazi Germany's mockery of religion, continues to stand empty.

The story, which is told in flashbacks, opens with a panning shot on seven crosses—one of which remains empty. A voice-over declares: "There is something in the human soul that sets men above the animals." The film then follows Heisler's desperate efforts to contact friends who can help him to leave the country. Pursued relentlessly by the Gestapo who broadcast his description and publish his picture in local newspapers, he is forced to remain on the run and seek help wherever he can find it. A truck driver who has given him a lift orders him out of his vehicle when he discovers his identity. His former sweetheart, now married to a Nazi officer, refuses him food and clothing.

Meanwhile, the German underground, a small but dedicated group, prepares for Heisler's escape. Its members collect some money, produce a false passport and arrange for transportation on a neutral vessel. At first, they wait for the hunted man to contact them; then they begin to seek out his old acquaintances whom he may have contacted. Marnel (Herbert Rudley), an old radical friend and leader in the underground, directs the search for Heisler.

The embittered fugitive soon learns that the spirit of human decency still prevails in Nazi Germany in the hearts and souls of some of its citizens. Paul (Hume Cronyn), an old friend, gives Heisler food and shelter, realizing the dangers he and his wife and children face in harboring a criminal. A seamstress at a theatrical costume shop gives him a new suit of clothes and secretly places money in one of the pockets. A Jewish doctor bandages Heisler's hand without reporting the incident. A factory worker (Paul Guilfoyle) who abhors the Nazi regime hides Heisler in a hotel room. A caring chambermaid (Signe Hasso) warns him of a Gestapo search. A delicatessen clerk, working with the undergound, brings him sandwiches and information about his escape route. When he realizes that all these strangers and friends have bravely risked their own lives to assist him, he softens his own cynicism. "God help the people who live on this earth and draw their comfort from it—and sometimes from each other," he says to the chambermaid before he leaves for the vessel which will take him to freedom. ■

Shadow of Terror (1945), PRC. *Dir.* Lew Landers; *Sc.* Arthur St. Claire; *Cast includes:* Richard Fraser, Grace Gillern, Cy Kendall, Emmett Lynn, Kenneth McDonald.

A routine World War II drama involving secret plans for the atomic bomb, the film features Richard Fraser as a research scientist who is assaulted and tossed out of a moving train. His papers are stolen by spies eager to get their hands on his new weapon. Grace Gillern, as the romantic lead, helps him to recover. Snapping out of a case of amnesia, he manages to save his plans for the bomb.

The original film never makes reference to the atom bomb by name or to the nature of the scientist's plans. The drama was finished before the two bombs were dropped over Japan. Seeing a way to exploit the atomic bomb, the studio secured government footage of test results of the new and powerful explosive and spliced it to the end of the film. A narrator then announced that this was the secret of Fraser's papers. Thus the studio was able to scoop other companies with its "topical" drama. ■

Shadows of Suspicion (1919), Metro. *Dir.* Edwin Carewe; *Sc.* Finis Fox; *Cast includes:* Harold Lockwood, Naomi Childers, Helen Lindroth, Kenneth Kealing, William Bailey.

Set in England at the beginning of World War I, the drama concerns British and German spies who want some secret papers. Harold Lockwood, as the hero, eventually foils the efforts of Sir John Rizzio (Bigelow Cooper), a secret agent who discovers the papers in the possession of the heroine (Naomi Childers). She had hidden them in her stocking, but they slipped down near her ankle where they became visible. Captain Leslie Peacock portrays the chief of Scotland Yard. See British Intelligence: World War I.

Harold Lockwood was a popular screen star of more than 100 early silents, playing opposite many famous actresses, including Mary Pickford. He died of influenza in 1918 at age 31, a year before the film, adapted from George Gibbs' 1915 novel *The Yellow Dove*, was released. ■

Shadows Over Shanghai (1938), GN. *Dir.* Charles Lamont; *Sc.* Joseph Hoffman; *Cast includes:* James Dunn, Ralph Morgan, Linda Gray, Robert Barrat, Paul Sutton.

The Sino-Japanese War furnishes the background for this tangled drama of greed, deception and murder. James Dunn portrays a reporter; Ralph Morgan, an arms dealer for China; Linda Gray, a White Russian schoolteacher; and Robert Barrat, a disgraced Russian agent. All are seeking the key to a mysterious treasure located somewhere in the U.S.

The film exemplifies how a typical Hollywood product, produced simply for entertainment, may end up, intentionally or otherwise, as a piece of propaganda. The basic plot, chiefly about a coveted treasure, skirts the political issues of the conflict—as did virtually all similar action and spy films of the period. But the stock scenes of the devastating Japanese air attacks on heavily populated Shanghai certainly must have influenced audiences, particularly concerning the actions of Japan. ∎

Shanghai Story, The (1954), Rep. *Dir.* Frank Lloyd; *Sc.* Seton I. Miller, Steve Fisher; *Cast includes:* Ruth Roman, Edmond O'Brien, Richard Jaeckel, Barry Kelley, Whit Bissell, Basil Ruysdael.

Ruth Roman, working as an undercover spy for the U.S., helps to smuggle out of Communist China vital military information in this implausible drama. To avoid suspicion, she becomes romantically involved with the chief of the Shanghai police, played by Marvin Miller. He places other Europeans and Americans under house arrest in a local hotel when he suspects one of them of spying. Among the suspects are Edmond O'Brien, as a doctor who has been in China for several years, and Richard Jaeckel, who portrays a sailor. It is these two Americans whom Roman entrusts with the secret information and helps to escape. O'Brien later returns to carry on a love affair with his savior. ∎

Sharpshooters (1938), TCF. *Dir.* James Tinling; *Sc.* Robert Ellis, Helen Logan; *Cast includes:* Brian Donlevy, Lynn Bari, Wally Vernon, John King, Douglas Dumbrille, C. Henry Gordon.

Brian Donlevy portrays an American newsreel cameraman who becomes embroiled in a conspiracy set in a fictitious country in this comedy drama. Donlevy, a heavy-drinking cameraman, scoops other photographers when he captures on film the assassination of the king of Metovania. He then journeys to that land to shoot pictures of the coronation of the prince. He soon discovers a plot against the young prince's life by conspirators who are attempting to gain control of the country. Donlevy foils their scheme, saves the prince's life and gets his pictures. Wally Vernon plays Donlevy's comic assistant. Lynn Bari provides the romantic interest for Donlevy and the handsome prince (John King), the latter eventually winning her. ∎

Shell 43 (1916), Triangle. *Dir.* Reginald Barker; *Sc.* C. Gardner Sullivan; *Cast includes:* H. B. Warner, Enid Markey, Jack Gilbert, George Fisher.

A World War I drama, the film includes numerous trench and battle sequences as well as a suspenseful story. A British spy (H. B. Warner) poses as an American war correspondent. He has a German pass that allows him to move freely on the battlefield. In the final scene the heroic agent sacrifices his own life to knock out a strategic target. Knowing it will mean his own death, he secretly telephones a message to British headquarters to "shell Pit 43."

One of the early war movies to feature a British subject as hero, American film studios seemed to have their own hierarchy of national heroes during the conflict. Americans were featured in the largest number of entries, followed by the British and then the French. For some unknown reason, other Allies, such as the Italians and Belgians, provided few screen heroes or heroines. See British Intelligence: World War I. ∎

Sherlock Brown (1922), Metro. *Dir.* Bayard Veiller; *Sc.* Lenore J. Coffee; *Cast includes:* Bert Lytell, Ora Carew, Sylvia Breamer, De Witt Jennings, Theodore von Eltz.

The U.S. Secret Service is called in to recover stolen plans for a high explosive in this comedy drama. Bert Lytell, who portrays a bumbling amateur detective, volunteers his talent to the cynical chief of the secret service. Lytell, it seems, has an uncanny skill for "smelling" clues. In this case, he picks up the scent of sandalwood which he attributes to the *femme fatale* and traces her to her cabin aboard a vessel where he retrieves the formula. He later solves the entire theft by exposing a financier as the chief spy who earlier stole the papers from an army lieutenant. Lytell finds time for a little romancing with the sister of the lieutenant. ∎

Lobby card for the World War II spy thriller *Sherlock Holmes and the Secret Weapon* (1942).

Sherlock Holmes and the Secret Weapon (1942), U. *Dir.* Roy William Neill; *Sc.* Edward T. Loew, W. Scott Darling, Edmund L. Hartmann; *Cast includes:* Basil Rathbone, Nigel Bruce, Lionel Atwill, Kaaren Verne, William Post, Jr., Dennis Hoey.

A. Conan Doyle's master sleuth was enlisted to help out during World War II, as were other popular private eyes who appeared in series during the world conflict. In this drama both the British government and Nazi agents are after a secret bombsight invented by Dr. Tobel (William Post, Jr.), a Swiss scientist. The film opens in Switzerland where German spies are watching the scientist's house. Holmes, disguised as an elderly bookseller, helps Tobel to elude the spies and escape to England.

Meanwhile, Professor Moriarty (Lionel Atwill), Holmes' archenemy, is again on the loose and working for the Nazis. He kidnaps Tobel, hoping to sell the bombsight to Germany. Tobel, however, in an effort to keep his invention entirely secret, has divided it into four parts and given each to a different scientist for production. The remainder of the

plot concerns a battle of wits between Holmes and Moriarty as each tries to recover the parts before the other does. The film is an updated version of Doyle's story titled "The Dancing Men," the title referring to a code of little figures drawn by the doctor.

Aside from the usual wartime propaganda ("Germany wanted the Tobel bombsight. We'll send them thousands—in R.A.F. planes," a British officer says), the dialogue alludes also to Holmes' drug addiction. In one scene where he is Moriarty's prisoner, Holmes reproaches his captor, who intends to shoot him, for his lack of originality and offers his own method for doing away with an enemy. "I should have you placed on an operating table, place a needle in your veins and slowly draw off your life's blood." Moriarty smiles and retorts, "The needle to the last, eh, Holmes?"

Perhaps the most important bombsight mentioned during World War II was the legendary Norden bombsight—a secret device heavily guarded by the U.S. military and much coveted by Nazi agents. Hermann Lang, an inspector at the Norden factory, one night removed the plans for the bombsight and copied them. He then turned the copy over to Nikolaus Ritter, the head of a German spy ring in America. Ironically, the German air force gained little benefit from its most prized acquisition. The Germans did not install the device in their bombers in time for their heavy raids over Britain. Later, the Luftwaffe made little use of the bombsight since its bombers were chiefly assigned a supportive and defensive role over Germany. See British Intelligence: World War II; Detectives and Spies; *Enemy Agent* (1940) ■

Sherlock Holmes and the Voice of Terror (1942), U. *Dir.* John Rawlins; *Sc.* Lynn Riggs; *Cast includes:* Basil Rathbone, Nigel Bruce, Evelyn Ankers, Reginald Denny, Thomas Gomez, Henry Daniell.

Sherlock Holmes and Dr. Watson, as well as other sleuths who starred in their own detective series, were occasionally diverted from their usual domestic crime chores and assigned to uncover subversive activities and enemy agents during World War II. Basil Rathbone and Nigel Bruce portray the famous team in this drama about a Nazi radio broadcast that is terrorizing the English citizenry. Holmes is hired by the British Inner Council to capture the Nazi agent responsible for the "voice of terror" broadcasts. Evelyn Ankers portrays a young woman whom Holmes hires to watch a suspect (Thomas Gomez). Reginald Denny plays a Nazi agent who has infiltrated the Inner Council. An interesting highlight of the plot occurs when Holmes, appealing to their sense of patriotism, enlists the aid of English underworld characters to track down the enemy agents. This is a well-paced film based on A. Conan Doyle's story *His Last Bow.*

The Inner Council referred to in the plot may well have been a thinly disguised pseudonym for Britain's Prime Minister Winston Churchill's wartime Inner Circle, as described by John Colville, Churchill's private secretary, in his 1981 book *Winston Churchill and His Inner Circle.* The prime minister was not the only Allied leader to have benefited from such an esoteric group.

President Franklin D. Roosevelt, who was as fascinated with the arcane world of espionage as his English counterpart, created his own private personal intelligence service composed of two branches. Roosevelt subsidized one out of special untraceable funds while private individuals financed the other.

This second branch is the more interesting. Originating in 1917 as a secret society that called itself the Room, the group was made up affluent New Yorkers who were fascinated with espionage activities. Reporting on several international areas before World War II, the group engaged in counter-espionage operations after the conflict erupted. Also, Roosevelt requested that the Room be responsible for protecting America's war industries against acts of sabotage and guarding the nation's southern border against its infiltration by enemy agents. See British Intelligence: World War II; Detectives and Spies. ■

Sherlock Holmes in Washington (1943), U. *Dir.* Roy William Neill; *Sc.* Bertram Millhauser, Lynn Riggs; *Cast includes:* Basil Rathbone, Nigel Bruce, Marjorie Lord, Henry Daniell, George Zucco, John Archer.

Sherlock Holmes and his assistant, Dr. Watson, journey to Washington, D.C., in this entry in the popular series. They are on the trail of an international spy ring. Both Holmes and the spies are searching for a very important document that has been reduced to microfilm and concealed in the cover of a book of matches, a fact that only Holmes is aware of. The master detective's expert sleuthing soon unravels the mystery and exposes the enemy agents.

As is typical of the series, Watson supplies some comic relief. "We had a carrier pigeon in the last war," he informs his friend. "The poor bird kept flying 'round and 'round in circles. . . . We found out later on it was cross-eyed." The film, updated to World War II, lacks the atmosphere of the earlier entries that are set in the latter part of the nineteenth century. However, the direction is fast-paced and the plot is satisfactory.

Several entries in the series, especially those with a World War II background, end with Holmes uttering a quotation or homily about democratic values, the glory of England or the struggle against totalitarianism. This film is no exception. As he and Watson leave Washington, Holmes recalls the words of Winston Churchill: "'It is not given to us to peer into the mysteries of the future. But in the days to come the British and American people will, for their own safety and the good of all, walk together in majesty, in justice and in peace.'" See Detectives and Spies. ■

Shifting Sands (1918), Triangle. *Dir.* Albert Parker; *Cast includes:* Gloria Swanson, Joe King, Harvey Clark, Leone Carton.

Gloria Swanson portrays a welfare worker who becomes entangled with German agents in this World War I drama. In the course of her charity work, she meets a wealthy philanthropist, played by Joe King, whom she falls in love with and marries. A dapper gentleman enters the couple's life whom Swanson doesn't recognize as her former landlord who had once had her arrested on a false charge of stealing his wallet. The visitor, played by Harvey Clark, is a German spy seeking to steal vital plans from the husband's safe. Swanson, who turns out to be working for the secret service, foils the agent's plot. ∎

Ship Ahoy (1942), MGM. *Dir.* Edward Buzzell; *Sc.* Harry Clork; *Cast includes:* Eleanor Powell, Red Skelton, Bert Lahr, Virginia O'Brien, William Post, Jr., Frank Sinatra.

This World War II spy musical features Tommy Dorsey and his orchestra, Eleanor Powell's dancing, Frank Sinatra's singing and Red Skelton's clowning. One would think that all this talent would culminate in a blockbuster movie, but the results prove otherwise. The plot concerns enemy spies (John Emery and Bernard Nedell) posing as American booking agents who hire Dorsey and his troupe to entertain aboard a ship. Their ulterior motive is to secretly transport a magnetic mine to Puerto Rico. Aboard the vessel are Red Skelton, who is trying to settle his nerves; secret service agents who suspect an enemy plot; and Bert Lahr, who is trying to woo Virginia O'Brien. Some comic moments arise as Skelton mistakenly gains possession of the suitcase containing the bomb. Before the American agents round up the spy ring, Sinatra gets a chance to sing a few numbers. Also, Powell performs her dance specialties, including tapping out a message in morse code. ∎

Ship Comes In, A (1928), Pathé. *Dir.* William K. Howard; *Sc.* Julien Josephson; *Cast includes:* Rudolph Schildkraut, Louise Dresser, Robert Edeson, Milton Holmes.

An immigrant's faith in America never wavers as he undergoes one adversity after another in this patriotic drama set during World War I. Rudolph Schildkraut (father of famous actor Joseph Schildkraut) portrays the Hungarian immigrant who happily works as a janitor in a government building. An anarchist cousin tries to influence him, but he will have none of this chatter against the land that he has adopted. When his time comes to receive his citizenship papers, he is so overjoyed that he has his wife bake the judge a cake. However, his villainous cousin conceals a bomb in the cake. It explodes and wounds the judge. Schildkraut is arrested and jailed. Meanwhile the unfortunate victim loses his son in the war. He is eventually released and returns to his janitorial duties.

The use of European immigrants as main screen characters was carried over from the previous decade when such films as Charlie Chaplin's *The Immigrant* were popular, especially in the cities which housed large populations of foreigners. It is doubtful whether the children of these immigrants, who made up a large portion of movie audience during the 1920s, were as absorbed by the subject matter as their parents had once been. See Anarchists in the U.S. ∎

Short Cut to Hell (1957). See *This Gun for Hire* (1942). ∎

Silencers, The (1966), Col. *Dir.* Phil Karlson; *Sc.* Oscar Saul; *Cast includes:* Dean Martin, Stella Stevens, Daliah Lavi, Victor Buono, Arthur O'Connell, Robert Webber.

Dean Martin portrays superspy Matt Helm in this light, entertaining drama about a Chinese-initiated plot to involve the U.S. in a global war. Victor Buono, as an agent of the Communist Chinese, plans to divert a U.S. missile and have it hit America's nuclear stockpile, thereby causing worldwide fallout. Helm outdoes James Bond as he battles his way to Buono's lair in a secret cave while avoiding assassination, sexual temptation and other obstacles. His chief weapon is his gun which fires backwards when held by a foe.

Stella Stevens portrays a bumbling beauty in whom Helm takes more than a casual interest. Daliah Lavi, as an adversary spy, proves a handful for the American agent. Cyd Charisse portrays a dancer murdered by the villains in the middle of one of her numbers. James Gregory plays Helm's oddball superior. Arthur O'Connell and Robert Webber play two underlings in the employ of Buono. The film, the first in a series of Matt Helm spy spoofs, is based on *The Silencers* and *Death of a Citizen*, two novels by Donald Hamilton. ∎

Silent Command, The (1923), Fox. *Dir.* Gordon Edwards; *Sc.* Anthony Paul Kelly; *Cast includes:* Edmund Lowe, Alma Tell, Bela Lugosi, Carl Harbough, Martin Faust, Gordon McEdward.

A spy story involving the mining of the Panama Canal, the film centers on an American navy officer (Edmund Lowe) who designs the plans for the mine fields. When he leaves the office located in the Canal Zone, spies try to steal the plans but are foiled when a fire breaks out and burns everything in the office. Not deterred by this, the enemy agents follow the officer to Washington and try again. This time he plays along with the gang while covertly working for the U.S. Secret Service. Meanwhile his wife believes that he has betrayed his country, until the end of the film when all turns out well. See Panama Canal. ∎

Silent Flyer, The (1926), U. *Dir.* William Craft; *Cast includes:* Malcolm MacGregor, Louise Lorraine, Thur Fairfax, Hughie Mack, Anders Rudolph, Edith Yorke.

A U.S. Secret Service agent foils the plans of villains to steal a revolutionary new airplane motor in this silent 10-chapter serial. Malcolm MacGregor, as secret agent Lloyd Darrell, journeys to a small Northwest community where an inventor (Anders Rudolph) is developing a silent airplane motor. Darrell soon falls in love with the inventor's daughter (Louise Lorraine). Meanwhile, the inventor and his daughter are plagued by a gang bent on appropriating the plans for their own benefit. This brings the agent, aided by his faithful dog, Silver Streak, into action for ten action-packed chapters, with such titles as "The Jaw of Death" and "Flames of Peril," before he uncovers the gang leader. ∎

Silent Mystery, The (1919) serial. *Dir.* Francis Ford; *Cast includes:* Francis Ford, Mae Gaston, Rosemary Theby, Elsie Van Name.

A fast-paced serial that blends the mystery format with the spy genre, the film concerns a stolen Egyptian jewel, a German spy and a strange murder. An American tourist in Egypt steals "The Eye of the World," a priceless jewel, after she learns that her once-wealthy husband is having financial difficul-

ties. The woman, obsessed by money, prods her daughter to enter into a marriage with a wealthy man who is then mysteriously murdered. The crime is covered up to appear as a suicide. But a curious U.S. government agent proves that the bridegroom did not take his own life. Meanwhile, the body and the valuable jewel have disappeared. There are enough suspects, including a suspicious-looking German spy, to further complicate matters. ∎

Silk-Lined Burglar, The (1919), U. *Dir.* Jack Dillon; *Sc.* Fred Myton; *Cast includes:* Priscilla Dean, Ashton Dearholt, Sam De Grasse, Sam Appel, Lillian West, Fred Kelsey.

The resourceful sweetheart of a U.S. Secret Service operator is determined to help him solve a difficult case in this World War I drama. Priscilla Dean portrays the heroine who hires Boston Blackie, a professional safecracker (Sam De Grasse), to assist her in obtaining evidence against a suspected German spy. The government agent (Ashton Dearholt) is hesitant to arrest the suspect without conclusive evidence. Since the U.S. has not yet entered the war against Germany, his arrest, if unfounded, may cause an international incident.

Dean and her accomplice enter the spy's quarters and find the evidence they need. But the suspect returns and catches them in the act. A fight ensues and the couple escape. The spy is finally arrested and the safecracker joins the secret service.

The film is based on Jack Boyle's popular fictional character Boston Blackie, a former criminal who works on the side of the law. In this drama, one of the earliest Boston Blackie films, he is billed in third place. Later he became the lead character in both silent and sound features. Many were straight mysteries, but on occasion the plot involved spies, as in this entry, and *Meet Boston Blackie* (1941), with Chester Morris in the role of the modern Robin Hood. See Detectives and Spies. ∎

Silver Car, The (1921), Vitagraph. *Dir.* David Smith; *Sc.* Wyndham Martyn; *Cast includes:* Earle Williams, Kathlyn Adams, Geoffrey Webb, Erick Mayne, Emmett King.

International and political intrigue dominate this drama set during World War I. Earle Williams portrays an American international jewel thief who enlists in the army to escape capture. He meets a young Englishman (Geoffrey Webb) who, like Williams, is using the service as a cover. Webb, the son of an earl, has been accused of forgery. Both have enlisted under pseudonyms. During battle Webb saves Williams' life, and the two men, thinking they will soon be killed, exchange confidences. Both, however, survive the war.

Following the armistice, Williams tries to locate his wartime buddy. He meets his friend's sister (Kathlyn Adams) and falls in love with her. He then learns that the earl is forced to retire because an unscrupulous foreign nobleman holds a political document that is detrimental to the earl, the girl's father. Williams journeys to the mythical principality of Malmatia and secures the paper after several harrowing exploits. He returns to England and marries his friend's sister. His army companion, suffering from the effects of the war, does not recall Williams' confession concerning his criminal background. ■

Sink or Swim (1920), Fox. *Dir.* Richard Stanton; *Sc.* Edward Sedgwick, Ralph Spence; *Cast includes:* George Walsh, Enid Markey, Joe Dowling, Charles Elder, James O'Shea.

Court intrigue in a mythical country ensnares a young American in this satirical comedy adventure. George Walsh portrays the young hero whose carefree life in the States compels his wealthy father to send him to Lithoonia on family business. Meanwhile, that country is about to erupt in a revolution instigated by the traitorous prime minister. Walsh intercedes in behalf of the beautiful princess who is about to lose her throne. He succeeds almost single-handedly in defeating the chief villain and his henchmen and preserving the title for the heroine. ■

Sky High (1922), Fox. *Dir.* Lynn Reynolds; *Sc.* Lynn Reynolds; *Cast includes:* Tom Mix, Eva Novak, J. Farrell MacDonald, Sid Jordan, William Buckley.

Cowboy star Tom Mix portrays an immigration bureau agent assigned to investigate a gang of smugglers operating in the vicinity of the Grand Canyon in this fast-paced action drama. The outlaws have been busy smuggling large numbers of illegal Chinese into the States. Mix maneuvers his way into the good graces of the gang so that he can uncover their operations and capture the elu-

sive chief. At one point he rescues the heroine who happens to be the ward of the leader. Although chiefly a western, the film employs an airplane and cars for added thrills. Much of the action involves chases and escapes along the ridges and cliffs of the Grand Canyon. ■

Sky High (1952), Lippert. *Dir.* Samuel Newfield; *Sc.* Orville Hampton; *Cast includes:* Sid Melton, Mara Lynn, Sam Flint, Doug Evans, Fritz Feld, Mark Crah.

A known saboteur's look-alike is enlisted by army intelligence to help in the capture of a gang of enemy agents in this weak service comedy. Sid Melton, as a slow-witted private stationed at an air force base, happens to resemble a dangerous spy. A U.S. intelligence officer, concerned about the possible theft of plans for a secret new airplane, orders Melton to pose as the saboteur so that he can gain the confidence of the other spies. The G.I.'s blundering eventually leads to the capture of the nest of agents. Mara Lynn portrays a waitress at the local base in this poorly conceived and executed comedy. ■

Sky High Saunders (1927), U. *Dir.* Bruce Mitchell; *Sc.* Bruce Mitchell; *Cast includes:* Al Wilson, Bud Osborne, Elsie Tarron, Frank Rice.

Al Wilson portrays a dual role in this inept melodrama about a gang of smugglers who use airplanes for their illegal enterprise. One brother, thought killed in France during World War I, works for smugglers. His twin, a member of the U.S. Air Patrol, kills his brother during a dogfight. He then assumes the dead man's identity and infiltrates the gang. Elsie Tarron, who plays the female lead, eventually learns of the switch but nevertheless falls in love with the air patrol officer. Frank Rice, who portrays a mechanic, handles the weak comedy routines. ■

Sky Liner (1949), Screen Guild. *Dir.* William Berke; *Sc.* Maurice Tombragel; *Cast includes:* Richard Travis, Pamela Blake, Rochelle Hudson, Steven Geray, Creg McClure, Gaylord Pendleton.

An F.B.I. agent is on the trail of a spy who is trading government documents to an unnamed foreign power in this mystery drama set chiefly aboard a passenger plane. Richard Travis portrays the government agent. Gaylord Pendleton is the spy traveling with his gal, played by Rochelle Hudson. Also aboard, among other passengers, is Steven Geray, as the secret agent representing the foreign country. After Pendleton is killed during the flight, Travis assumes official control of the investigation, which ends in a climactic shoot-out with Geray the loser. Pamela Blake, as the airline hostess, serves chiefly in a decorative capacity. ∎

Lobby card for *Sky Murder* (1940), the last entry in MGM's Nick Carter series featuring Walter Pidgeon as the detective.

Sky Murder (1940), MGM. *Dir.* George B. Seitz; *Sc.* William R. Lipman; *Cast includes:* Walter Pidgeon, Donald Meek, Kaaren Verne, Edward Ashley, Joyce Compton, Tom Conway.

The weakest and last of the three Nick Carter detective series starring nonchalant Walter Pidgeon as the master sleuth, this World War II spy entry concerns a group of espionage agents. A senator asks Carter to help in the capture of enemy agents who have already murdered a suspected spy aboard a plane and have targeted another victim, played by Kaaren Verne. The routine plot and sleuthing contribute little suspense or action to further events, except to the demise of the series. Once again, Donald Meek, that wonderful character player, adds some comic relief. Tom Conway, in a minor role, was to emerge shortly as the star of his own detective series in the role of the Falcon. ∎

Sky Parade, The (1936), Par. *Dir.* Otho Lovering; *Sc.* Brian Marlow, Byron Morgan, Arthur Beckhard; *Cast includes:* Jimmie Allen, William Gargan, Katherine DeMille, Kent Taylor, Grant Withers, Sid Saylor.

Foreign agents attempt to steal a robot plane invented by three former World War I heroes in this action drama aimed at a juvenile audience. William Gargan, Kent Taylor and Robert Fiske portray the ex-air aces who continue their flying careers as barnstormers and commercial pilots. After the trio successfully develop an airplane that can be controlled from the ground, a gang of spies, led by Grant Withers, tries to get its hands on the invention. Action includes several fist fights and flying stunts. Katherine DeMille provides some minor romantic interest, and Sid Saylor contributes to the comic relief. Jimmie Allen, a popular radio star of the period, plays himself in the last half of the film, contributing to the exciting climax. ∎

Sky Patrol (1939), Mon. *Dir.* Howard Bretherton; *Sc.* Joseph West, Norman S. Parker; *Cast includes:* John Trent, Marjorie Reynolds, Milburn Stone, Jackie Coogan, Jason Robards, Bryant Washburn.

Another entry in the "Tailspin Tommy" series based on the comic strip character created by Hal Forrest, this airplane drama concerns the smuggling of ammunition across the U.S. border. John Trent as the title hero, Milburn Stone as Trent's sidekick, and Marjorie Reynolds as a stewardess are the three mainstays of the series. They eventually frustrate the schemes of the leader of the smugglers (Leroy Mason) and his gang. Jackie Coogan, former child star of the silents, portrays the son of a colonel who leads a school of young cadets interested in flying. Young Coogan, who displays a fear of guns, is shot down and reported missing. Tailspin Tommy, in charge of training the cadets, searches for the missing student and discovers a suspicious airship as well as the smugglers. ∎

Smashing the Spy Ring (1939), Col. *Dir.* Christy Cabanne; *Sc.* Arthur T. Horman, Dorrell McGowan, Stuart McGowan; *Cast includes:* Ralph Bellamy, Fay Wray, Regis Toomey, Walter Kingsford, Ann Doran, Warren Hull.

Enemy agents attempt to sabotage the production of U.S. government military supplies in this low-budget pre-World War II drama. Ralph Bellamy, as a special agent assigned to the case, poses as a scientist suffering from amnesia. Supposedly in possession of a secret poison-gas formula, he enters the hospital where the spies are located. He eventually puts an end to the spy network. Fay Wray plays the sister of a government agent who has been killed trying to apprehend the gang. Walter Kingsford portrays the leader of the saboteurs whose main mission is to steal government military equipment plans. Regis Toomey appears as Bellamy's sidekick. ∎

Smiles (1919), Fox. *Dir.* Arvid E. Gillstrom; *Sc.* Ralph H. Spence; *Cast includes:* Jane and Katherine Lee, Ethel Fleming, Val Paul, Carmen Phillips, Charles Arling.

A film designed to exploit the popularity of the impish Lee sisters, this World War I comedy concerns their helping to capture a nest of German spies. Involved in the simple story is a young hero whose romantic advances are rejected by the aunt of the young sisters. She thinks he is a slacker. The young man, working under cover, is actually an operative with U.S. intelligence and is on the trail of enemy agents. When the spies kidnap the heroine, he pursues them and engages them in a wild battle. Finally, the children appear by parachute and help him rescue his future wife and arrest the spies. Most of the laughs come from the children's slapstick antics. ∎

Society Smugglers (1939), U. *Dir.* Joe May; *Sc.* Arthur T. Horman, Earl Fenton; *Cast includes:* Preston Foster, Irene Hervey, Walter Woolf King, Frank Jenks, Fred Keating, Regis Toomey.

The Treasury Department places two of its special operatives inside a suspected diamond smuggling ring in an effort to gain evidence against the illegal operation in this standard drama. Preston Foster, as the chief agent, assigns Irene Hervey to seek employment with a luggage firm that Foster believes is a front for the smugglers. Walter Woolf King, as the head of the gang, cleverly arranges for winners of a slogan contest to be awarded with a European vacation and to journey with special luggage which conceals the diamonds.

Foster devises a plan to have another of his agents (Regis Toomey) act as one of the winners. However, the gang gets wise to the Treasury agent who is murdered during the trip to Europe. Foster, with his other able assistant, Hervey, finally gets the necessary evidence to convict King and his smugglers. The film, which ends in an exciting shoot-out, was adapted from the novel *Key Woman* by Joseph Steele. ∎

Sofia (1948), Film Classics. *Dir.* John Reinhardt; *Sc.* Frederick Stephani; *Cast includes:* Gene Raymond, Sigrid Gurie, Patricia Morison, Mischa Auer, John Wengraf, George Baxter.

A small group of Americans, conducting undercover activities behind the Iron Curtain, rescue several atomic scientists from the Reds in this far-fetched Cold War drama of intrigue set in the Balkans. Gene Raymond portrays a tough ex-O.S.S. agent who is a major part of the operation which frees key scientists destined for the U.S. Sigrid Gurie, as one of the rescued scientists, just happens to be Raymond's former sweetheart. Patricia Morison, as a nightclub singer, is a double agent who exchanges information with both Western and East-bloc spies. This was one of the first spy dramas to be filmed in Cinecolor. See Office of Strategic Services. ∎

Sol Madrid (1968), MGM. *Dir.* Brian Hutton; *Sc.* David Karp; *Cast includes:* David McCallum, Stella Stevens, Telly Savalas, Rip Torn, Pat Hingle, Ricardo Montalban.

A U.S. secret agent poses as a drug buyer in an effort to smash a drug-smuggling operation involving the Mafia and other dealers based in Mexico in this fast-paced drama. David McCallum, as the government agent, is first assigned to find a former member of the mob who has stolen half-a-million dollars from the crime bosses. McCallum must try to persuade the man on the run (Pat Hingle) to give evidence against the Mafia. To help him find Hingle, the agent has Hingle's mistress (Stella Stevens) lead him to her former lover.

The remainder of the film takes place in and around Acupulco where McCallum masquerades as a drug dealer to help him infiltrate the operations. Ricardo Montalban portrays a local Mexican contact. Telly Savalas plays a small-time heroin pusher. Rip Torn is the drug kingpin. Paul Lukas, a leading screen personality during the 1930s and 1940s, appears as an elder statesman of the Mafia. The film, based on the novel *Fruit of the Poppy* by Robert Wilder, concentrates more on plot and character development than on gadgetry—an almost obligatory element of the spy dramas of the 1960s. ∎

Soldier, The (1982), Embassy. *Dir.* James Glickenhaus; *Sc.* James Glickenhaus; *Cast includes:* Ken Wahl, Klaus Kinski, William Prince, Alberta Watson, Jeremiah Sullivan.

Tartar leader Akim Tamiroff (2nd from r.) tries unsuccessfully to get Michael Strogoff's mother (Fay Bainter) to identify her son, a courier for the czar, in *The Soldier and the Lady* (1937).

Soviet agents, posing as terrorists, threaten to blow up half the world's supply of Middle East crude oil unless the Israelis pull out of the West Bank in this well-mounted but humorless action drama. The U.S. President threatens Israel with U.S. troops, but fails to force an Israeli withdrawal from the West Bank. He then sends in The Soldier—a C.I.A. superspy given carte blanche in dealing with world crises—to deal with the Soviet agents. Ken Wahl, as the expressionless agent, hopscotches around the globe in an effort to ply his brand of professional tactics against villains—with results that end in violence and bloodshed. Klaus Kinski portrays the chief culprit who steals the U.S. plutonium used as a threat to the Saudi Arabian oil. Jeremiah Sullivan portrays Wahl's fellow agent. Alberta Watson plays an attractive Israeli secret agent. William Prince portrays the U.S. President. See Central Intelligence Agency; K.G.B.; Mossad. ■

Soldier and the Lady, The (1937), RKO. *Dir.* George Nicholls, Jr.; *Sc.* Mortimer Offner, Anthony Veiller; *Cast includes:* Anton Wal-

brook, Elizabeth Allan, Margot Grahame, Akim Tamiroff, Fay Bainter, Eric Blore.

Based on *Michael Strogoff*, Jules Verne's novel of czarist Russia during the Tartar revolt of 1870, the film stars international actor Anton Walbrook in his American debut. He portrays Michael Strogoff, courier to the czar, who is sent on a special mission by Czar Alexander II to the Czar's brother. Carrying the plans for the defeat of the Tartars, Strogoff, traveling incognito, suffers a series of harrowing experiences before he reaches his mission. Others try to prevent him from completing his rendezvous, including an attractive spy (Margot Grahame) who works for the Tartar leader (Akim Tamiroff). After narrowly escaping a Tartar attack upon a barge and almost being permanently blinded by the Tartar chieftain, he reaches the Czar's brother in time for the Russian troops to defeat the enemy hordes in a spectacular battle.

American, French and German silent versions of the novel had appeared previously. The earliest feature was a Selig production released in 1914 that starred Jacob Adler, a popular actor of the Yiddish stage. RKO purchased the rights to the 1926 French adaptation and skillfully inserted many of the more exciting action scenes into its own film. ■

Soldiers of the Storm (1933), Col. *Dir.* D. Ross Lederman; *Sc.* Charles Condon, Horace McCoy; *Cast includes:* Regis Toomey, Anita Page, Barbara Weeks, Robert Ellis, Wheeler Oakman.

Regis Toomey, as an undercover agent for the U.S. border patrol, trails of a gang of smugglers who are using Mexico as a base for their operations in this action drama. Toomey poses as a stunt flier to throw off any suspicions of his real purpose. Following several flying sequences, a couple of murders and the rescue of a young woman whom the smugglers want to eliminate, Toomey helps in rounding up the culprits. Anita Page portrays the daughter of a politician. ■

Solomon King (1974), Sal/Wa. *Dir.* Sal Watts, Jack Bomay; *Sc.* Sal Watts; *Cast includes:* Sal Watts, "Little Jamie" Watts, Claudia Russo, Felice Kinchelow, Samaki Bennett, Louis Zito.

A C.I.A. agent helps a former Green Beret fighter carry out a raid against insurgents in a Middle East sheikdom in this inept action drama. Sal Watts, who portrays a California nightclub owner, seeks to avenge the murder of his ex-girlfriend (Claudia Russo). When Watts, once with the Green Berets, learns that the killers' headquarters are in an unnamed Middle East country, he summons his Vietnam buddies and his brother ("Little Jamie" Watts) to join him in his venture. Louis Zito, as the C.I.A. agent, joins the small raiding party in their bloody attack. See Central Intelligence Agency. ■

Somewhere in France (1916), Triangle. *Dir.* Charles Giblyn; *Cast includes:* Howard Hickman, Louise Glaum, Joseph Dowling, Fanny Midgley, Jerome Storm, George Fisher.

Based on the 1915 novel by Richard Harding Davis, the drama opens in Paris during World War I. The mistress of a French air force captain steals a set of fortification plans of the city he has drawn. She sells them to the Germans and advances her career in German intelligence in Berlin. Meanwhile the French captain, who is arrested and found guilty of irresponsibility, commits suicide. His brother, who vows revenge, enters the spy's employ when she returns under the guise of a French countess. He exposes her spy operations and she is arrested. See German Intelligence: World War I. ■

Son of a Sailor (1933), FN. *Dir.* Lloyd Bacon; *Sc.* Ernest Pagano, Al Cohn, Paul Gerrard Smith, H. M. Walker; *Cast includes:* Joe E. Brown, Jean Muir, Thelma Todd, Johnny Mack Brown, Frank McHugh.

Joe E. Brown stars in this service comedy about a wacky sailor whose absurd antics get him into hot water with his buddies and superiors. He finagles a 24-hour pass and spends his day in port trying to get a date for the evening. One charming young woman he meets happens to be an admiral's granddaughter (Jean Muir). Unaware of this fact, he boasts about his close association with navy officials. She then invites him to dinner where his supposed "friends" are gathered.

He gets himself involved in other comic misadventures, including boarding an abandoned vessel that is about to be bombed in target practice, challenging a champion fighter in an exhibition boxing match and sparring with a rough butler. He accidentally redeems himself by capturing a spy, a guest at the admiral's home, who has stolen the plans for a secret automatic-pilot device from a lieutenant's room. The last scene shows Brown aboard his fighting ship being decorated for bravery and promoted. Johnny Mack Brown portrays an officer who is in love with Muir. Thelma Todd, as the spy's sultry accomplice, attempts to seduce Brown while her partner steals the plans. ■

Song of Love, The (1924), FN. *Dir.* Chester Franklin, Frances Marion; *Sc.* Frances Marion; *Cast includes:* Joseph Schildkraut, Norma Talmadge, Arthur Edmund Carewe, Laurence Wheat, Maude Wayne, Earl Schenck.

The drama, set in French-ruled Algeria, stars Norma Talmadge as a dancer who attracts the fancy of a belligerent tribal chief. He is bent on driving the foreigners from North Africa in a holy war. A French secret agent (Joseph Schildkraut) is dispatched to defuse the explosive situation. He not only foils the Arab leader's plans but wins the love of Talmadge as well. There are several action sequences between the native dissidents and the colonials. The film was adapted from Margaret Peterson's novel *Dust of Desire.*

Aside from the obvious and hackneyed romantic plot, the bellicose tribal chief suggests the real-life exploits of Abd el-Kader, an Algerian Muslim leader. Attempting to stem the flow of French colonists into his homeland, he led a holy war against them in the mid-1800s. After defeating the French in two wars, he was finally beaten in a third engagement by an overwhelmingly superior force. ∎

S.O.S. Coast Guard (1937), Rep. *Dir.* William Witney, Alan James; *Sc.* Franklyn Adreon, Barry Shipman; *Cast includes:* Ralph Byrd, Bela Lugosi, Maxine Doyle, Herbert Rawlinson, Richard Alexander, Lee Ford.

A crazed inventor develops a highly destructive disintegrating gas that threatens the international community in this 12-chapter serial. U.S. Coast Guard Lieutenant Terry (Ralph Byrd) is assigned to prevent the inventor (Bela Lugosi) from selling his deadly gas to a foreign power. The gas, which can be placed in small bombs, ten of which has enough power to annihilate a major city. Maxine Doyle portrays a curious reporter who more often hinders than helps Byrd foil a host of agents working for the inventor. Made chiefly for the juvenile market, the serial offers the usual fast action, chases and plenty of fist fights. Ralph Byrd, who had played the title role in the serial *Dick Tracy* earlier that same year, was to be plagued by the identification. Unable to shake the Tracy image, he returned to make several more Tracy serials and a handful of feature films, chiefly as the square-jawed comic-strip detective. ∎

South of Panama (1941), PRC. *Dir.* Jean Yarbrough; *Sc.* Ben Roberts, Sidney Sheldon; *Cast includes:* Roger Pryor, Virginia Vale, Lionel Royce, Lucian Prival, Duncan Renaldo.

A weak drama about international spies determined to steal a secret formula for invisible paint, the film gets bogged down in routine melodrama and stereotyped characters. Roger Pryor portrays the hero who foils the plot of the foreign agents and woos the heroine, played by Virginia Vale, in this low-budget film. Duncan Renaldo, a relatively minor character in this B drama, later starred in his own series of westerns, the Cisco Kid. In the 1950s Renaldo repeated the role in a television series which brought him greater recognition. Co-screenwriter Sidney Sheldon later became a best-selling novelist. ∎

A member of an international spy network plies his trade as his gang tries to steal a secret formula in *South of Panama* (1941).

Southern Yankee, A (1948), MGM. *Dir.* Edward Sedgwick; *Sc.* Harry Tugend; *Cast includes:* Red Skelton, Brian Donlevy, Arlene Dahl, George Coulouris, Lloyd Gough, John Ireland.

Red Skelton portrays a bungling bellhop who daydreams about catching Confederate spies for the U.S. Secret Service in this Civil War comedy. Working in a St. Louis, Missouri, hotel, he spends more time nettling a Union colonel to employ him as a secret agent than he does at his job. The colonel, however, has more serious concerns. The South's most successful spy, known as the Gray Spider, has infiltrated the North's top brass and has been stealing all of its military maps and plans.

Skelton, while delivering a major's uniform to one of the hotel rooms, stumbles upon the officer's true identity. He is the notorious Gray Spider. When the spy (George Coulouris) returns to his room, a scuffle ensues and Skelton accidentally knocks the spy unconscious and assumes his identity. He then notifies the Union colonel and the spy is arrested. The colonel then sends the reluctant Skelton, who would rather catch spies than impersonate one, behind enemy lines with false battle plans.

The comic predicaments depend chiefly on false identities, mix-ups, chases and slapstick. There are some clever moments, including one scene in which Skelton, caught in the middle of a battle, half-clothes himself in a Yankee uniform while his other side displays a Confederate uniform. Carrying flags of both armies, he nonchalantly parades between both forces who cheer his bravery. When the wind reverses the flags, both armies begin to fire upon him. Verbal humor, for the most part, is weak, although there is one bright spot when the exasperated Union colonel tries to spell out Skelton's dual mission: to turn over the false map to a Confederate officer and give a secret paper to a fellow agent. "The paper's in the pocket of the boot with the buckle, and the map is in the packet in the pocket of the jacket," the officer explains. Naturally, this befuddles our hero.

Other cast members help to move the farce along. Arlene Dahl, as a Southern belle and part-time spy, falls in love with Skelton, whom she mistakes for the real Gray Spider. Brian Donlevy plays a war profiteer and Dahl's suitor. Jealous of her attention to Skelton, Donlevy tries desperately to remove his competition. John Ireland, as a Confederate captain in league with Donlevy, is continually frustrated by Skelton's antics.

Sylvan Simon, who actually directed the film, was taken off the credits by the studio when he objected to reshooting minor scenes unnecessarily. According to an interview with Red Skelton, the studio, fearful of bringing in the picture under budget, ordered more retakes. The executives were afraid that the bankers would insist that future films adhere to this lower budget. Director Edward Sedgwick was then assigned the task of taking the comedy over the budget. Silent screen comedian Buster Keaton, who made the classic Civil War comedy, *The General* (1927), helped to create several of the comic routines for Skelton. ■

Soviet spies in the U.S. Hollywood has concocted an assortment of Soviet-agent types operating within America's borders. They include those Americans influenced by greed or politics, refugees blackmailed to protect their families behind the Iron Curtain, Soviet spies recently arrived to accomplish a singular assignment and, perhaps the most pernicious of all, the Soviet spy planted in the U.S. years earlier who has assimilated into American society.

Large-scale Soviet surveillance of American activities began well before the Cold War which followed in the wake of World War II. A Soviet trading company, known as Amtorg, was founded in New York in the mid-1930s. Although it was a legitimate commercial business dealing with major American enter-

prises and involving millions of dollars, it also provided cover for hundreds of agents who posed as employees. These Soviet "workers" were dispersed to various cities where they recruited other agents, spied on military and industrial installations and purchased important documents and information which were then relayed to Moscow. In spite of sporadic exposés about Amtorg's harboring spies, the U.S. government dismissed these incidents as "minor."

The concept of Soviet spies thoroughly trained at home and transplanted to the U.S. to live quiet lives until called into service has its roots in reality. "Little America," a Soviet training school in the Ukraine, resembles a small American city. Instructors and recruits speak only English, use American money in simulated American stores and read American periodicals. Students may spend as much as five years here before they receive their U.S. assignment.

Several spy films allude to this unique training program. One of the earliest is *Flight to Tangier* (1953), about a Soviet agent sent to the U.S. in 1945 to establish his American citizenship; later, he attempts to carry out a plot designed to label the Americans as warmongers. *Man on a String* (1960), based on the true experiences of Hollywood producer Boris Morros, briefly depicts a Communist training program for spies destined for the U.S. In the thriller *No Way Out* (1987) Kevin Costner, as a highly respected U.S. naval officer working in the Pentagon, in reality is a Soviet agent who has been specially trained to play the role of an American. *Defense Play* (1988) opens with such a training program in progress somewhere in the Soviet Union. Young Soviet agents look, talk and dress like Americans as their military instructors observe them from a glass-enclosed booth. The otherwise minor drama *Little Nikita* (1988), with River Phoenix as the unaware son of ostensibly loyal American parents, explores this theme in more depth. The hapless teenager suddenly learns that his mother and father are trained Soviet agents who have been under cover in the U.S. for 20 years.

One of the most serious C.I.A. breaches in security was executed by a spy posing as a defector. Karl Koecher received three years' training as an agent in his native Czechoslovakia. He defected to the West in 1965 and within a few months emigrated with his wife to the U.S. He went to work for the C.I.A. in

1973 after receiving his Ph.D. in philosophy from Columbia University and becoming an American citizen. Along with turning over secret documents to the Soviets, he exposed the identity of a crucial C.I.A. contact in Russia who ended up committing suicide. Koecher and his wife in 1986 became part of an exchange agreement for Soviet dissident Natan Sharansky.

However, early Cold War films, in their haste and zest to expose the Red Menace, chiefly depicted Soviet agents in stereotyped terms reminiscent of the Axis screen spies of World War II. They threatened and bullied, sometimes murdered their own fellow agents and took women and children as hostages. They usually ended up facing a hail of bullets or perishing in some other horrible way that met with audience approval. Rarely were they allowed to express their ideology or talk about their personal lives. Even more rarely do they turn informant, as in *Project X* (1949), a low-budget drama about Soviet agents assigned to steal atomic secrets. They are exposed by one of their own party members who cooperates with U.S. government investigators.

Refugees were a vulnerable target in these early Cold War dramas. *Walk East on Beacon* (1952), for example, which is set in Boston, concerns a Soviet plot to steal secret scientific information from a refugee scientist (Finlay Currie). Agents threaten to kill his son who is living in Europe. Other innocents fell prey to Soviet spies. In *I Married a Communist* (1949), which lapses into an old-fashioned gangster melodrama, Robert Ryan, as an ex-Communist, is warned by his former party bosses that no one "quits" the party. They want him to foment labor trouble. *The Red Menace* (1950), a weak drama, shows how a variety of naive Americans, including a student and a black, are duped by Communists. In *The Destructors* (1968) John Ericson, as one of a Communist chief's cohorts, is a Korean War hero who has temporarily turned traitor as a result of Communist brainwashing.

Sometimes Hollywood blended the crime drama with the spy theme. In *A Bullet for Joey* (1955), for example, a Communist secret agent hires a former American gangster (George Raft) to kidnap an atomic physicist. *The Girl Who Knew Too Much* (1969) concerns Communist conspirators who are on the verge of gaining control of a powerful underworld syndicate for the purpose of weakening American trade.

Other films depict American scientists who turned to the Soviets for various reasons. *Walk a Crooked Mile* (1948) focuses on Soviet agents bent on stealing America's atomic secrets. They are assisted by a traitorous American scientist. In *The Thief* (1952) Ray Milland portrays a Washington-based American nuclear scientist who turns traitor.

More recent films have tended to soften the image of Soviet agents, depicting the more violent ones as renegades, acting independently. In *Telefon* (1977), for example, a hard-line Communist fanatic (Donald Pleasence), who is against a U.S.-Soviet move toward detente, tries to instigate a war between the two world powers. Charles Bronson, as another Russian agent, is assigned to stop him. In *Little Nikita* (1988) a ruthless and dangerous Soviet agent is killing fellow agents in an attempt to blackmail the U.S.S.R. He demands $200,000 or he will continue to murder other agents in the U.S. A top Soviet spy is assigned to bring in the renegade.

Allegations about spies in the U.S. working for the Soviet Union have occasionally surfaced during the late 1980s and as late as 1990. K.G.B. defector Major Victor Ivanovich Sheymov, for example, said at a news conference (March 2, 1990) that "two sources" in the State Department fed various information to the Soviets during the 1970s. Sheymov, who had come to the U.S. in 1970 after working as a cipher specialist for the K.G.B., has been an American citizen since 1985. ∎

Space Master X-7 (1958), TCF. Dir. Edward Bernds; Sc. George Worthing Yates, Daniel Mainwaring; Cast includes: Bill Williams, Lyn Thomas, Robert Ellis, Paul Frees, Joan Barry, Thomas B. Henry.

This science-fiction suspense drama concerns the search by two U.S. security agents for a woman carrying a deadly alien organism which threatens mankind. Brought back from Mars during a research mission by a space satellite, the organism kills the scientist (Paul Frees) after he discovers its presence. It escapes from the laboratory by way of Lyn Thomas, who portrays the scientist's girlfriend. Bill Williams and Robert Ellis, as the U.S. agents, are assigned to find Thomas before the organism contaminates others. Moe Howard, better known to audiences as one of the Three Stooges comedy team, adds some comedy relief in his portrayal of a cab driver. ■

Spanish-American War (1898).

Just as Turkey was considered the "sick man of Europe" at the end of the nineteenth century, the Spanish Empire in the Americas was in a similarly debilitating position at the same time. Although Spain was able to subjugate the colonial peoples of Cuba, Puerto Rico and the Philippines, it was unprepared for conflict with a major world power—which the United States had become.

U.S. intelligence during this period was not sophisticated, but it proved effective against Spain. Captain Andrew Rowan was chief of the map section of the Military Information Division of the U.S. Army. On the eve of the war he was dispatched to Cuba together with a group of Cuban rebels and landed in that country on April 24, 1898. Rowan established contact with rebel General Garcia in Oriente Province and made plans to synchronize U.S. military operations with the rebels. Garcia also furnished the American with local maps.

Navy Lt. Victor Blue joined rebel General Maximo Gomez in the central provinces of Cuba; Gomez, like Garcia, provided valuable local military data.

Prior to the war, U.S. Captain Martin Hellings had molded a group of American Western Union telegraphers in Cuba into an espionage network. When Spanish Admiral Cervera telegraphed the Spanish forces in Havana that he was bringing his fleet into the harbor in Santiago, the Western Union telegraphers intercepted the message and relayed it to American forces in Key West, Florida. U.S. ships of the North Atlantic Fleet immediately set sail for Santiago and blocked Cervera's fleet in the harbor.

Following his Declaration of War against Spain on April 22, 1898, President McKinley dispatched Admiral George Dewey to the Philippines whereupon the Americans devastated the Spanish fleet in Manila Bay. While Dewey lay siege to Manila, Spanish Admiral Manuel de la Camara prepared another fleet at Cadiz, Spain, for attack upon Dewey's forces. The quickest route to the Philippines lay through the Suez Canal. Meanwhile, paid American spies reported the progress of the Spanish fleet along its route. Lt. William Sims of the Office of U.S. Navy Intelligence employed all sorts of agents, including Italians, French aristocrats and retired Swedish Army officers, from Madrid to the Canary Islands to the Suez Canal.

The Spanish espionage effort during the war was centered in Montreal where Lt. Ramon Carranza located his network. Prior the the war Carranza had used the Pinkerton Detective Agency in the U.S. to spy on Cuban emigrés. In Canada, Carranza hired Frank Mellor, a private detective, who was to join the American army, together with other Canadians in Spanish employ. After landing in Cuba, Mellor and the other agents were to cross Spanish lines and report their findings.

U.S. Secret Service agents had been following Carranza from Washington where he had been naval attaché before the outbreak of hostilities to Montreal. Carranza was observed contacting George Downing, an English immigrant to the U.S. Downing's mail was intercepted, confirming he had passed secret naval war plans to the Spanish. When Carranza's espionage activities were proven to neutral Canada, he was expelled for violating that country's laws. Mellor and his agents were simultaneously picked up on the American side of the border by the U.S. Secret Service.

Unfortunately, these colorful espionage events were largely overlooked in the few spy films about the war. Instead, the dramas relied on conventional plots and characters. In *Lucille Love, the Girl of Mystery* (1914), an early silent serial, an archvillain steals military plans from an army lieutenant stationed in the Philippines. Two disappointing action dramas were produced about Andrew Rowan's mission in Cuba: a silent version titled *A Message to Garcia* (1916), featuring a female protagonist who assists Rowan, and the sound remake, *A Message to Garcia* (1936). Wallace Beery received top billing and dominated the screen instead of John Boles, who portrayed Rowan. In *Santiago* (1956), set on the eve of the war, a pretty Cuban agent persuades a mercenary American gunrunner (Alan Ladd) to get involved in Cuba's struggle for independence against Spain. The film opens in Tampa, Florida, the "jumping-off place for contraband shipments to Cuba," Ladd delivers rifles and gunpowder to Cuban agents. ■

Speed King (1923), Goldstone. *Dir.* Gordon Jones; *Cast includes:* Richard Talmadge, Virginia Warwick, Mark Fenton, Harry Van Meter.

Acrobatic screen personality Richard Talmadge plays a dual role in this action drama about foreign intrigue involving two fictitious European countries. As a famous American motorcycle racer, Talmadge is invited to compete in a foreign land. Once he arrives, a group of secret agents representing a rival nation pays him to impersonate the king whom he closely resembles. Unknown to Talmadge, the traitors are using him to gain some territory for a neighboring power. Once the American racer learns the truth, he swings into action and saves the kingdom for the rightful ruler. At one point Talmadge is captured and sentenced to death for impersonating the king, but the ruler rescues his look-alike in the nick of time. ∎

Spies Like Us (1985), WB. *Dir.* John Landis; *Sc.* Dan Aykroyd, Lowell Ganz, Babaloo Mandel; *Cast includes:* Chevy Chase, Dan Aykroyd, Mark Stewart, Sean Daniel, Bruce Davison, William Prince.

Two incompetent U.S. intelligence agents, unaware that they are being used as decoys to distract the Soviets, end up as heroes when they prevent a U.S.-Soviet nuclear war in this occasionally funny comedy. Chevy Chase and Dan Aykroyd, as two bumbling government employees seeking to advance themselves from their humdrum jobs, take an examination for the Foreign Service Department and are caught cheating. To their surprise, they are selected for special training as spies and sent by parachute near the Afghan border on a secret mission. They are unaware that they are only decoys while their superiors have sent two experienced agents to take control of a mobile Soviet missile launcher in the area. Following several misadventures, including their encounter with a band of Afghan freedom fighters, their escape from a pair of Russian agents and their meeting up with the actual spy team, they manage to help complete the mission.

The film starts off menacingly enough, showing the Soviets installing their most powerful rocket in a remote forest on their border. A U.S. spy satellite spots the weapon and sets off the series of misadventures involving Chase, who has some diplomacy skills, and Aykroyd, a code-breaker with language abilities. Perhaps the most outlandish sequence is Chase's attempts at cheating during the examination. He has answers written on the inside of a phony eye patch, on a long sheet of paper hidden inside his mouth, and on notes stuffed in his pockets—all of which immediately raise the ire of the proctor. Some of the verbal gags are on target. After rigorous training at a special combat school for spies, our two reluctant heroes have second thoughts about their upcoming mission and approach their superior officer. "We'd like to go home now," Chase announces, "so thanks for the bruises and you can keep the stool samples." Later, when Aykroyd observes a pretty American doctor (Donna Dixon), whom they had met earlier, carrying a special aluminum case, he describes it to Chase: "It's a highly intelligent piece of hardware." "So she's a high-class intelligent piece," Chase concludes.

Much of the comedy comes at the expense of the military, represented here by a trigger-happy general (Steve Forrest). When he first learns about the missile launcher and the State Department's plans to send in spies to activate it so that U.S. can destroy it in space, Forrest is ecstatic. "We must make no mistake this time," he warns. "Our whole way of life hangs in the balance." Later, when American technology fails to blow up the Soviet missile, Forrest, prepared for such an emergency, presses the appropriate buttons to launch a nuclear war against the Soviet Union. "History illustrates conclusively," he explains, "that naive wishing for peace is the surest possible way to encourage an aggressor." Finally, he shows disappointment when Aykroyd, at the Soviet launch site, is able to deflect the missile so that it can be destroyed. ∎

Spirit of '17, The (1918), Par. *Dir.* William Taylor; *Sc.* Julia Ivers; *Cast includes:* Jack Pickford, G. H. Geldert, Edythe Chapman, L. N. Wells, Charles Arling, Virginia Ware.

A group of twelve-year-old boys, hungry for excitement and adventure, uncover a plot by German spies to stir up dissent among miners in this patriotic drama set during World War I. The goal of the enemy agents is to have the mine put out of commission, thereby crippling American war production. Young Jack Pickford (Mary's brother) plays the leader of the youngsters. He calls upon the residents of a veterans' home to help him capture the alien agents. Based on a story by Judge Willis Brown of the Chicago Juvenile Court, the film was advertised as a "red, white and blue story . . . vibrant with patriotism."

Several World War I dramas dealing with the home front focused on the importance of labor in the war effort. In *The Road to France* (1918) the hero breaks up a German plot to foment a strike at a shipyard. *Safe for Democracy* (1919) attacks members of the International Workers of the World, a radical union of the period, equating them with foreign agents trying to sabotage war production. See Labor Unrest. ∎

Splendid Hazard, A (1920), FN. *Dir.* Arthur Rossen; *Cast includes:* Henry B. Walthall, Rosemary Theby, Norman Kerry, Ann Forrest, Thomas Jefferson.

Agents of the U.S. Secret Service become involved in this strange drama which concerns a mysterious figure who asserts that he is a descendant of Napoleon Bonaparte. The deranged character, portrayed by Henry B. Walthall, intends to regain the throne of France. Supported by a loyal group of followers, he seeks the lost emperor's treasure, a search that takes him to France, the U.S. and finally to Corsica. Unfortunately for the pretender, he is killed in a duel before he can prove his case. Rosemary Theby plays a young woman who falls in love with Walthall. But his obsession with his destiny leaves him emotionally unresponsive to her overtures. ∎

Splendid Sinner, The (1918), Goldwyn. *Dir.* Edwin Carewe; *Cast includes:* Mary Garden, Hamilton Revelle, Anders Randolph, Henry Pettibone, Roberta Bellinger.

An American Red Cross nurse agrees to deliver a document to the Allies during World War I and pays for her heroism with her life in this drama. Mary Garden, as the mistress of a rich German (Anders Randolph), decides to leave her lover after a quarrel. She meets a handsome young physician (Hamilton Revelle) who falls in love with her and they marry. They move to New York where the husband falls on hard times. His wife, desperate to help him, visits a gambling house and wins substantial sums of money. The establishment is owned by her former lover who wants to renew their relationship, but the happily married woman refuses. The German vindictively reveals Garden's past to her husband who, in a moment of anger, leaves her. He enlists in the Canadian army and is sent to France. His wife, meanwhile, joins the Red Cross. Assigned to a hospital in a section of France which is occupied by the Germans, she meets her husband. He asks her to carry an important document through enemy lines. She agrees and is captured. As she faces a firing squad, she receives a note from her former German lover that he would spare her life if she resumes her former relationship with him. She destroys the note and is shot. ∎

Springfield Rifle (1952), WB. *Dir.* Andre DeToth; *Sc.* Charles Marquis Warren, Frank Davis; *Cast includes:* Gary Cooper, Phyllis Thaxter, David Brian, Paul Kelly, Lon Chaney, Phil Carey.

A Union officer (Gary Cooper) masquerades as an outlaw to discover who is stealing government horses in this Civil War action drama. A western cavalry post is plagued by a gang of rustlers who steal the mounts as they are being shipped to Union troops and sell them to the South. A Union colonel contrives a plan that cashiers Cooper out of the service on charges of cowardice. Cooper's wife (Phyllis Thaxter) and son are not aware of the scheme that allows Cooper to join the outlaws and eventually round up the miscreants, particularly the commander of the army post (Paul Kelly), who is in reality a Southern sympathizer. David Brian plays the leader of the rustlers. The title refers to the new model of rifle that Cooper tests during his exploits and that was to become standard army issue. The film, set in 1864, describes the origins of the Army Intelligence Department. ∎

Spy, The (1914), Universal. *Dir.* Otis Turner; *Sc.* James Dayton; *Cast includes:* Herbert Rawlinson, Edna Maison, Ella Hall, William Worthington, Edward Alexander, Rex De Rosselli.

Based on James Fenimore Cooper's novel about the American Revolution, the silent drama tells the story of a member of George Washington's household who works as a spy for the Commander in Chief. To protect the true identity and activities of the young man as he journeys back and forth across British lines, even Washington's own men do not know of the subterfuge. When they capture him, they think he is spying for the British and plan to execute him at one point in the story. The film has several rousing battle scenes.

Cooper's central character was allegedly based on an actual person. John Jay, the famous lawyer and judge, recounted to his friend Cooper the exploits of a secret agent assigned to gather information about British activities. ■

Spy, The (1917), Fox. *Dir.* Richard Stanton; *Sc.* George Bronson Howard; *Cast includes:* Dustin Farnum, Winifred Kingston, William Burress, Charles Clary, William E. Lowry, Howard Gaye.

The story takes place just prior to America's entry into World War I. Dustin Farnum portrays a frivolous young American who becomes aware that numerous German spies have infiltrated all aspects of life in the U.S. He decides to enlist in the secret service and is sent to Berlin to locate a book containing the names of German spies in America. With the aid of a young German woman who falls in love with him, he obtains the valuable book and turns it over to the American ambassador. But the couple are caught and tortured. Revealing nothing, they are sentenced to death. As they walk to their doom, they regret nothing. The idea for the film was probably prompted by a series of newspaper stories alleging a growing danger from German spies in the country. German spies were blamed for a series of mysterious explosions at munitions warehouses and elsewhere during the war. ■

Spy Chasers (1956), AA. *Dir.* Edward Bernds; *Sc.* Bert Lawrence, Jerome S. Gottler; *Cast includes:* Leo Gorcey, Huntz Hall, Bernard Gorcey, Leon Askin, Sig Ruman, Veolo Vonn.

The Bowery Boys tangle with foreign agents from the mythical land of Truania in this weak entry of their comedy series. Sig Ruman, who often plays villainous roles in spy dramas, appears as the king of the above country who is incognito in New York biding his time until he can return in safety. Meanwhile, schemers opposed to his return kidnap his daughter. Leo Gorcey and Huntz Hall, the mainstays of the Bowery Boys, stumble around engaging in their usual antics with Gorcey spouting aphorisms and Hall mugging his way through as stooge for Gorcey. They end up rescuing the pretty captive, after

which the king rewards the boys for their gallant efforts. ■

Spy comedies. The spy comedy became popular during World War I and has continued to entertain audiences until the present day. Except for Charlie Chaplin's *Shoulder Arms* (1918) and a few others, war comedies in general were not usually made until after the conflict. Major and minor studios offered their top screen personalities as well as many minor talents to the spy comedy genre. The popular Lee Sisters appeared in several spy comedies. In *Doing Their Bit* (1918) they are shipped to America from Ireland to live with an uncle who owns a munitions plant. They soon help to expose a group of spies who are plotting against the factory. *Smiles* (1919) has the children help in the capture of more foreign agents. George Walsh portrays a navy reject in *I'll Say So* (1918) who gets mixed up with some German spies on the Mexican border.

Spy comedies became a Hollywood staple during World War II. *All Through the Night* (1941), starring Humphrey Bogart, is a comedy drama about spies and hoodlums in New York City. The plot involves Nazi agents who plan to blow up a battleship in a local harbor. The East Side Kids in such low-budget entries as *Bowery Blitzkrieg* and *Flying Wild*, both released in 1941, and *Junior Army* and *Let's Get Tough!*, both 1942, engage in their usual low comedy as they clash with foreign agents. MGM's singing star Jeanette MacDonald and Robert Young journey to the Middle East in *Cairo*, a 1942 spy spoof, where MacDonald opens a secret pyramid by reaching the note of high C. In *Call Out the Marines* (1942) Victor McLaglen and Edmund Lowe repeat their familiar roles as Captain Flagg and Sergeant Quirt (using different names)— a pair of brawling leathernecks. In *The Lady Has Plans* (1942) Paulette Goddard is mistaken for a spy who has been temporarily tattooed with secret plans. Nazi and British agents attempt to undress her in an effort to read the alleged secrets.

By 1943 leading comedians of stage, screen and radio were making spy comedies. Laurel and Hardy in *Air Raid Wardens* (1943), after being rejected by the draft board, manage to stumble upon and capture a nest of Nazi agents. Stan and Ollie again become entangled in intrigue in *The Big Noise* (1944) when some spies plot to steal a superbomb. *Margin for Error* (1943), with its original premise of assigning Jewish policemen to guard a German consulate in New York, features Milton Berle as one of the officers. Bob Hope brought his one-liners and his portrayal of the reluctant hero to a string of successful comedies, including *My Favorite Blonde* (1942), *They Got Me Covered* (1943), *My Favorite Brunette* (1947) and *My Favorite Spy* (1951).

Spy comedies starring major comics continued well into the postwar years. Danny Kaye as a G.I. in *On the Double* (1961) is called upon to impersonate a British general whom he happens to resemble. Kaye becomes entangled with the general's chauffeur (Diana Dors) who turns out to be a German spy.

The basic plots were often similar—the awkward, reluctant hero thrown headlong into some intrigue, or accidentally stumbling onto a sinister plot, who somehow manages to triumph. He is not as clever as his plotting adversary. He is not as skilled with weapons as his opponents. But somehow he survives. Perhaps it is his instinct for survival, or his sense of moral justice, or his last-minute surge of rash courage which helps us identify with him.

These comedies do not portray a very complimentary picture of the U.S., since these inept heroes, who bear the brunt of the jokes, are often Americans. However, there are certain consolations. The comedy film, of course, is not an American phenomenon. Other nations have their own bumbling heroes. Also, within the context of spy comedies, other characters in addition to the hero are satirized, burlesqued and mocked. The pompous, the arrogant and the vain, all worthy targets of comedy, are universal. Comedy is democratic.

Finally, a nation that can laugh at itself reflects a people who have long nurtured the roots of security, confidence and freedom. "How do you expect to win the war with an army of clowns?" asks Schultz, a German guard in *Stalag 17*. "We sort of hope you'll laugh yourselves to death," an American prisoner of war quips. ■

Spy dramas: the silents. Plots about spies, double agents, enemy aliens and international intrigue have been with us since the birth of the American movie industry at the turn of the century. Ranging from crude silent one-reelers to sophisticated romantic dramas, spy films cover a variety of wars and world conflicts and take place in many countries. They generally contain the usual ingredients of other dramas—romance, adventure, suspense and, to a lesser degree, political intrigue. As a genre, they follow certain conventions. Heroes or heroines match wits with master spies who control a network of underlings. Secret weapons, military plans or important figures are the typical targets of unscrupulous domestic or foreign agents. Often, the fate of a nation hangs in the balance.

The themes of war, loyalty, greed and paranoia dominate the spy drama. Events may point to preparedness as the safest road for a nation, even if agents must steal another country's military plans. These films test the loyalties of their heroes and heroines. Agents are always on the prowl for the weak who are willing to accept money in exchange for information. National fear may set off a chain of unlikely events that seem to infringe upon one's freedoms—all for national security reasons, as in the spy films that emerged during the Cold War of the 1950s.

American spy films have ranged far and wide in their attempt to bring entertainment to their audiences. One of the earliest spy dramas, "The Hand of Uncle Sam" (1910), concerns an American in an unnamed foreign country who is accused of spying. He is rescued from a firing squad at the last minute when the Secretary of War sends a torpedo boat to the rescue. The real spy is captured and put to death. Several pre-World War I spy movies used the Civil War as background. In the one-reel short, "The Girl Spy Before Vicksburg" (1911), a daughter of the South disguises herself as a member of a Union convoy and destroys a powder wagon. A fisherman in "The Gray Sentinel" (1913) volunteers to act as a spy for the Confederates who are trying to run a Union blockade. Civil War films involving intrigue continued into the sound era, adding little to the genre and even less about the nature of the conflict. *Only the Brave* (1930), for example, tells of a Union captain (Gary Cooper) who volunteers as a spy. He purposely allows himself to be caught with false plans designed to mislead the Confederate general staff. In *Secret Service* (1931), based on William Gillette's popular Civil War play, Richard Dix, as a Union captain, dons a Confederate uniform to spy upon the enemy. The drama also appeared as a silent film in 1919.

Almost as many spy dramas about World War I were produced as those about the second global conflict. In *My Country First* (1916), one of the earliest, a Kaiser-like German spy attempts to steal the formula for a powerful explosive. *Somewhere in France* (1916) was one of the earliest World War I dramas to feature a female spy. After stealing secret plans from her French lover, Louise Glaum rapidly advances within the ranks of German intelligence. Dustin Farnum, as a U.S. Secret Service agent in *The Spy* (1917), journeys to Berlin to obtain a book which lists all the secret agents operating in America. He succeeds in finding the book and turns it over to the proper authorities but is later caught and sentenced to death as a spy. *Paws of the Bear* (1917), a romantic spy drama set chiefly in Belgium, concerns a young Russian agent (Clara Williams) and her American counterpart (William Desmond).

Sometimes spies were uncovered most unexpectedly and in the most unlikely places. Jack Mulhall, as an American prisoner of war interned in a German camp in *Flames of Chance* (1918), discovers that a letter from the States, when held near a candle, contains secret writing. Enemy agents in America, he realizes, are sending messages via this route to Germany. In *No Man's Land* (1918) a German agent on a remote Pacific island uses a wireless to feed information about Allied shipping to enemy raiders.

According to American films, the home front was no guarantee of safety from enemy machinations. As early as 1915 films were dramatizing the threat of spies on American shores. *Over Secret Wires* depicts German spies contacting submarines about American shipping off the coast of Oregon. By 1916 foreign agents were working in Washington trying to steal the formula for a high explosive, according to the drama *Paying the Price*. In *Miss Jackie of the Army* (1917) Marguerita Fischer, as the young heroine, overhears spies planning to blow up a troop train. Director Francis Ford in *Who Was the Other Man?* (1917) also portrays a stalwart secret service agent in hot pursuit of the "Black Legion," a nefarious group of saboteurs. Dorothy Dalton, as the promiscuous wife of an English captain in *The Dark Road* (1917), has an affair with an art connoisseur who in reality is a German spy. He learns from her husband's letters about secret troop movements and relays the information to his headquar-

ters. German spies set out to steal the plans for a new American rifle in *The Kaiser's Shadow* (1918) until they are foiled by U.S. Secret Service agent Thurston Hall and French spy Dorothy Dalton.

The year 1918 was a banner one for domestic spy dramas. Gloria Swanson, in such films as *The Secret Code*, *Shifting Sands* and *Wife or Country*, specialized in roles which depict her as a vulnerable female who is forced to spy for German agents. A similar fate befell Peggy Hyland, portraying a senator's wife in *Her Debt of Honor*. A German agent (Frank Schiller), after having an affair with her, tries to gain vital information for his own country. In *The Border Wireless* William S. Hart foils the plans of German agents to relay the location of General Pershing's troopship on its way to France. Cowboy star Tom Mix uncovers a plot by German spies to take over a tungsten mine in *Mr. Logan, U.S.A.*. Policeman Glenn White in *Love and the Law* stumbles across a plot by foreign agents to blow up a troop train. America's shipbuilding industry becomes the target of German spies in *The Road to France*. Jack Mulhall in *Madam Spy* impersonates a female agent so that he can capture a gang of spies. German agents attempt to destroy the sugar plantations of Hawaii in *The Marriage Ring*, with Enid Bennett, Robert McKim and Jack Holt. A pacifist wife in *Stolen Orders* steals secret information from her admiral husband to further the cause of her organization. In the romantic drama *Suspicion* the lonely wife of a research scientist has an affair with a German, unaware that he is a spy. England is the setting for *The Man Who Wouldn't Tell*, a drama involving the British secret service. In *Claws of the Hun*, with Charles Ray, German spies attempt to steal highly secret papers from an American munitions plant. Lewis Stone, as an English officer in *Inside the Lines* (1918), prevents the Germans from blowing up Gibraltar and crippling a large part of the English navy anchored there. Ralph Forbes appeared in a 1930 remake.

The war may have ended in 1918, but the conflict continued in the steady stream of spy dramas and comedies that appeared during the next two decades. Carlyle Blackwell, as an American secret agent in *Love in a Hurry* (1919), poses as a muleteer aboard a tramp steamer. In reality a New York millionaire who had unknowingly sold precious war matériel to German agents, he vows to expose the entire gang. *The Highest Trump* (1919), one of the earliest war films to focus on the use of airplanes in combat, features Earle Williams in a dual role. *Dangerous Days* (1920) takes place on the eve of World War I. German agents are bent on subverting the production of American munitions manufacturers. In 1921 the first of three screen versions of E. Phillips Oppenheim's popular novel *The Great Impersonation* appeared. A German agent who closely resembles an Englishman travels to Britain to replace his look-alike. A variation of the plot occurs in *Nazi Agent* (1941), starring the distinguished veteran actor Conrad Veidt. He appears in the dual role of twin brothers, one a loyal German-American and the other a Nazi spy. In *The Hidden Code* (1920) the inventor of a high explosive tattoos the secret formula on his daughter's shoulder. *Secret Orders* (1926) concerns enemy agents in the U.S. trying to learn about troop sailings. In *The Great Deception*, released the same year, an Englishman (Ben Lyon) educated in Germany becomes a double agent working for England. The plot anticipates *The Counterfeit Traitor* (1962), starring William Holden and Lilli Palmer.

It is difficult to measure the effects of these films on American audiences. They must have created a good deal of suspicion toward certain foreigners and concern about the potential vulnerability of the nation's secrets. ∎

Spy dramas: the talkies. The advent of sound no doubt helped the spy genre, which depends on dialogue more than the combat film. Stories of male and female spies, often having to choose between love and duty, filled the screen in dramas about World War I. George O'Brien, as an English spy in *True Heaven* (1929), falls in love with Lois Moran, a German agent. In *This Mad World* (1930) Basil Rathbone, as a French spy, decides to visit his mother living behind German lines. He falls in love with a German officer's wife who informs on him. Marlene Dietrich, as a streetwalker, is persuaded to pose as a German spy in *Dishonored* (1931). However, her new career is short-lived when she falls in love with an enemy agent (Victor McLaglen) and effects his escape. A military court sentences her to death for placing love before duty. In *The Gay Diplomat* (1931) Ivan Lebedeff portrays a handsome Russian officer. His reputation with women inspires Russian

intelligence to assign him to Bucharest to track down a female spy.

This romantic theme continued throughout the 1930s. Greta Garbo starred in *Mata Hari* (1932), based on the exploits of the most famous female spy. She succumbs to the same fatal flaw as Dietrich and pays the same heavy price. Constance Bennett, as a Russian agent in *After Tonight* (1933), falls in love with Austrian counterspy Gilbert Roland. In *Madame Spy* (1934) Fay Wray, as a Russian agent, marries the chief of the Austrian diplomatic service. *Lancer Spy* (1937), with George Sanders and Dolores Del Rio, provides a noteworthy culmination to the espionage dramas of World War I since it contained many of major elements of the genre. In a reversal of the Oppenheim plot mentioned above, Sanders plays a dual role—an English agent who doubles for a captured German officer and is sent back to Germany. Dolores Del Rio, as a German spy, falls in love with him.

Upon a second viewing, World War I spy dramas of the 1930s appear uniquely romantic and charming as the female spies more often than not choose love over duty. The lush settings and evocative atmosphere are often inaccurate but visually enjoyable. The gowns and hair styles, especially, seem more in tune with the Depression era than with the World War I years. The cat-and-mouse games between the male spy and his female counterpart from the enemy country appear quaint by today's standards.

American studios produced only a handful of spy dramas set in the politically turbulent 1930s. Rarer still were direct references to Hitler's National Socialism or Mussolini's and Franco's Fascism. The U.S. government, wishing to remain neutral in Europe's intensifying storm, frowned upon any film that criticized another country. Hollywood readily complied, not wishing to lose its lucrative foreign markets. *Cipher Bureau* (1938) features Leon Ames as the head of the counter-espionage cipher bureau. The agency is set up to foil hostile nations from sending secret messages to their agents in the U.S. In *The Spy Ring* (1938), with William Hall and Jane Wyman, unidentified enemy agents plot to steal the U.S. Army's latest anti-aircraft weapon.

World War II spy dramas began with a powerful, forthright exposé of German infiltration in the U.S. *Confessions of a Nazi Spy* (1939) stars Edward G. Robinson as an F.B.I.

agent who helps to unravel the web of spies. That same year Anna Sten played a European refugee in *Exile Express* pursued by foreign spies who need her to decipher a secret formula. The following year director Alfred Hitchcock turned out *Foreign Correspondent*, starring Joel McCrea, Laraine Day and George Sanders. More sophisticated but just as anti-German as its predecessors, the plot concerns an American reporter (McCrea) who becomes entangled in international intrigue in Europe. In *Flying Blind* (1941), with Richard Arlen and Jean Parker, foreign agents try to steal a newly developed transformer for use in fighter aircraft.

As soon as America entered the war, Hollywood studios cast their major stars in a variety of spy plots set in foreign lands. The atmospheric *Journey Into Fear* (1942), with Joseph Cotten, Dolores Del Rio and Orson Welles, spins a tale of intrigue involving munitions smuggling and Nazi spies aboard a vessel bound for Turkey. In *Berlin Correspondent* (1942) Dana Andrews, as an American radio correspondent in Berlin, comes into possession of highly secret Nazi war information. Robert Cummings in Alfred Hitchcock's suspenseful *Saboteur* (1942) portrays an innocent factory worker who is accused of destroying an aircraft plant. He eludes the police and pursues Norman Lloyd, the real saboteur, across the continent to clear his own name. Joan Crawford and Fred MacMurray, as American newlyweds honeymooning in Europe in the implausible but entertaining *Above Suspicion* (1943), are asked to spy for the Allies. That same year, George Raft in *Background to Danger* matches wits with Nazi and Russian agents in Turkey. Fritz Lang's *Ministry of Fear* (1944), about spies operating in England, overflows with intrigue, paranoia and deception—characteristics of *film noir*. Ray Milland, as a helpless victim, echoes another characteristic of the genre: "I wonder if you know what it means to stand all alone in a dark corner." *The Conspirators* (1944), set in Lisbon, features Hedy Lamarr as a young Frenchwoman married to a German official. Paul Henreid portrays a Dutch guerrilla leader hunted by the Nazis.

The low-budget studios, usually concerned with economics, found that spy stories were cheaper to produce than combat films which required larger casts, more special effects and larger sets. Most of these dramas pertained to the home front. Low-budget films, which also came from the major studios, continued throughout the war years and beyond. J. Edward Bromberg in *The Devil Pays Off* (1941) uncovers a plot involving a shipping tycoon who plans to sell his fleet to a potential enemy of the U.S. *Underground Agent* (1942) features Bruce Bennett as a government agent trying to prevent defense plant secrets from falling into enemy hands. *Black Dragons* (1942) features Bela Lugosi as a Nazi doctor bent on a trail of revenge after he is betrayed by the Axis powers. In *Busses Roar* (1942), featuring Richard Travis, a saboteur is foiled in his attempt to ignite an oil field as a signal to a Japanese submarine. *Spy Ship* (1942), with Craig Stevens and Irene Manning, concerns a network of spies who trade American military secrets about American ship departures to the enemy. In *Spy Train* (1943) Richard Travis steps off the bus and boards a train with fellow passengers, including Nazi agents. The flag-waving *Submarine Alert* (1943) features Richard Arlen as a foreigner and Wendy Barrie as a federal agent. Both help to prevent enemy agents from signaling a Japanese submarine off the Pacific coast. These dramas followed the conventions of the genre, rarely offering anything innovative in plot or theme.

Some of these B features were set elsewhere although they were all made in Hollywood's back lots. Often the exotic sets were more appealing than the routine plots. *Secret Agent of Japan* (1942), with Preston Foster and Lynn Bari, concerns espionage in an international settlement in Shanghai. Jon Hall dons a cloak of invisibility in *Invisible Agent* (1942) to create havoc among Nazi and Japanese leaders in Berlin. Special agent Robert Lowery in *Lure of the Islands* (1942) investigates enemy activity somewhere in the Pacific. The Pacific was also the setting of *Prisoner of Japan* (1942) where Japanese agents operating from an island threaten American warships. Leo Carrillo, Andy Devine and Don Terry teamed up in *Danger in the Pacific* (1942) to locate Nazi arms hidden on another island. The trio teamed up again for *Escape From Hong Kong* (1942), about German spies and an undercover agent (Marjorie Lord) working for British intelligence in Hong Kong. In *Half Way to Shanghai* (1942), set in Burma in 1942, Nazi agents attempt to get maps of Chinese defenses and ammunition depots. *Secrets of Scotland Yard* (1944), with Edgar Barrier, explored some of the methods employed by the Yard to break enemy codes. *Storm Over Lisbon* (1944), with Vera Hruba Ralston, Richard Arlen and Erich von Stroheim, told a familiar tale filled with the usual spies and other assorted villains.

Espionage at home was a popular subject for dramas from both major and minor studios. As early as 1940, foreign agents in *The Hidden Enemy* are trying to steal American secrets, specifically a metal two-thirds lighter than aluminum. Charles Farrell, as a G-man, poses as a Nazi agent in *The Deadly Game* (1941) so that he can round up a spy network. Saboteurs cause a series of fatal plane crashes in *Federal Fugitives* (1941) before Neil Hamilton puts a stop to them. Teenagers do their share at home in *Down in San Diego* (1941) by breaking up a spy ring at a naval base.

The home front as the setting for World War II spy dramas reached its peak in 1942. In *Dangerously They Live* hospital intern John Garfield rescues a recently arrived British agent (Nancy Coleman) from the clutches of Nazi spies. In *The Dawn Express*, also known as *Nazi Spy Ring*, Nazi agents attempt to steal the secret of a new type of gasoline known as "Formula 311" in this low-budget drama. A high explosive is the prize sought by secret agents in *Powder Town*, starring Edmond O'Brien as an eccentric scientist. Hollywood is the background for *Foreign Agent*, a 1942 drama in which Nazi spies have a double mission in the film capital. They desire the plans for a special light filter and attempt to persuade citizens to resist the war effort. Hitchcock's influence can be seen in several spy dramas in which an innocent person gets involved in a spy ring. Both Richard Carlson in *Fly by Night* (1942) and Robert Preston in *Pacific Blackout*, released the same year, face this dilemma.

As World War II continued to dominate the headlines and the thoughts of all Americans, movie audiences began to tire of war films and preferred escapism. Hollywood replied by producing fewer combat and spy films. *They Came to Blow Up America* (1943) concerns eight German saboteurs who are put ashore off Long Island, ultimately caught and brought to trial. In *Appointment in Berlin* (1943) George Sanders, secretly enlisted into the British secret service, poses as a German collaborator and journeys to Berlin. Character actors J. Carrol Naish and John Carradine were enemy agents in several low-budget

films, including *Waterfront* (1944), in which they both appear at their meanest as agents of the Nazis. *The House on 92nd Street* (1945), considered by many critics as one of the best spy dramas to emerge from World War II, reveals in semi-documentary style the story of how the F.B.I. prevented major military secrets, including the formula for the atomic bomb, from falling into the hands of Nazi agents operating in New York City.

Some wartime features combined the crime genre with the spy film. In *Dangerous Partners* (1945), for example, James Craig and Signe Hasso portray a couple who try to bilk an insurance company out of an inheritance, which is also coveted by a Nazi spy. *Quiet Please, Murder*, another crime-spy film with George Sanders, has Nazis involved with counterfeit copies of rare books. *Sabotage Squad* concerns a bookie, rejected by the draft, who sacrifices his life to prevent the destruction of an airplane factory. Finally, crime dominates the subject matter of *Main Street After Dark* (1944), a cautionary tale of a gang of pickpockets and small-time crooks who prey upon unwary servicemen. The crime-spy blend continued into the postwar period with such films as *The Safecracker* (1958), directed by and starring Ray Milland. Portraying the title character, Milland is released from an English prison by British intelligence and assigned to steal a list of Nazi agents from a Belgian chateau.

At times, the heroes of these home-front spy dramas were servicemen. In *The Marines Come Through* (1943) Wallace Ford plays a leatherneck hero who prevents Nazi agents from stealing a secret bombsight.

As with World War I spy movies, those of the Second World War continued well into the postwar period. *Cloak and Dagger* (1946), starring Gary Cooper as an American scientist and Lilli Palmer as an Italian partisan, involves Nazi Germany's experiments with atomic energy. That same year *O.S.S.*, starring Alan Ladd, and *13 Rue Madeleine*, with James Cagney, describe how American secret agents operated behind German lines during the war. Ray Milland, as a British agent in the wartime romantic drama *Golden Earrings* (1947), seeks refuge with a gypsy caravan. Marlene Dietrich, as a gypsy, falls in love with him. The highly entertaining and urbane *Five Fingers* (1952), starring James Mason as a suave valet to the English ambassador in Turkey and free-lance spy who sells photographed secrets to the Nazis, added a fresh approach and a sense of realism to the spy drama. *The Counterfeit Traitor* (1962), another highly acclaimed espionage drama, stars William Holden as an American businessman who poses as a Nazi sympathizer for British intelligence. Lilli Palmer, as an idealistic anti-Nazi agent who falls in love with Holden, is captured and executed by the Germans. *A Face in the Rain* (1963) featured Rory Calhoun in the familiar plot about an American agent who parachutes behind enemy lines and is pursued by Nazis.

Occasionally, films dealt with unrepentant postwar Nazis. In *Rendezvous 24* (1946) unconverted Nazi scientists after the war experiment with atomic energy which they plan to use to blow up major cities. *The Devil Makes Three* (1952), with Gene Kelly as a U.S. intelligence agent, concerns a secret plot hatched in postwar Germany to resurrect the Nazi party.

Spies played major roles in films about foreign revolutions and other wars. In *Conspiracy* (1939), which obliquely extols the virtues of democracy, an American (Allan Lane) gets mixed up with a revolution in a Central American country where the dictator is finally deposed. *The Fallen Sparrow* (1943), starring John Garfield, deals with events that occurred during the Spanish Civil War. Two years later Charles Boyer starred in *Confidential Agent*, another tale of intrigue about the Spanish Civil War. The Korean War figures in *Tokyo File 212* (1951), a story about Communist spies operating in Tokyo and influencing the outcome of the war.

Historical films were apt topics for spying. Jon Hall in *Brave Warrior* (1952) portrays an American agent whose mission is to ferret out those who are inciting the Indians to side with the British on the eve of the War of 1812. George Montgomery, as a British scout in *The Pathfinder* (1952), is assigned to spy on a French fort during the French and Indian War in this adventure based on James Fenimore Cooper's novel. The Napoleonic Wars furnish the backdrop for *Sea Devils* (1954), starring Yvonne De Carlo as a British spy and Rock Hudson as a smuggler. Hudson eventually rescues De Carlo, and they both escape with the plans for a French invasion.

Almost invariably (except for occasional entrepreneurs like James Mason), screen spies in most films from the early silent era through the early post-World War II decades were steadfast in their determination to serve their country, regardless of the many dangers. They sometimes were diverted by romantic interludes but returned ultimately to their assigned tasks. Enemy agents, just as dedicated to their causes, were relentless in their pursuits. Propaganda intruded often—by way of dialogue, speeches and incidents—as the heroes and heroines carried the war relentlessly to the enemy's back yard.

The movie spy has changed over the years. He has advanced from amateur to professional. World events and shifting values have made him cynical and ruthless. His weapons have become more sophisticated and deadly. More ambivalent and complex than his earlier counterpart, he is capable of suddenly switching sides, engaging in immoral or unethical practices or simply concluding a case by following his own private morality. In essence, he embodies the moral relativism and incongruities of modern twentieth-century man. "Have you noticed," a Soviet spy (Paul Scofield) muses to his American counterpart (Burt Lancaster) in *Scorpio* (1973), "that we are being replaced by young men with . . . a dedication to nothing more than efficiency? . . . Hardware men with highly complex toys and, except for language, not an iota of difference between the American model and the Soviet model."

Simultaneously, other cynical films about political intrigue and assassination appeared in the wake of the deaths of the Kennedys and Martin Luther King. Such downbeat dramas as *Executive Action* (1973) and *The Parallax View* (1974) suggested other nightmarish conspiracies. Led by specific or unknown influential forces, their insane world of power manipulation, political murder and paranoia often overwhelmed the protagonist, regardless of his courage and moral decency. See also Detectives and Spies; Women as Spies. ■

Spy Hunt (1950), U. *Dir.* George Sherman; *Sc.* George Zuckerman, Leonard Lee; *Cast includes:* Howard Duff, Marta Toren, Philip Friend, Robert Douglas, Philip Dorn, Walter Slezak.

This drama deals with an attempt to expose an assassination plot in an unnamed democratic European nation. Marta Toren portrays an agent who tries to smuggle some incriminating film about the assassination attempt out of the country. She hides it in the collar of a black panther. Howard Duff, as the innocent owner of two panthers, quickly falls in love with the female spy whom he helps to keep the film from falling into enemy hands. Meanwhile other agents (Philip Friend, Philip Dorn, Robert Douglas), desperate to retrieve the film, pursue Toren and Duff in this suspenseful tale. The film is based on the novel *Panther's Moon* by Victor Canning. ■

Spy in the Green Hat, The (1966), MGM. *Dir.* Joseph Sargent; *Sc.* Peter Allan Fields; *Cast includes:* Robert Vaughn, David McCallum, Jack Palance, Janet Leigh, Leticia Roman, Eduardo Ciannelli, Allen Jenkins.

Edited from entries in "The Man From U.N.C.L.E." television series, this theatrical version concerns a plot to change the course of the Gulf Stream. Jack Palance portrays the chief villain who wishes to wreak havoc on the U.S. Secret agents Napoleon Solo (Robert Vaughn) and Illya Kuryakin (David McCallum), Solo's assistant, are assigned to put an end to Palance's scheme. Janet Leigh, as one of Palance's agents, comes close to doing away with Solo's sidekick. An unabashed take-off on the James Bond series, this light film offers some of its own satire on gangster melodramas of the 1930s and includes some of the character players of that genre—sinister Eduardo Ciannelli, small-time hoodlums Allen Jenkins and Vince Barnett, and neurotic Elisha Cook, Jr. ■

Spy in the Sky (1958), AA. *Dir.* W. Lee Wilder; *Sc.* Myles Wilder; *Cast includes:* Steve Brodie, Sandra Francis, Andrea Domburg, George Coulouris, Bob De Lange, Hans Tiemeyer.

A U.S. intelligence agent is assigned to find a missing German scientist somewhere in Vienna in this weak drama made in Holland. The scientist (Hans Tiemeyer) has escaped from the Soviet Union, where he had been employed in that country's space program. Steve Brodie, as the secret agent concerned as much about his love life as his assignment, gets distracted by and mixed up in several romances with Sandra Francis and Andrea Domburg before he can accomplish his mission. The perennial villain and character actor George Coulouris portrays the head of the Communist spy network opposing the American agent. Brodie finally gains possession of the German scientist's important papers after he engages in several chases and some gun-

play. This poorly plotted and conceived film was adapted from the novel *Counterspy Express* by A. S. Fleischman. ■

Spy Ring, The (1938), U. *Dir.* Joseph H. Lewis; *Sc.* George Waggner; *Cast includes:* William Hall, Jane Wyman, Jane Carleton, Leon Ames, Ben Alexander, Don Barclay.

An army base is the setting for intrigue and romance in this weak drama. Enemy agents plot to steal the U.S. Army's latest anti-aircraft machine gun. Jane Carleton, as a blonde *femme fatale*, has already been responsible for the death of one army officer in her attempt to secure the secret plans. William Hall portrays the hero, a captain and star polo player, whose games are interrupted by the intrigue. He eventually foils the scheme by setting up a trap during a polo match. He captures the spies and wins the heroine (Jane Wyman) in this low-budget film. ■

Spy Ship (1942), WB. *Dir.* B. Reeves Eason; *Sc.* Robert E. Kent; *Cast includes:* Craig Stevens, Irene Manning, Maris Wrixon, Michael Ames, Peter Whitman, John Maxwell.

An enemy agent (Irene Manning) sells information about American ship departures to foreign spies in this drama that takes place prior to the attack on Pearl Harbor. The plot concerns a network of spies who trade American military secrets to the enemy in this well-paced, low-budget film. Manning, as an heiress who conceals secret documents in her antiwar lecture notes, is killed off about midway into the plot. There is a rousing gun battle at the conclusion of this remake of a 1934 Warner Brothers feature titled *Fog Over Frisco* with Bette Davis. ■

Spy Smasher (1942) serial, Rep. *Dir.* John English, William Witney; *Sc.* Ronald Davidson, Norman Hall, William Lively, Joseph O'Donnell, Joseph Poland; *Cast includes:* Kane Richmond, Sam Flint, Marguerite Chapman, Hans Schumm, Tristram Coffin.

A 12-chapter World War II serial, the plot has the title hero, played by Kane Richmond, battling Nazi agents. The chief villain (Hans Schumm), known only as the Mask, controls a spy network in America actively engaged in various acts of espionage and sabotage, including destroying planes and stealing secret weapons. Spy Smasher, replete with cape and airplane goggles, manages to thwart the

Mask's treacherous acts in each episode. Richmond has a twin brother who eventually sacrifices his life to save his hero-brother. The Mask meets a fitting and sensational end when his submarine collides with a mine. See Serials. ∎

Spy Train (1943), Mon. *Dir.* Harold Young; *Sc.* Lewis Schwabacher, Wallace Sullivan, Bart Lytton; *Cast includes:* Richard Travis, Catherine Craig, Chick Chandler, Evelyn Brent, Thelma White, Gerald Brock.

The chief setting of this weak World War II drama is a train. Various passengers search for a mysterious black bag that is supposed to contain Nazi documents but instead holds a time bomb. The hero and heroine are played by Richard Travis and Catherine Craig, while Chick Chandler portrays a photographer. The German spies are blown up by their own device at the conclusion of this inept film. ∎

Spy With My Face, The (1966), MGM. *Dir.* John Newland; *Sc.* Clyde Ware, Joseph Calvelli; *Cast includes:* Robert Vaughn, Senta Berger, David McCallum, Leo G. Carroll, Michael Evans, Sharon Farrell.

Robert Vaughn, as a not-so-secret agent Napoleon Solo, once again battles the villainous organization trying to dominate the world in this expanded version of a "Man From U.N.C.L.E." television entry. This time around, the rogues, led by their chief, Darius Two, kidnap Solo and replace him with an exact double. Their purpose is to gain access to a secret superweapon. It seems that the world powers, anticipating an attack from outer space in the future, have built a powerful counterweapon which is heavily guarded in an underground hideaway somewhere in Switzerland. Darius' plan is to have Solo's double steal the combination that activates the weapon. Then his enemy agents will storm the facility, capture the weapon and, through it, control the world. Darius' diabolical plan almost succeeds until Solo escapes and foils the scheme.

Strongly influenced by the James Bond films of the period, this spy spoof tries to capture the comic tone and high production values of the British series. Location shooting includes Washington, D.C., the Austrian Alps and Switzerland. Senta Berger, as an attractive and seductive enemy agent, and Sharon Farrell, as a sexy airline stewardess, provide Solo with some romantic diversions. Michael

Evans, as the villain Darius, has his lighter moments. Using a hidden camera, he and one of his henchmen observe Solo about to engage in lovemaking. He shuts the camera off, announcing: "There's a time when prying ends and a sense of morality begins." David McCallum, repeats his role as Illya Kuryakin, Solo's sidekick, while Leo G. Carroll returns as the chief and supervisor of Section One of U.N.C.L.E. (United Network Command for Law Enforcement). Carroll played a similar role in Hitchcock's comedy-thriller *North by Northwest* (1959), which strongly influenced the spy-film cycle of the 1960s. See "The Man From U.N.C.L.E." ∎

S*P*Y*S (1974), TCF. *Dir.* Irwin Kershner; *Sc.* Mal Marmorstein, Laurence J. Cohen, Fred Freeman; *Cast includes:* Elliott Gould, Donald Sutherland, ZouZou, Joss Ackland, Kenneth Griffith, Vladek Sheybai.

An obvious attempt to exploit the commercial success of Robert Altman's black comedy *M*A*S*H* (1970), which also starred Gould and Sutherland, this anemic satire on international satire focuses on two inept C.I.A. agents. Gould and Sutherland foul up the defection of a Soviet ballet dancer and bring down upon themselves the anger of both the Agency and the Russians. The remainder of the film concerns their attempts to elude their pursuers as they become involved French revolutionaries. Chases and other attempts at comic routines don't help the film. ∎

Spy's Fate, The (1915), Lubin.

The U.S. Secret Service becomes interested in some secret papers concerning an industrial smelting process in this undistinguished drama. The plot involves two competing smelting companies and several spies, including a woman operative representing the U.S., another woman spy of a foreign power, one male agent working for a competitive company and another male government agent. The two American agents eventually bungle their way through incidents on their path to solving the mystery. ∎

Stalag 17 (1953), Par. *Dir.* Billy Wilder; *Sc.* Billy Wilder, Edward Blum; *Cast includes:* William Holden, Don Taylor, Otto Preminger, Robert Strauss, Harvey Lembeck.

Director Billy Wilder blends comedy with drama in his film about captured American air crews in a German prisoner-of-war camp during World War II. William Holden portrays a cynical sergeant, a loner whose scrounging and trading with the guards leads his fellow prisoners to suspect that he is an informer. After two American prisoners have been killed trying to escape and another exposed for sabotaging a troop train, the occupants of Stalag 17 suspect that one of their own is an informer. Holden, after he is beaten up by his fellow prisoners, fixes his sights on learning the identity of the real informer. He discovers that an American-educated German spy has been planted in the barracks and is secretly passing information to the camp commandant by placing messages in a hollow of a chess piece. When Holden explains to the others how they have been betrayed, they decide to use the informer as a decoy while Holden and a lieutenant make their escape. That same night the men toss the informer out of the barracks and, before he has a chance to identify himself, the guards, thinking he is trying to break out, shoot him down. Meanwhile, during all the confusion, the two Americans cut through the barbed wire and fade into the darkness of the night.

The film, which is often sardonic, provides plenty of comedy, contributed chiefly by Robert Strauss, who plays "Animal," and Harvey Lembeck, as Harry Shapiro, to relieve the tense moments. In the final sequence Shapiro can't figure out why Holden would put his own life in danger. "I'd like to know what made him do it," he wonders out loud. "Maybe he wanted to steal our wire cutters," Animal replies. "Did you ever think of that?" Otto Preminger stepped out of his usual director's role to portray the arrogant camp commandant. Sig Ruman, as Schultz, the imitable guard, also adds to the humor. The prisoners frequently make him the butt of their jokes. "How do you expect to win the war with an army of clowns?" he asks. "We sort of hope you'll laugh yourselves to death," a prisoner quips. Peter Graves plays the covert German-born informer who wins the confidence of the Americans. Don Taylor portrays a captured lieutenant whom the Gestapo wants for blowing up a German train. Director and co-screenwriter Wilder adapted the work from the successful stage play by Donald Bevan and Edmund Trzcinski. ■

Stamboul Quest (1934), MGM. *Dir.* Sam Wood; *Sc.* Herman Mankiewicz; *Cast includes:* Myrna Loy, George Brent, Lionel Atwill, C. Henry Gordon, Mischa Auer.

Myrna Loy portrays one of Germany's most effective spies in this sophisticated World War I drama. Responsible for the demise of Mata Hari, who made the fatal mistake of falling in love with one of her victims, Loy scoffs at the thought of committing the same error. George Brent portrays an American medical student who loses his heart to Loy. He follows her to Turkey where she has been assigned to ferret out a Turkish officer (C. Henry Gordon) who is collaborating with the British. She resists Brent's charms at first but soon succumbs.

However, her liaison with the Turkish officer stands in the way of their romance. Brent criticizes her country's tactics. "I know what war is," he reassures her. "You go out and fight. You shoot and get shot. That's what war is. You don't use women as weapons." Loy refuses to give up her assignment. When he asks her whether that includes having an affair with the officer, she replies that she is not sure. Her superior (Lionel Atwill), aware that Brent's jealousy is interfering with her mission, steps in. He informs her that Brent has been killed by a firing squad. Loy, thinking herself responsible for her lover's death, has a mental breakdown and spends the remainder of the war in a convent. While she is recovering, Brent visits her and the two lovers are reunited.

The film is unique in at least two respects. Not only does the drama evoke sympathy for a German spy, it also allows the same German spy to triumph. These were unthinkable elements in Hollywood during and immediately following World War I (with one eye on its lucrative foreign markets) and almost as disconcerting in the period dominated by the rise of Nazism in Germany. A foreword points out the differences between espionage and counter-espionage, concluding that where the former may be glamorous, the latter work is not. The character portrayed by Myrna Loy was based on the exploits of Anna Maria Lesser, Germany's actual top woman spy during World War I, also known as "Fraulein Doktor." A film of this title, released in 1969, was one of several made of her wartime adventures. ■

State Department—File 649 (1949), Film Classics. *Dir.* Peter Stewart; *Sc.* Milton Raison; *Cast includes:* Virginia Bruce, William Lundigan, Jonathan Hale, Frank Ferguson, Richard Loo, Philip Ahn.

William Lundigan portrays a member of the American foreign service who is sent to strife-torn China as the "eyes and ears" of the U.S. in this post-World War II drama. The U.S. foreign office suspects that something is brewing in the northern provinces of China concerning an aggressive Mongolian warlord chief (Richard Loo) and his ties with his "friends to the north." Lundigan is assigned to the post of vice consul in a northern village but arrives too late to be of any use. Aided by a "highly efficient spy network," the warlord moves into the area, declares martial law and places all Westerners under house arrest in the U.S. quarters. He plans to free his hostages once the Chinese government officially recognizes him as prince of the entire region.

Following some brutal actions on the part of the warlord and his soldiers, Lundigan decides on a plan of his own to rid the province, and China, of the aggressor. He plants some dynamite in the warlord's trailer. He then volunteers himself as the sole hostage when the warlord, upon suspecting retaliation from Nationalist China's army, hastily retreats. During the journey, Lundigan learns that the warlord has an army waiting in the north. Outfitted with tanks and planes, the warlord intends to strike in force against the Chinese government. Lundigan verbally attacks the ambitious Mongolian who retaliates by shooting the American. But Lundigan manages to blow up the trailer before he dies, killing the warlord and thereby preventing a war.

The slow-paced film, which is dedicated "to the foreign service of the United States," is helped by the use of Cinecolor. Virginia Bruce plays a fellow agent who falls in love with Lundigan. Philip Ahn, as the warlord's second in command, gives a convincing performance as a loyal aide to his leader's mad dreams. The title refers to William Lundigan's file. ∎

Steel Fist, The (1952), Mon. *Dir.* Wesley Barry; *Sc.* C. K. Kivari; *Cast includes:* Roddy McDowall, Kristine Miller, Harry Lauter, Rand Brooks, Byron Foulger, Kate Lawson.

A student somewhere behind the Iron Curtain hides from the police after precipitating a riot in this Cold War drama. Roddy McDow-

all portrays the youth who seeks shelter with the underground following his protest against new labor edicts. He is taken to a village near the border where he finds shelter with a sympathetic brother and sister. He falls in love with the girl, played by Kristine Miller, who helps him cross the border. Harry Lauter plays the brother in this suspenseful, low-budget tale. The film is based on the story "Flight to Freedom" by Phyllis Parker. ∎

Step by Step (1946), RKO. *Dir.* Phil Rosen; *Sc.* Stuart Palmer; *Cast includes:* Lawrence Tierney, Anne Jeffreys, Lowell Gilmore, George Cleveland, Jason Robards.

Another post-World War II drama about a group of unrepentant Nazis attempting to restore the party to its former glory, this low-budget film features Lawrence Tierney and Anne Jeffreys as an innocent couple being pursued by the F.B.I., police and secret agents. Tierney, as a marine veteran, and Jeffreys, as a secretary to a senator, are accused of stealing secret government documents. They flee from the police and government agents and hide in a motel managed by George Cleveland, who contributes some comic relief. Meanwhile several Nazis, played chiefly by Lowell Gilmore and Jason Robards, want the coveted documents that have accidentally fallen into Tierney's possession. The remainder of the film consists of chases and other action sequences before the plot is unraveled. See Nazi Subversion: Post-World War II. ∎

"Stirring Days in Old Virginia" (1909), Selig.

A Civil War drama set in the spring of 1865, this short silent film revolves around a Confederate captain assigned to a secret mission while Union troops are camped on his Virginia plantation where his wife resides. The film includes rather realistic battle scenes for 1909 as well as portrayals of Generals Grant and Lee. ∎

Stolen Orders (1918), State Rights. *Dir.* Harley Knoles, George Kelson; *Sc.* Charles Whittaker; *Cast includes:* Montagu Love, Carlyle Blackwell, Kitty Gordon, Madge Evans, June Elvidge, George MacQuarrie.

A World War I drama, the film centers on secret information which is in possession of an American admiral. His wife (Kitty Gordon), who has a passion for gambling, is lured by German spies to a casino where she accumulates large debts. The enemy agents persuade her to steal the sealed orders from her husband in return for covering up her losses. When the admiral's brother, a U.S. Navy lieutenant (Carlyle Blackwell), discovers that one of the spies (Montagu Love), a former jewel thief, plans to deliver the papers to Germany by way of a dirigible, he follows them in a hydroplane. Love's daughter (June Elvidge), who happens to be the lieutenant's girlfriend, accompanies her father in the dirigible. Also aboard is an old enemy of the young woman's father. The two men engage in a struggle and fall overboard to their deaths. Elvidge parachutes to safety, carrying the packet of important documents, and returns them to her pursuing fiancé. The film is an adaptation of *Sealed Orders*, a 1913 English melodrama by Cecil Raleigh and Henry Hamilton. ■

Stolen Treaty, The (1917), Vitagraph. *Dir.* Paul Scardon; *Sc.* Helmer Walton Bergman; *Cast includes:* Earle Williams, Corinne Griffith, Denton Vane, Robert Gaillard, Bernard Seigel, Billie Billings.

A U.S. Secret Service agent is assigned to recover a stolen treaty between the fictitious European country of Zorania and the U.S. in this drama of intrigue, deceptions and diplomacy. Earle Williams, as the government agent, poses as a society playboy, meets the vacationing Prince Zarl of Zorania at a party. The prince (Denton Vane) actually is on a secret mission to negotiate a treaty with the U.S. Later, Williams learns in Washington that the treaty has been stolen. The thief wants $15 million for its return.

Williams persuades his girlfriend (Corinne Griffith) to help him in his efforts to retrieve the important document. It seems that a suspect, Farnelli, is involved. She manages to meet the suspect, and Williams enters upon the scene, chloroforms Farnelli and tears off his disguise which reveals the prince. He admits stealing the treaty as a ploy to help him pay off his accumulated gambling debts. ■

Stopover Tokyo (1957), TCF. *Dir.* Richard L. Breen; *Sc.* Richard L. Breen, Walter Reisch; *Cast includes:* Robert Wagner, Joan Collins, Edmond O'Brien, Ken Scott, Reiko Oyama, Larry Keating.

Communist agents in Japan attempt to create chaos by assassinating the U.S. High Commissioner while he attends a peace rally in this slow-paced drama based on John P. Marquand's novel. Robert Wagner, as a U.S. counterintelligence agent, has the difficult job of protecting the unmanageable commissioner who disregards the threats upon his life. Edmond O'Brien, as the chief conspirator, has problems annihilating Wagner, who finally succeeds in getting rid of the bomb meant for the commissioner. Joan Collins provides the romantic attraction of both Wagner and Ken Scott, a fellow agent. She rejects Wagner who, she feels, is too involved with his job. Solly Makamura portrays a Japanese agent killed in the line of duty by O'Brien and leaves behind a young daughter. ■

Storm Over Lisbon (1944), Republic. *Dir.* George Sherman; *Sc.* Doris Gilbert, Dane Lussier; *Cast includes:* Vera Hruba Ralston, Richard Arlen, Erich von Stroheim, Otto Kruger, Eduardo Ciannelli, Mona Barrie.

A routine wartime drama of intrigue set in World War II Lisbon, the film gives top billing to Vera Hruba Ralston as a seductive nightclub dancer. The club is owned by an unscrupulous Nazi sympathizer (Erich von Stroheim) who trades in lives and military information. Richard Arlen portrays an American correspondent who is about to leave for the States with highly secret documents on film. Stroheim plots to prevent Arlen from getting the information through. Eduardo Ciannelli plays Stroheim's murderous henchman in this familiar tale filled with the usual spies and other assorted villains. ■

Stranger, The (1946), RKO. *Dir.* Orson Welles; *Sc.* Anthony Veiller, John Huston (uncredited); *Cast includes:* Edward G. Robinson, Loretta Young, Orson Welles, Philip Merivale, Richard Long, Martha Wentworth.

An escaped Nazi war criminal, wanted by the Allied War Crimes Commission, hides out in a small New England village in this suspenseful World War II drama. Edward G. Robinson, as a U.S. government agent, tracks down the mass murderer (Orson Welles) to the village and employs psychological warfare against him. Welles, who has gone under cover as a professor and becomes an accepted member of the peaceful community, marries a highly respected local resident and headmaster's daughter (Loretta Young). He is temporarily threatened with exposure when another former Nazi arrives to visit him. "I'll stay hidden until the day that we strike again," the unrepentant Welles confides to his friend. But when he learns that all war crimes charges against the man were dropped suddenly and that he was followed to the village, Welles suspects a trap. He kills his friend to avoid any links to him.

Robinson's suspicions about Welles are confirmed, especially when he discovers the body of the murdered man. Welles' wife, meanwhile, knows nothing of her husband's past and refuses to believe the charges when she is told. The cat-and-mouse game between the hunter and the hunted continues until the wife learns that Welles has planned to kill her. In a melodramatic sequence filled with ominous shadows, low-key lighting and various camera angles, Welles tries to kill his wife by weakening a ladder step leading to the village clock tower. When his plan fails, he attempts to hide from the authorities in the same tower where he soon becomes impaled on the sword of one of several moving life-size statues—a grotesque gargoyle—a final, sensational sequence filled with baroque visual images.

Orson Welles, who had directed the sensational and controversial *Citizen Kane* (1941), became anathema to Hollywood studios, especially after his two box-office flops—*The Magnificent Ambersons* (1942) and *Journey Into Fear* (1943). Studio moguls, who considered him personally difficult to get along with and financially extravagant, never again gave him control of production costs. RKO cautiously had him direct and star in *The Stranger* only after he agreed to follow an existing script and a stringent editing schedule. He agreed and turned out this flawed but visually interesting drama—a work that he later regarded as his worst film. See Nazi Subversion: Post-World War II. ∎

Strategy of Terror (1969), U. *Dir.* Jack Smight; *Sc.* Robert L. Joseph; *Cast includes:* Hugh O'Brian, Barbara Rush, Neil Hamilton, Frederick O'Neal, Will Corry.

A fanatical right-winger plots to assassinate four United Nations functionaries in this bland political drama edited from a two-part television presentation. Neil Hamilton, as the superpatriot, believes the U.N. is a subversive organization undermining the greatness and power of America. Barbara Rush portrays a newspaper reporter who accidentally blunders upon Hamilton's conspiracy. Hugh O'Brian, as the local police detective, eventually foils the plot with the help of Rush. The pair provide some romantic interest. Frederick O'Neal, as an African under-secretary to the U.N., is one of Hamilton's potential targets in this overly preachy tale that extols the world organization as perhaps the last hope for peace among nations. ∎

Submarine Alert (1943), Par. *Dir.* Frank McDonald; *Sc.* Maxwell Shane; *Cast includes:* Richard Arlen, Wendy Barrie, Nils Asther, Roger Pryor, Abner Biberman.

Enemy agents threaten American shipping off the Pacific coast in this routine World War II drama. Richard Arlen plays a radio engineer who discovers a network of spies sending radio signals to a Japanese submarine that is responsible for several sinkings. The script, using one of the oldest plot devices, has Arlen publicly disgraced so that he can infiltrate the spy nest. (Just one year earlier director John Huston utilized the same ploy in *Across the Pacific* with Humphrey Bogart playing the discredited officer who worked his way into a group of Japanese agents.) Wendy Barrie portrays an F.B.I. agent in this weak film. ∎

Submarine Base (1943), PRC. *Dir.* Albert Kelley; *Sc.* Arthur St. Claire, George Merrick; *Cast includes:* John Litel, Alan Baxter, Fifi D'Orsay, Eric Blore, Iris Adrian.

An American gangster on the lam hides out on a remote island off the coast of Brazil where he collaborates with Nazi agents in this low-budget World War II drama. The fugitive (Alan Baxter) helps to refuel German submarines that prey upon Allied shipping. John Litel, as a former police officer and survivor of a sunken vessel, recognizes Baxter. Eventually, Baxter betrays the enemy agents and is killed. Fifi D'Orsay portrays the daughter of a local innkeeper who falls for Baxter. The film offers little in the way of battle scenes. ∎

Subterfuge (1969), Commonwealth. *Dir.* Peter Graham Scott; *Sc.* David Whitaker; *Cast includes:* Gene Barry, Joan Collins, Richard Todd, Tom Adams, Suzanna Leigh, Michael Rennie.

An American C.I.A. agent is assigned to ferret out a British double agent operating in England in this uninteresting, slow-paced drama, a joint British-U.S. production. Gene Barry portrays the American. Joan Collins portrays the estranged wife of one of the suspects. During the course of the story, Collins' young son is kidnapped, adding complications. Marius Goring portrays a Soviet undercover agent. Suzanna Leigh plays his seductive assistant. Other British agents suspected as the traitor include Richard Todd, who portrays a womanizer; Colin Kitteridge, a chief of security; and Tom Adams, Collins' pouting husband. ■

Sultan's Daughter, The (1944), Mon. *Dir.* Arthur Dreifuss; *Sc.* M. M. Raison, Tim Ryan; *Cast includes:* Ann Corio, Charles Butterworth, Tim Ryan, Edward Norris, Irene Ryan, Fortunio Bonanova.

A World War II musical involving American bands, chorus girls and German agents, the film stars Ann Corio in the title role. Charles Butterworth plays her sultan-father who tries to stop his daughter from dealing with Nazi agents. They want to buy out her oil properties. Edward Norris portrays an American entertainer stranded in the desert. Fortunio Bonanova, as a scheming underling of the Sultan, is in league with the German agents in this routine but harmless tale. ■

Sundown (1941), UA. *Dir.* Henry Hathaway; *Sc.* Barre Lyndon, Charles G. Booth; *Cast includes:* Gene Tierney, Bruce Cabot, George Sanders, Harry Carey, Sir Cedric Hardwicke, Joseph Calleia, Carl Esmond.

Bruce Cabot and Gene Tierney star in this World War II adventure drama set at a remote British outpost in East Africa. Cabot plays a dedicated and idealistic local administrator who understands and is respected by the local natives. George Sanders is assigned to help Cabot learn where and how a neighboring tribe is getting arms. It seems that the Nazis are intent on fomenting trouble for the British. Gene Tierney, as a sultry Eurasian owner of a string of trading posts, is working as a British agent. When she learns that a mineralogist, who is a Nazi spy traveling under a false Dutch passport, is the chief supplier of the weapons, she decides to accompany him to his secret supply depot. Cabot follows, learns where the hiding place is and sends back word to Sanders. The climax is a rousing battle in which Sanders is mortally wounded. "People of all Churches pulling together—that's strength—that's all we need," he says to Cabot before he dies. Rationalizing his choice of the army as a career rather than the Church, he concludes: "They're both the basis of civilization. The Church holds it together and the army defends it."

The scene then shifts to a bomb-damaged church in England where Sanders' father, a bishop (Sir Cedric Hardwicke), speaks to his congregation, which includes Tierney and Cabot. "Mourn not for the brave," he says. "They live in the indestructible splendor of all eternity." He continues with a patriotic plea for victory:

> Fly high your flag upon the hill,
> Keep bright your faith and hold until
> Our England wins, and win she will.
> Who waits with faith waits with victory.

The film was made before the U.S. had entered the war and during England's darkest hour. World War II had begun its second year, and the sympathies of the American public, which saw one nation after another crumble before the Nazi war machine, were clearly with the British. *Sundown* was Hollywood's—and America's—tribute to a brave, embattled nation standing alone like a bastion against the forces of dictatorship sweeping across Europe. ■

Sunset Pass (1929), Par. *Dir.* Otis Brower; *Sc.* J. W. Rubin, Ray Harris; *Cast includes:* Jack Holt, Nora Lane, Jack Loder, Chester Conklin.

Jack Holt, as a U.S. government agent, goes under cover to capture a gang of rustlers in this better-than-average silent western drama. Masquerading as a convict, he makes the proper contact during his stay in prison to get him into the gang upon his release. He develops a close relationship with the leader. Holt also romances the leader's sister (Nora Lane). When the showdown comes between Holt, who reveals his true identity, and the gang, his new-found friend decides to end his career in a gunfight. Holt eases the sister's pain by telling her that her brother sacrificed his life to help carry out the law. Western writer Zane Grey's story, from which the screenplay originated, served as the basis for two sound films with the same title—one released by Paramount in 1933 and another by RKO in 1946. ■

Lobby card for Suzy (1936), a World War I drama with Jean Harlow as the wife of British officer Franchot Tone (c.).

Suspicion (1918), State Rights. *Dir.* John M. Stahl; *Sc.* Thomas Bedding; *Cast includes:* Warren Cook, Wilmuth Merkyl, Grace Davison, Mathilda Brundage, Alma Dore, John O'Keefe.

A weak World War I romantic drama, the film concerns a married doctor engaged in military research for the U.S. government who suspects his partner of having an affair with his wife. Spurred on by local gossip, the doctor (Warren Cook) grows more suspicious of his partner (Leonard White), who is also his nephew, and his wife (Grace Davison). When a German agent who is trying to steal the doctor's secret papers exits from the wife's bedroom, the husband thinks the stranger is his partner and accuses his wife of being unfaithful. Distraught by the unfounded charges, she takes poison but recovers. A U.S. Secret Service agent soon appears and explains that the intruder was a German spy trying to steal the doctor's papers. The embarrassed husband then apologizes to his wife and business partner. ■

Suzy (1936), MGM. *Dir.* George Fitzmaurice; *Sc.* Dorothy Parker, Alan Campbell, Horace Jackson, Lenore Coffee; *Cast includes:* Jean Harlow, Franchot Tone, Cary Grant, Lewis Stone, Benita Hume, Inez Courtney.

Jean Harlow, as an American chorus girl stranded in England, faces more than her share of adversity in this implausible World War I romantic drama based on the novel by Herbert Gorman. She meets and marries a struggling Irish inventor (Franchot Tone) who is employed at a factory owned by a German woman. When he begins to suspect his employer of consorting with German agents, she sends a fellow spy (Benita Hume) to kill him. Harlow witnesses the shooting and is accused by their landlady of committing the act. Thinking that her husband is dead, she escapes and leaves for Paris.

Working as a café singer, she meets a French air ace (Cary Grant), falls in love and marries him. Grant returns to the fighting, and Harlow remains in his home to care for his aging father (Lewis Stone). Suddenly

Tone, who was only wounded by the spy, appears in France as a British officer and accuses Harlow of being unfaithful. Grant, meanwhile, has been having an affair with a woman who is the same German spy who earlier had shot Tone. When Harlow and Tone expose her as an enemy agent, she fatally shoots Grant and escapes. "No one must know how he died," says Harlow, as the self-sacrificing wife to the very end. To preserve Grant's war-hero image, Tone then crashes an airplane onto the grounds of the mansion and places Grant's body next to the wreck, thereby making it appear that the Frenchman died in battle.

The contrived and sentimental plot focuses on light repartee and romance while subjugating the war to the background. "You know what a stabilizer is?" Tone earnestly asks Harlow early in the film. "Well," the Broadway showgirl replies, "it's something to do with horses, isn't it?" The film ends with a eulogy given by Grant's squadron commander to the dead hero's fellow airmen. "Whatever memorial may be erected to him one day, his real memorial is in the hearts of the French people. . . . We can cling, during the meaningless horrors or war, to the selfless courage of men like him. That courage purifies war."

Several effective air battles appear in the film, some of which have been lifted from other features. The incident involving the plane crash has also been borrowed. In *The Eagle and the Hawk* (1933), another World War I air drama with Cary Grant, Grant takes the body of air ace Fredric March, who has committed suicide, up in a plane and crashes it to make it seem as though March was killed in action. ◼

Swat the Spy (1918), Fox. *Dir.* Arvid Gillstrom; *Sc.* Raymond Schrock; *Cast includes:* Jane Lee, Katherine Lee, Charles Slattery, P. C. Hartigan, Florence Ashbrooke.

A World War I comedy drama about enemy agents, the film centers on the Lee sisters' father who has discovered a more powerful explosive. The scientist (Charles Slattery) is so wrapped up in his experiments that he is unaware that most of his household employees are German agents who are planning to steal the formula. The scientist, learning that his wife is pregnant, tells his two impish little daughters that he has written a letter asking for a baby brother for the two girls. The sisters, who have been preoccupied with taunting the household of spies, decide that they don't want the new addition. They enter the father's laboratory and steal the letter, which is actually the formula for the new explosive. The girls unknowingly upset the plans of the butler-spy, who decides to steal the invention. After a comical chase, he is finally captured by U.S. Secret Service agents. The scientist acknowledges his mischievous daughter for saving the formula. ◼

T

Taint, The (1914), Eclectic. *Dir.* Sidney Olcott; *Cast includes:* Helen Francis, Edward José, Ruby Hoffman, Chreighton Hale, Louis Hendricks, Sam Ryan.

A woman falsely accused of murder and sentenced to prison sees the hand of justice years later in this drama. Helen Francis, as the innocent victim, had been an assistant to a biologist when she met her employer's secretary (Edward José). Francis becomes pregnant, but the secretary refuses to marry her. When the biologist learns of his cowardly act, she threatens him with exposure. During a quarrel he kills her and places the blame on Francis, who is found guilty and hauled off to prison. Her baby is sent to live with a farm family. Years later when Francis gains an early release after preventing a prison break, she gets a job as a secret agent. While tracking down a spy who is trying to steal government documents from an industrialist, she discovers the spy is the father of her child. He is eventually killed when a train is derailed. Meanwhile her son, whom she hasn't seen in years, is engaged to the industrialist's daughter. The mother is then reunited with her son. Although no director is credited, we may assume that producer Sidney Olcott, who occasionally directed his productions, probably did double duty on this drama. ■

Tall Target, The (1951), MGM. *Dir.* Anthony Mann; *Sc.* George Worthing Yates, Art Cohn; *Cast includes:* Dick Powell, Paula Raymond, Adolphe Menjou, Marshall Thompson, Ruby Dee, Will Geer.

A group of conspirators plots to assassinate newly elected President Abraham Lincoln in this tense drama set in 1861 before the Civil War. Dick Powell, as a New York police officer who had earlier worked as Lincoln's bodyguard, learns of the plot and alerts his superiors. When they make light of the threat, Powell resigns from the force and investigates the possible assassination attempt on his own. He discovers one of the potential conspirators aboard a Baltimore-bound train. Following several confrontations, a murder and other incidents of intrigue, Powell is able to foil the scheme. A Northern army officer (Adolphe Menjou) is involved in the conspiracy along with a young Southerner (Marshall Thompson) who intends to carry out the actual assassination. Lincoln and Allan Pinkerton, the famous detective, are portrayed in cameo roles by Leslie Kimmell and James Harrison respectively. See American Civil War: Intelligence and Covert Actions.

The incidents in the film are loosely based on the infamous Baltimore Plot of 1861. Although Maryland stood with the North in the Civil War, there was a great deal of pro-Southern sentiment in the state. Therefore, when talk of a plot to assassinate newly elected President Lincoln reached New York City Police Superintendent John Kennedy, he judged it serious enough to dispatch detective David Bookstaver to investigate.

At about the same time, the president of the Philadelphia, Wilmington and Baltimore Railroad, Samuel Felton, learned of secessionist plans in Maryland which included destruction of railroad lines in and around Washington in an effort to isolate the capitol from the rest of the North. Felton hired the detective Allan Pinkerton to check.

Pinkerton moved to Baltimore where he made the acquaintance of Cypriano Fernandini, an Italian immigrant. Apparently the new immigrant so completely assimilated into the environment that he integrated the Southern hatred for Lincoln into his own psyche. Pinkerton learned that Fernandini was part of a plot to assassinate the President-elect.

Lincoln was due to arrive in Philadelphia on February 22, 1861, to dedicate the new American flag which now included the state of Kansas. The President was then scheduled to travel to Baltimore on the Northern Central Railroad, move by open carriage for a mile to the Baltimore and Ohio Railroad Station and then would travel to Washington by train. Surprisingly, considering that time of strife, there was no effort to hide Lincoln's movements, the record of which was published in the local press. The plotters' plans called for intercepting the President on his one-mile carriage drive.

The conspirators were hoping to incite the secessionist-minded Palmetto Guards and the National Volunteers to join in a general uprising. The pro-Southern sympathies of Baltimore Police Chief George Kane was also factored in.

Pinkerton reached Lincoln the day before the scheduled assassination and explained the situation; the detective pleaded with the President to return immediately to Washington. President Lincoln tended to dismiss Pinkerton's advice until the plot was confirmed by an independent source.

Detective Bookstaver, who had been assigned by Police Superintendent Kennedy, had gone "undercover" and discovered details of the same plot. He reported it to a member of General Winfield Scott's staff who, in turn, forwarded the report to Lincoln via Frederick Seward, the son of William Seward, Lincoln's choice for secretary of state. Authenticated by this second source, the story was believable and Lincoln decided to return to Washington immediately. The plotters were never prosecuted. ■

Tampico (1944), TCF. *Dir.* Lothar Mendes; *Sc.* Kenneth Gamet, Fred Niblo, Jr., Richard Macauley; *Cast includes:* Edward G. Robinson, Lynn Bari, Victor McLaglen, Marc Lawrence, Mona Maris, Robert Bailey.

A routine World War II espionage drama, the film stars Edward G. Robinson as the captain of an oil tanker. Victor McLaglen portrays his first mate. During their journey in the Gulf of Mexico, their vessel rescues a group of survivors whose ship was torpedoed by a German U-boat. Lynn Bari portrays one of the survivors. The plot then takes the principal characters to Tampico where espionage activities seem to run rampant. ■

Tangier (1946), U. *Dir.* George Waggner; *Sc.* M. M. Musselman, Monty F. Collins; *Cast includes:* Maria Montez, Preston Foster, Robert Paige, Louise Allbritton, Kent Taylor, Sabu.

Exotic Tangier furnishes the setting for this otherwise tepid tale of intrigue involving a hunt for a Latin Nazi collaborator and murderer. Maria Montez, as a Spanish dancer, wants to learn the identity of the quisling who has murdered one of her relations. Robert Paige, as a correspondent who has fallen into disfavor, seeks to regain his reputation by breaking an international story. Sabu portrays a native guide and adds humor to his role. Preston Foster, as the collaborator, masquerades as the police chief of Tangier and meets a particularly brutal end when he is killed in a violent elevator crash. ■

Tangier Incident (1953), AA. *Dir.* Lew Landers; *Sc.* George Bricker; *Cast includes:* George Brent, Mari Aldon, Dorothy Patrick, Bert Freed, Dan Seymour.

A plot concocted by a trio of atomic scientists to sell important information to the Communists forms the background of this routine drama. George Brent, as an American intelligence agent, masquerades as a black market profiteer in Tangier to stop the transfer of the secrets. Mari Aldon plays a Communist spy posing as a wealthy American. Dorothy Patrick portrays an innocent who becomes entangled in the web of intrigue. Veteran character actor Dan Seymour, often seen in other dramas with exotic settings, plays the chief of the Tangier police. See Cold War. ■

Target (1985), WB. *Dir.* Arthur Penn; *Sc.* Howard Berk, Don Peterson; *Cast includes:* Gene Hackman, Matt Dillon, Gayle Hunnicutt, Victoria Fyodorova, Ilona Grubel, Herbert Berghof.

A semi-estranged son rediscovers his ex-C.I.A. agent father when their mother/wife is kidnapped in this drama. Gene Hackman, as the former agent, is now a respectable businessman leading a quiet, dull life. His son (Matt Dillon), a college dropout, knows nothing about his father's past life as a secret agent. Their strained relationship puts pressure on each. When Hackman's wife disappears during her vacation in France, he journeys to France to investigate. Dillon insists on going along to help. Once in Europe, Hackman learns from Taber, an old friend and C.I.A. chief at the U.S. embassy, that his wife has been kidnapped. Also, unidentified assassins attempt to kill Hackman. It is then he reveals to his astonished son his past work with the C.I.A.

They next journey to Hamburg where Hackman contacts his former lover and soon learns that his wife is in the hands of an East German agent who wants revenge for his own family's murder. Hackman travels to East Germany and confronts the agent, now an invalid, who accuses the American of breaking the unwritten code of going after another agent's family. Hackman denies this, suggesting that other forces are at work. Eventually they discover that Taber, the C.I.A. chief, in reality is a double agent who killed the German's wife and children to protect his own cover. Hackman rescues his wife and takes her and their son away from the abandoned airfield where she had been held captive. The East German then kills Taber and himself.

One of the few American espionage dramas to portray a C.I.A. agent in a favorable light (Hackman is fair and honest, a protector of home and family), the film also explores the father-son relationship and the multiple meanings of the word "family." Hackman risks everything to find his wife. The East German seeks revenge for the murder of his family. Taber uses the word "family" to link all past and present members of the C.I.A. When Taber is about to cold-bloodedly kill a lower-echelon C.I.A. agent, the condemned man utters: "But we're family!" See Central Intelligence Agency. ■

Target Hong Kong (1952), Col. *Dir.* Fred T. Sears; *Sc.* Herbert Purdum; *Cast includes:* Richard Denning, Nancy Gates, Richard Loo, Soo Yong, Ben Astar, Michael Pate.

An American soldier of fortune interferes with a Communist plot to take over Hong Kong in this Cold War drama. Richard Denning plays the American who has just lost thousands of dollars in a Hong Kong gambling house. The owner of the establishment recruits him to fight for the Chinese Nationalists. Meanwhile, she doesn't realize she is being used by the Communists. Nancy Gates, as the adopted daughter of the gambling house owner, provides the romance in this low-budget film. ■

Target Unknown (1951), UI. *Dir.* George Sherman; *Sc.* Harold Medford; *Cast includes:* Mark Stevens, Alex Nicol, Robert Douglas, Don Taylor, Gig Young.

This World War II drama explores some of the methods used by German intelligence to extract military information from unsuspecting Allied prisoners of war. The film begins with an exciting American bombing raid over German-held territory. One of the bombers is hit, and the captain (Mark Stevens) orders the crew to bail out. The men are captured and taken in for interrogation supervised by a clever German colonel who believes significant information can be assembled from small bits of seemingly unimportant facts. When Stevens suspects their ploy, the Germans decide to switch tactics and use Stevens' own character traits against him. "An earnest soldier . . . patriotic," concludes one officer. "With pride in his country and his weapons," adds another. "That pride may very well be the chink in his armor."

The Nazis eventually learn from their prisoners that a major fuel dump is the next target. They order the fuel moved and send every available fighter plane aloft to meet the Allied bombers. As Stevens and his crew are being shipped to a permanent prison camp, he and two comrades escape, contact the French underground and transmit a message to England warning of the German trap. Gig Young, as a German officer raised in America, poses as an understanding sympathizer whom Stevens confides in. He even criticizes the brutality of the Gestapo. "Those Gestapo men," he confides to Stevens, "they put no signatures to the Geneva Convention." To gather more information, the German command places another English-speaking German posing as a fellow American prisoner in captivity with Stevens. When Stevens learns his identity, he calls the Nazi a "traitor." "You're the traitor," the German explains. "You and that stupid crew of yours. You know what you've done? You've given us a first-rate briefing on your Cambrai raid." See German Intelligence: World War I. ■

Tartu (1943), MGM. *Dir.* Harold S. Bucquet; *Sc.* John Lee Mahin, Howard Emmett Rogers; *Cast includes:* Robert Donat, Valerie Hobson, Glynis Johns, Walter Rilla, Martin Miller, David Ward.

British intelligence sends an army officer behind German lines to destroy a poison gas plant in this entertaining World War II adventure. Robert Donat, as the patriotic volunteer, is first seen deactivating unexploded bombs that have fallen on London. Told to report to headquarters, he is asked, because of his chemistry background, to take on a dangerous assignment in Nazi-occupied Czechoslovakia where German scientists are completing work on a deadly poison gas. Of course, he accepts gracefully.

Donat, posing as a dapper Rumanian chemist who is willing to cooperate with the Germans, is parachuted into Czechoslovakia. He infiltrates the otherwise impregnable underground chemical plant as a collaborating foreign worker where he eventually drops small time bombs into various ducts. Suspense builds when the Nazis discover his true purpose, forcing him to battle his way to safety. Valerie Hobson, as a friend of the Nazis, in reality is a spy for the Czech underground. She helps Donat escape across the Channel to England. Walter Rilla portrays a vicious Nazi officer who is enamored of Hobson.

MGM made the conventional wartime propaganda film in England with a chiefly British cast. The studio wanted Donat, after his Oscar-winning performance in *Goodbye, Mr. Chips*, in another of its features. Donat, who had turned down various scripts for four years, finally agreed to make this picture, alternately titled *The Adventures of Tartu*. ■

Tarzan's Desert Mystery (1943), RKO.

Dir. William Thiele; Sc. Edward T. Lowe; Cast includes: Johnny Weissmuller, Johnny Sheffield, Nancy Kelly, Otto Kruger, Joseph Sawyer, Lloyd Corrigan.

Nazi agents attempt to foment trouble for a peaceful sheik in this World War II entry in the "Tarzan" series. Tarzan, Boy and Cheetah travel across a desert in search of a rare medicine when they meet an American entertainer (Nancy Kelly). She is on her way to warn the sheik about the Nazi plot. Other complications arise when Tarzan is accused of stealing a prize horse and Kelly is jailed on a murder charge. But the king of the jungle resolves all by the end of the film. Otto Kruger plays a Nazi agent. ■

Telefon (1977), UA.

Dir. Don Siegel; Sc. Peter Hyams, Stirling Silliphant; Cast includes: Charles Bronson, Lee Remick, Donald Pleasence, Tyne Daly, Alan Badel, Patrick Magee.

A hard-line Communist fanatic, who opposes a U.S.-Soviet move toward detente, tries to instigate a war between the two world powers in this suspenseful drama based on Walter Wager's novel. It seems that a handful of die-hard Soviet politicos, opposed to their government's present course, activate some of their agents planted in the U.S. years ago to destroy strategic American military installations. Having been hypnotized by way of drugs, the robot-like spies respond only to certain telephone messages from their superiors. The K.G.B., following its government's present policy of detente with the West, seeks to prevent the dissident agents from instigating a nuclear war.

Charles Bronson, as a secret agent for the K.G.B. with the rank of major, is assigned to travel to the U.S. and stop the deliberate and politically dangerous acts of sabotage. Lee Remick portrays another Soviet agent, already installed in the U.S., whom Bronson's superiors assign to work with him. In reality, Remick is a double agent employed by the C.I.A. Donald Pleasence, as the maverick Soviet agent, eludes K.G.B. agents in the Soviet Union and escapes to the U.S. where he begins to carry out his destructive plot. Using a prearranged trigger-code, consisting of lines from Robert Frost's poem "Stopping by Woods on a Snowy Evening," he telephones each undercover agent who then proceeds on a suicidal mission of sabotage.

The relationship between Bronson and Remick at first remains purely professional. Bronson, concerned only with the gravity of his assignment, rejects Remick's romantic parries. But her charm and sexuality soon melt away his coldness. A romance blossoms as they pursue Pleasence and bring to an end the threat of war. Some of the Cold War cynicism (both the C.I.A. and K.G.B. intend to assassinate Bronson after he completes his assignment) is mollified by the optimistic ending with its facile metaphor of the detente theme. The two agents ask their respective governments to allow them to fade into obscurity where they will live in romantic bliss.

Much of the dialogue is intelligent and helps in the exposition of the plot. Early in the film, Bronson's immediate superior explains that after the U-2 incident in which an American spy plane was shot down over the Soviet Union, the Soviets introduced Operation Telefon. Fearing that war between the U.S. and the Soviet Union was inevitable, the latter developed "a network of the finest deep-cover agents any nation ever produced. They were to infiltrate, burrow deep and prepare to strike in the event of nuclear war." Still earlier, the basic plot is only suggested during an interview when Bronson is recalled to active duty. "Tell me, major," the head of the K.G.B. (Patrick Magee) asks, "in all the world, who is the most secret agent?" "Anyone who manages to stay secret," Bronson replies. "But there is an even more ideal agent," Magee explains, referring to the drugged, deep-cover operatives installed in the U.S. "One who doesn't know he is an agent." See Soviet Spies in the U.S. ∎

Television Spy (1939), Par. *Dir.* Edward Dmytryk; *Sc.* Horace McCoy, William Lipman, Lillie Hayward; *Cast includes:* William Henry, Judith Barrett, William Collier, Sr., Richard Denning, John Eldredge, Dorothy Tree.

The latest developments in television transmission become the target of foreign agents in this low-budget World War II spy drama. William Henry, as a young engineer, discovers a way to extend the range of television's conventional 50-mile limit. Immediately, spies realize the importance of this development in time of war and plot to steal it. Anthony Quinn and Morgan Conway portray members of the spy ring. Veteran film actor William Collier, Sr. plays the financier who backs the engineer. Judith Barrett appears as the female lead.

The film is undistinguished except for being one of the earliest to acknowledge the potential of the new medium of television, heretofore used mainly as a gimmick in serials. Morgan Conway, one of the heavies, went on to play the role of the popular comic-strip detective Dick Tracy whenever Ralph Byrd absented himself from the part. ∎

Terminal Entry (1986), Intercontinental. *Dir.* John Kincade; *Sc.* David Mickey Evans, Mark Sobel; *Cast includes:* Edward Albert, Paul Smith, Yaphet Kotto, Heidi Helmer, Patrick Labyorterux, Yvette Nipar.

A radical Middle East terrorist leader orders suicide hit squads to the U.S. to assassinate major political leaders in this far-fetched action drama. Edward Albert as Capt. Danny Jackson, the heroic leader of a government strike team, is assigned to stop the terrorists on the southern border. The nation becomes aware of the threat through a news telecast.

"We have 250 freedom fighters in the United States," announces the terrorist leader in an interview. "We seek martyrdom. Death is a salvation for us." This is a particularly perilous time with the President holding an international conference of major world leaders in Washington.

Meanwhile, a group of bored teenagers, some of them determined computer hackers, accidentally break into a program titled "Terminal Entry," which they think is a highly technical war game. In reality, it is the command post of the terrorist organization operating in the Southwest. To become participants in the game, the youngsters must issue assignments to members of a terrorist group. As a lark, the innocent players order the assassination of the Russian delegate. Later, they call upon all the terrorists to assemble at the cabin the teenagers are using. When they discover that the assassination was carried out, they realize their lives are in danger.

However, Albert and other strike teams, who have picked up the message on their computer, proceed to the cabin to battle the terrorists. A violent fire-fight ensues in which the suicide squads are finally annihilated and the young boys and their girlfriends rescued. Yaphet Kotto, as the senior officer of the U.S. strike teams patrolling the border, joins Albert in many of the shoot-outs. ∎

Texas Pioneers (1932), Mon. *Dir.* Harry Fraser; *Sc.* Harry Fraser; *Cast includes:* Bill Cody, Andy Shufford, LeRoy Mason, Sheila Manners, John Elliott, Frank Lackteen.

A U.S. Army officer poses as a malcontent so that he can join a gang of outlaws who are suspected of selling guns to hostile Indians in this familiar western drama set in and around an army post. Bill Cody portrays the soldier who works his way into the gang's confidence. Meanwhile the cavalry, on spurious information, rides out of the fort to help a wagon train, leaving the post open to an Indian attack. However, all ends well, with Cody exposing the leader of the gunrunners after besting him in a personal fight. Sheila Manners plays the female lead. ∎

Texas to Bataan (1942), Mon. *Dir.* Robert Tansey; *Sc.* Arthur Hoerl; *Cast includes:* John King, Dave Sharpe, Max Terhune, Marjorie Manning, Budd Buster, Ken Duncan.

One of several B westerns released during World War II to update its plot to reflect contemporary events, the film blends conventional cowboy action with Axis sabotage. John King, Dave Sharpe and Max Terhune, as the Range Busters, are charged with delivering a herd of cattle to the army for shipment to the Philippines. However, a Japanese spy, masquerading as a Filipino cook at the ranch where the trio are employed, attempts to sabotage their mission. Ventriloquist Terhune provides some forced comedy relief, and Marjorie Manning adds a slight romantic angle to the tale. ■

That Man Bolt (1973), U. *Dir.* Henry Levin, David Lowell Rich; *Sc.* Quentin Werty, Charles Johnson; *Cast includes:* Fred Williamson, Byron Webster, Miko Mayama, Teresa Graves, Satoshi Nakamura, John Orchard.

Fred Williamson, as an international courier who transports syndicate money, gets mixed up with murder and sexy women in Las Vegas, Los Angeles and Hong Kong in this inept, cliché-ridden action drama. When Teresa Graves, one of Williamson's bed partners, is murdered in Las Vegas, he decides to avenge her death. This brings him into conflict with Satoshi Nakamura, who heads a global crime operation. A kung-fu expert, Williamson battles his way to his goal by fighting a kung-fu champion, eluding government agents and participating in car chases. Niko Mayama portrays another of Williamson's romantic interests. Byron Webster plays a government agent. John Orchard portrays his assistant. ■

Then There Were Three (1961), Parade. *Dir.* Alex Nicol; *Sc.* Frank Gregory, Allan Lurie; *Cast includes:* Alex Nicol, Frank Latimore, Barry Cahill, Sid Clute, Frank Gregory, Michael Billingsley.

A handful of American soldiers, separated from their main unit, attempt to make it back to their lines in this suspenseful World War II drama set in Italy. One of the G.I.s, however, is actually a Nazi spy assigned to kill an important Italian guerrilla leader. Suspicions are tossed around as the Americans try to discover which one of their number is the German. The assassination plot is eventually foiled in this low-budget but tightly directed film. ■

There Are No Villains (1921), Metro. *Dir.* Bayard Veiller; *Sc.* Mary O'Hara; *Cast includes:* Viola Dana, Gaston Glass, Edward Cecil, De Witt Jennings, Fred Kelsey.

The U.S. Secret Service has problems with one of its agents who hesitates to testify against a suspected opium smuggler in this suspenseful drama. Viola Dana portrays the recalcitrant agent. Reporting to her chief, she admits she is having difficulties getting evidence against a leading opium smuggler. But she suspects King, a pleasant young man, of working for the smuggler. She hopes he will lead her on the proper trail. She returns to the case and befriends the young man who soon conquers her heart. She then refuses to incriminate him in the smuggling operation.

When her secret service boss affirms that he will force her to give evidence against King at his trial, she decides to marry the suspect so that she will not be compelled to testify against her husband. Following several complications, including efforts by the police to prevent the wedding ceremony, the couple are married. Everything is straightened out when the bride and her chief learn that King also is a secret service agent assigned to the San Francisco office and working on the same case. The smuggler leader is arrested, and the young couple go off on a much-deserved honeymoon. ■

They Came to Blow Up America (1943), TCF. *Dir.* Edward Ludwig; *Sc.* Aubrey Wisberg; *Cast includes:* George Sanders, Anna Sten, Ward Bond, Dennis Hoey, Sig Ruman.

An F.B.I. agent (George Sanders) poses as a loyal Nazi in this World War II drama of espionage and sabotage. Eight German saboteurs who are put ashore off Long Island are eventually caught and brought to trial. Through flashback sequences, the film depicts how the eight were trained for their assignments. Ward Bond portrays an F.B.I. chief who leads the hunt for the enemy agents while Anna Sten plays a member of the German underground in love with George Sanders. To allay the fears of its audiences, the film, released during the war, was careful to include a foreword informing its audiences that the incidents were not based on any factual events. However, a similar circumstance, known as the Pastorius Project, actually occurred during the war.

Lt. Walter Kappe, a German intelligence officer, dreamed up the Pastorius Project. In

George Sanders (c.) poses as a sympathetic German to help the F.B.I. locate a group of Nazi saboteurs. *They Came to Blow Up America* (1943).

1942 he recruited eight German-Americans and brought them back to Germany for demolition training. Their mission was to sabotage aluminum production facilities in the Northeast so as to disrupt aircraft production. If they succeeded, the saboteurs were directed to destroy bridges and water reservoirs in the New York metropolitan area.

Four agents were discharged from a German submarine at Amangansett, Long Island, on the evening of June 12, 1942; the remaining four were brought by a second German submarine to a beach area outside Jacksonville, Florida, and dropped off on the evening of June 16, 1942. Apparently losing his nerve, one of the saboteurs, George Dasch, with the consent of a second agent, Peter Burger, surrendered to the F.B.I. Dasch revealed the extent of the Pastorius Project as well as the names and locations of the other agents.

President Roosevelt acted immediately, and on July 2, 1942, he appointed a secret military court to hold trial. All of the agents were judged guilty of attempted sabotage during wartime; six were hanged immediately.

Dasch was sentenced to 30 years in prison while Burger received life imprisonment. Following the war, when passions had abated, President Truman released both survivors and ordered them returned to Germany. ■

They Dare Not Love (1941), Col. Dir. James Whale; Sc. Charles Bennett, Ernst Vajda; Cast includes: George Brent, Martha Scott, Paul Lukas, Egon Brecher, Roman Bohnen.

George Brent portrays an anti-Nazi leader who flees his native Austria on the eve of World War II. Arriving in America, he meets another Austrian refugee (Martha Scott), whom he had met previously while crossing the Atlantic. She and her father, who have opened a Viennese restaurant, are engaged in aiding fellow refugees. Brent decides to make a deal with German agents operating in the U.S. He will surrender to the Gestapo if they will release a handful of prisoners. Scott joins him aboard the ship which will take him back to Austria and warns him of a Nazi betrayal. They are married by the captain and eventually freed when the vessel is intercepted by a British warship when war is declared.

The film is another Hollywood propaganda film, released before America's entry into the war, assailing the oppression and ruthlessness of Nazi Germany. The basic plots of these features were not as far-fetched as some would imagine. Movie audiences encountered a continuous stream of newspaper and magazine articles that attested to the unfortunate plight of numerous refugees who fled from religious and political persecution in lands dominated by Nazi rule. ■

They Got Me Covered (1943) Par. *Dir.* David Butler; *Sc.* Harry Kurnitz; *Cast includes:* Bob Hope, Dorothy Lamour, Lenore Aubert, Otto Preminger, Eduardo Ciannelli.

Bob Hope plays a bungling reporter in this World War II spy comedy. As a correspondent for an international news agency early in the war, he bungles several major assignments such as the Rothstein murder, the Munich bombing and Hitler's invasion of Russia. His agency boss restrains himself from committing mayhem on the returning incompetent. "You've wrecked my nervous system, ruined my reputation; you've cost me money, customers and good will!" he cries. "Does that mean you're dissatisfied with my work, chief?" Hope asks.

The hapless reporter relocates in Washington, hoping to regain his reputation by uncovering enemy agents. He soon becomes entangled in a network of Nazi spies, including an updated Mata Hari (Lenore Aubert) and the group's ruthless leader (Otto Preminger). With the help of Dorothy Lamour and various branches of the government, Hope brings the foes to justice. The film is not one of the comedian's best works, but it provides several good one-liners. ■

They Live in Fear (1944), Col. *Dir.* Josef Berne; *Sc.* Michael Simmons, Sam Ornitz; *Cast includes:* Otto Kruger, Clifford Severn, Pat Parrish, Jimmy Carpenter, Erwin Kalser, Danny Jackson.

A World War II propaganda drama that calls for tolerance toward refugees, the plot centers on a young emigrant who escapes to America to free himself of Nazi oppression. Ironically, the boy finds the same intolerance in his newly adopted home. German agents seek him out and threaten the lives of his family who have remained behind. Clifford Severn portrays the persecuted teenager. Otto Kruger appears as the only principal adult in this tale about oppressive forces in the U.S. A unique theme for its time, especially in pointing out that not all Germans were Nazis, the story is not developed sufficiently to lift it out of its low-budget status. ■

Saboteurs plan to kill an army intelligence colonel as Allan Lane and Sally Eilers, both working under cover, look on and wonder how to save the officer. *They Made Her a Spy* (1939).

They Made Her a Spy (1939), RKO. *Dir.* Jack Hively; *Sc.* Michael Kanin, Joe Pagano; *Cast includes:* Sally Eilers, Allan Lane, Fritz Leiber, Frank M. Thomas, Theodore von Eltz.

This espionage drama opens with a series of sabotage acts flashing across the screen. In the last of these, a young army officer is about to demonstrate to his superior a military device he has developed when an unexpected explosion kills both men. The young officer's sister (Sally Eilers) decides to join the U.S. Army's Military Intelligence Division to help uncover the spy ring responsible for her brother's death. After trying to dissuade her, the chiefs of staff give her a chance. The colonel in charge warns her that they are up against an "organization powerful and cunning, guided by a brilliant brain."

Posing as a disgruntled civil service worker who has recently been dismissed, she makes contact with a suspected spy network using a restaurant for its cover. She is accepted into the inner circle when she proves she can deliver a copy of a treaty the spy leader wants. A reporter (Allan Lane), posing as a member of the spy ring, and Eilers soon become friends. However, she thinks he is an enemy agent. With her help, all the spies are soon rounded up except the leader, whom no one has seen. Fortunately, Eilers knows his voice from a telephone conversation. The master spy is a respected member of a Washington committee investigating the intelligence bureau. When he realizes he is about to be exposed, he tries to escape. He temporarily eludes the government agents by hiding atop the Washington Monument. When he is followed there, he jumps to his death rather than face a trial. This climactic sequence also includes some of the flag-waving dialogue indicative of the film. "Every time I look out at Washington," the chatty elevator operator at the famous site admits, "I kind o' get the feeling that all this is permanent, that it's strong, that it's here to stay." ∎

They Saved Hitler's Brain (1963), Crown International. *Dir.* David Bradley; *Sc.* Richard Miles; *Cast includes:* Audrey Caire, Walter Stocker, Carlos Rivas, John Holland, Dani Lynn, Marshall Reid.

An international conspiracy of unrepentant Nazis, led by the preserved brain of Hitler, plots to conquer the world in this inane low-budget drama. A group of Nazis, operating from its base in a fictitious South American country, obtains a deadly gas formula powerful enough to fell entire armies. Before the leaders can release the weapon, they have to make certain there is no antidote. After assassinating several U.S. agents and another scientist, the conspirators' henchmen kidnap American Professor Coleman, who has been working on the formula. His daughter and son-in-law, a government agent, follow him to South America where they join forces with others to foil the world-domination scheme.

Much of the film is laughable. One particular sequence has two Nazi storm troopers carrying around the head of a twitching Hitler encased in glass. Another, epitomizing the low production values of the film, shows a crowded nightclub with a total of about four or five tables filled with patrons who are outnumbered by entertainers and staff. Aside from the ludicrous and disjointed plot, the dialogue ("Surely, a few Nazis can't upset the world," "So you're the superior ones—the slappers of women, the torturers of old men") is sophomoric. See Nazi Subversion: Post-World War II. ∎

Thief, The (1952), UA. *Dir.* Russell Rouse; *Sc.* Clarence Greene, Russell Rouse; *Cast includes:* Ray Milland, Martin Gabel, Rita Gam, Harry Bronson, John McKutcheon, Rita Vale.

A Washington-based American nuclear scientist turns traitor in this unusual Cold War drama which has no spoken dialogue but retains its sound effects. Ray Milland portrays the turncoat who, working with foreign agents, photographs certain secret papers and turns the film over to the enemy. When government officials discover a security leak, Milland and his cohorts scheme to leave the country. Milland journeys to New York where he is followed to the Empire State Building by an F.B.I. agent who is then killed. Milland, shaken by this unexpected murder, surrenders to the F.B.I.

The innovative technique of unfolding the tale without spoken dialogue is interesting at the beginning but soon grows annoying. However, there are moments when the effect heightens the suspense, especially when telephones ring or other sounds intrude upon events. See Soviet Spies in the U.S. ∎

Thin Man Goes Home, The (1944), MGM. *Dir.* Richard Thorpe; *Sc.* Robert Riskin, Dwight Taylor; *Cast includes:* William Powell, Myrna Loy, Lucile Watson, Gloria De-Haven, Anne Revere, Helen Vinson, Harry Davenport.

Amateur sleuth Nick Charles (William Powell) and his wife Nora (Myrna Loy) get mixed up with murder and an espionage ring in this fifth entry in the popular detective series. Nick casually returns home to visit his parents (Harry Davenport, Lucile Watson) who never wanted their son to be a detective. His stay is suddenly interrupted when a visitor requests his help involving some skull-duggery. This seemingly unimportant incident soon leads to the visitor's murder, a mysterious group of paintings and an espionage plot on the part of foreign agents who are seeking to steal the plans for a new propeller being developed at a local defense plant. Following several more killings, Nick's perceptive detective work and some witty dialogue, the amateur sleuth solves the case, exposes the spy ring and uncovers its leader (Lloyd Corrigan), prancing around as one of the town's most noble citizens.

With this entry, it became apparent that the series was thinning out. Only one more film followed—*The Song of the Thin Man* (1947).

The Thin Man series, which began in 1934 based on characters created by Dashiel Hammett, almost single-handedly launched a new genre—the sophisticated detective comedy. *The Thin Man*, the unpretentious first and best entry, so delighted its audiences that the surprised studio, which set out to make a simple, quick, inexpensive detective yarn, was practically forced to provide sequels. ■

Thing We Love, The (1918), Par. *Dir.* Lou Tellegen; *Sc.* Harvey Thew; *Cast includes:* Wallace Reid, Kathlyn Williams, Tully Marshall, Mayne Kelso, Charles Ogle, Billy Elmer.

German agents attempt to destroy an American munitions plant in this standard World War I drama. Wallace Reid, as a vice-president of the firm, suspects that the company president (Tully Marshall) is secretly sympathetic to the German cause. Marshall has secretly agreed to destroy the plant in exchange for a large sum of money from the Germans. Reid, discovering Marshall's motives, masquerades as one of the workers and professes loyalty to Germany. He is accepted as a German agent and assigned to plant a bomb that will destroy the factory. Although he is arrested by a detective, Reid exposes the entire plot and proves that the president was part of the conspiracy.

Five years after the film was released, the handsome and popular screen star Wallace Reid died from drug and alcohol abuse. Suffering head injuries resulting from a train crash, he was given morphine to relieve the pain. He soon became addicted and, in 1922, was forced to give up his promising screen career. He entered a sanitarium where he succumbed the following year. ■

13 Frightened Girls (1963), Col. *Dir.* William Castle; *Sc.* Robert Dillon; *Cast includes:* Kathy Dunn, Murray Hamilton, Joyce Taylor, Hugh Marlowe, Khigh Dhiegh, Charlie Briggs.

The daughter of an American diplomat gets involved in the world of espionage in this inept and silly drama set in London and in a Swiss boarding school. Teenager Kathy Dunn, as the precocious daughter, chances upon a political murder while she is vacationing in London. She quickly notifies a C.I.A. agent (Murray Hamilton), whom she secretly admires. Once enmeshed in the shadowy world of intrigue, she begins to collect information

from several embassies. Her father's position allows her easy access to numerous files. She soon becomes known in espionage circles as "Kitten," a notorious secret agent, and is pursued by various factions. Finally, Hamilton has to journey to her Swiss school to rescue her from impending danger. ■

13 Rue Madeleine (1946), TCF. *Dir.* Henry Hathaway; *Sc.* John Monks, Jr., Sy Bartlett; *Cast includes:* James Cagney, Annabella, Richard Conte, Frank Latimore, Walter Abel.

A suspenseful World War II drama of espionage involving the O.S.S. (Office of Strategic Services), the film concerns one of the agency's secret missions behind enemy lines. A team of three agents undergoes vigorous training in preparation for the special assignment. Finally, the three men are sent into France to investigate Germany's rocket-launching sites. One of the team (Richard Conte), however, is a double agent, a Nazi spy who has been raised in the U.S. Conte deliberately sabotages one of the team's parachutes and the unfortunate agent falls to his death.

When the team's supervisor and chief agent (James Cagney) discovers the deception, he decides to parachute into France and complete the mission. After Cagney accomplishes his assignment, he is captured by Conte, who has him tortured to learn the exact location of the forthcoming Allied invasion. Meanwhile, the London intelligence office, where Cagney's boss (Walter Abel) is located, learns of the agent's capture. Allied commanders order a squadron of bombers to attack the Gestapo headquarters where Cagney is being held, hoping to kill him before he is forced to talk. The final scenes show a defiant Cagney undergoing brutal interrogation at the hands of Conte's henchmen as Allied bombs fall on the infamous 13 Rue Madeleine. The film opens and closes with the following words inscribed on the O.S.S. headquarters building: "What is past is prologue"—anticipating the continuation of U.S. intelligence under the aegis of the C.I.A., set up in 1947, just two years after the O.S.S. was dissolved.

The drama, adapted from the novel *The Tiger Among Us* by Leigh Brackett, was produced by Louis De Rochemont, who gave the production the same sense of immediacy and high production values as his earlier productions. He was responsible for a popular series of shorts titled "The March of Time," which ran from the 1930s through the war years. He also produced the highly successful semi-documentary spy drama *The House on 92nd Street* (1945). See Jedburgh Operations; Office of Strategic Services; Operation Overlord. ■

German nurse Eva Marie Saint helps captured American officer James Garner escape from Nazis in the World War II drama *36 Hours* (1964).

36 Hours (1964), MGM. *Dir.* George Seaton; *Sc.* George Seaton; *Cast includes:* James Garner, Eva Marie Saint, Rod Taylor, Werner Peters, John Banner.

A captured American officer is tricked by the Germans into revealing the actual invasion plans of the Allies in this suspense- ful World War II drama set on the eve of the Normandy invasion. James Garner, as Major Jefferson Pike, an officer with U.S. intelligence, is drugged by German agents while he is on a special mission in Lisbon. He is transported to Germany and made to believe that he has been suffering from amnesia for six years. He discovers the Nazi scheme only after he mentions Normandy but proceeds to confuse his interrogators about the location of the invasion. His revelation occurs when he notices that a cut on his finger, which he had gotten only days before his amnesia, has still not healed. To confirm his suspicions, he checks some books strewn around in the hospital and notices none have been printed after the war.

Rod Taylor, as Major Walter Gerber, a German psychiatrist, believes he can get the vital information from Garner without using physical torture as advocated by an S.S. officer. Raised in the U.S. until age 16, Gerber devises an elaborate plot to convince Pike that he is recuperating at an American hospital.

Gerber poses as an American doctor trying to help the American officer recover from his amnesia and has filled the surroundings with English-speaking staff and American paraphernalia. When Gerber learns that his experiment has failed and that his own life is in danger, he helps his patient to escape into Switzerland.

Eva Marie Saint portrays a concentration camp victim who volunteers to help the psychiatrist. She is chosen because of her nursing background and her ability to speak English. Gerber promises to keep her out of the dreaded camp if his experiment succeeds. When the American discovers he has been tricked by the Germans, she decides to help him. She escapes with Pike.

Werner Peters, as Otto Schack, the ambitious S.S. officer, portrays the major villain in the drama. Gerber, who opposes his strong-arm tactics, describes him as an "ignorant, heel-clicking storm trooper." Suspicious of intellectuals, Schack warns the doctor about the consequences of failure. "Do you really think this scheme will succeed?" "I'll stake my reputation on it," the doctor replies. "You have staked more than your reputation, doctor, much more," the S.S. officer adds menacingly.

Early in the film there is much dialogue about the intricacies and convoluted world of espionage and intelligence. At an Allied strategy meeting of intelligence officers several days before the invasion, the group is convinced that the Germans expect the assault to take place in northern France, at Calais. But one U.S. colonel wants more confirmation. "We've got to find out if they're playing games with us," he says, asking Pike about his Lisbon contact. "He's only a clerk in the German embassy," Pike explains. "I don't think he's working for German intelligence, but I think they know he's working for us. Whenever they want to mislead us, they make it easy for him to find some false information." All agree that Pike should make one last trip to Lisbon to find out from his contact where Germany expects the Allied landings to take place. The session ends on a note of levity, with one officer commenting on the elaborate precautions intelligence has taken to throw the Germans off guard: "We've got that actor reviewing troops in Gibraltar—impersonating General Montgomery." The title refers to the limited time the psychiatrist has to extract the information from the American major. The film is based in part on "Beware of the Dog," a short story by Roald Dahl. See Operation Overlord. ■

This Gun for Hire (1942), Par. *Dir.* Frank Tuttle; *Sc.* Albert Maltz, W. R. Burnett; *Cast includes:* Veronica Lake, Robert Preston, Laird Cregar, Alan Ladd, Tully Marshall, Mikhail Rasumny.

Treason and international intrigue over a secret chemical formula shape the plot of this icy drama based on Graham Greene's novel *A Gun for Sale*. Alan Ladd, as a hired gun who carries out his assignment only to be betrayed by the treacherous Laird Cregar, seeks revenge on the man who hired him. Meanwhile Ladd meets an attractive blonde singer (Veronica Lake) whose patience and sympathy manage to reach the otherwise cold killer. An edgy romance develops as the police hunt for the hired killer. Cregar is part of a plot to sell a newly developed formula to the Japanese. Ladd, in his blind revenge, foils Cregar's plans at the cost of his own life. Robert Preston portrays a police detective and Lake's fiancé. Tully Marshall, as an elderly tycoon, exemplifies the corrupt, Machiavellian financier who would sell out his country for money and power.

The film catapulted Alan Ladd to stardom. As a steely-eyed, amoral killer who lives an empty and lonely life in sleazy rooms, he thaws under Lake's influence. Sexy Veronica Lake, who perhaps typified the 1940s Hollywood leading ladies, is as tough and wisecracking as she is emotionally vulnerable. *Film noir* conventions include themes of greed and betrayal and scenes drenched with low-key lighting. Paramount released a remake of the tale in 1957 titled *Short Cut to Hell*, directed by James Cagney and featuring Robert Ivers, Georganna Johnson and William Bishop. ■

This Is My Affair (1937), TCF. *Dir.* William A. Seiter; *Sc.* Allen Rivkin, Lamar Trotti; *Cast includes:* Robert Taylor, Barbara Stanwyck, Victor McLaglen, Brian Donlevy, Sidney Blackmer, John Carradine.

President McKinley assigns a U.S. Navy officer to expose a syndicate of bank robbers in this historical drama set in the early 1900s. Robert Taylor, as the secret agent, goes under cover and gains the confidence of some of the thieves who are operating from a music hall in the Midwest. Here he meets Barbara Stanwyck, who portrays the half-sister of one of the culprits (Brian Donlevy). Meanwhile, McKinley is assassinated. He was the only other person who knew of Taylor's special mission. When Taylor is captured, along with other members of the gang, he cannot prove that he was commissioned by the late President. Stanwyck, who has fallen for Taylor, appeals to Theodore Roosevelt, McKinley's successor, on behalf of Taylor, who has been convicted and sentenced to hang. Victor McLaglen portrays Donlevy's partner and has an eye for Stanwyck. This leads to several clashes with Taylor. ■

This Mad World (1930), MGM. *Dir.* William DeMille; *Sc.* Clara Beranger, Arthur Caesar; *Cast includes:* Basil Rathbone, Kay Johnson, Louise Dresser, Veda Buckland, Louis Natheaux.

A World War I drama starring Basil Rathbone, the grim plot was so depressing that it failed at the box office. Rathbone portrays a French spy who decides to visit his mother living behind German lines. He meets and falls in love with Kay Johnson, who plays a disguised countess and wife of a German officer. When she learns his real identity, he threatens to shoot her if she exposes him. In the choice between love and duty, he selects the former while she chooses the latter. She informs on him and he is executed. The repentant informer then decides to take her own life. The film is based on the play by Francois de Curel. Director William DeMille was the older brother of producer-director Cecil B. DeMille. ■

Threads of Destiny (1914), General. *Dir.* Joseph W. Smiley; *Sc.* William H. Clifford; *Cast includes:* Evelyn Nesbit Thaw, Bernard Siegel, Marguerite Risser, William Cahill, Joseph W. Smiley, Marguerite Marsh.

A drama of intrigue set in both Russia and the U.S., the story concerns the hapless exploits of Miriam Grunstein, a young Russian Jewess. Her mother is killed during a massacre, and her father, a political prisoner, is exiled to Siberia. More tragedy is about to befall Miriam when her honor is threatened by Romanoff, the lascivious head of Russia's secret police. Warned by her dying father, Miriam seeks the help of other local Jews who effect her escape to America. Years later she is happily married to an Arizona rancher, a Russian emigré. Suddenly Romanoff appears on the

Czar's business. He threatens to expose Miriam, who then turns to a group of local nihilists. Fearing that the Russian has been sent to spy upon them, they plot to kill him. Their plan succeeds, and Miriam is saved to continue her new life in America. ■

Three Days of the Condor (1975), Par. *Dir.* Sydney Pollack; *Sc.* Lorenzo Semple, Jr., David Rayfiel; *Cast includes:* Robert Redford, Faye Dunaway, Cliff Robertson, Max von Sydow, John Houseman.

An innocent C.I.A. employee is tossed into a complex web of intrigue, treachery and betrayal in this suspenseful drama based on James Grady's novel *Six Days of the Condor.* Robert Redford, as a "reader," a low-level researcher for the C.I.A., uncovers a plot within the secret organization. While he is out buying lunch for his colleagues, they are all murdered by unknown assassins. When the leaders of the killers learn that their hired gunmen missed Redford, they put out a "contract" on his life. On the run, Redford kidnaps an innocent bystander (Faye Dunaway) and hides out in her apartment while he tries to unravel the mystery.

Cliff Robertson, as Redford's immediate superior, is under orders to have him killed. Max von Sydow portrays a professional assassin hired by a renegade agent responsible for the murders to track down Redford. When they finally meet, the assassin, no longer interested in his prey, warns Redford to disappear, perhaps to Europe, and become an independent agent. He warns Redford that his life may still be in danger and explains that confidence in one's own precision is the only thing worth fighting for.

John Houseman, as one of the C.I.A. chiefs in on the conspiracy, laments how the role of espionage has changed from World War II to today's political uncertainties. He had worked under Col. William "Wild Bill" Donovan, head of the Office of Strategic Services (O.S.S.), during World War II. "Do you miss that kind of action?" an agent asks Houseman. "No," he replies mournfully, "I miss that kind of clarity."

After Redford disentangles the secret plot, he meets with Robertson. "Do we have plans to invade the Middle East?" he asks. "We have games," Robertson replies. "We play games." When Redford responds with disgust, his superior explains the political expediencies. "It's simple economics. Today it's oil. In 10 or

15 years, food, plutonium. What do you think the people will want us to do then?" "Ask them!" the idealistic Redford returns. "Not now—then," Robertson continues. "Ask them when they're running out. Ask them when there's no heat in their homes and they're cold. Ask them when their engines stop. Ask them when people who have never known hunger start going hungry." Redford, to protect his own life, explains that he has spilled the whole story to the *New York Times.* "You've done more damage than you know," Robertson exclaims. "I hope so," Redford replies as he walks away. See Central Intelligence Agency. ■

Three Faces East (1926), PDC. *Dir.* Rupert Julian; *Sc.* C. Gardner Sullivan, Monte Katterjohn; *Cast includes:* Jetta Goudal, Robert Ames, Henry Walthall, Clive Brook, Edythe Chapman.

Based on the play by Anthony Paul Kelly, the film concerns a network of German spies operating in London during World War I, the chief of whom poses as a butler employed in the home of an important British war official. Jetta Goudal portrays a secret agent who is attracted to a young British officer (Robert Ames). Clive Brook plays the master spy. The film, which was remade in 1930 and again in 1940 under the title *British Intelligence,* includes several brief battle scenes.

By the 1920s, Hollywood studios were softening their image of the German. In war films released during the conflict and for one or two years after, enemy officers and their underlings almost invariably engaged in rape and pillage, burned and bayoneted babies and enslaved the children of captive nations. In all three versions of *Three Faces East* and many other war dramas released several years after the armistice, the Germans began to be depicted as suave and sophisticated, often undetectable in manner and dress from the heroes. See British Intelligence: World War I. ■

Three Faces East (1930), WB. *Dir.* Roy Del Ruth; *Sc.* Oliver H. P. Garrett, Arthur Caesar; *Cast includes:* Constance Bennett, Erich von Stroheim, Anthony Bushell, William Courtney, Crauford Kent, Charlotte Walker.

This World War I drama, a remake of a 1926 silent film based on a 1918 melodrama, stars Constance Bennett as a British agent who maneuvers her way into German headquarters to learn the identity of a leading spy working in England. Erich von Stroheim is the master German spy working as a butler of Dutch descent in the home of Sir Winston Chamberlain. Menacing submarines off the coast of England and secret radio transmitters threaten American ships heading toward England. The climactic scene is also a surprising one. Bennett shoots the butler in the back as he attempts to send information to a German submarine. This is one of the earliest instances of a hero or heroine shooting a villain in the back. A third film version appeared in 1940 titled *British Intelligence* starring Margaret Lindsay. ▪

Three Kinds of Heat (1987), Cannon. *Dir.* Leslie Stevens; *Sc.* Leslie Stevens; *Cast includes*: Robert Ginty, Victoria Barrett, Shakti, Sylvester McCoy, Barry Foster, Jeannie Brown.

A U.S. government agent, a New York cop and a Hong Kong law officer join forces on a special Interpol mission to find and put an end to the sinister career of an international gangster in this weak action drama. Robert Ginty portrays the special agent, Victoria Barrett the female cop from the Big Apple and Shakti the Oriental policewoman. The story shifts from New York to London as the trio close in on Sylvester McCoy, the chief villain who leads them on a merry chase until the noisy climactic battle staged in a warehouse filled with explosives. The production is below par for writer-director Leslie Stevens, who turned out several notable television series, including *The Outer Limits*. ▪

Three Musketeers, The (1921), UA. *Dir.* Fred Niblo; *Sc.* Edward Knoblock; *Cast includes*: Douglas Fairbanks, Leon Barry, George Seigmann, Eugene Pallette, Boyd Irwin, Marguerite De La Motte, Adolphe Menjou, Nigel de Brulier.

Alexander Dumas' famous tale about intrigue in 17th-century France offered the popular and exuberant Fairbanks an opportunity to star in his most ambitious film up to that year. He surrounded himself with a host of other talented actors and actresses and relatively huge sets that almost dwarfed his appearance as the gallant D'Artagnan. Nevertheless, his efforts were not in vain, for the film grossed more than $1.5 million and retains its place as one of the best of many adaptations of the novel.

The story begins in 1625 in the French court of Louis XIII (Adolphe Menjou), "teeming with plot and counterplot, faction and cabal, enmity and jealousy," as a title card explains. Cardinal Richelieu (Nigel de Brulier), an iron-willed, powerful, ambitious figure, considers Queen Anne (Mary MacLaren) a barrier to his future goals. He decides to discredit her in the eyes of King Louis by suggesting she is having an affair with England's Duke of Buckingham (Thomas Holding). When his spies report that the queen has given a rare diamond buckle to the duke as a farewell token, the cardinal devises an intricate plot. He knows that the king had given the buckle to Anne as a gift, so he convinces Louis to request that the queen wear it at an upcoming ball.

The remainder of the plot concerns the queen's efforts—by way of D'Artagnan and his friends, the three musketeers—to get the buckle back from the duke in time for the festivities. Richelieu dispatches his agents and troops to prevent D'Artagnan from accomplishing his mission. Fairbanks engages in enough acrobatics—dueling with the cardinal's soldiers, leaping from windows and eluding his foes—to keep his fans happy and the intricate plot moving. Several years later he made a sequel titled *The Iron Mask* (1929), also silent. Many other American and foreign versions of the novel followed over the next few decades, including an RKO release in 1936 with Walter Abel in the Fairbanks role, a 1939 Fox film with Don Ameche and an MGM Technicolor adaptation in 1948 with Gene Kelly emulating Fairbanks' acrobatics. In addition, the intrigue about the love-gift and its return was transformed into a contemporary setting in the 1930 spy drama *Last of the Lone Wolf*, with Bert Lytell playing a modern-day D'Artagnan. ▪

Three Stooges in Orbit, The (1962), Col. *Dir.* Edward Bernds; *Sc.* Elwood Ullman; *Cast includes*: The Three Stooges, Carol Christensen, Edison Stroll, Emil Sitka, George N. Nelse, Rayford Barnes.

Larry, Moe and Curly-Joe (Larry Fine, Moe Howard, Joe De Rita) ply their comic antics in this slapstick farce about Martian spies trying to steal a secret weapon from its inventor. The weapon combines the advantages of a tank, submarine and rocket. Character comedy actor Emil Sitka, who appeared in more than three dozen shorts and features with the

Three Stooges, portrays the inventor. Carol Christensen and Edison Stroll provide the romance, but the bulk of the film is dominated by the visual comedy of the trio.

Curly (Jerry Howard), the original member of the comedy team, had become ill and was replaced in 1947 by an older brother, Shemp Howard, who died in 1955. Joe Palma and Joe Besser, veteran performers in their own right, each filled in temporarily until Joe De Rita joined Larry and Moe. ■

Three the Hard Way (1974), AA. *Dir.* Gordon Parks, Jr.; *Sc.* Eric Bercovici, Jerry Ludwig; *Cast includes:* Jim Brown, Fred Williamson, Jim Kelly, Sheila Frazier, Jay Robinson, Charles McGregor.

A secret organization made up of white racists plots to rid the U.S. of its black population in this inept and silly action drama. Three popular black performers—Jim Brown as a recording producer, Fred Williamson as a public relations expert and Jim Kelly as a karate-school owner—take on the Fascist group in a series of violent shoot-outs, car chases and hand-to-hand battles.

Jay Robinson portrays Monroe Feather, the effete head of the sinister organization. "We have a scientific institution here," he explains to one of his victims. "We seek humane solutions to social disorders. The ultimate purpose is a cleansing—a purification—of the races on this continent, particularly in this great nation of ours." To this end he dispatches three teams, each carrying a jar of highly toxic poison liquid that affects only blacks. The underlings head for three cities—Detroit, Washington and Los Angeles—where they are to drop the solution into the city water supply. In the meantime, each of our three heroes journeys to a different city to foil the genocidal plan.

The film exemplifies the black exploitation dramas that were popular in the 1970s. A blend of James Bond type of sleuthing, violent confrontations, superhero stunts, garish sets and a sound track of rock music, they offered pure escapism at the expense of logic and credible characterization. ■

Through Thick and Thin (1927), Lumas. *Dir.* B. Reeves Eason, Jack Nelson; *Sc.* Edward J. Meagher; *Cast includes:* William Fairbanks, George Periolat, Ina Anson, Ethel Shannon, Art Ortego.

A U.S. Secret Service agent is assigned to find and round up a gang of drug smugglers operating south of the border in this routine drama that provides plenty of action. William Fairbanks, as the government agent, masquerades as a tough guy once he reaches Mexico. When he meets up with the gang, he overpowers one their strongest members and is accepted into the group. He then meets the daughter (Ethel Shannon) of one of the smugglers. He quickly falls in love with her while suspecting her father of being the leader. However, Fairbanks later learns that the man, in reality, is a detective trying to get evidence against the smugglers. Fairbanks rescues the daughter and effects the capture of the gang. ■

Thunder Island (1963), TCF. *Dir.* Jack Leewood; *Sc.* Don Devlin, Jack Nicholson; *Cast includes:* Gene Nelson, Fay Spain, Brian Kelly, Miriam Colon, Art Bedard, Antonio T. Martino.

Plotters attempt to assassinate an exiled dictator in this little drama filmed in Puerto Rico. Gene Nelson, as the assassin who belongs to a group of idealists, bungles the assignment. The group wants the intended target killed because they fear his return to power. Fay Spain and Brian Kelly portray a married couple whose marriage is coming apart. Nelson unintentionally heals their troubles. Miriam Colon portrays a member of the idealistic assassins. ■

Treachery and double treachery are about to occur in the Malayan jungle where Nazis are trying to halt rubber production. *Tiger Fangs* (1943).

Tiger Fangs (1943), PRC. *Dir.* Sam Newfield; *Sc.* Arthur St. Claire; *Cast includes:* Frank Buck, June Duprez, Duncan Renaldo, J. Farrell MacDonald, Howard Banks, J. Alex Havier.

Famous animal tamer and circus performer Frank Buck leads a United Nations team into the Malayan jungle to investigate an outbreak of attacks by man-eating tigers in the region in this low-budget World War II film. They discover the particularly deadly creatures have been drugged by Nazi agents to attack the rubber plantation workers. The spies hope to curtail the production of rubber, essential to the Allied war effort. June Duprez plays an attractive biologist while Dan Seymour portrays the heavy in more ways than one in this routine tale.

Historically, the film is implausible in its premise. The rubber-producing areas mentioned in the plot had already fallen into Japanese hands early in the war. Therefore, it was highly unlikely that any plantations had to be prevented by the enemy from producing the vital war material for Allied countries or that scientists representing the United Nations would have been sent into enemy territory. ■

Tigress, The (1914), Famous Plays and Players. *Sc.* Aaron Hoffman; *Cast includes:* Olga Petrova.

Olga Petrova portrays a wife and mother who suffers the loss of her family when she rejects the advances of a powerful official in this four-reel drama set in a fictitious land that suspiciously resembles Russia. The politico effects the husband's murder, has Petrova's child taken away from her and imprisons the mother. Petrova escapes and makes her way to the U.S. Embittered by her horrible experiences and losing faith in all societies, she joins an international network of spies. Meanwhile, two Americans adopt her daughter. They return to America where one is soon appointed to a diplomatic post. He has in his possession important fortification plans. Spies steal the papers and intend to turn them over to the captain of a foreign warship lying off the Atlantic coast. When Petrova learns that the diplomat is one of the Americans who rescued her child, she returns the plans. The spies have other, stolen, secret documents which they turn over to the captain. Petrova reveals this information to the diplomat who notifies the proper authorities. Using the threat of coastal defense guns, the diplomat prevents the foreign ship's departure until the documents are returned. ■

Till We Meet Again (1936), Par. *Dir.* Robert Florey; *Sc.* Edwin Justus Mayer, Brian Marlow, Alfred Davis, Morton Barteaux; *Cast includes:* Herbert Marshall, Gertrude Michael, Lionel Atwill, Rod LaRocque, Guy Bates Post, Torben Meyer.

Two lovers who are separated by the war end up as secret agents on opposite sides in this World War I drama. Herbert Marshall portrays an English actor who is in love with a Viennese actress (Gertrude Michael). The war interferes with their wedding as each is called to duty to act as a spy. The film includes a few brief scenes of the war itself, but these are chiefly stock shots. The couple, who engage in the usual cat-and-mouse game of espionage, are permitted at the end of the film to escape to neutral territory to continue their romance. The film, based on the play *The Last Curtain* by Alfred Davis, has been noted for its accurate period atmosphere, an element often neglected in the Hollywood spy dramas of the 1930s. ■

Till We Meet Again (1944), Par. *Dir.* Frank Borzage; *Sc.* Lenore Coffee; *Cast includes:* Ray Milland, Barbara Britton, Walter Slezak, Lucile Watson, Mona Freeman.

A downed American flier is aided by the French underground and a novitiate nun in this World War I romantic drama adapted from the play by Alfred Maury. Ray Milland portrays a happily married pilot who is given important documents by the French Resistance to take back to England. An unworldly convent girl (Barbara Britton) poses as his wife to help him get through Nazi lines. An affectionate relationship develops between the two as Milland explains his deep love for his wife and Britton begins to understand more about life outside the Church. Later, she is caught by the Nazis who plan to send her to a German brothel. A local French mayor and collaborator (Walter Slezak), horrified by the brutal decision, kills her before the sentence can be carried out. ■

Time to Die, A (1983), Almi. *Dir.* Matt Cimber; *Sc.* John Goff, Matt Cimber, William Russell; *Cast includes:* Edward Albert, Jr., Rod Taylor, Rex Harrison, Linn Stokke, Raf Vallone, Cor Van Rijn.

A World War II veteran plots revenge against those Nazis who murdered his wife in this dark drama set in Europe in the late 1940s. Edward Albert, as Michael Hogan, the avenging husband, receives help from a C.I.A. agent (Rod Taylor). However, Taylor's motives are far from altruistic. His purpose is to delay Albert's efforts in finding and harming von Osten, one of his targets, played by Rex Harrison, who is being cultivated by the C.I.A. as West Germany's future chancellor. Linn Stokke provides some romantic interest for Albert. Despite its atmosphere of deception and betrayal, reminiscent of the *film noir* cycle of the 1940s, the drama remains static and uninteresting. The film was completed in 1979 under its original title *Seven Graves for Grogan.* ■

To Be or Not to Be (1942), UA. *Dir.* Ernst Lubitsch; *Sc.* Edwin Justus Mayer; *Cast includes:* Jack Benny, Carole Lombard, Robert Stack, Lionel Atwill, Felix Bressart, Sig Rumann.

With Mel Brooks' 1983 adaptation of Lubitsch's black comedy available, it is interesting to take another look at the original. It was made during the early, bleak years of World War II, not the best occasion to release a farce about the fall of Poland to the Nazis. The film encountered another dark cloud. One of its stars, Carole Lombard, died before its release. The story concerns a troupe of Polish actors, led by a vain actor (Jack Benny) and his wife (Lombard), who are in Warsaw when the Nazis invade. When their theater is closed by the conquerors, the players become involved in espionage and a final escape to freedom. Mayer's witty and tight script and Lubitsch's expert direction overcome minor criticisms of the film. Benny gave the finest performance of his film career and Lombard was as beautiful and sparkling as ever. The supporting actors contributed much to the dark humor. Sig Rumann, as Nazi officer "Concentration Camp" Erhardt ("I do the concentrating, they do the camping"), pans Benny's performance of *Hamlet*: "What he did to Shakespeare, we are doing now to Poland." Felix Bressart is excellent as an old-time actor who wishes only to play Shylock.

Director Lubitsch was criticized at the time for his insensitivity in making this film which his contemporaries considered to be in bad taste. His critics complained that the comedy diminished the global war, with all its ramifications, to a poor joke. One even labeled the film as "propaganda for Goebbels." Today's audiences will wonder what all the fuss was about. ■

To Be or Not to Be (1983), TCF. *Dir.* Alan Johnson; *Sc.* Thomas Meehan, Ronny Graham; *Cast includes:* Mel Brooks, Anne Bancroft, Tim Matheson, Charles Durning, José Ferrer.

A remake of the Ernst Lubitsch black comedy about a troupe of Polish performers under Nazi occupation, the film retains the basic plot but adds color, several musical numbers and the Brooks style of wit and slapstick. Mel Brooks repeats Jack Benny's original role as Bronski, the head of the theatrical company. Anne Bancroft, as his wife (and his spouse in real life), takes up a backstage romance with a Polish pilot (Tim Matheson). Charles Durning plays an incompetent local Gestapo chief who falls for the charms of Bancroft. José Ferrer portrays a German spy posing as a Polish patriot.

Some additions to the original include the song "Sweet Georgia Brown" sung in Polish and the Nazi persecution of a homosexual backstage dresser. Whether Brooks improved on the original film may depend on the individual's appreciation of the director's sense of humor. ■

To Have and Have Not (1944), WB. *Dir.* Howard Hawks; *Sc.* Jules Furthman, William Faulkner; *Cast includes:* Humphrey Bogart, Walter Brennan, Lauren Bacall, Hoagy Carmichael, Dan Seymour, Marcel Dalio.

Howard Hawks' World War II drama about the resistance of the Free French against the Vichy government in Martinique stars Humphrey Bogart as Harry Morgan. Morgan, who operates a fishing boat, smuggles resistance leaders to the Free French on the Caribbean island. At first, he is reluctant to get politically involved. "I don't understand what kind of war you're fighting," he remarks to one of the resisters. Later, when Vichy officials, led by character actor Dan Seymour, start pushing him around, he takes a stand against them.

Bogart gets unusually strong support from others in the cast, especially Lauren Bacall in her first screen role. As "Slim," a sultry café singer who falls for Bogart, she manages to steal more than one scene from her future husband. The now famous "whistle" scene has become a screen classic. Her singing was dubbed by Andy Williams. Walter Brennan has the role of Bogart's alcoholic sidekick. Hoagy Carmichael, as a café entertainer, contributes some singing and piano playing.

Lobby card for the World War II drama *To Have and Have Not* (1944) with Humphrey Bogart (2nd from r.), Lauren Bacall (r.) and Walter Brennan (c.).

The film, in many respects, is reminiscent of *Casablanca*. It even has some of the same actors (Bogart, Dan Seymour, Dalio) and similar dialogue. "I'm glad you're on our side," a French patriot says to Bogart, echoing the words of Paul Henreid, the freedom fighter in *Casablanca*. Henreid's defiant and optimistic conviction that, even if all the leaders are caught, "thousands will rise in their places," is repeated in the later film by another resistance leader. "There's always someone else. That is the mistake the Germans always make with people they try to destroy. There will be always someone else." Hoagy Carmichael replaces Dooley Wilson as the ubiquitous piano player and singer. Bogart again represents a neutral America that, when confronted with injustice and tyranny, will side with the forces of liberty. Even the melodramatic ending in which Bogart kills one of the officials and helps a resistance leader and his wife escape their pursuers is unabashedly duplicated.

Nelson Rockefeller, in charge of the American Affairs Committee at the time, learned about Hawks' production, which was based on Ernest Hemingway's novel. To stave off any objections from the Latin American countries, he persuaded Hawks to switch the setting from Florida-Cuba to Martinique. Hawks and Warners agreed and also changed the author's original plot which dealt with the smuggling of Chinese into the U.S. See Vichy France. ■

To Live and Die in L.A. (1985), MGM/UA.

Dir. William Friedkin; *Sc.* William Friedkin, Gerald Petievich; *Cast includes:* William H. Peterson, Willem Dafoe, John Pankow, Debra Feuer, John Torturro, Darlane Fleugel, Dean Stockwell.

A U.S. Secret Service agent, obsessed with avenging his partner's murder, tracks down an elusive counterfeiter in this chiefly implausible drama about sleazy characters on both sides of the law. William H. Peterson portrays the vindictive agent who breaks all the rules in his pursuit of counterfeiter and killer Willem Dafoe. Peterson and his new partner (John Pankow) go undercover as two

Palm Beach dealers in bogus money and set up a deal with Dafoe, who demands $30,000 up front. Since their department never allots more then $10,000 for this type of scheme, Peterson must find another method of raising the money. When he learns from one of his informants (Darlane Fleugel) that a man dealing in stolen diamonds is carrying $50,000 in cash, he persuades his partner to help him steal the money to finance the sting involving Dafoe.

The two agents kidnap the courier at the airport and drive him to a deserted area under a highway where they proceed to rob him. But the heist turns sour when the man is killed by strangers who have followed the agents. Later, after a harrowing car chase on a crowded elevated highway which leaves dozens of wrecked trucks and cars in its wake, the two agents learn the victim was an F.B.I. operative working under cover. Peterson remains untouched by the death he has caused while Pankow begins to crack under the strain. Still determined to entrap the counterfeiter, Peterson again convinces his partner to help him continue with the operation against Dafoe. In the final showdown Peterson is killed and Pankow is left to hunt down the counterfeiter who burns to death in his warehouse. Pankow then returns to his dead partner's sexy informant and tells her she is now working for him.

The film, based on the novel by Gerald Petievich, is difficult to accept on its own terms. Too many holes in the plot (Peterson's first partner goes alone to investigate Dafoe's warehouse, an exciting but unrealistic car chase, Peterson recapturing one of Dafoe's couriers who has escaped the agent's custody) strain credibility. In addition, there is no likable or sympathetic character the audience can identify with. Peterson allows his personal vendetta against Dafoe to cloud his judgment and subvert the law. Pankow, who knows his partner's tactics are wrong and illegal, is too weak to resist him; instead, he becomes Peterson's alter and sinks into the mire that was once his partner's world in the surprising, cynical ending. ∎

To the Ends of the Earth (1948), Col. *Dir.* Robert Stevenson; *Sc.* Jay Richard Kennedy; *Cast includes:* Dick Powell, Signe Hasso, Maylia, Ludwig Donath, Vladimir Sokoloff, Edgar Barrier.

An international ring of fanatical conspir-ators plots to dominate the world by making its peoples dependent upon opium in this well-paced, suspenseful drama that encompasses several continents. Dick Powell, as a U.S. government narcotics agent, suspects that the worldwide operation has been in business as early as 1935 and traces the drug-smuggling organization to such remote regions as Shanghai, Egypt and Cuba. Signe Hasso, as a governess in China for a pretty and charming orphan, provides Powell with his prime suspect as the ringleader. He finally uncovers the gang's byzantine operation of smuggling the drug through U.S. customs and exposes it real leader, the not-so-innocent orphan, played by Maylia. Vladimir Sokoloff portrays a Chinése official in this intriguing tale. ∎

To the Victor (1948), WB. *Dir.* Delmer Daves; *Sc.* Richard Brooks; *Cast includes:* Dennis Morgan, Viveca Lindfors, Victor Francen, Bruce Bennett, Dorothy Malone, Tom D'Andrea.

A group of conspirators, made up chiefly of Nazi collaborators, plots an assassination in this drama set in post-World War II France. Their purpose is to protect one of their associates who is being tried for war crimes. Their target is the defendant's wife—a possible witness. Dennis Morgan, as an ex-G.I. who is steeped in illegal black market activities, rescues Viveca Lindfors, who portrays the traitor's wife. They find solace in each other's love and vow to rededicate their lives. Lindfors gives damaging testimony against her husband, and Morgan turns over a new leaf. The film was shot partially in Paris and on Normandy's Omaha beach strewn with the debris of war, a symbol of the lovers' past wrecked lives. ∎

To Trap a Spy (1966), Arena/MGM. *Dir.* Don Medford; *Sc.* Sam Rolfe; *Cast includes:* Robert Vaughn, David McCallum, Lucian Paluzzi, Patricia Crowley, Fritz Weaver, Will Kuluva.

The popularity of the British-produced James Bond spy series in the early 1960s prompted American film and television producers to join the bandwagon. "The Man From U.N.C.L.E." quickly established itself as a T.V. staple and ran for several seasons. Additional footage was added to the original pilot program and released theatrically as *To Trap a Spy.* The familiar plot concerns a secret organization's attempt to gain control of an African republic. The conspiracy includes the assassination of the country's president and his chief advisers. However, Robert Vaughn, as Napoleon Solo, is assigned to foil the scheme. Patricia Crowley portrays an innocent housewife who helps him carry out his mission. David McCallum, repeating his television role, appears as Illya Kuryakin, Solo's sidekick. Other series episodes were converted for theatrical release, including *The Spy With My Face*, also released in 1966. See "The Man From U.N.C.L.E." ∎

Tobruk (1966), U. *Dir.* Arthur Hiller; *Sc.* Leo V. Gordon; *Cast includes:* Rock Hudson, George Peppard, Nigel Green, Guy Stockwell, Jack Watson, Leo Gordon, Heidy Hunt.

This World War II action drama concerns a special British force made up of commandos and German-born Jews on a special mission to destroy General Rommel's fuel supply and hold a key position at Tobruk until the British navy arrives. The plan calls for the Jews, who speak German fluently, to pose as Nazi soldiers and the British as prisoners of the "Nazis" so that they can infiltrate German lines. Hudson stars as an English major. George Peppard portrays the Jewish commander while Nigel Green plays the colonel in charge of the column of 90 men. The plot provides for plenty of action as the infiltrators, using flame-throwers and other weapons, destroy the fuel dump and battle the German defenders in this rousing tale.

The film includes a subplot involving the anti-Semitic feelings of Hudson and Green which are manifested in their attitudes toward Peppard. Unfortunately, this dramatic potential is never fully realized. ∎

Tokyo File 212 (1951), RKO. *Dir.* Dorrell McGowan, Stuart McGowan; *Sc.* Dorrell and Stuart McGowan; *Cast includes:* Florence Marly, Robert Peyton, Tainosuke Mochizuke, Byron Michie.

When Communist activities in Tokyo begin to affect the progress of the Korean War, U.S. Army intelligence decides to send in one of its top operatives in this standard drama. The American agent (Robert Peyton), masquerading as a writer, visits the local Tokyo night spots, including several less-respectable dives, in his search for the spy ring. His journey allows the director to exploit the talents of several local entertainers. Florence Marly

plays a seductive international spy who eventually redeems herself by sacrificing her life to prevent an assassination. In general, the film is a rather murky anti-Communist propaganda tale allegedly based on official army intelligence files. See Korean War: Intelligence and Covert Actions. ∎

Lobby card for *Tokyo Joe* (1949), a post-World War II drama with Humphrey Bogart as an ex-G.I. who foils a smuggling racket involving war criminals trying to return to Japan.

Tokyo Joe (1949), Col. *Dir.* Stuart Heisler; *Sc.* Cyril Hume, Bertram Millhauser, Walter Doniger; *Cast includes:* Humphrey Bogart, Alexander Knox, Florence Marly, Sessue Hayakawa, Jerome Courtland, Gordon Jones.

Humphrey Bogart portrays an ex-G.I. who returns to Japan after World War II and is drawn into a smuggling racket. Co-owner of a nightclub, he discovers that his prewar wife has married someone else. He begins an airline freight line as the first step in his determination to win her back. Sessue Hayakawa, as the leader of a secret group of agents who wish to smuggle war criminals back to Japan, finances Bogart's freight line. He then blackmails the American into the smuggling scheme by kidnapping Bogart's little daughter. Bogart, however, cooperates with government officials and effects the arrest of several major Japanese war criminals. But he pays with his life during the rescue of his daughter. Florence Marly portrays his wife. Alexander Knox plays her husband. ∎

Tokyo Rose (1945), Par. *Dir.* Lew Landers; *Sc.* Geoffrey Homes, Maxwell Shane; *Cast includes:* Lotus Long, Byron Barr, Osa Massen, Don Douglas.

A World War II action drama, the film concerns the famous female broadcaster and an escaped G.I.'s plan to capture her. Byron Barr portrays an American prisoner of war who is selected by the Japanese for a radio interview with Tokyo Rose, a purveyor of propaganda for the Japanese. He escapes from his captors during the excitement of an air raid and finds time to destroy the radio station. He manages to contact the Japanese underground whom he convinces to assist him in kidnapping Rose. They succeed in their mission following several close scrapes with soldiers and reach the coast where an American submarine is scheduled to pick them up.

The true story of Tokyo Rose proved more fascinating than the film with its implausible plot. Iva Toguri was a Japanese-American who was visiting Japan in 1941 when Pearl Harbor was bombed. Unable to return to the United States, she spent the war years in Japan and married a Portuguese.

Mrs. D'Aquino was hired by the Japanese Broadcasting Corporation as a propaganda broadcaster. She spoke excellent English and her 15-minute show was specifically beamed to American troops in the Far East. She originally introduced herself as "Anna" and then switched to "Orphan Ann." Her programs were mostly propaganda and were designed to lower the morale of American troops. In between jazz and other musical selections, she intimated that the wives and girlfriends of American troops were being unfaithful with the 4-Fs (those rejected by the draft) back home; she also suggested that the war in the Pacific was outside American interests and that Americans need not be fighting there. "Orphan Ann's" broadcasts were widely heard, but despite her best efforts to undermine the fighting spirit of American troops, her radio shows were greeted with amusement.

Although there were between ten and twelve various women broadcasting propaganda to American troops on the Japanese radio network—they were known collectively as Tokyo Rose—Iva D'Aquino was the most prominent. Whereas the others were native Japanese with good command of English, she was an American national.

Following the war, most of her fellow pro-pagandists melted into their Japanese background; D'Aquino, however, refused to renounce her American citizenship. She was arrested by the occupation authorities and charged with treason. She argued that she was trapped in Japan during the war and was just "doing a job" to support herself. The judge didn't buy her defense and sentenced her on October 6, 1949, to ten years in prison and a $10,000 fine. She served six years and was released because of good behavior.

Iva, however, persisted in trying to obtain a full pardon. She was eventually successful when President Nixon, on his last day in office, January 19, 1977, issued her a presidential pardon. She fared much better than her British counterpart, Lord Haw-Haw, who broadcast for the Nazis and was eventually executed as a traitor. See Lord Haw-Haw. ■

Tompkins, Peter. See *The Pigeon That Took Rome* (1962). ■

Tonight We Raid Calais (1943), TCF. *Dir.* John Brahm; *Sc.* Waldo Salt; *Cast includes:* John Sutton, Annabella, Lee J. Cobb, Beulah Bondi, Blanche Yurka.

A German munitions plant is the target of an Allied air strike in this World War II drama. An English agent (John Sutton) is assigned to infiltrate Nazi lines and illuminate the factory so that Allied bombers can destroy it. A young Frenchwoman (Annabella) is reluctant to help the British, whom she blames for her brother's death during an R.A.F. attack on French ships. But once she witnesses the brutality of the Nazis, who kill her parents, she realizes who the true enemy is. French farmers, led by Blanche Yurka, fire the fields near the plant, thereby lighting the way for the R.A.F. in this unexceptional film. ■

Top Secret! (1984), Par. *Dir.* Jim Abrahams, David Zucker, Jerry Zucker; *Sc.* Jim Abrahams, David Zucker, Jerry Zucker; *Cast includes:* Val Kilmer, Lucy Gutteridge, Christopher Villiers, Omar Sharif, Peter Cushing, Jeremy Kemp.

The writer-director trio of the highly successful *Airplane!* (1980) are less effective with this fatuous comedy about a rock star who gets mixed up in political intrigue in East Germany. Anachronisms add to the plot absurdities. The villains are Nazis while the allies are members of the French Resistance. Val Kilmer portrays the Presley-like hero who becomes embroiled in a conspiracy to unite the two Germanys.

The script has moments that are genuinely clever and funny. East Germans read a newspaper called "The Oppressor." Omar Sharif, as an anti-East German secret agent complete with trenchcoat, approaches his possible contact, a blind street peddler. To identify himself, Sharif gives the first part of a secret message: "Do you know any good white basketball players?" "There are no good white basketball players," the blind man acknowledges. There is an inventive underwater fight between hero and villain—with the setting that of a western saloon. The last sequence is a spoof of World War II espionage films in which the heroine chooses to remain behind to fight the invaders who have occupied her country while her lover leaves by plane. "As long as a single man is forced to cower under the iron fist of oppression," heroine Hillary (Lucy Gutteridge) affirms, "as long as a child cries out in the night or an actor can be elected President, we must continue the struggle."

Similar to their earlier film, the writers-directors unabashedly toss in gags and comic routines in the most unexpected places, but somehow they are not as snappy or outrageous as their earlier work. The basic idea of a spoof on the Elvis-style musicals and the spy genre (particularly, Fritz Lang's 1946 espionage drama *Cloak and Dagger*) is a clever one. Unfortunately, most of the material doesn't live up to the promise. ∎

Top Sergeant Mulligan (1928), Anchor.
Dir. James Hogan; Sc. Francis Fenton; Cast includes: Donald Keith, Gareth Hughes, Wesley Barry, Lila Lee.

A World War I comedy, the film centers on an entertainer (Wesley Barry) who, while trying to recruit young men for the service, finds himself in the army. Sergeant Mulligan (Donald Keith) makes Barry's life miserable. Once in France, Barry and another doughboy (Wade Boteler) become romantically involved with a French girl who is actually a male German spy. They are assigned to capture the enemy agent but are themselves caught. They are shipped to Berlin where they accidentally catch the spy they were originally sent to get. But the war has ended, and when they return to their unit with their captor, all they get for their troubles is heckling from their fellow soldiers. ∎

Topaz (1969), U. Dir. Alfred Hitchcock; Sc. Samuel A. Taylor; Cast includes: Frederick Stafford, John Forsythe, Tina Hedstrom, Dany Robin, Claude Jade, Philippe Noiret.

French and American intelligence join forces to investigate the Soviet Union's involvement in Cuba in this Hitchcock spy thriller. Frederick Stafford portrays a French secret agent who agrees to help the C.I.A. discover the Soviet Union's interest in Cuba and the Russian mole in N.A.T.O. He seeks the help of a fellow spy (Roscoe Lee Browne) who infiltrates a group of Cubans in New York. Browne reports to Stafford who, accompanied by his anti-Castro girlfriend (Karin Dor), journeys to Cuba. There she enlists the aid of two trusted Cubans to photograph Soviet long-range missiles being unloaded from a cargo vessel. They are captured but manage to hide the film, which Dor surreptitiously turns over to Stafford before he leaves Cuba for the U.S. One of Castro's underlings learns of her betrayal and kills her.

Stafford returns to France after delivering the film to U.S. agents. He then discovers that the double agent with the French intelligence service is his own friend who commits suicide when he is charged with treason. The film is based on Leon Uris' novel which, in turn, was a fictionalized account of the experiences of Philippe de Vosjoli, a French spy. This was not one of Hitchcock's better films, perhaps because of its extensive plot details or lack of Hitchcockian surprises. ∎

Torn Curtain (1966), U. Dir. Alfred Hitchcock; Sc. Brian Moore; Cast includes: Paul Newman, Julie Andrews, Lila Kadrova, Hansjoerg Felmy, Tamara Toumanova, Wolfgang Kieling.

A distinguished American nuclear physicist poses as a defector as a means of getting vital formula equations from his East German counterpart in this generally disappointing Cold War suspense drama. Paul Newman, as the ersatz defector, is accompanied by his assistant and girlfriend (Julie Andrews), on a trip to Norway to attend a scientific convention. Unknown to Andrews, Newman makes plans to defect to East Berlin. When she learns from a travel agent that he has booked a seat on a flight to East Berlin, she decides to follow him.

The remainder of the plot concerns Newman's efforts to wrest the parts of the formula from the Communist physicist while Newman unsuccessfully tries to get his assistant to return to the West. Soviet security personnel soon grow suspicious of the American's motives when one of their agents disappears. After Newman wrings the scientific information from the professor—something to help Newman complete work on an American anti-missile missile—he and Andrews begin their suspenseful but drawn-out escape to the West.

Earlier in the film Carolyn Conwell, as the wife of a peasant farmer, helps Newman do away with a member of the secret police who has been following the American. After a prolonged struggle underscored by a sense of sadistic horror, they finally manage to place the agent's head in a gas oven until he stops breathing. Ludwig Donath portrays the egotistical physicist whom Newman tricks into supplying the necessary data. Donath engages in a duel of wits with the American and, in an outburst of frustration, exclaims: "You have told me nothing! You know nothing!" Donath finally realizes he has revealed important secrets to the American. Lila Kedrova, as a pathetic Polish refugee looking for an American sponsor to help her leave the Eastern bloc, aids the couple in their escape. David Opatoshu portrays the head of an underground group of East Germans dedicated to helping others flee to the West.

Hitchcock supplies some suspense and perverse humor ("Cuban," a Communist security chief remarks, referring to a cigar, "Your loss, our gain"), but the production falls below his better work. In one sequence he returns to one of his more familiar settings—a crowded theater—where Communist guards are searching for Newman and Andrews. In a not-too-original ploy, Hitchcock has the American scientist create a diversion by shouting, "Fire!" so that he and his assistant can escape their pursuers. ■

Toughest Man Alive (1955), AA. *Dir.* Sidney Salkow; *Sc.* Steve Fisher; *Cast includes:* Dane Clark, Lita Milan, Anthony Caruso, Ross Elliott, Myrna Dell, Thomas Henry.

A U.S. government agent goes under cover to break up a gun-smuggling ring supplying arms to Central American revolutionaries in this routine drama. Dane Clark, as the special agent, masquerades as a notorious gunrunner in an effort to learn the identity of the leaders who are overseeing the entire operation. Lita Milan, posing as a café singer, is actually a revolutionary seeking to purchase weapons for an impending uprising in her country. Ross Elliott portrays Clark's co-agent while Myrna Dell plays Elliott's wife. Anthony Caruso, as the villain Clark is impersonating, appears suddenly near the end of the tale and almost ruins the undercover agent's efforts to expose the gunrunners. ■

Trader Tom of the China Seas (1954) serial, Rep. *Dir.* Franklin Adreon; *Sc.* Ronald Davidson; *Cast includes:* Harry Lauter, Aline Towne, Lyle Talbot, Robert Shayne, Fred Graham.

Foreign agents smuggle contraband arms and ammunition to dissident groups bent on revolution in a fictitious Asian country in this unoriginal 12-episode serial. When the United Nations learns that an unnamed foreign power is behind the revolution, the world body assigns Trader Tom, played by Harry Lauter, to investigate. Our hero must undergo the usual fights and escapes, battles with natives and spies, before he resolves the potentially explosive political situation in Burmatra, an otherwise peaceful coastal nation. To save production costs, the studio borrowed heavily from stock footage of earlier serials. Released near the end of the serial cycle, this entry was not alone in suffering from this practice. Television proved too great a competitor, and the genre succumbed in 1956. ■

Trail of the Octopus, The (1919) serial, Hallmark. *Dir.* Duke Worne; *Sc.* J. Grubb Alexander; *Cast includes:* Ben Wilson, Neva Gerber, Howard Crampton, Allen Garcia, Marie Pavis.

A Chinese cabal, pursuing world control, sends out secret agents to obtain a mysterious scientific discovery that would help the group toward that end. This 15-chapter serial offers many of the conventions of the genre, including chases, climactic entrapments and an inscrutable masked figure known only as "Monsieur X." An American scientist, to protect the discovery, distributes nine daggers to fellow scientists around the world. The blades are part of a complex key which, when inserted into a special lock, open the secret buried in a hidden cave. Howard Crampton portrays the American scientist who is murdered after making the strange scientific breakthrough. Neva Gerber, as his daughter, seeks the help of a master detective (Ben Wilson). They both experience a series of close calls and adventures before the mystery is finally resolved. ∎

Trapped (1949), EL. *Dir.* Richard Fleischer; *Sc.* Earl Felton, George Zuckerman; *Cast includes:* Lloyd Bridges, John Hoyt, Barbara Payton, James Todd, Russ Conway, Bert Conway.

The U.S. Treasury Department cracks down on a gang of counterfeiters flooding the country with bogus bills in this familiar but well-paced drama. The government releases a former counterfeiter, played by Lloyd Bridges, hoping that he will lead government agents to the gang that is using his plates in their operation. John Hoyt portrays a secret agent who goes under cover to gain the confidence of the counterfeiters. At one suspenseful point, just as he is about to crack the case, his cover is blown. Barbara Payton portrays Bridges' old flame. The counterfeiting ring, led by James Todd, is finally smashed. ∎

Trapped in the Sky (1939), Col. *Dir.* Lewis D. Collins; *Sc.* Eric Taylor, Gordon Rigby; *Cast includes:* Jack Holt, Ralph Morgan, Paul Everton, Katherine DeMille, C. Henry Gordon, Sidney Blackmer.

Foreign agents attempt to gain possession of a newly designed noiseless airplane in this slow-paced pre-World War II action drama. To purchase the rights to the invention, the spies must convince the U.S. government, which is testing the high-speed aircraft, that the plane is a failure. To that end, they sabotage the test flight which leads to the death of an army officer. Jack Holt, as the victim's superior officer, arranges both to accept the blame and for his own court-martial so that he can infiltrate the spy network. He soon uncovers the scheme, including the traitorous inventor who has been conspiring with the foreign agents. Katherine DeMille plays the romantic lead. Popular screen villain C. Henry Gordon portrays the head of the spies. ∎

Treason (1917), Bluebird. *Dir.* Allen Holubar; *Sc.* Robert Lee Weigert; *Cast includes:* Allen Holubar, Lois Wilson, Dorothy Davenport, Joseph Girard, George Pearce, Edward Hearn.

A telegraph operator and recently recognized hero of a fictitious country temporarily turns traitor after he is humiliated. Allen Holubar, as the hero in this drama, intercepts and

kills a spy who has sneaked across the border of Holubar's nation. The wounded hero is promised a promotion for his acts. Meanwhile, his rival in love (Edward Hearn), a government official, betrays Holubar, who is disgraced. Embittered by this turn of events, Holubar is persuaded by a spy to steal his country's new military code. Suddenly he is awarded his promised promotion. Realizing the mistake he has made, he rushes to the border and retrieves the secret code from the spy. Lois Wilson portrays Holubar's beloved and provides the romantic object of the two rivals. ∎

Treason (1918), Mutual. *Dir.* Burton King; *Sc.* J. Clarkson Miller; *Cast includes:* Edna Goodrich, Howard Hall, Mildred Clair, Clarence Heritage, Stuart Holmes.

A wife, jealous of her husband's ardor to his work in developing a new explosive, foolishly steals the formula and entrusts it to a local romeo in this World War I drama. Edna Goodrich portrays the envious wife who discovers too late that her suitor is in reality a German spy who has only used her to obtain the secret formula. When she learns that the government is counting on her husband's discovery, she goes to the spy's home to retrieve it. A struggle ensues between them, but she is saved by her husband (Howard Hall) and a U.S. Secret Service officer (Clarence Heritage) who promptly arrests the German agent. The scientist then joins the army, and his wife volunteers as a nurse in the Red Cross. ∎

Trenchcoat (1983), Disney. *Dir.* Michael Tuchner; *Sc.* Jeffrey Price, Peter Seaman; *Cast includes:* Margot Kidder, Robert Hays, David Suchet, John Justin, David Faraldo, Ronald Lacey.

Margot Kidder portrays an aspiring mystery writer who journeys to Malta for a vacation and to gather material for story in this forced comedy. Instead, she soon finds herself involved in a real murder, a plot by Arab agents to locate a missing drug shipment and a terrorist conspiracy. A suspicious-looking character, thinking the Malta police are after him, hides a coded map in a rack of picture postcards. Kidder accidentally picks it up along with a handful of other cards. When the man returns to the rack and finds his map gone, he follows Kidder and makes several attempts to get his property back. The remainder of the film concerns Kidder's narrow escapes from various groups and her confrontations with the police and a motley array of villains.

Unaware that she is living in her own fantasy world, Kidder sees each person she meets as a potential character in her forthcoming mystery story. "I feel sorry," she muses to herself about a date (Robert Hays), "for a guy who spends all of his time in a fantasy world." Hays, working as an undercover agent for the Nuclear Regulatory Agency, is on the trail of a cache of plutonium that terrorists are searching for. Kidder, however, thinks Hays is part of a scheme to murder her. The couple eventually fall in love and capture an elderly Irish couple who are part of the terrorist group. English actor John Justin, who had played romantic leads in the 1940s, appears as a finicky hotel owner who feels threatened by Kidder's misadventures and erratic behavior. ■

Trials of Alger Hiss, The (1980), History on Film. *Dir.* John Lowenthal.

Using chiefly interviews and records that had been suppressed for more than 25 years, John Lowenthal produced this intelligent documentary that raises several questions about the original evidence that convicted Alger Hiss in January 1950. Those interviewed range from Robert Stipling, investigator of the House Un-American Activities Committee (H.U.A.C.), jurors and witnesses to F.B.I. agents and Hiss himself. Others who were unavailable or refused to go before the camera (Richard Nixon) appear in the film by way of stock newsreel footage. Hiss speaks out mainly against Whittaker Chambers, his main accuser, and questions his motives and emotional stability. The documentary gives plenty of background information, including references to the Depression, World War II and the Cold War.

The dramatic Hiss-Chambers confrontation had all the makings of a grade B espionage movie. The characters included a Phi Beta Kappa graduate of Harvard Law School; an admitted Communist agent for the U.S.S.R.; an ambitious young congressman who would soon become President of the United States; and, waiting on the periphery, Senator Joseph McCarthy, who orchestrated the hunt for Communists in the State Department.

Alger Hiss, following his graduation from Harvard Law School in 1929, clerked for Su-preme Court Justice Oliver Wendell Holmes and served in the Agriculture, Justice and State Departments; he served for a short while as secretary-general of the United Nations after its beginning in 1945. In short, Hiss represented all the qualities—privilege, "fellow-traveler" and Eastern intellectual—disparaged by Senator Joseph McCarthy.

Whittaker Chambers had been an editor at *Time* magazine. During his testimony before the House Un-American Activities Committee in 1948, he identified Hiss as a member of a Communist cell in the 1930s. Chambers claimed that Hiss had provided him with highly confidential State Department records which were then turned over to the Soviet Union. The Congressional witness testified that he had used his typewriter to copy certain information provided to him by Hiss and that other information was on filmstrips. Hiss denied the charges before the House Committee. Richard Nixon was the young Congressman on committee who eventually became President.

Chambers then repeated his charges publicly, where he was not protected by the Congressional shield of immunity, and thus dared a lawsuit. Hiss responded in court. Hiss and Chambers both testified before a grand jury and repeated their Congressional performance. Hiss was indicted on two counts of perjury. His first trial in 1949 resulted in a hung jury. However, Alger Hiss was convicted during his second trial and was sentenced in 1950 to five years in prison. He eventually was released in 1954 after serving three years and eight months at the Lewisburg, Pennsylvania, federal prison. ■

Trouble With Spies, The (1987), DEG-HBO. *Dir.* Burt Kennedy; *Sc.* Burt Kennedy; *Cast includes:* Donald Sutherland, Ned Beatty, Ruth Gordon, Lucy Gutteridge, Michael Hordern, Robert Morley.

Donald Sutherland portrays a bumbling, novice British agent whose superiors deliberately send him on a false mission and into the arms of Soviet spies in this inept comedy. When the top brass at the agency learn that the Soviets have developed a special truth serum they intend to use on captured agents, the British assign Sutherland to an island to find a missing fellow agent. If the Soviets capture him, they will learn nothing, since Sutherland knows nothing. The innocent agent, taking his mission seriously, signs into a hotel and meets an array of strange characters, including his counterpart, a Soviet spy. They soon discover that they are being exploited by their respective governments and decide to join forces to create havoc with each other's intelligence agencies. The film, completed in 1984 but not released until 1987, is based on *Apple Pie in the Sky*, a novel by Marc Lovell. ■

True Heaven (1929), Fox. *Dir.* James Tinling; *Sc.* Dwight Cummins; *Cast includes:* George O'Brien, Lois Moran, Phillips Smalley, Oscar Apfel, Duke Martin.

A World War I drama, the film stars George O'Brien as an English officer stationed at first in Belgium where he meets a bar girl (Lois Moran) who is a spy for the Germans. She is friendly with all the Allied officers from whom she can obtain information. O'Brien and Moran fall in love. Later, he is assigned as a spy to infiltrate German headquarters. The lovers meet again and spend the night together. Torn between her love for her country and her feelings for the Englishman, she succumbs to the former and reports him to her superiors. He is sentenced to face a firing squad but is saved at the last moment when news of the armistice arrives. The film includes several battle sequences although the bulk of the drama revolves around the love story. ■

23 1/2 Hours' Leave (1919), Par. *Dir.* Henry King; *Sc.* Agnes C. Johnstone; *Cast includes:* Douglas MacLean, Doris May, Thomas Guise, Maxfield Stanley, Wade Boteler.

Set chiefly in an army camp during World War I, this service comedy concerns a general's daughter who is aided by an otherwise mischievous sergeant in her search for German spies. Douglas MacLean portrays the young sergeant who spends most of his time devising pranks. Doris May portrays the pretty heroine. Using well-proven conventions of stage comedy, the plot depends mainly on farce and mistaken identity. MacLean doesn't know that May is the general's daughter until it is too late. ■

Two Lovers (1928), UA. *Dir.* Fred Niblo; *Sc.* Alice D. G. Miller; *Cast includes:* Ronald Colman, Vilma Banky, Noah Beery, Nigel de Brulier, Virginia Bradford, Helen Jerome Eddy.

Vilma Banky, as the innocent niece of a treacherous Spanish duke, agrees to spy for him in this drama of intrigue and adventure set in the Netherlands in 1572. Spain holds the Flemish people in a tyrannical vice. However, signs of resistance soon appear. The duke (Noah Beery), determined to raze the city of Ghent, needs proof of internal treason before he could get the king of Spain to agree with his plan of destruction. He convinces his niece that her spying would help to end further bloodshed. To achieve this allegedly noble end, she agrees to marry the son of an influential family.

Meanwhile Ronald Colman, disguised in black leather, becomes a champion of the Flemish people by fighting the abuses of the occupiers. Known as "Leatherface" because of his attire, he kills Banky's young husband who was about to brutally attack a defenseless barmaid. Later, Colman and Banky fall in love. But when she discovers his secret identity, she informs her uncle, thinking she is helping the cause of peace. She then learns the truth—that the duke is preparing to destroy Ghent. She allies her cause with the downtrodden Flemish and rides to warn them. The people rise up and reclaim their land. The character of Leatherface, in appearance and deed, was very similar to that of Zorro, an earlier masked avenger made famous on the silent screen by Douglas Fairbanks. The film was adapted from the novel by Baroness Orczy. ■

Two-Man Submarine (1944), Col. *Dir.* Lew Landers; *Sc.* Griffin Jay, Leslie T. White; *Cast includes:* Tom Neal, Ann Savage, J. Carrol Naish, Robert Williams, Abner Biberman, George Lynn.

Enemy agents attempt to force the secret of the penicillin drug from Americans in this implausible World War II drama. Japanese and Nazi spies combine their sinister talents and harass a group of American researchers working in the Pacific. Ultimately, the nefarious agents are foiled as they go to their deaths aboard a submarine. Tom Neal and Ann Savage portray the hero and heroine in this low-budget film. ■

Two Tickets to London (1943), U. *Dir.* Edwin L. Marin; *Sc.* Tom Reed; *Cast includes:* Michele Morgan, Alan Curtis, C. Aubrey Smith, Barry Fitzgerald, Tarquin Olivier, Mary Gordon.

A fugitive tries to clear his name in this

weak drama set in England during World War II. Accused of treason by navy officials for aiding enemy submarines to sink troop transports, the former first mate (Alan Curtis) escapes his captors during a train wreck. With the help of another passenger whom he saves (Michele Morgan), he heads for London to prove his innocence. All is resolved by the end of the film, including the romance between the hero and heroine. Dooley Wilson portrays an entertainer, similar to his role in *Casablanca*, and livens things up with his singing. ■

Two Weeks to Live (1943), RKO. *Dir.* Malcolm St. Clair; *Sc.* Michael L. Simmons, Roswell Rogers; *Cast includes:* Chester Lauck, Norris Goff, Franklin Pangborn, Kay Linaker, Irving Bacon, Herbert Rawlinson.

Radio personalities Lum and Abner (Chester Lauck and Norris Goff) bring their homespun humor to the screen in this weak but inoffensive comedy involving a Nazi spy ring. Abner's charts get confused with those of another patient during a medical examination and he is given two weeks to live. He and Lum journey to Chicago where they undergo a series of misadventures, including being cheated by city slickers, performing perilous stunts to retrieve the funds they lost and be-

coming entangled in a bomb plot by enemy agents. Abner, of course, learns about the mix-up in the doctor's records. The pair made a series of low-budget comedies for RKO, but they never achieved the popularity on screen that they had on radio. ■

Two Yanks in Trinidad (1942), Col. *Dir.* Gregory Ratoff; *Sc.* Sy Bartlett, Richard Carroll, Henry Segall, Jack Henley; *Cast includes:* Pat O'Brien, Brian Donlevy, Janet Blair, Donald MacBride, Roger Clark, John Emery.

Two American racketeers end up in the army in Trinidad and capture a Nazi agent in this mundane service comedy drama that takes place on the eve of Pearl Harbor. A tough hoodlum (Pat O'Brien) joins the army to avoid a fellow gangster (Brian Donlevy) after a falling out between the two former friends. Donlevy and two of his cronies follow O'Brien into the service where the two adversaries continue their feud. When they hear that the Japanese have attacked Pearl Harbor and then discover a plot by a Nazi spy involved in the transportation of oil, the two rivals join forces to foil the enemy. Comic character actor Donald MacBride plays their harassing sergeant. See Pearl Harbor. ■

U

U-Boat Prisoner (1944), Col. *Dir.* Lew Landers; *Sc.* Aubrey Wisberg; *Cast includes:* Bruce Bennett, Erik Rolf, John Abbott, Robert Williams, John Wengraf, Kenneth MacDonald.

An American sailor poses as a Nazi spy in this implausible World War II action drama that reportedly is based on the actual experience of Archie Gibbs, a seaman detained aboard a German submarine. Gibbs (Bruce Bennett) assumes the identity of a Nazi whose ship has been sunk. He is picked up by a German U-boat whose officers believe his story. Gibbs is then quartered with a group of prisoners whom he takes into his confidence. He overpowers some of the submarine crew, causes a torpedo to be destroyed and saves the prisoners. The film contains an abundance of patriotic dialogue. ∎

Unafraid, The (1915), Par. *Dir.* Cecil B. DeMille; *Cast includes:* Rita Jolivet, House Peters, Page Peters, Billy Elmer, Lawrence Peyton, Theodore Roberts.

Page Peters portrays a Montenegran aristocrat who is on a secret mission for Austria in this drama about treason. Rita Jolivet, as a rich young American, falls in love with the nobleman and joins him on his journey home where they intend to marry. But the aristocrat's brother, Count Stefan (House Peters), kidnaps the prospective bride before the ceremony and, taking her to his castle, coerces her to marry him. The new bride soon learns that Page Peters intended to marry her only for her wealth. Besides, he turns out to be a traitor to his country. She soon discovers that it is House Peters whom she loves. The film is based on *The Unafraid*, a 1913 novel by Eleanor M. Ingram. ∎

Uncertain Glory (1944), WB. *Dir.* Raoul Walsh; *Sc.* Laszlo Vadnay, Max Brand; *Cast includes:* Errol Flynn, Paul Lukas, Jean Sullivan, Lucile Watson, Faye Emerson.

A criminal finds redemption in this offbeat, slow-paced World War II drama. About to be guillotined for murder, the condemned man (Errol Flynn) is saved at the last moment by an air raid of Allied planes. The bombing and resulting confusion allow him to escape his executioners. Later, he is captured in a small village miles from Paris by a French police inspector (Paul Lukas), his long-time nemesis. Before they leave for Paris, the wily Flynn persuades the policeman to allow him to impersonate a saboteur wanted by the Nazis who are about to execute 100 French hostages. The sentimental inspector, although suspicious of his prisoner's intentions, agrees to the terms. Flynn, who explains that he would rather die in front of a firing squad than by guillotine, then cajoles his captor to give him a few days of life before he surrenders to the Gestapo.

Meanwhile, the relatives of the hostages desperately seek ways to save their loved ones. "Martyrs are fools who die because they want to," a distraught mother announces. "My son wants to live." The local priest tries to quell their distress. "A saboteur has struck a blow for France," he explains. "Would you have him give himself up?" "Is he worth more than a hundred lives?" the mother questions. "Anything that maintains a free spirit," the priest replies, "is worth more than life." The wartime propaganda extends to other characters. Flynn, never intending to fulfill his part of the agreement, escapes from Lukas and takes with him a young and pretty villager (Jean Sullivan). Riding on back of a farmer's horse-drawn cart, Flynn asks the farmer to go faster. The man says of his horse: "She's like France—too old to beat, too tough to die." "What keeps her going?" Flynn asks. "Courage," the driver replies.

Sullivan's courage and the old farmer's faith are too much for the escaped convict's conscience. Flynn reports to Lukas in Paris and both men walk to Gestapo headquarters where Flynn turns himself in to free the hostages. ■

Under Cover (1916), Par. *Dir.* Robert G. Vignola; *Sc.* C. D. Hobart; *Cast includes:* Hazel Dawn, Owen Moore, William Courtleigh, Jr., Ethel Fleming, Frank Losee, Ida Darling.

A U.S. Secret Service agent poses as a smuggler to get evidence against a corrupt customs official in this simple drama based on the play by Roi Cooper Megrue. Owen Moore portrays the agent who goes under cover. Frank Losee, as the crooked customs man, blackmails a young woman (Hazel Dawn) whose sister has stolen some jewels, to spy for him. Forced to accept the task to protect her sister from arrest, Dawn is to report on the activities of Moore, an alleged smuggler. Problems arise when Dawn is romantically attracted to her prey. Later, when Losee confronts Moore, the latter offers the customs official a large bribe, which he accepts. At that moment, Moore reveals his true identity and places Losee under arrest. Dawn is ecstatic that the man she loves is not a smuggler. ■

Under False Colors (1917), Pathé. *Dir.* Emile Chautard; *Cast includes:* Jeanne Eagels, Frederick Warde, Robert Vaughn, Anne Gregory, Carey Hastings.

Jeanne Eagels portrays a Russian countess in this drama set during the early days of the Russian Revolution. She escapes with the help of an American. The ship she is sailing on is torpedoed, but again she manages to escape. She assumes the identity of an American woman, a fellow passenger who perishes as a result of the sinking. The remainder of the film concerns her involvement with a group of revolutionaries fighting to establish freedom in Russia, and an American millionaire (Frederick Warde) who is financing the struggle.

American film studios were quick to exploit the Russian Revolution as a screen topic. This drama was one of the earliest and set the generally anti-revolutionary tone for those films to follow. D. W. Griffith, for example, several years later in his 1921 historical drama about the French Revolution, *Orphans of the Storm*, attacks the upheaval in Russia in his opening titles, warning his audiences against the evils and dangers of "Bolshevism." ■

Undercover Agent (1939), Mon. *Dir.* Howard Bretherton; *Sc.* Milton Raison; *Cast includes:* Russell Gleason, Shirley Deane, J. M. Kerrigan, Maude Eburne, Oscar O'Shea, Selmer Jackson.

A counterfeiting ring dealing in bogus sweepstakes tickets leads a U.S. postal worker to ferret out the illegal scheme in this low-budget drama. Russell Gleason, as an ambitious post office employee, investigates on his own time so that he can get back in the good graces of his superiors. He had earlier prevented a local pawnshop stickup, but because he carried a gun while off duty, his bosses criticized him. He finally helps the U.S. Postal Inspection Service round up the counterfeiters. Shirley Deane plays the female lead. J. M. Kerrigan, as a former Shakespearean actor, portrays Deane's father and adds to the human interest of an otherwise standard plot. ■

Undercover Girl (1950), UI. *Dir.* Joseph Pevney; *Sc.* Harry Essex; *Cast includes:* Alexis Smith, Scott Brady, Richard Egan, Gladys George, Edmon Ryan, Gerald Mohr.

A New York policewoman-trainee volunteers to help investigate a California drug-smuggling operation in this routine but suspenseful drama. Alexis Smith, as the female cop, gladly accepts the assignment, since the smugglers were responsible for her police officer-father's murder. She journeys to the coast, where she joins forces with the Los Angeles police. She then poses as a drug buyer and is partially accepted by the gang. However, others in the mob suspect her. Scott Brady, as a police officer working on the case with Smith, soon becomes attracted to the undercover agent. Edmon Ryan, as a discredited doctor, acts as a front for the smugglers so that he can raise enough money for his son's medical education. ■

Undercurrent, The (1919), Select. *Dir.* Wilfrid North; *Sc.* William Addison Lathrop; *Cast includes:* Guy Empey, Betty Blythe,

Charles A. Stevenson, Betty Hutchinson, Eugene Strong.

Russian agents spread dissent and propaganda among Americans in the hope of eventually bringing about a world revolution in this anti-Communist drama. Guy Empey portrays a returning World War I veteran who joins a group of Bolsheviks. He soon grows disillusioned with the organization and denounces its cause. Betty Blythe plays a Russian agent who, learning that the authorities are about to arrest her, shoots a fellow provocateur and then turns the weapon upon herself. Before making his screen debut in this film, Guy Empey, a real-life war veteran, had gained a certain degree of popularity with the publication of *Over the Top*, a book about his war experiences.

The anti-Red theme of gullible Americans being duped by Communist ideology who later try to extricate themselves reappeared in films with some regularity during the Cold War that followed World War II. *The Red Menace* (1949), for example, shows how several naive Americans are duped by Communists, while in *I Married a Communist*, released the same year, Robert Ryan, as an ex-Communist, is warned by his former party bosses that no one "quits" the Party. See Palmer Raids; Red Scare of 1919–1920. ∎

Underground (1941), WB. *Dir.* Vincent Sherman; *Sc.* Edwin Justus Mayer, Oliver H. P. Garrett; *Cast includes:* Jeffrey Lynn, Philip Dorn, Kaaren Verne, Mona Maris, Peter Whitney.

Another in a series of Hollywood dramas intended to expose the ruthlessness of the Nazi regime, the film pays tribute to a small band of Germans who resist their government's policies. Philip Dorn, as a leader in the German underground, broadcasts from mobile radio stations to bring the truth to the German people. Jeffrey Lynn portrays a dedicated Nazi soldier who inadvertently turns in his own brother to the Gestapo. Realizing too late the realities of what Nazism represents, he replaces his brother in the underground as Dorn goes to his death.

The film presents the usual anti-Nazi propaganda of the period, including allusions to the dreaded concentration camps and didactic speeches. "Freedom will prevail," Lynn exclaims in a final illegal broadcast, "and peace on earth will reign when this medieval darkness will be only a memory. . . . This is

our fight: to bring light where there is darkness." The following quotation from Shakespeare hangs on the wall of the brothers' home and suggests the theme of the drama:

> What stronger breastplate than a heart untainted!
> Thrice be he armed that hath his quarrel just,
> And he but naked, though locked up in steel,
> Whose conscience with injustice is corrupted.

Historically, there remained in Germany throughout the war a small group of strategically placed civilians and officers whose anti-Nazi sympathies led them to supply Allied agents with useful military information. As early as the 1930s, while Hitler was busy formulating his military strategies, the British Secret Intelligence Service received repeated warnings from these Germans about Nazi battle orders, development of new weapons and mobilization plans. Fred Zinnemann's drama *The Seventh Cross* (1944) depicts some of the work of the anti-Nazi German underground during the mid-1930s. ∎

Underground Agent (1942), Col. *Dir.* Michael Gordon; *Sc.* J. Robert Bren, Gladys Atwater; *Cast includes:* Bruce Bennett, Leslie Brooks, Frank Albertson, Julian Rivero, George McKay, Rhys Williams.

Enemy agents attempt to listen in on vital secrets at a defense plant in this low-budget World War II drama. A government agent (Bruce Bennett) is assigned to prevent any breach of secrecy at the plant. After he devises a method to foil the enemy's plans, he proceeds to round them up. Rhys Williams plays the head of the spy network. Leslie Banks portrays Bennett's recently hired assistant in this routine tale. ∎

Unexpected, The (1914), Balboa.

The U.S. Secret Service finds it is having difficulties in gathering evidence against a gang of smugglers and therefore calls upon one of its female operatives to act as a spy. She poses as an artist and befriends some local mountaineers. One young man falls in love with her. Meanwhile the spy sends information by way of carrier pigeon to her superiors. When the gang is eventually rounded up, the secret agent protects the young mountain man who has innocently become involved with the smugglers. ∎

Unexpected Places (1918), Metro. *Dir.* E. Mason Hopper; *Sc.* Albert S. LeVino, George D. Baker; *Cast includes:* Bert Lytell, Colin Kenney, Louis Norrison, Edythe Chapman, Rhea Mitchell.

German spies make repeated attempts to gain possession of important documents in this drama set during World War I. The search for the papers results in the murder of an innocent servant and the poisoning of an English lord who has carried the documents across the ocean to America. Bert Lytell portrays a quick-witted reporter who uncovers the German plot to steal the papers. He retrieves them and thus becomes the target of enemy agents. Rhea Mitchell, as the lord's cousin, becomes entangled in the mystery when she mistakes the reporter for the lord. She is kidnapped by the spies who are willing to trade her for the coveted papers. The reporter manages to free her, but the couple is pursued by the gang of spies. The police finally capture the culprits. The film is based on the short story by Frank R. Adams. ∎

Unseen Enemy (1942), U. *Dir.* John Rawlins; *Sc.* Roy Chanslor, Stanley Rubin; *Cast includes:* Leo Carrillo, Andy Devine, Irene Hervey, Don Terry, Turhan Bey.

Leo Carrillo portrays a stepfather desperate enough to betray his country in this low-budget drama that takes place on the eve of the attack on Pearl Harbor. He turns traitor so that he can help his stepdaughter who is forced to work in a waterfront café. He sells his services to enemy agents who hire a crew for a Japanese ship designed to attack American merchant vessels. Andy Devine plays a government agent who is aided by a Canadian intelligence officer (Don Terry). Carrillo's charge, played by Irene Hervey, also assists in foiling the plot and capturing the spies. Carrillo sacrifices his life in an act of redemption. ∎

Unwritten Code, The (1944), Col. *Dir.* Herman Rotsten; *Sc.* Leslie T. White, Charles Kenyon; *Cast includes:* Ann Savage, Tom Neal, Roland Varno, Howard Freeman, Mary Currier, Bobby Larson.

A Nazi spy plots to free German prisoners of war interned in the U.S. in this implausible World War II drama. Roland Varno portrays a Nazi who assumes the identity of a British officer killed in action. He enters the U.S. as an Allied hero while secretly plan-

Army sergeant Tom Neal helps to hunt down a Nazi spy who plans to free German prisoners of war in *The Unwritten Code* (1944).

ning to free his fellow Germans. He is eventually killed by the camp guards. Tom Neal plays an American army sergeant while Ann Savage provides the romantic interest. ∎

Up Romance Road (1918), Mutual. *Dir.* Henry King; *Sc.* Stephen Fox; *Cast includes:* William Russell, Charlotte Burton, John Burton, Joseph Belmont, Emma Kluge.

German spies plot to blow up a warehouse of military supplies destined for the Allies in this World War I drama. William Russell and Charlotte Burton portray an engaged couple who are both wealthy and bored. Craving excitement, they allow themselves to be kidnapped by enemy agents who lock up the couple in the German ambassador's home. It is here they eavesdrop on the plot of the German spies. Russell escapes and, in a mad dash by automobile, manages to arrive at the warehouse in time to prevent the sabotage. ∎

U.S. intelligence: World War I. In typically optimistic and democratic fashion, the United States had no central, organized intelligence establishment to speak of at the onset of World War I.

The Federal Bureau of Investigation, established in 1908, initially provided research services for the Department of Justice. The latter organization soon developed its own Bureau of Investigation and assumed major control of domestic counterintelligence. One of the Bureau's agents, William Neuhoffer, a recent German immigrant, penetrated the German intelligence network in Mexico. Neuhoffer provided information which led to the arrest of some of the terrorists who, on

July 30, 1916, blew up two million pounds of munitions on Black Tom Island in New York City's harbor.

The Justice Department was also charged with the immense task of keeping surveillance on more than one million aliens, the vast majority of whom were law-abiding immigrants awaiting their citizenship. Only a small number of spy films referred directly to this agency. For example, *The Burden of Proof* (1918) shows the chief of the Department of Justice investigating the theft of important documents.

Although the Bureau of Investigation's staff was increased from 300 to 400, the task appeared impossible to its director, Bruce Bielaski. The American Protective League, a civic-minded organization, offered its assistance to the director who unfortunately accepted. The League's members were a band of amateur busybodies who eventually harassed innocent citizens and instigated illegal wiretaps and arrests.

In 1915 President Wilson ordered the U.S. Secret Service to keep the German and Austrian embassies under surveillance. Frank Polk, the second in command at the Department of State, assumed responsibility for coordinating the results of the secret service investigations with British intelligence. With carte blanche, the U.S. Secret Service tapped the telephone lines and intercepted the mail of the German and Austrian embassies in Washington and New York City. Dr. Heinrich Albert, the German commercial attaché, had the temerity to take a public elevated train on July 24, 1915, and had the misfortune to forget his bag on the train. A secret service agent who had been following Albert pounced on the bag and provided the U.S. and Great Britain with one of the great coups of the war. (Dr. Albert is portrayed as a loathsome character in the 1918 wartime serial *The Eagle's Eye*.)

German business ventures, including some dummy corporations intended to siphon off war matériel from the Allies and others offering employees exorbitant wages to encourage worker dissatisfaction in other corporations, were uncovered. After due consideration, the Justice Department determined that none of these business undertakings were illegal. Nevertheless, the story was leaked to the newspapers and the Germans suffered a strong public relations loss.

At times the secret service attempted to cooperate with local police forces throughout the U.S. In one of those rare instances in which such coordination actually took place, New York City police provided the secret service with enough information to lead to the arrest, on October 24, 1915, of a German demolitions expert, Robert Fay, who was suspected of a number of bombings in the New York metropolitan area. Circumstantial evidence gathered through Fay's arrest led to Captain Franz von Papen, the German military attaché, who was declared *persona non grata* and expelled from the U.S. Although von Papen traveled back to Germany via Great Britain under an American safe-conduct pass, the British seized his trunks and documents upon arrival at Falmouth. The confiscated documents implicated a number of German espionage agents. Picking up the trail back in New York City, the secret service raided the offices of the new German military attaché, Wolf von Igel, who had succeeded von Papen and discovered records of additional German espionage agents operating in America.

Army intelligence in 1914 was basically concerned with Mexico and bandit leader Pancho Villa. Three-quarters of the U.S. Army was moved to the Mexican border. Problems in Europe only peripherally concerned the Army. U.S. military intelligence units in Mexico were there primarily to keep tabs on our southern neighbor and only gathered substantial data on German businesses and espionage in that country as an afterthought. The Office of Naval Intelligence, on the other hand, believed Japan might be our primary enemy in the Pacific and began to develop contingency plans for a war against Japan, which showed an unusual interest in Mexico.

Spy films about Mexican-American border conflicts began to appear even before America's entry into World War I and continued throughout the conflict. In *For the Honor of Old Glory* or *Carrying the Stars and Stripes Into Mexico* (1914), a Mexican spy infiltrates the U.S. Army as a second lieutenant and leads his colonel and regiment into a trap in Mexico. *The Key to Yesterday* (1914) has a U.S. agent (Carlyle Blackwell) operating in Mexico during that country's revolution. American agents in *The Love Thief* (1916) try to prevent Mexican guerrillas from buying arms in the U.S.

America's entry into World War I in 1917

brought a large infusion of money and personnel into army and navy intelligence. A Military Intelligence Unit was established within the War College of the army under General Van Deman. The restructuring of army and navy intelligence units led to closer cooperation between the State Department and British intelligence, but it came too late to increase our general strategic intelligence capacity.

On the European mainland General Pershing created G-2, an army intelligence unit which provided specific field intelligence. G-2 launched agents who furnished reports on troop strength, terrain and enemy counterintelligence. G-2 also intercepted enemy radio and telephone communications and ran an effective cryptanalysis division. Several spy films dealt with intelligence activities at the front. *Called to the Front* (1914), for example, concerns a U.S. agent assigned to deliver important documents to the Russians. In *Berlin via America* (1918) actor-director Francis Ford, brother of director John Ford, portrays an American agent who infiltrates Germany's elite flying corps. In *The Kaiser's Finish* (1918) Earl Schenck, as a secret agent, impersonates the Kaiser's illegitimate son in an attempt to assassinate the Crown Prince. The behind-enemy-lines dramas continued to appear well after the armistice. In *Her Man o' War* (1926) U.S. intelligence sends two doughboys, posing as deserters, behind enemy lines to find a route to a big gun that is preventing an Allied attack.

U.S. agents appeared on American screens in a variety of plots during and after the war. In *Daughter Angele* (1918) U.S. intelligence, suspecting spies are signaling German submarines from an innocent-looking mansion, sends in one of its agents. *I Want to Forget* (1918) has a patriotic American wife (Evelyn Nesbit) volunteering her services as a spy for her country. While assigned to secure valuable papers from a suspected German spy, she assists in his capture. Feather-brained Billie Burke is mistaken for a German spy in the comedy *In Pursuit of Polly* (1918), but she is soon rescued by a U.S. government agent. An American secret agent poses as a German spy in *The Kaiser's Shadow* (1918) to protect the secret plans for a new type of rifle. In *The Hun Within* (1918) a U.S. agent helps to prevent the destruction of a troopship and round up a spy network.

Films about the conflict released long after the war had ended continued to feature American agents foiling the villainous plots of foreign and domestic spies. Earle Williams in *The Highest Trump* (1919) plays a dual role. When his twin brother, a German agent, is killed, Williams, working for the U.S. government, replaces him and is accepted as a German spy. The fear of American boys helplessly going to a watery grave as the result of their troopship being sunk by a German submarine was one of the most effective images Hollywood could conjure up. Several films exploited this anxiety. In the comedy drama *Friendly Enemies* (1925) U.S. agents round up German spies responsible for the sinking of one such transport ship. In *Convoy* (1927) Dorothy Mackaill is called upon by the U.S. Secret Service to uncover a spy who is leaking information to the enemy about troop transport departures.

Although many films about World War I concerned U.S. operatives battling espionage agents and saboteurs at home and abroad, most dramas and comedies released during the conflict featured civilian heroes and heroines—men from all walks of life loyal to the war effort, patriotic women who innocently stumbled upon a spy plot, children who were caught up in the war fervor of the period. Hollywood helped to both create and reflect the perception of a mighty war machine geared up to battle and crush any aggressor. See German Intelligence: World War I; U.S. Secret Service. ■

U.S. intelligence: World War II. "We know of new methods of attack, the Trojan Horse, the fifth column that betrays a nation unprepared for treachery. Spies, saboteurs and traitors are the actors in this new tragedy." President Franklin D. Roosevelt broadcast this warning to the American people on May 26, 1940, during one of his radio fireside chats. Upon hearing of covert operations during World War II, most Americans today immediately associate those activities with the Office of Strategic Services (O.S.S.), organized by General William J. Donovan. But the battle against foreign and domestic spies began long before America's entry into the war, and it was waged quite effectively by the F.B.I., under the direction of J. Edgar Hoover, and other government agencies.

German espionage in America during the 1930s focused chiefly on economic and technological information that could be useful to

Hitler's military program. Spies had such contacts as a Swiss-born U.S. Army captain, a draftsman among naval architects and several employees in aircraft plants. Ironically, much of the material gathered by Nazi agents was openly available to anyone who sought such information. In fact, according to the American embassy in Berlin, by 1934 American salesmen operating in Germany were busily engaged in selling airplane engines, gyro compasses, automatic pilot apparatus and anti-aircraft control systems to the Nazis. Also, agreements between German and American companies allowed for an open exchange of the latest developments in such areas as formulas for explosives, the processing of butyl rubber and the manufacture of airplane engine starters.

Hoover in 1937 had been authorized by President Roosevelt to conduct antisubversive surveillance. The bureau enlisted a number of German expatriates, including a certain William Sebold. Sebold had been born in Germany and, under F.B.I. tutelage, became a double agent. As a result of Sebold's activities, the F.B.I. in 1940 arrested 32 German agents operating in the U.S. and brought German espionage here to a halt.

While the U.S. was engaged in tracking down and arresting foreign agents before entering World War II, Hollywood studios, always on the prowl for melodramatic topical issues, kept many of its players, especially those with foreign accents, busily employed in a string of spy dramas and comedies. Films released prior to America's entry into the conflict usually hesitated to identify the national origins of their foreign spies. The studios, attempting to remain neutral, did not want to alienate any of their lucrative foreign markets. American audiences, however, drew the obvious conclusions. The foreign accents of these nefarious agents often suggested their Teutonic backgrounds. *Cipher Bureau* (1938) features Leon Ames as the head of the counter-espionage cipher bureau, an agency set up to foil hostile nations from sending secret messages to their agents in the U.S.

Dozens of spy films released after Japan's attack on Pearl Harbor dealt with threats of espionage and sabotage on the home front—with more than 75 released in 1942 alone. Most of these dramas differentiated between U.S. and Axis intelligence preparations. American agencies usually acted defensively,

sending out their operatives only to halt a rash of sabotage acts or prevent the theft of vital documents or a secret weapon. On the other hand, aggressive and well-entrenched German and Japanese agents were often seen in prewar America laying the foundation for future espionage. Once the U.S. entered the conflict, films showed these enemy networks unleashing their attacks upon defense plants, munitions dumps, shipyards and other military targets. *Joe Smith, American* (1942) features Robert Young as a World War II airplane technician who is captured and tortured by German agents. Finally, federal agents help him to retrace his steps to the enemy hideout.

American intelligence operations behind enemy lines did not take the offensive until the Office of Strategic Services was established. The O.S.S. was the dream and brainchild of one man. While on a presidential mission to England in 1940, William Donovan met with Prime Minister Churchill and his chief of the British Secret Intelligence Service in the Western Hemisphere, William Stephenson. Stephenson persuaded the American of the need for the U.S. to centralize intelligence operations into one agency. Upon returning to Washington, Donovan persuaded President Roosevelt to establish such an agency. In 1942 the President appointed Donovan the Coordinator of Information.

J. Edgar Hoover, as reigning director of the F.B.I., resented this invasion of what he considered his "turf," and a jurisdictional war began. For a while it appeared that Hoover would get his way as usual. However, this time Hoover lost and Donovan's office, which was now known as the O.S.S., was transferred to the joint chiefs of staff. (Eventually the O.S.S. evolved into the Central Intelligence Agency.) Donovan's creation provided full-service intelligence. It gathered data, sifted through the information, extrapolating hypotheses, and acted upon the conclusions. The O.S.S. thus placed agents in the field, interviewed returning overseas travelers, cooperated with emigré groups, and intercepted mail, radio and telegraph communications. Recognized scholars in the various disciplines were hired and the facilities of the Library of Congress were put at the disposal of Donovan's staff.

The most celebrated department of the O.S.S. was the Special Operations Branch. Groups of from 20 to 40 men were dropped behind enemy lines and fought with local partisans. Other, smaller, sections of five to six men gathered information and often trained local partisans in guerrilla tactics. These exploits, with their intrinsic dramatic and suspense potential, were highly romanticized in Hollywood reenactments. In *The Enemy General* (1960) Van Johnson, as an American agent in the O.S.S., is assigned to smuggle a Nazi officer out of Europe and escort him safely to England. *A Face in the Rain* (1963) concerns an American agent who has parachuted behind enemy lines into Italy. It was agents such as these who provided intelligence for the American and British airplanes to accurately bomb the German rocket installations at Peenemunde in Germany and the oil fields in Rumania. *Operation Crossbow* (1965) presents a fictionalized version of agents penetrating German rocket sites.

U.S. intelligence regarding the Pacific zone and Japan emerged from a completely different series of events. The navy had been concerned with the military threat posed by Japan ever since the Russo-Japanese War of 1904. Accordingly, the Office of Naval Intelligence compiled, in 1912, a strategy for potential war with Japan entitled War Plan Orange. Through the 1920s and 1930s the navy nurtured a group of specialists in Japanese history, language and military tactics. The Office of Naval Communications' Code and Signal Section maintained surveillance on Japanese military, diplomatic and electronic communication. In 1940 William Friedman, a cryptologist who was the director of the army's Signal Intelligence Service, broke Code Purple, the secret Japanese communications code. Despite this impressive intelligence coup, neither the navy nor the army predicted the Japanese attack on Pearl Harbor.

As a result of this surprise attack, the War Department reorganized military intelligence. Subsequently, the navy's new Fleet Radio Unit, Pacific Fleet, intercepted and decoded a top-secret message to Japanese naval commanders indicating that Admiral Yamamoto would be making a one-day inspection tour of naval bases in the Solomon Islands on April 18, 1943. Navy intelligence was divided about killing Yamamoto. On the one hand, the interception of his plane might indicate to the Japanese that the Americans had broken their code; on the other hand, Yamamoto's death would lower Japanese morale, especially so because he had launched

the surprise attack on Pearl Harbor. The commander of the U.S. Pacific Fleet, Admiral Nimitz, decided to go with the plan. He dispatched eighteen P-38 fighters from Guadalcanal; they flew low over the ocean to avoid Japanese radar and successfully intercepted and shot down Yamamoto's bomber and escort. Navy operations put out a cover story indicating that some Australians had spotted the Japanese bomber and that the Americans were ignorant of the important dignitary on the airplane. The Japanese bought the story and never suspected that their code had been broken. *China Venture* (1953), apparently, used the incident in their fictionalized version. The plot concerns a small group of U.S. Marines and navy men who are assigned by naval intelligence the task of bringing in for questioning a Japanese admiral whose plane had crashed off the China coast.

Captain Joseph Rochefort, a cryptologist, was the supervisor of the navy's Code and Signal Section of the Office of Naval Communications. The Signal Section, by careful analysis of Japanese radio communication, was able to provide the navy with the Japanese combat plan before the Battle of Midway, thereby giving the U.S. its greatest naval victory in World War II.

Films of espionage relating to World War II appeared well after the conflict had ended although their number began to decrease dramatically. *Close-Up* (1948) concerns a gang of ex-Nazis under cover in New York who are trying to destroy newsreel clips which provide damaging evidence against one of its members.

Since there was no longer any need to embellish the contents with anti-Axis propaganda, these dramas often focused on other plots such as betrayal or stories based on actual incidents. *I Was an American Spy* (1950) re-enacted the true experiences of Claire Phillips during World War II. *Operation Secret* (1952) concerns a former American agent and a traitor in the French underground. ∎

U.S. Secret Service. In 1915 a U.S. Secret Service agent retrieved a briefcase crammed with documents that the German commercial attaché, had forgotten on a train. The Germans' bogus companies in the U.S., used as cover for enemy agents, were revealed, and the Secretary of the Treasury disclosed the story to the press. The incident, which revealed to the world the extent of German espionage, exemplifies only one of the many functions of the secret service.

When the U.S. began printing paper currency in 1862, it was faced with an unprecedented number of counterfeiters. Subsequently, in 1865, Congress established the secret service, whose function it was to stop the counterfeiters. The term "secret service" has been used in a general way by writers such as the 19th century American playwright William Gillette and, later, those who contributed scripts to film studios. Several Civil War dramas depict activities of Secret Service agents, but these operatives, obviously, were not actually official members of the agency.

At times, the U.S. Secret Service extended its activities beyond the scope initially envisioned by Congress. This was probably inevitable, for there was no other federal police organization until the creation of the F.B.I. in 1908. Although the agency was never authorized to conduct foreign intelligence operations, it was used for that purpose during the Spanish-American War and World War I. In 1906 Congress designated the protection of the President as an additional function of the agency. In *The Kidnapping of the President* (1980) an arrogant C.I.A. chief demands that his agency handle the abduction of a U.S. President. He frustrates the more expert efforts of secret service chief William Shatner, who is burdened with negotiating with terrorists while he is trying to free the President.

Eventually the U.S. Secret Service was authorized to protect the President's family, the Vice-President, the President-elect and, in 1968, the major presidential candidates. *Assassination* (1987) illustrates this latter function. When mysterious assassins make various attempts on the life of the First Lady (Jill Ireland), Charles Bronson, as a dedicated and professional U.S. Secret Service agent, is assigned to protect her.

Several spy dramas set during the Civil War include heroes who are members of a more general secret service. *Secret Service* (1919), based on William Gillette's famous Civil War play, features Robert Warwick as a Union secret service agent who is assigned the task of helping to bring about the fall of Richmond. Comedian Ted Healy, who introduced the Three Stooges comedy team to the stage and ultimately to the screen, plays a trouper in a medicine show who is in reality

working for the Union secret service in *Operator 13* (1934).

President Wilson enlarged the scope of the secret service when World War I erupted in 1914. He assigned the agency to investigate any violations of neutrality. Agents uncovered sundry examples of espionage and counterespionage. Several war dramas about secret service agents began to appear. In *Called to the Front* (1914), for example, a U.S. Secret Service officer and wireless operator (Arthur Finn) must deliver important documents to the Russians. Thomas Chatterton, as a U.S. Secret Service agent in the two-reel drama "Over Secret Wires" (1915), uncovers a plot involving German spies who are signaling their U-boats about American shipping off the coast of Oregon. Actor-director Francis Ford portrays an American flier employed by the secret service in *Berlin via America* (1918). In *The Kaiser's Shadow* (1918) Thurston Hall, as a secret service agent, poses as a German spy to unmask the leader of an espionage network.

Hollywood occasionally returned to melodramatic plots about counterfeiting, the crime the agency was originally assigned to handle. The famous magician, Harry Houdini, portrays *Haldane of the Secret Service* (1923) and battles a gang of Chinese counterfeiters. In *The Custard Cup* (1923) a U.S. Secret Service agent poses as a member of a counterfeit gang so that he can get enough evidence to put the culprits behind bars. The U.S. Secret Service goes after a gang who made off with a set of treasury bank-note engraving plates in *Code of the Secret Service* (1939), an incredibly inept drama featuring Ronald Reagan. Jack Holt, in the serial *Holt of the Secret Service* (1942), battles a master counterfeiting ring that threatens the stability of the U.S. economy. A U.S. Secret Service agent poses as an underworld hired gun so that he can infiltrate a gang of counterfeiters in the low-budget drama *The Counterfeit Killer* (1968). Counterfeiters and secret service agents have clashed on screen as recently as 1985 in *To Live and Die in L.A.*, a violent drama that added psychological overtones to the genre by providing its villain (Willem Dafoe) with a disturbed personality.

Hollywood studios drafted some of their two-fisted male players as secret service agents and sent them after the smuggling racket, another popular screen topic. A U.S. Secret Service agent uncovers a gang of rumrunners operating between Cuba and Massachusetts in the comedy drama *The Game Chicken* (1922). Robert Ellis in *Forbidden Cargo* (1925) portrays a U.S. Secret Service agent stationed in the Bahamas to put a stop to rumrunners operating in the area. *A Gentleman of Quality* (1926) pits the U.S. Secret Service against a gang of silk smugglers. Bert Lytell, working for the U.S. Secret Service, masquerades as an underworld character in an effort to expose a group of jewel smugglers in *Alias the Lone Wolf* (1927).

Periodically, films depicted secret service agents battling the drug problem. U.S. Secret Service agents take on a gang of opium smugglers operating in Hong Kong in *The Warning* (1928). Agent Jack Holt in *Behind the Mask* (1932) goes under cover to expose a drug syndicate.

Film studios kept the secret service busy battling a host of other lawbreakers. The U.S. Secret Service uncovers a plot on the part of the Latin-speaking countries of the world to take control of the U.S. in *Elusive Isabel* (1916). The head of the U.S. Secret Service poses as a gentleman of leisure as a ploy to catch The Hawk, an international jewel thief, in *The Hunting of the Hawk* (1917). J. Warren Kerrigan in *The Best Man* (1919) portrays a U.S. Secret Service agent who is assigned to recover an important secret government code that has been stolen. The U.S. Secret Service assigns an army captain (Edward Langford) to investigate a growing Communist threat on New York's Lower East Side in *The Volcano* (1919). In *Golden Silence* (1923) the secret service seeks to put an end to a series of mail robberies. Matt Moore, masquerading as a buffoonish character, turns out to be a U.S. Secret Service agent who saves members of an international conference from an assassin in *Diplomacy* (1926). The film ends with a tribute to all secret service agents who protect and defend the integrity of international law and diplomacy. In the serial *Flying G-Men* (1939) U.S. Secret Service airmen, led by Robert Paige, help to foil a plot by a network of spies who threaten the U.S. with invasion.

Sometimes the agent's mission involved other lands. *The Love Thief* (1916), inspired by contemporary incidents along the Mexican border, involves U.S. Secret Service agents who are trying to prevent Mexican guerrillas from buying American arms. Secret service agents from the U.S., England and France are assigned to prevent a saboteur from blowing up the Panama Canal in *Marie Galante* (1934).

Surprisingly, U.S. Secret Service films often featured heroines as agents. Even the multitude of World War II espionage films could not match the number of women who worked under cover for the secret service. *The Unexpected* (1914) was one of the earliest film to feature a female member of the agency. When the secret service finds it is having difficulties in gathering evidence against a gang of smugglers, it calls upon one of its female operatives to infiltrate the band. A U.S. Secret Service agent (Vola Vale) in *The Bond Between* (1917) is assigned to investigate a suspected art smuggler; instead, she finds herself helping him to prove his innocence. In *The Mollycoddle* (1920) heroine Ruth Renick portrays a secret service agent assigned to get evidence against a smuggling operation. When she is captured by villain Wallace Beery, Douglas Fairbanks, as the title character, comes to her rescue. Ethel Grey Terry in *The Penalty* (1920) portrays a U.S. Secret Service agent assigned to investigate a master criminal operating in San Francisco. Jack Holt, as *The Lone Wolf* (1924), teams up with Lucy Shannon, a U.S. Secret Service agent, to protect coveted secret papers that contain military plans of the U.S.

A handful of World War I spy dramas featured female members of the secret service. Gloria Swanson, working under cover as a U.S. agent, foils a German spy's scheme in *Shifting Sands* (1918). Evelyn Brent in *Secret Orders* (1926) portrays a telegrapher who joins the U.S. Secret Service. In *Convoy* (1927), a World War I sea drama, a young woman (Dorothy Mackaill) is called upon by the U.S. Secret Service to help uncover a spy. ∎

V

Valley of Hunted Men, The (1928), Pathé. *Dir.* Richard Thorpe; *Sc.* Frank I. Ingraham; *Cast includes:* Buffalo Bill, Jr., Kathleen Collins, Alma Rayford, Gascar Apfel, Frank Griffith.

Buffalo Bill, Jr. portrays a member of the U.S. border patrol in this western drama about a gang of smugglers operating in Mexico. Growing impatient with bureaucratic ineptness and delay of the service in putting an end to the smugglers' activities, our hero decides to play a lone hand. The gang is smuggling guns south of the border and importing rum to the U.S. Bill's plan is to force them out of their Mexican sanctuary so they can be rounded up.

He crosses the border, enters the band's hideaway and provokes them to give chase. Meanwhile he finds time to romance a young woman being held by the outlaws. Complications arise when the daughter of one of the smugglers falls in love with him but is rebuked. The gang gives chase as our hero lights some pre-arranged fire signals to alert the U.S. border unit. The outlaws ride into the trap and are apprehended. ■

Valley of Hunted Men, The (1942), Rep. *Dir.* John English; *Sc.* Albert DeMond, Morton Grant; *Cast includes:* Bob Steele, Tom Tyler, Jimmie Dodd, Anna Marie Stewart, Budd Buster, Hal Price.

Several westerns released during World War II updated their plots to include espionage agents and saboteurs bent on subverting America's war efforts. One such entry in the popular "Three Mesquiteers" western series concerns an escaped Nazi. He poses as the nephew of a German refugee, now a patriotic American, who has developed a new method of producing rubber—a vital wartime product. The hero trio (Bob Steele, Tom Tyler and Jimmie Dodd), known as the Three Mesquiteers, do some hard riding and straight shooting before they bring the Nazi spy to justice.

This western series had a continual change of members. Earlier participants included John Wayne during his B western period, beefy Ray Corrigan, ventriloquist Max Terhune and silent screen player Raymond Hatton as the old-timer. Wayne's last appearance as a Mesquiteer was in *New Frontier*, released in 1939, the year that brought him fame in John Ford's classic *Stagecoach*. ■

Vanquished, The (1953), Par. *Dir.* Edward Ludwig; *Sc.* Winston Miller, Frank L. Moss, Lewis R. Foster; *Cast includes:* John Payne, Coleen Gray, Jan Sterling, Lyle Bettger, Willard Parker, Roy Gordon.

A Confederate veteran returns home after spending time as a prisoner of war in a Union camp in this post-Civil War drama based on the novel by Karl Brown. The veteran (John Payne) has secretly been assigned to expose corruption in his home town, a condition brought about by the infamous Reconstruction period. Working under cover, he soon learns that the civil administrator (Lyle Bettger), who has moved into Payne's former mansion, is behind most of the crooked dealings. To gain proof against Bettger, Payne signs up as his tax collector, much to the dismay of his girlfriend (Coleen Gray) and the other townspeople. After the usual setbacks and typical fights and shoot-outs, Payne straightens out the local problems. ■

Venetian Affair, The (1967), MGM. *Dir.* Jerry Thorpe; *Sc.* E. Jack Neuman; *Cast includes:* Robert Vaughn, Elke Sommer, Felicia

Farr, Karl Boehm, Boris Karloff, Edward Asner.

International agents scheme to sabotage the efforts of major world powers to bring about peaceful coexistence between the East and West in this slow-paced drama set during the Cold War. When a bomb kills more than a dozen diplomats at a Venice peace conference, each side suspects the other. Robert Vaughn, as a former C.I.A. agent now employed as a reporter for an international news agency, is assigned to cover the story. He soon finds himself entangled in a web of intrigue spun by the C.I.A. and international spies. His former C.I.A. chief (Edward Asner), now in charge of the Venice office, suspects Vaughn's wife (Elke Sommer) of being a Communist spy. He recruits the ex-C.I.A. agent to track her down.

Meanwhile, a sinister and ruthless spy (Karl Boehm) who sells his services to any power, has developed a dangerous mind-altering drug that turns its victims into helpless puppets. Boehm, who drugged an American diplomat at the ill-fated conference, was responsible for the bombing. A political analyst (Boris Karloff) has learned about Boehm's secret drug and plans to expose him at the next peace conference. This sets off a search for Karloff's report by Boehm's henchmen, Asner and Vaughn. The reporter recovers the papers and appears in the nick of time at the next diplomatic meeting to prevent another disaster.

The film, based on Helen MacInnes' novel, ends with Asner about to read Karloff's report to various representatives of the major powers. "A week ago," he begins, "when peaceful coexistence among our countries seemed a possibility, a violent act was perpetrated by factions in Peking, dedicated to uncompromising ideologies. A mind-controlling drug that is capable of changing the brain's nerve cells and of robotizing a human being. . . ." ∎

Via Wireless (1915), Pathé. *Dir.* George Fitzmaurice; *Sc.* Ouida Bergère; *Cast includes:* Gail Kane, Bruce McRae, Paul McAllister, Harry Weaver, Brandon Hurst.

A patriotic drama set during World War I, the story concerns a U.S. Navy lieutenant and an architect, rivals in the invention of a big gun that the War Department wants for coastal defense. The architect sabotages the officer's gun so that it fires with disastrous results. Following several melodramatic incidents, the villain is exposed.

The film was not without its propaganda value at a time when the American public was in the midst of a heated debate between advocates of pacifism and those who cried out for preparedness. President Wilson appears briefly in an early portion of the film as an advocate of appropriate coastal defenses. The film is based on the 1908 play by Paul Armstrong and Winchell Smith. ∎

Vichy France. When France fell to the Germans early in World War II, Premier Reynaud resigned and was replaced by a World War I hero, Marshall Petain, who immediately signed an armistice with Germany. In contrast to his Eastern policies, Hitler offered liberal terms to the French: France south of the Loire would be free of German troops and could manage its own internal affairs; northern France and the coastline, however, would be occupied and administered by Germany. French naval vessels had to be disarmed but could remain under the control of the French government which was established at Vichy.

The Vichy government, except for some minor protests against German charges for its army of occupation, collaborated with the victors. The French Empire fell into line and accepted Petain's authority. (Such wartime films as *Casablanca* and *To Have and Have Not* reflect this collaboration.) The war seemed over for most, but not all, Frenchmen. An obscure brigadier general, Charles de Gaulle, who had escaped from France to London, refused to lie down. Since France lacked any other figurehead, the British government recognized him as the leader of the French government-in-exile which became known as the Free French. He broadcast to the French people on June 18, 1940, insisting that a battle, not the war, had been lost. Despite this bravado, only several hundred French troops responded to his call.

At this point, de Gaulle failed to establish any control over the elements of the French Empire; the British remained extremely concerned regarding the disposition of the French fleet. Admiral Darlan, the commander of French naval forces, had secretly instructed his officers to sink their ships rather than permit them to be seized by Hitler. The British, unaware of Darlan's instructions, initiated their own actions. They seized control of French vessels in British ports and, in Alexandria, they reached agreement with the French admirals to disarm their ships in port. After some hesitation, on July 3, Churchill ordered his own naval command to open fire on French naval vessels in the port at Mers-el-Kebir near Oran. Nearly 1,400 French sailors were killed and one battle cruiser and two battleships were crippled or destroyed.

American films during the war occasionally alluded to the struggle between the Vichy French and the Free French. *Casablanca* (1942) mirrored the effects of oppressive Nazi control, Vichy collaboration and the numerous intrigues and acts of espionage that occurred despite the watchful eyes of both these forces. The conflict culminates in the final sequence when a corrupt French official (Claude Rains), in an act of redemption, takes sides against the Vichy regime, symbolically shown when he drops a bottle of Vichy water into a waste basket. Warner Bros., having succeeded in using Rick's café in *Casablanca* as a microcosm of the warring nations, turned a French ship into a symbol of embattled France in *Passage to Marseilles* (1944), as elements of Free France overcome the traitorous Vichy forces aboard the freighter. *To Have and Have Not*, another Warner drama released in 1944, told about the resistance of the Free French against the Vichy government in Martinique. The film, in many respects, repeats the plot of *Casablanca* and includes some of the same actors (Bogart, Dan Seymour, Dalio) and similar dialogue. "I'm glad you're on our side," a French patriot says to Bogart, echoing the words of Paul Henreid, the freedom fighter in *Casablanca*. Humphrey Bogart again portrays a neutral American who finally decides to help the Free French underground after Vichy officials start pushing him around. ∎

Vietnam War: intelligence and covert actions. It was one of those ironic circumstances of history that a wounded Vietnamese whom an American medical team saved from death in 1945, Ho Chi Minh, evolved into the North Vietnamese leader of the forces opposing the American intervention in Vietnam. The Office of Strategic Services (O.S.S.) during World War II had trained sabotage teams of Vietminh, as the Communist guerrillas were then known, and had participated with the Vietminh and French in joint commando raids against Japanese installations.

After the war the Vietminh captured control of Annam, Cochin China and Tonkin and fought the French for authority over the rest of Vietnam. The Vietminh emerged as Communists and infiltrated saboteurs into South Vietnam who terrorized the local inhabitants into recognizing the Communists as a *sub rosa* government. Local officials were assassinated in an attempt to undermine the central government in Saigon.

America was drawn into the Vietnam conflict following the disastrous French defeat at the hands of the North Vietnamese at the Battle of Dien Bien Phu on May 7, 1954, which led to France's subsequent withdrawal from Vietnam. Fearing Communist expansion, freed from the drain of the Korean War which had ended in 1953 and impressed by the C.I.A.'s "domino theory" which maintained that the fall of Indochina would eventually lead to the fall of other Southeast Asian countries, President Eisenhower in 1955 dispatched a U.S. Military Advisory Group to South Vietnam.

Major Edward Lansdale, the C.I.A. station chief in Manila, had been transferred to Vietnam the previous year and assumed the role of chief of the Military Mission in Saigon. Lansdale was successful in defeating the Huk/Communist uprising in the Philippines and in electing Ramon Magsaysay president in 1953. The C.I.A. hoped that Lansdale would repeat in Vietnam his previous success in the Philippines. Lansdale threw American support behind Emperor Bao Dai's prime minister, Ngo Dinh Diem. The American organized Diem's presidential guard and assisted in the writing of the Constitution of South Vietnam. He brought along the Filipinos who had defeated the Huks at home and were familiar with counter-insurgency techniques. They organized the Freedom Company, a private not-for-profit corporation. They sent sabotage teams into North Vietnam and identified Communist agents in the South. The group organized Village Self-Defense Corps and assisted in road-building and construction of hospitals. Although Lansdale attempted to prod President Diem toward democratic reforms, the latter, a staunch Roman Catholic, refused to institute popular changes and continued his anti-Buddhist policies. Once Lansdale understood that Diem was alienating the majority of the population, he threw in the towel early in the war in 1956 and left South Vietnam. *The Quiet American* (1958), based on Graham Greene's novel, was a fictionalized account of some of his experiences in Vietnam. Audie Murphy portrayed Lansdale.

Concomitant with the increasing role of American troops in Vietnam came a shift of intelligence-gathering from the C.I.A. to the U.S. Army. Major General Joseph McChristian, assistant chief of staff of the U.S. Military Assistance Command, organized the analysis of radio communication, interrogation of prisoners, air reconnaissance and analyses of seized documents.

Both army and navy forces tested a cornucopia of electronic military devices. Infrared scanners were used. A "people-sniffer" which could detect urine and human perspiration was developed by the army. Unattended ground sensors were dropped onto the Ho Chi Minh Trail, a jungle road over which the North Vietnamese infiltrated men and matériel to the South; the UGSs, as these devices were known, embedded themselves into the ground and detected the vibrations of men and vehicles. The air force introduced Remotely Piloted Vehicles, drones which photographed enemy territory.

One of the most radical programs introduced by the C.I.A. during the Vietnam War was the Phoenix Program. Vietcong defectors, encouraged by an offer of amnesty, often identified their former comrades. Posters were distributed offering rewards for those so identified, and local villagers were encouraged to inform on their neighbors. The Provincial Reconnaissance Units of the South Vietnamese government would then pick up the suspects and often imprison or execute them without benefit of trial. The abuses inherent in the program and its subsequent public exposure by former C.I.A. agent Frank Snepp in his book *Decent Interval* compelled its discontinuation in 1971. It has been estimated that 20,000 Vietnamese were killed as a direct result of the Phoenix Program.

The C.I.A., the U.S. Military Assistance Command and the Army of the Republic of South Vietnam each supported its own intelligence apparatus. They shared some intelligence data and up to 1967 provided the same analysis of enemy guerrilla strength. In 1966 Samuel Adams, a C.I.A. analyst, visited Vietnam and, using the same data, claimed that previous reports had underestimated enemy strength by one half. Whereas earlier analyses had judged Vietcong and North Vietnamese forces in South Vietnam to be 260,000, Adams concluded that it was 500,000. In view of President Johnson's political difficulties at home with the growing antiwar movement, the inference that a still greater American commitment of troops was needed to counter the increasing number of enemy troops was politically unpalatable. Adams' report was scrapped and C.I.A. Director Helms approved the lower estimate. Adams subsequently charged, in a C.B.S. television interview in 1982, that General Westmoreland, chief of the U.S. Military Assistance Command, had personally disguised the true figure of enemy strength. Westmoreland sued for libel but failed to win a judgment.

Like the Korean conflict, the Vietnam War inspired few spy dramas. If the former is to be called, as a few historians have suggested, the "forgotten war," then the Vietnam conflict must go down in the chronicles as the war most Americans did not want to be reminded of. About one decade after the conflagration, several action dramas began to appear pitting such superheroes as Sylvester Stallone and Chuck Norris, successfully wielding superweapons, against hordes of Asian Communists. As the nation's wounds began to heal, these popular escapist, revisionist depictions of the war were soon replaced by more serious personal dramas such as *Platoon* (1986) and *Born on the Fourth of July* (1989). The spy drama, however, remained rare. One film which takes place during the conflict is *Operation CIA* (1965), with Burt Reynolds portraying a C.I.A. agent who is sent to Saigon to investigate the murder of a fellow agent. Masquerading as a professor of agriculture, he meets his contact (Kieu Chinh) who tells Reynolds of a plot to assassinate the U.S. ambassador. In *The Losers* (1970), a low-budget, highly fictitious exploitation film, the U.S. government hires a motley gang of motorcyclists to rescue a C.I.A. agent whom the North Vietnamese are holding captive in Cambodia. One of the most acclaimed films dealing with covert actions during the war was *Apocalypse Now* (1979). Martin Sheen portrays a U.S. intelligence officer sent "unofficially" into Cambodia by his superiors to "terminate" the command of Kurtz (Marlon Brando), a megalomaniac American officer whose military tactics are disapproved of by the top brass. ■

Nancy Coleman and Michael O'Shea become prisoners of a right-wing extremist organization trying to spread chaos in the U.S. *Violence* (1947).

Violence (1947), Mon. *Dir.* Jack Bernhard; *Sc.* Stanley Rubin, Louis Lantz; *Cast includes:* Nancy Coleman, Michael O'Shea, Sheldon Leonard, Peter Whitney, Emory Parnell, Pierre Watkin.

A secret organization, specializing in spreading disorder and violence, caters to discontented veterans in this above-average cautionary drama. Masquerading as patriots, the group, calling itself United Defenders, exploits its members by having them commit acts of violence. Nancy Coleman, as a reporter for a picture magazine, goes under cover in an effort to expose the group. Michael O'Shea, as another investigator with similar objectives, joins her in uncovering the subversive activities. Sheldon Leonard, Peter Whitney and Emory Parnell, as the major villains, provide several perilous situations for the pair of investigators. See Black Legion. ■

Virginia City (1940), WB. *Dir.* Michael Curtiz; *Sc.* Robert Buckner; *Cast includes:* Errol Flynn, Miriam Hopkins, Randolph Scott, Humphrey Bogart, Frank McHugh, Alan Hale.

This Civil War drama opens in 1864, with the South facing economic bankruptcy and military defeat. The only hope for the Confederacy is a daring and desperate scheme proposed by an army officer (Randolph Scott). He plans to secretly transport $50 million in gold from Virginia City mine owners whose sympathies lie with the South. Errol Flynn portrays a Union intelligence officer who volunteers to stop the suspected wagon train of gold from reaching Confederate lines. Miriam Hopkins, as a Confederate spy who poses as a saloon singer in Virginia City, falls in love with Flynn.

Dialogue and incidents suggest the ironies of the war. Hopkins, about to journey to Virginia City as a spy, comments to Scott, a fellow secret agent, that their roles demand "treating friends like strangers and enemies like friends." Later, Scott orders her to lead Flynn into a trap because the Union spy may endanger their entire plan. "So I must lead him quietly and unsuspectingly to his death," Hopkins muses, "because I am a woman. That's only something a woman can do." However, Flynn, after he is captured, escapes and saves the remnants of the Southern families from being wiped out by a band of Mexican bandits. Scott is mortally wounded by the bandits.

Released during World War II, but before America's entry into the conflict, the film appealed in its ending for a unified nation. When he is court-martialed for not revealing where he has hidden the gold, Flynn explains his actions. "Their leader hoped that someday their gold would return to the South, where it belongs, to help them rebuild their homes and restore some of their pride." Nevertheless, he is sentenced to death. Hopkins visits President Lincoln on the eve of the armistice and pleads for Flynn's life. The President promises to pardon Flynn and asks Hopkins to give her Southern friends the following message: "Tell them we're now one people, united by blood and fire. From this day forward our destiny is indivisible." See American Civil War: Intelligence and Covert Actions. ■

Virtuous Men (1919), S-L Films. *Dir.* Ralph Ince; *Sc.* Ralph Ince, Arthur H. Sawyer; *Cast includes:* E. K. Lincoln, Grace Darling, Clara Joel, Robert W. Cummings, John P. Wade.

Saboteurs plot to destroy a shipyard which is producing special ships for the U.S. government in this drama. Their plans, however, are foiled by a young supervisor (E. K. Lincoln) who has recently joined the firm. Following several confrontations with the gang, he finally helps in their capture. Grace Darling appears as the daughter of the firm's president. Robert W. Cummings portrays the sinister leader of the plotters. Irving Brooks plays a member of the U.S. Secret Service. ■

Voice of Terror, The. See *Sherlock Holmes and the Voice of Terror* (1942). ■

Volcano, The (1919), Pathé. *Dir.* George Irving; *Cast includes:* Leah Baird, Edward Langford, W. H. Gibson, Jacob Kingsbury, Harry Bartlett.

A controversial propaganda drama about a Communist conspiracy, the film concerns bomb plots, Red agitators and a New York schoolteacher-heroine who becomes embroiled with the conspirators. Leah Baird portrays the heroine who naively joins the Communist movement in hopes of bettering the lives of children on the Lower East Side of New York. Suspended from her job by the superintendent, she is convinced by one of the leaders of the agitators (Jacob Kingsbury) to join the group.

The U.S. Secret Service assigns an army captain (Edward Langford) to investigate the growing Communist threat in the area. He visits Baird's home to tell her that her brother, who had saved the captain's life during World War I, is returning. Meanwhile he falls in love with her. The Communist leader, jealous of the blossoming romance, incites Baird against the captain, leading to a plot to assassinate him along with Governor Alfred E. Smith, Attorney General Alexander Palmer, and others. However, Baird's brother and a handful of other soldiers appear and disrupt the conspiracy. She realizes her mistake and marries the captain. See Palmer Raids; Red Scare of 1919–1920.

The film was a timely one, since New York City, where the story takes place, had undergone a bomb scare that resulted in a sensational trial. Controversy plagued the production from the beginning. Local Jewish newspapers labeled it anti-Semitic. The studio was forced to alter some of the dialogue in the title cards and characters' names. The hero, a captain in the U.S. Secret Service, was given a more Jewish-sounding name—Nathan Levison. Alexis, a major villain, takes time out to explain that he is not a Jew but a Bolshevik. Several important political figures, who had previously endorsed the film, withdrew their support, including Franklin Delano Roosevelt, then Assistant Secretary of the Navy, and Governor Alfred E. Smith. The latter, however, appeared in a cameo role signing a bill to prohibit the display of the red flag. ■

Voyage to the Bottom of the Sea (1961), TCF. *Dir.* Irwin Allen; *Sc.* Irwin Allen, Charles Bennett; *Cast includes:* Walter Pidgeon, Joan Fontaine, Barbara Eden, Peter Lorre, Robert Sterling, Michael Ansara.

The commander of a U.S. atomic submarine, trying to save the planet from overheating, faces problems from a saboteur operating within his vessel in this suspenseful undersea drama. Earth, it seems, is being overheated by a celestial blaze at the rate of several degrees per day. Walter Pidgeon, as the troubled commander who is unable to contact the President, must assume responsibility for his plan to fire a Polaris missile into space at the deadly fire, thereby destroying its destructive capabilities. Other countries, as well as the United Nations, oppose his decision. Joan Fontaine, as a saboteur aboard the submarine, tries to foil Pidgeon's attempts. However, he finally launches the missile and accomplishes his mission. ■

W

WAC From Walla Walla, The (1952), Rep. *Dir.* William Witney; *Sc.* Arthur T. Horman; *Cast includes:* Judy Canova, Stephen Dunne, George Cleveland, June Vincent, Roy Barcroft, Allen Jenkins.

Singer-comedienne Judy Canova foils an espionage plot in this service comedy romp. Hailing from a western military-oriented family, she joins the Women's Army Corps by accident and soon becomes embroiled with enemy agents who are trying to filch information concerning guided missiles. Judy's escape from the villains and her assistance in their capture are the highlights in this frenetic comedy. Our heroine is also trying to win the affections of a lieutenant, played by Stephen Dunne. Irene Ryan plays Judy's feather-brained sergeant. The film is worth seeing for some of the popular character actors of the 1930s, such as badman Roy Barcroft and comic Allen Jenkins. ■

Walk a Crooked Mile (1948), Col. *Dir.* Gordon Douglas; *Sc.* George Bruce; *Cast includes:* Louis Hayward, Dennis O'Keefe, Louise Allbritton, Carl Esmond, Onslow Stevens, Raymond Burr.

Soviet agents are determined to obtain America's atomic secrets in this Cold War drama. A California atomic plant is the subject of investigation when authorities discover that important documents have disappeared. The spies are aided by a traitorous American scientist, a highly placed member of the Lakeview Nuclear Project. Dennis O'Keefe, as an investigator for the F.B.I., joins forces with Louis Hayward of Scotland Yard. They eventually bring the spy network to justice in this weak drama that was shot at various locales for authenticity.

Released shortly after the press began to question the loyalty of leading American nuclear physicists, the film added to the mounting Cold War hysteria. See Cold War; Soviet Spies in the U.S. ■

Walk East on Beacon (1952), Col. *Dir.* Alfred Werker; *Sc.* Leo Rosten, Virginia Shaler, Emmett Murphy; *Cast includes:* George Murphy, Finlay Currie, Virginia Gilmore, Louise Horton, Karel Stepanek, Peter Capell.

The F.B.I. investigates Soviet espionage in the Boston area in this Cold War drama unfolded in semi-documentary style. Based on J. Edgar Hoover's *Reader's Digest* article, "The Crime of the Century," the film depicts the undercover work done by the F.B.I. in exposing a Soviet plot to steal secret scientific information from a refugee scientist, played by Finlay Currie. Communist agents threaten to kill his son who is living in Europe. He reports his dilemma to federal agents, and the pursuit of the spy ring begins.

George Murphy portrays the chief of the agents assigned to the case. He utilizes hidden cameras, lip readers and television to track the Red network which extends from Boston to Washington. The F.B.I. then provides disinformation to keep the scientist's son alive. The goal of the Communists was to get information about Project Falcon, a scheme for the ultimate weapon—a space station to orbit around the earth. To add to the realism, the film was shot on location and includes stock footage demonstrating investigative methods of the F.B.I.

There is at least one unintentionally funny scene in the film. U.S. agents have been filming every person who visits Virginia Gilmore's apartment. After several weeks of surveillance, the processed films reveal her wildly kissing a Soviet agent. Her passions

Scotland Yard investigator Louis Hayward joins F.B.I. agent Dennis O'Keefe (both standing) in unmasking a Communist spy ring trying to steal America's atomic secrets in the Cold War drama *Walk a Crooked Mile* (1948).

obviously aroused, she seizes her lover's hair, ears, neck, then pulls him down out of the camera range. F.B.I. chief Murphy shuts off the projector. "Poor kid," he mutters, "doesn't she know she's being used?" See Cold War; Federal Bureau of Investigation; Soviet Spies in the U.S. ∎

Wanted: Dead or Alive (1987), New World. *Dir.* Gary Sherman; *Sc.* Michael Patrick Goodman, Brian Taggert, Gary Sherman; *Cast includes:* Rutger Hauer, Gene Simmons, Robert Guillaume, Mel Harris, William Russ, Susan McDonald.

The C.I.A. hires a former agent to track down and capture a dangerous Arab terrorist who has been responsible for numerous indiscriminate killings in the Los Angeles area in this excessively violent drama. Rutger Hauer, as the ex-C.I.A. man now self-employed as a bounty hunter, accepts the contract because the terrorist (Gene Simmons) had earlier killed Hauer's buddies. The contract includes a $50,000 bonus for

bringing in the Arab alive. However, unknown to Hauer—and his C.I.A. friend who delivers the offer—the agency chief has set up Hauer as bait for the terrorist, who would like to kill the ex-agent.

Hauer figures out the double-cross after a gun battle with some of Simmons' Arab minions. To elude the C.I.A. during his hunt for the terrorist leader, Hauer asks his pal, a police officer (William Russ), to impersonate him and distract the C.I.A. agents who are watching Hauer. Russ, acting as decoy, then boards Hauer's boat which explodes moments later. Hauer, more determined than ever, pursues the terrorists to a chemical plant where they plan to blow up the works, thereby killing 30,000 people. The C.I.A. and police arrive and a gunfight ensues. Hauer captures Simmons and places a hand grenade in the terrorist's mouth. He then turns him over to the C.I.A. chief, turns down the $50,000 bonus and pulls the pin. Hauer appeared in a similar film, *Nighthawks* (1981), this time playing the villain—a terrorist mercenary who stalks the major world cities to ply his trade. ■

War and the Woman (1917), Pathé. *Dir.* Ernest C. Warde; *Sc.* Philip Lonergan; *Cast includes:* Florence La Badie, Ernest C. Warde, Tom Brooke, Wayne Arey, Grace Henderson, Arthur Bower.

A drama about the effects of war on a young couple, the film does not designate a particular war or which country has sent an invading army. Florence La Badie portrays the heroine, the daughter of foreign-born parents. When she discovers that her stepfather is a traitor, she leaves his home. She helps a pilot (Wayne Arey) whose plane has just crashed. The two strangers soon fall in love and marry. War is declared while the couple are on their honeymoon, and Arey is told to report for duty. La Badie, left alone, is taken prisoner when the enemy invades and captures the couple's home. Meanwhile, her husband receives permission to search for her. He infiltrates enemy lines in time to rescue his wife who has dynamited the house with enemy officers inside. The couple then flies to safety in his airplane. President Wilson is portrayed peripherally. ■

War criminals. *Hotel Berlin* (1945) ends with the following message scrolling up the screen: "Our purpose is not to destroy the German people—but we are determined to disband all German armed forces . . . bring all war criminals to just and swift punishment— wipe out the Nazi Party and Nazi laws from the life of the German people—Germany must never again disturb the peace of the World." The signatures of Winston Churchill, Franklin Roosevelt and J. Stalin appear at the bottom. But almost as these noble words disappeared from America's movie screens, so did many of the top Nazi war criminals.

Some Allied military branches carelessly— sometimes deliberately—allowed Nazi war criminals to escape. Officers in charge cited political and other expediencies for their actions. The case of one such criminal, Klaus Barbie, the "Butcher of Lyons," may well be representative. Early in World War II Barbie worked for Germany's SS in the Netherlands. In 1942 he was transferred to Lyons, France, where he was appointed head of the Gestapo. It was in that capacity that he earned his niche in history. He supervised the interrogation of thousands of Jews and war prison-

ers and personally tortured and executed many of them. He specialized in tracking down members of the French Resistance and directed the execution of their leader, Jean Moulin.

Although American forces captured him at the end of the war, the U.S. protected and employed him in its battle against "international Communism." The U.S. government, embarrassed when it had to admit that he was on its payroll, did not turn him over to French authorities. Instead, Barbie was aided in his escape to South America where he lived in Peru and later in Bolivia using the name of Klaus Altmann. International pressures on the government of Bolivia eventually were instrumental in his extradition to France in 1983 where he had already twice been sentenced to death in absentia.

When Barbie was captured, the time limit specified by the statute of limitations for war crimes had already run out, and the French authorities had to find new grounds for indictment. They included the arrest and deportation to concentration camps of a number of groups of people, including 44 Jewish children hiding at a farmhouse at Izieu, a suburb of Lyons; 86 Jewish members of relief organizations; and 650 mostly Jewish men and women only days before the Allies liberated Lyons. Most of the prisoners eventually died at Auschwitz.

Jacques Verges, Barbie's defense lawyer, claimed that his client was tried because his side had lost the war, insisting there were no moral grounds for trying Barbie. The defendant refused to recognize the authority of the court and chose not to attend court sessions during the trial. The jury, unimpressed with the defense, found Barbie guilty on all charges and sentenced him to life in prison.

American spy films about war criminals generally fall into two categories—those released during the years immediately following the war and those which appeared much later. Those in the former group retained the idealism and sense of justice that grew out of the struggle against totalitarianism. In addition, these dramas envisioned the war criminal as a potential threat to world peace and security. They featured noble main characters who dedicated themselves to bring these unrepentant Nazis to justice. In *Cornered* (1945), for example, high-ranking Nazis who have escaped prosecution by the Allies have settled in Argentina and are busily engaged in planning the next war. "They are even more than war criminals fleeing a defeated nation," an idealistic lawyer (Morris Carnovsky), working with an organization committed to prosecute the suspects, exclaims. "They do not consider themselves defeated." In *The Stranger* (1946) Edward G. Robinson, as a member of the Allied War Crimes Commission, hunt an escaped Nazi criminal (Orson Welles) in a small New England village. "I'll stay hidden until the day that we strike again," the unrepentant Nazi confides to a fellow German.

Film like *Rogues' Regiment* (1948), which focused on the search for the fictitious Martin Bruner, a ruthless Nazi war criminal who has escaped justice at the Nuremberg trials, echoes similar sentiments. The final sequence includes these ringing words by a narrator: "The last steps of Martin Bruner upon that scaffold are a warning to the world that such men must not march again." These dramas had the Allies relentlessly trying to expose the crimes of the top Nazis. In *Sealed Verdict* (1948) Ray Milland, as a U.S. Army prosecutor of Nazi war criminals, learns that one such defendant (John Hoyt) may take his own life before the sentence is carried out, and thus become a martyr to other unrepentant Nazis. Milland prevents the attempted suicide by dislodging a poisonous vial from a scar in the Nazi's cheek.

By the 1970s, following the disillusionment with the Vietnam War and exposés concerning the questionable practices of such intelligence agencies as the C.I.A., spy films adopted a cynical tone, which was reflected in plots about war criminals. In *Marathon Man* (1976) William DeVane, as a U.S. intelligence agent, collaborates with a wanted Nazi war criminal (Laurence Olivier) who, for his own safety, occasionally informs on other Nazi war criminals. *The Salamander* (1981) features Anthony Quinn, as a former World War II partisan fighter and hunter of war criminals. While governments ignore the lessons of the past, Quinn remains a solitary man of conscience trying to prevent a fascist coup in present-day Italy. In the drama *A Time to Die* (1983), featuring Edward Albert, Jr., Rod Taylor and Rex Harrison, and set in post-World War II Europe, a Nazi war criminal is being cultivated by the C.I.A. as West Germany's future chancellor.

Espionage films about war criminals have followed the same path of other spy dramas whose subject matter, characters and themes have changed to reflect the political exediencies, events and, above all, realities of their period. The following lines, once again from *Hotel Berlin*, seem sadly prophetic: "This time we shall be anti-Nazis," a German officer says, preparing to escape to the U.S., "poor refugees who have escaped from Germany. . . . Americans forgive and forget easily." ∎

War of 1812: intelligence and covert actions.

The state of organized espionage on both combatants' sides in the War of 1812 was the mirror image of that which existed during the American Revolution: whereas in the earlier war the Americans had been better organized and had entered the war with an existing espionage apparatus, the British were now better prepared. The British army, ever since the Revolution, had continued to collect intelligence in the U.S.

The Americans lacked the most basic knowledge of their potential enemy north of the border. They didn't even possess maps of Canada; they had no knowledge of British troop strength and were not aware of the feelings of Indians on the border. This last deficiency is reflected in *Brave Warrior* (1952), an action drama set on the eve of the War of 1812. Jon Hall portrays an American agent assigned to uncover traitors who are inciting the Indians to join the British side. Although in the film Tecumseh, chief of the Shawnees, helps Hall, in reality the Shawnee sided with the British against the Americans.

Americans, resentful of earlier British rule, sent to Congress in 1811 a group of Western and Southern legislators known as the "War Hawks" who were dedicated to expanding the Union into Canada and Florida. With the votes of these War Hawks, President Madison was able to override the opposition of the New England Federalists and have Congress vote a declaration of war against Great Britain on June 1, 1812.

Prior to the outbreak of hostilities, the Crown-appointed governor of Canada had dispatched a former American officer, John Henry, to the New England states to gauge the depth of pro and antiwar opinion. Henry journeyed through Vermont and Massachusetts in the years 1809, 1810 and 1811. He discovered a great deal of pro-British feelings—enough to encourage him to concoct a scheme whereby New England would be split from the rest of the U.S. and would join Canada. The plan never got very far, and Henry sold his stratagem to President Madison.

When American General Hull invaded Canada at the outbreak of war, the British commander, General Brock, was able to feed his opponent false information which exaggerated British troop strength in Canada. General Hull was misled and, unwilling to risk defeat, pulled his forces back to Detroit. The initiative then passed to Brock, who soon laid siege to Detroit. Although British forces were roughly the same size as the besieged Americans, Brock, by means of a ruse, deceived Hull into surrendering Detroit. The British commander had managed to place a false report with Hull to the effect that 5,000 Indians were going to join in the siege of Detroit, and the general believed it.

The Treaty of Ghent, signed in 1814, brought a peace between the U.S. and Great Britain which neither signatory believed would last very long. The U.S. acquired the port of Mobile in Florida while the British were able to turn their full attention to the war against Napoleon on the Continent.

Few spy films cover these facts. Several other historical dramas concern different aspects of the War of 1812. *The Buccaneer* (1938) recounts, in part, the Battle of New Orleans. The film points out that General Andrew Jackson and his backwoodsmen were a poor match for the well-trained, well-armed British soldiers until the pirate Jean Lafitte and his men join the fray. In *Magnificent Doll* (1946), a fictionalized biography of Dolly Madison, the gallant patriot, played by Ginger Rogers, saves important government documents from falling into the hands of the British during the War of 1812. The film strays from fact for the sake of fancy. *Mutiny* (1952), an action drama with Mark Stevens and Angela Lansbury, is set during the War of 1812 and based on an actual incident. The plot concerns American patriots seeking to transport much-needed gold bullion from France. ■

"Warfare in the Skies" (1914), Vitagraph. *Dir.* Frederick A. Thomson; *Sc.* Frederick A. Thomson; *Cast includes:* Earle Williams, Edith Storey.

A young aviator of an unnamed European nation falls in love with a young American who also attracts the attention of a nobleman, another flier. When a revolution threatens the nation, both rivals enlist on the side of the Loyalists, but the nobleman switches allegiances to the rebels and proceeds to drop bombs from his airplane. The young patriot takes his plane aloft and crashes into the traitor's airship. The wounded hero is captured by the revolutionary forces and hospitalized. When his sweetheart is captured as a Loyalist spy and faces a firing squad, the American, who has escaped his captors, once again takes to the air and rescues her.

This was one of the earliest films about air warfare to be released during World War I although the story did not deal directly with that conflict. J. Stuart Blackton, one of the triumvirate who controlled Vitagraph, was later to turn out several forceful war movies. If his works seem anti-German, it is probably because Blackton was born in England. Convinced that his original homeland was fighting to save civilization, he believed that the U.S. should support Britain. ■

Warning, The (1928), Col. *Dir.* George B. Seitz; *Sc.* Lillian Ducey; *Cast includes:* Jack Holt, Dorothy Revier, Pat Harmon, Frank Lackteen, Norman Trevor.

U.S. Secret Service agents and double agents dominate this melodrama about a gang of opium smugglers operating in Hong Kong. Jack Holt portrays an elusive ship owner and member of the gang of smugglers who, in reality, is working for the secret service. Meanwhile, another agent (Dorothy Revier) is being held captive by one of the smugglers. Holt cleverly effects her escape without revealing his true identity. Later, she arranges for the capture of the gang but is betrayed by her partner who is working with the smugglers. Revier is again taken prisoner. With the help of a machine gun and some hand grenades, Holt once again rescues Revier while fighting off the gang. Following the demise of the smuggler, Holt reveals to Revier that he is a fellow agent. The climactic action sequence, with the lone Holt battling almost impossible odds, in many respects anticipates the Rambo action dramas starring Sylvester Stallone. ■

Washington, George (1732–1799). Nathan Miller in his history, *Spying for America*, names George Washington "America's first spymaster." The general employed numerous espionage techniques during the American Revolution, including, among others, the use of covert actions, reconnaissance, disinformation and conventional spying.

After the actual outbreak of war, General Washington, needing a more professional reconnaissance unit, turned to Lt. Col. Thomas Knowlton, a veteran of the French and Indian Wars. Knowlton's Rangers, as they were known, scouted behind enemy lines and provided significant intelligence regarding the geography of the territory in dispute.

Joshua Mersereau, a native of New York City, along with his two sons and brother, reported British troop movements on Staten Island directly to Washington. They deliberately leaked disinformation to British intelligence. In time, the "Mersereau Ring" expanded to include non-family members. It was finally absorbed by a unit in the Continental Army operated by Colonel Elias Dayton. Dayton is believed to have planted a "mole" within the British army itself; his agents were stationed in Manhattan and Staten Island. Captain Benjamin Tallmadge ran another espionage apparatus known as the "Culper Ring"; he also reported directly to Washington.

Washington himself was the head of the Patriot's intelligence network. Hercules Mulligan, one of the general's New York spies, learned of two British assassination attempts on Washington and thus saved his life. *Washington at Valley Forge* (1914), a silent drama about General Washington during the American Revolution, conjures up an incident at an inn in which a local heroine overhears a plot to kill the general while he is asleep. *The Spy* (1914), based on James Fenimore Cooper's novel about the American Revolution, tells the story of a member of George Washington's household who works as a spy for the general.

In the winter of 1777, the Continental Army, bivouacking in Morristown, New Jersey, was badly demoralized. At the time, it only required a determined British assault to break the back of the Revolution. Washington planted disinformation with British intelligence that he was planning to attack them on two fronts—in New York City and Philadelphia—and thus convinced the British to regroup in defensive positions.

Washington's agents were able to deceive British General Clinton into believing that Continental troops were planning an attack on the British stronghold of New York City. Clinton naturally remained in New York and was unable to assist Cornwallis at Yorktown, Virginia, where the actual attack took place. The combined French and American forces thus defeated Cornwallis on October 19, 1781. Minor skirmishes continued, but the British defeat at Yorktown marked the virtual end of the war. Great Britain turned to its interests on the Continent and signed the Peace of Paris which recognized American independence. Two historical dramas recount Cornwallis' capitulation in fairly accurate terms—the silent film *Janice Meredith* (1924) and *The Howards of Virginia* (1940), with Cary Grant and Martha Scott. See American Revolution: Intelligence and Covert Actions. ■

Washington at Valley Forge (1914), U.

Dir. Francis Ford, Grace Cunard; *Sc.* Francis Ford, Grace Cunard; *Cast includes:* Francis Ford, Grace Cunard, Harry Schumm, Peter Leon, Ernest Shields, Harry Edmondon.

A silent drama about General Washington during the American Revolution, the film covers a lot of territory. It depicts some of the causes leading to the uprising of the colonies, several battles and an incident at an inn in which Betty (Grace Cunard), a local heroine, overhears a plot to kill the general, played by director-screenwriter Francis Ford (John's older brother), while he is asleep. Betty tells her lover, who is actually a British spy, about the plot, expecting him to seek help. Instead, he reports to the Hessians. But Betty's brother overhears his conversation and learns the truth about his deception. Meanwhile, she exchanges rooms with Washington and is mortally wounded by the spy that night. She lives long enough to expose her ex-lover as the traitor.

Assassination plots upon Washington's life had actually occurred. Washington, as the head of the Patriot's intelligence network during the Revolution, had several secret agents continually report to him directly. Hercules Mulligan, one of his New York spies, learned about two British assassination attempts on Washington and thus saved his life.

An epic of sorts within its own limitations (four reels), the film reenacts several historical incidents, including Paul Revere's ride and the heroic actions of the Minutemen. It also introduces some of the major figures of the American Revolution, including Lafayette. See American Revolution: Intelligence and Covert Actions. ■

Washington, D.C. The nation's capital has been the focus of several wartime spy comedies and dramas. Some features concentrated on the country's early conflicts. In *Barbary Pirate* (1949), a film concerning America's troubles with Mediterranean principalities, hero Donald Woods uncovers a traitor in Washington who has been supplying the pirates with information concerning the cargo of American ships.

Washington became the setting for films about imaginary and actual wars during the 20th century. Once America entered World War I, film studios depicted Washington as a hotbed of spy activities. For example, Kitty Gordon, as an adventuress in *As in a Looking Glass* (1916), is blackmailed by foreign agents into stealing secret government plans from a Washington official. According to the drama *Paying the Price* (1916), foreign agents were already working in Washington trying to steal the formula for a high explosive even before America's entry into the war. Gloria Swanson, as a neglected wife of a senator in *Secret Code* (1918), is falsely accused of passing military secrets to the Germans.

World War II brought profound changes to Washington, transforming the city from a provincial southern town with its casual pace to a bustling, overcrowded, wheeling-and-dealing political nerve center. This transformation, so aptly described in David Brinkley's 1988 book *Washington Goes to War*, was reflected in films set in the capital during the war. They encompassed both comedies and dramas, sometimes blending the two genres. *Careful, Soft Shoulders* (1942), a comedy set in wartime Washington, stars Virginia Bruce as a bored socialite who gets mixed up with Nazi agents. However, most comedies about wartime Washington narrowed their themes to the confusion and crowded conditions that beset the capital.

Low-budget World War II spy dramas occasionally used the capital as their background. In *The Lone Wolf Spy Hunt* (1939) Warren William, as the title character, foils a Washington spy network determined to steal secret anti-aircraft plans. In *Pacific Rendezvous* (1942)—which has nothing to do with its title—Lee Bowman, as a navy officer and code expert, captures a Nazi spy ring operating in the capital. Sherlock Holmes and Dr. Watson

(Basil Rathbone and Nigel Bruce) travel to the U.S. to investigate an international spy ring in *Sherlock Holmes in Washington* (1943). *Ladies of Washington* (1944) features Anthony Quinn as an enemy agent trying to obtain military secrets from government worker Sheila Ryan.

Virtually all of these films were made in Hollywood studios. Stock footage of Washington supplied establishing shots and backgrounds. Movie audiences, many of whom in those less-traveled times seldom ventured beyond their state, got the opportunity to see their capital. The climactic scene of *They Made Her a Spy* (1939), a drama about enemy agents operating in the U.S., takes place atop the Washington Monument. "Every time I look out at Washington," a chatty elevator operator admits, "I kind o' get the feeling that all this is permanent, that it's strong, that it's here to stay." He undoubtedly reflected the wartime patriotic spirit of many filmgoers who, while sitting in darkened theatres, saw the same grand vistas.

As the Cold War heated up and Hollywood began exploring Soviet attempts at subversion in the U.S. and other conspiracies, real or imagined, Washington again served as background for some of these dramas. However, a more critical movie audience that had outgrown rear-projection shots as a result of television shows like "I Spy" which traveled to different locales, demanded on-location shooting. This was reflected in such films as *No Way Out* (1972) and *All the President's Men* (1976). ■

Wasp, The (1918), World. *Dir.* Lionel Belmore; *Cast includes:* Kitty Gordon, Rockcliffe Fellowes, Charles Gerry, Sadee Burbank, William Calhoun, Edward Roseman.

German spies plot to destroy a munitions factory in this World War I comedy drama. Kitty Gordon, as the rich daughter of an industrial magnate, refuses to marry her father's business partner. Following a heated argument, she leaves and has her recently hired chauffeur (Rockcliffe Fellowes) take her and her maid for a drive. A German agent, planning to blow up her father's munitions plant, captures the trio. Gordon discovers a tunnel that the spy has dug that leads to the factory. She manages to untie her maid and send her for help. The police arrive, capture the spy and rescue Gordon and the chauffeur who turns out to be a rich football star at

Yale. Her father accepts the young man as his future son-in-law. ■

Watch on the Rhine (1943), WB. *Dir.* Herman Shumlin; *Sc.* Dashiell Hammett, Lillian Hellman; *Cast includes:* Bette Davis, Paul Lukas, Geraldine Fitzgerald, Lucile Watson, Beulah Bondi, George Coulouris.

Based on Lillian Hellman's anti-Fascist play, this World War II drama stars Paul Lukas as Kurt Muller, an anti-Nazi resistance leader and Bette Davis as his strong-willed and devoted wife. They journey to prewar America from their native Germany only to encounter elements of Fascism in this seemingly peaceful land. Lukas, a former engineer, forsakes his career and personal safety to fight against tyranny. A veteran of the Spanish Civil War where he fought against Franco, he now struggles against the forces of Hitler. When a fellow passenger aboard a train asks him what his trade is, he replies, "I fight against Fascism." Bette Davis, as his patient and loving wife, understands his passion and reassures him that she has never had any regretful moments about their political struggles. Lucile Watson plays Davis' doughty and headstrong mother who has been insulated from world politics. "Well," she remarks after a harrowing encounter with a Fascist guest in her own home, "we've been shaken out of the magnolias." George Coulouris plays a Rumanian count and blackmailer. A parasite swept to American shores from the backwash of European decadence, he willingly trades in human lives to fill his pockets.

Herman Shumlin, who directed the stage version as well as the film, underscores the theme that Fascism may permeate the most tranquil American home. "You don't know what it's like to be frightened," Muller says to his wife's family in America. "Unfortunately, you'll have to learn." His wife later echoes a similar warning. "The world has changed, and some of the people in it are dangerous. It's time you knew that." Shumlin pays tribute to men like Kurt Muller, who have the courage to fight totalitarianism regardless of the dangers. When Muller once again prepares to go to Germany where there is a price on his head, his mother-in-law asks, "Must it always be your hands?" "For each man his own hands," Muller explains. "Each can find his own excuse." The film, however, seems overly didactic by today's standards, especially some of Muller's long speeches to his son as he, Muller, is about to depart. ■

Watched (1974), Penthouse. *Dir.* John Parsons; *Sc.* John Parsons; *Cast includes:* Stacy Keach, Harris Yulin, Bridget Pole, Turid Aarstd, Valeri Parker, Denver John Collins.

A U.S. government agent becomes paranoid during his assignment in this drama that tries to examine the conflict between official surveillance and an individual's right of privacy. Stacy Keach, as a no-nonsense agent who works by the book, suspects that he is being framed. This soon drives him into a state of paranoia. He believes a fellow agent (Harris Yulin) has been pursuing him. At one point, Keach is not certain whether Yulin has been killed. Francis Ford Coppola's *The Conversation*, released earlier the same year and starring Gene Hackman, offers a more intense study of paranoia and surveillance. ■

Waterfront (1944), PRC. *Dir.* Steve Sekely; *Sc.* Irving Franklyn, Martin Mooney; *Cast includes:* John Carradine, J. Carrol Naish, Maris Wrixon, Edwin Maxwell, Terry Frost, John Bleifer.

J. Carrol Naish portrays the leader of a group of Nazi agents while masquerading as an innocent eye doctor in this low-budget World War II drama. John Carradine plays a hired gunman working for Germany. Maris Wrixon provides the romantic interest. Her beau is suspected of the murder of her boss, but all ends well for the couple. ■

We're in the Navy Now (1926), Par. *Dir.* Edward Sutherland; *Sc.* Monty Brice; *Cast includes:* Wallace Beery, Raymond Hatton, Chester Conklin, Tom Kennedy, Donald Keith.

A quasi-sequel to the commercially successful *Behind the Front* (1926), Wallace Beery and Raymond Hatton team up again for this sea farce set during World War I. As in the earlier film in which the crafty Hatton takes advantage of dimwitted Beery, this time Hatton, as Beery's scheming fight manager, skips off with the loser's purse. Beery spots him one day during a navy recruiting parade and gives chase until the boys get inducted into the service by mistake. Following several misadventures and antics aboard ship where they are continually in trouble with their superiors, they manage—by accident—to capture a spy as well as save a convoy of ships.

The pair made one more war comedy as a team, *Now We're in the Air*, released the following year. ▪

We've Never Been Licked (1943), U. *Dir.* John Rawlins; *Sc.* Norman Reilly Raine and Nick Grinde; *Cast includes:* Richard Quine, Noah Beery, Jr., Anne Gwynne, Martha O'Driscoll, William Frawley.

Richard Quine plays a double agent in this World War II drama of intrigue and deception. As a student at Texas A & M and the son of a military officer who has graduated from the famous agricultural and military university, Quine becomes unpopular with fellow students when he takes up the Japanese cause. He is dismissed from the school when officials learn that he has given Japanese agents a secret formula. Quine returns to Japan where he had lived for a number of years and broadcasts Japanese propaganda to the U.S. and elsewhere. Quine, however, is secretly sending military information to American intelligence. Having the trust of Japanese officials, he joins a bombing mission, overpowers a pilot and crashes the plane into a Japanese aircraft carrier at the cost of his own life.

Large segments of the film were shot on the campus of Texas A & M, with its thousands of students participating in several scenes. The plot is similar to that of *Appointment in Berlin*, released the same year, in which George Sanders flees to Germany, gains the trust of the Nazis and secretly broadcasts military information to England. He also loses his life in the last sequence. ▪

When Hell Broke Loose (1958), Par. *Dir.* Kenneth G. Crane; *Sc.* Oscar Brodney; *Cast includes:* Charles Bronson, Richard Jaeckel, Violet Rensing, Robert Easton, Eddie Foy, III, Avrid Nelson.

An American soldier in Germany during World War II helps to foil an assassination plot against General Eisenhower in this drama. Charles Bronson, as a reluctant G.I. who only entered the service to beat a prison rap, meets a young German woman (Violet Rensing) with whom he falls in love. She reveals to him, and later to American authorities, that her brother (Richard Jaeckel), a member of the Nazi underground, is part of a plot to kill the American military leader.

Bronson had appeared in several earlier features in minor roles under his real name, Charles Buchinsky. This was one of his earliest films in which he received top billing. The plot uses a familiar device of several World War II dramas. English-speaking Nazi soldiers, dressed in American uniforms, infiltrate Allied lines to create confusion. German Colonel Otto Skorzeny led such a group during the Ardennes Offensive. See German Intelligence: World War II. ▪

When the Redskins Rode (1951), Col. *Dir.* Lew Landers; *Sc.* Robert E. Kent; *Cast includes:* Jon Hall, Mary Castle, John Ridgely, Pedro de Cordoba, James Seay, Sherry Morland.

The French and Indian War provides the background for this historical drama. The story takes place in 1753 in Virginia. The British, who are trying to enlist the aid of the Delaware Indians to fight against the French, are having difficulties because of the interference of a French spy (Mary Castle). She charms Jon Hall, the son of the chief of the Delawares (Pedro de Cordoba), as part of her plot. But Hall soon learns of her real intentions. In an attempt to give the plot a semblance of authenticity, the script writers have added the figure of George Washington, who is portrayed by James Seay. Several action sequences involve skirmishes between the Indians and the militiamen. ▪

Where There's Life (1947), Par. *Dir.* Sidney Lanfield; *Sc.* Allen Boretz, Melville Shavelson; *Cast includes:* Bob Hope, Signe Hasso, William Bendix, George Coulouris, Vera Marshe, George Zucco.

Bob Hope portrays a contented disk jockey who is thrust into the role of heir-apparent to a fictional kingdom in this fast-paced comedy. When Bolshevik conspirators assassinate the king of Barovia, a committee journeys to New York to persuade Hope, who is the rightful heir to the throne, to return with them to their strife-torn land. Hope, at first, is reluctant, but when he feasts his eyes upon their voluptuous general (Signe Hasso), he consents. However, the small group of loyalists is plagued by a band of murderous conspirators determined to prevent their return. Hope is also being hunted by the policemen-brothers of his fiancée (Vera Marshe) who want him to fulfill his marital vows to their sister. Veteran villain George Coulouris portrays the chief enemy agent. ▪

Which Way to the Front? (1970), WB. *Dir.* Jerry Lewis; *Sc.* Gerald Gardner, Dee Caruso; *Cast includes:* Jerry Lewis, Jan Murray, John Wood, Kaye Ballard, Steve Franken, Robert Middleton.

Jerry Lewis plays a neurotic tycoon who is rejected by the draft board in this weak comedy set during World War II. Determined to do his share in the conflict, he hires a trio of other 4-Fs and, with several of his servants, organizes a motley guerrilla unit. They journey to Italy aboard his yacht where Lewis captures a Nazi general, impersonates a German officer and does a Chaplinesque dance with Hitler. Other popular personalities of the period who appear in this generally unfunny film include Sidney Miller, Kaye Ballard, Paul Winchell and Jan Murray. ∎

"While America Sleeps" (1939). See Spy Films: the Talkies. ∎

Whip Hand, The (1951), RKO. *Dir.* William Cameron Menzies; *Sc.* George Bricker, Frank L. Moss; *Cast includes:* Carla Balenda, Elliott Reid, Edgar Barrier, Raymond Burr, Otto Waldis, Michael Steele.

Former Nazis, now aligned with the Communist cause, are experimenting secretly with germ warfare in the Wisconsin mountains in this suspenseful little drama set during the Cold War. Elliott Reid, as a magazine writer and photographer vacationing in Wisconsin, grows suspicious about incidents occurring at a well-guarded hideaway. Inquisitive about a nearby mysterious lodge and a lake once alive with fish and now barren, he journeys across the body of water to investigate. The sister (Carla Balenda) of a local doctor joins him. They discover that a group of Communists, composed chiefly of unrepentant Nazis, are developing a germ-warfare weapon. The couple are taken prisoner but are soon rescued by F.B.I. agents who are tipped off about the conspirators' plot. Raymond Burr and Otto Waldis portray some of the villains in this intriguing tale. See Nazi Subversion: Post-World War II. ∎

White Circle, The (1920), Par. *Dir.* Maurice Tourneur; *Sc.* Jules Furthman, John Gilbert; *Cast includes:* Janice Wilson, John Gilbert, Spottiswoode Aitken, Harry B. Northrup, Wesley Barry.

Members of a secret society based in Italy seek revenge on their banker who has gambled away their funds in this drama set in 1860. Huddlestone, the English banker, fearing the consequences of his actions, escapes with his daughter to Scotland. Agents of the "White Circle" follow him there and assassinate him. Meanwhile, two gentlemen become interested in the victim's daughter (Janice Wilson). Northmour (Harry B. Northrup), a villainous figure, had agreed to help the banker in return for Wilson's hand in marriage. The party meets Cassills (John Gilbert), soon to become the hero of the plot. After much intrigue and evasion of the alien agents, Cassills and the daughter find happiness. Northmour withdraws from the scene, choosing adventure and freedom over marriage and domesticity. The film is based on Robert Louis Stevenson's *The Pavilion on the Links.* ∎

Who Goes There? (1917), Vitagraph. *Dir.* William P. S. Earle; *Sc.* Robert W. Chambers; *Cast includes:* Harry Morey, Corinne Griffith, Arthur Donaldson, Mary Maurice, Anne Brody, Stanley Dunn.

Based on the 1915 novel by Robert W. Chambers, the drama takes place in Belgium during World War I. An American of Belgian descent (Harry Morey) is captured by the Germans and forced to bring back from England a female spy (Corinne Griffith) who has a secret code. If he does not return with her, a group of Belgian hostages will be killed. He carries out the mission but turns over the code to British agents. On the journey back to Belgium he and the spy fall in love although she is betrothed to the German officer (Arthur Donaldson) who sent Morey to England. ∎

Who Is Number One? (1917) serial, Par. *Dir.* William Bertram; *Cast includes:* Kathleen Clifford, Cullen Landis.

A 15-episode serial filled with mysterious enemy agents, an unnamed avenger and numerous superweapons, the plot concerns a former inventor whose life and the lives of his loved ones are being threatened by an unknown group. Kathleen Clifford, as the heroine of the serial and ward of Graham Hale, the inventor, returns from Europe to live in the home of her benefactor. She soon becomes the target of the inventor's enemies who steal his plans for a supersubmarine. Ensuing chapters include the introduction of railway tanks, special weapons, other paraphernalia and submarine battles designed to keep the serial interesting. A romance develops between the ward and Hale's courageous son (Cullen Landis) who rescues Clifford from several dangerous situations. ■

Who Was That Lady? (1960), Col. *Dir.* George Sidney; *Sc.* Norman Krasna; *Cast includes:* Tony Curtis, Dean Martin, Janet Leigh, James Whitmore, John McIntire, Barbara Nichols.

A chemistry professor, caught by his wife kissing a student, tells his spouse that he is working for the F.B.I. and eventually gets mixed up with real spies in this farce based on Norman Krasna's play *Who Was That Lady I Saw You With?*. Tony Curtis, as the scholarly transgressor whose wife (Janet Leigh) is now threatening him with divorce, asks his television-writer pal (Dean Martin) for advice. Martin concocts a tale that Curtis was romancing the pretty student, suspected of spying, as part of his undercover assignment for the government. However, Curtis and Martin soon become entangled in a real intrigue involving enemy agents and the F.B.I. ■

Who Was the Other Man? (1917), U. *Dir.* Francis Ford; *Sc.* William Parker; *Cast includes:* Francis Ford, Mae Gaston, Beatrice Van, Duke Worne, William T. Horne.

The Black Legion, a secret German spy ring, threatens the U.S. in this World War I drama of intrigue. Francis Ford portrays an American who closely resembles a German agent. The German's contact mistakes Ford for the spy and hands him a photo of another agent (Beatrice Van) whom he is to meet aboard a vessel. Ford, realizing what is occurring, decides to keep the appointment and expose the spies for the benefit of his country. The steamer arrives in New York City where Van and Ford report to the Legion headquarters. The couple are assigned to steal valuable plans. Van succeeds in drugging the courier, but Ford makes off with the plans. He returns to the spies' den, intent on capturing the entire group. To his surprise, his German look-alike appears and unmasks Ford. A battle ensues with Ford losing to overwhelming odds. The police arrive in time to save him and round up the spies.

U.S. intelligence must have been perturbed at the conclusion of this film when audiences learned that the head of the spy network was a traitorous member of the U.S. Secret Service. The term "Black Legion" later served as the name of an actual racist organization, fashioned in the mode of the Ku Klux Klan, that terrorized Detroit in the 1930s. See Black Legion. ■

Who's Your Servant? (1920), RC. *Dir.* (Unlisted); *Sc.* Julian Johnson; *Cast includes:* Lois Wilson, Yukio Aoyama, Andrew Robeson, Albert Morrison, William Scott.

Set in post-World War I Washington, this drama concerns a Japanese spy's efforts to steal secret plans from a U.S. Navy officer. The spy, operating under cover as a servant in the officer's household, overhears his master mention that he is in possession of these important documents. The servant then conspires to obtain the papers for his own country. Lois Wilson, as the naval officer's daughter, helps to foil the spy's plans.

At least one critic (*Variety*) attacked the film for its poor timing. The writer charged that international efforts toward establishing a lasting peace, in progress at the time, might be hampered by the drama's suggestions of Japanese duplicity. See Japanese War Scare of 1907. ■

Wicked Dreams of Paula Schultz, The (1968), UA. *Dir.* George Marshall; *Sc.* Burt Styler, Albert E. Lewin, Nat Perrin; *Cast includes:* Elke Sommer, Bob Crane, Werner Klemperer, Joey Forman, John Banner, Leon Askin.

A popular East German athlete, preparing for the Olympic Games, eludes a lecherous propaganda minister and defects to the West by pole-vaulting over the Berlin Wall in this comedy. Elke Sommer, as the Olympic star, faces other problems after her escape when C.I.A. and Communist agents get involved in her defection. Bob Crane, as a sleazy black marketer, hides her in the home of his friend, a C.I.A. agent, only to return her to Communist agents the next day in exchange for a payoff. But he falls in love with her and decides not to go through with the deal. Sommer, who learns of the betrayal, is disillusioned and returns to the East. Crane realizes the harm he has caused her and smuggles himself into East Berlin to apologize to her. Dressed in drag, he manages to meet her and the two escape to the West. Joey Forman portrays the C.I.A. agent. Werner Klemperer plays the leering propaganda minister. See Defection. ■

Wife or Country (1918), Triangle. *Dir.* E. Mason Hopper; *Sc.* Charles Wilson; *Cast includes:* Harry Mestayer, Gloria Swanson, Jack Richardson, Gretchen Lederer, Charles West.

The wife of an important member of the Justice Department, played by Gloria Swanson, becomes entangled with German spies. When she pleads with the leader of the agents to release her from these activities, he refuses. Eventually the group is caught and the woman takes her own life. Swanson should have known better. She had two other indiscreet involvements with German agents the same year. In *The Secret Code* she plays the wife of a senator who is almost compromised by her liaisons with German spies. And in *Shifting Sands* a spy attempts to blackmail her into stealing vital plans from her husband's safe. ■

Wife Takes a Flyer, The (1942), Col. *Dir.* Richard Wallace; *Sc.* Gina Kaus, Jay Dratler; *Cast includes:* Joan Bennett, Franchot Tone, Allyn Joslyn, Cecil Cunningham, Roger Clark, Lloyd Corrigan.

A broad spoof on Nazi officialdom and German occupation, the film stars Joan Bennett as a Dutch woman seeking a divorce and Franchot Tone as a downed British flier who poses as Bennett's eccentric husband. Allyn Joslyn portrays a Nazi major in charge of occupation forces in Holland who moves into Bennett's house where Tone is hiding. Situation and verbal comedy, much aimed at poking fun at the Nazis, carry the film. Eventually, Tone "borrows" a German plane and escapes with Bennett to England. ■

Wild Horse Rustlers (1943), PRC. *Dir.* Sam Newfield; *Sc.* Joe O'Donnell; *Cast includes:* Bob Livingston, Al St. John, Linda Johnson, Lane Chandler, Stanley Price, Frank Ellis.

Nazi agents try to foil the U.S. Army's attempts to meet its quota of horses in this western drama set during World War II. The plot revolves around an honest ranch foreman, played by Lane Chandler, whose long-lost twin brother shows up as a German spy. The brother, raised in Germany and indoctrinated in Nazi ideology, impersonates his American counterpart. Bob Livingston, as the hero, does some hard riding and shooting before the saboteurs are corralled. Linda Johnson plays the female lead. Veteran character actor Al St. John provides some of the laughs. Other humor, unintentional, results from the inane portrayal of the spies as a dimwitted lot. ■

Wild Pair, The (1987), Trans World. *Dir.* Beau Bridges; *Sc.* Joseph Gunn; *Cast includes:* Beau Bridges, Bubba Smith, Lloyd Bridges, Gary Lockwood, Raymond St. Jacques, Danny De La Paz.

A local policeman and an F.B.I. agent join forces to smash a drug operation that is supporting a right-wing paramilitary group in this action drama. Bubba Smith, as the socially conscious cop who works with ghetto kids, and Beau Bridges as the agent, are tossed together against their will to track down a major drug dealer (Raymond St. Jacques) who takes orders from the leader (Lloyd Bridges) of an extreme right-wing organization. The F.B.I. agent masquerades as a drug buyer and takes off with the dealer's supply. He is eventually caught, brought to the paramilitary base and tortured. When he is about to be murdered, Smith smashes in and frees his partner. They both engage in a violent battle with the gang. The base is destroyed and Smith kills the right-wing leader. The all-too-familiar climactic fight includes the use of grenades, automatic weapons and an armored car. ■

Winged Mystery, The (1917), Bluebird. *Dir.* Joseph De Grasse; *Sc.* William Parker; *Cast includes:* Franklyn Farnum, Claire Du Brey, Rosemary Theby, Charles Hill Mailes, Sam De Grasse, T. D. Crittenden.

Twin brothers born in America and raised in Germany take different political paths when World War I erupts in this silent drama saddled with an improbable plot. Louis and August (both played by Franklyn Farnum), argue violently about their respective allegiances. Louis remains supportive of his native America while August joins the German army. The latter steals his twin brother's passport and, with his wife (Claire Du Brey), a German spy, sails for New York. The couple rent a home in Long Island, invite a group of wealthy partygoers to join them and suddenly hold the guests for ransom. August then sends messages by carrier pigeons to the families of his hostages. However, the pigeons are traced back to the German couple's residence and the police surround the place, demanding the kidnappers' surrender. August and his wife decide to battle it out with the law, and in the ensuing gunfight, the Germans are killed.

The drama, an early anti-German propaganda film released only months following America's entry into the war, is unique in more than one respect. The spy film of the period usually concerned some important document or secret weapon that enemy agents would try to steal. The use of extortion by the couple, a far-fetched device in 1917, was one such innovation. A second was the portrayal of twin brothers fighting on opposite sides of a conflict, a device further developed in subsequent decades. It was most effectively employed in *Nazi Agent* (1942), with Conrad Veidt portraying two brothers, one a patriotic German-American and the other a German official and fanatical Nazi. ∎

American navy pilot Edward Norris proves who's boss to Nazi officer Henry Guttman on a remote Pacific island. *Wings Over the Pacific* (1943).

Wings Over the Pacific (1943), Mon. *Dir.* Phil Rosen; *Sc.* George Sayre; *Cast includes:* Inez Cooper, Edward Norris, Montagu Love, Robert Armstrong, Henry Guttman, Ernie Adams.

A World War I veteran and his pretty daughter have their idyllic life on a Pacific island disrupted by events of the Second World War in this drama. Montagu Love plays the old-timer who witnesses the disruption of his peaceful island by a German pilot (Henry Guttman) and an American navy flier (Edward Norris). Guttman finds oil on the island and relays the information to the Japanese. Meanwhile, Norris falls in love with the veteran's daughter (Inez Cooper). Robert Armstrong portrays a Nazi agent. Hero

Norris ends up defeating the Japanese and Nazi elements in this low-budget film.

Monogram was one of several secondary studios that helped to fill the movie screens of wartime America with action and spy "quickies." The sharp contrast between these dramas and those produced by such major studios as MGM, 20th Century-Fox and Paramount can be seen in the size of the cast, the sets and the principal players. ∎

"Winning Coat, The" (1909), Biograph. *Dir.* D. W. Griffith; *Sc.* D. W. Griffith.

A short, one-reel silent drama, the story concerns a young courtier who is expelled from the court by his king. It seems he has violated a royal order prohibiting him from seeing the young woman he loves. She is a member of the queen's entourage. The banished lover soon discovers a plot to assassinate the queen, foils it and is restored into the good graces of the king. ∎

Winning Girl, The (1919), Par. *Dir.* Robert Vignola; *Sc.* Will M. Ritchey; *Cast includes:* Shirley Mason, Theodore Roberts, Harold Goodwin, Lincoln Steadman, Clara Horton.

A young heroine captures a German spy, saves an airplane factory, wins the man of her dreams and rehabilitates her lethargic father in this World War I comedy drama. Shirley Mason portrays the vivacious daughter of a depressed father who has given up on life. He had earlier lost the family fortune and felt cheated that Mason, his first born, was not a boy. Employed in a local airplane plant to help keep her family from poverty, she meets and falls in love with an army pilot (Niles Welch) whose mother owns the factory. Mason accidentally stumbles across a German saboteur about to destroy the plant and foils his plot. By the end of the film she helps her father regain his confidence and faith in the value of work. ∎

Winter Kills (1979), Avco. *Dir.* William Richert; *Sc.* William Richert; *Cast includes:* Jeff Bridges, John Huston, Anthony Perkins, Sterling Hayden, Eli Wallach, Dorothy Malone.

Another attempt at dramatizing a conspiracy against a U.S. President, this entry, based on Richard Condon's novel, lacks cohesion and general suspense. Jeff Bridges, as the young brother of a President who had been slain 19 years earlier, seeks out the assassins.

John Huston portrays the patriarch-father of the victim. Dorothy Malone, as Bridges' mother, is an incurable alcoholic. Anthony Perkins portrays Huston's eccentric intelligence officer. Sterling Hayden, as a tycoon, harbors militaristic plans in this convoluted plot. ■

Without Hope (1914), Sawyer. *Dir.* Fred Mace; *Sc.* Elaine Sterne; *Cast includes:* Marguerite Loveridge, Mary Charleson, Caroline Rankin, Kathleen Hammond, Catherine Proctor, Harry Kendall.

A young waitress, adopted by some wealthy young women as part of a Big Sister organization, is taken to a resort where she foils the plans of foreign spies in this comedy. Marguerite Loveridge, as the orphan-waitress, accompanies her benefactresses to a resort where an inventor (William Mandeville) and his daughter also are guests. Mandeville has developed a formula for noiseless gunpowder. Meanwhile, Catherine Proctor, as a foreign agent accompanied by a fake count, plots to steal the formula for her own unnamed country. The ex-waitress, however, recognizes the phony count from her former employment and exposes him. ■

Wolves of Kultur (1918) serial, Pathé. *Dir.* Joseph A. Golden; *Cast includes:* Leah Baird, Charles Hutchinson, Betty Howe, Sheldon Lewis, Mary Hull, Edmund Dalby.

German spies hatch a series of nefarious plots against the U.S., including the theft of plans for a newly constructed submarine, in this World War I serial. Leah Baird, as the stalwart heroine, vows vengeance on the enemies of her country who have killed her father. Working with members of the U.S. Secret Service, she becomes entangled in the enemies' plots and is often captured. However, she manages to escape each time and foils their immediate plans—until the next chapter. The serial offers the obligatory chases, heroics and perils. See Serials. ■

Woman Disputed, The (1928), UA. *Dir.* Henry King, Sam Taylor; *Sc.* C. Gardner Sullivan; *Cast includes:* Norma Talmadge, Gilbert Roland, Arnold Kent, Michael Vavitch, Boris De Fas, Gustav von Seyffertitz.

A prostitute serves her country in this romantic drama set in Austria chiefly during World War I. Norma Talmadge portrays a woman of the streets whom an Austrian and a Russian officer decide to salvage. They set her up as a respectable woman, both eventually falling in love with her. She chooses the Austrian officer (Gilbert Roland). The Russian (Arnold Kent) is left only with hatred for Roland. Kent then leads a Russian invasion of the Austrian town and captures a spy masquerading as a priest. Kent promises to release the priest if Talmadge willingly gives herself to him. When she refuses, the spy convinces her that his escape will help deliver vital information to the Austrians. She reluctantly surrenders herself to Kent. After the Austrians retake the town, Roland learns about her affair with Kent and treats her with contempt. But when he discovers the truth from the dying Kent about her patriotic sacrifice, he forgives her. The film is based on the novel by Dennison Cift. ■

Woman of Experience, A (1931), RKO. *Dir.* Harry Joe Brown; *Sc.* John Farrow; *Cast includes:* Helen Twelvetrees, William Bakewell, Lew Cody, ZaSu Pitts, H. B. Warner.

A World War I drama closely resembling others of this genre, including *Dishonored*, released earlier the same year, the film stars Helen Twelvetrees as a prostitute-spy. The role is similar to that which Marlene Dietrich played in the earlier work. When Twelvetrees finally exposes an enemy agent (Lew Cody), he commits suicide. She is wounded and told she has but six months to live. William Bakewell, as her lover Karl, marries her despite his mother's warnings about the former spy's questionable background. But because of her service to her country, she is cleared by Franz Josef himself. The drama, based on the stage production titled *The Registered Woman* by John Farrow, is set in wartime Vienna. ■

Woman on the Index, The (1919), Goldwyn. *Dir.* Hobart Henley; *Sc.* Edward Gheller; *Cast includes:* Pauline Frederick, Wyndham Standing, Willard Mack, Ben Hendricks, Jere Austin.

A young woman's happiness is threatened by ghosts from her past in this drama involving the diplomatic service, the underworld and the U.S. Secret Service. Pauline Frederick portrays the tortured heroine who had earlier married a criminal. Her husband committed suicide when the police closed in on him. Fellow gang members blamed Frederick for his death, but the police, faced with insufficient evidence, acquitted her. Several years have passed and she has established a new life for herself in Washington as the wife of a government official (Wyndham Standing).

Her former arresting officer (Ben Hendricks), who has advanced to U.S. Secret Service chief, asks her to help entrap a Russian agent (Willard Mack). An unsavory figure, the spy discovers her past life and blackmails her to steal important plans. However, he is exposed by his own Japanese servant who is another secret service agent in disguise. The Index in the title refers to the Police Index, a list of suspected criminals. The film is based on a 1918 play by Lillian Trimble Bradley and George Broadhurst. ▪

Woman the Germans Shot, The (1918), Plunkett & Carroll. *Dir.* John G. Adolfi; *Cast includes:* Julia Arthur, Creighton Hale, J. W. Johnston, William Tooker, Thomas Brooks, George Le Guere.

American stage actress Julia Arthur portrays the role of nurse Edith Cavell in this World War I silent drama. The film depicts the English heroine's life from early childhood until her capture and execution by the Germans. Nurse Cavell aided wounded Allied and German soldiers in Belgium and remained at her post even when the enemy advanced and overran the dressing station where she worked. The Germans placed her before a firing squad for helping Allied soldiers to escape. Her biography was retold in a sound version in 1939, titled *Nurse Edith Cavell.* ▪

Womanhood, the Glory of the Nation (1917), Vitagraph. *Dir.* J. Stuart Blackton, William P. S. Earle; *Sc.* Helmer W. Bergman; *Cast includes:* Alice Joyce, Harry T. Morey, Joseph Kilgour, Naomi Childers, Walter McGrail.

A young American decides to act as a spy for her country after the U.S. is invaded by a foreign power in this propaganda drama that advocates preparedness. Alice Joyce portrays a tourist who, returning to the U.S. from the Orient, learns that her homeland, deficient in military forces and weaponry, has been invaded. She returns with the newly appointed Minister of Energies (Harry T. Morey). During her travels Joyce had met Count Dario (Joseph Kilgour), an officer of the foreign invaders and an admirer of hers. She meets him in New York and joins forces with him as a

means of gaining military information. Meanwhile Morey and his forces invent a new weapon, a "Firebug," which helps to defeat the enemy. The Count is killed by his own father for betraying the cause while the true lovers, Joyce and Morey, are reunited.

Action sequences include airships laying waste to lower New York City, sea battles and trench warfare. Many of these sequences were produced by using models and miniatures. A controversy raged about America's future role in World War I. The public was divided between pacifists and those who advocated preparedness. Vitagraph released this propaganda drama supporting the latter group. This was one of several films of the period that promoted preparedness as the proper course for the nation. ▪

Women as spies. War may be a man's business, but the art of espionage, in American films and in real life, was often assigned to women. Dramas and comedies have depicted countless examples of how the distaff side helped, directly or indirectly, to defeat the enemy. Women began playing significant roles in war films as early as 1908. Julia Richards, as "Barbara Frietchie," bravely defends the American flag during the Civil War. This was the first of four screen adaptations of John Greenleaf Whittier's famous poem.

Films about women as spies reached their peak in the early 1930s. Within a few years this theme almost disappeared from the screen as men were entrusted to the craft of spying and women trailed along either as their assistants or love objects. Women as agents regained some popularity with the advent of World War II, but the films were only a pale reminder of those evocative romantic relics that appeared earlier.

Female spies became a staple of Civil War dramas. Two Civil War films reenacted the undercover work of Pauline Cushman, a real-life Union spy. Selig released *Pauline Cushman, the Federal Spy* in 1913. MGM's 1934 drama *Operator 13* starred Marion Davies as a Union spy who works alongside Cushman, portrayed by Katherine Alexander. In "The Girl Spy Before Vicksburg" (1911) the heroine of this short silent feature disguises herself as a member of a munitions convoy and destroys the powder wagon. Grace Cunard in "In the Fall of '64" (1914) portrays a Southern belle who poses as a slow-witted boy to gain access to Union quarters where her beau is being held captive as a spy. She manages to extinguish a candle, allowing her lover to escape in the ensuing darkness. She later steals the enemy's battle plans and crosses into Confederate territory. Bessie Barriscale, as a young Confederate woman willing to sacrifice her life for the South in *Madam Who?* (1918), engages in the dangerous act of espionage. In *Court Martial* (1928) Betty Compson portrays the leader of a band of rebel marauders.

Sound films occasionally continued to employ Civil War settings. Miriam Hopkins in *Virginia City* (1940) portrays a Confederate spy who poses as a saloon singer to help get a gold shipment through Union lines. *Ride a Violent Mile* (1957), reversing the background of the spy, has Union agent Penny Edwards posing as a dancer in a western saloon while she busies herself investigating Confederate activities. Finally, in the comedy *Advance to the Rear* (1964) Stella Stevens portrays a Confederate spy.

During World War I, films of the home front included heroines who uncovered spy rings that threatened the nation. Other dramas portrayed them as innocent dupes influenced by sophisticated enemy agents. When faced with the dilemma of choosing between country and their loved one, some women opted for the former while others stuck by their man. Whatever the heroine's frailties, the film studios were careful to eschew describing her as frivolous or cowardly.

World War I films paid tribute to women by placing them in a variety of sacrificial roles. *As in a Looking Glass* (1916) was one of the earliest World War I dramas to tell of a wife who is killed by enemy agents after she has destroyed vital papers about to fall into the wrong hands. In *Daughter Angele* (1918) Pauline Starke, another popular actress of the period, poses as an orphan girl as a ploy to gain entrance into a mansion and help capture a German agent signaling to enemy submarines.

Silent war-related films produced after World War I presented the more conventional female screen images, including that of spy. Marion Davies in *The Dark Star* (1919) portrays a secret agent in World War I and gains access to vital plans containing the locations of Turkish fortresses. Betty Compson in *New Lives for Old* (1925) volunteers to serve as a spy and is assigned to have an affair with a suspected officer who is ultimately convicted as a traitor.

The sound period often added a touch of sophistication to the genre. Marlene Dietrich for a time dominated the screen as the worldly woman who faced danger with a smile, even at the cost of her own life. In *Dishonored* (1931) she portrays an Austrian spy who falls in love with the secret agent she has helped to capture. She sets him free and faces a firing squad for her act of love. Greta Garbo made a similar film one year later in which she plays the infamous and alluring spy *Mata Hari*. Myrna Loy in *Stamboul Quest* (1934) portrays Germany's master spy. She is responsible for the demise of Mata Hari who made the fatal mistake of falling in love with one of her victims.

Women were the principals in a host of similar films, including, among others, *Madame Spy* (1934) with Fay Wray, *Operator 13* (1934) with Marion Davies and *They Made Her a Spy* (1939) with Sally Eilers. Sometimes they were prostitutes called upon to serve their country as spies, as was Norma Talmadge in *The Woman Disputed* (1928), Marlene Dietrich in *Dishonored* (mentioned above) and Helen Twelvetrees in *A Woman of Experience* (1931).

World War II produced its share of spy films with women as secret agents. Ilona Massey in *International Lady* (1941) plays a dangerous spy in this cautionary tale about the enemy within. Her unusual method of contacting Nazi U-boats and providing them with vital shipping and air force information consists of her using tonal phrasings and musical notes in her songs during her radio broadcasts. In *Spy Ship*, released the following year, Irene Manning portrays a secret agent who sells information about ship departures to the enemy. Lola Lane, as a Russian agent in *Miss V From Moscow* (1943), considered one of the worst films ever made, is sent to Nazi-occupied Paris to pose as a German spy whom she happens to resemble. Virginia Bruce in *Action in Arabia* (1944) portrays a special agent assigned to stop Nazi spies from destroying the Suez Canal. Constance Bennett and Gracie Fields place their lives in peril when they decide to join the French Resistance and are hunted by the Nazis in *Paris Underground* (1945).

Claire Phillips joined the ranks of such real-life spies as Pauline Cushman and Mata Hari, whose exploits, fictitious or otherwise, appeared in films. Some of her World War II experiences were reenacted in *I Was an*

WORLD WAR I

American Spy (1951), with Ann Dvorak playing the title role.

In more recent times women have appeared on screen as C.I.A. agents. Rosalind Russell in *Mrs. Pollifax—Spy* (1971) portrays a widow who volunteers her services to the C.I.A. to act as a spy for her country. She soon finds herself a captive of Communist agents in this anemic spy spoof. Linda Fiorentino in *Gotcha!* (1985), like Dietrich, Garbo and Loy in earlier films, ends up romantically involved with her prey. Diane Keaton in the murky drama *The Little Drummer Girl* (1984) portrays a pro-Palestinian English actress who is persuaded to act as an Israeli spy—with the predictable romantic complications. Some post-World War II spy films placed women in roles usually reserved for their male counterparts. *In Like Flint* (1967) has James Coburn, as a special agent, assigned to foil the attempts of a secret organization of women planning to take control of the world in this spoof of the spy genre.

American film studios unintentionally may have helped to advance the role of women in these spy comedies and dramas. By being placed in perilous and competitive positions and forced to rely on their own resources and skills, women were lifted out of their more conventional, stereotyped roles in film and society. When Marlene Dietrich in *Dishonored* (1931) remarks: "I'm not afraid of life, although I'm not afraid of death either," she is expressing the same courage as the bravest soldier in the trenches. Although many of the plots were pure fiction, those in the audience could not help but take notice of the changing role of women. In this sense, these films influenced and accelerated, rather than reflected, social change.

Women in the Night (1948), Film Classics. *Dir.* William Rowland; *Sc.* Robert St. Clair, Edwin Westrate; *Cast includes:* Tara Birell, William Henry, Virginia Christine, Richard Loo, Gordon Richards, Benson Fong.

This low-budget exploitation drama depicts the treatment of women prisoners by the Axis powers near the end of World War II. The film purportedly is based on case histories found in the files of the United Nations Information Office. The plot includes scenes of women forced to provide sexual favors for Nazi officers at their club in Shanghai. The Japanese also get into the act of degrading their female captives. The film includes a subplot involving secret agents and a mysterious secret weapon known as the "Cosmic Death Ray." ■

Wonder Man, The (1920), S-L Films. *Dir.* John G. Adolfi; *Sc.* Joseph W. Farnham; *Cast includes:* Georges Carpentier, Faire Binney, Florence Billings, Downing Clarke, Robert Barrat.

A member of the French secret service, assigned to recover stolen post-World War I contracts between French and American agents, poses as a guest of an American social club. Georges Carpentier portrays the French agent. During his investigation he becomes infatuated with a millionaire's daughter (Faire Binney). Among other members of the social group are the culprits, one of whom suspects the Frenchman. After an exciting boxing match with his love rival (Robert Barrat), Carpentier winds up the case and wins the affection of Binney, who earlier had judged the Frenchman a coward. Carpentier, a full-fledged French war hero and European heavyweight champion, was popular with the American public during the post-World War I years. He received a contract for three films. ■

World for Ransom (1954), AA. *Dir.* Robert Aldrich; *Sc.* Lindsay Hardy; *Cast includes:* Dan Duryea, Gene Lockhart, Patric Knowles, Reginald Denny, Nigel Bruce, Marian Carr.

An international criminal kidnaps an English nuclear scientist and threatens to turn him over to the Soviets if Britain does not pay the ransom in this cloak-and-dagger drama set in Singapore. Dan Duryea, as a soldier of fortune who is in love with the wife of one of the kidnappers, decides to find the missing scientist while he eludes British intelligence and the police. He eventually locates the victim, rescues him and kills the kidnapper-husband (Patric Knowles). Marian Carr, as Knowles' wife, ends up rejecting Duryea when she learns about her husband's death. Gene Lockhart, as the brains behind the kidnapping scheme, hires Knowles to carry it out. Reginald Denny portrays the chief of military intelligence. ■

World War I. See British Intelligence: World War I; German Intelligence: World War I; U.S. Intelligence: World War I. ■

World War II. See British Intelligence: World War II; German Intelligence: World War II; U.S. Intelligence: World War II. ∎

Wrath of God. See *Black Sunday* (1977). ∎

Wrecking Crew, The (1968), Col. *Dir.* Phil Karlson; *Sc.* William McGivern; *Cast includes:* Dean Martin, Elke Sommer, Sharon Tate, Nancy Kwan, Nigel Green, Tina Louise.

Another in the Matt Helm spy series based on the novels of Donald Hamilton, this entry concerns the theft of one billion dollars in gold, which threatens the stability of the world currency. Once again Dean Martin, as the casual Helm, is assigned to find the mastermind behind the plot. A British agent, played by Sharon Tate, is delegated to help Martin in his investigation. Nigel Green, as the mastermind behind the grand theft, is assisted by Elke Sommer and Nancy Kwan, both of whom add erotic interest to the comic unraveling. John Larch replaces James Gregory as Martin's superior. The film generally continues the standards set by the previous entries, which include high production values, an entertaining script and above-average performances. Director Phil Karlson, who turned out the first Helm entry, *The Silencers*, returns to the fold. ∎

Wrong Is Right (1982), Col. *Dir.* Richard Brooks; *Sc.* Richard Brooks; *Cast includes:* Sean Connery, George Grizzard, Robert Conrad, Katharine Ross, G. D. Spradlin, John Saxon.

Director-writer Richard Brooks' fast-paced offbeat satire on America's morals, television and political and cultural leaders manages to hit its targets as often as it misses. The initial plot concerns an Arab ruler who threatens to hand over two small nuclear weapons to a radical revolutionary unless U.S. President Lockwood resigns. The Middle East leader has learned that the President had earlier authorized the Arab ruler's assassination. The bombs will be exploded in Israel and New York if the demands are not met.

Sean Connery, as a highly popular television news commentator, is powerful enough to demand the attention of various world leaders. George Grizzard portrays President Lockwood, a wishy-washy leader incapable of making decisions. John Saxon and Katharine Ross portray C.I.A. agents. The intelligence agency comes under heavy fire in the script as an amoral group of misfits ready to manipulate anyone to gain its ends. Leslie Nielson, as the President's prancing rival in the forthcoming election, has won over the hard-hats. The film is based on *The Better Angels*, a novel by Charles McCarry. See Central Intelligence Agency. ∎

XYZ

Yank in Libya, A (1942), PRC. *Dir.* Albert Herman; *Sc.* Arthur St. Claire; *Cast includes:* H. B. Warner, Walter Woolf King, Joan Woodbury, Parkyakarkus, Duncan Renaldo, George Lewis.

A World War II drama about an American war correspondent who uncovers a Nazi gun-smuggling ring in Libya, the film is short on action or war sequences. Walter Woolf King plays the curious reporter while veteran actor H. B. Warner portrays a local British consul. Radio comedian Parkyakarkus supplies the much-needed comic relief in this low-budget tale. ∎

Walter Woolf King (r.), as an American war correspondent, poses as an Arab to uncover a Nazi gun-smuggling ring in Libya. *A Yank in Libya* (1942).

"Yankee Doodle in Berlin" (1919), Lesser. *Dir.* F. Richard Jones; *Cast includes:* Bothwell Browne, Ford Sterling, Mal St. Clair, Marie Provost, Bert Roach.

A Mack Sennett World War I comedy short, the film centers on an American flier, portrayed by Bothwell Browne, who is sent to Berlin to get strategic war maps from the Kai- ser. Browne, dressed as a woman, has the German leaders competing for his attentions in this zany comedy. ∎

Yankee Pasha (1954), U. *Dir.* Joseph Pevney; *Sc.* Joseph Hoffman; *Cast includes:* Jeff Chandler, Rhonda Fleming, Mamie Van Doren, Lee J. Cobb, Bart Roberts.

The days of the Barbary pirates, prior to the Tripolitan War (1800–1805), dominate this adventure drama about an American frontiersman who journeys to Morocco to rescue a New England woman with whom he has fallen in love. Rhonda Fleming plays the beautiful captive who is sold into the harem of a Moroccan womanizer (Bart Roberts). Jeff Chandler, as the transplanted backwoodsman, poses as a rifle instructor for a local chieftain's guards while he searches for Fleming. When he locates her, U.S. sailors from a recently docked ship help him storm the Moroccan chieftain's fortress for the climactic battle and rescue. A sea battle occurs earlier in the film when a pirate ship attacks the American vessel with Fleming and her father aboard. Lee J. Cobb plays a sultan.

Based on a novel by Edison Marshall, the film is set in 1800, on the eve of the Tripolitan War. Until that conflict, the U.S. and other nations were forced to pay tribute to Moroccan pirates for the privilege of sailing the Mediterranean. The power of these pirates is reflected in the arrogance of one of the local Moroccan sultans who boasts: "Every American is our slave, or why else do they pay us tribute?" Later in the film an American captain voices his disgust in this system of tribute and anticipates the ensuing war. "Someday we'll be able to sail through the Mediterranean without our government having to buy our safety." ∎

Yankee Pluck (1917), World. *Dir.* George Archainbaud; *Sc.* Willard Mack; *Cast includes:* Ethel Clayton, Edward Langford, Johnny Hines, Montagu Love, Eric Wayne.

Japanese agents attempt to steal the plans for an anti-submarine device in this mild drama that takes place before America's entry into World War I. A young American navy lieutenant (Edward Langford) invents an electric tower which can neutralize the capabilities of submarines. While he waits for U.S. government approval, Japanese agents pressure the father of the inventor's sweetheart to steal the plans. But the daughter (Ethel Clayton) foils the plot just in time. The young officer sells his invention to the government and forgives his future father-in-law. See Japanese War Scare of 1907. ■

Yellow Cargo (1936), Grand National. *Dir.* Crane Wilbur; *Sc.* Crane Wilbur; *Cast includes:* Conrad Nagel, Eleanor Hunt, Vince Barnett, Jack LaRue, Claudia Dell, Henry Strange.

The U.S. Immigration Service assigns two of its agents to investigate a gang of smugglers operating in Los Angeles in this light drama. Using Catalina Island as a transfer point, members of the gang, posing as movie producers, smuggle illegal aliens, disguised as a group of extras, into the U.S. Conrad Nagel, as one of the government agents, masquerades as an extra to learn more about the illegal activities. Meanwhile the second agent, portrayed by Eleanor Hunt, poses as a newspaper reporter and accompanies Nagel on the journey. She is assisted by a photographer (Vince Barnett) who provides the comic relief. The trio suffer through some narrow escapes before the smugglers are rounded up. ■

Yellow Dog, The (1918), U. *Dir.* Colin Campbell; *Sc.* Elliott J. Clawson; *Cast includes:* Frank Clark, Clara Horton, Will Machen, Arthur Hoyt, Frank Hayes.

German agents and sympathizers plot to set fire to an American shipyard in this drama set during World War I. A local village patriot (Arthur Hoyt) organizes a group of boys to ferret out the "yellow dogs," or German sympathizers, who are spreading pro-German propaganda throughout the community. One young member of this newly organized unit, "Nosey" White (Antrim Short), overhears two men plotting to destroy some ships

which have been contracted to the government to transport supplies to Allied forces. White tells his father who then brawls with the spy. The man, about to set fire to the vessels, is shot and his accomplice jailed.

The film inspired a nationwide movement of anti-"yellow dog" clubs composed of patriotic youths. They were encouraged to expose any pro-German sympathizers or other unpatriotic citizens who threatened the war effort. Local and state officials were quick to take part in organizing these groups.

The term "yellow dog" originated in the 1890s and referred to something entirely different from its meaning in the above film. It was applied to labor contracts in which workers were forced to pledge that they would not join any union. Eugene V. Debs, the renowned American Socialist, founded two powerful American railroad unions: the Brotherhood of American Firemen and the American Railway Union. The latter union replaced the former with one giant labor organization for all railroad workers.

The American Railway Union in 1893 found itself locked in a life-or-death struggle with the Pullman Company; the rail line had cut union salaries by one-third without suffering any special losses of its own. Debs called a strike of over 100,000 railroad workers in an effort to force Pullman to rescind its policy. Despite the fact that Debs had guaranteed no interruption of mail service, Pullman was able to obtain an injunction against the strike in court on the grounds of a possible dislocation of mail service.

With the injunction of the Federal Circuit Court of Chicago in its pocket, Pullman hired 5,000 strikebreakers, deputized them as federal marshals and gave them weapons. President Cleveland was convinced by Attorney-General Olney, who was at the time serving on the board of directors of the railroad, to commit several thousand federal troops, ostensibly to protect life and property but actually to break the strike. Governor Altgeld of Illinois refused to accept the presence of federal troops but was overruled by the Federal Circuit Court of Chicago.

Debs refused to call off the strike, was arrested and sent to jail for six months. In the meantime, 70 workers were wounded, 33 killed and several hundred arrested. The strike was crushed and the new or rehired workers were forced to sign a "yellow-dog" contract in which they promised never to join a union. With this devastating experience in mind, Debs became a Socialist. Under capitalism, he believed, government would inevitably side with the bosses against the workers. He therefore abandoned efforts at reforming capitalism from within and, in 1897, founded the American Socialist Party, the American Social Democracy. ■

Yellow Typhoon, The (1920), FN. *Dir.* Edward José; *Sc.* Monte Katterjohn; *Cast includes:* Anita Stewart, Ward Crane, Donald MacDonald, Joseph Kilgour, George Fischer.

The plot of this drama concerns two sisters, one good (Hilda) and the other evil (Berta). Both are played by Anita Stewart. Berta abandons her husband, a navy engineer (Donald MacDonald), and settles in the Orient where she gains her infamous reputation as The Yellow Typhoon. She collaborates with a villainous saboteur to steal a protective device for submarines which her husband has invented. Her partner kills the engineer but fails to obtain the plans, now in the possession of a lieutenant commander (Ward Crane).

Berta's sister Hilda, a U.S. Secret Service agent, is aboard the same ship carrying two enemy agents and the officer who is transporting the blueprints to Washington. He doesn't fully trust Hilda. But his suspicions are finally laid to rest when she interferes with her sister's attempts to steal the plans. The two culprits are killed in a skirmish with the police. Hilda and the navy officer, who have fallen in love with each other, arrive in Washington with the plans. The film is based on the novel by Harold MacGrath. ■

"You Nazty Spy" (1940), Col. *Dir.* Jules White; *Cast includes:* The Three Stooges, Dick Curtis, Don Beddoe.

Larry, Moe and Curly, better known as the Three Stooges, made more than a hundred shorts for Columbia. Some released during World War II were spoofs on Hitler and the Nazis. In this zany little gem Moe is appointed the dictator of Moronica, with Curly as an incompetent general and Larry portraying a leading dignitary, both of whom assist Moe in the affairs of state. Moe's impersonation of Der Fuhrer is too broad to be effective. ■

Young Eagles (1930), Par. *Dir.* William A. Wellman; *Sc.* William S. McNutt, Grover Jones; *Cast includes:* Charles "Buddy" Rogers, Jean Arthur, Paul Lukas, Stuart Erwin, Frank Ross.

A World War I aviation drama, the film costars Jean Arthur as an American spy posing as a German. An American flier (Charles Rogers) who has fallen in love with her becomes disillusioned when he learns that she has run off with a German aviator. Once she gains the necessary information, she transmits it to American authorities. Rogers, of course, forgives her when he discovers the truth. The film provides several air battles, none of which compared to those in *Wings* (1927), which also starred Rogers and made by the same director. Some of the footage was borrowed from *Wings*. The German, played by Paul Lukas, was treated with more sympathy than he would have been had this drama been made during the war. The film has been singled out as the first 1930s drama with a World War I background. ■

Zaharoff, Sir Basil (1849–1936). The archetype of arms dealers of the last decade of the 19th century and the first two decades of the 20th century—mysterious, powerful and well-connected—was Sir Basil Zaharoff.

Despite investigations by the French Chamber of Deputies in 1922, the British House of Commons in the same year and an American Senate Committee investigation in 1934, little is known about this "mystery man of Europe." Whatever information there is has been pieced together by rumor and innuendo.

Historians have presumed that he was of Greek or Russian origin. At one point he earned his living as a "torch," setting fires and then robbing his victims. He later worked as a pimp and drug dealer. Always ambitious, he established in 1877 a relationship with Nordenfeldt, the Scandinavian armaments manufacturer, and became its chief salesman. He soon owned a controlling interest in that company as well as other arms manufacturers in Britain, France, Austria and Germany.

He was quick to exploit the always festering dispute between Greece and Turkey, first selling Greece one submarine and then turning around and, using fear and psychology, selling two submarines to the Turks. When the Russians objected to foreign control of their shipbuilding conglomerate, Zaharoff undertook the task of assembling a Turkish shipbuilding industry. He persuaded Nordenfeldt to merge with the British firm of Vickers and, during the Boer War, sold British arms to both the Boers and the British. The weapons he delivered to Spain were used in Cuba to kill American troops. Turkish arms and mines used in the Dardanelles during World War I to kill British troops came from the British firm of Vickers. Continuing in this non-discriminatory manner, Zaharoff sold arms to both sides during the Russo-Japanese War (1904–1905) and World War I.

During the 1920s his wealth was estimated in the hundreds of millions of dollars. His interests expanded into oil through the Anglo-Persian Oil Company which had a connection with the British government. Rumors suggested he obtained control of the Principality of Monaco in 1923 by buying a large share of stock from Prince Louis of Monaco who needed money.

Zaharoff's principal defender in Britain was Prime Minister Lloyd George while in France his advocate was Premier George Clemenceau. To the critical observer at the end of the 20th century, it seems inconceivable that a man who sold British arms used to kill British troops in the Boer War and World War I was awarded the Knight's Grand Cross of the British Empire and that a man who sold weapons to the Germans during World War I received the French Grand Cross of the Legion of Honor.

A handful of films employ characters that strongly resemble Zaharoff and usually present him unfavorably. For example, the villains in *The Great Impersonation* (1935), based on E. Phillips Oppenheim's novel, are members of an international cartel, merchants of death who foment conflicts around the world so that they can sell their munitions. Edmund Lowe portrays the dual role of Englishman and spy who exposes the sinister ring, including the brains behind the organization (Charles Waldron). In *Bulldog Drummond at Bay* (1937) agents who represent the "mystery man of Europe," an ominous international arms dealer, kidnap the inventor of a new weapon when they fail to obtain it through legitimate means. ■

Zotz! (1962), Col. *Dir.* William Castle; *Sc.* Ray Russell; *Cast includes:* Tom Poston, Julia Meade, Jim Backus, Fred Clark, Cecil Kellaway, Zeme North.

Soviet spies try to learn the secrets of a California professor's magical powers in this weak comedy. A former archaeology student at an ancient site sends Tom Poston, as a professor of ancient English languages, a coin which, Poston soon discovers, contains mystical powers. Harassed by his dean who thinks Poston has psychiatric problems and a rival colleague who wants the chairmanship of their department, Poston decides to take the coin to the Pentagon. But officials there don't believe him. The Russians, however, hear about Poston and his magic coin and assign secret agents to investigate. They kidnap his niece and girlfriend whom they will exchange for the secrets of the coin. Using the coin, Poston tricks them and frees the hostages. In the struggle the coveted coin falls into a sewer where it disappears forever. The spies are rounded up, and Poston returns to his college where he gains the chairmanship post over his rival. The film is based on the 1947 novel by Walter Karig. ■

Appendix A
List of Topics Treated as Separate Entries

American Civil War: Intelligence and Covert Actions

American Revolution: Intelligence and Covert Actions

Anarchists in the U.S.

André, John

Andrews' Raid

Arnold, Benedict

Bancroft, "Brass"

Black Legion

Black September

Bond, James

Brainwashing

British Intelligence: World War I

British Intelligence: World War II

British Spy Films

Burma

Central Intelligence Agency

Cold War

Copperheads

Cushman, Pauline

Defection

Detectives and Spies

Donovan, William J. "Wild Bill"

Double Agents

Federal Bureau of Investigation

Fifth Column, The

German Intelligence: World War I

German Intelligence: World War II

Gouzenko, Igor

Hale, Nathan

Heydrich, Reinhard

House Un-American Activities Committee

Japanese War Scare of 1907

Jedburgh Operations

K.G.B.

Korean War: Intelligence and Covert Actions

Labor Unrest

Latin America

Le Quenx, William Tufnell

Lisbon

Lord Haw-Haw

Man From U.N.C.L.E. series

Mata Hari

Mengele, Josef

Morgan, John Hunt

Mosby, John Singleton

Mossad

Nazi Subversion: post-World War II

Northwest Conspiracy

Office of Strategic Services

Operation Nordpol

Operation Overlord

Palmer Raids

Panama Canal

Pearl Harbor

Philby, Harold "Kim"

Philippines

Appendix B
List of Spy Serials

Adventures of the Flying Cadets	(1943)	Neal of the Navy	(1915)
Batman, The	(1943)	Patria	(1916)
Blackhawk	(1952)	Pearl of the Army	(1916)
Dick Tracy's G-Men	(1939)	Phantom Creeps, The	(1939)
Don Winslow of the Coast Guard	(1943)	Radar Patrol vs. Sky King	(1950)
Don Winslow of the Navy	(1942)	Red Barry	(1938)
Drums of Fu Manchu	(1940)	Robinson Crusoe of Clipper Island	(1937)
Eagle's Eye, The	(1918)	Secret Agent X-9	(1945)
Flying G-Men	(1939)	Secret Code, The	(1942)
G-Men vs. the Black Dragon	(1943)	Secret Kingdom, The	(1916)
Holt of the Secret Service	(1942)	Secret of the Submarine, The	(1916)
Junior G-Men of the Air	(1942)	Secret Service in Darkest Africa	(1943)
King of the Mounties	(1942)	Silent Mystery, The	(1919)
King of the Royal Mounted	(1940)	Spy Smasher	(1942)
King of the Texas Rangers	(1941)	Trader Tom of the China Seas	(1954)
Lucille Love, the Girl of Mystery	(1914)	Trail of the Octopus, The	(1919)
Mandrake the Magician	(1939)	Who Is Number One?	(1917)
Masked Marvel, The	(1943)	Wolves of Kultur	(1918)
Million Dollar Mystery	(1914)		

Appendix C
Spy Films:
Awards and Nominations

Appendix D
Spy Films About
Political Assassinations

Arabesque	(1966)	Manchurian Candidate, The	(1962)
Assassination	(1987)	Miniature, The	(1910)
Chinatown Squad	(1935)	My Official Wife	(1914)
Commando	(1985)	Mysterious Mr. Moto	(1938)
Day of the Dolphin	(1973)	Navy Blues	(1937)
Devil's Chaplain, The	(1929)	Operation CIA	(1965)
Domino Principle, The	(1977)	Operation Daybreak	(1976)
Dreamscape	(1984)	Operation Manhunt	(1954)
Eiger Sanction, The	(1975)	Orient Express	(1934)
Espionage	(1937)	Parallax View, The	(1974)
Executive Action	(1973)	Passport to Destiny	(1944)
Falcon's Brother, The	(1942)	Paws of the Bear	(1917)
Four Men and a Prayer	(1938)	Pursuit to Algiers	(1945)
Girl Nihilist, The	(1908)	Russian Roulette	(1975)
Hangmen Also Die	(1943)	Scarlet Oath, The	(1916)
Hard Contract	(1969)	Scorpio	(1973)
Hitler—Dead or Alive	(1942)	Secret Kingdom, The	(1916)
Journey to Freedom	(1957)	Sharpshooters	(1938)
Kaiser's Finish, The	(1918)	Sky Murder	(1940)
Killer Elite, The	(1975)	Solomon King	(1974)
King's Game, The	(1916)	Spy Hunt	(1950)
Last Train From Bombay	(1952)	Stopover Tokyo	(1957)
Lincoln Conspiracy, The	(1977)	Strategy of Terror	(1969)
Little Miss Rebellion	(1920)	Tall Target, The	(1951)
London Blackout Murders	(1942)	Terminal Entry	(1986)
Love and Money	(1982)	Three Days of the Condor	(1975)
Man Hunt	(1941)	Thunder Island	(1963)
Man Who Knew Too Much, The	(1956)	To the Victor	(1948)

Appendix E
Spy Films Listed by Their Related War

ALGERIAN-FRENCH WARS (1830–1847)

Song of Love, The	(1924)

AMERICAN CIVIL WAR (1861–1865)

Advance to the Rear	(1964)
Arizona Bushwhackers	(1968)
Black Dakotas, The	(1954)
Copperhead, The	(1920)
Court Martial	(1928)
Dan	(1914)
Fastest Guitar Alive, The	(1967)
Five Guns West	(1955)
General, The	(1927)
Girl Spy Before Vicksburg, The	(1911)
Gray Sentinel, The	(1913)
Great Day in the Morning	(1956)
Great Locomotive Chase, The	(1956)
Hands Up	(1926)
Heart of Lincoln, The	(1915)
Held by the Enemy	(1920)
In Old Kentucky	(1909)
In the Fall of '64	(1914)
Lincoln Conspiracy, The	(1977)
Little Yank, The	(1917)
Madam Who?	(1918)
May Blossom	(1915)
Only the Brave	(1930)

Operator 13	(1934)
Railroad Raiders of '62	(1911)
Ransomed or a Prisoner of War	(1910)
Rebel City	(1953)
Redhead and the Cowboy, The	(1950)
Ride a Violent Mile	(1957)
Sam Davis, The Hero of Tennessee	(1915)
Secret Service	(1919)
Secret Service	(1931)
Southern Yankee, A	(1948)
Springfield Rifle	(1952)
Stirring Days in Old Virginia	(1909)
Virginia City	(1940)

AMERICAN REVOLUTION (1775–1783)

Benedict Arnold and Major André	(1909)
Borrowed Plumage	(1917)
Governor's Daughter, The	(1909)
Heart of a Hero, The	(1916)
Scarlet Coat, The	(1955)
Spy, The	(1914)
Washington at Valley Forge	(1914)

THE COLD WAR (1946–1980s)

Action of the Tiger	(1957)
Alaska Patrol	(1949)
Arctic Flight	(1952)

Assignment—Paris	(1952)	I Married a Communist	(1949)
Atomic City, The	(1952)	I Was a Communist for the FBI	(1951)
Avalanche Express	(1979)	Ice Station Zebra	(1968)
Beast of Yucca Flats, The	(1961)	Iron Curtain, The	(1948)
Big Jim McLain	(1952)	Jet Pilot	(1957)
Blackhawk	(1952)	Journey to Freedom	(1957)
Blindfold	(1966)	Knock on Wood	(1954)
Bowery Battalion	(1951)	Kremlin Letter, The	(1970)
Bullet for Joey, A	(1955)	Lisbon	(1956)
Capture That Capsule!	(1961)	Little Nikita	(1988)
Carolina Cannonball	(1955)	Man on a String	(1960)
Chairman, The	(1969)	Man on a Tightrope	(1953)
Clipped Wings	(1953)	Manchurian Candidate, The	(1962)
Cloak and Dagger	(1984)	Mrs. Pollifax—Spy	(1971)
Counterspy Meets Scotland Yard	(1950)	My Son John	(1952)
Daniel	(1983)	Nasty Rabbit, The	(1965)
David Harding, Counterspy	(1950)	Never Let Me Go	(1953)
Dead to the World	(1962)	Night People	(1954)
Defense Play	(1988)	No Time for Flowers	(1952)
Destructors, The	(1968)	No Way Out	(1987)
Dimension 5	(1966)	On Company Business	(1980)
Diplomatic Courier	(1952)	Operation Manhunt	(1954)
Don't Drink the Water	(1969)	Osterman Weekend, The	(1983)
Escape From East Berlin	(1962)	Outrageous Fortune	(1987)
Falcon and the Snowman, The	(1985)	Panic in the City	(1968)
Fantastic Voyage	(1966)	Paris Playboys	(1954)
Fearmakers, The	(1958)	Pickup on South Street	(1953)
Firefox	(1982)	Prize, The	(1963)
Five Steps to Danger	(1956)	Project X	(1949)
Flame of Stamboul	(1951)	Red Menace, The	(1949)
Flight to Tangier	(1953)	Red Snow	(1952)
Flying Saucer, The	(1950)	Romanoff and Juliet	(1961)
Foreign Intrigue	(1956)	Russian Roulette	(1975)
49th Man, The	(1953)	Savage Drums	(1951)
Geisha Girl	(1952)	Savage Mutiny	(1953)
Girl in the Kremlin, The	(1957)	Scorpio	(1973)
Girl Who Knew Too Much, The	(1969)	Secret Ways, The	(1961)
Gog	(1954)	Security Risk	(1954)
Gotcha!	(1985)	Shanghai Story, The	(1954)
Guilty of Treason	(1950)	Sky High	(1952)
Hammerhead	(1968)	Sofia	(1948)
Hong Kong Confidential	(1958)	Soldier, The	(1982)
Hopscotch	(1980)	Spies Like Us	(1985)
Hunt for Red October, The	(1990)	Spy Hunt	(1950)

Spy in the Sky	(1958)			
SPYS (S*P*Y*S)	(1974)			
Steel Fist, The	(1952)			
Stopover Tokyo	(1957)			
Subterfuge	(1969)			
Tangier Incident	(1953)			
Target Hong Kong	(1952)			
Telefon	(1977)			
Thief, The	(1952)			
Time to Die, A	(1983)			
Top Secret	(1984)			
Topaz	(1969)			
Torn Curtain	(1966)			
Trials of Alger Hiss, The	(1980)			
Trouble with Spies, The	(1987)			
Venetian Affair, The	(1967)			
WAC From Walla Walla, The	(1952)			
Walk a Crooked Mile	(1948)			
Walk East on Beacon	(1952)			
Where There's Life	(1947)			
Whip Hand, The	(1951)			
Who Was That Lady?	(1960)			

CRIMEAN WAR (1854–1856)

Charge of the Lancers (1954)

CUBAN REVOLUTIONS

Cuba (1979)
Bright Shawl, The (1923)
Santiago (1956)

FRENCH AND INDIAN WAR (1754–1763)

Pathfinder, The (1952)
When the Redskins Rode (1951)
Seats of the Mighty, The (1914)

FRENCH INDO-CHINA WAR (1946–1954)

Rogues' Regiment (1948)
China Gate (1957)
Quiet American, The (1958)

Wicked Dreams of Paula Schultz,
The (1968)
World for Ransom (1954)
Zotz! (1962)

FRENCH REVOLUTION (1789–1799)

Reign of Terror (1949)

GLORIOUS REVOLUTION (1688–1689)

Fighting Blade, The (1923)

IRISH-ENGLISH WARS

Outsider, The (1980)

ISRAELI WARS

Ambassador, The (1984)
Judith (1966)

KOREAN WAR (1950–1953)

Back at the Front (1952)
Bamboo Prison, The (1954)
Prisoner of War (1954)
Tokyo File 212 (1951)

MEXICAN REVOLUTION (1910–1921)

Key to Yesterday, The (1914)
Love Thief, The (1916)

MEXICAN WAR OF 1846–1848

For the Honor of Old Glory (1914)

NAPOLEONIC WARS (1803–1815)

Eagle of the Sea (1926)
Fighting Eagle, The (1927)
Fighting O'Flynn, The (1949)
Sea Devils (1953)

RUSSIAN REVOLUTION (1917)

British Agent (1934)
Scarlet Lady, The (1928)
Under False Colors (1917)

RUSSO-TURKISH WAR (1877–1878)

Michael Strogoff (1910)
Michael Strogoff (1914)
Soldier and the Lady, The (1937)

SANUSI ANTI-BRITISH REVOLT
  (1915–1917)

Flame of the Desert   (1919)

SEVEN WEEKS WAR (1866)

Salome, Where She Danced   (1945)

SINO-JAPANESE WAR (1937–1945)

Burma Convoy   (1941)
China Girl   (1942)
International Settlement   (1938)
Night Plane From Chungking   (1943)
North of Shanghai   (1939)
Shadows Over Shanghai   (1938)

SPANISH-AMERICAN WAR (1898)

Message to Garcia, A   (1916)
Message to Garcia, A   (1936)

SPANISH CIVIL WAR (1936–1939)

Blockade   (1938)
Confidential Agent   (1945)

VIETNAM WAR (1956–1975)

Apocalypse Now   (1979)
Losers, The   (1970)
Operation CIA   (1965)

WAR OF 1812 (1812–1814)

Brave Warrior   (1952)

WORLD WAR I (1914–1918)

Adele   (1919)
Adventures of Kitty Cobb, The   (1914)
After Tonight   (1933)
Alien Enemy, An   (1918)
American Buds   (1918)
Arms and the Girl   (1917)
Arms and the Woman   (1916)
As in a Looking Glass   (1916)
Berlin via America   (1918)
Better 'Ole, The   (1926)

Birth of a Race, The   (1918)
Blue Envelope Mystery, The   (1916)
Body and Soul   (1931)
Bonds of Honor   (1919)
Border Wireless, The   (1918)
British Intelligence   (1940)
Burden of Proof, The   (1918)
Caillaux Case, The   (1918)
Called to the Front   (1914)
Claws of the Hun   (1918)
Come On In   (1918)
Convoy   (1927)
Crimson Wing, The   (1915)
Crucible of Life, The   (1918)
Cup of Fury, The   (1920)
Dangerous Days   (1920)
Daredevil, The   (1918)
Dark Road, The   (1917)
Dark Star, The   (1919)
Darling Lili   (1970)
Daughter Angele   (1918)
Daughter of Destiny   (1918)
Daughter of Uncle Sam, A   (1918)
Dishonored   (1931)
Doing Their Bit   (1918)
Doomed Battalion   (1932)
Draft 258   (1918)
Dugan of the Dugouts   (1928)
Eagle's Eye, The   (1918)
Eagle's Wing, The   (1916)
Eternal Temptress, The   (1917)
Ever in My Heart   (1933)
Fair Pretender, The   (1918)
False Faces, The   (1919)
Firefly of France, The   (1918)
Flames of Chance   (1918)
Follow the Girl   (1917)
Friendly Enemies   (1925)
From Two to Six   (1918)
Gay Diplomat, The   (1931)
Girl of Today, The   (1918)
Girl Philippa, The   (1917)
Good-bye Kiss, The   (1928)
Gray Parasol, The   (1918)

Great Deception, The	(1926)	Luck and Pluck	(1919)
Great Impersonation, The	(1921)	Madame Spy	(1918)
Great Love, The	(1918)	Madame Spy	(1934)
Greatest Power, The	(1917)	Man Who Won, The	(1919)
Ham and Eggs at the Front	(1927)	Man Who Wouldn't Tell, The	(1918)
Her Country First	(1918)	Mare Nostrum	(1926)
Her Debt of Honor	(1918)	Marriage Ring, The	(1918)
Her Man o' War	(1926)	Marriages Are Made	(1918)
Highest Trump, The	(1919)	Mata Hari	(1932)
Hillcrest Mystery, The	(1918)	Mata Hari	(1985)
His Birthright	(1918)	Men of the Sky	(1931)
His Daughter Pays	(1918)	Message of the Mouse, The	(1917)
Hotel Imperial	(1927)	Miss Jackie of the Army	(1917)
Hotel Imperial	(1939)	Mothers of Men	(1920)
Hun Within, The	(1918)	Mr. Grex of Monte Carlo	(1915)
Huns Within Our Gates	(1918)	Mr. Logan, U.S.A.	(1918)
I Married a Spy	(1938)	Mrs. Slacker	(1918)
I Want to Forget	(1918)	My Country First	(1916)
I'll Say So	(1918)	Mystic Faces	(1918)
In Again—Out Again	(1917)	New Lives for Old	(1925)
In Pursuit of Polly	(1918)	No Man's Land	(1918)
In the Diplomatic Service	(1916)	Now We're in the Air	(1927)
Inside the Lines	(1918)	Nurse Edith Cavell	(1939)
Inside the Lines	(1930)	On Dangerous Ground	(1917)
Intrigue, The	(1916)	On the Jump	(1918)
Ivory Snuff Box, The	(1915)	Over Secret Wires	(1915)
Joan of Plattsburg	(1918)	Over the Top	(1918)
Kaiser's Finish, The	(1918)	Passport to Hell, A	(1932)
Kaiser's Shadow, The	(1918)	Patria	(1916)
Kultur	(1918)	Patriotism	(1918)
Lafayette, We Come!	(1918)	Paws of the Bear	(1917)
Lancer Spy	(1937)	Paying the Price	(1916)
Last Outpost, The	(1935)	Pearl of the Army	(1916)
Law Unto Herself, A	(1918)	Price of Applause, The	(1918)
Leap to Fame	(1918)	Price of Malice, The	(1916)
Legion of the Condemned	(1928)	Prussian Cur, The	(1918)
Lest We Forget	(1918)	Reckoning Day, The	(1918)
Light of Victory, The	(1919)	Recoil, The	(1917)
Little Patriot, A	(1917)	Rendezvous	(1935)
Little Wildcat	(1922)	Riley of the Rainbow Division	(1928)
Littlest Scout, The	(1919)	Road Through the Dark, The	(1918)
Love and the Law	(1919)	Road to France, The	(1918)
Love in a Hurry	(1919)	Romance of the Air, A	(1918)
Love Light, The	(1921)	Royal African Rifles, The	(1953)

Safe for Democracy	(1918)	Who Goes There?	(1917)
Salvation Joan	(1916)	Who Was the Other Man?	(1917)
Sawdust Doll, The	(1919)	Wife or Country	(1918)
Scotland Yard	(1930)	Winged Mystery, The	(1917)
Sea Flower, The	(1918)	Winning Girl, The	(1919)
Seas Beneath, The	(1931)	Wolves of Kultur	(1918)
Secret Code	(1918)	Woman Disputed, The	(1928)
Secret Game, The	(1917)	Woman of Experience, A	(1931)
Secret of the Submarine, The	(1916)	Woman the Germans Shot, The	(1918)
Secret Orders	(1926)	Womanhood, the Glory of the Nation	(1917)
Shadows of Suspicion	(1919)	Yankee Doodle in Berlin	(1919)
Shell 43	(1916)	Yankee Pluck	(1917)
Shifting Sands	(1918)	Yellow Dog, The	(1918)
Ship Comes In, A	(1928)	Young Eagles	(1930)
Silk-Lined Burglar, The	(1919)		
Silver Car, The	(1921)		
Smiles	(1919)	WORLD WAR II (1939–1945)	
Somewhere in France	(1916)	Above Suspicion	(1943)
Spirit of '17, The	(1918)	Across the Pacific	(1942)
Splendid Sinner, The	(1918)	Action in Arabia	(1944)
Spy, The	(1917)	Adventures of the Flying Cadets	(1943)
Spy's Fate, The	(1915)	Air Raid Wardens	(1943)
Stamboul Quest	(1934)	All Through the Night	(1941)
Stolen Orders	(1918)	Ambush Bay	(1966)
Suspicion	(1918)	American Guerrilla in the Philippines	(1950)
Suzy	(1936)	Angry Hills, The	(1959)
Swat the Spy	(1918)	Appointment in Berlin	(1943)
Thing We Love, The	(1918)	Armored Command	(1961)
This Mad World	(1930)	Assignment in Brittany	(1943)
Three Faces East	(1926)	Atlantic Convoy	(1942)
Three Faces East	(1930)	Back to Bataan	(1945)
Tigress, The	(1914)	Background to Danger	(1943)
Till We Meet Again	(1936)	Batman, The	(1943)
Top Sergeant Mulligan	(1928)	Beasts of Berlin	(1939)
Treason	(1917)	Behind the Eight Ball	(1942)
Treason	(1918)	Berlin Correspondent	(1942)
True Heaven	(1929)	Betrayal From the East	(1945)
23 1/2 Hours' Leave	(1919)	Betrayed	(1954)
Unexpected Places	(1918)	Big Noise, The	(1944)
Up Romance Road	(1918)	Black Dragons	(1942)
Via Wireless	(1915)	Black Parachute, The	(1944)
War and the Woman	(1917)	Blue, White and Perfect	(1941)
Wasp, The	(1918)	Bombay Clipper	(1942)
We're in the Navy Now	(1926)		

Jewels of Brandenburg	(1947)	Northern Pursuit	(1943)
Joan of Ozark	(1942)	On the Double	(1961)
Joan of Paris	(1942)	Once Upon a Honeymoon	(1942)
Joe Smith, American	(1942)	One Night in Lisbon	(1941)
Journey Into Fear	(1942)	Operation Crossbow	(1965)
Jungle Heat	(1957)	Operation Daybreak	(1976)
Junior Army	(1942)	Operation Secret	(1952)
Junior G-Men of the Air	(1942)	O.S.S.	(1946)
Keep 'Em Sailing	(1942)	Pacific Blackout	(1942)
King of the Cowboys	(1943)	Pacific Rendezvous	(1942)
King of the Mounties	(1942)	Paris Calling	(1941)
King of the Royal Mounted	(1940)	Paris Underground	(1945)
King of the Texas Rangers	(1941)	Passage to Marseilles	(1944)
Ladies of Washington	(1944)	Passport to Alcatraz	(1940)
Lady Has Plans, The	(1942)	Passport to Destiny	(1944)
Last Blitzkrieg, The	(1958)	Passport to Suez	(1943)
Little Tokyo, U.S.A.	(1942)	Phantom Plainsman, The	(1942)
London Blackout Murders	(1942)	Phantom Raiders	(1940)
Lucky Jordan	(1942)	Phantom Submarine, The	(1941)
Lure of the Islands	(1942)	Pigeon That Took Rome, The	(1962)
Madame Spy	(1942)	Powder Town	(1942)
Make Your Own Bed	(1944)	Pride of the Army	(1942)
Malaya	(1949)	Prisoner of Japan	(1942)
Man at Large	(1941)	Private Snuffy Smith	(1942)
Man Hunt	(1941)	Pursuit to Algiers	(1945)
Margin for Error	(1943)	Quiet Please, Murder	(1942)
Marines Come Through, The	(1943)	Raid on Rommel	(1971)
Masked Marvel, The	(1943)	Raiders of the Lost Ark	(1981)
Master Race, The	(1944)	Remember Pearl Harbor	(1942)
Meet Boston Blackie	(1941)	Reunion in France	(1942)
Ministry of Fear	(1944)	Revenge of the Zombies	(1943)
Miss V From Moscow	(1943)	Rio Rita	(1942)
Moritori	(1965)	Roar of the Press	(1941)
Mr. Dynamite	(1941)	Sabotage	(1939)
Murder in the Air	(1940)	Sabotage Squad	(1942)
Murder on the Waterfront	(1943)	Saboteur	(1942)
Murder Over New York	(1940)	Safecracker, The	(1958)
My Favorite Blonde	(1942)	Samurai	(1945)
My Favorite Spy	(1942)	Scarlet Clue, The	(1945)
Mystery Sea Raider	(1940)	Sealed Cargo	(1951)
Mystery Ship	(1941)	Secret Agent of Japan	(1942)
Nazi Agent	(1942)	Secret Agent X-9	(1945)
Nick Carter, Master Detective	(1939)	Secret Code, The	(1942)
Nightmare	(1942)	Secret Command	(1944)

Secret Door, The (1964)

Secret Enemies (1942)

Secret Invasion, The (1964)

Secret Service in Darkest Africa (1943)

Secret War of Harry Frigg, The (1968)

Secrets of Scotland Yard (1944)

Secrets of the Underground (1943)

Seven Miles From Alcatraz (1942)

Shadow of Terror (1945)

Sherlock Holmes & the Secret Weapon (1942)

Sherlock Holmes & Voice of Terror (1942)

Sherlock Holmes in Washington (1943)

Ship Ahoy (1942)

Sky Murder (1940)

Sky Patrol (1939)

South of Panama (1941)

Spy Ship (1942)

Spy Smasher (1942)

Spy Train (1943)

Stalag 17 (1953)

Storm Over Lisbon (1944)

Submarine Alert (1943)

Submarine Base (1943)

Sultan's Daughter, The (1944)

Sundown (1941)

Tampico (1944)

Target Unknown (1951)

Tartu (1943)

Tarzan's Desert Mystery (1943)

Television Spy (1939)

Texas to Bataan (1942)

Then There Were Three (1961)

They Came to Blow Up America (1943)

They Dare Not Love (1941)

They Got Me Covered (1943)

They Live in Fear (1944)

They Made Her a Spy (1939)

Thin Man Goes Home, The (1944)

13 Rue Madeleine (1946)

36 Hours (1964)

This Gun for Hire (1942)

Tiger Fangs (1943)

Till We Meet Again (1944)

To Be or Not to Be (1942)

To Be or Not to Be (1983)

To Have and Have Not (1944)

Tobruk (1966)

Tonight We Raid Calais (1943)

Trader Tom of the China Seas (1954)

Two-Man Submarine (1944)

Two Tickets to London (1943)

Two Weeks to Live (1943)

Two Yanks in Trinidad (1942)

U-Boat Prisoner (1944)

Uncertain Glory (1944)

Underground (1941)

Underground Agent (1942)

Unseen Enemy (1942)

Unwritten Code, The (1944)

Valley of Hunted Men, The (1942)

Watch on the Rhine (1943)

Waterfront (1944)

We've Never Been Licked (1943)

When Hell Broke Loose (1958)

Which Way to the Front? (1970)

Wife Takes a Flyer, The (1942)

Wild Horse Rustlers (1943)

Wings Over the Pacific (1943)

Women in the Night (1948)

Yank in Libya, A (1942)

You Nazty Spy (1940)